THE
NEW BOOK
OF
KNOWLEDGE

THE
NEW BOOK
OF
KNOWLEDGE

Scholastic Library Publishing, Inc.
Danbury, Connecticut

VOLUME 9

I

ISBN 0-7172-0540-1 (set)

The publishers wish to thank the following for permission to use copyrighted material:
Charles Scribner's Sons, an imprint of Macmillan Publishing Company, for "One Monday Morning" by
    Uri Shulevitz, copyright © 1967 by Uri Shulevitz.
Basic Books, Inc., Publishers, for *Frames of Mind: The Theory of Multiple Intelligences* by Howard
    Gardner, copyright © 1983 by Howard Gardner.

I, the ninth letter in the English alphabet, is a descendant of the ancient Phoenician and Hebrew letter *yod* and the Greek letter *iota*. In Phoenician speech the word *yod* probably meant "hand," and many language scholars believe that an earlier version of the letter may have represented a hand or the palm of a hand. *Yod* looked like this: ℈

When the Greeks adapted the Phoenician alphabet, they renamed the letter *iota*. The Greeks pronounced the *iota* like the I in *marine*. Eventually the letter took on a straighter form, and by 403 B.C. it looked like this: |

The Romans learned the Greek alphabet from the Etruscans, who ruled in Rome from the end of the 7th to the end of the 6th century B.C. But in the Roman alphabet the I sometimes stood for an I vowel sound, sometimes for a Y consonant. The Y sound of the letter eventually passed into a J sound similar to the sound heard in *jewel*—so the letter I was used for the sound of J, too. The I still had this double use when the Romans gave their alphabet to western Europe. It continued to be used for both sounds in English until the 17th century, when I and J became two separate letters.

In English we usually pronounce the letter I by opening the lips and placing the tongue behind the lower front teeth. The main sounds of the letter in English are the short I, as in the word *wit,* and the long I, as in the word *tide*. The English I is also sometimes pronounced like a Y, as in the word *onion,* or like the U in *turtle,* as in the word *stir*.

The letter I serves as a word referring to the speaker, as in "I am John Smith." In English grammar it is the first person singular pronoun. In chemistry I stands for the element iodine. It is the symbol for one in the Roman numeral system. The letter I is also found in many abbreviations. On maps it often stands for island. In many organization names, such as ITU (International Typographical Union), it stands for the word international.

Reviewed by MARIO PEI
Author, *The Story of Language*

See also ALPHABET.

Ii · 1

SOME WAYS TO REPRESENT I:

The **manuscript** or printed forms of the letter (left) are highly readable. The **cursive** letters (right) are formed from slanted flowing strokes joining one letter to the next.

The **Manual Alphabet** (left) enables a deaf person to communicate by forming letters with the fingers of one hand. **Braille** (right) is a system by which a blind person can use fingertips to "read" raised dots that stand for letters.

The **International Code of Signals** is a special group of flags used to send and receive messages at sea. Each letter is represented by a different flag.

International Morse Code is used to send messages by radio signals. Each letter is expressed as a combination of dots (•) and dashes (––).

In the plays of Henrik Ibsen, individual ideals often conflict with social values. In *A Doll's House*, Nora leaves her unhappy marriage to seek self-fulfillment.

IBSEN, HENRIK (1828–1906)

The Norwegian poet and playwright Henrik Ibsen is one of the great figures of world literature. His plays, which often emphasize an individual's search for meaning, influenced the development of modern drama.

Ibsen was born on March 20, 1828, in Skien, Norway. His father, a wealthy merchant, lost his fortune when Henrik was 8. At 15, Henrik became a druggist's apprentice in the small town of Grimstad. The pay was so low that he could afford little clothing or food. He read, wrote poetry, and studied Latin, hoping to pass the university entrance exams. A friend sent one of his poems to a paper, and it was published. Another friend paid for the publication of Ibsen's first play, *Catilina* (1850).

Ibsen left Grimstad for Christiania (now Oslo) in 1850 and took the university exams, but his grades in Greek and arithmetic were not good enough. For nine months he and two friends published a liberal, satirical weekly. His play *The Warrior's Barrow* was performed successfully that winter, and he was asked to compose a prologue (introductory speech) for a musical festival benefiting the Norwegian Theater in Bergen. When the famous violinist Ole Bull, founder of the theater, heard the prologue, he appointed Ibsen theater poet and stage manager.

Ibsen's first popular success was *The Feast at Solhaug* in 1856. The next year he was asked to direct the Norwegian Theater in Christiania. He married Susannah Thoresen in 1858. Their only child, Sigurd, was born in 1859. The theater went bankrupt in 1862, and Ibsen borrowed from his friends in order to keep on writing. The success of *The Pretenders* in 1864 brought him a government grant to travel abroad. He began *Brand* in Ariccia, Italy. After its publication in 1866, the Norwegian government granted Ibsen a lifelong pension. Before the grant went into effect, however, Ibsen's extreme poverty and an attack of malaria drove him nearly to suicide.

Ibsen wrote about Norway but he could not live there. He was bitter about his countrymen's lack of understanding of his work. He lived instead in Italy and Germany. The German youth idolized him. His plays were the sensations of every season. *The Pillars of Society* (1877) played in five Berlin theaters simultaneously in 1878. *A Doll's House* (1879) provoked violent discussions. Great actresses played its heroine, Nora, in all the capitals of the world. Public performances of *Ghosts* (1881) were forbidden in Germany, but *An Enemy of the People* (1882) became the most talked-about play of the year. The unhappy ending of *Hedda Gabler* (1890) also aroused controversy.

Ibsen's seriousness of purpose, his close observation of the life around him, and the infinite pains he took to rewrite increased his powers with every play. His plays fall into three groups: (1) poetic, idealistic dramas, such as the romantic *Peer Gynt* (1867); (2) plays that attempted to reform social conditions; the greatest of these, *Ghosts* (1881), inspired the naturalistic problem play in all modern literatures; and (3) psychological dramas that were studies of single individuals; the first of these, *The Wild Duck* (1884), was a pioneer of the modern symbolical play. All the plays have as their theme the conflict between the moral ideals of the individual and the moral traditions of society. Ibsen believed that the individual should remain true to himself under all circumstances.

In 1891 Ibsen returned to Norway to live—Christiania's most distinguished citizen. Two of his last works, *The Master Builder* (1892) and *When We Dead Awaken* (1899), are largely autobiographical. He died on May 23, 1906. His monument in Oslo bears no name or inscription. It simply has a carving of a miner's hammer, an apt symbol for a man who dug ever deeper into human experience.

Reviewed by REGINALD L. COOK
Middlebury College

ICARUS. See GREEK MYTHOLOGY (Profiles).

ICE

In our world, ice is one of the most common substances. Nearly one tenth of the earth's land is covered with ice. In earth's history there has been less ice than now, and at times there has been more. During the Ice Age, a period that ended about 8,000 years ago, ice covered nearly one third of the earth's land.

Ice is part of our everyday life in many ways. Some people are familiar with ice as part of a winter storm. Others gaze at distant ice-topped mountains, while some people may live in a land molded and carved by ice. Sometimes ice is helpful. Ice is valuable as a refrigerant for keeping food fresh. It may be used to cool parts of the body before surgery. And most everyone knows the fun of skating and skiing on ice and snow. But ice can also be harmful. When the temperature falls and the water in plants and animals turns into ice, the tissue is usually destroyed. Very few people like driving on icy roads during a winter storm. And when huge masses of floating ice, called icebergs, drift into the ocean, they can be a deadly hazard to ships.

▶ HOW ICE FORMS

Ice forms on the earth's surface in two ways: It may start as snow that slowly changes into ice, or it may form by the freezing of water.

Ice From Snow

In most places where it snows in winter, the air temperatures in spring and summer are high enough to melt all of the snow that has fallen. However, in very high mountain areas and in the polar regions, some snow still remains at the end of the summer. Because some snow remains unmelted each year, the thickness of snow in these areas gradually increases over the years.

Falling snow consists of six-sided crystals, full of air bubbles. It is only about one third to one tenth as heavy as water. But as the snow lies on the ground, it changes slowly. The weight of the snow on top presses on the snow near the bottom. As the crystals become more and more rounded, they pack together more closely, and the snow becomes denser and heavier.

As time passes and more snow accumulates, the lower layers are buried deeper and deeper.

Ice crystals, which occur in a variety of six-sided forms, fall through the atmosphere, clustering together to form snowflakes.

The air bubbles in the crystals no longer join together, and the densely packed material is called ice. How long it takes for snow to turn into ice depends on the snow accumulation rate, the air temperature, and the weight of the snow in the upper layers. It may take several hundred years, or in places where there is usually some melting and refreezing to speed along the change to ice, it may take just a dozen years.

Ice from Water

Whether it is in lakes or ponds or in an ice cube tray, water forms ice in the same way. Heat flows from the warm water into the cooler air. As the surface water looses heat, it cools until it reaches 39°F (4°C). At that temperature, water is at its heaviest. The heavy water at the top sinks and pushes warmer and lighter water up from below. The new surface water also cools, sinks, and pushes more bottom water to the surface.

The up and down movement continues until all the water is at 39°F (4°C). When the water at the top cools below this point, it becomes lighter and so stays at the surface. Then the water starts to freeze and form ice. The ice is even lighter than the cooled water and floats at the surface. In a lake or pond, the water at the bottom remains at 39°F (4°C), which makes it

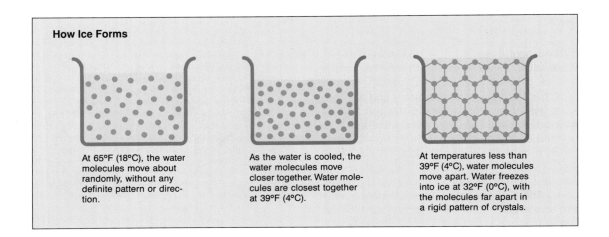

How Ice Forms

At 65°F (18°C), the water molecules move about randomly, without any definite pattern or direction.

As the water is cooled, the water molecules move closer together. Water molecules are closest together at 39°F (4°C).

At temperatures less than 39°F (4°C), water molecules move apart. Water freezes into ice at 32°F (0°C), with the molecules far apart in a rigid pattern of crystals.

possible for the plants and animals to live there. If ice were heavier than water, ponds and lakes would start freezing at the bottom and few living things could survive in them.

Properties of Ice

No matter how ice is formed, it shares some common qualities. Ice is hard, and it is transparent (except when it contains air bubbles and appears white). It is lighter than an equal amount of water (so it will float whether it is on a river or in a cold drink), because it occupies more space than the water it came from.

Freezing and Melting. Fresh water freezes in normal conditions at 32°F (0°C), usually called the freezing point. But if the water contains other chemicals, such as the salt in seawater, it does not freeze until it reaches a lower temperature. The freezing point for seawater is about 28°F (-2°C). This is why it is quite common for trucks to spread salt over icy roads—it lowers the freezing point to below the air temperature so the ice will melt.

The melting point of ice (or the freezing point of water) can also be changed with pressure. When ice-skating, all of a person's weight is concentrated on a very small area. The pressure immediately under the skates is

very high, usually high enough to lower the freezing point to below the local air temperature. The ice under the skate melts so that the person is really skating along on a very thin layer of water. As soon as the person moves forward, the pressure is removed and the melting point returns to 32°F (0°C). As the skates pass by, the water refreezes.

The Flow of Ice. Ice in an ice cube looks like a perfectly normal, hard solid. However, it is not a simple solid at all. If one presses an ice cube between two metal plates and gradually increases the pressure, the ice will spread out sideways. This sideways movement is called **creep**, or **flow**. The rate of flow changes with pressure. The greater the pressure, the faster the flow.

The same thing happens in nature. In an area where snow is accumulating—more snow falls in winter than melts in summer—the ice remains almost motionless until it becomes 200 to 300 feet (61 to 91 meters) thick. Then the pressure on the lower layers is great enough to cause movement. Slowly, the ice will start to flow downhill at a measurable rate. When a natural mass of ice moves under its own weight, it is called a **glacier**. Relatively small, thin glaciers on nearly flat ground may move only a few inches a year, while huge glaciers may move half a mile a year.

▶ ICE ON THE EARTH: GLACIERS

Scientists divide glaciers into groups according to their temperature (temperate or cold), or they may group glaciers according to their location and shape as valley glaciers, ice caps, ice sheets, and ice shelves.

What started out as a dirty snowball, grew to several miles wide, and can only be seen every 76 years?

Halley's Comet. Scientists playfully call comets "dirty snowballs" because the very center of a comet's head, the nucleus, forms from a mixture of ice and dust.

Above: Wedge-shaped cracks called crevasses make winter travel across ice sheets or glaciers dangerous.
Right: A river of ice flows through the mountains and fills the valleys of Alaska's Columbia Glacier.

Valley Glaciers

Valley glaciers are glaciers that carve out mountain valleys. They can be seen as white rivers of ice flowing down high mountain valleys in many parts of the world. These glaciers can be very large; some in the Himalaya Mountains are 60 miles (97 kilometers) long.

As the ice flows through the rises and hollows of the valleys, the surface ice on the glacier is often stretched and may crack. The cracks are called **crevasses** and are one of the greatest dangers in crossing glaciers and ice sheets, especially when they are hidden under a surface covering of new snow. Usually crevasses on temperate glaciers (where the ice temperature is not much below the freezing point) are not more than 100 feet (30 meters) deep. But in Greenland and the Antarctic they may be as deep as 150 feet (46 meters).

Ice Caps and Ice Sheets

When a high mountain plateau is covered with a dome of ice, it is called an **ice cap**. As an ice cap grows, it stretches across the plateau, spilling out in all directions. It may grow to cover larger and larger areas until a vast area of land is completely covered by the glacier. Then it is called an **ice sheet**.

Spectacular ice sheets cover most of Antarctica and Greenland. The Greenland Ice Sheet covers an area of about 700,000 square miles (1.8 million square kilometers). That is an area almost three times as large as Texas. The Antarctic Ice Sheet covers an area of nearly 5.4 million square miles (14 million square kilometers). That is an area one and a half times as large as the United States.

The ice sheets rise and fall as they cover the land. Near the middle of Greenland, the surface of the ice sheet is about 10,000 feet (3,000 meters) above sea level; and in Antarctica the surface of the ice sheet reaches about 13,000 feet (4,000 meters) above sea level. The ice sheet also covers land that is below sea level. In some areas, the bottom of the ice is 3,281 feet (1,000 meters) or more below sea level.

Ice Shelves

When an ice sheet flows across a seacoast and extends onto the sea forming a high ice cliff, it is called an **ice shelf**. An ice shelf floats on the sea, but it is still attached to the land. The coasts of Antarctica are fringed by ice shelves. The largest are the Ross and the Filchner ice shelves. Each is as big as Texas. The Ross Ice Shelf, more than 1,000 feet (300 meters) thick, moves forward at speeds of

Top: Valley and outlet glaciers drain into the Ross Ice Shelf, helping to make it the world's largest body of floating ice. The shelf has an airfield and several research stations on it.

Bottom: The harp seal lives in the cold waters below the frozen surface of the sea. A layer of blubber beneath its skin helps to keep this water mammal warm.

about .5 mile (about 1 kilometer) a year.

Huge flat-topped icebergs form when chunks of the ice sheet break off, or **calve**, and plunge into the sea. One of the biggest icebergs ever recorded was 2,883 square miles (7,500 square kilometers). It was more than twice the size of Rhode Island!

▶ **MEASURING THE ICE**

Scientists use different ways to measure the earth's ice depending on what they want to find out about the ice. Some measurements tell scientists how thick the ice is. Other measurements tell how fast the ice moves, and still others tell how old the ice is.

Snow Accumulation. Altitude and air temperature affect snow accumulation. As a glacier flows downhill, the ice reaches warmer altitudes and the amount of melting increases. Some of the water soaks into the glacier and refreezes, but the rest either evaporates into the air or runs off as **meltwater** (water from melted snow and ice). For the glacier to remain the same size, the total amount of melt-

ing must be the same as the total amount of snow and ice accumulation. Melting increases and glaciers become smaller when the average air temperature increases for a number of years (as it has since about 1870). If all the earth's ice were to melt, sea levels would rise about 200 feet.

Snow accumulation is measured in two ways. The easier way is to erect poles that measure the snow as it piles up against them. The other method is to dig pits or to drill into the ice and remove cores of it. Then the snow layers can be studied.

In some glacial areas the air temperature rises in the summer. The surface snow melts slightly and then it refreezes, forming a layer of crystals that are rounded and cemented together. These clearly marked layers, called **annual layerings**, enable scientists to measure the accumulation of snow for each year.

There are also annual layerings in glacial areas where there is very little melting or none at all. In these areas the snow crystals that fall in the winter, when it is colder, are different from those that fall in the summer. The different patterns created by the crystals form recognizable layers that can be measured.

Although scientists may measure the rate of snow accumulation at many places on a glacier, they are still unable to get an accurate measure of the amount of ice that is lost in the form of icebergs. So scientists often do not know whether the ice sheets are growing, shrinking, or staying the same.

Measuring Depth. The thickness of ice can be measured in two ways. In the seismic

Above left: After a core of ice is cut into sections, the sections will be melted and a laboratory analysis made of their oxygen content. *Above:* In the process of calving, giant blocks of ice break away from an ice shelf to form icebergs.

method, explosives are put into holes drilled down into the ice. When the explosives are set off, the force of the explosion compresses the surrounding ice. The compression sets up shock waves that travel in all directions. Waves travel through the surface layers of the ice and down to the solid surface beneath the ice. When the waves hit the solid surface, they are reflected back to the surface of the ice. There the waves are picked up by instruments that measure the rate and time the waves took to travel through the ice. From these measurements, the distance the waves traveled from the surface below to the surface of the ice can be found, giving scientists the thickness of the ice.

Radio waves are also used to measure the thickness of ice. A plane flying over the ice sends out bursts, or pulses, of radio waves. Some of the waves reflect off the surface of the ice, but the rest pass through the ice and are reflected back by the underlying rock. Instruments measure the time it takes the reflected waves to return to the plane and from that information the thickness is computed.

Measuring Age. Scientists use ice cores not only to examine the depth of the ice and to compute its age, but also to get information about the past climate. The most common method uses the air that was contained in the snow when it first fell. The air becomes trapped in the ice and remains there no matter how deeply the ice is buried.

Scientists measure the amounts of the two common forms of oxygen, O^{16} and O^{18}, at various depths along the ice core. The changes in the amounts of the two types of oxygen are used to find the temperature that existed when the snow fell. From the samplings, the yearly variation of air temperature can be found and the thickness of the annual layers established. The thickness measurements are used to calculate the age of the ice at various depths.

From the Vostok station, high on the ice sheet of eastern Antarctica, Russian and French scientists have recovered an ice core 5,000 feet (1,500 meters) long. The annual accumulation of snow at that site is very low, so a core of that length penetrates through long periods of time. Scientists studying the core have found the ice at the bottom of the core to be about 120,000 years old. This core does not even reach halfway to the bottom of the ice sheet, where the ice may well be half a million years old!

People who live in Arctic climates have always been interested in ice because of its effect on the plants and animals in the area. In many ways, their survival depends on understanding the ice. But scientists study ice to find out about the earth's past and future. Glaciers are a kind of outside earth-science laboratory. Most important, however, people are just naturally curious about their home planet.

COLIN BULL
Dean Emeritus, The Ohio State University

See also ANTARCTICA; GLACIERS; GREENLAND; ICE AGES; ICEBERGS.

A rock weighing over 500 tons (454 metric tons) was deposited by a retreating glacier near the Grand Canyon's Inspiration Point.

ICE AGES

One third of the small planet is buried under miles-thick ice that stretches out from the polar ice caps. The rest of the planet is cooled by the ice. Only regions farthest from the ice are even barely warm. Oceans are narrow. Much of their water has been sucked up by the giant mountains of ice now covering half of what was once ocean surface.

If you were on a starship, would this be a place to visit? Would you expect to find life? Land your imaginary starship near the edge of the ice and get ready for a surprise. This planet is bursting with life—on land, in the seas, and in the air. Among the creatures are some two-legged ones that may be intelligent . . .

What is this planet? It is Earth just a few thousand years ago, and the two-legged creatures are our ancestors. Earth is experiencing an ice age—a period when thick sheets of ice spread over large regions of the planet.

▶ THE MYSTERY OF THE MOVING ROCKS

People living in the high mountain region along the border between France and Switzerland were the first to report that Earth was once covered with much more ice than there is today. High in the mountains, they had seen the giant masses of ice, called glaciers, move and change in size.

They were also the first to explain something that had been puzzling geologists (scientists who study Earth's land and its history). Huge granite boulders were found scattered along the slopes of limestone mountains. Scientists called the strange rocks **erratics**, or wanderers. The mountain people thought that the glaciers had been larger in the past, moving like rivers of ice through the mountains and valleys and carrying the granite erratics. When the ice melted, the rocks were left on the mountain slope—the only sign that the glaciers had been there.

In the early 1800's, two Swiss scientists, Ignatz Venetz and Johann (Jean) de Charpentier, tried to convince their fellow scientists that the ice had carried the erratics. Other scientists found their idea hard to believe. If Venetz and Charpentier were right, it would mean that glacial ice had moved hundreds or thousands of miles from the tops of mountains or the cold regions in the far north to spread over the valley floors.

It was almost twenty years later that another Swiss scientist, Louis Agassiz, conducted experiments that would prove that the giant ice fields had moved. He also showed that the Alpine glaciers had carried huge amounts of rock—a mixture of sand, gravel, mud, and boulders. When the glaciers melted, this rock mixture was left behind. This material is called **glacial till**.

Agassiz learned to recognize erratics and other signs marking the passage of glaciers. Solid rock surfaces were scratched and polished by the ice as it flowed over them. Ridges of rock, called **moraines**, had been left at the ends and sides of glaciers as they retreated. Material collected by the glaciers was deposited over the land in smooth egg-shaped mounds, called **drumlins**, and cone-shaped hills, called **kames**. Rivers and lakes formed as the melted ice filled the valleys and channels cut through the soil by glaciers. All these signs told Agassiz that the glaciers had once been much larger.

▶ FINDING THE ICE AGE

Agassiz saw glacier signs all over northern Europe. Later when he moved to the United States, he saw glacier signs there too. He concluded that there was a time when glaciers covered vast regions of the North.

Since the discoveries Agassiz made, scientists have learned that there were several periods of time when vast regions were covered by ice, each lasting a few million years. The most recent one began about 165 thousand years ago. It is the greatest ice age we know about.

During the most recent period, ice in North America extended all the way through Canada to the United States. Ice reached Wisconsin, swept over New York City, and traveled down the Rocky Mountains and coastal mountains to California and New Mexico. The spreading ice sheets pushed south through Europe to the middle of the continent; the city of Moscow and parts of Germany and Poland were also buried under the ice. Immense amounts of water were trapped in the ice, and the sea level dropped 400 feet. Venice, Italy, a seaport today, was 150 miles from the sea. The lands of Ireland, Britain, and France were all joined, as were North America and Asia.

Ice ages come and go in vast patterns of advance and retreat of the glaciers and ice caps. The advances of ice are called **glacial** stages; the retreats are called **interglacial** (between the glaciers) stages.

Right: Glacial till, a mixture of rocky debris, is spread over a Colorado field once covered with ice. *Below:* Snakelike ridges of rock, called moraines, form at the ends and along the sides of a glacier as it retreats.

Most of the 4.6 billion years Earth has existed, the climate has been warm. There was little or no ice anywhere. But scientists know of at least seven ice eras, long periods marked by advances and retreats of ice. An ice era may last as long as 65 million years. The past 65 million years, the time since the extinction of the dinosaurs, is considered an ice era. During that period there have been half a dozen periods, or epochs, of about 2 or 3 million years when the ice advanced, separated by longer times when there was much less ice.

Within the ice epoch, advances of the ice are the ice ages, which are separated by interglacials. There were four or five ice ages in the last ice epoch, but there were about 20 smaller advances and retreats. The exact dates when ice ages and interglacials occurred are much in dispute. **Oceanographers** (scientists who study the ocean) use samples of the ocean floor to study periods of Earth's history. Based on their studies, oceanographers think the last interglacial ended around 120,000 to 126,000 years ago. Other scientists have evidence from the land that it ended about 147,000 years ago. Recent evidence from studying corals suggests that the date might be anywhere from 122,000 to 130,000 years ago, which supports the oceanographers. Using these findings, geologists have

PLEISTOCENE ICE AGE

Stage	United States Description	European Description
(Fourth Interglacial?)	(Recent)	
Fourth Glacial stage	Wisconsin	Würm
Third Interglacial	Sangamon	Riss-Würm
Third Glacial stage	Illinoian	Riss
Second Interglacial	Yarmouth	Mindel-Riss
Second Glacial stage	Kansan	Mindel
First Interglacial	Aftonian	Günz-Mindel
First Glacial stage	Nebraskan	Günz

put the coldest part of the most recent ice advance at 21,000 years ago.

When scientists name the ice ages, they use the names given to the major time divisions of Earth's history. Each division of time is marked by certain kinds of rock and fossils. We are living in the time division known as the Pleistocene epoch. As the most recent ice age occurred mainly during this epoch, which began about 2 million years ago, it is sometimes called the Pleistocene Ice Age.

▶ LIFE IN THE ICE AGE

The Ice Age shaped the world we know today. Animals and plants changed to fit with the colder climate. Even where it was not much colder, such as near the equator, the climate changed. Ocean temperatures around

Glaciers dragged along rock and other materials. When the ice melted, the rock was left behind in long smooth mounds, called drumlins, and cone-shaped hills, called kames.

the world were lower. Half of the world's ocean water was covered with ice. There was also less rainfall. Thick forests needing large amounts of water to grow were replaced by grasslands, which required less water.

A few places that are dry today had abundant rainfall during the Ice Age. The American Southwest received enough rainfall to nourish giant lakes, including one where Death Valley (a desert) is today. Much of the Great Plains, an area stretching across the west central part of North America, is grassland today. But during the Ice Age it was lush forest. In Europe, however, there was almost no forest land.

Where there was no ice or only seasonal ice, plants and animals thrived. Some of them would be familiar today. Most of the plants, as well as the small animals, were similar to the ones living today in regions with the same kinds of climate.

Animals of the Ice Age

The large animals of the Ice Age are quite different from animals living today. For one thing, many were very large. There were giant beavers, kangaroos 10 feet (3 meters) tall, and

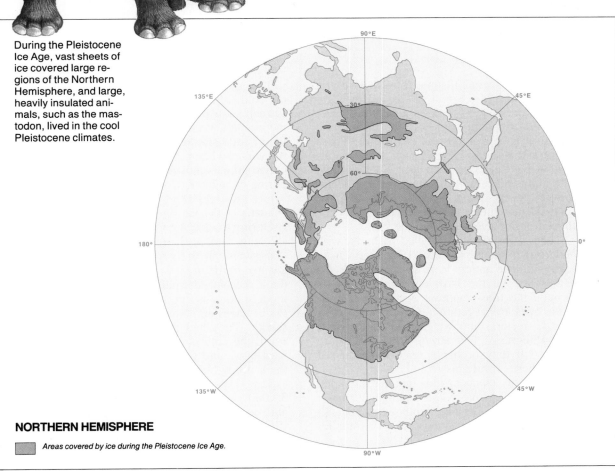

During the Pleistocene Ice Age, vast sheets of ice covered large regions of the Northern Hemisphere, and large, heavily insulated animals, such as the mastodon, lived in the cool Pleistocene climates.

NORTHERN HEMISPHERE

Areas covered by ice during the Pleistocene Ice Age.

As the society of the Cro-Magnons developed, so did the tools they made. The many different kinds of tools they created, such as (left to right) harpoons and fishhooks, scrapers, and batons, helped them survive the ice ages.

armadillos 7 feet (2 meters) long. Bison with horns measuring 6.5 feet (2 meters) from tip to tip lived then, as well as a relative of the two-toed sloth that could rear up on its hind legs to a height of 20 feet (6 meters). These large animals were plant eaters. Giant carnivores (meat eaters), such as cave lions and saber-toothed cats with long stabbing teeth, preyed on the plant eaters. Other animals, such as giant vultures and dire wolves, flocked to feed on the leftovers from the kills.

There were giant deer called Irish elk, with antlers that spread 12 feet (3.7 meters) from tip to tip. The antlers were so large some scientists believe the Irish elk could not pass through the forest without becoming tangled in the trees and vegetation. Cave bears 10 feet long (3 meters) and weighing 1,500 pounds (680 kilograms) had strong teeth and sharp claws, but they probably lived on a diet of mostly berries and grasses.

Herds of elephant-like creatures called mammoths and mastodons roamed the land. The largest type of mammoth was about 13 feet (4 meters) tall. The mastodon was smaller at about 10 feet (3 meters).

The animals were well suited to living in the cold. Many of them had thick furry coats to keep them warm. During Ice Age summers, the animals ate huge amounts of food, which their bodies stored as fat, to help them survive the winter when food was not so easy to find. Other animals moved south to the forest areas during the winter.

Humans in the Ice Age

During the Ice Age, our ancestors faced the challenges of a changing climate. Neanderthals were an early people who were well adapted to life in the Ice Age. Scientists do not think the Neanderthal is a direct ancestor of modern humans but rather like a close cousin to our ancestors. Neanderthals were short and stocky. They had large noses, which helped warm the cold air they breathed. Faced with hard tasks and limited tools, they developed thick strong bones.

The last Neanderthals vanished about 35,000 years ago. Although scientists are not able to explain how the Neanderthals vanished, they have found clues to how they lived. Neanderthals gathered plants to eat and also were superb hunters. They took care of the old and ill, and they buried their dead.

About 40,000 years ago, people who were just like modern humans appeared in Europe. There is increasing evidence that these people, often called Cro-Magnons, lived in Africa much earlier than they lived in Europe. They were not physically adapted for the Ice Age environment as the Neanderthals were. But they were much more advanced culturally. Most built shelters to live in. They also used tools to make weapons for hunting game. Art, such as paintings of animals on cave walls, bone carvings, and modeled clay objects, was produced by Cro-Magnons. All people on Earth today appear to be their descendants.

Conditions during the Ice Age helped humans travel to many different areas of the world. Asia and North America were joined by land between Siberia and Alaska. Northwest Alaska was not covered by glaciers, so it was an attractive hunting and fishing ground for people in icebound Siberia.

The lower sea level enabled humans to travel to Australia: At the height of the Ice Age, the islands of Indonesia were, for the most part, connected by land to Asia. Only thin ribbons of water separated the islands, which formed stepping stones of land to Australia. It was a fairly simple matter for humans to cross the strips of water. Bone fragments place the time they reached Australia as at least 60,000 years ago.

When the ice began to retreat about 12,500 years ago, the way was opened for the people from Alaska to move into the remainder of North America. Because Central America connects North and South America, there were also some people who traveled from North America to South America.

▶ **THE GREAT ICE AGE EXTINCTION**

Near the end of the Ice Age, most of the large animals no longer existed. In some cases, the changing climate was the cause. However, many scientists think there may have been a different cause for many of the changes in the animal populations. One reason scientists suspect a different cause is that most of the extinctions took place shortly after the arrival of northern hunters.

These hunters, from Alaska and connecting lands, were named Clovis people. Their characteristic arrowheads, or Clovis points, have been found across most of North America. Often they are found embedded in the long-buried bones of huge Ice Age animals. Some think the Clovis people were such good hunters they killed whole populations of animals, such as mammoths. Animals that preyed on the mammoths then died out, or became extinct, because the Clovis people had killed all their food.

The hunter theory can also account for some animals (such as the brown bear and the American bison) becoming physically smaller,

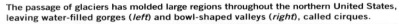

The passage of glaciers has molded large regions throughout the northern United States, leaving water-filled gorges (*left*) and bowl-shaped valleys (*right*), called cirques.

and it explains why animals in places where hunting is allowed are not as large as the same kind of animals in protected nature reserves: Hunters kill the largest animals first. The smaller animals that escape being killed tend to produce the same-sized offspring. Soon the whole hunted population consists of smaller animals.

By 10,000 years ago, the plants and animals we have today were all that remained in Europe and North America. However, there were no horses or camels in North America. The Spanish explorers brought horses from Europe in the 1500's. Some got free and are the ancestors of the wild horses of today's West. In the 1800's, the U.S. Army brought camels to the southwestern desert. A few wild camels still roam parts of Arizona and New Mexico.

▶ TAKING EARTH'S TEMPERATURE

The first **glaciologists** (people who study glaciers) such as Venetz, Charpentier, and Agassiz used physical evidence to support their Ice Age theories. They looked for scratches in rocks caused by glaciers. They examined the huge rocks that were moved by glaciers. They studied the glacial patterns of moraines and drumlins and the kinds of lakes typically formed by glaciers. However they were only able to establish that there had been one ice age; they did not realize there had been other ice ages. The early scientists saw only one ice age because the last one wiped out most traces of the earlier ones.

Scientists have developed new methods to learn about ice-age climates. One way is to study the ice and snow from the past. To get a sample, scientists bore into a glacier using a drill with a hollow cylinder. When the drill is brought up, a cylinder of ice, called a core, fills the hollow within the drill.

Recognizable layers in the core show differences in the amount of ice and snow that can be matched up to changes in the weather. Some winters receive more snow than others. When more snow falls each winter than melts in summer, the glacier grows larger. When less snow falls than melts, the glacier shrinks. While measuring layers in glaciers is useful, as time goes by the layers begin to blend together. After about 100,000 years, scientists cannot tell much about past climates from the ice layers in glacier cores.

Another method of studying ancient climates looks at the kinds of plants, animals, and other small creatures living in various climates. Although fossils of whole plants are hard to find, many flowering plants produce large amounts of pollen, which is blown over

The solid rock surface beneath a moving glacier is polished and scratched (*below*) and gouged out (*right*) by the loose rock carried along in the bottom of the ice.

A micrograph display (*far right*) of the shells of tiny one-celled animals (forams). A sediment core (*right*) taken from the ocean has a dark layer containing cold-water foram shells and a lighter layer containing warm-water foram shells.

large regions. Almost any rock formed from mud or sand has plant pollen in it— that is if it was formed after the start of flowering plants (at least 120 million years ago). Scientists assume that plants thriving in cold weather today would have thrived in the cold weather of the past. So when pollen from those plants is found in rock formations, it means that the climate must have been cool. When pollen from hot-weather plants is found in rock formations, it means the climate must have been hot when the rock formed.

Because the pollen method is only good for the past 120 million years, scientists looked for a better way to study climate changes of ancient times. In the 1920's, Wolfgang Shott observed that some types of tiny sea creatures called **foraminifera** (or **forams**) lived only in warm water, while others lived only in cold water. Each type of foram has its own distinctive hard shell. Even after hundreds of thousands of years, scientists could tell whether ancient water had been warm or cold during a particular time period by the types of foram shells left on the ocean bottom.

A process much like drilling for an ice core is used to get the foram shells. A hollow drill is sunk into the ocean bottom to collect a core of the ocean's sand and mud. The layers of soil are examined to see whether the shells they contain are cold-water forams or warm-water forams. With this method, the changes in the ancient climate from warm to cold and back to warm could be found, but not the actual temperatures.

The search continued for a better way to find out what the temperatures were in the past. About 1950 another method was found that also used forams, but in a different way

—this time, the shells of the forams were analyzed to determine what kinds of oxygen were present.

Oxygen is the most common element on Earth. There are two kinds of oxygen in the air we breathe. One kind is light oxygen, called O^{16}. The other oxygen, O^{18}, is heavier, and it is also rarer. The ocean also contains large amounts of oxygen. Most of it is O^{16}, but there is also a little of the heavier O^{18}.

The shells of forams are made of a chemical containing oxygen. The oxygen is absorbed from seawater. As the water becomes warmer, more of the heavier oxygen is absorbed. As it becomes colder, more of the lighter kind is used by the forams. When a sea core is taken, the amounts of O^{16} and O^{18} found in the forams are studied. The past temperature of the water can be calculated by using the amounts of oxygen in the shells, along with information about the salt content of the seawater. Finally, comparing the varying amounts of oxygen found in the forams at different levels in the core supplies information about the number of times the land had been covered with glaciers.

▶THE CAUSE OF ICE AGES

Shortly after Agassiz convinced others that Earth had once been buried under huge ice sheets, people began to wonder what had caused the ice. One of the first to offer an explanation was a French mathematician named Joseph A. Adhémar. In 1842, he suggested that the Ice Age was brought about by astronomical events—that the slow, regular changes in Earth's orbit and its tilt and spin were responsible for changing Earth's climate.

Adhémar concluded that about 11,000 years ago, northern winters were much colder because the Northern Hemisphere was the farthest away it could be from the sun. He also predicted that after about another 11,000 years, when the distance from the sun was again at its greatest, there would be another ice age. Adhémar's theory seemed reasonable at first. But as more information about the ice ages appeared, scientists were able to establish that ice ages did not come approximately every 22,000 years.

Other scientists revised Adhémar's theory. James Croll, a Scottish scientist, predicted that every 100,000 years when Earth's path took it the farthest from the sun, there would be an ice age 11,000 years long in the North. This would be followed by an ice age of 11,000 years in the Southern Hemisphere. Then another 100,000 years would pass without an ice age. Croll's ideas were also accepted, at first. But as the dating methods for the ice ages were developed, it was clear that an ice age did not develop every 100,000 years.

A Yugoslavian scientist, Milutin Milankovitch, further refined Adhémar's work. After years of study, Milankovitch developed mathematical formulas to describe the relationship of the changes in Earth's tilt, orbit, and spin to the changes in Earth's climate. He calculated that these three factors work together to vary the amount of sunshine reaching the Northern Hemisphere. According to Milankovitch, the amounts of sunshine were varied enough to allow the advance of great ice sheets across the continents.

As time went on, new information about the dates of the ice ages did not always support the predictions made by Milankovitch. However, many scientists use the relationship he described between Earth and the sun as part of other theories. A more recent theory combines that relationship with the interaction between the ocean and the atmosphere to explain the changes in glacial cycles.

▶ IS THE ICE ABOUT TO RETURN?

Predicting when or if great amounts of ice will once again cover Earth depends on which theory is used. If the Milankovitch theory is correct, the ice should not return for 3,000 to 7,000 years. Some believe we are in an interglacial period that has already lasted 11,000 years. Because the last four interglacial periods lasted between 8,000 and 12,000 years, they believe that the ice will return soon.

All predictions are affected by many other factors. Earth's crust is broken into large slow-moving sections called plates. These plates carry the continents along as they move. The changing positions of continents and large islands influence where ice forms. These movements also cause changes in mountain ranges and ocean currents. Both mountain ranges and ocean currents affect the climate in specific regions. If they cool the climate in regions that are already cold, such as polar areas, glaciers will form.

Certain gases in the atmosphere, especially carbon dioxide, influence the climate. These gases are called greenhouse gases because they trap the sun's heat the way a greenhouse does. Evidence from bubbles trapped in glaciers suggest that the amount of carbon dioxide was very low during the last glacial periods. Today, human activity is putting more carbon dioxide and other greenhouse gases into the atmosphere. This could cause the climate to become warmer, thus preventing another glacial period. On the other hand, a warmer climate might result in changes that could be as devastating as another ice age. If all the ice around the world were to melt, the sea level would rise about 200 feet (61 meters). Lands around the world would be flooded. Many islands would be lost. Whole cities would disappear under the water.

Measurements of various kinds have indicated that Earth has been cooling down for the past 6,000 years. The cooling is very gradual and for decades or even centuries at a time, temperatures rise rather than fall. Temperatures have been measured for many years by weather stations around the world, and so far, the temperatures of the 1980's and 1990's have been the highest recorded. However, some measurements made by weather satellites do not show the development of any long-term trend of cool or warm temperatures.

Will we have another ice age soon? It is difficult to predict correctly whether it will rain next week. No one can be sure about ice ages either. But if humans have not changed the climate too much, just as we know it will rain sometimes in the future, we can be certain that another ice age will come.

BRYAN BUNCH
President, Scientific Publishing

See also CLIMATE; EARTH, HISTORY OF; GEOLOGY; GLACIERS; ICE; OCEANOGRAPHY.

A noise like thunder fills the air as the huge chunks of ice breaking away from the Columbia Glacier in Alaska crash into the sea.

An iceberg, which may take several years to melt as it drifts along on ocean currents, towers above a vessel traveling in nearby icy waters.

ICEBERGS

From a distance it looks like a white mountain rising majestically out of the ocean. It is an iceberg—a floating island of freshwater ice. Icebergs are chunks broken off from the great masses of land ice called glaciers. Most icebergs in the Northern Hemisphere come from Greenland. Icebergs in the Southern Hemisphere come from Antarctica.

Icebergs vary greatly in size, but what is seen is only a part of the iceberg. Most of its mass, about $9/10$ to $7/8$, is hidden under the water. Some icebergs are relatively small. They may be about 300 feet (91 meters) long and rise 10 feet (3 meters) out of the ocean. The largest North Atlantic iceberg measured 4 miles (6.4 kilometers) long. Icebergs from the Antarctic tend to be bigger and have flatter tops than icebergs in the North Atlantic. The biggest iceberg ever recorded was found in the Antarctic. It was 200 miles (322 kilometers) long and 60 miles (97 kilometers) wide—bigger than the country of Belgium or the state of Vermont.

How Icebergs Form.   Most of Greenland and Antarctica are covered by glaciers year round. Glaciers also cover some parts of Alaska. They are formed by layers of packed ice and may be thousands of feet thick. Glaciers are pulled forward to lower ground by gravity. Finally, their front ends, or **tongues**, reach down to the sea. At the coast, the tips of the tongues break off, plunge into the ocean, and become icebergs. This process is called **calv-**

ing. When calving occurs, a loud cracking noise fills the air. Sometimes a low rumbling can be heard for hours before the ice actually breaks; then comes a hissing as air escapes from bubbles bursting in the ice along the break.

Glaciers calve throughout the year. Just as many icebergs break off in the winter as in the summer. But in the winter, their passageway to the ocean may be blocked by frozen seawater. Icebergs pile up behind the sea ice until spring. When sea ice melts and breaks up in spring, a whole fleet of icebergs may sail out into the open ocean. Because of fog and the release of so many icebergs, spring is a particularly dangerous time for shipping. Many shipping companies take more southerly routes at this time of year.

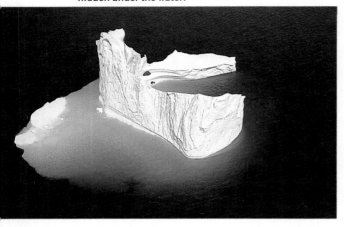

Only a small part of an iceberg is visible above the water's surface. Most of its bulk (about nine-tenths) is hidden under the water.

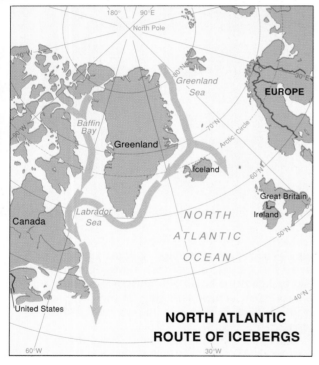

NORTH ATLANTIC ROUTE OF ICEBERGS

The Melting of an Iceberg. Icebergs start to melt and break up almost as soon as they are afloat. Icebergs from the Northern Atlantic drift along the Greenland and Labrador currents south into the warmer waters of the Gulf Stream. Many move into shipping lanes. Antarctic icebergs float north into more temperate climates, where they melt. They rarely get far enough north to interfere with shipping.

As icebergs drift into warmer and warmer water, cracks appear and become filled with water from the melting iceberg. When this meltwater freezes at night, it expands and widens the cracks. Finally, icebergs melt down to bergy bits, chunks about the size of a house. Many make so much noise as they float along in the ocean they are called growlers.

Patrolling the Ocean. It is difficult to tell precisely how far an iceberg extends under the surface from what can be seen above the ocean. In a thick fog, during a storm, or at night, icebergs can be deadly, as they were on the night of April 14, 1912. This is the date of the sinking of the British ship *Titanic*. It was the biggest and supposedly the safest ship ever built, but it sank on its first voyage, from England to New York City. The *Titanic* hit an iceberg that tore six narrow gashes in its hull. It sank about 2½ hours later. More than 1,500 people were lost in the icy seas.

After the sinking of the *Titanic*, an international conference was called to find a way to prevent such disasters. As a result of the conference, the International Ice Patrol was formed. The United States Coast Guard maintains the International Ice Patrol, and countries whose ships sail the North Atlantic contribute to the cost. The ice patrol has been charting icebergs in the North Atlantic shipping lanes since 1914. It transmits information about the location and approximate size of sighted icebergs. Since the International Ice Patrol was started, no lives have been lost due to icebergs in the patrolled area.

Using Icebergs. Experts have looked for ways to use icebergs for several decades. Although it was never completed, a plan was developed during World War II to use icebergs as natural aircraft carriers. The international community has considered ways to harvest the great amounts of fresh water trapped in icebergs. Eventually a workable plan may be developed to tow icebergs to water-poor nations. Once there, the iceberg could be melted to provide a plentiful source of fresh water.

REBECCA B. MARCUS
Author, *First Book of Glaciers*
Reviewed by A. L. LONSDALE
Lieutenant Commander
United States Coast Guard

See also ICE; ICE AGES.

Fast and easy to handle, the DN is one of the most popular single-seating iceboats.

ICEBOATING

Iceboating is the sport of sailing on ice—often at high speeds. Whether it is sailing purely for pleasure or in competition, iceboating is an exciting sport. Skilled iceboaters can reach speeds of almost four times the prevailing wind speed, sailing across the ice at more than 100 miles (160 kilometers) an hour.

An iceboat is a small craft similar to a sailboat. It is fitted with sharp blades on the bottom of the hull, or body, of the boat. The blades let the boat travel swiftly and smoothly across the ice. Areas with large bodies of water and cold winter temperatures are ideal for iceboating, which is also called ice yachting. In the cold-weather climates of the northern United States (particularly New York, New Jersey, and the Great Lakes region) and northern European nations, it is a popular sport.

▶THE START OF ICEBOATING

Iceboating has a long history. Some experts believe it may be traced back to a period of over 4,000 years ago, when primitive man may have attached bone runners to sleds. The sleds were powered by the force of the wind against sails attached to the sleds. The first iceboats as we know them were most likely used in the Netherlands during the 1600's. Iron runners were placed on sailboats in order to travel along frozen canals, transporting people and goods.

The first iceboats in the United States were probably built or imported from Europe by Dutch settlers, who sailed them along frozen stretches of the Hudson River. After the Civil War, iceboating enthusiasts formed clubs, such as the Poughkeepsie Ice Yacht Club (1865) and the Hudson River Ice Yacht Club (1870).

In the 1930's, more people were drawn to the sport with the introduction of small, lightweight, and less expensive iceboats such as the iceboat called a skeeter. The sport remains popular today, with about 8,000 iceboaters in the United States and about 2,000 in Europe. The International Skeeter Association is the most popular iceboating organization today.

▶TYPES OF ICEBOATS

Iceboats generally have long, narrow hulls made of wood, aluminum, or fiberglass. Most boats are between 16 and 22 feet (5 and 7 meters) long. Iceboats have room for one or two persons who sail in a sitting or semi-reclining position. There are two chief kinds of iceboats in use today: (1) the triangular iceboat with three runners, and (2) the oval, rounded-bottom boat known as the scooter.

Most iceboats are steered by a steering runner, called a rudder. The rudder is placed either at the rear, or stern, of the boat on a stern-steerer, or at the front, or bow, of the boat on a bow-steerer. The first iceboats were stern-steerers. In America, stern-steerers, called Hudson River type boats, were large boats up to 70 feet (21 meters) long. The huge sails they carried were as large as 1,000 square feet (93 square meters).

Bow-steerers were built beginning in the 1920's, when the emphasis in iceboat construction was on strength and lightness. Many bow-steered iceboats consist of a small triangular platform with a single runner in front and two runners in back. The advantage of steering with a front rudder is that it helps to prevent side-slipping. The bow-steered design continues to be the most popular iceboat design today, with the skeeter and the DN, named for the Detroit News Craftsmen's Shop, the most popular versions.

Another type of iceboat, the scooter, has no rudder at all. The inventors of the scooter needed a craft that could cross ice and patches of open water to rescue people or transport goods. The scooter has a rounded bottom, to which metal runners are attached, and is steered by moving the sails.

▶ SAILING AN ICEBOAT

Equipment. Iceboating requires warm clothing and special shoes with spikes (creepers) attached to help iceboaters grip the ice. Heavy sweaters, jackets, gloves, and hats are essential to guard against frostbite. Some iceboaters also wear knee and elbow pads. Goggles are needed to protect against snow and flying ice, and a helmet is necessary to protect the head in case of an accident.

On the Ice. When ideal conditions for iceboating occur, which may be only a few days each season, iceboaters are out on the ice in great numbers. Iceboats run best on clear, glass-smooth ice. The iceboater begins by pushing the boat with the sail let out. As the boat gathers speed, the iceboater runs alongside, then jumps into the boat and pulls in the sail to increase the boat's speed. Iceboats are sailed in much the same way as sailboats, using steering techniques, called tacking and jibing, that use the wind and the sails to change the direction of the boat.

Safety precautions are an essential part of iceboating. Before any sailing, boats are checked to see that they are in good condition and securely assembled. Careful iceboaters learn the characteristics of their boats and the skills to manage them, such as how to stop quickly by either sailing into the wind or dropping the sail and moving in small circles. Probably the most important safety measure for an iceboater to follow is: Never leave an iceboat with its sail up unattended. Whenever they are sailing, iceboaters must be on the alert for other sailors or people on the ice. Safety measures in iceboating include looking ahead (especially before changing direction), giving other boats the room they need to maneuver, and staying away from crowded areas when traveling at high speeds.

A technique known as hiking may pose special hazards. To hike in an iceboat is to lift the windward runner up off the ice and sail on two runners only. This maneuver, which is used in racing, increases the boat's speed, but can lead to an accident. If the hike is too high, the boat may tip over.

Open water is another hazard iceboaters may face. As temperatures increase during the day, enough ice may melt in a certain area to create open water, and iceboaters must take great care to avoid sailing into it.

▶ ICEBOAT RACES

Once the nimble bow-steerers were introduced, they quickly replaced the large, slow stern-steering iceboats in popularity. Today the stern-steerers are no longer produced. However, there are some stern-steerers that have been maintained or restored. These can still be raced, but there are very few competitions open to them.

Sanctioned iceboating competitions are organized for bow-steerers according to classes based on specification such as type, sail size, mast height, and number of sailors. The Northwestern Ice Yachting Association and the Eastern Ice Yachting Association have organized divisions for skeeters, DN, Nite, Renegade, and Arrow iceboats.

Iceboat races are usually held on a course marked out by buoys about a mile (1.6 kilometers) apart. Racing iceboats do not sail directly downwind because they cannot reach top speeds in that way. Instead, they sail across the wind, which allows them to reach much higher speeds.

STEPHEN C. TURNER
Author, *Great Beginnings:
Olympics to Superbowl*

ICE CREAM

Ice cream is one of the world's most popular desserts and snack foods. It is a frozen food made mostly of cream, milk, sugar, water, and flavorings. Its appeal comes from the different flavors available and the ways in which ice cream can be served—in dishes, cones, sundaes, milkshakes, sodas, cakes, and many other fun and interesting ways.

▶ HOW ICE CREAM IS MADE

Ice cream was once considered a delicacy because it was so difficult to make. The ingredients used to be shaken by hand in a pan surrounded by salt and ice until the mixture cooled and became firm. About 1846, a hand-cranked freezer was developed, which was difficult to operate but was still easier to use than the pan method. The continuous freezer (a fast industrial freezer) was developed in the 1920's, which made the manufacture of ice cream quick and economical. It soon became easier to buy packaged ice cream at a store than to make it at home.

Today ice cream is made in factories from a liquid mix of milk, cream, sugar, and sometimes eggs. Stabilizers are added to prevent large ice crystals from forming and to keep the ice cream from melting too quickly. Emulsifiers are added to give the ice cream a smooth texture.

The mix is pasteurized to reduce bacteria, and homogenized to distribute the milk-fat particles evenly throughout. Then it is cooled as it flows over refrigerated pipes into a vat, where it "ages" for 3 to 4 hours. Then it is quickly frozen at a temperature of about 22° F ($-6°$ C). Air is whipped into the mix as it freezes to make the ice cream smoother. The amount of air mixed in—called overrun—also determines how dense, or heavy, the ice cream becomes. In the United States, a gallon (3.8 liters) of ice cream is required by law to weigh at least 4.5 pounds (2 kilograms). Ice creams with low overrun, or less air, are considered by many people to be of higher quality.

Before freezing, liquid flavorings, such as vanilla, are added to the ice cream. Fruits and nuts are added partially frozen. While it is still fairly soft, the ice cream is packaged. Machines fold, fill, and close the cartons or cups that you buy in the store. The process of freez-

Ice cream is one of the world's most popular foods. "Plain old vanilla" is the most requested flavor.

ing is finished as the ice cream travels on a conveyor belt inside a cold tunnel. From the tunnel the ice cream is stored in a hardening room at temperatures as low as $-30°$ F ($-34°$ C). Then it is loaded onto refrigerated trucks and carried to stores and restaurants.

▶ STORING AND SERVING ICE CREAM

Ice cream may be stored in a home freezer for several months. (The colder the temperature, the longer the ice cream can be stored.)

Who invented the ice cream cone?

Ernest A. Hamwi, an immigrant to the United States from Damascus, Syria, had a booth at the 1904 Louisiana Purchase Exposition in St. Louis, Missouri. Hamwi sold zalabia, a crisp pastry baked on a waffle iron and served with sugar or other sweets.

Next to Hamwi's booth was an ice cream vendor. At that time, ice cream was served in dishes. But one hot day the ice cream vendor ran out of clean dishes. Hamwi quickly rolled one of his warm waffles into the shape of a cone, which hardened in a few seconds as it cooled. He offered it to his neighbor, who put the ice cream in it and handed it to an eager customer. And that is how the ice cream cone was born.

Before serving, let the ice cream soften for a few minutes. Once the carton has been opened, wrap it in foil or plastic to keep the ice cream from absorbing odors and to prevent a skin from forming on the surface. Melted ice cream should not be refrozen.

▶THE FOOD VALUE OF ICE CREAM

Ice cream is a nutritious food. Like milk, it contains protein, calcium, phosphorus, and vitamin A. The U.S. Food and Drug Administration requires that ice cream contain at least 20 percent milk solids. Ice cream, however, contains sugar and is higher in calories than milk, so it should be substituted for milk only as a special treat.

▶OTHER FROZEN DAIRY PRODUCTS

Ice cream has many companion products. **French ice cream** (frozen custard) has had egg yolks added to the ice cream mix. **Ice milk** is a frozen dessert that is very much like ice cream but has less milk fat (from 2 to 7 percent). Ice milk and **soft ice cream** are not frozen as long as regular ice cream. These products are often sold at roadside stands.

U.S. government regulations say that vanilla ice cream must contain at least 10 percent milk fat, but in many ice creams, the percentage is higher. **Gelato** is the Italian word for "frozen." It is used in the United States to refer to a very rich ice cream with a low overrun and a cooked egg-custard base. Some frozen products, such as **mellorine** and **tofutti**, taste like ice cream, but their fat content comes from vegetable sources instead of milk.

Sherbets are another product of the industry. They are often flavored with fruits or fruit juices, which give them a tart flavor, and they contain some milk products. The milk-fat content of sherbet is not much more than 1 percent, but there is a high sugar content. **Ices** are similiar to their first cousins, the sherbets, but no milk ingredients are added.

▶HISTORY

The history of ice cream is a mystery. No one knows exactly where or when people began to eat it. One story tells how the Roman emperor Nero sent slaves to the mountains to bring back snow, which was served to him sweetened with honey and fruit pulp. We do know that Marco Polo tasted flavored ices during his famous travels in Asia because he brought back the recipes when he returned to Italy in 1295.

Recipes for flavored ices spread from Italy to the rest of Europe in the 1500's. The chefs of kings constantly experimented with new combinations to please their masters. At some point, cream and butter were added to the recipes, and the new dish was called "cream ice."

It is not known exactly when ice cream was first made in the United States. One of the earliest-known American references to ice cream was in a tavern's advertisement in a New York newspaper in 1786. Dolley Madison, wife of President James Madison, was the first to serve ice cream in the White House in the early 1800's. Throughout the 1800's, "ice cream socials" became a popular way to entertain friends. Everyone helped shake the pans or turn the crank of the freezer, and homemade peach or strawberry ice cream was the reward for their hard work. Today people can still have fun making ice cream at home with electric or hand-cranked ice cream machines.

GLENN WITTE
International Association of Ice Cream
Manufacturers

See also DAIRYING AND DAIRY PRODUCTS.

Families have enjoyed making ice cream at home since 1846, when the hand-cranked freezer was invented.

Ice hockey has been called the world's fastest team sport. The main objective of the game is to score a goal by shooting a puck into the other team's net.

ICE HOCKEY

Hockey has been called the world's fastest team sport. The game is played on ice by two teams of six players. The basic objectives of hockey are simple: Shoot a small rubber disk, called a puck, into the other team's net, and prevent the opponent from scoring goals.

A goal is scored when the puck is shot or deflected legally across the goal line. The last offensive player to touch the puck is credited with the goal and up to two other players can be awarded assists on the play.

▶THE HOCKEY RINK

Hockey is played on an oval sheet of ice usually 200 feet (61 meters) long and 85 feet (26 meters) wide. A wall roughly 3 feet (1 meter) high, known as the boards, surrounds the ice surface. Above the boards, Plexiglas panels keep the puck in play and protect spectators from flying pucks. Hockey was played first on natural ice, but now most standard rinks have artificial ice surfaces.

In European and Olympic hockey, the ice surface is larger—200 feet (61 meters) long by 100 feet (30.3 meters) wide. This places a greater emphasis on passing and reduces the physical contact between players.

The ice surface is divided into three zones, which are marked by two blue lines 60 feet (18 meters) from each goal. The middle of the rink is called center ice, or the neutral zone. The end in which a team has its goal is its defensive zone, while the other end is its offensive zone.

There is a red line at center ice and goal lines, which are also red, at each end. In front of each goal is a semicircle 12 feet (3.7 meters) wide by 4 feet (1.2 meters) deep called the crease. If an attacking player is in the crease when a goal is scored, the goal does not count.

▶RINK EQUIPMENT

The goal is made of metal pipe 2 inches (5 centimeters) in diameter, 4 feet (1.2 meters) high, and 6 feet (1.8 meters) wide. It is covered by strong netting to catch the puck when a goal is scored. Until the late 1980's, pipes sunk into the ice held the goal firmly in place, making the goal almost unmovable when a player collided with it. Magnetic anchors now allow the net to move when hit hard by a player, reducing the risk of injury.

Teams have 18 skaters and 2 goalies in uniform for each game. Players' benches are just behind the boards along the sides of the rink. The timekeepers sit in a special area, usually close to the penalty box.

A bell, horn, or siren signals the end of each of the three 20-minute periods. In addition to the game clock, the scoreboard often has small clocks to show the times of penalties. A goal judge sits behind the boards in back of each net and indicates that a goal has been scored by switching on a red light.

▶ PLAYING EQUIPMENT

Each hockey organization has its own rules governing the equipment worn by players. The skates, pants, shin guards, elbow pads, shoulder pads, gloves, helmets, and sticks must meet the organization's standards.

A standard ice hockey rink is shown with dimensions, goals, markings, and players' positions. Between the blue lines is the neutral zone, divided in half by a red center line. The game is started or restarted after a referee's call in the face-off circles and spots (in red).

10 ft (3 m)

goal cage
goal crease
12 ft (3.7m)
end zone face-off circle
30 ft (9 m)
60 ft (18 m)
blue line
30 ft (9 m)
200 ft (61 m)
center face-off circle
center line (red line)
left wing
right wing
center
face-off spot
30 ft (9 m)
blue line
left defense
right defense
60 ft (18 m)
goal line
goalie
6 ft (1.8 m)
10 ft (3 m)
85 ft (26 m)

As the game of hockey developed, hockey equipment has kept pace. Ice skate blades were once attached to the bottom of boots. Now the skate and blade are one unit. Hockey pants were once constructed of canvas lined with felt. Felt was also used in shoulder and shin pads. Modern hockey equipment is made from high-tech materials that are not only lightweight and durable but also afford greater protection. Hockey pants are made of nylon. Plastic and foam are used in pads, shin guards, and gloves, which are light, flexible, and very strong.

The stick and puck have changed little. Hockey sticks were once made from a single piece of wood. Now they are often constructed from laminates (layers of wood) and covered with fiberglass to add strength. Aluminum shafts with replaceable wooden blades have also gained popularity. The stick must not exceed 53 inches (135 centimeters) in length from the heel to the end of the handle. The blade, which is usually curved, may not be more than 14.8 inches (37.5 centimeters) long, nor more than 3 inches (7.6 centimeters) high. The puck is a hard rubber disk 1 inch (2.5 centimeters) thick and 3 inches (7.6 cen-

Ice hockey players require considerable protective equipment because of the speed and force of the game. The equipment worn by forwards and defensive players (*opposite page A*) is usually streamlined. It may include a helmet and face mask (1), chest protector and shoulder pads (2), elbow pads (3), gloves (4), hip and thigh pads (5), knee pads and shin guards (6), skates (7), and hockey stick (8).

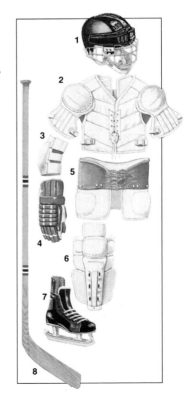

timeters) in diameter. It may not weigh less than 5.5 ounces (156 grams) or more than 6 ounces (170 grams).

Goalies wear special chest and arm protection; large leg pads, which can be no more than 10 inches (25.4 centimeters) wide; and special gloves. A catching glove is similar to a first baseman's mitt in baseball. A backhand glove, called a blocker, has a rectangular pad used to deflect the puck. Goalies' skates have longer blades and steel toes for protection from the puck. A full helmet with wire face mask has become increasingly popular, but some face masks are molded from rubber and plastic. The goalie's stick has a straight blade 4.5 inches (11.4 centimeters) high.

▶ THE PLAYERS

Since 1911, ice hockey has been played with six players: a goalie, two defensemen, center, left wing, and right wing. Before then, teams had a seventh player on the ice as well. This player was called a rover. Captains and alternate captains, designated by the letters C and A on their jerseys, are the only players allowed to speak to the referee about the interpretation of a rule.

Because of the fast pace and the physical demands of the sport, substitutions can be made at any time during a game. However, no more than six players are allowed on the ice at one time.

▶ BASIC SKILLS

Because hockey is played on ice skates, it is one of the few sports that requires a learned form of movement. A player's skating ability it crucial to success in the sport. Poor skating ability has kept players with strong skills in other parts of the game from making the top hockey leagues.

Stickhandling, passing the puck, team play, an instinct for the game, and a commitment to winning are also important.

Since a season lasts up to nine months in the professional leagues, physical conditioning is a fundamental part of hockey training. Players now train during the off-season to build up stamina and endurance.

Skating. The average player may skate 3 miles (5 kilometers) during a game and reach speeds of 20 miles (32 kilometers) per hour. Hockey players have improved as skaters over the years because of better skating instruction

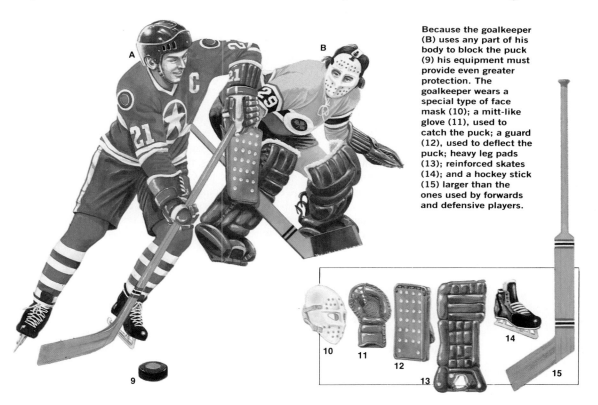

Because the goalkeeper (B) uses any part of his body to block the puck (9) his equipment must provide even greater protection. The goalkeeper wears a special type of face mask (10); a mitt-like glove (11), used to catch the puck; a guard (12), used to deflect the puck; heavy leg pads (13); reinforced skates (14); and a hockey stick (15) larger than the ones used by forwards and defensive players.

programs for young players. It is very important for players to be able to start and stop quickly, to turn in both directions, and to skate backward swiftly. A player must also combine skating skills with puck handling skills. In training players, European hockey specialists use soccer, gymnastics, and special exercises that enhance balance and agility, to develop strong skating.

Shooting. Scoring goals is the essence of hockey. In order to make a good shot, a player must have a stick of the proper length, weight, and "lie." The lie is the angle at which the handle meets the blade.

The slap shot is used often. It propels the puck at a high rate of speed. The puck is hit with the blade of the stick in a movement much like a golf swing. However, many coaches and players prefer the wrist shot, because of its greater accuracy and quicker release. The backhand, a reverse wrist shot, is less powerful. However, this shot has a high success rate because it often catches the goalie off guard.

Shots to the low and high corners of the net are the most difficult for the goalie to stop. Most goals are scored from the "slot," the area directly in front of the net.

Passing and Stickhandling. Controlling the puck with the stick is another fundamental hockey skill. The ability to make an accurate pass and to receive a pass while skating at fast speeds is very important in hockey, where team play is emphasized. The puck travels faster than a player can, so passing is a more effective means of moving the puck than stickhandling.

Checking

Checking. Checking is the most popular defensive skill and can take several forms. A defender can use his body to throw an opponent off balance and force him to lose control of the puck. A defender can also check an opponent with his stick as long as he does not break the rules. The poke check is difficult but useful for stealing the puck in open ice.

▶**HOW TO PLAY**

The game consists of three 20-minute periods with a 12- to 15-minute intermission between them. To start the game, the referee drops the puck at center ice between the two opposing centers. This is called a face-off. Each center tries to gain possession of the puck and build an attack toward the other team's goal.

A face-off at center ice is also used to resume play whenever a goal is scored or a

Face-Off

new period is opened. A face-off can also occur (most often on one of the circles shown on the rink diagram) if a foul is committed, if the puck leaves the playing surface, or if a whistle stops play for an offside or icing (see "Fouls and Penalties" section).

The "transition game" is an important strategic element of hockey. A team must be able to switch immediately from defense to offense when it gains possession of the puck. If a team is slow in making the transition, it loses its advantage by allowing its opponent to set up its defense.

At almost every level of organized hockey there are three officials on the ice: the referee, who is in charge of the game, and two linesmen, who signal icings and offsides. Off-ice officials include the timekeepers, scorekeepers, and goal judges.

PLAYING RULES

Hockey rules are basically consistent throughout the world, though this was not always the case. At one time in international hockey, the attacking team could not bodycheck beyond the center red line. Bodychecking rules are now standardized worldwide.

Fouls and Penalties. There are six types of penalties—minor, bench minor, major, misconduct, match, and penalty shots. **Minor** penalties (two-minute removal from the ice to the penalty box) are given for such offenses as charging (taking more than two strides before checking an opponent), delay of game, elbowing, high-sticking (checking with the stick above the shoulders), holding, hooking, interfering with an opponent who was not last in possession of the puck, slashing an opponent with the stick, spearing, or tripping.

Penalty Box

Bench minors are called for such violations as having too many men on the ice.

Major penalties (banishment from the ice for five minutes) are given for more serious offenses, such as fighting and trying to injure an opponent. Players who receive minor or major penalties cannot be replaced on the ice, so their team must play shorthanded. This gives an opponent the opportunity for a power play for the duration of the penalty.

Misconduct penalties (banishment from the ice for ten minutes or the duration of the game) are given mainly for abuse of officials. The player involved must sit in the penalty box for ten minutes, but the team can replace him with another player. Game misconducts may be given to a player who continues to break the rules, who becomes the third man in a fight, or who spears or butt-ends an opponent. This player goes to the locker room for the remainder of the game. He can also be replaced on the ice.

Match penalties (banishment for the remainder of the game and automatic suspension) are rare and are usually given to a player who deliberately injures or head-butts an opponent. Another player takes his place on the penalty bench and serves a major penalty term. The offending player may not compete until his case is decided by league officials.

The **penalty shot** is a free shot on goal. It is usually awarded when a player is tripped or hooked from behind when there are no opponents, other than the goalie, between the offensive player and the goal. On the penalty shot, the puck is placed at center ice. All players except the shooter and the goalie must stand aside. The shooter has the choice of shooting from a distance or skating in close to try to feint (trick) the goalie out of position.

Icing the Puck. When the defensive team shoots the puck from its own half of the ice to relieve pressure from the opposition, and if the puck crosses the red line at the far end of the rink, it is said to have been iced. The puck is then brought back and faced off in one of the two circles in the defending team's end of the rink. Play does not stop if a shorthanded team ices the puck.

Offsides. An offside is a passing play in which the puck is shot across two lines, or a play in which a player crosses the blue line into the attacking zone ahead of the puck. The position of the player's skates determines the offside. An offside is not called if the players who have crossed the blue line ahead of the puck are out of the zone before an attacking player touches the puck.

Goal Scoring. A goal is scored only when the entire puck has crossed the goal line into the net area. If the referee loses sight of the puck, particularly in goal-area scrambles, play is stopped and a faceoff results.

Goal Scoring

Ice hockey is believed to have originated in Canada in the mid-1800's. Early players, as shown in this engraving, attached the skates to their shoes with straps.

▶ HISTORY OF THE GAME

Origins. History books vary on the origins of ice hockey, Canada's national sport. The general agreement seems to be that British soldiers in Kingston, Ontario, played the first hockey games on the frozen surface of Lake Ontario in 1855. Claims have been made in Russia that *bandy*, which resembles field hockey on ice, was played in the early 1800's and was the forerunner of ice hockey.

Around 1875, students at McGill University in Montreal compiled the first rules of the game. Teams from different cities played against each other under the McGill rules, and loosely structured leagues sprang up.

Lord Stanley's Cup. Hockey was flourishing in Canada in the 1890's when Lord Stanley arrived as governor-general from Britain. He was intrigued by the game and in 1893 donated a silver cup to be awarded to the amateur champions of Canada. The original trophy cost Lord Stanley $48.33. Ironically, he was recalled to Britain before the first Stanley Cup was awarded in 1894.

Teams and Leagues. Hockey teams in New York played against Canadian teams for the first time in 1899, and in 1909 the professional National Hockey Association (NHA) was formed with four teams. Beginning in 1912, the Stanley Cup was awarded to the champions of professional rather than amateur hockey. The National Hockey League replaced the NHA in 1917. Since then, the NHL has held the Stanley Cup tournament.

From 1942 to 1967, the NHL had six teams: the Toronto Maple Leafs, New York Rangers, Montreal Canadiens, Boston Bruins, Detroit Red Wings, and Chicago Blackhawks. In 1967 the addition of the Philadelphia Flyers, Pittsburgh Penguins, Minnesota North Stars, Los Angeles Kings, St. Louis Blues, and Oakland Seals expanded the league.

The league changed even more during the 1970's. The Vancouver Canucks and Buffalo Sabres were added in 1970. The Atlanta (now Calgary) Flames and the New York Islanders

The Stanley Cup

STANLEY CUP CHAMPIONS*

1917 Seattle Metropolitans	**1947** Toronto Maple Leafs	**1976** Montreal Canadiens
1918 Toronto Arenas	**1948** Toronto Maple Leafs	**1977** Montreal Canadiens
1920 Ottawa Senators	**1949** Toronto Maple Leafs	**1978** Montreal Canadiens
1921 Ottawa Senators	**1950** Detroit Red Wings	**1979** Montreal Canadiens
1922 Toronto St. Patricks	**1951** Toronto Maple Leafs	**1980** New York Islanders
1923 Ottawa Senators	**1952** Detroit Red Wings	**1981** New York Islanders
1924 Montreal Canadiens	**1953** Montreal Canadiens	**1982** New York Islanders
1925 Victoria Cougars	**1954** Detroit Red Wings	**1983** New York Islanders
1926 Montreal Maroons	**1955** Detroit Red Wings	**1984** Edmonton Oilers
1927 Ottawa Senators	**1956** Montreal Canadiens	**1985** Edmonton Oilers
1928 New York Rangers	**1957** Montreal Canadiens	**1986** Montreal Canadiens
1929 Boston Bruins	**1958** Montreal Canadiens	**1987** Edmonton Oilers
1930 Montreal Canadiens	**1959** Montreal Canadiens	**1988** Edmonton Oilers
1931 Montreal Canadiens	**1960** Montreal Canadiens	**1989** Calgary Flames
1932 Toronto Maple Leafs	**1961** Chicago Blackhawks	**1990** Edmonton Oilers
1933 New York Rangers	**1962** Toronto Maple Leafs	**1991** Pittsburgh Penguins
1934 Chicago Blackhawks	**1963** Toronto Maple Leafs	**1992** Pittsburgh Penguins
1935 Montreal Maroons	**1964** Toronto Maple Leafs	**1993** Montreal Canadiens
1936 Detroit Red Wings	**1965** Montreal Canadiens	**1994** New York Rangers
1937 Detroit Red Wings	**1966** Montreal Canadiens	**1995** New Jersey Devils
1938 Chicago Blackhawks	**1967** Toronto Maple Leafs	**1996** Colorado Avalanche
1939 Boston Bruins	**1968** Montreal Canadiens	**1997** Detroit Red Wings
1940 New York Rangers	**1969** Montreal Canadiens	**1998** Detroit Red Wings
1941 Boston Bruins	**1970** Boston Bruins	**1999** Dallas Stars
1942 Toronto Maple Leafs	**1971** Montreal Canadiens	**2000** New Jersey Devils
1943 Detroit Red Wings	**1972** Boston Bruins	**2001** Colorado Avalanche
1944 Montreal Canadiens	**1973** Montreal Canadiens	**2002** Detroit Red Wings
1945 Toronto Maple Leafs	**1974** Philadelphia Flyers	**2003** New Jersey Devils
1946 Montreal Canadiens	**1975** Philadelphia Flyers	**2004** Tampa Bay Lightning

*Since 1917 the NHL has held the Stanley Cup tournament, a best-of-seven series between conference champions. An influenza epidemic ended the 1919 series after five games. A labor dispute between players and team owners caused the 2004–05 season to be canceled.

were admitted in 1972. Two years later, the Washington Capitals and Kansas City Scouts joined the league. The Seals moved to Cleveland and were then merged with the North Stars. The Scouts became the Denver Rockies for several seasons before settling in New Jersey as the Devils.

When the World Hockey Association (WHA) dissolved in 1979, its four surviving teams (the Edmonton Oilers, Hartford Whalers, Quebec Nordiques, and Winnipeg Jets) joined the NHL. By the 1993–94 season, five more teams—the San Jose Sharks, Ottawa Senators, Tampa Bay Lightning, Florida Panthers, and Anaheim Mighty Ducks—had been added, giving the league 26 teams. Then, in 1993, the Minnesota North Stars became the Dallas Stars. Two years later, the Quebec Nordiques became the Colorado Avalanche, and the Winnipeg Jets became the Phoenix Coyotes in 1996. In 1997, the Hartford Whalers became the Carolina Hurricanes.

In 1998, the NHL realigned the organization of its teams, with both the Eastern and Western Conferences expanding from two to three divisions. That year also saw the addition of a new team, the Nashville Predators. The Atlanta Thrashers joined the league in 1999. Two more teams, the Columbus Blue Jackets and

NATIONAL HOCKEY LEAGUE		
EASTERN CONFERENCE		
Atlantic Division	**Northeast Division**	**Southeast Division**
New Jersey Devils	Boston Bruins	Atlanta Thrashers
New York Islanders	Buffalo Sabres	Carolina Hurricanes
New York Rangers	Montreal Canadiens	Florida Panthers
Philadelphia Flyers	Ottawa Senators	Tampa Bay Lightning
Pittsburgh Penguins	Toronto Maple Leafs	Washington Capitals
WESTERN CONFERENCE		
Central Division	**Northwest Division**	**Pacific Division**
Chicago Blackhawks	Calgary Flames	Anaheim Mighty Ducks
Columbus Blue Jackets	Colorado Avalanche	Dallas Stars
Detroit Red Wings	Edmonton Oilers	Los Angeles Kings
Nashville Predators	Minnesota Wild	Phoenix Coyotes
St. Louis Blues	Vancouver Canucks	San Jose Sharks

the Minnesota Wild, began play in the year 2000.

The Olympics. Hockey became an official Olympic Winter Games sport in 1920. The Canadian team has won six gold medals. In 1936, Great Britain was awarded its only gold medal. The U.S. team won the gold medal in 1960 at Squaw Valley, California, and in 1980 at Lake Placid, New York. The Soviet team won seven gold medals. In 1992, the Unified Team, made up of players from the republics that made up the former Soviet Union, won the gold medal at Albertville, France. In 1994,

A jubilant U.S. ice hockey team celebrated its victory in the 1980 Olympic Winter Games. The U.S. players upset the highly favored team from the Soviet Union.

For information on Wayne Gretzky, see the feature in this article.

Phil(ip) Esposito (1942–) was an eight-time All-Star during his 18 years in the NHL. Playing for the Chicago Blackhawks, Boston Bruins, and New York Rangers, he also led the league in scoring five times (1969, 1971–74) and was named MVP twice (1969, 1974). In 1978 he won the Lester Patrick Award for his valuable contributions to U.S. ice hockey. He retired in 1981 and was elected to the Hockey Hall of Fame in 1984.

Gordon (Gordie) Howe (1928–) was known as Mr. Hockey. He played 26 seasons in the NHL—25 with the Detroit Red Wings and one with the Hartford Whalers. Howe was a six-time MVP (1952–53, 1957–58, 1960, 1963) and led the league in scoring six times (1951–54, 1957, 1963). Howe also played five seasons in the World Hockey Association (WHA)—four with the Houston Aeros and one with the New England Whalers. He was inducted into the Hockey Hall of Fame in 1972.

Gordie Howe

Robert Marvin (Bobby) Hull (1939–), a left wing known for his devastating slap shots, played 15 seasons for the Chicago Blackhawks in the NHL. During his NHL career, he was the first player to score 50 or more goals in more than one season. He was also a three-time leading scorer (1960, 1962, 1966), a twelve-time All-Star, and a two-time MVP (1965–66). Hull joined the Winnipeg Jets of the WHA in 1972 and remained with them when they became part of the NHL in 1979. He joined the Hartford Whalers in 1979 for his last season in the NHL. Bobby Hull was inducted into the Hockey Hall of Fame in 1983.

Guy Lafleur (1951–) was a two-time MVP (1977–78) and three-time scoring champion (1976–78) who played for the Montreal Canadiens, the New York Rangers, and the Quebec Nordiques. He was the youngest player to score 400 career goals and 1,000 career points. Lafleur was also the first player to score 50 or more goals six seasons in a row. He was inducted into the Hockey Hall of Fame in 1988.

Mario Lemieux (1965–) played his entire career for the Pittsburgh Penguins, helping them win two Stanley Cup championships (1991–92). After being named Rookie of the Year in 1985, Lemieux was a three-time MVP (1988, 1993, 1996) and led the NHL in scoring six times (1988–89, 1992–93, 1996–97). Lemieux was diagnosed with Hodgkin's disease in the early 1990's, and a few years later missed an entire season due to a back ailment. He

Sweden won its first gold medal. Women's hockey became an official Olympic sport in 1998, and the United States team won the first gold medal.

▶ **INTERNATIONAL COMPETITION**

Ice hockey is played in more than thirty countries and has been a popular international sport since the 1920's. The International Ice Hockey Federation (IIHF) in Switzerland governs international play and stages the annual world championship.

Period of Growth. During the early 1970's, international ice hockey began an exciting period of enormous growth. Many players went to other countries to play, which led to an exchange of hockey strategies and techniques. As a result of the international player movement, eight stars from the Soviet Union joined NHL teams during the 1989–90 season.

Summit Series. The "Summit Series" in 1972 fueled the explosion in international hockey. The national team of the Soviet Union faced off against Team Canada, a national squad of NHL All-Stars. The Canadian team was expected to win the eight-game series easily, but Team Canada barely won the series four games to three, with one tie.

The stars of the WHA played the Soviets in 1974, and this time the Soviets won easily. These two series inspired an increasing number of international games between the NHL, WHA, and teams from the Soviet Union, Sweden, Czechoslovakia, and Finland.

Player Exchange. The exchange of players between the game's two "camps"—the NHL and the European countries where hockey is a major sport—has contributed greatly to international hockey. By the late 1980's, more than 600 Canadian players and a few from the United States were playing in West Germany, Switzerland, Austria, Italy, France, the Netherlands, and Britain. Many Russians, Czechs, Slovaks, Swedes, and Finns have become exceptional players in the NHL.

Varied Styles. As international hockey competition expanded and players increas-

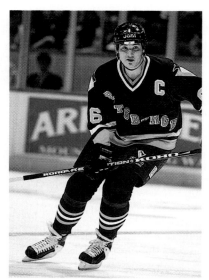

Mario Lemieux

Howarth William (Howie) Morenz (1902–37), often called the Babe Ruth of Hockey and the Canadien Comet, played for the Montreal Canadiens, the Chicago Blackhawks, and the New York Rangers. A three-time All-Star (1930–32), he was also the league's MVP three times (1928, 1931–32). His career came to an abrupt end in 1937 when he died of complications from a broken leg suffered during a game. Morenz was elected to the Hall of Fame in 1945.

Robert Gordon (Bobby) Orr (1948–) played twelve seasons (not including the 1978–79 season he missed with an injury) in the NHL for the Boston Bruins and the Chicago Blackhawks. After winning the Calder Memorial Trophy as best rookie in 1967, Orr went on to win the James Norris Memorial Trophy as the best defensive player eight times (1968–75). He was also the first player to win the MVP award three times in a row (1970–72) and the first defensive player to win the Art Ross Trophy for most points scored in a season (which he did in 1970 and 1975). Orr was elected to the Hall of Fame in 1979.

Maurice Richard (1921–2000) was called the Rocket for his incredible speed on the ice. Richard spent his entire 18-year career with the Montreal Canadiens, help-

Maurice Richard

retired in 1997 and was inducted into the Hockey Hall of Fame less than six months later when it waived its standard three-year waiting period for eligibility. Lemieux and a group of investors bought the Penguins in 1999, and in 2000 he came out of retirement to play for his old team once again.

ing them to eight championship seasons (1944, 1946, 1953, 1956–60) while playing on 14 All-Star teams. In 1947, he was named the league's MVP. Richard retired from the NHL in 1960 and was elected to the Hockey Hall of Fame the following year.

ingly moved to other countries, the vast differences between the style of hockey played in the NHL and in the European countries diminished. North American hockey had emphasized individual effort over total team play, especially in Canada. But the Europeans had taken a very scientific approach, stressing team play and hockey fundamentals. They employed a more sophisticated approach to training than the North American professionals, using other sports, notably soccer, to prepare athletes for hockey.

Throughout the 1970's and the 1980's, increasing numbers of coaches studied each other's methods. NHL teams began to use the European, especially Russian, training ideas. These included off-ice conditioning programs and emphasizing team-play strategies. The European teams started to allow a more individualistic style to emerge. The result was a mixed style of play. The game became more systemized, allowing players to use their individual skills more than traditional team play did.

Some Champion Teams. The Montreal Canadiens, who won the Stanley Cup four consecutive years from 1976 to 1979, combined the best aspects of the two approaches, with strong individual players and good team play. The New York Islanders, four-time winners from 1980 to 1983, played a very traditional, defensively oriented game. The Edmonton Oilers won the Stanley Cup four times in five years from 1984 to 1988.

The legendary Soviet national team of the 1980's was led by defensemen Viacheslav Fetisov and Alexei Kasatonov, and forwards Igor Larionov, Sergei Makarov, and Vladimir Krutov. Nicknamed the Green Five because of the color of their practice uniforms, they dominated the world's hockey scene for a decade, winning everything except the two Canada Cup tournaments. These Russian stars moved to the NHL for the 1989–90 season.

▶ **NHL STARS**

The National Hockey League has had many exceptional players during its history.

WAYNE GRETZKY

Wayne Gretzky has been called the greatest player in the history of ice hockey. In fact, he was nicknamed the Great One for the remarkable skills he displayed and the records he set during his 20 years in the NHL.

Gretzky was born in Brantford, Ontario, on January 26, 1961. His talent for hockey was evident by the time he was 10 years old. Playing for his hometown team, he set an age-group record (which still stands) by scoring 378 goals. By the time Gretzky was 14, fans eagerly sought his autograph.

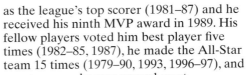

He turned professional in 1978 and joined the Indianapolis Racers of the World Hockey Association (WHA). Later that year, Gretzky was traded to the WHA's Edmonton Oilers, where he was named Rookie of the Year. He remained with the Oilers when they joined the NHL in 1979.

Gretzky did not wait long to make his mark in the new league. In his first season, he set a record for single-game assists by a rookie, became the youngest player to score 50 or more goals in one season, and won his first of eight straight MVP awards (1980–87).

As he moved from the Oilers to the Los Angeles Kings, the St. Louis Blues, and finally the New York Rangers, Gretzky continued his amazing accomplishments. He won seven Art Ross Trophies in a row as the league's top scorer (1981–87) and he received his ninth MVP award in 1989. His fellow players voted him best player five times (1982–85, 1987), he made the All-Star team 15 times (1979–90, 1993, 1996–97), and he was named most gentlemanly player five times (1980, 1991–92, 1994, 1999). In 1998, Gretzky was named the Greatest Hockey Player of All-Time by *The Hockey News.*

At the end of his career, Gretzky held an amazing number of NHL records, including the following:

- most goals, career (894)
- most goals, season (92)
- most points, career (2,857)
- most points, season (215)
- most assists, career (1,962)
- most assists, season (163)
- most playoff goals, career (122)
- most playoff points, career (382)
- most assists in playoffs, career (260)
- most assists in playoffs, season (31)
- most 100-or-more-point seasons (15)
- only player to score 200 points or more in a single season (four times)

In honor of Gretzky's achievements, the Hockey Hall of Fame inducted him in 1999 without the standard three-year waiting period after a player retires—one of only a handful of players to be so honored. In 2000, the NHL retired his famous uniform number 99. No player on any NHL team would ever wear that number again.

Such players of the past as Howie Morenz, Maurice Richard, Gordie Howe, Bobby Hull, Bobby Orr, Guy Lafleur, and Ray Bourque stand out for their performances. For more information on some of the NHL's stars, see the profiles accompanying this article. For information on Wayne Gretzky, one of the greatest players in NHL history, see the feature accompanying this article.

Some great new NHL players emerged during the 1990's. Mario Lemieux, sometimes considered second only to Wayne Gretzky as the sport's greatest player, dominated the 1990's. Outstanding Russian players such as forward Alexander Mogilny also made their mark. Other stars included right wing Brett Hull, center Steve Yzerman, defensemen Eric Lindros and Paul Coffey, and goaltender Patrick Roy. Right wing Jaromir Jagr was widely considered the best player in the NHL by 2000.

FRANK ORR
Sportswriter, *The Toronto Star*
Author, *The Story of Hockey*

ICELAND

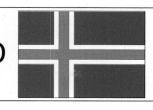

Iceland is an island nation of Europe, located in the North Atlantic Ocean between Europe and North America. Although its northernmost point touches the Arctic Circle, Iceland is less frigid than the name implies. It has green valleys, woodlands, and farmlands, as well as towering glaciers.

Seafarers from Norway founded Iceland's first permanent settlement about the year 874. Little more than a century later, Icelanders founded colonies in Greenland, about 180 miles (290 kilometers) to the west. Much of what is known about the region's early history has been learned from its famous sagas—epic tales written in the Middle Ages that are still read and enjoyed today.

▶ PEOPLE

Iceland is inhabited by about 271,000 people. Most of them are descendants of the Vikings—Norwegians and other Scandinavians who settled on the island in the late 800's—and of Celtic peoples from Viking colonies in the British Isles. For more information, see the article VIKINGS in Volume U-V.

Language. The modern Icelandic language is directly derived from Old Norse, the language of the Vikings. Because Iceland was isolated from the outside world for many centuries, the language has survived almost unchanged.

Religion. About 95 percent of Icelanders belong to the Evangelical Lutheran Church, the state church. A small number belong to other Protestant denominations and the Roman Catholic Church. Still some others follow the Old Norse religion, worshiping such gods as Odin and Thor.

Education and Libraries. Education is compulsory for children between the ages of 6 and 15. Iceland has eleven colleges and one university, the University of Iceland, located in Reykjavík, the capital. Iceland's main academic library is located on the university campus.

Food. Fish, along with lamb, has always been an important part of the Icelanders' diet. A favorite dish, especially at Christmastime, is *hangikjöt*

Clockwise from left: **Most Icelanders are descended from the Vikings. The picturesque city of Reykjavík is Iceland's capital. Swimming is a favorite national pastime.**

Although Iceland's name suggests an entirely frozen landscape, the island has many green valleys and flowing rivers.

(smoked lamb). Other typical Icelandic foods include *hardfiskur* (dried fish) and a low-fat milk curd called *skyr*.

Customs. The Old Icelandic calendar divided the year into only two seasons, winter and summer. Therefore, Icelanders celebrate the First Day of Summer on the Thursday of the third week of April—even though this is long before summer weather actually arrives. Icelanders celebrate their National Day on June 17, the anniversary of the founding of the modern Republic of Iceland in 1944.

Icelanders still maintain their ancient naming customs. Instead of family surnames, they have patronymics—names drawn from the father's first name. So if a man named Jon has a son named Petur, he will be called Petur Jonsson; and if Jon has a daughter named Kristin, she will be Kristin Jonsdóttir. Women do not take their husbands' names on marriage, but keep their own patronymic.

Sports. Icelanders are avid swimmers. Because the sea is generally too cold for swimming, many towns have heated public swimming pools. Handball and soccer are the most popular spectator sports.

▶ **LAND**

During the Ice Age, all of Iceland was covered by a sheet of glacial ice that eroded away the rock to form Iceland's many spectacular valleys, fiords, and mountain ridges. The glaciers gradually retreated as the climate grew warmer, but 12 percent of Iceland is still hidden by glaciers. The largest of them, Vatnajökull, covers an area of 3,200 square miles (8,300 square kilometers), which is nearly three times the size of the state of Rhode Island.

Largely a mountainous country, Iceland has an average elevation of some 1,640 feet (500 meters) above sea level. The lowland areas are found mainly in the south and west, where most of the people live.

The island was produced by volcanic activity, although some regions of the island are no longer volcanically active. In 1963, an eruption on the sea floor led to the birth of a new island, Surtsey, and in 1971, a new volcano burst into life in the Vestmannaeyjar (Westman Islands) off the southern coast, destroying part of a town. Iceland's highest peak, Mt. Hvan-

Iceland

nadalshnúkur, is a volcano, although inactive. Relatively small earthquakes occur regularly in the volcanic regions. The most active volcano, Mount Hekla, last erupted in 2000.

Natural hot water is found in many places in Iceland, where the Earth is heated by volcanic energy. In some cases, the hot water bursts from the Earth in a gush or spout. The word "geyser" comes from Geysir, Iceland's largest spouting hot spring, which sends spouts of boiling water nearly 200 feet (60 meters) into the air.

Rivers, Waterfalls, and Coastal Waters. Iceland is entirely surrounded by the North Atlantic Ocean. The country's longest river, the Thjórsá, is 143 miles (230 kilometers) long. Its largest lake, Thingvalla, covers an area of 32 square miles (83 square kilometers). Many of Iceland's rivers form beautiful waterfalls. The most notable among them are Dettifoss (Falling Falls) in the north and Gullfoss (Golden Falls) in the south.

Climate. Iceland's climate is relatively mild because of the warming influence of the North American Current, which flows along its southern coast. The average temperature in December is around the freezing point. The average temperature in June is 52°F (11°C). The climate is windy and changeable. Precipitation is heavier in the south than the north. The Vestmannaeyjar islands, off the southern coast, receive an average of 63 inches (1,600 millimeters) of rain and snow a year, while Akureyri in the north is relatively dry, averaging 19 inches (483 millimeters).

Natural Resources. Although Iceland has almost no mineral resources, it has other valuable natural resources. These include its fishing grounds, geothermal energy (stores of natural hot water in the Earth in the volcanic areas), and hydroelectric power, generated by harnessing the energy of waterfalls and rivers. Geothermal en-

ergy is used to heat most of Iceland's homes and other buildings. Hydroelectric sources provide all of Iceland's electricity.

▶ **ECONOMY**

Icelanders enjoy one of the highest standards of living in the world. But unlike other Western countries, Iceland's economy is largely dependent on a single commodity—fish.

Services. A growing number of Icelanders are employed in the service sector. Of the total workforce, about 20 percent work for the government and another 20 percent are employed in other services. Iceland's wild and

Fishing vessels docked in Reykjavík harbor indicate the importance of fishing to Iceland's economy.

unspoiled environment attracts an increasing number of visitors, increasing the importance of tourism.

Fishing and Agriculture. Historically the basis of the Icelandic economy, fishing and fish processing still account for more than 70 percent of Iceland's export income. For this reason, Iceland strictly protects its exclusive fishing zone and applies a quota system to avoid overfishing. Despite the importance of Iceland's fisheries, only 11 percent of the workforce is employed in fishing and fish processing.

Iceland's farmers, who traditionally bred sheep, have been diversifying into other kinds of animal husbandry (cattle, pigs, chickens) and arable farming. The two most important crops are potatoes and turnips. Planting new forests is a high priority, with large areas of land being planted with seedlings every year.

An Icelandic farmer shears a sheep for its wool, which is used primarily to make warm clothing.

Manufacturing. Manufacturing accounts for a very small sector of the Icelandic economy. Among the few industrial products are aluminum and ferrosilicon.

Trade. Fish and fish products are Iceland's main exports. Because of the lack of manufacturing, the country must import cars, household equipment, and most other consumer items, as well as many foodstuffs. Iceland's main trading partners are members of the European Union, followed by the United States and Japan.

Transportation. There are no railroads in Iceland, but the Ring Road links the coastal areas of the country. Because heavy snows may make entire regions inaccessible by road in winter, regular air services are maintained to all corners of the country. Icelandair is the national airline.

Communication. Iceland has one state-run television station and radio station and several additional commercial stations. Three daily newspapers, *Dagur*, *Dagbladid Visir*, and *Morgunbladid*, are published.

▶ **MAJOR CITIES**

Almost every town and village in Iceland began as a coastal fishing community. More than half of Iceland's population lives in the capital, Reykjavík, and its neighboring communities. The largest town after Reykjavík is Akureyri, with a population of about 15,000.

Reykjavík, the capital, is where Iceland's first settler, Ingólfur Arnarson, made his home in 870. Originally a farm, it developed into a village in the 1800's. With a population of 105,000, Reykjavík is the center of government, education, business, and culture. The name "Reykjavík" means "Smoky Bay," in reference to the clouds of steam that rise from its hot springs.

▶ **CULTURAL HERITAGE**

Icelanders gained a place in literary history through their sagas, written between the 100's and 1300's. The sagas are epic tales of love, feuds, revenge, and tragedy, many of them based upon true stories. Some, such as *Njal's Saga*, are regarded as classics of world literature. The most renowned Icelandic writer of the 1900's was novelist Halldór Laxness (1902–98), who won the Nobel Prize for literature in 1955.

Literature was for many centuries almost the only art form practiced in Iceland. Music, painting, sculpture, theater, and dance did not begin to develop until the 1800's. Today, Iceland's cultural activities include art shows, plays, and concerts. An international arts festival is held in Reykjavík every other year.

▶ **GOVERNMENT**

Iceland is a democratic republic. The president, elected for a 4-year term, performs the mainly ceremonial duties of a head of state.

Every June 17, Icelanders celebrate National Day with choir singing and other festivities.

Governmental power rests with a prime minister, who leads the majority political party or coalition of parties in the Althing, the one-house parliament, whose 63 members are elected for 4-year terms.

Iceland's national constitution dates from 1944, the year in which the island gained full independence from Denmark.

▶ HISTORY

Iceland was named by Floki Vilgerdarson, a Norwegian who attempted to settle there around the year 860. He gave up and went home, but not before he named the island for the drift ice he saw filling one of the fiords.

In 874, Ingólfur Arnarson became the first permanent settler, establishing a farm at Reykjavík. He was followed by other Norwegians, and in 930 the Icelandic chieftains and their representatives established their own nation, the Old Commonwealth. It was governed by the Althing, the world's first democratic parliament. Chieftains from all regions of the country gathered each summer at Thingvellir ("the plain of the assembly") in the southwest, to make laws and to judge legal cases. In 1000, the Icelanders adopted Christianity, abandoning the old Norse gods they had previously worshiped. Some Icelanders later settled in Greenland, under the leadership of Erik the Red.

Foreign Rule. Beginning in the 1100's, Iceland was beset by strife and civil war. As a result, in 1262 the Icelanders agreed to accept Norwegian rule. Iceland, along with Norway, came under Danish rule in 1380. Denmark then governed Iceland for more than five centuries.

The island's economy declined severely after a royal monopoly on trade was declared by the Danish king in 1602, limiting commerce to a few individuals. Natural disasters struck in 1783 and 1784, when the volcano Laki erupted, causing the death of one-fifth of the population.

In the 1800's, under the leadership of the brilliant scholar and politician Jón Sigurdsson, the Icelanders began to campaign for their independence.

Independence. Iceland was granted a constitution under the Danish crown in 1874, home rule in 1904, and self-government in 1918. But Iceland remained subject to the King of Denmark until the foundation of the modern republic in 1944, during World War II. During that war, British and American troops were stationed in Iceland to prevent its occupation by Germany. Iceland joined the North Atlantic Treaty Organization (NATO) after the war ended in 1945. However, it had no armed forces and remains dependent on the United States for its defense.

Recent Events. Because Iceland's economy is so dependent on the sea, it has tried to keep other nations from fishing in its coastal waters. The so-called "cod wars" between Great Britain and Iceland caused a temporary break in diplomatic relations between the two countries in 1976. The legislature banned the entry of nuclear weapons into Iceland in 1985.

Olafur Ragnar Grimsson, president since 1996, was re-elected in 2000 and 2004. Independence Party leader David Oddsson, who had served as prime minister since 1991, was succeeded by Progressive Party leader Halldor Asgrimsson in 2004.

ANNA YATES
Freelance Journalist

On a beautiful winter day, recreational skaters of all ages flock to a pond in New York's Central Park to enjoy one of the most popular winter sports.

ICE-SKATING

For more than 1,000 years, people have skated on frozen lakes, canals, and rivers. Ice-skating first started as a means of transportation in areas with long months of winter. It was not long before ice-skating was not only used as a means of transportation, but also as a means of recreation. Skating as a sport was developed in the Netherlands and spread to northern European countries—with the help of King Charles II. He brought the sport of skating with him when he returned to London from exile in the Netherlands. Soon ice-skating was a leisure pastime of the upper class. Although it may have started as a sport of the upper class, today skating is enjoyed by many different people throughout the world—as a recreation activity and as a competitive sport.

There are several different types of skating, each with its own special equipment. The two main types of competitive ice-skating are figure skating and speed skating. Figure skating combines grace, strength, and accuracy as skaters perform acrobatic leaps and trace graceful patterns on the ice. Speed skating is a sport in which skaters race on an oval track. Speed skaters may race alone against the clock or against other skaters on the ice. Ice hockey is a competitive sport that also requires excellent skating skills. For more information, see the article ICE HOCKEY in this volume.

▶ICE-SKATING EQUIPMENT

Proper equipment is essential for ice-skating. Ice-skating boots should fit snugly but not too tightly, and the blades should be kept sharp. Because figure skating, speed skating, and ice hockey are very different sports, they require different equipment.

Figure skates are made so that skaters can perform acrobatic maneuvers. They have high tops to support the skater's arch and ankle, and a blade that is only slightly longer than the boot. This blade is usually about ⅛ inch (3 millimeters) thick and 12 inches (30 centimeters) long. The front of the blade has sawlike teeth called **toe rakes**, or **toe picks**. The toe rakes bite into the ice to help skaters perform certain spins and jumps. The bottom of the blade is grooved to create an inside and outside edge. These edges allow a figure skater to maneuver easily, and are used in almost all basic maneuvers, such as starting, gliding, and stopping.

Speed skates are designed to allow skaters to start quickly and maintain high speeds on the ice. The skates have low, flexible boots ending just above the ankle, and the blade is long, thin, and straight. It extends in front of the toe of the boot, and usually measures about $\frac{1}{32}$ inch (0.8 millimeters) wide and 12 to 18 inches (30 to 45 centimeters) long. The blade is ground completely flat on the bottom.

Ice hockey skates have low boots that are quite tough, in order to protect a skater's feet during the rough game of hockey. The blade is thin and is usually shorter than a speed-skating blade.

Ice skaters generally wear warm, comfortable clothing. The clothing should be loose so movement is not restricted. Thin wool or cotton socks keep a skater's feet warm without hindering the flow of blood.

▶ SAFETY ON THE ICE

Learning to skate requires an understanding and practice of good safety habits. If you are skating outdoors on a natural ice surface, the greatest danger is the risk of falling through the ice. Ice that is less than 4 inches (10 centimeters) thick may not support the weight of a skater, and it is almost impossible to judge how thick ice is just by looking at it. For this reason, you should never skate alone on natural ice. Make sure you only skate in areas, such as park rinks, that are approved skating areas. Any designated skating area should have a ladder and a rope available for rescue purposes. Obstructions such as tree limbs and roots, or deep snow are also hazards to watch for when skating on a natural ice surface.

The greatest danger when skating on an indoor ice rink is generally that of colliding with other skaters. Before you start skating, learn the rules of the rink. These rules generally stress being careful to skate in the direction of travel and to avoid crossing the path of other skaters.

Beginning skaters, whether on natural ice or on indoor rinks, need to have the right equipment and to practice good safety habits.

Types of Ice Skates

Figure skates have curved blades with sawtoothed tips that grip the ice during sharp turns, spins, and jumps.

Speed skates have long, thin, lightweight blades for quick starts and fast speeds throughout a race.

Hockey skates have short, pointed blades curved at each end for quick starts and stops and fast turns.

LEARNING TO SKATE

Most beginners use figure skates while learning how to skate—because of the high top that provides ankle support and the blade that allows more maneuverability than speed or hockey skates. Once beginners have learned the basic skating movements on figure skates, the same movements can be practiced using speed skates or hockey skates.

It is very important to lace your boots properly before you start skating. Lace the boots somewhat loosely at the toe and tightly in front of the ankle. This will give the ankle extra support. The lacing should be looser again near the top of the boots. In general, boots should fit snugly, but not tightly enough to cut off blood circulation or prevent the ankle from flexing forward.

The first thing to do when learning to skate is to get your balance. Keep your head up and do not bend forward. Your arms should be at your waist and your hands relaxed. Keep your feet together, slide them back and forth a bit, and try to glide along on both feet. Your first steps on the ice may be frightening, but with each step you will improve. You will soon get used to the feeling of being on skates.

After you are able to glide, you can begin **stroking**. Bend slightly forward at the waist. Push off from the front part of the blade on either foot. (Do not push off from the toe picks.) If you are pushing off with your right foot, bend your right knee as you begin to stroke and straighten it as you end your glide. Do the same for the left foot.

You must also learn to stop. Glide in a straight line with your feet about 18 inches (46 centimeters) apart. Then force your heels apart and point your toes together to make a **snowplow** position. This will bring you to a slow stop. A more experienced skater may use the **hockey stop**. Here the skater leans back with bent knees and quickly lifts and turns both skates sideways. The blades will skid sideways on the ice and bring the skater to a quick stop.

After you can skate forward and backward, you must also be able to turn. The best way to turn is by using a **crossover**. This is a movement in which your free foot (the foot not on the ice) passes in front of your skating foot. Then your free foot is placed on the ice and your weight shifted to it. For example, if you wish to turn to the right while skating on the right foot, bring the left foot in front of the right. Shift your weight gradually until the left foot crosses over the right and touches the ice on the inside edge.

The left foot now carries the weight, and the right foot can be lifted off the ice. Bring it up beside the left and shift your weight to the right foot, gradually bringing it back down on the ice. Bring your left foot up and cross it in front as before. Repeat these moves around a large circle and hold each edge as long as you can. Practice crossing over backward as well as forward to both right and left.

▶COMPETITIVE SKATING

Competitive skating is practiced by many dedicated skaters. The two chief kinds are figure skating and speed skating.

Figure Skating

Figure skating is distinguished by its emphasis on carefully controlled and exacting turns and curves. There are three main categories of figure skating: singles skating, pair skating, and ice dancing.

Singles Skating. The programs performed in competitive singles skating are divided into two parts: the original program and free skating.

In a 1989 competition, figure skater Midori Ito of Japan became the first woman to complete a triple-axel jump, spinning three and a half times in the air before landing.

Daring lifts are part of a pair-skating couple's performance (*left*). The ice-dancing couple (*above*) skates in a graceful pattern of steps that resemble those used in ballroom dancing.

The original program consists of eight acrobatic moves of jumps, spins, steps, and combinations of jumps and spins. All skaters perform the same specified movements, but they arrange their own programs—deciding the order of the maneuvers and choosing the music to which they will perform them. Skaters are limited to a time period of 2 minutes and 40 seconds. They are judged on the basis of both technical skill in performing the maneuvers and artistic creativity in coordinating the program with music.

Free skating consists of combinations of jumps, spins, and other acrobatic movements selected and arranged by the skaters themselves. Judges score competitors on the basis of their technical merit, creativity in coordinating maneuvers with music, and the overall difficulty and variety of the free skating.

Before 1990, single-skating competitions also featured programs of compulsory figures,

which tested a skater's ability to trace exact figures on the ice. Beginning in 1990, however, compulsory figures were eliminated from world figure-skating championships by the International Skating Union.

Pair Skating. Pair skating is one of the most acrobatic forms of skating. It consists of a man and a woman skating a program of their own devising. Skating together, the man often lifts, throws, and spins the woman, much as a male dancer would do in a ballet. The couples try to create an impression of grace, harmony, and teamwork. The skaters sometimes separate from each other, but they perform most of their moves in unison. As in figure skating, pair-skating competition consists of two main parts—the original program and free skating.

There are two basic styles of pair skating. In **mirror** skating, the couple skates face-to-face, almost as in ballroom dancing. In **shadow** skating, the skaters perform their movements at the same time, one skater shadowing the other. All pair-skating routines alternate these two styles. Routines often begin with shadow skating, then shift to mirror skating as the couple prepares for a lift or jump.

Skating champions Bonnie Blair of the United States (*below*) and Uwe-Jens Mey of Germany (*right*) smashed the world and Olympic records for the men's and women's 500-meter speed-skating events during the 1988 Winter Olympics.

Ice Dancing. Ice dancing is an elegant form of skating that combines skating with ballroom dancing. While it is similar to pair skating, it differs in that ice dancers rarely separate from each other, and no maneuvers are permitted in which the man lifts the woman high above the ice. The emphasis in ice dancing is on close coordination among dancers rather than on acrobatic maneuvers.

In competition, ice dancers must perform compulsory dances, free dances, and original set-pattern dances. Compulsory dances have definite patterns that must be skated exactly. Free dances are created by the couple. The timing must be exact, and the dances must follow certain rules, such as each dancer must have one skate on the ice at all times. Dances are judged on the skaters' technical ability as well as on their originality in creating combinations of new or known dance movements.

Speed Skating

Speed skating is a sport in which skaters race various distances on oval ice tracks. Speed skaters do not perform lifts, jumps, or other acrobatic maneuvers. The speed skater is an athlete whose main concerns are technique and speed. Top speeds in races may be as high as 35 miles (58 kilometers) per hour.

Speed-skating technique is generally dependent on three factors: balance, rhythm, and drive. Speed skaters try to keep their bodies relaxed as they race. They lean forward over the ice, keeping their heads up and their eyes looking straight ahead as they push their legs back and forth to gain speed on the ice.

A good skating rhythm results from a steady, flowing motion of the arms and legs. Most speed skaters swing their arms as they race, which helps to maintain balance and increase the power of each stroke. The drive comes from the pushing of the legs during each stroke. Speed skaters try to bend their knees deeply to create the long strokes that result in powerful forward pushes.

Competitive speed skating involves three types of races: long-track, or Olympic-style skating; pack skating; and short-track skating. Men and women race separately in speed-skating races.

Long-Track Skating. This is the most popular kind of speed skating in international competition. Two skaters race around a two-lane track that measures 437 yards (400 meters) around. Men's races are usually 500, 1,000, 1,500, 5,000, and 10,000 meters long. Women's races are 500, 1,000, 1,500, 3,000, and 5,000 meters long.

Pack Skating. Pack skating is the most popular kind of speed skating in the United States. A group of skaters start together in pack skating. They compete against one another in a series of heats, or races. Those who win advance to the final races.

Short-Track Skating. This type of speed skating consists of individual races and relay races held on tracks that are shorter than Olympic-style tracks. The tracks are usually the size of hockey rinks. In individual races, small groups of skaters race against one another. In relay races, two four-member teams compete to see which team can place one of its skaters across the finish line first. One member from each team skates until he or she is replaced by a teammate.

▶ **THE OLYMPICS**

The history of Olympic skating events begins with the first Olympic Winter Games, held in 1924 in Chamonix, France. The Winter Games have been held every four years since then except for the years 1940 and 1944, when they were canceled due to the events of World War II.

Both figure skating and speed skating became official Olympic events in 1924. Men and women competed in figure skating, but at first only men competed in speed skating. Women's competition in speed skating began in 1960. Ice dancing became an official Olympic event in 1976.

The Norwegian skater Sonja Henie became the first world-famous figure-skating star, winning Olympic championships in 1928, 1932, and 1936. Other famous women figure skaters who won Olympic medals include Tenley Albright, Carol Heiss, Sjoukje Dijkstra, Peggy Fleming, Beatrix Schuba, Dorothy Hamill, Anett Pötzsch, Katarina Witt, Kristi Yamaguchi, and Oksana Baiul.

One of the most famous male figure-skating champions of the mid-1900's was the American skater Dick Button, who won the

Above: Sonja Henie of Norway was ice-skating's first great star. Her exceptional skill and revolutionary techniques, combined with her appealing personality, brought popularity to the sport. *Below:* A Dutch ice skate from the early 1800's.

Olympic championship in 1948 and 1952. Button became famous for his flying leaps high above the ice. Another American skater, Hayes Alan Jenkins, won the Olympic title in 1956. His brother David won the Olympic gold medal in 1960. A famous British skater, John Curry, won the Olympic gold medal in 1976.

Other Olympic gold medalists in men's skating include Manfred Schnelldorfer, Wolfgang Schwarz, Ondrej Nepela, Robin Cousins, and Scott Hamilton.

▶ **THE HISTORY OF SKATING**

Nobody knows exactly when or where ice-skating began, but archaeological evidence shows that it has an extremely long history. The earliest remains of skates were uncovered among Roman ruins in London. These remains, which date back to about 50 B.C., show that ancient people made shoes from leather and skate blades from animal bones.

Bonnie Blair (1964–   ), born in Cornwall, New York, left her mark on Olympic history during her career as a speed skater. She won her first gold medal at the 1988 Games in the 500-meter race. At the 1992 Games, in addition to winning the 1,000-meter race, she became the first woman to repeat as champion in the 500-meter event. At the 1994 Games, she again won both the 500- and 1,000-meter races. Blair was named *Sports Illustrated*'s Sportswoman of the Year in 1994 and retired the following year.

Brian Boitano (1963–   ) was born in Sunnyvale, California. In 1982 he became the first skater to successfully perform the triple axel jump. Afterward, Boitano was U.S. figure-skating champion four straight years (1985–88) as well as Olympic and world champion in 1988. He was elected to the World Figure Skating Hall of Fame in 1996. In that same year Boitano choreographed and directed the television special *A Skating Romance*.

Kurt Browning (1966–   ) was born in Alberta, Canada. He won three different ice-skating competitions four times each: the world championship (1989–91, 1993); the Canadian championship (1989–91, 1993); and the Canadian professional championship (1995–98). He also was a three-time world professional champion (1995–97) and a two-time U.S. professional champion (1996, 1998). Browning was elected to the Canadian Figure Skating Hall of Fame in 1998.

Dick Button (1929–   ) was born in Englewood, New Jersey.

Ekaterina Gordeeva and Sergei Grinkov

Scott Hamilton

In 1948 he became the first American to win an Olympic gold medal in figure skating, and he won an additional Olympic gold medal in 1952. He was U.S. champion seven times (1946–52) and world champion five times (1948–52). Button was one of the original inductees into the World Figure Skating Hall of Fame in 1976 and was also inducted into the U.S. Olympic Hall of Fame in 1983.

Ekaterina Gordeeva (1971–   ) and **Sergei Grinkov** (1967–95), both born in Moscow, Russia, were a highly successful and popular figure-skating pair. They began skating together at a young age and married in 1991. During their amateur and professional careers they collected an impressive record: world champions four times (1986–87, 1989–90), world professional champions three times (1991–92, 1994), European champions three times (1988, 1990, 1994), and Olympic gold medal winners twice (1988, 1994). Their career and life together came to a tragic end in 1995 when Grinkov died suddenly of a heart attack during a practice session. Gordeeva resumed her skating career the following year, performing solo.

Dorothy Hamill (1956–   ), born in Chicago, Illinois, was among the first great women skaters from the United States. During her amateur years, Hamill was a three-time U.S. figure-skating champion (1974–76) and world and Olympic champion in 1976. She continued her dominance of the sport after turning professional, reigning as the world professional champion for five straight years (1983–87). She was elected to the United States Figure Skating Hall of Fame in 1991.

Other remains found in Europe show that northern Europeans made skates from leather and animal bone, probably beginning as early as the 1100's.

In the 1300's, people began making skates of iron blades set in wood blocks. Such skates were used during the winter months in the Netherlands to travel on frozen canals. Many people believe that the English word "skates" is derived from the Dutch word *schaats*.

In the 1500's, metal blades began to be attached to shoes with screws. Such skates were used by the Dutch to win an important battle in 1572: Dutch soldiers, wearing skates with iron blades, were able to move quickly and outmaneuver the Spanish troops attacking the city of Amsterdam.

In the 1600's, skating became a popular recreational activity in many parts of Europe. Settlers from Europe eventually introduced skating to North America when they settled there. By the 1700's, the practice of hollow grinding blades was begun, and blades gradually became curved rather than flat.

Ice-skating in the United States became widely popular during the 1800's. In 1849 the first American skating club was established in Philadelphia. In 1850, also in Philadelphia, the first all-steel skates were created by E. W. Bushnell. The use of steel in skates made them lighter and stronger than iron skates and increased their popularity.

Skating also increased in popularity thanks to the invention of refrigeration. Artificial ice

Scott Hamilton (1958–) was raised in Bowling Green, Ohio. He was the U.S. and world figure-skating champion for the same four years (1981–84) and also won the gold medal at the 1984 Olympics. He was elected to the U.S. and the World Figure Skating Halls of Fame in 1990. Despite some health issues, including a bout with cancer in 1997, Hamilton continued to skate and produce skating shows.

Eric Heiden (1958–), born in Madison, Wisconsin, was one of the most dominant speed skaters in the history of the sport. In 1977 he became the first American man to win the world speed-skating championship. At the 1980 Olympic Games he set five records as he won every speed-skating event, becoming the first athlete to win five individual gold medals in a single Olympics. He was elected to the Amateur Speedskating Union Hall of Fame in 1989.

Sonja Henie (1912–69) was born in Oslo, Norway. She revolutionized figure skating by bringing a greater degree of athleticism and dance to the sport. In 1927, at the age of 15, she won the first of ten consecutive world championships. She also won three Olympic gold medals (1928, 1932, 1936). Henie's skill and presence on the ice led to a successful acting career in films throughout the 1930's and 1940's. She retired in 1960 and was one of the first skaters to be elected to the World Figure Skating Hall of Fame in 1976.

Michelle Kwan (1980–) was born in Torrance, California. She was a nine-time U.S. champion (1996, 1998–2005), a five-time world champion (1996, 1998, 2000-01, 2003), and world professional champion in 1998. In addition, she was named *Skating* magazine's Skater of the Year seven times (1994, 1996, 1998–99, 2001–03)—the only skater to receive that honor more than once. Kwan also won silver medals in the U.S. championships (1994–95, 1997), the world championships (1997, 1999, 2002), and the Olympics (1998). In 2002, she won the bronze medal at the Olympic Games.

Tara Lipinski (1982–), born in Philadelphia, Pennsylvania, was only 15 years old when she made Olympic history: At the 1998 Games, she became the youngest figure skater to win a gold medal. She was also the youngest skater to win both the U.S. and the world championships, which she did a year earlier. Lipinski was named Female Athlete of the Year by the United States Sports Academy in 1998, the same year she turned professional. In 1999 she became the youngest world professional figure-skating champion of all time.

Katarina Witt (1965–) was born in Karl-Marx-Stadt in the former East Germany. One of the most mesmerizing figure skaters of recent times, Witt was a four-time world champion (1984–85, 1987–88) and a six-time European champion (1983–88). In addition, she won gold medals in the 1984 and 1988 Olympic Games. Witt began acting in films and television in the 1990's, and in 1990 she won an Emmy Award for her outstanding performance in the television special *Carmen on Ice.* She was elected to the World Figure Skating Hall of Fame in 1995.

Kristi Yamaguchi (1971–), born in Hayward, California, was one of America's most popular and accomplished figure skaters. She was the world professional figure-skating champion four times (1992, 1994, 1996–97), world champion twice (1991–92), and winner of the gold medal at the 1992 Olympic Games. She was also named Skater of the Year in 1996 by *American Skating World* magazine. In 1998 Yamaguchi was elected to the U.S. Figure Skating Hall of Fame and the World Figure Skating Hall of Fame.

Kristi Yamaguchi

rinks began to be built in many different places. Such rinks made skating a year-round activity and introduced the sport to places that had no natural ice. About 1870, an American ballet dancer and teacher, Jackson Haines, greatly influenced skating techniques by blending dance movements with ice-skating. Haines is generally regarded as the man who introduced modern figure skating to Europe.

In 1892 the International Skating Union was formed. Also in that year, the first speed-skating and figure-skating competitions were held, in Vienna, Austria.

By the early 1900's, ice-skating had become a popular spectator sport and entertainment. Ice shows often toured the United States and Europe. In 1915, Irving Brokaw, a successful businessman and ice-skating promoter, brought an ice-skating comedy to New York. *Flirting at St. Moritz* was immensely popular, and its leading skater, Charlotte Oelschlagel, became well known in New York.

The Olympic Winter Games, first held in 1924, are now broadcast on television throughout the world. The Olympic competitions in figure skating, speed skating, and ice dancing have introduced the world of ice-skating to millions of people throughout the world.

STEPHEN C. TURNER
Author, *Great Beginnings:
Olympics to Superbowl*

See also ICEBOATING; ICE HOCKEY; OLYMPIC GAMES; ROLLER-SKATING.

IDAHO

*In the 1800's, a Colorado politician estab-
lished a mining company in a place he called
Idaho. He invented the name himself, but for
many years people mistakenly believed it was
an Indian word. Then, to promote his growing
empire and attract investors, he nicknamed the
place Gem of the Mountains. Today, due to the
state's enduring mineral wealth, Idaho's official nickname is the Gem State.*

State flag

Idaho is one of the six states that make up
the Rocky Mountain region of the United
States. It is a land of startling beauty. Jagged
mountains, vast forests, broad plains, crystal-
blue lakes, and swift rivers make up its wild
and enchanting landscape.

Idaho lies in the Pacific Northwest. The
Rocky Mountains sweep through much of
the state, dominating lands covered largely by
evergreen forests. Melting snowfields feed
thousands of streams that flow down from
the mountains into deep canyons. Plains and
desert regions cover most of southern Idaho.

Idaho's rugged landscape makes it difficult
for large cities to develop, and most Idahoans
prefer it that way. They live in an uncrowded,
unspoiled country that people from other
places consider a vacationland. About 1.3
million people live in Idaho, placing it among
the least populous states in the union. Boise,
the state's capital and largest city, lies in a fertile valley in southwestern Idaho. Most of
Idaho's larger cities have grown up in this region, known as the Columbia Plateau, on the
Snake River Plain.

The Idaho region has been inhabited for
some 12,000 years. Native Indian tribes include the Nez Percé in the north and the
Shoshoni in the south. White people first explored Idaho less than 200 years ago. In 1805,
Meriwether Lewis and William Clark came
through the region on a scientific expedition.
They managed to find a way to cross Idaho,
which was a very difficult task.

Soon afterward, Canadian beaver hunters
explored the area and set up fur-trading
posts. Sharp competition developed between
the British-Canadian and American fur trappers, causing a border dispute between Great
Britain and the United States. The issue was
settled in 1846 and Idaho became a United
States possession. In 1863, Congress orga-

nized Idaho as a territory. The region's population continued to grow, and in 1890, Idaho
became the nation's 43rd state.

Idaho is unusually rich in mineral resources. Profitable silver and gold mines have
operated in the forested mountain areas for
more than a century. The Coeur d'Alene mining district in the northern Panhandle is un-
matched in the United States in the
production of silver. It also produces large
amounts of lead and zinc.

Heavy industry never developed in Idaho
because the state has no oil fields and no coal
or iron mines. Farming developed after 1900,
when several large irrigation projects were
completed. Tourism began to flourish following the 1936 opening of Sun Valley, a ski resort in the Sawtooth Mountains.

Today the state's economy is largely based
on trade, light industry, services, tourism, and
the variety of Idaho's natural resources.
Among the goods manufactured are processed foods, chemicals, and electronic products. Abundant forestlands support a valuable
lumber industry. Livestock feed on Idaho's
expansive rangelands. The state's most valuable crops include sugar beets, wheat, barley,
and, of course, the potatoes for which Idaho
has become famous.

**Idaho's Sawtooth National Recreation Area features
hundreds of spectacular lakes and mountains (*top*) and
herds of pronghorn, or American antelope (*right*). It is
an ideal place for trout fishing (*far right*) and other
activities.**

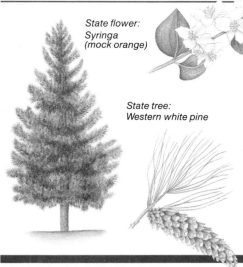

State flower:
*Syringa
(mock orange)*

State tree:
Western white pine

FACTS AND FIGURES

Location: Northwestern United States; bordered on the north by Canada, on the south by Nevada and Utah, on the east by Montana and Wyoming, and on the west by Washington and Oregon.

Area: 83,574 sq mi (216,456 km²); rank, 14th.

Population: 1,293,953 (2000 census); rank, 39th.

Elevation: *Highest*—12,662 ft (3,859 m), at Borah Peak; *lowest*—710 ft (216 m), on the Snake River.

Capital: Boise.

Statehood: July 3, 1890; 43rd state.

State Motto: *Esto Perpetua* ("May it endure forever").

State Song: "Here We Have Idaho."

Nickname: Gem State.

Abbreviations: ID; Ida.

State bird:
Mountain bluebird

► **LAND**

Idaho is the most northwesterly of the Rocky Mountain states. It has an odd shape, somewhat like a chair. The long, narrow part of Idaho in the north is called the Panhandle.

Land Regions

Idaho connects three major land regions of the western United States—the Rocky Mountains, the Columbia Plateau, and the Basin and Range Province.

The Rocky Mountains. The largest natural region in Idaho is made up of mountains that extend from Montana's Rocky Mountains west into Oregon and Washington. They cover most of the north and central parts of the state.

Idaho's mountain region includes about twenty different ranges. The Rocky Mountains bordering Montana and Wyoming are part of the northern and middle Rockies. Farther west tower the Lemhi and Lost River ranges, where Borah Peak, the state's highest point, is located.

Most of the mountains in central Idaho, however, are quite different. They were formed when rivers carved deep canyons through the Columbia Plateau. These mountains are named for the river systems that run through them —Coeur d'Alene, Clearwater, and Salmon.

Similar glacial trenches farther north created the Selkirk and Cabinet mountains.

The Continental Divide runs through the Beaverhead Mountains, along part of the Idaho-Montana boundary. Idaho's Middle Rocky Mountains include parts of two ranges, the Teton and the Wasatch ranges.

The Columbia Plateau is a large Pacific Northwest region that stretches across the southern part of the state. Ages ago the land in this area was very rugged. Then came a long period when volcanoes erupted and huge amounts of lava flowed from great cracks in the earth. The lava filled in canyons and buried mountains. The area is now mostly flat to rolling, but some mountainous areas remain.

The Basin and Range Province, in the southeast, is made up of a small part of Bear River's basin. Several high ridges also reach into the Columbia Plateau. They include Cache Peak and Bannock Mountain.

Rivers and Lakes

The Snake River is Idaho's most important river. It flows in a great arc across the southern part of the state. Most of the state is drained by the Snake and its tributaries, the Salmon, Clearwater, Payette, and Boise rivers.

All of the rivers in the Panhandle area flow toward the Columbia River. Among these are the St. Joe, Kootenai, Pend Oreille, Spokane, and Coeur d'Alene rivers. In the Basin and Range Province, the principal river is the Bear. It drains into Great Salt Lake in Utah. A number of these rivers have spectacular waterfalls.

The mountainous uplands of Idaho are dotted with hundreds of lakes. Most of these lakes were created by melting glaciers many thousands of years ago. The two largest are Pend Oreille and Coeur d'Alene. Bear Lake in southeastern Idaho is shared with Utah.

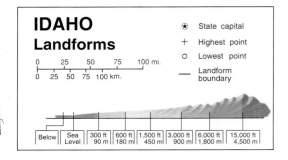

IDAHO
Landforms

| 0 | 25 | 50 | 75 | 100 mi. |

| 0 | 25 | 50 | 75 | 100 km. |

⊛ State capital
+ Highest point
○ Lowest point
— Landform boundary

| Below | Sea Level | 300 ft 90 m | 600 ft 180 m | 1,500 ft 450 m | 3,000 ft 900 m | 6,000 ft 1,800 m | 15,000 ft 4,500 m |

(Map labels: SELKIRK MTS., Kootenai R., CABINET MTS., Pend Oreille, Lake Pend Oreille, COEUR D'ALENE MTS., Coeur d'Alene R., Coeur d'Alene L., St. Joe R., Dworshak Res., CLEARWATER MTS., 710 ft. (216 m), Clearwater, River, BITTERROOT RANGE, SEVEN DEVILS MTS., HELLS CANYON, Salmon, River, Brownlee Dam, Snake R., Rocky Mountains, SAWTOOTH MTS., SALMON RIVER MTS., 12,662 ft. (3,859 m), LEMHI RANGE, LOST RIVER RANGE, BEAVERHEAD MTS., CENTENNIAL MTS., Payette R., Boise, Boise River, Craters of the Moon Nat'l Mon., Columbia Plateau, OWYHEE MTS., Bruneau R., Snake, River, Shoshone Falls, American Falls Res., Bear R., Basin and Range, Bear Lake)

Climate

Warm air from the Pacific Ocean keeps Idaho's climate relatively mild. The high ranges of the Continental Divide often stop blizzards and cold air that come from Canada and the Arctic regions. The average temperature in Boise in January is 30° F (−1° C); in July it is 75° F (24° C).

The most humid parts of the state are in the Panhandle and the Rocky Mountains. Some areas there receive an annual precipitation of more than 40 inches (1,000 millimeters). The driest part of Idaho is the Snake River Plain, where the average annual precipitation is less than 10 inches (250 millimeters). At the higher elevations, most of the precipitation is in the form of snow. Very little snow falls on the lowlands, however.

Idaho's growing season is longer in the west than in the east. Frost-free growing seasons for crops range as high as 180 days in Boise Valley, where some specialty crops take a long time to mature.

Plant and Animal Life

About 40 percent of Idaho is forested. Northern Idaho has the world's largest stand of western white pine, Idaho's state tree. Other important trees include the yellow pine, lodgepole pine, Douglas fir, western larch, Engelmann spruce, and western red cedar. The Indians used to hollow out canoes from giant red cedars, which rival the California redwoods in size and age.

Crops thrive in the rich lava soils of the Columbia Plateau, whose broad plains cover most of northwestern and southern Idaho.

Wildlife is abundant in Idaho. Some of the most common large animals are elk, deer, moose, bears, coyotes, antelope, mountain sheep, and goats. There are also bobcats and cougars. There used to be wolves, but they have moved out of all but a few wilderness areas. Some five hundred species of birds, many of them migratory, thrive in Idaho. Canada geese, with populations sometimes in the millions, nest there undisturbed. Idaho's lakes and streams are well known for their trout and whitefish. Salmon breed in large numbers in the Salmon River and its tributaries, although dams and pollution now threaten them.

Left: The Snake River cascades over the rim of Shoshone Falls. *Below:* Red-tailed hawks and other birds nest in the Snake River Birds of Prey Natural Area.

Natural Resources

Idaho's soils offer plenty of variety to farmers and ranchers. The mountain soils are thin and not very fertile, but forests can thrive in them. The soils of the Columbia Plateau are made up of lava and windblown materials that are very productive when irrigated.

Minerals of commercial value are found throughout the state. Lead, silver, and zinc deposits are especially important, along with gold, copper, and phosphate. The greatest concentration of mineral wealth is in the Panhandle, particularly in the silver mines of the Coeur d'Alene district. In addition, the phosphate deposits of southeastern Idaho are among the largest in the United States.

One of Idaho's most valuable resources is the water in its rivers and streams. Dams on the rivers have created huge reservoirs, which store water for irrigation and hydroelectric power. Without these irrigation systems, southern Idaho would have remained largely uninhabited.

▶ PEOPLE

Idaho, like the rest of the Mountain States, is sparsely settled. Most of its residents live in the rich farmlands watered by the Snake River. Other population centers are in the lumbering, agricultural, mining, and tourist regions in the Panhandle.

People from many places have settled in Idaho, but the majority are of European ancestry. The most common heritages are British, German, Irish, and Scandinavian, which account for nearly 85 percent of Idaho's population. Other groups of European origin include the French, Dutch, and Basques. The Basques, who originated from the Pyrenees Mountains in southwestern Europe, came to Idaho in substantial numbers after 1900. They have prospered and maintained their cus-

The ancestors of Idaho's various people include northern Europeans (*left*), Basques (*right*), and Bannock and Shoshoni Indians (*bottom*).

toms in southern Idaho, particularly in Boise. Hispanic-Americans make up the fastest-growing ethnic group, and their cultural programs and events have become notable. Idaho has fewer numbers of Asian- and African-Americans.

All of Idaho's native Indian tribes have retained their identities, and their population numbers are comparable to those in the days before white settlement. Except for a Pend Oreille group that relocated in Montana, the Indians continue to live on Idaho reservations or in similar settlements. Many other Idahoans claim at least some Indian ancestry.

Education

Idaho has a number of institutions of higher learning. Among the state-supported schools are the University of Idaho in Moscow, Idaho State University in Pocatello, Boise State University in Boise, and Lewis-Clark State College in Lewiston. In addition, there are community colleges in Coeur d'Alene and Twin Falls. Among Idaho's private liberal-arts colleges are College of Idaho in Caldwell, Northwest Nazarene College in Nampa, and Ricks College in Rexburg.

Libraries, Museums, and the Arts

Cultural opportunities that were once limited to large metropolitan centers now reach a number of remote areas. Public and academic libraries are available in most cities and towns, and the Idaho state library extends service to rural areas as well. Two state historical museums (both part of an Idaho State Historical Society educational program), an ethnological museum in Twin Falls, and a natural history museum in Pocatello interpret state

The University of Idaho in Moscow is a state-supported institution of higher education. Founded in 1889, it is Idaho's oldest university.

history and science with modern displays and programs. A number of local county historical museums also offer high-quality exhibits.

Community symphony orchestras, including The Boise Philharmonic, two opera companies (Boise and Idaho Falls), two choral groups (Boise and Lewiston), and a professional ballet company (Boise) provide opportunities for cultural entertainment. There are, in addition, several theatrical companies, including the Boise Shakespearean Company.

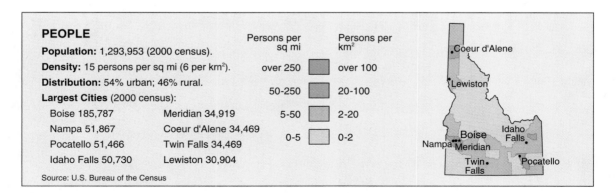

PEOPLE

Population: 1,293,953 (2000 census).

Density: 15 persons per sq mi (6 per km²).

Distribution: 54% urban; 46% rural.

Largest Cities (2000 census):

Boise 185,787	Meridian 34,919
Nampa 51,867	Coeur d'Alene 34,469
Pocatello 51,466	Twin Falls 34,469
Idaho Falls 50,730	Lewiston 30,904

Source: U.S. Bureau of the Census

Persons per sq mi	Persons per km²
over 250	over 100
50-250	20-100
5-50	2-20
0-5	0-2

►ECONOMY

The industries and products of Idaho are closely related to its natural resources. Manufacturing largely involves the processing of products that come from Idaho's farms, forests, and mines. Industries based on high technology have come to the state recently.

Services

Services make up the largest segment of Idaho's economy. They account for 60 percent of the gross state product (GSP). The GSP is the total market value of the state's goods and services. Financial services, including banking, insurance, and real estate, make up about 16 percent of the GSP. Wholesale and retail trade combined also make up 16 percent. General services, such as health, business, and tourism, account for another 15 percent. Government, which includes the administration of public schools and hospitals, accounts for 13 percent.

Manufacturing and Construction

Manufactured products account for approximately 16 percent of the GSP. Most of Idaho's factories are engaged in the processing of food, minerals, and forest products and the manufacture of chemicals and electronics products. The leading food processed in Idaho is the potato. Many products can be made from potatoes, from frozen french fries to starch. Sugar beets, meats, and dairy products also are processed. In addition, Idaho has several large phosphate plants that produce fertilizers and chemicals. Laser printers for computer printing are also manufactured in Idaho. The construction of roads, bridges, buildings, and the like accounts for approximately 3 percent of the GSP.

PRODUCTS AND INDUSTRIES

Manufacturing: Food products, lumber and other forest products, chemicals, electronic products.

Agriculture: Livestock, potatoes, wheat, sugar beets, barley, dairy products.

Minerals: Silver, phosphate rock, gold, sand and gravel, lead, zinc, molybdenum.

Services: Wholesale and retail trade; finance, insurance, and real estate; business, social, and personal services; transportation, communication, and utilities; government.

Percentage of Gross State Product* by Industry

- Manufacturing — 16%
- Finance, insurance, and real estate — 16%
- Wholesale and retail trade — 16%
- 15% — Business, social, and personal services
- 13% — Government
- 11% — Transportation, communication, and utilities
- 9% — Agriculture
- Mining 1%
- Construction 3%

*Gross State Product is the total value of goods and services produced in a year. Source: U.S. Bureau of Economic Analysis

---

Idaho grows more potatoes than any other state. Processing potatoes (*left*) and raising cattle (*below*) are basic to the state's economy.

Left: Wheat is one of Idaho's most profitable crops. *Right:* The production of lumber and other forest products is one of the state's major industries.

Transportation and Communications

A national transportation system connects many parts of Idaho to other states, but there are no direct interstate highways between north and south. Railroads also cross the state east to west, but not north to south. A system of forest roads penetrates some timbered ridges, but a central wilderness area dominates Idaho's mountain country. Road construction is forbidden there, as the people take great pride in preserving their wilderness heritage.

The state's busiest airport is in Boise, the capital. Many northerners, however, find it easier to use the airport across the Washington border, in Spokane. Many people in the southeast find the airport in Salt Lake City, Utah, more convenient.

Idaho publishes nearly a dozen daily newspapers, including Boise's *Idaho Statesman*, Idaho Falls' *Post-Register*, and Lewiston's *Tribune*, and an even greater number of weekly newspapers. Radio and television stations broadcast throughout the state. All totaled, transportation, communications, and public utilities make up 11 percent of the GSP.

Agriculture and Forestry

Idaho's farm products account for about 9 percent of the GSP. Of this number, nearly 40 percent comes from livestock, 20 percent from potatoes, and 12 percent from wheat. Idaho leads the nation in the production of commercial trout and Russet Burbank potatoes (or "Idaho potatoes"), which are excellent for baking. Other valuable crops include sugar beets, seed crops (corn, alfalfa, and clover), mint for chewing gum, barley, hops, onions, prunes, and cherries.

Idaho has a significant lumber industry. Close to one hundred sawmills make all kinds of lumber products from Idaho timber. In addition, one of the world's largest paper mills is located in Lewiston.

Mining

Silver, phosphate rock, lead, and zinc rank highest in value among the minerals produced in the state. Idaho is one of the country's leading producers of these minerals, as well as of abrasive garnet, antimony, and vanadium. Other minerals (all metals) that add to Idaho's income from mining include gold, cobalt, copper, tungsten, and molybdenum. The amounts produced from year to year depend on the demand.

Besides phosphate rock and abrasive garnet, Idaho produces various profitable nonmetallic minerals, such as sand and gravel, stone, and pumice. Abrasive garnet is used for polishing. Pumice is a light, spongy stone thrown up by volcanoes. It is used for cleaning and polishing.

Gemstones can be found in all parts of the state. Beautiful fire opals come from Gem County near Emmett. Adams County has rubies, sapphires, and many pink garnets. Other areas have quartz, agates, jasper, and onyx. Some of the stones are mined commercially. But many are found by people who explore by themselves.

Places of Interest

Cataldo Mission, near Cataldo, is Idaho's oldest standing structure. The mission was built about 1850 by three Jesuit missionaries and a band of Coeur d'Alene Indians. They built the structure without nails, using heavy timbers, handmade boards, willow branches, and mud. The building has been restored as a National Historic Landmark.

City of Rocks, a national reserve, is located south of Burley, six miles (10 kilometers) from the Utah border. It contains many large, strangely shaped monuments that were carved out of granite rocks by wind and water. They reminded the gold-rush prospectors of turtles, elephants, dragons, and other fantastic creatures. One group of spires rises to great heights from the floor of the basin. From a distance, it looks like a city's skyline.

Craters of the Moon National Monument, southwest of Arco, contains a vast number of strange volcanic formations of cinder cones, craters, caves, and weird piles of rocks. The astonishing landscape has the appearance of the moon, as seen through a telescope.

Crystal Falls Cave, near St. Anthony, is just one of Idaho's many remarkable caves. It is a huge cavern with ice formations along its corridors. It also has a frozen river and a frozen waterfall.

Hells Canyon National Recreation Area contains North America's deepest gorge. Located between Lewiston and Boise along the Oregon border, the canyon was carved through volcanic rock by the Snake River. Of exceptional geologic interest are Seven Devils Mountains, which form the eastern walls of Hells Canyon. In some places they measure as high as 7,900 feet (2,400 meters). The spectacular view from Heaven's Gate Lookout extends into four states.

Nez Perce National Historic Park, located near Lewiston, is the only national park that lies completely in Idaho. The culture and history of the Nez Percé Indians is preserved there. It contains two dozen prehistoric villages and historic sites relating to Lewis and Clark.

Sawtooth National Recreation Area, managed by the U.S. Forest Service, is located in central Idaho in the mountains, northwest of Sun Valley. The region is larger than the state of Rhode Island. It contains hundreds of spectacular lakes and peaks, and about 28 percent of the area is wilderness.

Shoshone Falls, near Twin Falls, also is in a Snake River gorge that was cut nearly 15,000 years ago by flood waters. Vertical cliffs tower over its 212-foot (65-meter) drop, a descent greater than Niagara Falls.

Snake River Birds of Prey Natural Area, 30 miles (48 kilometers) from Boise, houses a collection of eagles, hawks, and falcons. Vertical cliffs, more than several hundred feet high over a deep gorge provide nesting sites for these hunting birds. Approximately 482,000 acres (195,059 hectares) of desert lands are reserved for their use.

Sun Valley, a major ski and summer resort, is located in the Sawtooth Mountains near Ketchum. Founded in 1936, it was one of the first American resorts of its kind. It has been the site of many national and international ski events.

State Parks. Idaho has dozens of state parks used for recreation. Among the largest and most popular are Farragut State Park on Pend Oreille Lake and Heyburn State Park on Lake Coeur d'Alene. For more information, contact Idaho State Parks and Recreation Department, Statehouse Mail, Boise, ID 83720

Below: Remarkable granite formations can be found in the City of Rocks. *Right:* Cataldo Mission, Idaho's oldest building, is a National Historic Landmark. *Below right:* Sun Valley is a world-class ski resort.

Boise is Idaho's state capital and most populous city. The city lies in a fertile valley at the foot of the Boise Mountains.

▶CITIES

Boise. Idaho's capital city lies in the Boise River valley in the southwestern part of the state. Its name is a French word that means "wooded." Boise is a regional marketing center and serves as headquarters for several corporations. Its major industries include the manufacture of electronic equipment. Boise is the only city in Idaho with a population greater than 100,000.

Idaho Falls. Located in the southeast on the Snake River, Idaho Falls has grown into a scientific and technological community that is noted for its municipal hydroelectric plant. Idaho Falls also serves as a tourist access point for traffic to Yellowstone National Park and Grand Teton National Park.

Pocatello. Located in a rich agricultural region of the southeast, Pocatello is Idaho's primary railway and industrial center and serves as a distribution center for crops, dairy products, and livestock. It also has several phosphate processing plants and is home to Idaho State University.

Pocatello was named for an Indian chief of the Shoshoni tribe. The city was established in 1882 not long after the railroads reached southeastern Idaho.

Nampa is an industrial and railroad center for southwestern Idaho. Its industries include publishing, the manufacture of electronic equipment, and food processing. One of the world's largest sugar beet processing plants is located in Nampa. Northwest Nazarene College is also located there.

▶GOVERNMENT

The constitution of the state of Idaho was adopted in 1889, about eight months before the territory was admitted to the union. There have since been more than 160 amendments. One in 1896 granted women the right to vote —24 years before a similar amendment was made to the United States Constitution.

The executive branch of Idaho's government consists of a governor and other executive officers. There is a governor's cabinet, which is made up of several departments, including labor, agriculture, law enforcement, and finance. Idaho's governor controls most, but not all, of the state's departments.

Idaho's legislature is made up of two bodies, the senate and the house of representatives. These bodies hold annual sessions to enact laws, which are subject to constitutional restrictions. A legislative council supervises a professional budgeting and auditing staff that helps prepare laws, raise taxes, and spend

GOVERNMENT

State Government
Governor: 4-year term
State senators: 42; 2-year terms
State representatives: 84;
 2-year terms
Number of counties: 44

Federal Government
U.S. senators: 2
U.S. representatives: 2
Number of electoral votes: 4

For the name of the current governor, see STATE GOVERNMENTS in Volume S. For the names of current U.S. senators and representatives, see UNITED STATES, CONGRESS OF THE in Volume U-V.

funds. Laws can also be enacted or repealed by popular vote.

The highest state court in Idaho is the Supreme Court. It is made up of five justices. The major trial courts in the state are called district courts. There are more than 30 of these, presided over by district judges. Appeals courts may review district-court decisions. Minor offenses may be judged by local magistrates in 75 precincts.

County offices are administered by three commissioners each. Law enforcement is also a local function managed by county sheriffs and city police. City governments are administered by mayors and city councils.

▶HISTORY

Indian tribes have lived in what is now Idaho for about 12,000 years. In the early 1800's, the various Indian groups there included the Coeur d'Alene and the Kutenai groups in the Panhandle, the Bannock and the Shoshoni in the south, and the Nez Percé in north central Idaho. All of these were friendly in their first contacts with white settlers. Trouble came only when settlers arrived in great numbers and began to take the land.

Discovery and Exploration

Members of the expedition of Meriwether Lewis and William Clark entered Idaho in August 1805, by way of the Lemhi Pass. Because they could not descend the Salmon River, they left Idaho and traveled north into Montana. One month later they again entered Idaho, this time over the Lolo Pass. They made their way to the Clearwater River and traveled down this river to Lewiston. From there they went on to the Pacific.

Fur traders and trappers were next to explore Idaho. Among the first fur traders was David Thompson, representative of a British company. Thompson founded a trading post, Kullyspell House, on the shores of Pend Oreille Lake in 1809. Later other trading posts were established in the south. In 1834, Nathaniel Wyeth, a Boston merchant, established Fort Hall near present-day Pocatello. Because it was located on the Oregon Trail, Fort Hall later became one of the main trading posts of the West. Fort Boise, near the mouth of the Boise River, was also established in 1834. By 1840 most of the valuable furs had been taken, and the trappers began to disappear.

INDEX TO IDAHO MAP

Aberdeen	(Bingham)	**C4**
American Falls •	(Power)	**C4**
American Falls Reservoir		**C4**
Arco •	(Butte)	**C4**
Ashton	(Fremont)	**D3**
Bellevue	(Blaine)	**B4**
Bitterroot Nat'l Forest		**B3**
Blackfoot •	(Bingham)	**C4**
Blackfoot Reservoir		**D4**
Boise✶	(Ada)	**A4**
Boise Nat'l For.		**B3, B4**
Bonners Ferry •	(Boundary)	**C4**
Buhl	(Twin Falls)	**B4**
Burley •	(Cassia)	**C4**
Cache Nat'l For.		**D4**
Caldwell •	(Canyon)	**A4**
Caribou Nat'l For.		**C4, D4**
Cascade •	(Valley)	**A3**
Cascade Reservoir		**A3**
Challis •	(Custer)	**B3**
Challis Nat'l For.		**B3, C3**
Chubbuck	(Bannock)	**C4**
Clearwater Nat'l Forest		**B2**
Coeur d'Alene •	(Kootenai)	**A2**
Coeur d'Alene Ind. Reservation		**A2**
Coeur d'Alene Lake		**A2**
Council •	(Adams)	**A3**
Craters of the Moon N. M.		**C4**
Dalton Gardens	(Kootenai)	**A2**
Driggs •	(Teton)	**D4**
Dubois •	(Clark)	**C3**
Duck Valley Ind. Reservation		**A4**
Dworshak Reservoir		**A2**
Eagle	(Ada)	**A4**
Emmett •	(Gem)	**A4**
Fairfield •	(Camas)	**B4**
Filer	(Twin Falls)	**B4**
Fort Hall Ind. Res.		**C4**
Fruitland	(Payette)	**A3**
Garden City	(Ada)	**A4**
Glenns Ferry	(Elmore)	**B4**
Gooding •	(Gooding)	**B4**
Grangeville •	(Idaho)	**A3**
Hailey •	(Blaine)	**B4**
Hansen	(Twin Falls)	**B4**
Hayden	(Kootenai)	**A2**
Heyburn	(Minidoka)	**C4**
Homedale	(Canyon)	**A4**
Idaho City •	(Boise)	**B4**
Idaho Falls •	(Bonneville)	**C4**
Inkom	(Bannock)	**C4**
Iona	(Bonneville)	**D4**
Jerome •	(Jerome)	**B4**
Kamiah	(Idaho)	**A2**
Kaniksu Nat'l For.		**A1, B1**
Kellogg	(Shoshone)	**A2**
Ketchum	(Blaine)	**B4**
Kimberly	(Twin Falls)	**B4**
Kuna	(Ada)	**A4**
Lake Lowell		**A4**
Lake Pend Oreille		**A1**
Lapwai	(Nez Perce)	**A2**
Lewiston •	(Nez Perce)	**A2**
Malad City •	(Oneida)	**C4**
McCall	(Valley)	**A3**
Meridian	(Ada)	**A4**
Middleton	(Canyon)	**A4**
Montpelier	(Bear Lake)	**D4**
Moscow •	(Latah)	**A2**
Mountain Home •	(Elmore)	**B4**
Mountain Home AFB	(Elmore)	**B4**
Murphy •	(Owyhee)	**A4**
Nampa	(Canyon)	**A4**
New Plymouth	(Payette)	**A4**
Nezperce •	(Lewis)	**A2**
Nezperce Ind. Reservation		**A2**
Nezperce Nat'l Forest		**B3**
Orofino •	(Clearwater)	**A2**
Osburn	(Shoshone)	**B2**
Palisades Reservoir		**D4**
Paris •	(Bear Lake)	**D4**
Parma	(Canyon)	**A4**
Payette •	(Payette)	**A3**
Payette Nat'l For.		**A3, B3**
Pinehurst	(Shoshone)	**A2**
Pocatello •	(Bannock)	**C4**
Post Falls	(Kootenai)	**A2**
Preston •	(Franklin)	**D4**
Priest Lake		**A1**
Priest River	(Bonner)	**A1**
Rathdrum	(Kootenai)	**A2**
Rexburg •	(Madison)	**D4**
Rigby •	(Jefferson)	**D4**
Rupert •	(Minidoka)	**C4**
Saint Anthony •	(Fremont)	**D4**
Saint Joe Nat'l Forest		**A2, B2**
Saint Maries •	(Benewah)	**A2**
Salmon •	(Lemhi)	**C3**
Salmon Nat'l For.		**B3, C3**
Sandpoint •	(Bonner)	**A1**
Sawtooth Nat'l Forest		**B4, C4**
Shoshone •	(Lincoln)	**B4**
Soda Springs •	(Caribou)	**D4**
Sugar City	(Madison)	**D4**
Targhee Nat'l For.		**C3, D4**
Twin Falls •	(Twin Falls)	**B4**
Wallace •	(Shoshone)	**B2**
Weiser •	(Washington)	**A3**
Wendell	(Gooding)	**B4**
Wilder	(Canyon)	**A4**
Yellowstone Nat'l Park		**D3**

• County Seat   Counties in parentheses   ✶ State Capital

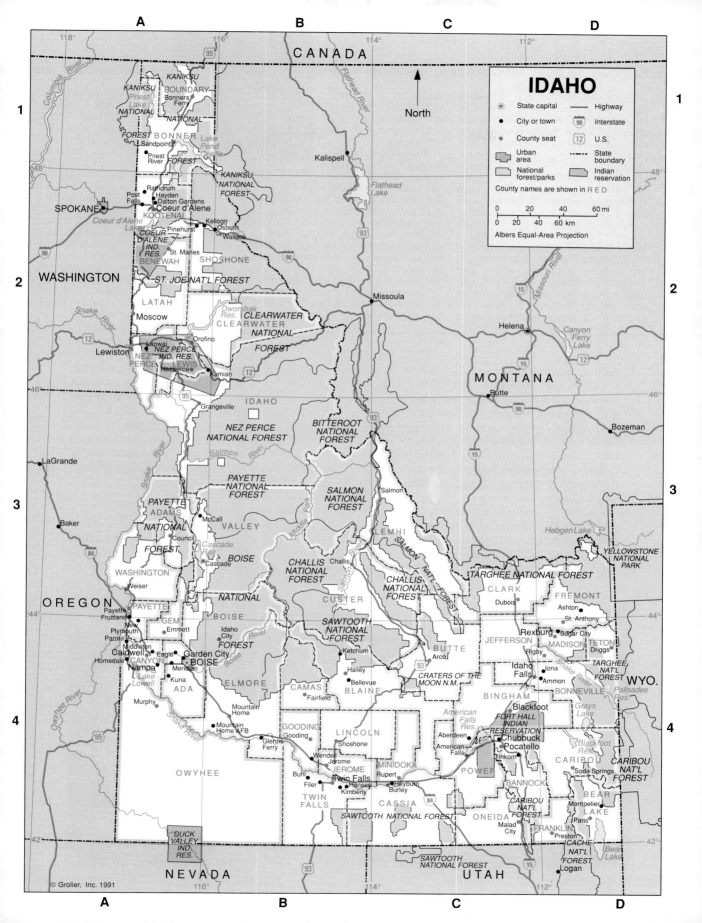

IDAHO

Symbol	Meaning	Symbol	Meaning
⊛	State capital	—	Highway
●	City or town	🛡90	Interstate
●	County seat	🛡12	U.S.

Urban area
National forest/parks
Indian reservation

State boundary

County names are shown in R E D

0   20   40   60 mi
0 20 40 60 km

Albers Equal-Area Projection

CANADA

North

WASHINGTON

OREGON

NEVADA

UTAH

MONTANA

WYO.

© Grolier, Inc. 1991

Famous People

William Edgar Borah (1865–1940), lawyer and political leader, became famous during his long service as U.S. senator from Idaho (1907–40). He was known especially for his ability as an orator and for his independent stand on important national issues. He was born in Illinois but went to Boise in 1890 to practice law.

Gutzon Borglum (1867–1941), born near Bear Lake, was a sculptor whose works are characterized by their power and enormity. His best-known creation is Mount Rushmore National Memorial in South Dakota. Out of the side of a mountain, Borglum carved the faces of four American presidents—George Washington, Thomas Jefferson, Abraham Lincoln, and Theodore Roosevelt. He began the project in 1927 and worked on it until his death. His other works include the large head of Lincoln at the U.S. Capitol building in Washington, D.C.

Vardis Fisher (1895–1968), born in Annis, was a writer whose novels have been praised for their historical accuracy. Among the best known are *Children of God*, about the history of the Mormons, and *The Mothers*, about the Donner party, a group of settlers from Illinois, many of whom tragically perished while trekking across the Sierra Nevada on their way to California in 1846–47. Fisher also wrote a 12-volume series of novels on spiritual and intellectual history called *The Testament of Man*.

Gutzon Borglum

Ernest Hemingway (1899–1961), a novelist, journalist, and short-story writer, spent the final year of his life in Ketchum. Many of Hemingway's stories were based on his own adventures. His most famous short story, "The Snows of Kilimanjaro," is based on his experiences in Africa. His novel *A Farewell to Arms* was based on his experiences in Italy during World War I. *The Sun Also Rises* reflects his and his generation's disillusionment after the war. In 1953 he won the Pulitzer prize for *The Old Man and the Sea*, a short novel. In 1954, he won the Nobel prize for literature. (A biography of Hemingway appears in Volume H.)

Settling the Territory

Idaho was originally part of the Oregon country—a vast area that included what is now Oregon, Washington, and part of Canada. When Oregon became a state in 1859, Idaho was included in the Washington territory. Shortly afterward, gold was discovered in Idaho, and people came to the area by the thousands. Congress created the Idaho territory in 1863.

The first permanent settlement in Idaho was established by Mormons at Franklin in 1860. Other permanent settlements, including Lewiston, Boise, and Soda Springs, were established between 1860 and 1870.

Gold rushes brought in fortune hunters from many different places, and they moved about often in their search for wealth. Some important gold towns declined rapidly and became Chinese mining camps after a few seasons. Chinese miners learned how to produce gold from places where no one else would bother to work. By 1870, more than half of Idaho's miners were Chinese.

Relations with the Indians

Idaho settlers had their share of conflicts with the Indians as they expanded into Indian territory. In 1877, U.S. troops were called in to force a Nez Percé band to relocate from

Left: Thousands of years ago, Indians carved these pictures into the rocks along the Snake River. *Below:* The discovery of gold in 1860 brought miners to Idaho in droves.

Walter Perry Johnson (1887–1946), considered one of the greatest right-handed pitchers in baseball history, began his career in Weiser, but he was born in Humboldt, Kansas. Johnson played for the Washington Senators from 1907 until 1927. He won 416 games (more than any other pitcher in American League history); struck out 3,508 batters (a record that lasted more than 50 years); and pitched a record number (110) major-league shutouts (seven were opening games). He was nicknamed "The Big Train" because of his size and overpowering fastball. Johnson was elected in 1936 as one of the five original members of the Baseball Hall of Fame.

Ernest Hemingway

Ezra Pound

Ezra Pound (1885–1972), a poet and literary critic, was born in Hailey, although he was raised in Pennsylvania. In 1908, he left the United States to live in London and Venice. His controversial long poem, *The Cantos*, is regarded by many as the most important long poem in modern literature. As a critic, Pound influenced the works of T. S. Eliot, William Butler Yeats, James Joyce, and others. He started the literary movement known as imagism.

Sacagawea (1787?–1812?) was a Shoshoni Indian slave, who accompanied the Lewis and Clark expedition west to the Pacific Ocean. She was born in Idaho, probably near Lemhi. In 1800 she was captured by Hidatsa Indians and carried to their village in North Dakota. There she was sold to a Canadian trader named Toussaint Charbonneau, who married her. Lewis and Clark employed Charbonneau as an interpreter, with the understanding that his wife would go with him. (For more information, see the article INDIANS, AMERICAN in Volume I.)

Oregon to a reservation in Idaho. The Indians, led by Chief Joseph, defeated the troops at White-Bird Canyon, but were later overcome on their retreat through Montana. Skirmishes with the Bannock Indians took place the following year, and they, too, were subdued and removed to reservations.

Labor Disputes

On July 3, 1890, Idaho was admitted to the union as the 43rd state. Soon after, the Coeur d'Alene mining district opened, but conflicts quickly arose between the miners, unions, and mine owners. These disagreements touched off a long series of strikes.

In 1899, disgruntled miners dynamited the Bunker Hill plant. To restore order, Governor Frank Steunenberg called in federal troops, which angered many of the miners. Steunenberg was assassinated six years later, and a famous trial followed. William E. Borah prosecuted labor leader and union organizer "Big Bill" Haywood and others for the crime. But the defense attorney, Clarence Darrow, won acquittal for the accused.

20th-Century Developments

In 1902 Congress passed an act that marked the beginning of large-scale irrigation in Idaho. The state was then able to reclaim vast areas of arid and partly arid lands, and agriculture soon became the state's chief source of income. Arrowrock Dam, completed in 1915, was built to provide water reserves for Boise Valley. Several large reservoirs also were constructed. Along with irrigation projects came the development of water power.

After 1919, a disastrous national farm depression slowed Idaho's growth, as did the worldwide economic depression that began in 1929. National recovery programs helped ease the state's unemployment and financial problems, but Idaho was severely afflicted.

In the 1930's, Idaho's economy started to improve as it shifted toward tourism and recreation. Outdoor recreation had been a long-standing Idaho attraction, and its continued popularity was assured with the opening of a ski and summer resort at Sun Valley in 1936.

In 1949, Idaho's National Reactor Testing Station opened near Arco. This was an event of worldwide importance, as it led to the development of nuclear power for commercial purposes. In 1955, Arco became the first village in the United States to be lighted (for one hour) by nuclear power.

Other construction milestones followed. In 1958, Brownlee Dam, the largest power plant on the Snake River, was placed in service. And in 1975, the Columbia-Snake River Inland Waterway was completed, making it possible for barges to travel between Lewiston and the Pacific Ocean. All of these advancements have helped Idaho's economy thrive.

MERLE WELLS
Idaho State Historical Society

IGUANAS

Although it looks like a small, fierce dinosaur with its claws and spines, this shy creature's main pleasure is lounging in the treetops nibbling on tender shoots and leaves. The green iguana, which is the largest lizard in the Americas, may weigh up to 30 pounds (13.6 kilograms) and reach a length of 6 feet (1.8 meters). Its whip-like tail makes up almost two thirds of its length. The green-scaled body has a crest of soft spines running along the middle of the back. Hanging on the throat is a fold of loose skin called a dewlap.

Green iguanas can be found basking in the sun of tropical and subtropical forests from Mexico to Brazil. They belong to the group of reptiles, called Squamata, that includes all lizards and snakes. Its large family includes horned and spiny lizards, chuckwallas, anoles, and basilisks. While most of its relatives live in the Americas, some live as far away as Madagascar and Fiji.

Iguanas and Their Young. Green iguanas court and breed in January or February. When an iguana mates or is being aggressive, parts of its body, such as the head and shoulders, change color. From its greenish color, the iguana changes to orange or pink.

About two months after breeding, the female digs a tunnel in soft ground and lays 20 to 90 round, white-shelled eggs in a chamber at the tunnel's end. Each egg is about 1 inch (2.5 centimeters) in diameter.

Sprawled out on branches, often high above the ground, iguanas warm themselves and feed on buds, leaves, and flowers. They may also eat small insects.

If the nest is not disturbed, the eggs hatch about five months after they are laid. The baby iguanas are about 10 inches (25 centimeters) long. Often, they leave the nest hole together and stay in groups. They clean one another, rub chins, and sleep together.

The young animals are bright green. As they get older, dark bands of scales begin to develop across the shoulders and tail. The iguanas grow rapidly. By the time iguanas are a year old, they are about 3 feet (about 1 meter) long. Although iguanas can live up to ten years, most are killed by predators before their second birthday.

The Life of an Iguana. Iguanas, like all reptiles, are cold-blooded: Their blood is the same temperature as the outside environment. They still need heat for their bodies to function normally, so much of their time is spent soaking up heat energy from the sun. During cold weather, the animals move to the forest floor and seek warm places under logs or in holes.

Each male iguana marks out its own territory. It produces a waxy, scented substance and leaves traces of it among the leaves and branches of its treetop home. It defends this territory against other male iguanas. Rising up on its front legs, it snaps its tail and hisses to scare off an intruding iguana. The best fighter has the largest territory—and mates with the most females.

The Iguana and its Environment. At one time the iguana flourished in the lowland forest, but much of the forestland has been cleared to raise crops and cattle. Animals and people eagerly hunt the iguana, killing almost 95 percent of the iguana population for food. Iguana meat is considered such a tasty treat that it is often called "chicken of the trees." The fat of the iguana is also used as a salve for burns.

Today, efforts are being made to establish iguana ranches in tropical forests. The successful breeding of captive iguanas will not only help save the threatened iguana, but it will also save the vanishing tropical forests.

JENNY TESAR
Author, *Introduction to Animals*

Reviewed by DOUGLAS FALK
Assistant Curator
New York Zoological Society

ILIAD

The *Iliad* is the earliest and most famous work of Greek literature. It is an **epic** (a long poem recounting heroic deeds) believed to have been composed by Homer, a poet who lived during the 700's B.C. Homer probably recited his poems from memory, and the *Iliad* may not have been written down until a later period.

The *Iliad* is divided into 24 parts, or books. It tells the story of events that happened during the Trojan War, which took place about 400 years before the time of Homer. According to legend, the war began when Paris, a son of the king of Troy, kidnapped Helen, wife of the king of Sparta. Homer's poem covers only a few weeks during the last year of the war.

The chief hero of the poem is the Greek warrior Achilles. "The wrath of Achilles is my theme," Homer says at the beginning of the poem. After quarreling with Agamemnon, the leader of the Greek army, Achilles refuses to fight. Without the help of Achilles and his men, the Greeks begin to lose the war. Agamemnon offers Achilles many gifts and begs him to rejoin the fighting, but Achilles refuses. Later, Achilles allows his friend Patroclus to fight wearing Achilles' own armor. Hector, the chief Trojan warrior, kills Patroclus and takes the armor. Seeking revenge, Achilles re-enters the battle and kills Hector. Achilles is restored to his honored position among the Greeks. He also grows in humanity when he gives back Hector's body to Hector's father, the aged king of Troy.

The *Iliad* ends with a truce, for the funerals of Hector and Patroclus. Stories of what happened afterward are found in Vergil's *Aeneid* (29–19 B.C.), with its story of the Trojan Horse, and Homer's *Odyssey*, which tells the adventures of another hero, Odysseus, on his long journey home from Troy.

The *Iliad* contains many moving scenes that show Homer's understanding of human relationships. The poem is also famous for its exciting battle scenes. Homer shows the horrors of war as well as the qualities of courage and self-sacrifice that it brings out in people.

The gods constantly take sides in the war, and they champion individual warriors. For example, Achilles' mother, the goddess Thetis, persuades Zeus to help the Trojans when her son is angry. She also brings him new armor after his is lost through the death of Patroclus. Some of the most humorous scenes show the gods among themselves. Often they behave like mortals, quarreling and fighting.

Homer's style is dramatic, noble, and realistic. Although he was a Greek, he treats the Trojans sympathetically and fairly. Another notable feature of Homer's style is the use of **epithets**, descriptive phrases that characterize persons and things. Achilles is "swift-footed"; the sea is "wine-dark"; the goddess Aphrodite is "laughter-loving."

The *Iliad* is a profound reflection of Greek thought and culture. It also influenced much world literature, not merely epic poetry. This influence is first seen among the Greeks themselves, especially writers of tragedy.

An excerpt from the *Iliad* can be found in GREECE, LITERATURE OF in Volume G.

URSULA SCHOENHEIM
Queens College
Reviewed by GILBERT HIGHET
Formerly, Columbia University

See also AENEID; HOMER; ODYSSEY; VERGIL.

The Greek warriors Achilles and Ajax are shown playing a game in this painting from a Greek vase made about 540 B.C. Achilles is the hero of Homer's *Iliad*.

ILLINOIS

Illinois was named by early French settlers for the Illiniwek Indians, its original inhabitants, whose name meant "superior men." The state has earned many nicknames in its recorded history. It is often called the Prairie State because it is located on the broad, rolling plains of the American Midwest. It has also been called the Corn State, because Illinois produces more corn than any other state except Iowa. But in 1955, Illinois adopted its official nickname—the Land of Lincoln—to honor its most famous adopted citizen, Abraham Lincoln, 16th president of the United States. Lincoln, who is known as the Great Emancipator, practiced law and began his political career in Illinois. Today he lies buried in Springfield, the state capital.

Illinois is a land of striking contrasts. Much of southern Illinois is thinly populated, tranquil countryside, while the northern part of the state is filled with the hustle and bustle of agribusiness and large-scale industries.

Illinois is one of the most economically prosperous states in the nation. It is a giant in manufacturing, commerce, and scientific research, and an important center of transportation. The vast farmlands that cover about 80 percent of the state make Illinois the nation's leading producer of soybeans and its second leading producer of corn.

Of all the fifty states, Illinois ranks fifth in population. Also, it is the most populous state in the Midwest. Located in northern Illinois is Chicago, the largest city in the state and the third largest city in the entire country. More than 50 percent of all Illinoisans live in Chicago's greater metropolitan area.

Thousands of famous people have called Illinois home. The state has claimed more than its fair share of Nobel prize winners. Scores of its writers, musicians, entertainers, and athletes have earned international acclaim. The state also has produced some of the world's foremost educators, journalists, religious leaders, scholars, social reformers, business leaders, and statesmen.

Many people call Illinois the Prairie State because grassy plains (*right*) cover so much of the landscape. It also is home, however, to Chicago (*opposite page*), the third largest city in the United States.

State flag

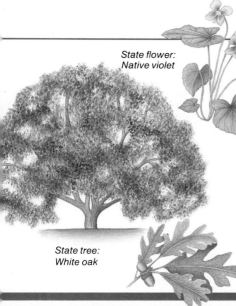

State flower:
Native violet

State tree:
White oak

FACTS AND FIGURES

Location: North central United States; bordered on the north by Wisconsin, on the south by Kentucky, on the east by Indiana, and on the west by Iowa and Missouri.

Area: 57,918 sq mi (150,007 km²); rank, 25th.

Population: 12,419,293 (2000 census); rank, 5th.

Elevation: *Highest*—1,235 ft (375 m), at Charles Mound; *lowest*—280 ft (85 m), on the Mississippi River in Alexander County.

Capital: Springfield.

Statehood: December 3, 1818; 21st state.

State Motto: *State sovereignty, national union.*

State Song: "Illinois."

Nicknames: Land of Lincoln (official); Prairie State; Corn State.

Abbreviations: IL; Ill.

State bird:
Cardinal

Left: About 80 percent of Illinois is covered by the Till Plains, a midwestern region that contains some of the nation's most productive farmland. Wheat (pictured here), corn, and soybean fields thrive in this region. *Below left:* The Fox River in northern Illinois is known for its beautiful valleys. Several small towns have grown up along its banks.

▶LAND

During the Ice Ages, glaciers overran Illinois and formed the land that exists today. Acting like huge bulldozers, the glaciers flattened hills and filled in valleys, leaving most of the land quite level. When the glacial ice melted, huge amounts of earth material, called till, were deposited. (Till is made up of clay, sand, gravel, and ground boulders.) These deposits, along with prairie grasses that had decayed over thousands of years, formed the basis for Illinois' rich, fertile farmlands. But still there are several areas of sharp bluffs (steep cliffs), hills and valleys, and exposed rocks and boulders.

Land Regions

Illinois' varied surface features make up five natural land regions. They are the Till Plains; the Driftless Area; the Great Lakes Plains; the Interior Low Plateaus; and the Gulf Coastal Plain.

The Till Plains. When the Ice-Age glaciers melted, they left thick till deposits over most of Illinois. Till deposits form a gently rolling land surface that is occasionally broken by low, broad ridges called moraines.

The Driftless Area. This small area in the extreme northwestern corner is the only part of Illinois that was not smoothed by glaciers. The streams that cut through this landscape have produced a rough, hilly surface. The section along the Mississippi River contains deep valleys and high bluffs. Located here is Charles Mound, which at 1,235 feet (375 meters), is the highest point in the state.

The Great Lakes Plains. In the extreme northeastern part of the state, along the shores of Lake Michigan, lie the Great Lakes Plains. This area once was the floor of an ancient lake. Today it is a fairly level area that is drained by the Chicago and Calumet rivers. It is surrounded by a wooded area called the Valparaiso Moraine.

The Interior Low Plateaus. Also known as the Shawnee Hills, this area stretches for about 75 miles (120 kilometers) across the southern part of the state. It is rugged and heavily forested and contains many steep bluffs and deep, narrow valleys.

The Gulf Coastal Plain. Covering the southernmost part of the state is the Gulf Coastal Plain, which extends southward to the Gulf of Mexico. This region contains Illinois' lowest point, which lies 280 feet (85 meters) above sea level on the Mississippi River.

Rivers and Lakes

Although the state lies inland, Illinois is like an island. It is almost completely surrounded by water. The mighty Mississippi River lies to the west, forming the border with Iowa; the Ohio River to the southeast forms the border with Kentucky; the Wabash River to the east forms nearly half of the border with Indiana; and Lake Michigan to the northeast provides Illinois with another 60 miles (100 kilometers) of shoreline. The Mississippi River drains about 98 percent of the state. Tributaries of this river include the Illinois, Rock, Kaskaskia, and Ohio rivers.

Illinois' lakes were formed by glaciers. The best known of these are the Fox, Grass, and Pistakee lakes, which make up a group called Chain-O'-Lakes. Several other lakes lie in the floodplains of major rivers. For example, Lake Peoria is a wide spot in the Illinois River. Artificial lakes have been created by building dams across some of the state's rivers. The largest of these, Lake Carlyle, covers more than 26,000 acres (10,500 hectares). These lakes are particularly important in central and southern Illinois because they provide water for the cities in those regions.

Climate

The climate in Illinois varies from north to south. Northern Illinois has hot, humid summers, and the average high temperature in Chicago in July is 85°F (29°C). Northern winters are cold. The average high temperature in Chicago in January is 33°F (1°C), just above freezing. Southern Illinois also has hot, humid summers, and the average high temperature in Cairo in July is 91°F (33°C). The winters are cold, but the temperature usually stays well above freezing. The average high temperature in Cairo in January is 45°F (7°C).

Annual precipitation ranges from less than 36 inches (900 millimeters) in Chicago, in the north, to more than 44 inches (1,120 millimeters) in Cairo, in the south. Most of the state's precipitation comes in the form of rain during the warmer months. Severe storms, such as tornadoes and hailstorms, occur most often in the spring. Thunderstorms are frequent in the summer. Snow covers the ground during much of the winter in the north, but there is little snow in the south.

Plant and Animal Life

Most of the land in Illinois is prairie on which wildflowers grow in abundance. The most common types found are bloodroot, dogtooth violets, Dutchman's breeches, and toothwort. In the 10 percent of Illinois that is forested, woodland trees grow. The most common of them are cottonwood, hickory, maple, oak, and walnut trees.

Many kinds of mammals roam wild in the state. The most common ones are beavers,

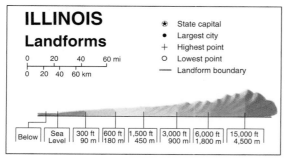

ILLINOIS Landforms

✳	State capital
•	Largest city
+	Highest point
○	Lowest point
—	Landform boundary

0 20 40 60 mi
0 20 40 60 km

| Below | Sea Level | 300 ft 90 m | 600 ft 180 m | 1,500 ft 450 m | 3,000 ft 900 m | 6,000 ft 1,800 m | 15,000 ft 4,500 m |

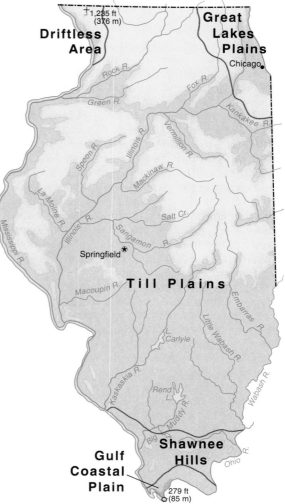

Left: Every August, children of all ages gather at the Illinois State Fair in Springfield, where they can enjoy live entertainment, carnival rides, and agricultural exhibitions. *Below:* When the weather permits, Illinoisans get together outdoors to relax, play games, and enjoy each other's company.

deer, gray and red foxes, minks, muskrats, opossums, rabbits, raccoons, squirrels, and skunks. Wild game birds are quite plentiful and include ducks, geese, pheasants, and quail. Waterfowl sanctuaries are maintained by the state along the Illinois and Mississippi rivers. Illinois' lakes and rivers, including Lake Michigan, support bass, buffalo fish, carp, catfish, perch, pike, and sunfish.

Natural Resources

Illinois' most important natural resources are its soils, minerals, water supplies, and forests. Since 1970, the state has been raising money to conserve and fight the pollution of these natural resources.

There are three major soil groups in the state—grassland soils, forest soils, and alluvial (floodplain) soils. The grassland soils in central and northern Illinois are rich and dark in color, caused by the decay of tall grass that once grew in the area. The forest soils are yellow to brown in color and are found mainly on the hills of southern and northwestern Illinois. They are less fertile than the grassland soils. Alluvial soils are located in the floodplains of the rivers and vary in fertility.

Illinois has a substantial amount of mineral wealth. The minerals are of three general types—the mineral fuels, the metallic minerals, and the nonmetallic, or earthy, minerals. Soft, or bituminous, coal beds lie beneath the surface of two thirds of the state. Illinois also has petroleum deposits in the southeast. Small deposits of lead and zinc are found in the south. Limestone, a source of crushed stone; sand and gravel; fluorspar, used to fluoridate water; and sandstone are found in various parts of the state.

The water resources of Illinois include its rivers and lakes and the underground supplies from deep wells. They furnish water for household and industrial uses and provide transportation and recreational facilities. Artificial lakes supply water to Bloomington, Decatur, and Springfield.

Most of the forests in the state are in the hills of southern Illinois. Many oak, hickory, maple, and cottonwood trees are harvested for lumber and firewood.

▶ PEOPLE

Illinois, with more than 12.4 million people, is the fifth most populous state in the country. It is also one of the most densely populated states, averaging 214 people per square mile (83 people per square kilometer).

Most of the original Illinois settlers were Anglo-Saxons from other states. In the 1800's came waves of European immigrants, mostly Germans and Irish. Later followed Italians, Poles, Hungarians, and Lithuanians. Many blacks came to Chicago from the South after the Civil War ended in 1865. In more recent history, Hispanic and other Latin Americans, Asians, and Russians have settled in Chicago.

More than 83 percent of the people of Illinois live in cities and towns, and more than 25 percent of all of them live within the Chicago city limits.

Libraries, Museums, and the Arts

Illinois has numerous cultural institutions with worldwide reputations for excellence. The Chicago Public Library is the largest library in the state. The John Crerar Library in Chicago is known for its science collections. The Newberry Library, also in Chicago, is noted for its special collections in history, music, and literature. The Illinois State Historical Library in Springfield has large collections pertaining to Abraham Lincoln, the Civil War, and state and local history.

Illinois, particularly Chicago, is an internationally acclaimed center for the arts. Among its most famous institutions are the Chicago Symphony Orchestra, the Lyric Opera of Chicago, and numerous leading museums. The Art Institute of Chicago contains collections of French, Dutch, Italian, and American masterpieces. The Field Museum of Natural History, in Chicago, has many famous exhibits, particularly in anthropology, botany, zoology, and geology. The Museum of Science and Industry, also in Chicago, has many exhibits, including some hands-on exhibits, on science, technology, and industry at work. The Illinois State Museum in Springfield has exhibits covering science, natural history, and the fine arts.

Education

Maintained by nearly 900 local school districts, public schools in Illinois educate more than 2 million pupils. In addition, there are some 325,000 students attending private and parochial (church-run) schools in the state.

Chicagoans are enthusiastic sports fans. The statuary lions outside the Art Institute of Chicago proudly displayed Chicago Bears football helmets to celebrate their 1986 Super Bowl championship win.

Illinois has many institutions of higher learning. The University of Illinois has an enrollment of about 65,000 on its Champaign-Urbana, Chicago, and Springfield campuses. It is one of the nation's largest state-supported universities. The Southern Illinois University system has campuses at Carbondale and Edwardsville. Other state universities are located in Charleston, Chicago, Springfield, Macomb, Normal, Park Forest South, and De Kalb. There are also about fifty two-year colleges in the state.

Well-known private colleges and universities in Illinois include the University of Chicago, De Paul University, Loyola University, and the Illinois Institute of Technology (all in Chicago) and Northwestern University in Evanston. Smaller schools in Illinois include Knox College in Galesburg, Bradley University in Peoria, Illinois Wesleyan University in Bloomington, Wheaton College in Wheaton, Augustana College in Rock Island, and Millikin University in Decatur.

PEOPLE

Population: 12,419,293 (2000 census).

Density: 214 persons per sq mi (83 per km²).

Distribution: 83% urban; 17% rural.

Largest Cities (2000 census):

Chicago 2,896,016	Naperville 128,358
Rockford 150,115	Peoria 112,936
Aurora 142,990	Springfield 111,454

Persons per sq mi	Persons per km²
over 250	over 100
50-250	20-100
5-50	2-20
0-5	0-2

Rockford • Chicago
Aurora • • Naperville
• Peoria
Springfield ★

Source: U.S. Bureau of the Census

The Chicago Mercantile Exchange is a marketplace where traders buy and sell contracts for perishable goods, such as eggs. It is the largest institution of its kind in the world.

▶ECONOMY

Once a predominantly agricultural state, today Illinois has an economy based primarily on service and manufacturing industries.

Services

About 73 percent of the Gross State Product (GSP), or the total value of goods and services produced in a year, is produced by the service industries of Illinois. Most of these industries are located in the Chicago area and include the following categories.

Wholesale and Retail Trade. This is the most important of the service industries. Wholesale trade includes the distribution of such items as food products, machinery, and motor vehicles. Retail trade includes selling products, such as in stores, restaurants, supermarkets, and automobile dealerships. The money earned by selling such products accounts for 18 percent of the total GSP and employs 24 percent of the state's entire work force.

Financial Services. Chicago is the financial capital of the Midwest. Its financial institutions include banks, insurance companies, and the Chicago Board of Trade, where grains and other commodities (economic goods) are traded by contract. Another Chicago financial institution is the Chicago Mercantile Exchange, where contracts are traded for livestock, eggs, and other perishable goods. These are the largest institutions of their kind in the world. Financial services account for 18 percent of the GSP but employ only 7 percent of the state's work force.

Government Services. These services include the maintenance of the state's schools, public hospitals, and military bases. State and local government services combined produce 9 percent of the total GSP and employ 14 percent of the state's work force.

Transportation and Communications Services. Since its early days, Illinois has been a great center for transportation and communication services. Today it is the center of a vast network of railroads, highways, waterways, and airways.

A large volume of freight crosses Illinois on highways and by railroad. Chicago is at the center of this activity and is the railroad center of the nation. Other large railroad centers are East St. Louis and Peoria. Interstate, federal, and state highways serve all sections of the state. Toll roads and expressways are especially important in the Chicago area, which is a major hub for trucking companies.

PRODUCTS AND INDUSTRIES

Manufacturing: Food products, non-electrical machinery, chemicals, fabricated metals, electric and electronic equipment, printing and publishing.

Agriculture: Corn, soybeans, hogs, cattle, dairy products, wheat, oats.

Minerals: Bituminous coal, petroleum, crushed stone, sand and gravel.

Services: Wholesale and retail trade; finance, insurance, and real estate; business, social, and personal services; transportation, communication, and utilities; government.

Percentage of Gross State Product* by Industry

Manufacturing 20%
Mining 1%
Agriculture 2%
Construction 4%
Government 9%
Transportation, communication, and utilities 11%
Business, social, and personal services 17%
Wholesale and retail trade 18%
Finance, insurance, and real estate 18%

*Gross State Product is the total value of goods and services produced in a year. Source: U.S. Bureau of Economic Analysis

Illinois is flanked by the two largest inland water systems in the United States. In the northeast corner is the Great Lakes system. It connects with the Atlantic Ocean by way of the St. Lawrence Seaway. On the western border of the state is the Mississippi River, which empties into the Gulf of Mexico. This river is the busiest waterway in the country.

Chicago is the airlines crossroads of the United States. The city has three airports, and one of them, O'Hare International, is among the nation's busiest commercial airports. More than 56 million people depart from and arrive there each year.

Every large town in Illinois has a newspaper, and many have daily papers. Chicago's major dailies are the *Chicago Tribune* and the *Chicago Sun-Times*. Other leading dailies in the state include *The Daily Pantagraph* (Bloomington), *The Journal Star* (Peoria), and *The Star-Journal Register* (Springfield). All of the larger cities have television and radio stations.

The transportation and communication service industries employ 6 percent of the state's workers and contribute 11 percent to the GSP.

Other Services. There are dozens of other industries that belong in the services category. They include health, legal, and social services; community, recreational, and tourism services; and personal services, such as hairstyling and dry cleaning. Together, they account for 17 percent of the GSP, and employ 23 percent of the state's work force.

Manufacturing and Construction

Most of the manufacturing in Illinois is done in the northern part of the state, especially in the Chicago area. Other important industrial centers are Rockford, Peoria, Rock Island, Moline, La Salle, Peru, Springfield, and the cities in the East St. Louis area. Construction occurs all over the state where roads, bridges, and buildings are built. Together, these two enterprises employ 23 percent of the state's work force and contribute 24 percent of the GSP.

Food Processing. The production of food items is the state's most important manufacturing enterprise, especially in the Chicago area. Many people work in industries that process soybeans and grains, particularly corn. Among the foods produced are baked goods, breakfast cereals, candies, sausages, and spices.

Machinery. Non-electrical machines are the second most important category of manufactured goods in the state. Illinois has long been a leading producer of farm machinery, construction and earth-moving equipment, freight cars, diesel engines, and other transportation equipment. The many factories in the state also turn out tools and dies, household and electrical appliances, pianos, and construction equipment.

Chemicals. The production of chemicals, the third most important manufacturing area, includes cleaning solutions and medicinal drugs. In addition, the production of fabri-

Illinois is one of the most prosperous states in the nation. About 20 percent of its economy is based on manufacturing, particularly food processing (*below*). In agriculture, the state ranks first in the production of soybeans and second in corn (*right*).

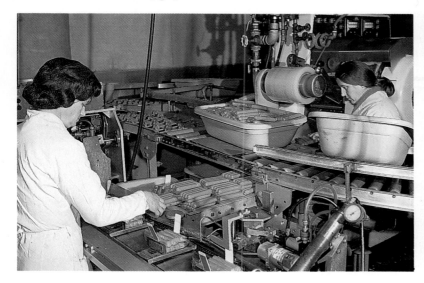

Places of Interest

Sir Georg Solti, music director of the Chicago Symphony Orchestra (1969–91).

Black Hawk Statue, Lowden Memorial State Park.

Lincoln's New Salem State Park, near Petersburg.

The Museum of Science and Industry, in Chicago.

Black Hawk State Historic Site is located on the Rock River in Rock Island. On the site is a statue commemorating Black Hawk, the Sauk warrior. In addition, the Hauberg Indian Museum there contains relics of the Sauk and Fox tribes and life-size dioramas.

Cahokia Mounds State Historic Site, near Collinsville, preserves what remains of an ancient Indian city that was first inhabited about 700 B.C. At the center is Monks Mound, the largest earthen mound in the New World.

Carl Sandburg Birthplace, in Galesburg, commemorates one of Illinois' greatest literary figures and preserves many of the Sandburg family's belongings. The home is representative of that of a typical working class family of the late 1800's.

Chicago contains a wide variety of important and interesting museums, cultural institutions, and historic sites. You can read more about these places in the CHICAGO article in Volume C.

Fort Kaskaskia State Historic Site, in Ellis Grove, overlooks the Mississippi River and the town of Kaskaskia, the first capital of Illinois. The fort was built by the French to protect themselves from the British during the French and Indian War. In 1766, the townspeople destroyed the fort, rather than have the British occupy it. Today only the foundation remains.

Lincoln-Herndon Law Offices, in downtown Springfield, is where Lincoln and his partner William Herndon maintained a law office in the 1840's and 1850's. There visitors may learn about Lincoln's professional life. Downstairs is a court, which has been restored to the way it appeared in the 1800's.

Lincoln Log Cabin, near Charleston, preserves the last home of Abraham Lincoln's parents, Thomas and Sarah Bush Lincoln. Farm life of the 1800's is recreated by park guides to give visitors a glimpse into the daily lives of the Lincolns and their neighbors.

Lincoln's New Salem, near Petersburg, is a reconstruction of the village where Abraham Lincoln lived as a young man. Park guides dressed in period costumes recreate the mood of the 1830's, and daily activities show what life was like in the 1830's, when Abraham Lincoln lived there.

Lincoln's Tomb is located in Oak Ridge Cemetery in Springfield. The tomb was dedicated in 1874, and Lincoln's remains were moved there in 1901. His wife, Mary, and three of his four sons also are buried there.

Ulysses S. Grant Home State Historic Site, in Galena, is the place where Grant returned after the Civil War. The house was a gift to him from the townspeople and is decorated with many of the Grant family's original furnishings. Galena itself is one of the best-preserved towns of the 1800's in the United States.

State Parks. For information on Illinois' state parks, contact the Illinois Department of Conservation, Office of Public Information, 524 South Second Street, Springfield, IL 62701-1787.

cated metal products, electric and electronic equipment, and printed materials is also important in Illinois.

Agriculture

The farms of the state employ 2 percent of the state's work force and contribute 2 percent of the GSP. There are some 21.6 million acres of farm land in Illinois devoted to raising crops. Illinois farmers grow many different crops, but they are best known for raising soybeans and corn. The state's soybean crop is the largest in the country, and the corn crop is second. Other grains grown in the state include rye, barley, oats, and popcorn. Farms near the large cities produce a variety of vegetables, and there are fruit orchards in many parts of the state.

Illinois ranks twelfth in the nation in raising livestock. Cattle and hogs have the highest market value. Sheep and poultry are also raised.

Mining

Mining employs 1 percent of the Illinois work force and contributes 1 percent of the GSP. Coal is the most important mineral. Most of the large coal mines are in the western and southern parts of the state. Soft coal is burned by the utility companies to generate electricity. Oil can be found in an area southwest of Springfield. Fluorspar can be found in southern Illinois. It is used in metal industries and to fluoridate drinking water.

▶ CITIES

Four out of every five people in Illinois live in a city. The state's most populous cities include Chicago, Rockford, Aurora, Naperville, Peoria, Springfield, and the twin cities of Champaign and Urbana.

Springfield. Illinois' capital city, Springfield is located in the central part of the state. It lies in the heart of the corn belt and is also an important coal-mining and industrial area. Pioneers from the south settled that region in 1818, the year Illinois became a state. The settlement was incorporated as a town in 1832 and became the state capital in 1839. Springfield is often associated with Abraham Lincoln because he made his home there for many years.

Chicago. Located on the southwestern shore of Lake Michigan, Chicago is the most

Springfield became Illinois' state capital in 1839. The capitol building shown above was completed in 1887. Earlier state capitals were located in Kaskaskia (1818–20) and Vandalia (1820–39).

important city in the Midwest. It is also the most populous city in Illinois and the third most populous city in the country. Half the people in Illinois live in Chicago's greater metropolitan area, and most of the state's industry and culture is centered there. You can read more about this city by reading the article CHICAGO in Volume C.

Rockford. The state's second most populous city, Rockford lies on the Rock River, and got its name from the ford in the river taken by the Galena-Chicago stagecoach line. Rockford was founded in 1834 and incorporated as a city in 1853. Today it is an agricultural marketing center. It is also the largest manufacturing center for screws and fasteners in the country and is one of the world's largest producers of machine tools.

Peoria. Settled in 1691, Peoria may be the oldest white settlement in Illinois. Located on the Illinois River in the heart of a rich agricultural basin, Peoria is named for the Indian tribe that lived there when the French explorers arrived. The flags of four nations have since flown over Peoria: France, Great Britain, Spain, and the United States.

Champaign-Urbana. These twin cities are home to the University of Illinois, the largest of Illinois' state-supported universities. The two towns are separately incorporated. Urbana was settled in 1822. Champaign was originally founded as West Urbana but became incorporated as Champaign in 1860.

▶ GOVERNMENT

Illinois' state constitution provides for a government made up of three branches. Each branch—the legislative, the executive, and the judicial—has specific duties assigned to it.

The legislative branch consists of the state legislature called the General Assembly. The General Assembly holds sessions every year to make the laws for the state. It is made up of two houses—a house of representatives and a senate. The house has 118 state representatives, who serve 2-year terms. The senate has 59 members, who serve either 2-year or 4-year terms.

The executive branch, headed by the governor, carries out the laws of the state. The governor appoints the heads of various state agencies. Executive officials are elected and include the governor, the lieutenant governor, the secretary of state, the attorney general, the treasurer, and the comptroller (the auditor of public accounts).

The judicial branch—the court system—is responsible for interpreting and applying the laws. There are three kinds of courts in the state: the state supreme court; the state appellate courts; and the state circuit courts. All judges are elected by the people.

The state supreme court has seven justices, who are elected to 10-year terms. The state's 36 appellate justices also serve 10-year terms. The circuit court justices (21 courts with a varying number of judges) serve 6-year terms.

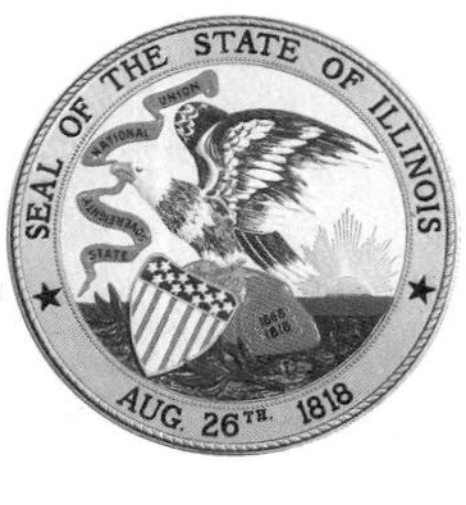

GOVERNMENT

State Government
- Governor: 4-year term
- State senators: 59; 2- or 4-year terms
- State representatives: 118; 2-year terms
- Number of counties: 102

Federal Government
- U.S. senators: 2
- U.S. representatives: 19
- Number of electoral votes: 21

For the name of the current governor, see STATE GOVERNMENTS in Volume S. For the names of current U.S. senators and representatives, see UNITED STATES, CONGRESS OF THE in Volume UV.

INDEX TO ILLINOIS MAP

Albion •	(Edwards)	E5
Aledo •	(Mercer)	C2
Alton	(Madison)	C5
Arlington Heights	(Cook)	F1
Aurora	(Kane)	E2
Belleville •	(St. Clair)	D5
Belvidere •	(Boone)	E1
Benton •	(Franklin)	E5
Bloomington •	(McLean)	D3
Bourbonnais	(Kankakee)	F2
Bradley	(Kankakee)	F2
Cahokia	(St. Clair)	C5
Cairo •	(Alexander)	D6
Cambridge •	(Henry)	C2
Canton	(Fulton)	C3
Carbondale	(Jackson)	D6
Carlinville •	(Macoupin)	D4
Carlyle •	(Clinton)	D5
Carmi •	(White)	E5
Carrollton •	(Green)	C4
Carthage •	(Hancock)	B3
Centralia	(Marion)	D5
Champaign	(Champaign)	E3
Charleston •	(Coles)	E4
Chester •	(Randolph)	D6
Chicago •	(Cook)	F2
Chicago Heights	(Cook)	F2
Cicero	(Cook)	F2
Clinton •	(De Witt)	E3
Collinsville	(Madison)	D5
Danville •	(Vermilion)	F3
Decatur •	(Macon)	E4
De Kalb	(De Kalb)	E2
Des Plaines	(Cook)	F1
Dixon •	(Lee)	D2
East Moline	(Rock Island)	C2
East Peoria	(Tazewell)	D3
East St. Louis	(St. Clair)	C5
Edwardsville •	(Madison)	D5
Effingham •	(Effingham)	E4
Elgin	(Kane)	E1
Elizabethtown •	(Hardin)	E6
Eureka •	(Woodford)	D3
Evanston	(Cook)	F1
Fairfield •	(Wayne)	E5
Freeport •	(Stephenson)	D1
Galena •	(Jo Daviess)	C1
Galesburg •	(Knox)	C3
Geneva •	(Kane)	E2
Golconda •	(Pope)	E6
Granite City	(Madison)	C5
Greenville •	(Bond)	D5
Hardin •	(Calhoun)	C4
Harrisburg •	(Saline)	E6
Harvey	(Cook)	F2
Havana •	(Mason)	C3
Hennepin •	(Putnam)	D2
Herrin	(Williamson)	D6
Hillsboro •	(Montgomery)	D4
Jacksonville •	(Morgan)	C4
Jerseyville •	(Jersey)	C4
Joliet •	(Will)	E2
Jonesboro •	(Union)	D6
Kankakee •	(Kankakee)	F2
Kewanee	(Henry)	D2
Lacon •	(Marshall)	D2
Lawrenceville •	(Lawrence)	F5
Lewistown •	(Fulton)	C3
Lincoln •	(Logan)	D3
Louisville •	(Clay)	E5
Macomb •	(McDonough)	C3
Marion •	(Williamson)	E6
Marshall •	(Clark)	F4
Mattoon	(Coles)	E4
McLeansboro •	(Hamilton)	E5
Metropolis •	(Massac)	E6
Moline	(Rock Island)	C2
Monmouth •	(Warren)	C3
Monticello •	(Piatt)	E3
Morris •	(Grundy)	E2
Morrison •	(Whiteside)	D2
Morton	(Tazewell)	D3
Mound City •	(Pulaski)	D6
Mount Carmel •	(Wabash)	F5
Mount Carroll •	(Carroll)	D1
Mount Prospect	(Cook)	F1
Mount Sterling •	(Brown)	C4
Mount Vernon •	(Jefferson)	E5
Murphysboro •	(Jackson)	D6
Naperville	(Du Page)	E2
Nashville •	(Washington)	D5
Newton •	(Jasper)	E5
Normal	(Mc Lean)	E3
North Chicago	(Lake)	F1
Oak Lawn	(Cook)	F2
Oak Park	(Cook)	F2
O'Fallon	(St. Clair)	D5
Olney •	(Richland)	E5
Oquawka •	(Henderson)	C3
Oregon •	(Ogle)	D1
Ottawa •	(La Salle)	E2
Park Forest	(Cook)	F2
Paris •	(Edgar)	F4
Paxton •	(Ford)	E3
Pekin •	(Tazewell)	D3
Peoria •	(Peoria)	D3
Peru	(La Salle)	D2
Petersburg •	(Menard)	D3
Pinckneyville •	(Perry)	D5
Pittsfield •	(Pike)	C4
Pontiac •	(Livingston)	E3
Princeton •	(Bureau)	D2
Quincy •	(Adams)	B4
Rantoul	(Champaign)	E3
Robinson •	(Crawford)	F4
Rock Falls	(Whiteside)	D2
Rockford •	(Winnebago)	D1
Rock Island •	(Rock Island)	C3
Rushville •	(Schuyler)	C3
Salem •	(Marion)	E5
Schaumburg	(Cook)	E1
Shawneetown •	(Gallatin)	E6
Shelbyville •	(Shelby)	E4
Skokie	(Cook)	F1
Springfield ✱	(Sangamon)	D4
Sterling	(Whiteside)	D2
Streator	(La Salle)	E2
Sullivan •	(Moultrie)	E4
Sycamore •	(De Kalb)	E2
Taylorville •	(Christian)	D4
Toledo •	(Cumberland)	E4
Toulon •	(Stark)	D2
Tuscola •	(Douglas)	E4
Urbana •	(Champaign)	E3
Vandalia •	(Fayette)	D5
Vienna •	(Johnson)	E6
Virginia •	(Cass)	C4
Waterloo •	(Monroe)	C5
Watseka •	(Iroquois)	F3
Waukegan •	(Lake)	F1
Wheaton •	(Du Page)	E2
Winchester •	(Scott)	C4
Woodstock •	(McHenry)	E1
Yorkville •	(Kendall)	E2

• County Seat Counties in parentheses ✱ State Capital

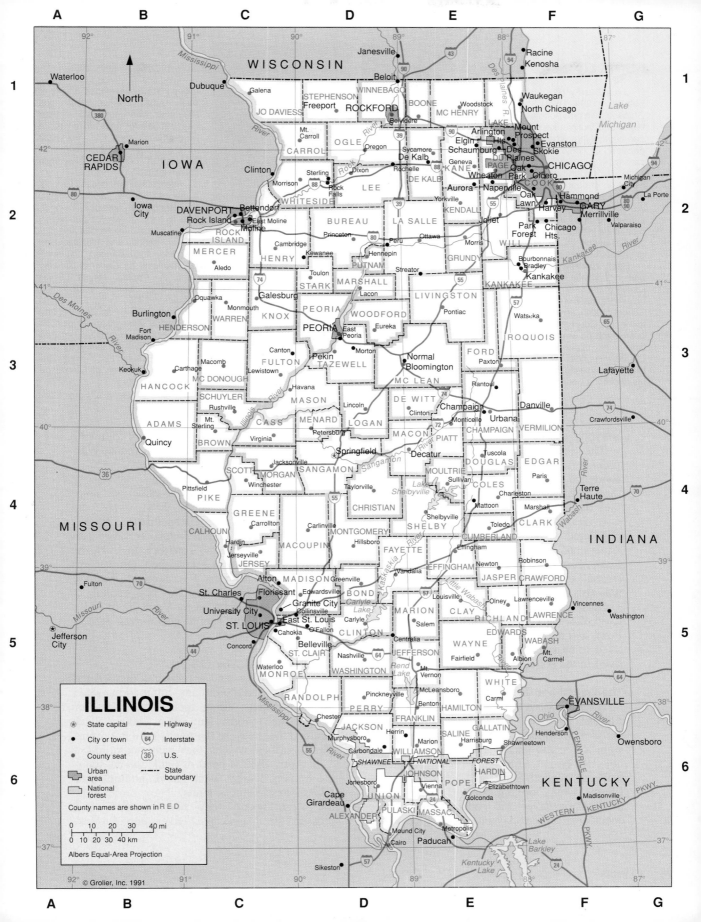

Famous People

Jack Benny (Benjamin Kubelsky) (1894–1974), born in Chicago, was a popular entertainer and violinist known for his penny-pinching character and deadpan comedy. He started his career in vaudeville in 1912. "The Jack Benny Show," first heard on radio in 1932, later became a popular television show (1950–64). Benny also appeared in many films, including *To Be or Not To Be* (1942). In 1957 he was given a special award by the National Academy of Television Arts and Sciences.

Harry Andrew Blackmun (1908–99), born in Nashville, Illinois, was an associate justice of the U.S. Supreme Court (1970–94). A graduate of Harvard University Law School (1932), he was appointed in 1959 to the U.S. Court of Appeals, Eighth Circuit, over which he presided until 1970. At the time of his appointment to the Supreme Court by President Richard Nixon in 1970, Blackmun was considered a moderate, but his decisions became increasingly liberal.

Katherine Dunham

Miles Davis

For example, he once supported capital punishment, but toward the end of his career he denounced the practice, calling it a "failed experiment." Blackmun is chiefly remembered for writing the majority opinion for the landmark case *Roe* v. *Wade* (1973), which held that a state could not pass a law prohibiting abortion.

Miles Davis (Miles Dewey Davis III) (1926–91), a jazz trumpeter, composer, and bandleader, was born in Alton. He began his career in the 1940's, playing a complex form of jazz called bop (or bebop) with Charlie Parker's jazz band and other

groups. Davis developed a style of music called cool jazz, which was smoother and more lyrical than bop, but he later returned to a more hard-driving style. In the late 1960's, Davis combined jazz with features of rock music in a style known as fusion.

Katherine Dunham (1910–   ), a modern dancer, choreographer, and ethnologist, was born in Joliet. She is best known for her repertoire of dances based on African and Caribbean ritual, dance, and folklore. She choreographed and danced in such Broadway musicals as *Cabin in the Sky* (1940) and *A Tropical Revue* (1943) and appeared as herself in the film *Stormy Weather* (1943). In the 1950's and 1960's, Dunham and her dance company toured the United States and Europe. In 1967 she founded a dance school and performing arts center for inner-city children in East St. Louis. Her writings include a memoir, *A Touch of Innocence* (1959).

▶ HISTORY

The Illinois region was once populated by prehistoric Indians called Mound Builders. Evidence from the discovery of thousands of their burial and temple mounds suggests that they lived there as early as 6500 B.C.

Eventually, the Illinois River valley was populated by the Illiniwek, a group of Native Americans that included the Cahokia, Kaskaskia, Moingwena, Michigamea, Tamaroa, and Peoria Indians. This tribal union was also known as the Illinois Confederacy.

Outside the Illinois River valley in the north lived the Sauk (or Sac), the Mesquakie (or Fox), and the Potawatomi. The Miami Indians lived in east central Illinois, and the Shawnee lived in the southeast.

The French and British in Illinois

The French were the first Europeans to see Illinois. In 1673, Louis Jolliet and Father Jacques Marquette traveled down the Mississippi River and later headed north on the Illinois River. In 1680 the French nobleman Robert Cavelier, Sieur de La Salle, explored Illinois while looking for the mouth of the Mississippi River. He founded Fort Crèvecoeur near present-day Peoria. In 1763 the region was turned over to the British following France's defeat in the French and Indian War.

Illinois Becomes the 21st State

Great Britain governed the American colonies and territories until 1781, when the Americans won their independence. Illinois became part of the Northwest Territory and later part of the Indiana Territory. In 1809, the Illinois Territory was established. On December 3, 1818, Illinois was brought into the union as the 21st state. The first capital, at Kaskaskia, was replaced by Vandalia in 1820. Then, in 1839, the capital was moved permanently to Springfield.

The Black Hawk War (1832)

Tensions over land agreements divided the new settlers and the Indians. Some Indians had signed treaties, selling their tribal lands for money and goods. But other Indians later claimed that because the treaties did not represent the tribes' wishes, they were not valid.

In April 1832, a band of Sauk and Mesquakie Indians, led by Black Hawk, attempted to retake these Illinois lands. They came from the west, where they had resettled, and crossed the Mississippi River into Illinois.

Benjamin David (Benny) Goodman (1909–86), born in Chicago, was a clarinetist and jazz bandleader. Known as the King of Swing, Goodman was one of the world's most popular bandleaders. He organized his own band in 1934 and conducted various jazz bands on tour. He also performed as a clarinet soloist with classical symphony orchestras. His autobiography is called *Kingdom of Swing*.

Daniel Hale Williams (1856–1931), a pioneer in the field of heart surgery, was born in Hollidaysburg, Pennsylvania. After receiving his M.D. from Northwestern University in 1883, he set up practice in Chicago, where he later founded (1891) Provident Hospital, the nation's first interracial hospital. In 1893, Williams performed a daring and successful surgical procedure to repair a wound to a patient's pericardium (the sac surrounding the heart). This was the first recorded operation of its kind. He also was the only African American to be named a charter member of the American College of Surgeons (1913).

Abraham Lincoln

Consult the Index and the article CHICAGO in Volume C to find more information in *The New Book of Knowledge* about the following people who were born in Illinois or are otherwise associated with the state:

ADDAMS, Jane	DOUGLAS, Stephen A.	MILLIKAN, Robert
BELLOW, Saul	EARP, Wyatt	Andrews
BLACK HAWK	FERMI, Enrico	PROXMIRE, William
BRYAN, William Jennings	FORD, Betty	REAGAN, Ronald
CLINTON, Hillary Rodham	FRIEDAN, Betty	SANDBURG, Carl
DARROW, Clarence	HEMINGWAY, Ernest	STEVENSON, Adlai, II
DISNEY, Walt	LINCOLN, Abraham	SULLIVAN, Louis
DOS PASSOS, John	MIES VAN DER ROHE,	
	Ludwig	

However, they soon met up with federal troops and Illinois militiamen.

The Indians were badly defeated in a battle at the mouth of the Bad Axe River, and Black Hawk was taken prisoner. On September 21, 1832, the surviving Indians gave up their claim to the Illinois lands in exchange for yearly payments and a reservation in what is now Iowa. This agreement was called the Black Hawk Purchase.

The Growth of Commerce and Industry

In 1825 the Erie Canal was completed, linking the Great Lakes in the Midwest with the Hudson River in the East. This new transportation route created a market in the East for Illinois' products, causing a boom in farming and industry.

When railroads came to Chicago in 1848, the city was already a major transportation center. The first railroad to open was the Galena and Chicago Union Railroad. It was followed in 1856 by the Illinois Central Railroad. Chicago became the transportation hub between east and west.

Illinois took its first steps toward becoming an industrial and agricultural giant in 1837, when John Deere made the first steel plow in Grand Detour. His plow made it easier to farm the endless acres of tough prairie soil, and opened up much of the state to agricultural development. In 1847 another important piece of farm equipment, the mechanical reaper, was developed in Chicago by Cyrus McCormick. The reaper speeded up harvesting the crops, saving the farmers time and money.

Illinois, Lincoln, and the Civil War

In 1858, Stephen A. Douglas, a U.S. senator from Illinois, ran for re-election to the Senate. His opponent in the race was Abraham Lincoln, a lawyer and former U.S. congressman from Springfield. Lincoln and Douglas met in seven Illinois locations to debate the issue of slavery. Lincoln lost the senatorial election, but in 1860 he won the election for president of the United States. Lincoln took office one month before the Civil War began.

During the war, Illinois favored the Union, and about 255,000 young men from the state served in the Union Army. The war created a great demand for products. Illinois grain was sold to the government to feed the Union soldiers, and the state became a leader in meat packing, food processing, and the manufacture of farm and transportation machinery.

The Haymarket Riot took place in Chicago on May 4, 1886. Anti-labor feelings later were roused because the demonstrating workers killed eight policemen.

The Great Chicago Fire (1871)

On the evening of October 8, 1871, a great tragedy occurred. A fire started in the barn behind Patrick O'Leary's house on DeKoven Street and raged for more than 24 hours across more than 3 square miles (8 square kilometers) of the city. Nearly 18,000 buildings, most of them made of wood, burned readily. The business district was destroyed. At least 300 people were killed and 90,000 left homeless.

Chicagoans began to rebuild immediately, and the city soon flourished again. Manufacturing output was second only to New York's, and Chicago became the center of the mail-order industry: Montgomery Ward opened his business there in 1872, and Sears, Roebuck and Company followed in 1893. Also, the world's first metal-supported skyscraper, the 10-story Home Insurance Building, was built in Chicago in 1885. The skyline would soon be filled with tall buildings.

Workers Revolt

In the late 1800's, Chicago became known for its labor disputes. The most famous of these was the Haymarket Riot of 1886. On May 3, a strike at the McCormick Harvester plant in Chicago had left six strikers dead. Workers gathered the following day in Haymarket Square at a protest rally. A labor sympathizer lobbed a bomb into the ranks of policemen, and shots were fired from both sides. Eight policemen and several bystanders were killed, and many more were injured.

Chicago During the Jazz Age

In 1918, many of New Orleans' great jazz musicians arrived in Chicago. When the southerners, such as Louis Armstrong, joined up with young Chicago musicians, such as Benny Goodman, Chicago-style jazz was born. But Chicago also had a dark side. Underworld criminals, notably Al Capone, supplied the city with illegal alcoholic beverages during the Prohibition years. The most notorious crime of the era took place on February 14, 1929, when Capone's men gunned down seven members of a rival gang in an incident known as the St. Valentine's Day Massacre.

Race riots also broke out on occasion. Tensions ran high, especially during the Great Depression of the 1930's, when millions of people lost their jobs, homes, and farms due to extremely hard economic times.

World War II

Throughout the United States' participation in World War II (1941–45), Illinois' defense factories and aircraft plants turned out tons of war materials to support the war efforts against Japan and Germany.

On December 2, 1942, the first controlled atomic reaction was set off under the stands of the football field at the University of Chicago. This experiment, supervised by Nobel prize winner Enrico Fermi, laid the groundwork for nuclear research and the development of the atomic bomb, which ended the war in the Pacific in 1945.

Postwar Developments

After the war, Illinois continued to prosper. In 1959, the opening of the St. Lawrence Seaway gave Chicago direct access to the Atlantic Ocean, further increasing the state's commerce. Large seagoing vessels finally could sail freely in and out of Chicago, and the city became a world port.

Illinois Today

The economy of Illinois has grown steadily over the years and has kept pace with trends in business and manufacturing. With its rich agricultural, industrial, and natural resources, Illinois is well prepared to meet the challenges of today's technological age.

THOMAS G. AYLESWORTH
Author, *Let's Discover the States Series*

See also CHICAGO.

Left: **A richly decorated initial takes up most of this page from the Lindisfarne Gospels, an illuminated manuscript created about A.D. 700. The complex patterns of interlaced lines are typical of early Irish and English illuminations.**

Above: **St. Luke is depicted in this page from a gospel book made during the late 900's for Otto III, a German ruler. Many illuminated manuscripts were made for kings, church leaders, and other wealthy people.**

ILLUMINATED MANUSCRIPTS

Illuminated manuscripts are handwritten books decorated with painted pictures or designs. They are usually thought of as an art of the Middle Ages, when beautifully decorated Bibles and prayer books were produced to glorify God and to teach religious doctrine. Often, gold leaf (a thin layer of gold) was added to the decoration, and the brilliant metal seemed to light up the pages of the manuscript. For this reason, the manuscripts were called "illuminated," from a Latin word that means "to light up."

Illustrated books have been made throughout the ages. Manuscripts decorated with drawings have been found in Egyptian tombs. It is believed that the ancient Greeks and Romans illustrated some texts, such as works on science and medicine. Some of the first elaborately decorated manuscripts were made in the eastern part of the Roman Empire, later called the Byzantine Empire, by professional scribes (copyists) and illuminators. By the 600's, the work of writing and illustrating religious manuscripts had been taken over by monks. The art of manuscript illumination spread throughout western Europe.

The monks worked in monasteries, in special rooms called **scriptoria**. At first, the monks simply copied the old manuscripts, but later they began to create new books. One

Above: A prayer book made for a French duke about 1415 contains calendar pages showing the signs of the zodiac and scenes of daily life. *Below:* An illuminated manuscript of the *Shah-nameh*, a famous Persian epic, was produced in the 1500's by an Islamic artist.

group of monks copied the text onto pages made of parchment or vellum, types of prepared animal skin. The manuscript was then given to illuminators, who decorated it using thick watercolor paints and gold leaf.

Some of the decorations in illuminated manuscripts were small pictures, called **miniatures** from the Latin word *minium*, or "red lead." Minium was often used as a pigment by early illuminators. (Today, the word "miniature" refers to any small picture.) The pictures did not always illustrate the text, and they did not always have religious subjects, such as images of saints or scenes from the Bible. Sometimes they depicted everyday scenes.

Other manuscript decorations were purely ornamental. Pages were bordered with designs that made a frame for the text. Some designs were based on plant or animal forms; other designs combined these forms with complex patterns of interlaced lines and geometric shapes. Often the first letter of a new section of text was enlarged and elaborately decorated. These initial letters sometimes filled an entire page.

During the 1100's, Europe's first universities were formed, and monasteries began to decline as centers of learning. Illuminated manuscripts were again created by artists working outside the church. Among these later manuscripts were collections of romances, books about animals and plants, and other nonreligious works. Then, in the 1400's, the printing press was invented. Hand-lettered manuscripts with hand-painted decorations gradually were replaced by printed books with illustrations, such as woodcuts or engravings, that could be reproduced along with the text.

Islamic Illuminated Manuscripts. Beautiful illuminated manuscripts were created by Islamic artists. Some of the finest Islamic manuscripts were produced in Persia from the 1300's to the 1700's. Because the Islamic faith discourages the making of images, much Islamic illumination consisted of abstract designs that did not represent people or things. Islamic artists also concentrated on **calligraphy**—the art of beautiful handwriting. Nonreligious art was less restricted, however, and Islamic books of stories, poems, and fables frequently were illustrated with likenesses of people.

Reviewed by GEORGE O. SIMMS
Author, *The Book of Kells: A Short Description*

ILLUSTRATION AND ILLUSTRATORS

The word "illustration" has several meanings, but it usually refers to any picture that accompanies a text. Illustrations can be drawings, paintings, or photographs, or they can take the form of maps, graphs, or charts. Some illustrations help explain the text or provide further information, while others are purely decorative.

▶ **EARLY ILLUSTRATIONS**

The earliest known manuscripts containing words and pictures were Egyptian scrolls. Scrolls were long sheets of papyrus (a paper-like material made from the stems of the papyrus plant) that were rolled up for storage. Papyrus scrolls were also used by the ancient Greeks. Between A.D. 100 and 400, scrolls were replaced by codices—manuscripts with pages made of parchment (prepared animal skins). Illustrated works of the poets Homer and Vergil are early examples of codices.

The invention of paper by the Chinese about A.D. 100 began a long tradition of fine illustration in both the eastern and western hemispheres. In China, brushes and diluted inks were used for writing characters and for making watercolor illustrations on paper. In the Islamic world, illustrators concentrated mainly on ornamental designs and on **calligraphy** (the art of beautiful handwriting). In Europe during the Middle Ages, monks copied holy texts onto parchment and illustrated them with beautifully painted pictures and designs. To read more about this art, known as manuscript illumination, consult the article ILLUMINATED MANUSCRIPTS, which appears on pages 77 and 78 of this volume.

Printed Illustrations. All early illustrations were unique, each one drawn and colored by hand. In the early 800's, however, the invention of the woodcut by the Chinese caused great changes in methods of illustration. An illustrator could now draw a picture on a piece of wood, cut away all the areas not drawn upon, ink the remaining raised section, and

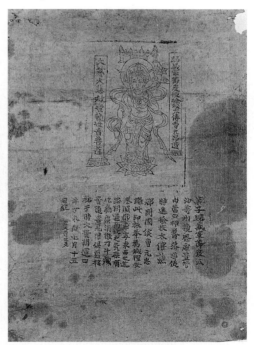

Upper left: An ancient Egyptian papyrus contains both words and pictures. *Above:* A Chinese illustration from the 900's is an early example of a woodcut. *Left:* A woodcut made in 1525 by the German artist Albrecht Dürer was used to illustrate a book on measurement.

print the image. Many copies of the original illustration could be made.

With the invention of the printing press about 1440, hand-lettered manuscripts were replaced by printed books. The first illustrations prepared to accompany the printed texts were woodcuts. Later, wood engraving was invented and became a popular technique for illustrating books. Unlike woodcuts, which are usually printed as black lines on a white background, a wood engraving usually is printed as white lines on a black background.

By 1500 artists such as Albrecht Dürer and Hans Holbein the Younger were producing intricate wood-block prints. Metal plates were also engraved to produce an image for print-

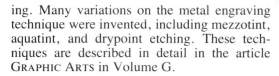

ing. Many variations on the metal engraving technique were invented, including mezzotint, aquatint, and drypoint etching. These techniques are described in detail in the article GRAPHIC ARTS in Volume G.

▶1700'S AND 1800'S

It is difficult today to imagine a world without photography or television. But until the mid-1800's, when modern photographic techniques were developed, the only means of visual communication was through painting and illustration. The public craved illustrated books, and illustrators of the 1700's and

1800's brought the art of illustration to new levels of excellence.

In England, William Hogarth and Thomas Rowlandson became famous for illustrations that depicted English society. William Blake wrote and illustrated some of the most beautiful poems of the period. He etched both text and image on the same plate so that the words became part of the design. John Tenniel, a successful political cartoonist, created memorable illustrations for *Alice's Adventures in Wonderland* (1865) and *Through the Looking-Glass* (1872), two children's books by Lewis Carroll.

In France during the 1800's, Honoré Daumier became famous for realistic newspaper illustrations that honestly depicted life in Paris. Another French illustrator, Gustave Doré, was best known for his illustration of classic literary works. Eugène Delacroix and

Henri de Toulouse-Lautrec were among the great French painters who turned to the art of illustration.

New Printing Techniques. The invention of photographic printing processes in the second half of the 1800's encouraged the spread of illustrated reading material. These processes, known as photoengraving and photolithography, involve photographing an image to obtain a negative, which is then transferred to a metal plate. The plate is developed, and the unexposed areas are etched away. The image that remains is inked and printed. (A further discussion of photoengraving and photolith-

ing a new need for illustrations. The American artist Winslow Homer was one of the best-known magazine illustrators in the United States. His wood-engraved images of the Civil War were first printed in *Harper's Weekly*.

Toward the end of the 1800's, the quality of some printed illustrations suffered from the misuse of faster, cheaper printing methods. The English writer and designer William Morris believed that book design could be improved by returning to early hand-printing processes such as the woodcut. His influence was felt all over Europe, and even today many illustrators still choose these early methods over modern printing techniques.

Opposite page, left to right: The lithographs of Honoré Daumier commented on aspects of French life. Images of the Civil War were captured in wood engravings by American artist Winslow Homer. *This page, top to bottom:* Illustrations by Arthur Rackham, Kate Greenaway, and Beatrix Potter added charm to children's story books.

ography appears in the article PRINTING in Volume P.)

The photographic image could be enlarged or reduced, allowing artists to make their original drawings in any size. Photographic printing processes also allowed more accuracy in reproducing the artist's original work. By 1900, a full array of colors and tones could be reproduced.

Along with improved reproduction processes came the development of high-speed printing presses. This allowed books and magazines to be produced quickly and cheaply. Illustrated magazines became popular, creat-

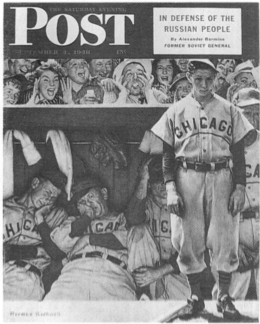

THE RISE OF ILLUSTRATED CHILDREN'S BOOKS

During the late 1800's and early 1900's, many illustrators began to focus their efforts on books for children. In England, Arthur Rackham and Edmund Dulac created beautiful illustrations for children's story books. Their pictures were filled with gnomes, fairies, goblins, and other fanciful creatures. Two other English illustrators were Kate Greenaway, who created charming watercolor illustrations of children, and Beatrix Potter, who wrote and illustrated *The Tale of Peter Rabbit* (1901) and many other books with animal characters. A noted French illustrator of the period was Bernard Boutet de Monvel, whose pictures accurately captured the moods and actions of young children.

In the United States, illustrators took advantage of the greater accuracy of photographic printing processes, producing beautiful full-color illustrations for a variety of children's books. Howard Pyle wrote and illustrated many well-known works, including *The Merry Adventures of Robin Hood* (1883) and four volumes of the stories of King Arthur and the knights of the Round Table. N. C. Wyeth illustrated many classic works of literature, bringing the stories to life with his depictions of adventure and romance.

MODERN ILLUSTRATION

The popularity of illustrated magazines, which had begun in the mid-1800's, continued throughout the first half of the 1900's. Many artists—including Charles Dana Gibson, Maxfield Parrish, Dean Cornwell, and Norman Rockwell—became famous for their magazine illustrations.

During the 1950's, magazines increasingly used photographs as illustrations, first in advertisements and later for stories and feature articles as well. This trend led to a decline in the importance of illustration art.

During the 1950's and 1960's, television began to replace illustrated magazines as a popular means of visual communication. As one major magazine after another stopped publishing, illustrators looked for other markets for their talents. Many found work in television, drawing storyboards (sketches used to guide the action) for commercials and television shows or creating the drawings for animated cartoons.

Other illustrators turned to book illustration. Paperback publishing had become a major industry after World War II (1939–45). Thousands of titles were printed, and almost every book had an illustration on its cover. Many artists gained fame for their illustrations of children's books. Books written and illustrated

Opposite page, left to right: Adventure tales were brought to life by the illustrations of N. C. Wyeth. Norman Rockwell's magazine illustrations celebrated ordinary Americans.

This page: Today's illustrators work in many areas. Illustrated children's books, such as those by Dr. Seuss, remain popular (*above*). Illustrators design book covers (*left*) and advertisements (*right*). Some illustrators use computers to create their art (*below*).

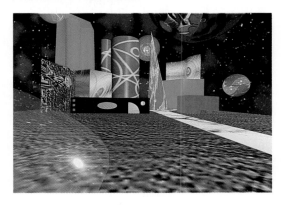

by Dr. Seuss (Theodore Geisel), including *The Cat in the Hat* (1957), have become world famous. Another American illustrator, Maurice Sendak, appealed to young imaginations with his illustrations for *Where the Wild Things Are* (1963) and other books.

In addition to book publishing, a host of new magazines specializing in sports, hobbies, fashion, travel, art, humor, and other topics provide work for illustrators. Advances in computer technology are also having an impact on illustration. Using special computer programs, artists can create full-color images directly on the computer screen and combine these images with text, all in one operation. Further development of this technology, known as "desktop publishing," may change the future role of illustrators in publishing.

WALT REED
President, Illustration House, Inc.
Author, *Great American Illustrators*

See also BOOKS; COMMERCIAL ART; ILLUMINATED MANUSCRIPTS.

The following page contains an illustrated feature that describes how a children's book illustrator works.

How a children's book illustrator works

An illustrator may write a story or may be asked by a publisher to illustrate someone else's story. In either case, in order to achieve the best results, the illustrator should have a strong feeling for the story.

Although a children's book appears to be simple, it takes a lot of careful planning.

The illustrator begins with a **storyboard.** The storyboard shows all the pages of the book, greatly reduced, on a single sheet of paper. The illustrator draws in rough but readable sketches that show only the essential elements of the pictures. The storyboard enables the illustrator to see the layout of the entire book, to study how the pages relate to one another, to review the book's overall composition, and to make adjustments.

The next step is making a **book dummy**, a booklet of blank pages that has the same number of pages as the actual book. At this stage, many illustrators prefer to use a small dummy, no larger than 3 by 4 inches, called a thumbnail dummy. The small size helps an illustrator to concentrate on the essential elements of the pictures and to avoid becoming sidetracked by details.

Using the storyboard as a guide, and with the text in mind, the illustrator makes sketches in the book dummy. Although the sketches are larger and slightly more detailed, they are still rough. The book dummy allows the illustrator to visualize the final book and to work out the progression of the pictures and their relationship to the words.

Next, the illustrator makes another book dummy that is the same size and shape as the finished book. This actual-size book dummy allows the illustrator to get the feel of the book in its entirety and to experience it as the reader would. At this stage, rough sketches are developed into detailed, finished sketches.

Then the illustrator traces the finished sketches onto fine paper or board. Although many techniques are available to illustrators, a combination of black line and color are most widely used to execute the final illustrations.

In order for the reader to enjoy a children's book, both the words and the pictures must be readable. All the picture elements, large and small, should be organized in a clear and pleasing way and should reflect the mood and feeling of the story.

URI SHULEVITZ
Author-Illustrator of *Writing With Pictures: How to Write and Illustrate Children's Books*

Double spread pencil sketch from the storyboard for One Monday Morning *by Uri Shulevitz.*

Rough sketch from the thumbnail dummy.

Finished sketch from the actual-size dummy.

On Tuesday morning the king, the queen, the little prince, and the knight came to visit me.

The final illustration in color as it appears in the printed book.

IMAGING, DIAGNOSTIC

For centuries, it was a mystery: What did the inside of the human body look like? How did it work? Doctors developed ideas about pain and disease and their treatment by examining the outside of the body. It wasn't until the 1800's that a way to "see" inside the body was discovered.

▶ THE FIRST IMAGE

It was in 1895 while experimenting with a simple device, called a cathode-ray tube, that the German physicist Wilhelm Conrad Roentgen discovered a new form of energy. To his astonishment, Roentgen found when he turned the tube on and placed his hand between the tube and a piece of chemically treated cardboard, he could see an image of the bones of his hand on the cardboard. He reasoned that unseen rays must have passed from the tube through his hand to make the image on the cardboard. Roentgen named the rays from this mysterious form of energy X rays, "X" standing for the unknown. Within months after his work became known, other doctors were using the X-ray procedure to diagnose broken bones and other ailments.

▶ X-RAY IMAGING

X rays are no longer a mysterious force; they are known to be very short wavelengths of electromagnetic radiation. The X-ray examinations performed today use the same process developed by Roentgen almost a hundred years ago. A person is placed between an X-ray source and an X-ray image recorder (a piece of film) and the X rays are passed through the body. An image is produced because the body is made up of all different kinds of tissues, and each kind of tissue allows a different amount of X rays to pass through to the film. Bone tissue is very dense and is able to stop more X rays than muscle and fat. So on X-ray film, bones appear white, while less dense tissues range from black to shades of gray. And the lungs, which are filled with air and thus readily allow X rays to pass through, appear almost black.

Although X rays are helpful in diagnosing disease, too much exposure to X rays can damage body tissue and cause cancer. Because of this danger, doctors set limits on the amount of X ray any one person receives during an examination.

▶ COMPUTED TOMOGRAPHY (CT)

In 1972, a new diagnostic tool was developed that combined the computer and X-ray techniques. British scientist Godfrey Hounsfield first documented this exciting new technique, calling it **computerized axial tomography** (CAT) scanning. Now it is simply called **computed tomography**.

When a CT image is made, a thin X-ray beam is passed through a very small, well-defined area of the body as it travels through a large tubelike machine. A series of detectors opposite the X-ray source collect the X rays that have passed through the body. Each time the tube revolves, the same small slice of the body is viewed from a different angle. The detectors then feed this information to a computer. The computer is able to store and compare the slices and then produce a cross-sectional image of what has been "seen." Although it was originally used to produce images of the brain, all parts of the body can now be imaged showing the subtle differences between bone and soft tissue detail.

▶ DIGITAL SUBTRACTION ANGIOGRAPHY (DSA)

Another imaging technique that uses X rays is **digital subtraction angiography**. The arteries of the heart and other body vessels (or ducts), such as the ducts within the liver, can be examined using DSA. DSA starts with the making of an X-ray image of the area to be examined. Then a radiopaque dye, a substance that does not allow the passage of X rays, is injected into the area's arteries or veins. As the dye is being injected, a second image is made. A computer compares the two images and produces a final image with everything

Early X-ray pictures, such as the one made by Roentgen of his wife's hand (*left*), are hazy images compared to the detailed, colored X rays now possible (*right*).

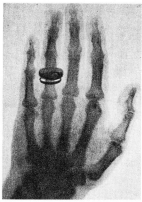 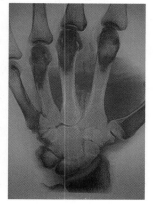

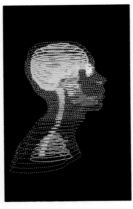

As the body is scanned, a variety of CT images, such as the cross-sectional image (*left*) and the three-dimensional image (*above*), can be produced.

waves) was used to search out underwater objects—submarines and icebergs.

Like sonar, sonography uses sound waves; but the fluid environment is the human body. High-frequency sound, or ultrasonic, waves are sent out from a device called a transducer, which acts as the source of the ultrasonic waves and the receiver of the waves. The transducer is placed against the skin and moved over the area to be studied. The waves penetrate the body, strike the structures within, and bounce back to the surface where they are captured by the transducer. A computer analyzes these echoes and builds an image that is projected onto the computer screen.

Sonography is used to image soft body structures such as the heart. Because it is considered to be a relatively safe form of imaging, it is the only recommended body scanning technique used on expectant mothers.

removed except the dye-filled vessels within the small well-defined area of interest.

▶ MAGNETIC RESONANCE IMAGING (MRI)

Many view the development of **magnetic resonance imaging** to be as important as the development of X-ray imaging. MRI uses powerful magnets placed in the outer walls of a tunnel-like machine to create a magnetic field. When a human body is placed in this magnetic field, the hydrogen atoms in the body become magnetized and line up in an organized pattern. Radio waves are released by the machine, changing the order of the hydrogen atoms. When the radio waves are turned off, the hydrogen atoms move back into order and emit an electrical signal. The signals are collected, fed to a computer, and used to produce an image.

Not only are the images more finely detailed than CT images but MRI better distinguishes between certain kinds of similar body tissues, such as the white matter and gray matter of the brain. Although not everyone can be placed in a magnetic field—the strong field can interfere with heart-pacing devices—there are no known harmful effects of MRI.

▶ SONOGRAPHY

The technique known as **sonography** owes its development to the use of sonar during the two world wars. During wartime, sonar (a system of underwater detection using sound

▶ RADIOISOTOPE IMAGING

Some types of imaging use **radioisotopes**, chemical elements that give off energy particles. Very small amounts of a radioisotope are combined with a substance the body processes, such as sugar or protein, and is then injected into the body. Because energy is given off, or emitted, by the radioisotope, its path through the body can be tracked by detectors. Information is gathered about where the chemical collects, how it is processed by the body, and how or if it is eliminated from the body. The information is fed into the computer and an image results.

Two types of imaging that use radioisotopes are **positron emission tomography** (PET) and **single photon emission computed tomography** (SPECT). Radioisotope imaging may be used to study the flow of blood through the body, the activity of specific organs, or the spread of tumor cells.

Diagnostic imaging has given new eyes to medicine—eyes that not only help diagnose disease but detect it at an early stage when preventative steps can still be taken. With each new technology the vision improves, bringing more understanding of the body and the chance for a longer, healthier life.

RONALD L. RAGLAND, M.D.
Chief, Neuroradiology
University of Massachusetts Medical Center

See also COMPUTERS (Computers in Medicine); DISEASES; X RAYS.

IMMIGRATION

Immigration is the voluntary movement of people from one country to another, usually with the aim of permanent settlement in the adopted country. A closely related term, emigration, refers to movement out of a country. Thus, when people depart from their homelands for new homes elsewhere, they are said to be emigrants. Once they arrive in their new countries, they are known as immigrants. People who flee their countries because of an immediate threat to their safety are usually referred to as refugees, since they seek refuge in other lands.

Immigration is one form of the broader movement of peoples called migration. Migration is as old as humanity itself. In prehistoric times, when humans lived largely by hunting, groups of people migrated, or moved from place to place, following the animals on which their existence depended. Even when settled communities based on farming developed, people continued this pattern of movement, for overpopulation, crop failure, or the pressure of neighboring peoples frequently made it necessary to cultivate new lands.

▶FACTORS IN IMMIGRATION

Major Causes. In more modern times, the major causes of immigration have included wars, social upheaval, economic calamities, and political and religious persecution. However, the single most compelling factor leading people to uproot themselves from their native lands and emigrate to foreign shores has

been the desire to find greater opportunities somewhere else.

Choice and National Borders. Immigration is considered to be a voluntary act, one of personal choice. Therefore, any forced migration of peoples, such as occurred during the centuries of the African slave trade, is not immigration. Nor is internal migration—the movement of people within a particular country—a form of immigration. Immigration usually involves the crossing of national borders. Internal migration most commonly takes place as people move from rural (country) areas to cities and from cities to suburbs, or when they travel from one region of a country to another because of economic conditions.

For many immigrants to the United States the first sight of their new homeland was the Statue of Liberty in New York Harbor. At nearby Ellis Island, some 17 million immigrants were processed between 1892 and 1954. Ellis Island now houses an immigration museum.

HISTORICAL BACKGROUND

Ancient Colonists. Forms of immigration existed in ancient times. The Greeks were among the earliest colonists, founding settlements in Asia Minor, Sicily, and the mainland of southern Italy at least 2,700 years ago. The Phoenicians (seafarers and traders from what is now Lebanon) also established themselves in the western Mediterranean Sea, and elsewhere, at about this time. Their greatest settlement, in North Africa, was aptly named Carthage, or "new town."

The Age of Discovery. The nature of immigration changed dramatically during the 1400's. This century marked the beginning of the great age of exploration and discovery, which led to the expansion of European power from the Mediterranean region to all of the world's inhabited continents. European navigators explored new lands in Africa and discovered new routes to the wealth of Asia. But while many of these areas offered opportunities for colonization for purposes of commerce and trade, few were suitable for large-scale settlement. The "discovery" by Europeans of the New World of the Americas, however, had the most far-reaching impact on the history of immigration.

The New World. Immigration to the Americas followed the epic voyage of discovery, in 1492, by Christopher Columbus, an Italian in the employ of Spanish monarchs. Spaniards quickly colonized the islands of the Caribbean Sea, what later became Mexico, Central America, and most of South America. The Portuguese founded settlements in what is now Brazil. English, French, Dutch, and smaller Swedish colonies were established in North America. The English colonies, scattered along the Atlantic Ocean coast of North America, were eventually to evolve into the United States.

The First Americans. The Europeans were not the first immigrants in the Americas, however. Thousands of years earlier, migrating peoples from northeastern Asia had crossed into North America by way of a land bridge (in what is now the Bering Strait), which then linked the two continents. Some of these people continued their migration southward, passing over the narrow connecting neck of Central America into South America. These earliest-known peoples in the Americas were the ancestors of the Indians.

See the article EXPLORATION AND DISCOVERY (Exploring North and South America) in Volume E. For information on the American colonies that became the United States, see COLONIAL LIFE IN AMERICA in Volume C and THIRTEEN AMERICAN COLONIES in Volume T. See INDIANS, AMERICAN in this volume. An article on slavery appears in Volume S.

IMMIGRATION TO THE UNITED STATES

The United States has rightly been called a nation of immigrants. In the little more than two hundred years of its existence, it has taken in more than 55 million people, from nearly every corner of the world. Many of these newcomers were welcomed by a growing nation, but others were viewed with suspicion and hostility. All contributed something to the United States; many contributed a great deal.

Beginnings. The first colonists in what would become the United States arrived in the 1600's. Some were adventurers, who sought to make their fortunes quickly in the New World. Others came to escape religious persecution or simply to be free to worship as they pleased. Most of the settlers, however, were ordinary people. They undertook the long, dangerous sea voyage, attracted by the plentiful land and hoping to find in a new country better economic opportunities than they could expect at home. Many of the early colonists were too poor to pay for their passage. They arrived in America as indentured servants, obligated to work a fixed number of years for masters who had paid their way.

Many of the early American colonists, too poor to pay for their passage, arrived as indentured servants.

SELLING WIVES TO THE PLANTERS.

Immigration to the United States from All Countries by Decades	
1821–30	143,439
1831–40	599,125
1841–50	1,713,251
1851–60	2,598,214
1861–70	2,314,824
1871–80	2,812,191
1881–90	5,246,613
1891–1900	3,687,564
1901–10	8,795,386
1911–20	5,735,811
1921–30	4,107,209
1931–40	528,431
1941–50	1,035,039
1951–60	2,515,479
1961–70	3,321,677
1971–80	4,493,314
1981–90	7,338,062
1991–98*	7,605,068

Source: U.S. Immigration and Naturalization Service, *Statistical Yearbook*

*Data for entire decade not yet available.

Above: A group of Eastern European immigrants ate their first Christmas dinner in the United States at Ellis Island in 1910. *Below:* Arriving immigrants had to pass a strict examination for infectious eye diseases.

Early Non-English Immigration. The original English settlers were followed by Scotch-Irish, Germans, and smaller numbers of French Huguenots (Protestants), Dutch, Scandinavians, and Swiss. A tiny community of Jews had originally settled in the Dutch colony of New Amsterdam (later renamed New York). By 1763 the colonial population had grown to about 2.5 million. Of this, about one third was non-English, including black slaves, most of whom were in the southern colonies.

Immigration slowed considerably during the American Revolution. The Napoleonic wars in Europe also made travel to America difficult. With the restoration of peace in 1815, immigration gradually increased. In 1820 the United States first began to keep an accurate record of the number of immigrants arriving each year.

A Great Wave. The mid-1800's saw a great new wave of immigration. In the years from 1845 to 1855, nearly 1.5 million Irish immigrants arrived in the United States, fleeing poverty and the famine caused by successive failures of the staple potato crop. During this same period, more than 1 million Germans came to America to escape the upheaval and political repression that followed the unsuccessful 1848 liberal revolution in Europe.

Many of the Irish settled in the Northeast. Most found work as laborers in the growing cities, or in the region's textile mill towns. The Germans settled mainly in the expanding Midwest, usually as farmers or workers in such cities as Cincinnati and St. Louis.

New European Immigrants. Immigration again declined during the U.S. Civil War (1861–65) but increased once more by 1870. Up until the 1880's, most immigrants to the United States had come from western or northern Europe. Beginning in about 1890, however, a second great wave of immigration

Immigration to the United States by Country of Origin 1820–1998	
Europe:	
Austria[1]	1,842,722
Belgium	216,297
Czech Republic and Slovakia[2]	153,307
Denmark	375,548
France	816,650
Germany	7,156,257
Greece	721,464
Hungary[1]	1,675,324
Ireland[3]	4,779,998
Italy	5,431,454
Netherlands	385,193
Norway[4]	758,026
Poland[5]	751,823
Portugal	521,697
Romania[6]	244,106
Russia[7]	3,830,033
Spain	299,825
Sweden[4]	1,257,133
Switzerland	369,046
United Kingdom	5,247,821
Yugoslavia[8]	183,538
Other European	224,297
Asia:	
China[9]	1,262,050
Hong Kong	398,277
India	751,349
Iran	233,860
Israel[10]	170,506
Japan[11]	517,686
Korea[12]	778,899
Philippines	1,460,421
Turkey	445,354
Vietnam[13]	699,918
Other Asian	1,647,611
Americas:	
Argentina[14]	153,699
Canada	4,453,149
Colombia[14]	399,892
Cuba[15]	885,421
Dominican Republic	810,201
Ecuador[14]	215,798
El Salvador	453,717
Haiti	375,938
Jamaica[16]	568,624
Mexico	5,819,966
Other American	2,708,424
Africa:	**614,375**
Oceania:	**250,206**
Origin Not Specified:	**290,679**

[1]Data for Austria and Hungary not available (NA) until 1861 and not separately until 1905. Data for Austria (1938–45) included in Germany. [2]Data NA until 1920. [3]Data prior to 1926 includes Northern Ireland. [4]Separate data for Norway and Sweden NA until 1871. [5]Data for Poland (1899–1919) included under Austria, Hungary, Germany, and Russia. [6]Data NA until 1880. [7]Includes the former U.S.S.R. (1922–91). [8]Includes today's Serbia and Montenegro, Bosnia and Herzegovina, Croatia, Macedonia, and Slovenia. [9]Includes Taiwan after 1957. [10]Separate data NA until 1949. [11]Data NA until 1861. [12]Separate data NA until 1948. [13]Separate data NA until 1952. [14]Separate data NA until 1932. [15]Separate data NA until 1925. [16]Separate data NA until 1953.

Source: U.S. Immigration and Naturalization Service, *Statistical Yearbook*

Top: Chinese immigrants first arrived in the United States in considerable numbers in the mid-1800's. They were welcomed at first as a source of cheap labor. But, as this illustration from a newspaper of the period shows, they aroused the hostility of white workers who saw the lower wages paid the Chinese as a threat to their own livelihood. Starting in 1882, Chinese immigration was suspended for more than 60 years. *Above:* Looking hopeful but apprehensive, an immigrant mother and child wait patiently at Ellis Island, about 1900.

began, mainly from southern and eastern Europe. The new immigrants included Italians, Slavs, Greeks, and eastern European Jews. For the Jews, religious oppression as well as economic reasons impelled their emigration.

Of the more than 3.5 million people who arrived between 1891 and 1900, a little more than half were new immigrants. From 1901 to 1910, the greatest decade of immigration in U.S. history, nearly 8.8 million people arrived. Of these, more than 70 percent were from southern and eastern Europe. A second great wave of more than 7.3 million immigrants arrived between 1981 and 1990; nearly half were from the Americas and more than one third were from Asia.

Many of the new immigrants entered the country at New York City. Between 1892 and 1954 they were received at a U.S. government facility on Ellis Island in New York Harbor. (The facility, closed in 1954, was reopened as a museum in 1990.) Other eastern coastal cities, including Boston, were also first homes of immigrants. Some of the immigrants moved inland, swelling the populations of cities such as Pittsburgh and Chicago. Others, more adventurous, crossed the country, settling at places along the way or on the West Coast.

So great was the flow of people to the United States during this period that in some

U.S. attitudes to European immigration often varied as well. A cartoon of 1850 (*above*) mocked the Irish and Germans who arrived in great numbers at that time. By contrast, "Welcome to All!" of 1880 showed Uncle Sam greeting new immigrants.

cities a majority of the population was made up of immigrants and their children. In New York City, one could walk for blocks hearing a variety of foreign languages and seeing newsstands filled with foreign-language newspapers.

Asian Immigration. Few Asians arrived in the United States until the mid-1800's. The growth of California after the discovery of gold in 1848 and the need for laborers to help build the transcontinental railroad spurred Chinese immigration. Japanese first arrived in the United States in the late 1800's and early 1900's. Most of the Japanese, as well as many Chinese, came as contract workers to farms on the West Coast or to plantations in Hawaii. Filipinos, from what was then the newly acquired U.S. territory of the Philippines, and other Asians also arrived in the United States during these years.

Problems of Adjustment. As strangers in a new land, many of the immigrants faced a difficult period of adjustment. Most immigrants tended to settle where people from the same country had established themselves earlier. Churches and clubs were often gathering places for people of the same ethnic origin. The rapid growth of foreign-language newspapers helped non-English-speaking newcomers to understand American ways. Public schools, in particular, encouraged the children of immigrants to adapt to American life.

Limiting Immigration. The first legislation restricting immigration of a particular ethnic group was aimed at the Chinese. At first welcomed as a source of cheap labor, they later aroused hostility among white workers, who saw the lower wages paid the Chinese as a threat to their own livelihood. In 1882 the U.S. Congress passed the Chinese Exclusion Act, which suspended new immigration by Chinese workers for ten years. The law was renewed repeatedly, before it was finally repealed in 1943.

The second group to be excluded was the Japanese. In 1907 the U.S. government reached a "gentleman's agreement" with Japan, which halted the flow of Japanese workers. The agreement remained in force until 1924. In addition to economic reasons, racial prejudice played a strong role in restricting Chinese and Japanese immigration.

Americans who wanted drastic curbs on immigration from southern and eastern Europe prevailed on Congress to pass legislation requiring a literacy test for newcomers. The law, passed in 1917, required immigrants over the age of 16 to be able to read and write at least one language. It did not have the desired effect of restricting southern and eastern European immigration, but later legislation did.

The Quota System. In 1921, Congress passed the Quota Act, which limited yearly immigration from any country to 3 percent of the number of persons of that nationality living in the United States in 1910. Three years later, Congress reduced the quota to 2 percent and changed the base year to 1890. This discriminated against southern and eastern Europeans because fewer of them had been in the United States in 1890. The National Origins Act of 1929 changed the base year to 1920 and set an annual total of 150,000 immigrants. It also prohibited immigration from Asia.

Some immigrants who contributed their talents to the United States. *Left:* Alexander Hamilton, first U.S. secretary of the treasury (Nevis, West Indies); Pierre Toussaint, being considered for canonization by the Roman Catholic Church (Haiti). *Right and below right:* Albert Einstein, scientist, who revolutionized the world of physics (Germany); Joseph Pulitzer, newspaper publisher and founder of the Pulitzer prizes (Austria-Hungary).

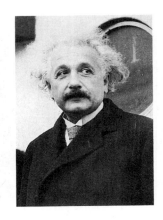

A mural by Ben Shahn depicts refugees (headed by Albert Einstein) who escaped to the United States just before the holocaust of World War II engulfed Europe.

After World War II, special laws allowed about 400,000 European refugees to come to the United States. Other laws allowed political refugees to enter during the 1950's and 1960's. Some were fleeing Communism in Eastern Europe, but most were refugees from the Communist regime in Cuba.

Re-opening the Golden Door. Although Congress opened the door to refugees, the quota system remained the basis of U.S. immigration law. Many people wanted the law changed because of its prejudice against certain nationalities. Finally, in 1965, Congress amended the law and abolished the national origins system. It then set up a system of preferences for immigration, giving priority to refugees and people who had special skills or close relatives in the United States. Ceilings were set for the number of immigrants from the Eastern Hemisphere and the Western Hemisphere. In 1978, Congress abolished these separate ceilings in favor of a worldwide total of 290,000 immigrants. Spouses and children of U.S. citizens were not counted as part of the total. As a result, many more Asians and eastern and southern Europeans were able to emigrate to the United States.

Illegal Aliens. Because immigration to the United States has been limited, many people have sought to enter illegally. The border between the United States and Mexico, in particular, is so easy to cross that it has proved impossible to halt the flow of Mexicans seeking to come to the United States. The U.S.

Top: Enrico Fermi, nuclear physicist (Italy); Jascha Heifetz, concert violinist (Russia/Lithuania). *Bottom:* I. M. Pei, architect (China); Louise Nevelson, sculptor (Russia/Ukraine).

Congress passed the Immigration Reform and Control Act in 1986 to reduce the flow of illegal aliens (people who enter a country without that government's permission). The law prohibited employers from hiring illegal aliens (except for some employers of seasonal farm workers) and also offered amnesty (freedom from prosecution) as well as legal status, to those who could prove they entered the United States before 1982. Furthermore, in 1996, Congress authorized a large increase in funds to help track down and deport illegal aliens.

The Newest Immigrants. In 1990, Congress raised the ceiling for the number of immigrants allowed to enter the country each year to 675,000, beginning in 1995. The newest immigrants to the United States are chiefly Asians and Latin Americans. Many of the Asian immigrants have come as refugees from Vietnam, Cambodia, and Laos following wars in Southeast Asia. Others have come from India, China, the Philippines and South Korea. Most of the Latin American immigrants have come from Mexico and from countries in the Caribbean, particularly the Dominican Republic, Jamaica, and Haiti. These newcomers are changing the ethnic makeup of the United States, which for so long was based mainly on European immigration.

In 1996, in order to cut the rising costs of social services, Congress again changed the immigration laws, making most legal immigrants ineligible for many benefits, including Supplemental Security Income, Medicaid, and food stamps.

▶ IMMIGRATION IN OTHER LANDS

Canada. The French and English were the chief European colonizers of what is now Canada. They first arrived in the region in the 1500's and 1600's, competing for its riches in fish and furs.

Immigration to this vast but lightly populated country was slow, consisting mainly of British settlers, until the end of the 1800's. Over the next twenty years, increasing numbers of Irish, Germans, Scandinavians, Ukrainians, and Russians arrived. Many helped build the railroads and settle the western plains. After World War II, Canada received refugees from Europe. It also has taken in immigrants from the Caribbean and refugees from Asia. Several million Canadians also have emigrated to the United States.

South America. Over the last 150 years, people from various European countries have emigrated to South America, adding to its basic Indian, Spanish, Portuguese, and some black African ethnic groups. Those "newer" immigrants have included Germans, French, Italians, British, and Eastern Europeans. Japanese, Chinese, and other Asians also have emigrated to South America. East Indians, originally brought as laborers, now make up more than half the population of the nation of Guyana. Many South Americans, in turn, have emigrated to the United States, especially in recent years.

Europe. Europe has been the site of countless migrations and other large population movements throughout its history. In modern times, the breakup of the Austro-Hungarian Empire after World War I redefined the map of Europe. The dislocation of World War II made refugees of many Europeans, including Eastern Europeans who fled to the West after

Left: The first British settlement in Australia was founded in 1788 at what is now Sydney Harbour. *Above:* Soviet Jewish immigrants kissed the ground after arriving in Israel in 1971. *Below:* These Vietnamese refugees fled to Hong Kong in 1989.

the installation of Communist governments in their countries.

Several of the former European colonial powers have absorbed peoples from their old African and Asian empires. Britain, in particular, has taken in blacks from the West Indies, East Indians, Pakistanis, and others. However, the British Nationality Act, which went into effect in 1983, has restricted immigration from the former colonies.

Africa. Europeans colonized virtually all of Africa but settled in significant numbers in only a few areas. The French established themselves in North Africa, particularly Algeria. British settlers farmed the fertile highlands of Zimbabwe (formerly Rhodesia) and other parts of southern Africa. The most hospitable land for Europeans proved to be what is now the Republic of South Africa. Originally colonized by the Dutch and British, it also received immigrants from other European countries as well from India.

Asia. Of all the nations of Asia, Israel stands out as a nation of immigrants. Created in the late 1940's as a homeland for dispossessed Jews, Israel, like the United States, has received immigrants from almost every corner of the globe. However, wars between Israelis and Arabs and among the Arabs themselves have forced many of the Middle Eastern peoples to become refugees.

Chinese and East Indians have emigrated to many areas of the world. They often arrived as contract laborers; many later became shopkeepers, and some became prosperous merchants. Many ethnic Chinese have lived in the countries of Southeast Asia. Indians settled in East Africa as well as South Africa.

Australia and New Zealand. The first-known inhabitants of Australia were the aborigines, who arrived thousands of years ago, probably from Asia. New Zealand was first settled by the Maori, a Polynesian people.

Colonization by Britain beginning in the late 1700's gave both countries a British outlook as well as the English language. Other European immigrants arrived after World War II. Underpopulated Australia has sought new immigrants. It long refused to accept Asians, but this policy was later abandoned.

Thus the story of immigration continues. It will probably never end so long as people seek a new life in a new land.

DAVID M. REIMERS
New York University
Revised by JEROME NEIBRIEF
Former Editor, *Lands and Peoples*

See also ALIENS; CITIZENSHIP; NATURALIZATION; REFUGEES.

IMMUNE SYSTEM

The invisible battle goes on day and night. There are many enemies lurking about, waiting to attack. On guard is a tireless army of defenders, posed and ready to fight. These defenders are part of the immune system—a remarkable system that protects the body from harmful invasions by foreign substances and disease-causing organisms.

▶ IMMUNITY

The body's ability to protect and defend itself against a foreign enemy agent is called immunity. There are several types of immunity. **Natural immunity** is a type of general inherited protection. A person is born with natural immunity, and it is species specific—for example, people do not get cat distemper and cats do not get human colds. **Active immunity** is the protection a person develops during his or her lifetime as the result of actually having been immunized against a disease. One way this can be done is by using vaccines to help an individual develop active immunity. Active immunity is long-lived and may even last a person's lifetime. **Passive immunity** is a temporary form of immunity that is borrowed from another source. It is short-lived, only lasting a matter of weeks. A baby receives passive immunity from its mother before it is born and after it is born from the mother's milk. Passive immunity protects the baby until it is old enough to have its "baby shots." Then the baby will build its own active immunity.

When the immune system sets up an attack against a foreign agent, it must first recognize which cells belong to the body and which do not so that it can selectively destroy the invader while protecting the healthy body cells. The immune system can tell the difference between what is self (the body's cells and tissue) from something that is foreign because of the chemical labels that appear on the outside surface of all body cells. The cells in a person's body have chemical **self** labels; each person has their own unique set of self labels. Invading agents also have chemical labels; each invading agent has **foreign antigen** labels.

Each foreign antigen has its own chemical configuration—just as each person has a unique set of human fingerprints. Because each foreign antigen has its own unique set of

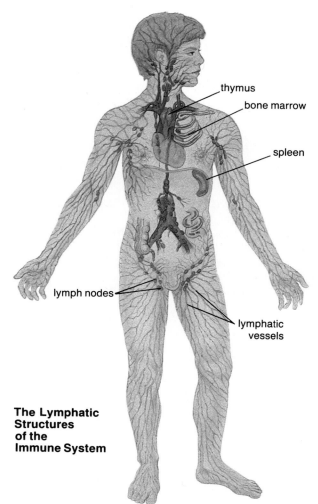

thymus

bone marrow

spleen

lymph nodes

lymphatic vessels

The Lymphatic Structures of the Immune System

The immune system is a defensive network spread throughout the body that protects us from infectious organisms and rids us of other harmful substances.

chemical fingerprints, the immune system is able to recognize the difference between foreign agents and develop a separate defense against each.

▶ THE IMMUNE RESPONSE

The immune response occurs in stages. When an organism invades the body, it must be recognized as foreign. Once it is recognized, it must be marked so that all the cells within the immune system will know that it is an invader and is attacking the body. Then the various troops of immune cells must be called to battle, a defense plan organized, and the defense begun. Finally, when the enemy has been defeated, a cease-fire must be sounded and the battle stopped.

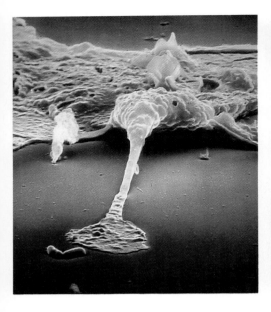

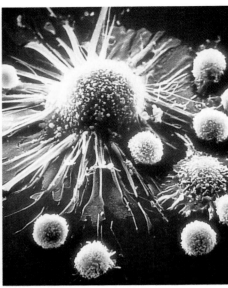

Far left: A macrophage patrolling the body for foreign invaders closes in on its target. Reaching out with an armlike extension, called a pseudopod, the macrophage will engulf the invading cell and then digest it. *Left:* Killer T cells recognize the foreign antigens on a cancer cell's surface and gather to attack the invader. The T cells will break down the cancer cell membrane and destroy the cell.

Immune Defenses

The immune system has two defense plans: nonspecific and specific. The **nonspecific defense** is used against all invaders. Nonspecific responses are only able to recognize the difference between self cells and foreign antigens. The response to the foreign antigens occurs quickly and does not require having had previous encounters with the outside invaders.

In a **specific defense**, the immune system recognizes the invader as one having previously attacked the body. Specific immune responses not only recognize self cells as different from foreign antigens; but they recognize the difference between the different kinds of foreign antigens.

Immune Cells and Molecules

The cells of the immune system fall into three groups: macrophages, natural killer cells, and lymphocytes. All types of cells are members of the white blood cell population and have their origin in bone marrow. These defender white cells account for one percent of the body's 100 trillion cells.

Macrophages. The macrophages are the first to the battleground and are part of a nonspecific defense. They swallow up and dispose of enemy agents, dead cells, and other debris. They are phagocytes, or "cell eaters." Not only do they ingest foreign substances, but macrophages also process harmful material so that it can be recognized as dangerous by other immune cells. These phagocytic cells constantly wander about, patrolling all the areas of the body. They are found in the bloodstream, tissues, and lymphatic system.

Natural Killer Cells. Natural killer cells are a group of special immune cells that are able to quickly identify and destroy a large variety of newly formed cancer cells, virus-infected cells, and fungi. These immune cells are nonspecific in their attack.

Lymphocytes. The lymphocytes follow the macrophages into battle against foreign invaders. Unlike the nonspecific macrophages, lymphocytes are part of a specific immune defense —they are programmed to recognize and destroy specific enemy agents. For example, one group of lymphocyte defenders is trained to recognize and protect against measles and another to protect against chicken pox.

There are two kinds of lymphocytes: T lymphocytes (T cells) and B lymphocytes (B cells). Although both types of lymphocytes are formed in the bone marrow, the T cells leave the bone marrow before they are fully developed and travel to the thymus gland. In the thymus gland, they mature and are programmed in the skills needed to function as a T cell. The B cells remain in the bone marrow to receive their B cell programming.

B Cells. When confronted with a specific enemy agent, some B cells are programmed to produce immune molecules called **antibodies** that recognize the chemical fingerprints of the foreign antigen. Each antibody is made up of long chains of smaller units in a pattern. The smaller units are amino acids, and it is their pattern that matches the chemical fingerprints of a specific foreign antigen—much like a lock and key match each other.

Antibodies do not attack the enemy directly. In battle with foreign invaders, some antibodies may call phagocytic cells to the battleground, mark the enemy so that it can be recognized and destroyed, or empty out the enemy cell by punching holes in its surface.

When the enemy agent has been defeated, other B cells store information about the invader for the future. If the foreign agent invades the body again, these memory B cells quickly recognize the foreign antigen and signal the production of antibodies to begin.

T Cells. There are four kinds of T cells: T helper cells, cytotoxic T cells, suppressor T cells, and memory T cells. The immune response begins with the command from the T helper cells. They recognize the invader, then call in and train other immune cells, including B cells and cytotoxic T cells. The cytotoxic (cell killing) T cells kill the enemy directly. T suppressor cells decide when the battle ends— they call a truce to the fighting and shut off the immune system. Memory T cells remain, ready to move quickly should the enemy invade again.

▶ORGAN TRANSPLANTS AND THE IMMUNE SYSTEM

Sometimes illness or an accident damages body tissue so much that it is no longer able to function normally. Then an operation, called a tissue graft, or transplant, may be performed to replace the damaged part. Healthy tissue, such as skin, may be taken from one part of the body and grafted to another part of the body. The body accepts the transplanted tissue because it has the same self label. Problems arise when the tissue or organs are taken from one person and transplanted to another. Then the immune system recognizes the transplant as foreign and launches an attack against it. When this happens, special drugs are used to lessen the immune system attack.

Although the body attacks cells that have a different self label, some self labels are chemically more similar than others and cause less of an immune response. The self labels are coded by genes inherited from each parent, so brothers and sisters are more likely to have similar, but not the same, self labels. The only people who would have the very same self labels would be identical twins, because they share the same genes.

▶DISORDERS OF THE IMMUNE SYSTEM

Sometimes the immune system works too hard and an allergic response results or it mistakes the body's own tissue for an invader and an autoimmune (self-immune) disease results. Other disorders result when cells in the immune system are attacked and destroyed by an organism, such as the AIDS virus, which destroys the T helper cell.

Allergies. Allergies are the result of an overactive immune system. In some people, the immune system mounts a large-scale attack against common environmental agents that should pose no threat to the body. Then unnecessary antibodies are produced against such things as house dust, animal dander, tree and weed pollens, and in some cases the chemical molecules in certain foods.

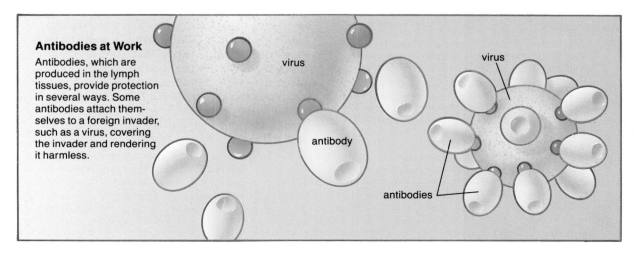

Antibodies at Work

Antibodies, which are produced in the lymph tissues, provide protection in several ways. Some antibodies attach themselves to a foreign invader, such as a virus, covering the invader and rendering it harmless.

virus

virus

antibody

antibodies

Autoimmune Disease. Autoimmune disease is a disorder of mistaken identity. It occurs when the body has difficulty distinguishing between self and foreign enemies. In rheumatoid arthritis, for example, the body's immune system acts as though parts of the knee, hand, or foot joints were foreign enemies, and it attacks them. The reason that some people develop an autoimmune disease and others do not is unknown. It is thought that some chemical agent or infectious organism may cause a change in the self label so that the immune system recognizes certain tissues as enemies.

AIDS. Acquired *i*mmune *d*eficiency *s*yndrome (AIDS) is a disease that destroys the immune system. The disease is caused by a virus called the *h*uman *i*mmuno-deficiency *v*irus (HIV). Like all other viruses, the HIV must seek out other living cells to infect and in which to reproduce; it is not able to live on its own. The AIDS virus seeks out the cells of the immune system, particularly T helper cells and macrophages, to infect.

Eventually the AIDS virus destroys the cell. Without the T helper cell, the immune system is unable to organize a defense plan to battle the invaders. Thus what are normally harmless organisms present in the environment can cause life-threatening infections in people who have AIDS.

▶ **IMMUNE DISCOVERIES**

Immunology, the study of the immune system, started long ago—even before people knew there was such a thing as the immune system! By the 1400's scientists had developed a primitive form of immunization. A powder made from dried smallpox scabs was inhaled as protection against getting smallpox.

Modern immunology really began with the work of two **immunologists**, the scientists who study the immune system. It was in 1796 that the first modern vaccination was developed by Edward Jenner, a country physician in England. He noticed that herdsmen and dairymaids who had been infected with cowpox, a mild viral disease affecting cows, did not get smallpox. Smallpox was a much more serious and often fatal disease. He used this information to develop a method of infecting people with cowpox to protect them from smallpox. The term **vaccination** (*vacca* meaning "cow") was used to describe Jenner's method.

The next important discovery was made almost one hundred years later by the French chemist-turned-biologist, Louis Pasteur. He discovered that chickens infected with a mild form of chicken cholera did not develop the more serious form of chicken cholera. To infect the chickens, Pasteur developed a weakened form of the disease-producing organism.

Since Pasteur's time, vaccines have been developed for a great many other diseases, including polio, measles, mumps, tetanus, whooping cough, and influenza. Immunologists have also developed methods to classify different types of blood and tissues, diagnose cancer, and examine genes and their effect on cell function.

▶ **NEW WEAPONS FOR THE FUTURE**

As they continue to study the immune system, scientists are able to develop new and powerful weapons against many infectious organisms. Vaccines, such as an experimental AIDS vaccine, are now being tested. Cells grown in the laboratory that produce huge amounts of specific antibodies, called monoclonal antibodies, are one of the newest manufactured warriors in the battle against cancer. And the link between behavior, such as exercise, and a more effective immune system is being explored.

CAROL MATTSON PORTH
Author, *Pathophysiology: Concepts of
Altered Health States*

See also AIDS; ANTIBODIES AND ANTIGENS; PASTEUR, LOUIS; VACCINATION AND IMMUNIZATION.

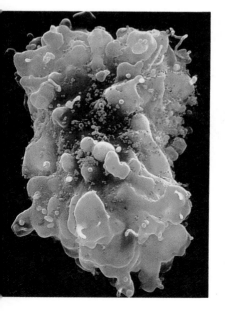

Hundreds of newly made, deadly AIDS viruses (tinted blue) emerge from an infected T helper cell. Each virus is ready to invade another cell, in which it will incorporate its own genes. The virus uses the cell's genetic machinery to produce its offspring, killing the cell in the process.

In 1868, President Andrew Johnson was tried by the Senate following his impeachment by the House of Representatives. After a two-month trial, he was acquitted by a single vote.

IMPEACHMENT

Impeachment is a legal action brought against a government official who has been accused of misconduct or criminal offenses. In the United States federal government, the House of Representatives can impeach an official by a majority vote. The impeached official then goes to trial in the Senate, with the chief justice of the U.S. Supreme Court acting as the judge. If two-thirds of the Senate finds the official guilty, he or she is removed from office. State governments also have impeachment powers, and most follow the same procedures as the federal government.

In the United States, a federal official may be impeached for treason, for taking bribes, or for "high crimes and misdemeanors." But is it a high crime for an official to oppose the policies of the political party in power?

The question came up when Supreme Court Justice Samuel Chase was impeached in 1804. He had been appointed to office by Federalists. When the Jeffersonians came to power, they thought Judge Chase was blocking their policies. The House impeached Chase, but the Senate declared him not guilty. This decision signaled that it was not an impeachable crime to oppose the party in power.

However, the issue came up again more than sixty years later when, for the first time in American history, the House impeached a president. Andrew Johnson became president in 1865 when Abraham Lincoln was assassinated. The Civil War had just ended and the country's biggest problem was reconstructing the devastated South. Because Johnson disagreed with the Congress over Reconstruction policies, the House impeached him. Johnson's Senate trial in 1868 lasted two months, but the Senate fell one vote short of the two-thirds majority necessary to convict him.

The question of impeaching a president arose again in 1974, during the Watergate scandal. Articles of impeachment against President Richard Nixon were approved by the House Judiciary Committee. The articles charged the president with obstruction of justice, abuse of power, and failure to comply with committee demands. But Nixon resigned his office before the full House had a chance to act on the impeachment charges.

In 1998, President Bill Clinton became the second president to be impeached, the result of a scandal over the president's personal involvement with a White House intern. On December 19, a House majority voted yes on two of four articles of impeachment—charges of perjury (lying under oath) and obstruction of justice (because most House members believed Clinton encouraged others to lie on his behalf). A Senate trial followed, and on February 12, 1999, Clinton was found not guilty on both charges.

Impeachment is a drastic action used only against officials whose offenses are serious. It occurs relatively infrequently in the United States, and few impeached officials are actually removed from office. But the legislative power to impeach is important because it protects the public against corrupt or otherwise unworthy government officials.

Reviewed by ERIC MCKITRICK
Columbia University

See also CLINTON, WILLIAM; JOHNSON, ANDREW; NIXON, RICHARD M.

IMPERIALISM

Imperialism is the term that describes one nation's dominance over another nation or territory. Most wars throughout history were caused by nations seeking to expand beyond their traditional borders. Nations built empires for various reasons. Some settled new lands to gain political prestige or economic opportunities for their growing populations. Others seized military bases in strategic places to protect themselves from foreign enemies. Others simply exploited the peoples and natural resources of less powerful regions to acquire wealth.

Some imperialists believed, however, that they had a duty to spread their forms of government, religion, and culture to those nations they considered less advanced or civilized. Some colonies benefited in many ways. For example, the imperial nations built roads and established schools and hospitals. Nevertheless, their interference permanently altered the ancient cultures and traditions of the natives.

▶ EARLY EMPIRES

Many empires developed in the pre-Christian era. These include the empire of the ancient Egyptians (beginning about 2,000 B.C.); the Chou dynasty in China (about 1,000 B.C.); the Assyrian Empire (in the 800's B.C.); and the Persian Empire (which reached its peak about 500 B.C.). Alexander the Great of Macedonia also created an enormous empire. By the time of his death in 323 B.C., his armies had swallowed up the Persian Empire and conquered all of the other lands between Greece and India.

The imperialist powers (*left to right*) Great Britain, Germany, Russia, France, and Japan greedily plot to divide China among them in this 1898 French cartoon. In the background, a Chinese mandarin is powerless to prevent the slicing of the pie.

The best known of the ancient empires, however, is the Roman Empire, which formally began in 27 B.C. The Romans conquered all of the lands bordering the Mediterranean Sea, eventually extending their advanced civilization as far north as Britain.

The Roman Empire was divided into two parts. The Roman Empire in the west, which was centered in Rome, collapsed in A.D. 476. Five hundred years later, during the Middle Ages, German rulers revived it to reunite the Christians of central Europe under one emperor. It was called the Holy Roman Empire, and it lasted until the early 1800's.

The Roman Empire in the east, known as the Byzantine Empire, lasted until 1453. In that year, Constantinople, its ancient capital, was seized by the Ottoman Turks, who had forged their own empire in the Middle East. When the Ottoman Empire reached its peak in the 1500's, it included most of southeastern Europe, northern Africa, and the Middle East.

Of all the empires in history, however, the largest was ruled by the Mongols. Genghis Khan began building this empire in the early 1200's. By the end of that century, under the rule of his grandson, Kublai Khan, it covered most of Asia and part of Europe.

▶ EMPIRE-BUILDING IN THE AGE OF DISCOVERY

Toward the end of the 1400's, a period of exploration began in Europe that helped bring it out of the Middle Ages. Improved navigational instruments helped explorers discover places in Africa, Asia, and the Americas, and superior weapons helped them overpower many of the peoples they encountered.

In the 1480's, the Portuguese set out to find a sea route to India. They sailed down the west coast of Africa, taking control of some of the lands along the way. Then in 1492, the Spanish, led by Christopher Columbus, began exploring the New World. The Spanish and the Portuguese soon settled and claimed most of present-day Mexico, Central America, and South America.

In the 1600's, other European nations began competing for empires all over the world. The Dutch grabbed rich territories in Asia to gain control over the profitable spice trade. They also set up colonies in South Africa and North America. The French acquired colonies too, including present-day Canada, which was particularly valuable for its furs.

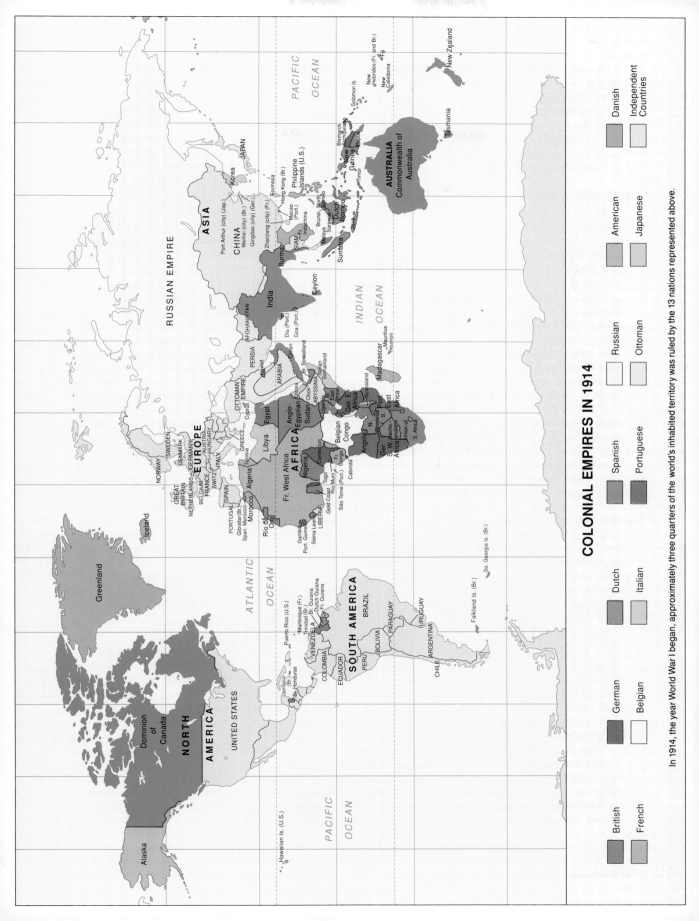

COLONIAL EMPIRES IN 1914

In 1914, the year World War I began, approximately three quarters of the world's inhabited territory was ruled by the 13 nations represented above.

British · **French** · **German** · **Belgian** · **Spanish** · **Portuguese** · **Russian** · **Ottoman** · **Dutch** · **Italian** · **American** · **Japanese** · **Danish** · **Independent Countries**

Map labels:

Alaska · Hawaiian Is. (U.S.) · Greenland · Iceland · Dominion of Canada · NORTH AMERICA · UNITED STATES · Puerto Rico (U.S.) · Jamaica (Br.) · Br. Honduras · Martinique (Fr.) · Trinidad (Br.) · Br. Guiana · Dutch Guiana · Fr. Guiana · VENEZUELA · COLOMBIA · ECUADOR · PERU · BOLIVIA · BRAZIL · PARAGUAY · URUGUAY · ARGENTINA · CHILE · SOUTH AMERICA · Falkland Is. (Br.) · So. Georgia Is. (Br.)

GREAT BRITAIN · NORWAY · SWEDEN · DENMARK · GERMANY · NETHERLANDS · BELGIUM · FRANCE · SWITZ. · AUSTRIA-HUNGARY · PORTUGAL · SPAIN · ITALY · GREECE · EUROPE · Gibraltar (Br.) · Span. Morocco

RUSSIAN EMPIRE · OTTOMAN EMPIRE · Cyprus (Br.) · PERSIA · AFGHANISTAN · ARABIA · Kuwait · Oman · ASIA · CHINA · Port Arthur (city) (Jap.) · Weihei (city) (Br.) · Qingdao (city) (Ger.) · Zhanjiang (city) (Fr.) · Korea · JAPAN · Formosa · Macao (Port.) · Hong Kong (Br.) · Philippine Islands (U.S.) · SIAM · Burma · INDIA · Ceylon · Diu (Port.) · Goa (Port.) · French Indochina · Brunei · North Borneo · Sarawak · Malaya · Sumatra · Dutch Borneo · Timor · New Guinea · Bismarck Arch. · Solomon Is. · New Hebrides (Fr. and Br.) · New Caledonia · Fiji · New Zealand · AUSTRALIA · Commonwealth of Australia · Tasmania

AFRICA · Morocco · Algeria · Tunisia · Libya · Egypt · Rio de Oro · Fr. West Africa · Gambia · Port. Guinea · Sierra Leone · LIBERIA · Gold Coast · Togo · Nigeria · Cameroon · Rio Muni · Fr. Congo · Cabinda · São Tomé (Port.) · Belgian Congo · Angola · N. Rhodesia · S. Rhodesia · Ger. S.W. Africa · Bechuanaland · S. Africa · Anglo-Egyptian Sudan · ABYSSINIA · Eritrea · Br. Somaliland · Italian Somaliland · Fr. Somaliland · Uganda · Br. East Africa · Ger. E. Africa · Nyasaland · Port. East Africa · Madagascar · Mauritius (Br.) · Reunion

ATLANTIC OCEAN · PACIFIC OCEAN · INDIAN OCEAN

In the 1660's, the British took over the Dutch territory in North America, and in 1763, they took Canada from the French. And despite their loss of the 13 American colonies after the Revolutionary War in 1783, the British continued to acquire new territories. They soon settled Australia and eventually went on to control one of the largest empires in history.

▶COLONIALISM IN THE 1800'S AND 1900'S

In the last few decades of the 1800's, major European powers stepped up their competition for overseas colonies. These colonies provided European industries with cheap labor, raw materials, and additional markets for European goods.

Great Britain, under the direction of Cecil Rhodes, seized large sections of Africa. It also took control of India from the East India Company. France, Germany, Italy, and Belgium also acquired colonies in Africa and Asia. China escaped a European conquest, in part because the imperial powers could not agree on how to divide it up between them.

The United States joined in the race for colonies after completing its westward expansion across North America. In 1898, after a war with Spain, it took over the Philippines and Puerto Rico and established a "sphere of influence" in Central America, where it acquired the Panama Canal Zone.

▶THE DECLINE OF COLONIALISM

World War I (1914–18), to a large degree, resulted from the colonial rivalries among the major European imperial powers. The victors held onto their overseas colonies and took over those belonging to the defeated countries. Germany, one of those defeated countries, soon tried to regain and expand its empire.

During World War II (1939–45), under the Nazi dictatorship of Adolf Hitler, Germany occupied, for a short time, a vast empire that included the bulk of Europe. At the same time, Japan seized an enormous empire in Asia, including a large portion of China. But their empire-building ended in 1945, when both countries were defeated in the war.

After the war, Great Britain, France, the United States, and other nations with big overseas empires had found it difficult and unprofitable to hold onto their colonies by force. Furthermore, they had fought World War II against imperial dictatorships, in the name of freedom—and naturally their own colonies wanted freedom for themselves. Thus the great empires began breaking up, sometimes peaceably, sometimes by violent struggle.

▶IMPERIALISM CHANGES FORM

In 1945, the United Nations, an international organization, was founded to promote peace among nations and help new countries develop their governments and economies. In Africa alone, more than forty countries emerged from imperial colonies. India became independent of Great Britain. The Philippines became independent of the United States. Even little islands in the Caribbean became self-governing. One by one, these new countries joined the United Nations, and it appeared that imperialism was dying out.

However, strong nations can impose their will on other countries without actually taking over their governments. In such cases, influence comes in the form of economic, and sometimes military, pressure. This form of domination is called **neoimperialism**.

The best example of a post-World War II neoimperialist empire was the former Soviet Union, which controlled by force half a dozen East European countries outside its borders. But in 1989, rebellion in these "Soviet satellites" started a process of disintegration, and by 1991 the Soviet empire had crumbled. The Soviets overthrew communism in favor of democracy, and more than a dozen Soviet satellites and republics declared independence.

▶IMPERIALISM TODAY

Imperialism was once regarded as something glorious, and countries were proud to spread their authority across the globe. Now most people think of it as menacing. In many countries, it is no longer popular to think that the strong have the right to use force or violence to take advantage of others. Today, partly due to the existence of the United Nations, it is much more difficult than it once was for the powerful nations to dominate the weaker ones.

ROBERT WESSON
Author, *The Imperial Order*

See also ANCIENT CIVILIZATIONS; EAST INDIA COMPANY; HOLY ROMAN EMPIRE; OTTOMAN EMPIRE; RHODES, CECIL; ROME, ANCIENT; UNITED NATIONS.

IMPETIGO. See DISEASES (Descriptions of Some Diseases).

Auguste Renoir portrayed a festive moment in *The Luncheon of the Boating Party* (1881). The informal, light-filled scene is characteristic of impressionist art.

IMPRESSIONISM

In Paris during the late 1860's, a small group of artists began to produce paintings that were beautiful to look at, but that were very different from most art of the period. The new paintings were lighter and more colorful than traditional paintings, and their subject matter often was informal. Many depicted scenes of sidewalk cafés, seaside resorts, and other popular spots. Others showed tranquil views of the French countryside. Most unusual of all was the artists' painting technique. Instead of mixing paint on a palette to create a range of color combinations, the artists daubed pure, unmixed pigments directly onto the canvas in what seemed to be a hodgepodge of brightly colored dashes.

The new form of painting, which came to be called impressionism, was the first modern art movement. Misunderstood at first, it later was widely accepted, changing the way artists painted and the way people looked at art.

▶FRENCH IMPRESSIONISM

Although impressionism later became an international art movement, it originated in Paris, the major European art center of the late 1800's. The first group of French impressionists consisted of about thirty artists, including Claude Monet, Auguste Renoir, Alfred Sisley, Camille Pissarro, Edgar Degas, and Berthe Morisot. A better-known and slightly older artist, Édouard Manet, worked with the group but did not exhibit with them. All the artists shared similar beliefs about art, although their individual styles differed.

The artists held their first exhibition in 1874, calling themselves an "anonymous group." The show drew a storm of criticism from the press and the public. One critic mockingly called the artists' work "impressionism," taking the term from the title of Monet's painting *Impression: Sunrise.* The critic meant that the paintings were only impressions, sketchy and incomplete. Later, supporters of the movement also adopted the name.

Style and Techniques. Impressionist paintings were unpopular at first mainly because they were so different from the paintings people were used to seeing. Traditional paintings often depicted people and scenes that were fa-

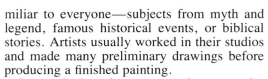

Two paintings of poplars by Claude Monet show how changing light affects color. Bright yellows highlight the sunlit trees at left; when in shadows, at right, the same trees are painted in shades of violet.

Édouard Manet influenced the impressionists but did not use their bright colors. *The Balcony* (1868) has strongly contrasting areas of light and dark tones.

miliar to everyone—subjects from myth and legend, famous historical events, or biblical stories. Artists usually worked in their studios and made many preliminary drawings before producing a finished painting.

Impressionists, in contrast, chose to paint ordinary people and everyday scenes. To them, the subject of a painting was not as important as the portrayal of light and color. For this reason, they preferred to work outdoors, painting quickly to capture rapidly changing qualities of light and atmosphere. Shapes were no longer carefully modeled and clearly outlined. Instead, they were painted as masses of vibrating color. Even shadows, usually painted gray or black, were tinged with color. Using what is called a "broken-color" technique, impressionist painters applied pure color to the canvas in many small brushstrokes. When viewed from a slight distance, the strokes of color seemed to merge, forming a complete image.

Each of the French impressionists used these techniques in different ways. Monet was especially interested in the effects of changing light on color and form. He frequently painted the same scene at different times of day. The changes in light and atmosphere caused the subject to look different in each painting.

Renoir portrayed the effects of flickering light by painting softened forms that appeared

The Bridge at Sevres (1877), by Alfred Sisley, captures the atmospheric conditions of a cloudy day by the water. A detail of the painting (*above*) shows the loosely painted brushstrokes that combine to form the image.

The Tub is a pastel drawing made by Edgar Degas about 1886. The informal subject matter, gracefully defined figure, and indoor setting are typical of the artist's style.

slightly out of focus. Manet did not use the bright colors of the impressionists, but his preference for everyday subjects greatly influenced the younger artists. Degas, too, painted informal subjects, such as women bathing and dancers stretching. Unlike other impressionists, he painted indoors and used outlines to define the shapes of his figures. (Biographies of each of the artists named above can be found in this encyclopedia.)

Although impressionism was considered to be a revolutionary art movement, earlier artists had experimented with similar techniques. The English painters John Constable and J. M. W. Turner skillfully portrayed light and atmosphere. The Spanish painters Diego Velázquez and Francisco Goya used color and brushwork to create the appearance of movement. The French artist Eugène Delacroix had observed that shadows contain elements of color. The work of all these artists influenced the impressionists, as did the forms and composition of Japanese woodblock prints.

▶SPREAD AND INFLUENCE OF IMPRESSIONISM

After 1875, impressionism became widely accepted and began to influence artists in other European countries. Prominent painters outside France, including the German artist Max Liebermann, the Italian artist Giuseppi De Nittis, and the English artist Wilson Steer, added elements of impressionism to their work.

By the end of the 1800's, impressionism had spread to the United States. Many Ameri-

Left: Allies Day, May 1917, by American impressionist Childe Hassam. *Right: Mont Sainte-Victoire* (1906), by postimpressionist Paul Cézanne, whose style led to cubism.

can artists, including Theodore Robinson, William Glackens, and Mary Cassatt, visited France and became closely associated with French impressionists. Cassatt, who studied with Degas, specialized in portraits of mothers and their children. (A biography of Cassatt appears in Volume C.) Among other American impressionists were Childe Hassam and John Henry Twachtman.

Postimpressionism. By 1890, impressionism had begun to fade as a movement. Differences in individual styles increased as artists moved in separate directions. Some artists wanted to preserve the bright color of the impressionists but create art with more structure, using strong outlines and solidly modeled forms. Others wanted to use color not just to capture an image but to express emotion. Together, the various styles that grew out of impressionism are called postimpressionism. Many important ideas in modern art developed from postimpressionism.

One of the postimpressionists, Georges Seurat, developed **pointillism**, a much more scientific version of the impressionist broken-color technique. His paintings were composed of many small dots of different colors calculated to produce an exact color effect. Another artist, Paul Cézanne, tried to demonstrate the solidity of objects by showing that they were made up of many intersecting planes (flat sur-

faces). Cézanne's technique led directly to the modern art style called cubism. It also influenced the development of abstract art. Abstract paintings may consist only of lines, planes, and other shapes. (A biography of Cézanne appears in Volume C.)

Other postimpressionists, such as Vincent van Gogh, Henri de Toulouse-Lautrec, and Paul Gauguin, were particularly interested in expressing emotion with color and design. Their work looked forward to the art movement known as expressionism, in which artists tried to reveal their inner feelings through their art. (Biographies of these three artists can be found in this encyclopedia.)

Impressionism in Literature and Music. Impressionist ideas also appeared in literature and music. Like impressionist artists, impressionist writers, such as Stéphane Mallarmé, and composers, such as Claude Debussy, tried to capture and portray in their work a fleeting moment in time. Elements in their works often seem disconnected and unformed. The parts are brought into an integrated whole by the imagination of the reader or listener, just as the separate strokes of color in an impressionist painting form a complete image in the eye of the viewer.

HOWARD E. WOODEN
Director Emeritus
The Wichita Art Museum

INCAS

The Incas, an American Indian people, were originally a small tribe in the southern highlands of Peru. In less than a century, during the 1400's, they built one of the largest, most tightly controlled empires the world has ever known. Their skill in government was matched by their feats of engineering. Roads, walls, and irrigation works constructed by the Incas are still in use today.

Spanish conquerors captured the Inca emperor in 1532 and began to break up the empire. But the Indian people of Peru never forgot their Inca heritage. Many, even now, believe that a new Inca king will someday arise to restore the glory of their ancestors.

▶SOCIAL ORDER

To fully appreciate the Inca achievement, it helps to visualize the difficult terrain of western South America. Along the coast are some of the world's driest deserts. Next to these flat coastal lands rise the jagged peaks of the Andes, whose eastern slopes are covered with rain forests. The native people of this varied region all lived under the rule of a single man, the emperor, addressed as "Chief Inca," "Son of the Sun," and "Lover of the Poor."

The Empire

The basic unit of Inca society was the village, or neighborhood, in which the residents thought of each other as at least distantly related. Marriage was within the neighborhood. Villages, as well as towns with two or more neighborhood units, were grouped into provinces. The empire as a whole was divided into four quarters, with the capital, Cuzco, at the center.

The Emperor. As a supposed descendant of the sun, the "Chief Inca" ruled by divine right. He ate from gold and silver dishes and never wore the same clothes twice. When messengers came before him, he remained hidden behind a screen. Like the pharaohs of Egypt, he took his own sister as his queen.

Established custom guaranteed that the emperor behave responsibly. He attended to the needs of his subjects and, to a limited extent, took part in public activities. When it was time for planting, the emperor himself broke the first clod of earth with his golden spade.

Nobles. The noble class came from Cuzco, home of the original Inca tribe. But as the empire grew, there were not enough nobles to fill all the offices. Men of ability, therefore, were chosen to form a second class of nobles. All men who were nobles, whether of the first

The remains of terraced hillsides and stone walls built by the Incas at Machu Picchu high in the Andes Mountains in southern Peru.

or second class, wore ear ornaments to set them apart from commoners.

The four nobles who governed the four quarters of the empire served as the emperor's council.

Labor Service. Instead of paying taxes, the Inca people performed regularly assigned labor on government lands. The produce of this labor was stored in warehouses used by the government, or by the people themselves in time of need.

The Quipu. The Incas kept precise records of what was in each warehouse. They also kept census records, in order to know how much labor service each community could give. Yet they had no writing, not even picture books as did the Aztecs. The Inca records were kept by means of knotted strings, called *quipus.*

The typical *quipu* (KEE-poo) had several strings attached to a main string. The group of knots farthest from the main string recorded units; the next group, tens; the next, hundreds; and so forth.

Language. Many different languages were spoken in ancient Peru. The Incas of Cuzco spoke Quechua (KETCH-wah). To unify the empire, they spread the language, and as a result Quechua became, and still is, the most widely spoken Indian language in the Americas.

Colonists and Armies. Another means of strengthening the empire was to make entire communities settle in new locations. Loyal to the emperor, these colonists could keep watch over newly conquered communities.

Conquest itself was accomplished by imperial troops, armed with stones that were hurled either singly by twirling a sling, or in groups attached to a system of connected strings. A weapon of stones connected in this manner is called a *bola.*

Almost all men, including the emperor, served in the army at one time or another. To be a warrior was every man's ideal.

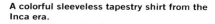
A colorful sleeveless tapestry shirt from the Inca era.

Way of Life

There are many gaps in our knowledge of Inca life. But we do have written accounts from several explorers and missionaries, as well as from two Incas: Garcilaso de la Vega and Waman Puma (Falcon Lion).

From these we know that most Incas lived in villages. Even Cuzco, the capital, was not a large city. Workers who supplied its needs lived in small settlements in the surrounding countryside.

Dress. When Inca people got up in the morning, they did not have to get dressed. They slept in their clothes. Women wore long gowns with a sash at the waist. Men wore loincloths and sleeveless shirts that hung almost to the knees. Both sexes wore sandals and long capes.

Food. The first meal of the day was at eight or nine in the morning. Most dishes were soups or stews. Beans, peppers, tomatoes, peanuts, and sweet manioc were used. But the more important foods were maize (corn) and potatoes. So-called Irish and Idaho potatoes actually originated in ancient Peru. Almost the only meat regularly used was guinea pig.

Work. Men, if they were not on military duty, worked in the fields. Women did spinning and weaving and took care of the home. Often, however, wives went to the fields and helped their husbands with the farming. Since there was no regular schooling (except for the children of nobles), most young people learned adult chores by watching their parents.

Some workers tended flocks of llamas. The llama, a relative of the camel, provided coarse wool for spinning and was used as a beast of burden. There were no wheeled vehicles, but a llama could carry 100 pounds (45 kilograms).

Shelter. The average house was a one-room structure of stone or mud brick, roofed with thatch. At night the whole family slept together on the floor. There were no mattresses (not even for the emperor). People doubled a huge blanket and crawled inside.

Religion

The most sacred shrine in Peru was the Temple of the Sun, in Cuzco. There was also a temple dedicated to the god of creation, Viracocha (wee-rah-KOH-chah). Other important deities were the Earth Mother and the spirit called Thunder, or God of the Weather.

People everywhere worshiped their ancestors. Each neighborhood kept a mummy, supposedly of the ancestor from whom all the living were descended. Mummies of the emperors were kept in palaces in Cuzco.

Feasts and the Calendar. The Incas developed an accurate calendar by observing the movements of the sun. By observing the moon, they divided the year into twelve months and planned their major religious feasts accordingly.

A feast celebrating the harvest was held in the month corresponding to May. June marked the great feast of the Sun. Rituals of planting were held in August. Sacrifices of guinea pigs and llamas were required on such occasions. Sometimes human beings were sacrificed.

Crafts and Engineering

The Incas were competent artists, but their works are valued less for beauty than for technical perfection. They are known not so much for sculpture and painting as for weaving, road and bridge construction, and stone masonry.

Textiles. Inca weaving rivaled the best work done in Europe. The finest cloth was a kind of tapestry, finished on both sides, with intricate designs in many colors. This was a woman's craft. Most other works were done by men.

Metalwork. The science of metallurgy was more advanced in Peru than anywhere else in the Americas. Deep mining was practiced, as well as a kind of smelting to remove metal from raw ore. Copper and tin were combined to produce bronze, which made stronger weapons and tools. Metalworkers also knew about casting, soldering, and riveting.

Masonry. Stone walls built by Incas were so perfectly fitted that even today a knife blade cannot be inserted in the joints. Stone buildings in Cuzco rose to heights of two and three stories.

Waterworks. Streams were rechanneled to bring in fresh water and carry off sewage. To irrigate fields in the highlands, hillsides were terraced, like the rice paddies of China.

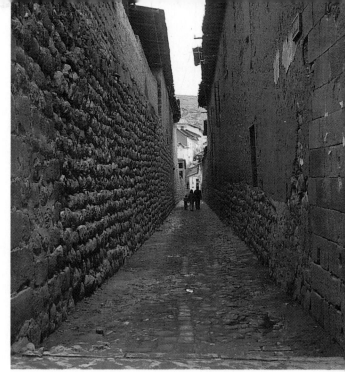

An ancient narrow street in Cuzco, Peru. Note the Inca stone wall on the left.

Roads. Roads connected all towns and villages with Cuzco. In the mountains the roads were built with retaining walls, switchbacks, culverts, and tunnels. Swift streams were crossed by suspension bridges.

Along the roads there were post houses, where runners waited to relay messages. Messengers carrying a *quipu* or a small package could travel 150 miles (240 kilometers) a day. It is said that in this way the emperor in Cuzco, high in the mountains, received fresh fish from the sea.

▶HISTORY

The record of civilization in western South America begins long before the Incas. About A.D. 500 there were great cultures flourishing along the seacoast and in the Andes. On the south coast of Peru the Nazca people produced textiles and colored pottery of much refinement. On the north coast the Moche crafted pottery that portrayed animals, plants, and human faces with a realism never equaled by the later cultures of Peru.

About A.D. 900 a civilization known as Chimu emerged on the north coast. The Chimu, who built a large walled city called Chan Chan, were one of the many peoples conquered by the Inca army in the 1400's.

Rise of the Incas

According to legend Cuzco was founded by a god-man called Manco Capac, whose father, the Sun, had sent him to civilize the world. From Manco descended a line of rulers known to later generations as emperors. It is doubtful, however, that the first six or seven could have been more than local chiefs.

Under the eighth chief, called Viracocha Inca, the rule of Cuzco was perhaps extended a few miles beyond its home valley. The history of the empire really begins with Viracocha Inca's son, called Pachacuti.

Pachacuti. During the reign of this great leader, the Incas added territory from the present border of Bolivia all the way north to central Ecuador. Understandably, it was Pachacuti who began many of the imperial policies described above. Under Pachacuti's son, Tupa Inca Yupanqui, the empire was extended southward to central Chile, so that it then spanned a distance of more than 2,500 miles (4,000 kilometers). The eleventh ruler, Huayna Capac, added only small territories in Ecuador and eastern Peru.

Spanish Conquest

When the conqueror Francisco Pizarro arrived in 1532, the Inca Empire was torn by a civil war. Huayna Capac's son Huáscar had been installed as emperor in Cuzco. But another son, Atahualpa, also claimed the throne and marched on Cuzco with his own army.

Taking advantage of the confusion, Pizarro captured Atahualpa. On Atahualpa's orders, Huáscar was murdered. Hoping to free himself, Atahualpa then offered to fill his prison cell with gold. Pizarro agreed, and llama trains began arriving with loads of gold objects. The incredible ransom was paid. But Pizarro had Atahualpa executed nevertheless.

Tupac Amaru. Although the Spaniards seized control of Peru, they could not extinguish the spirit of rebellion. A leader known as Tupac Amaru, last of the royal Incas, established a shadow empire in the eastern mountains and was not conquered until 1572. Two hundred years later another Tupac Amaru led a revolt in the southern highlands. Tupac Amaru II was caught and executed in 1781.

Inca Heritage

Quechua, the language of the Incas, is still widely spoken in Ecuador, Bolivia, and north-

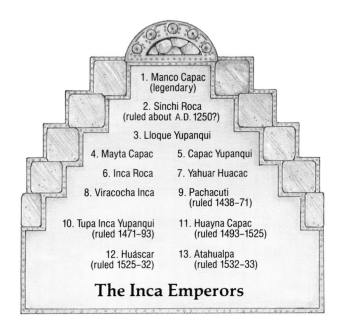

1. Manco Capac (legendary)

2. Sinchi Roca (ruled about A.D. 1250?)

3. Lloque Yupanqui

4. Mayta Capac   5. Capac Yupanqui

6. Inca Roca   7. Yahuar Huacac

8. Viracocha Inca   9. Pachacuti (ruled 1438–71)

10. Tupa Inca Yupanqui (ruled 1471–93)   11. Huayna Capac (ruled 1493–1525)

12. Huáscar (ruled 1525–32)   13. Atahualpa (ruled 1532–33)

The Inca Emperors

west Argentina. In Peru it is the native language of approximately half the population. Most of the Quechua people of Peru live in the highlands. However, in recent years many have migrated to Lima and other coastal cities, where they live in crowded neighborhoods.

Inkarrí. The memory of the Incas remains alive. Modern legends say that an Inca ruler will yet return, bringing a better life for the Quechua. Sometimes this hero is called Amaru (from Tupac Amaru), more often Inkarrí (from Inca and the Spanish word *rey*, meaning "king").

In the 1960's and 1970's the Peruvian government took steps to improve conditions for the Quechua people and to give the Inca heritage more prominence in national life. Quechua was made an official language of Peru, together with Spanish. The portrait of Tupac Amaru II now appeared on Peruvian paper money. And government officials made speeches to Quechua audiences, proclaiming, "Inkarrí is here!"

At the same time, schoolchildren in Peru were being taught to recite the names of the Inca emperors—the way young people everywhere learn multiplication tables and the alphabet. Some Peruvians can recite all 13 names in a single breath.

JOHN BIERHORST
Author, *The Mythology of South America*
See also INDIANS, AMERICAN (The Andean Nations).

INCOME TAX

Part of the money people earn is paid to the government as an income tax. Most forms of income—wages, business profits, interest from savings accounts, and earnings from investments—are taxed. The income tax is paid by individuals and by businesses from small shops to giant corporations.

For governments in the United States, Canada, and many other countries, the income tax is the biggest source of **revenue**, or money received. It is also one of the easiest taxes to collect. Often, before giving workers their paychecks, an employer will **withhold**, or take out, a portion of the workers' wages to pay to the government toward their annual income taxes. That way, most of the income taxes the workers owe are paid as they earn their salaries, and the government receives a steady flow of money.

▶ HOW THE TAX BEGAN

As long as people have had governments, they have had some form of income tax. In ancient times, money was not widely used, but grain was considered income, and people gave part of their crops to the government. Ancient Greeks and Romans imposed a form of tax on money earned by citizens. The first modern income tax was adopted by the British Parliament in 1799. The United States imposed an income tax in 1862 to help pay for the costs of the Civil War. In 1894 the United States Supreme Court declared income taxes unconstitutional. Because the revenues it provided were needed, however, Congress was urged to amend the Constitution to make the tax legal. In 1913 the 16th Amendment went into effect, and that year Congress imposed an income tax on individuals and corporations. Many changes have been made in the law since then, but the tax remains.

▶ PURPOSE OF THE TAX

Governments provide services that cannot be done by individuals, such as building roads, defending against foreign attacks, protecting national boundaries and forests, and providing mail services. The main purpose of the income tax is to raise money so that governments can pay the costs of these services and the salaries of the people who perform them. (Government workers also pay income taxes on the money they earn.) The costs of law enforcement, the courts, education, space exploration, and even weather reports are at least partly paid for by income taxes.

The government uses part of the money to provide social services, such as health care, supplemental old-age pensions, benefits for the unemployed, food stamps, welfare payments, and housing, as well as public works projects, such as road building, that create jobs. In Sweden and other European democracies, the use of the income tax is very important. Tax rates are higher in these countries than in the United States and their governments spend more on social services.

Most taxes are **graduated**, or progressive. That is, people who earn high wages generally pay a bigger part of every dollar to the government than people who earn low wages. People who earn more are asked to pay a higher percentage. Also, some taxpayers are allowed to **exempt** (exclude) a part of their income or **deduct** (subtract) certain expenses from it. For example, some taxpayers can deduct the amount they give to charity.

▶ MULTIPLE TAXATION

A person's income may be taxed more than once. In the United States and Canada, people pay income taxes to the federal government. In addition, many American states and all Canadian provinces impose their own income taxes. Some American city and county governments collect income taxes as well. Some of these cities tax income earned in that city, no matter where the taxpayer lives. As a result, a worker can owe an income tax to the city in which he or she works, and also owe income taxes to the city, state, and country where he or she resides. Nearby, another person might live and work in a city and state that has no income tax. This person would pay an income tax only to the federal government.

By April 15 every year, each worker fills out at least one form called a federal tax **return**, and sends it to the Internal Revenue Service (IRS). If the amount of tax withheld during the year is more than the tax owed, the taxpayer will receive a refund from the IRS.

Reviewed by LEONARD SLOANE
Author, *The New York Times Book of Personal Finance*

See also TAXATION.

INDEPENDENCE.   See Missouri (Cities).

Every Fourth of July, spectacular fireworks displays help Americans celebrate the day the United States declared its independence from Great Britain.

INDEPENDENCE DAY

Independence Day—the Fourth of July—is the holiday when Americans celebrate the birthday of the United States of America. It commemorates the day in 1776 when the American colonists declared their independence from Great Britain. By adopting the Declaration of Independence, the Second Continental Congress announced to the world that "these United Colonies are, and of right ought to be, free and independent states."

The first celebration of American independence took place on July 8, 1776, in Philadelphia. The ceremony began with a public reading of the Declaration outside the State House (now called Independence Hall). That evening, Philadelphians celebrated with bonfires, a parade, and the firing of cannons. From the tower of the State House, the Liberty Bell rang out, and the coat of arms of the King of England was taken down. The Declaration of Independence greatly boosted the morale of the Continental Army, which was then in its second year of fighting the British Redcoats in the Revolutionary War (1775–81).

John Adams, who signed the Declaration and later became the nation's second president, thought that Americans should celebrate a "great anniversary festival." In a letter to his wife, Abigail, he wrote, "It ought to be commemorated as the day of deliverance, by solemn acts of devotion to God Almighty. It ought to be solemnized with pomp and parade, with shows, games, sports, guns, bells, bonfires, and illuminations, from one end of this continent to the other, from this time forward forevermore." The first anniversary of Independence Day was celebrated in Philadelphia in 1777. It included all of the pomp and parade Adams had envisioned.

In 1788, several years after the Americans had won the Revolutionary War, a more elaborate celebration was held. That year the anniversary occurred just two weeks after the new Constitution of the United States was ratified. There was a large parade, a speech, and a dinner, during which many toasts were proposed. These toasts were addressed to "The People of the United States," "General Washington," and "The Whole Family of Mankind."

The idea of celebrating the Fourth of July grew over the years. Every year on that day the soldiers who fought in the Continental Army made it a tradition to gather and tell stories about the war and rejoice in their victory over the British. As people moved west during the 1800's, they spread the idea of celebrating the Fourth of July to new towns and territories.

It was not long before the whole country celebrated the Fourth. At sunrise all over the nation gun salutes were fired and bells rung. Flags were flown from buildings, from homes, and along the streets. Many shop windows were decorated with red, white, and blue, the colors of the American flag. Parades were followed by public readings of the Declaration of Independence. National songs were sung,

---

EVENTS THAT TOOK PLACE ON THE FOURTH OF JULY

1776 The Second Continental Congress adopted the Declaration of Independence.

1802 The United States Military Academy at West Point opened.

1817 Construction on the Erie Canal began.

1826 Former presidents John Adams and Thomas Jefferson died.

1828 Construction on the nation's first railroad, the Baltimore and Ohio, began.

1848 The cornerstone of the Washington Monument in Washington, D.C., was laid.

1884 The Statue of Liberty was formally presented to the United States by France.

1946 The United States granted independence to the Republic of the Philippines.

1960 The first 50-star flag was flown.

1976 The bicentennial (200-year) anniversary of the United States was celebrated.

and speeches were made. By 1941, Congress had declared the Fourth of July a national legal holiday.

Over the years, the Fourth of July has become associated with many activities. For some, it marks the true beginning of summer fun. Beaches, parks, and amusement areas typically are filled with holiday crowds. People go on picnics, where they run races and play softball and other outdoor games. But mostly, the Fourth of July has come to represent fireworks. In the evenings on the Fourth, in most communities around the country, large, colorful displays of firecrackers, rockets, sparklers, Roman candles, and pinwheels explode across the skies, bringing delight to children and adults alike.

At one time, however, fireworks caused so many accidents and injuries that the public demanded legislation to ensure a "safe and sane Fourth." Many states outlawed the private sale of fireworks, and today, public fireworks displays are sponsored and controlled by local communities, clubs, and businesses so that everyone may enjoy them in safety.

Reviewed by RICHARD B. MORRIS
Columbia University

See also DECLARATION OF INDEPENDENCE.

INDEPENDENCE HALL

Independence Hall in Philadelphia is the official birthplace of the United States of America. It was there that the Second Continental Congress chose George Washington as Commander in Chief of the Continental Army (1775), the Declaration of Independence was signed (1776), and the Constitutional Convention drafted a constitution for the United States government (1787).

Independence Hall, originally a meeting place for the Pennsylvania Assembly, was called the Pennyslvania State House. Construction was completed in the 1740's, although lawmakers began meeting in the unfinished Assembly Chamber as early as 1736.

In May 1775, one month after the Revolutionary War began, the Second Continental Congress met in the Assembly Chamber of the State House to draft a declaration of independence from Great Britain. On July 4, the Declaration of Independence was signed and four days later was read to the public, for the first time, from the State House Yard. The State House Bell, now called the Liberty Bell, rang out in celebration.

During the early years of the Revolutionary War, the British occupied Philadelphia and used the State House as a prison and a hospital. When the American Congress returned in 1778, they found the hall "filthy" with "the inside torn much to pieces." The hall was cleaned, and Congress again began meeting there. Nearly a decade later, in 1787, a convention was held there to draft a new

Philadelphia's Independence Hall is one of the most significant buildings in the United States. The Declaration of Independence was signed there in 1776.

constitution for the newly independent country. On September 17, the Constitution was signed and ready for ratification by the states.

Sometime in the 1800's, people began referring to the State House as Independence Hall. Today people come from all over the world to visit this historic site, which is now part of Independence National Historical Park. The Liberty Bell, which once stood in a room on the ground floor of the State House tower, now can be seen in Liberty Bell Center, not far from its original home.

Reviewed by HOBART CAWOOD
Independence National Historical Park

See also LIBERTY BELL.

INDEXES AND INDEXING

The index is the key that unlocks the contents of a book. It guides the reader to the exact page on which particular information is found. The first indexes included only general topics. Topics were not arranged in alphabetical order until the 1600's. Today a book written to provide information is considered of little value unless it is carefully indexed to show the exact location of every fact and subject and each person, place, and event discussed in its pages. Modern indexes, alphabetically arranged, are placed at the back of a book or in the final volume of some series of books.

Heading, Entry, and Subheading. The word or proper name used to indicate the subject indexed is called the **heading**. The heading, together with the number of the page or pages in the text on which the information about it is found, is called the **entry**. The usefulness of an index depends on the choice of the words selected as headings. These words must accurately describe the contents of the book, and they must be words that are familiar to the index user. They must be specific, logical, and definite terms that have only one meaning. There must be a separate heading for each subject mentioned in the book. Each topic must be listed under the same heading each time it appears. It cannot be scattered under different words of similar meaning.

A particular word useful in one index may be too general a term for the index of another book or too specific for a third. A bird guide will not use the heading "birds" in its index. It will list only the names of the particular species of birds it describes. The index of a book about world geography will not include the name of a village too small to be in the text. The index of a book on outer space written before the United States' first space flight will not list John Glenn.

If there are many references to one subject, **subheadings** will be used under a main heading for that subject. Subheadings bring together into one place different types of information on the subject. They identify and locate the information. In some indexes the subheadings form a kind of study guide to the topic.

Subheadings usually are placed in alphabetical order below the main heading. With this arrangement they can be seen clearly. They may be listed one subheading to a line or in paragraph form.

> **Advertising**, 306–13
>   magazines, 309
>   marketing, 308
>   newspapers, 310
>   public relations, 312–13
>   radio and television, 311
>   selling, 307

> **Advertising**, 306–13; magazines, 309; marketing, 308; newspapers, 310; public relations, 312–13; radio and television, 311; selling, 307

Cross-References. There are two types of guideposts, called **cross-references**, that make all indexes easier to use. The first is the "see" reference. This directs the reader away from a term not used as an entry and to the entry where the information will be found. The other is the "see also" reference. It directs the reader to additional and related information that will be found in another place.

The "see" reference is necessary because different people think of the same subject in different ways. Insofar as possible, the index includes all the terms that might be used to describe a topic listed. Under each term there appears a "see" reference to the word chosen for the entry. Many things, some people, and some places are known by more than one name. Ping-Pong is a game that some people play. Others call the game table tennis. The index will include both names and use a "see" reference under the one that is not the entry.

> **Ping-Pong** see Table tennis
> **Table tennis or Ping-Pong**, 212

Samuel Langhorne Clemens and Mark Twain are two names for the same person. Some books put information about him under one name, some under the other. However, the "see" reference will show the name under which the information will be found.

> **Clemens, Samuel Langhorne** see Twain, Mark
> **Twain, Mark** (Samuel Langhorne Clemens), American writer, 482
>   *Huckleberry Finn, The Adventures of*, 510
>   *Tom Sawyer, The Adventures of*, 318

By following up the "see" references, a user will be sure to find the information he or she wants. When an index is not well supplied with "see" references, it is sometimes necessary to look in several places before the term chosen for the entry can be found.

Some words found in indexes are so closely connected that it is difficult to separate completely the information they cover. "Athletics," "Games," and "Sports" are such words. The exact information the reader wants may appear under only one of the three. A "see also" reference can be used to bring the three terms together.

Athletics
   gymnastics, 202
   physical education, 394
   track and field, 282–84
   See also Games; Sports
Games, 222–26
   billiards, 112–13
   bowling, 214–16
   chess, 312–13
   table tennis, 212
   See also Athletics; Sports
Sports
   archery, 218–20
   baseball, 312–16
   golf, 412–14
   skiing, 214–16
   soccer, 220–22
   See also Athletics; Games

"See also" references are also helpful in guiding the reader away from a general heading when the material he or she wants is listed under a specific heading.

Kinds of Indexes. There are indexes to newspapers, to magazines, and to books. Some magazines publish indexes once a year or every six months and issue them to subscribers who request copies. *National Geographic* and *Consumer Reports* are among those magazines that do. Other indexes cover the material in many magazines. The *Readers' Guide to Periodical Literature*, published since 1900, makes available the information contained in nearly 200 popular magazines of general interest, mostly from the United States. It indexes articles by main subjects and by authors, but not usually by title. Published every two to four weeks, its information is quickly available. There are quarterly and annual cumulations of the monthly issues, in which all the entries are interfiled and bound in one volume.

Other magazine indexes specialize in particular types of information. Magazines of interest to teachers are covered by the *Education Index*. Magazines of interest to farmers and to scientists concerned with the production of food are covered by the *Agricultural Index*. These indexes list the magazines included in them. In addition, useful instructions, abbreviations, and explanations are provided at the beginning of each volume.

The largest index to many books is the *Cumulative Book Index*. It lists by author, title, and subject practically all books printed in English. It includes the publisher and the price of each book as well. The CBI, as it is often called, is published monthly except for August. Like the magazine indexes, it is cumulated annually. The CBI, which began as the *United States Catalog*, is a part of the national bibliography, a record of book publication.

The most useful indexes to books of a particular kind are those to plays, to poetry, and to quotations. Many plays and poems are published in collections, and it is difficult to know which collection will contain a certain selection. An index to plays shows in what book each listed play can be found. A poetry index does the same thing for each poem it includes. An index to quotations makes it possible to find a passage from the writings or speeches of particular persons. It also helps in finding quotations on certain subjects.

Some indexes are never in book form. The index of the books in a library may be in the form of a card catalog, a list printed on microfilm, or a computer listing. Companies index business records in computer files. Some people use card files for indexing recipes and for friends' addresses.

MARY KENT GRANT
Reviewed by EDWIN B. COLBURN
Vice-President and Chief of Indexing Services
The H. W. Wilson Company

See also REFERENCE BOOKS.

INDIA

India is a nation that dominates the vast region known as the South Asian subcontinent. With more than 1 billion people, it is the world's second most populous country (after China) and the world's largest democracy. Shaped roughly like an upside-down triangle, India stretches from the high Himalaya mountains in the north to the island nation of Sri Lanka in the south.

India's history dates back at least 4,500 years, to when the Indus River civilization, one of the world's first settled communities, developed there on the fertile plains of the Indus River. Over the centuries, many different peoples invaded India and took control of its vast natural resources. The last outsiders to rule India were the British, whose administration, known as the Raj, lasted more than 150 years. India finally became a modern, independent nation in 1947, after World War II. In that year the British withdrew from the subcontinent after dividing most of the region into the two nations of India and Pakistan.

▶ PEOPLE

India has been a melting pot of varied ethnic groups since the beginning of its history. However, the majority of its people are of

Below: The Taj Mahal at Agra stands as a memorial to the love an Indian ruler had for his wife. It was built in the 1600's by the emperor Shah Jahan as a tomb for his wife Mumtāz Mahal.

Dravidian and Indo-Aryan ancestry. The Dravidians have lived in India since prehistoric times. The Indo-Aryans first arrived in the subcontinent about 1500 B.C. The two peoples differed in appearance, language, and customs. The Indo-Aryans spoke a language related to the modern European languages, and their religious beliefs evolved into Hinduism. The Indo-Aryans became the dominant people of India, particularly in the north. Southern India remained principally Dravidian.

Language

The major languages of India can be divided into two broad groups. Those of northern, western, and eastern India are derived from ancient Sanskrit, an Indo-European language and the sacred language of Hinduism. They include Hindi, Assamese, Bengali, Gujarati, Kashmiri, Marathi, Oriya, Punjabi, Sindhi, Urdu, and Hindustani. The languages of the south—Kannada, Malayalam, Tamil, and Telugu—belong to the Dravidian family, although they have been influenced by Sanskrit. Kashmiri and Urdu also contain many words from Arabic and Persian.

Hindi, the national language, is spoken by about 30 percent of the population. Most educated Indians speak English as well as Hindi and their regional language. Indian children are taught both their regional language and Hindi in the primary and lower secondary levels of school. Later they may also learn English, Sanskrit, or Persian.

India is a large country with a vast population. *Opposite page:* A young man from the state of Rajasthan in the northwest, and a mother and daughter from Karnataka in the south. *Below:* A mounted guardsman at the president's residence in New Delhi, the capital. *Right:* An elderly Sikh from Punjab. *Far right:* A Hindu boy from the state of Maharashtra. *Center:* Muslims in Delhi. *Lower right:* A young woman from Kashmir.

Religion

Nearly all the world's major religions are represented in India. The vast majority of the people (about 81 percent) are Hindus.

Hinduism has four essential beliefs. Hindus believe in God (or gods who are manifestations of a single god or universal spirit) as the creator and sustainer of the universe. They believe in an inner self that is eternal, which ultimately merges with God. They believe in the moral responsibility (dharma) of people for their actions (karma), because they have a will of their own and determine their own actions. Finally, Hindus believe in reincarnation (rebirth). They believe that people must go through a series of births, deaths, and rebirths to atone for their sins before they can achieve liberation (merging with God). The nature of one's rebirth is largely determined by one's actions in an earlier life.

Islam, the religion of Muslims and India's second largest religion, is practiced by about 12 percent of the population. Other religious groups include Christians, Sikhs, Buddhists, and Jains. India also has smaller communities of Parsis (Zoroastrians) and Jews. For more information, see the separate articles HINDUISM, ISLAM, BUDDHISM, JUDAISM, ZOROASTRIANISM, and RELIGIONS OF THE WORLD in the appropriate volumes.

Education

Education in India is the responsibility of both the states and the central government. In almost all states, schooling is compulsory for all children between the ages of 6 and 14. The system provides for eight years of primary education, two years of lower secondary education, and two years of higher secondary education. The students who graduate from the higher secondary schools may be admitted to one of India's more than one hundred universities and

Religion has long played a vital role in India, and some places of worship have existed for centuries. *Below right:* This is one of the many famous Hindu temples located in the state of Tamil Nadu in the south. Hindus are India's largest religious group. *Right:* A Muslim kneels in prayer at a mosque. Muslims make up the second largest religious group. *Below:* The Golden Temple at Amritsar is the holiest shrine of India's Sikhs, a smaller religious group.

thousands of colleges. The largest of these is the University of Delhi.

India has made great strides in education since independence. It has more than doubled the literacy rate, although it is still only about 50 percent. In addition, many of the village elementary schools have only one teacher. And because of the shortage of trained teachers, a large-scale expansion of schools has been difficult.

The Caste System

The distinctive Indian institution known as the caste system, in which heredity determines one's social class, developed from the early Aryan custom of separating people according to the work they did. The original system included four castes. Brahmins—members of the highest caste—were priests. Kshatriya were soldiers and leaders of government. Vaisya were traders and farmers. Sudra were artisans and laborers.

A fifth group, the Dalits (meaning "the oppressed"), later developed. They were called "untouchables," because they were outside the bounds of caste—or outcasts. The use of the term "untouchable" was outlawed at independence, and since 1951 many Dalits have benefited from government affirmative action programs. In 1997, as India celebrated 50 years of independence, K.R. Narayanan became the first president elected from the Dalit caste. Nevertheless, discrimination against the Dalits remains strong, particularly in rural areas.

Although the caste system is less rigid than it once was, the country's social structure is still strongly influenced by it, and members of the same caste usually live in the same neighborhoods. An Indian born into a low-caste family cannot change to a higher caste by education or wealth.

Family Life

Family ties are very strong in India. The Indian family is made up not only of a husband and wife and their children but also includes a large extended family. Sons bring their wives to their parents' home to bring up their children. Often the extended family also includes grandsons and their wives and children. Daughters and granddaughters remain in the family until they marry and then become part of their husband's extended fam-

Top: India has made great strides in education. Since independence in 1947, it has more than doubled its literacy rate (the percentage of people able to read and write). *Above:* Village schools, however, often suffer from a shortage of teachers and classrooms. *Right:* Indian marriages are traditionally arranged by the couple's parents. The bride and groom see little of each other before the wedding ceremony.

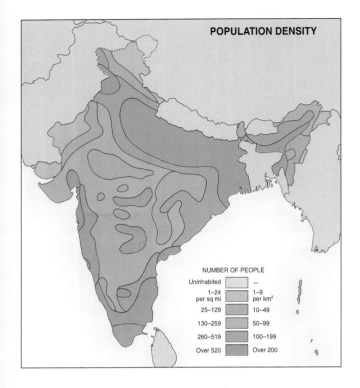

POPULATION DENSITY

NUMBER OF PEOPLE

Uninhabited		—	
1–24 per sq mi		1–9 per km²	
25–129		10–49	
130–259		50–99	
260–519		100–199	
Over 520		Over 200	

Homes

Indian homes vary in different parts of the country, depending on climate and the availability of building materials. A more expensive house may be built of brick with wooden doors and a tile roof. The house may have many rooms or just a few, and it may have one or two stories. The home of a poorer person is generally built of mud and straw with a thatched roof. It usually consists of a single story with only one or two rooms.

The majority of houses in the country have an interior courtyard around which the rooms are built. Sometimes there is an open court in front of the house, where women sit to prepare vegetables for cooking, children study their lessons, men have their hair cut, and peddlers bring wares to show. At night farmers keep cattle or other animals in one of the rooms that open on the courtyard.

In a Hindu home the kitchen is considered a sacred room. If the house does not have a separate kitchen, the cooking may be done in one corner of a large room that is also used for other purposes. The family sits on

ily. Marriages are usually arranged by the parents of the bride and groom. Dating takes place only among Westernized Indians.

Traditionally men took care of family money matters and the family's relations with the outside world. Women managed the household. All members of the family respected the authority of the elders, particularly of the oldest male, in outside matters. Women had a great deal of authority in matters affecting the running of the household. Neither men nor women interfered with each other's duties.

In the traditional extended family, all the property was held together, and all able members worked together for the benefit of the entire group, including those too old or too sick to care for themselves. After the death of the head of a family, a very large extended family would split apart, as sons started new families of their own.

In recent years, the extended family system has begun to break up as a result of new employment opportunities in the cities. Couples and their children may move away to look for jobs. Family members, however, still consider the family home their center, to which they return regularly.

Above: Villages are home to nearly two-thirds of India's people. This village is typical of those in the northern state of Uttar Pradesh. Left: Bullocks are the chief work animals. They are seen here drawing water for irrigation.

Rural Life

India is largely a nation of villages. Nearly two-thirds of the population lives in one of thousands of villages. For many, the village is both the center of farming activities and a social center.

In the western part of the Gangetic Plain of northern India, villages are large and grouped closely together. In the eastern part there are scattered villages, each made up of a few homes. In the Ganges Delta region of West Bengal, villages are made up of small groups of scattered houses, usually built on raised blocks above high flood level. In Rajasthan and the Deccan region where the land is dry, houses are built close together near the few available sources of water.

Some Indian villages may have only a few hundred people, while others may have several thousand inhabitants. Some of the large villages have small shops. Generally, however, villagers do most of their buying and selling at nearby market towns or at the weekly market.

Most Indian homes in rural areas have little furniture. In northern Indian houses, many beds are made from rice straw covered with a rug. In southern Indian homes, a simple mat may serve as the bed. Each house has only a few bare essentials, such as copper and earthenware pots for cooking, carrying water, and storing grain. A nearby lake, pond, or river supplies water for livestock and domestic use. Drinking water comes from wells.

the floor mat for meals, which are eaten in or near the kitchen. People outside the family and members of the family who have not performed the ritual of bathing do not enter the kitchen section of the orthodox Hindu house.

In the homes of the poorer families, food is cooked on a little clay stove (*chula*) in one corner of the room, or in a little alcove. Food is eaten with the tips of the fingers from a bowl or tray. Hands are washed before and after eating. Poverty is widespread in India. More than one-third of the population cannot afford an adequate diet.

Most well-to-do families have a separate room for worship. Only after bathing and changing into a clean garment may one enter the "worship room." The daily bath is an important ritual among Indians. A bath may be taken near an outside well, at a tap in the house, or in rivers or lakes.

Religious holidays are observed throughout the year by India's various faith groups. Among Hindus, celebrations may include bathing in the Ganges River, which is considered sacred.

The standard of living in Indian villages is low. To bring medical care to the rural population, health centers have been established in many areas. Each of these centers includes four to six hospital beds and is staffed with a doctor, several nurses, and midwives to assist women in childbirth. The more remote villages are served by roving health units made up of a doctor and a nurse traveling in a medical van.

Food and Drink

Indian food differs from region to region, although wheat and rice are staples. Most Indians do not eat beef, and chicken and lamb are expensive. Therefore, most people eat fruit and vegetables with rice or flat bread called chapati. A typical meal includes dal, a mixture of lentils or other legumes mixed with spices. Indians use a wide variety of spices, such as ginger, cloves, coriander, cardamom, turmeric, and cinnamon, to create complex flavors. Most Indians favor tea as a beverage.

Festivals

The great variety of religious beliefs and cultural traditions accounts for the large number of festivals in India.

Dasahara, one of the chief festivals of India, celebrated in September or October, symbolizes the triumph of good over evil. In Delhi, Dasahara celebrations are climaxed with the burning of giant images of legendary demons made of bamboo and papier-mâché and stuffed with firecrackers. In Mysore, in southern India, a parade is led by the governor of the state riding on a richly decorated elephant.

Divali, the Festival of Lights, is celebrated in October or November. All homes are lit with lamps or candles to show great joy and attract good luck.

Ramadan, the ninth month of the Islamic year, is observed by Indian Muslims as a sacred month during which they fast every day from dawn to sunset. The Id al-Fitr festival marks the end of the month of Ramadan and is celebrated as an especially joyful event.

Christians throughout India celebrate Christmas. In some northern Indian villages, groups of Christians sing native Christmas carols to the accompaniment of musical instruments.

Holi, a Hindu festival, is observed in February or March. It honors the god Krishna.

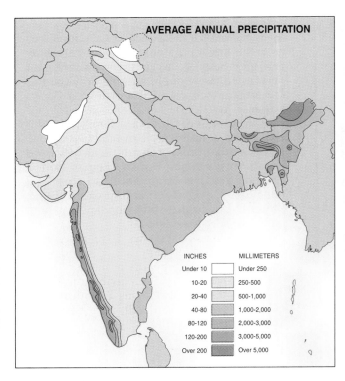

AVERAGE ANNUAL PRECIPITATION

INCHES	MILLIMETERS
Under 10	Under 250
10-20	250-500
20-40	500-1,000
40-80	1,000-2,000
80-120	2,000-3,000
120-200	3,000-5,000
Over 200	Over 5,000

The birthday anniversary of Guru Nanak, the founder of the Sikh religion, is celebrated with great joy, as is the birthday of Guru Gobind Singh, a Sikh religious leader.

Independence Day (August 15) is observed by people all over India with a sense of national pride, but Republic Day (January 26) celebrations in New Delhi, the capital, are the most impressive.

▶ LAND

In area, India is the world's seventh largest country. It is bordered on the east by Bangladesh and Myanmar; on the west by Pakistan; and by Nepal, China (including Tibet), and Bhutan on the north. The state of Jammu and Kashmir in the extreme north, which is claimed by India, has long been the subject of hostile boundary disputes among India, Pakistan, and China. (For more information, see the article on Kashmir in Volume JK.)

Land Regions

India has three main land divisions: the Himalaya mountain system in the north; the Gangetic Plain of the Indus, Ganges, and Brahmaputra rivers; and the peninsula of southern India.

The Himalayas. The great mountain wall of the Himalayas stretches for some 1,500 miles (2,400 kilometers) across northern and northeastern India. The Himalayas consist of three parallel ranges—the Great Himalayas, the Lesser Himalayas, and the Outer Himalayas. At their western end stands another lofty mountain range, the Karakoram. Another range, the Ladakh, spans northern India and Pakistan.

The Great Himalayas and Karakoram have an average elevation of more than 20,000 feet (6,100 meters). Karakoram contains K2 (or Mt. Godwin Austen), the world's second highest mountain peak. It is situated in a part of Kashmir controlled by Pakistan. At 28,250 feet (8,611 meters), K2 ranks second only to Mt. Everest, on the border between Tibet and Nepal. The world's third highest peak, Kanchenjunga, on the border between the Indian state of Sikkim and Nepal, rises to 28,169 feet (8,586 meters).

The mountains of the Lesser Himalayas, though smaller, also reach considerable heights. They are crossed by numerous large valleys, some of which are fertile and of great

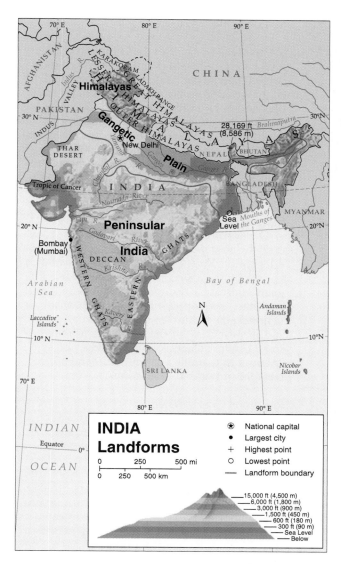

INDIA Landforms

⊛ National capital
• Largest city
+ Highest point
○ Lowest point
— Landform boundary

0   250   500 mi
0   250   500 km

15,000 ft (4,500 m)
6,000 ft (1,800 m)
3,000 ft (900 m)
1,500 ft (450 m)
600 ft (180 m)
300 ft (90 m)
Sea Level
Below

scenic beauty. Indians who can do so visit hill stations (mountain resorts) here, such as Simla and Darjeeling, to escape the intense summer heat of the plains.

The low foothills of the Outer Himalayas lie between the Lesser Himalayas and the Gangetic Plain. (For more information, see the article on the Himalayas in Volume H.)

The Gangetic Plain. The lowlands of the Gangetic Plain (or northern plains) stretch in a wide arc across India. This is the country's most productive and densely populated region. All three of the great rivers that water these lowlands—the Indus, the Ganges, and the Brahmaputra—are fed by the permanent snows and glaciers of the Himalayas.

Peninsular India. Southern India consists of a vast wedge-shaped peninsula covered mostly by a plateau called the Deccan. The plateau is separated from the Gangetic Plain by many hills and is bounded on the east and west by two low mountain ranges—the Eastern Ghats and the Western Ghats. The average elevation of the Eastern Ghats is about 2,000 feet (610 meters), although in some places the mountains rise to almost three times that height. The Western Ghats are more rugged, with elevations of 3,000 to 5,000 feet (900 to 1,500 meters).

The northwestern part of the Deccan is covered by vast lava flows from ancient volcanoes. Successive lava flows created what is known as the Deccan Traps, which look like giant staircases. They are actually weathered step-like, flat-topped hills, and they are a major scenic feature of the region.

The west coast of the peninsula is a land of small fishing villages, coconut palms, and spice gardens. In the hills a few miles inland are coffee, tea, and rubber plantations.

Rivers and Coastal Waters

Much of India is surrounded by major bodies of water—the Arabian Sea to the west, the Indian Ocean to the south, and the Bay of Bengal to the east.

The name "India" is derived from the Indus River, one of the great rivers of Asia. The greater part of the Indus basin now lies in neighboring Pakistan.

To Hindus, the Ganges is the most sacred of India's rivers. Its headwaters rise in the Great Himalayas, near the peak of Nanda Devi. The Ganges enters the plain through a gorge (opening) in the Outer Himalayas in the state of Uttar Pradesh. It flows due east, turns south, and with the Brahmaputra River flows through the nation of Bangladesh, finally emptying into the Bay of Bengal. (For more information, see the article on the Ganges River in Volume G.)

The Brahmaputra River sweeps around the eastern end of the Himalayas through a deep gorge. It flows through a region of tea gardens and rice fields in the state of Assam. From Assam it flows south into Bangladesh and then empties into the Bay of Bengal.

The Narmada, Tāpi, Kāveri, and Godavari rivers cross the Deccan plateau. Like the Ganges, the Narmada, Kāveri, and Godavari

India is a land of great contrasts. *Opposite page, top:* The Himalayas, the world's highest mountains, stretch like a wall across northern and northeastern India. *Opposite page, bottom:* India's southwestern coast has a lush green landscape and a semitropical climate. *Above:* South India contains areas of fertile land. *Right:* The Thar Desert in northwestern India includes large sand dunes and rock formations.

are sacred rivers of India. The Kāveri, also known as Dakshina Ganga (or Ganges of the South), is the second most sacred river of India. It has been harnessed for irrigation and hydroelectric power and supplies power to many areas in the state of Karnataka. The banks of the Narmada are lined with Hindu shrines and temples.

Climate

To understand the climate of India, one must understand the monsoon wind system. In winter, when the landmass is cooler than the surrounding water, the prevailing winds of the monsoon move from the subcontinent toward the ocean. These land winds are generally dry, and therefore no rain falls over most of India in winter. In summer, when the landmass is warmer than the surrounding water, the monsoon winds move deep into the subcontinent from the Bay of Bengal and the Arabian Sea and bring much rain. The summer monsoon usually starts about the middle or end of June, with very heavy rain and violent thunder and lightning. Throughout the period between June and September, the southwest winds of the summer monsoon bring rain to most parts of India. The northwest winds of the winter monsoon bring rain only to the southeastern coast.

Temperatures vary widely from north to south. In January the days are generally warm and the nights cold. The average January temperature is less than 55°F (13°C) in the Punjab in northwestern India and about 75°F (24°C) in the state of Tamil Nadu. April and May, when the sun is directly overhead, are the two hottest months of the year. The average temperature for May is more than 100°F (38°C) in northwestern India and over 85°F (29°C) in the Ganges delta in east central India.

The amount of rainfall also varies greatly from region to region. It ranges from less than 10 inches (250 millimeters) a year in parts of the very dry northwest to over 450 inches (11,430 millimeters) at Cherrapunji in Meghalaya in the northeast. Cherrapunji is one of the wettest spots on Earth.

Years when rainfall is unusual may be disastrous for the people of India. It can result in drought in one region and floods in another, with the loss of lives and the destruction of crops and property.

Natural Resources

India is rich in natural resources, particularly minerals. Its deposits of iron ore and coal are among the world's largest. Most of India's iron ore is mined in the states of Bihar and Orissa. Coal, found mainly in West Bengal and Bihar, provides much of India's industrial energy needs. Petroleum is also being produced in greater amounts.

Indian mines produce large quantities of mica, manganese, copper, bauxite (aluminum ore), chromite (chromium ore), ilmenite (titanium ore), zinc, and other minerals essential to modern industry. Gold and silver are mined in Karnataka state. India also produces diamonds, emeralds, and other gems.

India's rivers provide the water resources for irrigation and hydroelectric power development. Underground waters are also an important source of water for agriculture. Forests cover over one-fifth of the country and are another valuable natural resource, producing timber and helping prevent the erosion (washing away) of soil.

▶ ECONOMY

Although India's economy was traditionally based on agriculture, it ranks today among the ten leading industrial nations. However, because of its enormous population, India's

INDEX TO INDIA POLITICAL MAP

Agartala ★	(Tripura)	F5
Agra	(Uttar Pradesh)	C4
Ahmadabad	(Gujarat)	B5
Aizawl ★	(Mizoram)	F5
Allahabad	(Uttar Pradesh)	D5
Amritsar	(Punjab)	B3
Asansol	(West Bengal)	E5
Bangalore ★	(Karnataka)	C8
Bhopal ★	(Madhya Pradesh)	C5
Bhubaneswar ★	(Orissa)	E6
Bombay (Mumbai) ★	(Maharashtra)	B6
Calcutta (Kolkata) ★	(West Bengal)	E5
Calicut	(Kerala)	B8
Chandigarh ★	(Chandigarh **UT**; Haryana; Punjab)	C3
Cherrapunji	(Meghalaya)	F5
Cochin	(Kerala)	C9
Coimbatore	(Tamil Nadu)	C8
Daman ★	(Daman and Diu)	B6
Darjeeling	(West Bengal)	E4
Dehra Dun ★	(Uttaranchal)	C3
Delhi ★	(Delhi **UT**)	C4
Dispur ★	(Assam)	F5
Gandhinagar ★	(Gujarat)	B5
Gangtok ★	(Sikkim)	E4
Gauhati	(Assam)	F4
Gulbarga	(Karnataka)	C7
Howrah	(West Bengal)	E5
Hyderabad ★	(Andhra Pradesh)	C7
Imphal ★	(Manipur)	G5
Indore	(Madhya Pradesh)	B6
Itanagar ★	(Arunachal Pradesh)	F4
Jabalpur	(Madhya Pradesh)	C5
Jaipur ★	(Rajasthan)	B4
Jammu ★	(Jammu and Kashmir)	B3
Jamshedpur	(Jharkhand)	E5
Kanpur	(Uttar Pradesh)	C5
Kavaratti ★	(Lakshadweep **UT**)	B9
Kohima ★	(Nagaland)	G5
Lucknow ★	(Uttar Pradesh)	D4
Ludhiana	(Punjab)	B3
Madras (Chennai) ★	(Tamil Nadu)	D8
Madurai	(Tamil Nadu)	C9
Meerut	(Uttar Pradesh)	C4
Mysore	(Karnataka)	C8
Nagpur	(Maharashtra)	C6
Nanded	(Maharashtra)	C6
Nashik	(Maharashtra)	B6
New Delhi ⊛	(Delhi **UT**)	C4
Panaji ★	(Goa)	B7
Patna ★	(Bihar)	E5
Plassey	(West Bengal)	E5
Pondicherry	(Pondicherry **UT**)	C8
Port Blair ★	(Andaman and Nicobar Islands **UT**)	G8
Pune	(Maharashtra)	B7
Raipur ★	(Chhattisgarh)	D6
Rajkot	(Gujarat)	A6
Ranchi ★	(Jharkhand)	E5
Shillong ★	(Meghalaya)	F5
Silvassa ★	(Dadra and Nagar Haveli **UT**)	B6
Simla ★	(Himachal Pradesh)	C3
Srinagar ★	(Jammu and Kashmir)	B3
Surat	(Gujarat)	B6
Trivandrum (Thiruvananthapuram) ★	(Kerala)	C9
Vadodara	(Gujarat)	B6
Varanasi	(Uttar Pradesh)	D5
Vijayawada	(Andhra Pradesh)	D7
Vishakhapatnam	(Andhra Pradesh)	D7

★ State Capital   States and Union Territories (**UT**) in parentheses   ⊛ National Capital

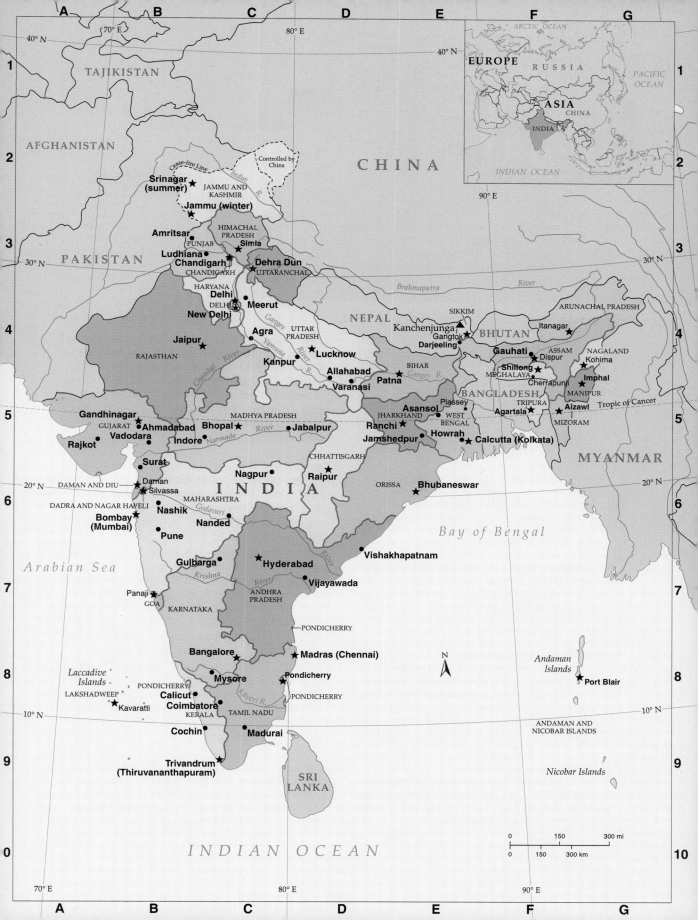

India's large deposits of coal and iron ore have helped the country become an important producer of steel. *Left:* This steel mill is located in West Bengal. *Below:* Rice is one of the country's staple foods. Most of the rice is cultivated in the Ganges River valley and along the southern coasts.

per capita income (average income per person) is less than $400 a year. Thus, in spite of a growing economy, it remains one of the world's poorest nations.

Services

Service industries account for 51 percent of India's total revenues. They include personal and business services, government, wholesale and retail trade, finance, insurance, real estate, transportation, communication, and utilities. Businesses related to tourism, such as hotels and restaurants, also provide much income.

Manufacturing

Indian industry developed rapidly after independence in 1947, spurred by government-sponsored five-year plans. Today it accounts for about 24 percent of the economy.

The manufacture of textiles, particularly cotton clothing and fabrics, has long been one of India's most important industries. Other industries include the production of chemicals, processed foods, steel, transportation equipment, cement, engineering machinery, and computer software. India also has a flourishing filmmaking industry.

Agriculture

Most of India's farmland is divided into small plots. Farm machinery is not widely used. Most farmers plant and harvest their crops by hand. However, new farming methods, more irrigation facilities, and new varieties of seeds have greatly increased food production in recent years.

India is one of the world's leading producers of rice, one of its staple foods. Most rice is grown in the Ganges River valley and along the coast of peninsular India. Wheat is grown in much of northern and central India. Cotton is grown in the southern and northwestern parts of the Deccan and in the Punjab. Sugarcane is grown on the Gangetic Plain.

Tea is grown on plantations in the far eastern state of Assam. Plantations in the south produce rubber, coffee, and spices, particularly pepper, cardamom, and mustard seed. Coconut groves in the southwest yield coir (coconut fiber) and copra (dried coconut meat). Bananas are grown in the river delta along the eastern coast. Other crops include jute (used to make burlap and twine), peanuts, oilseeds, and various grains.

The manufacture of textiles, especially cotton clothing and fabric, is one of India's largest and most important industries.

Communication

India has nearly 250 radio broadcast stations and more than 550 commercial television stations. Major daily newspapers include *Hindustan Times*, *Indian Express*, and *Deccan Herald*. Computer use has grown as the number of Internet service providers (ISP's) has increased.

▶ MAJOR CITIES

India has numerous cities with populations of 1 million or more. Many others are rapidly approaching the 1 million figure. Several rank among the great cities of the world.

New Delhi, India's capital, is a modern city with more than 7 million people. Along with Old Delhi, it makes up the city known collectively as Delhi. For more information, see the article on Delhi in Volume D.

Bombay (Mumbai), India's largest city, has a metropolitan area population of more than 15 million. Situated on the west coast, it is distinguished by its many skyscrapers. Bombay is

Foreign Trade

India imports more goods from other countries than it exports abroad. Necessary imports include crude oil, machinery, and fertilizers. Most of these goods are purchased from the United States, the Benelux countries (Belgium, the Netherlands, and Luxembourg), the United Kingdom, Saudi Arabia, Japan, and Germany.

India's primary exports include textiles, gems and jewelry, engineering equipment, chemicals, software, and tea. Many of these goods are bought by the United States, the United Kingdom, Germany, and Japan.

Transportation

India has vast transportation systems. There are nearly 40,000 miles (64,400 kilometers) of railway track and more than 2 million miles (3,220,000 kilometers) of roadways (although only one-third of them are paved). Buses and bicycles are widely used by commuters, as automobiles remain a luxury.

The chief mode of transportation in rural India is the bullock cart. The bullock (or steer) is also the chief work animal on farms.

India has more than half a dozen fine ports and harbors, easing the transport of goods by ship and boosting foreign trade. Oil and natural gas are transported by a network of pipelines. The country has nearly 450 airports. International airports are located in Bombay (Mumbai), Delhi, Madras (Chennai), Calcutta (Kolkata), and Bangalore. The national airline is Air India.

Delhi, India's third largest metropolis, has a population of more than 7 million. It is made up of two cities, Old Delhi and New Delhi, the capital.

India's major port and commercial center as well as a key industrial center. It is also the center of the nation's thriving film industry. For more information, see the article on Bombay (Mumbai) in Volume B.

Calcutta (Kolkata), the capital of the state of West Bengal, is India's second largest city. Nearly 12 million people are packed into the city and its industrial suburbs. As the hub of eastern India, it is also a center of commerce and industry. The city's museums focus on Indian life and history. However, Calcutta is also a city of great poverty, and its streets teem with poor and homeless people. For more information, see the article on Calcutta (Kolkata) in Volume C.

Cows, traditionally viewed as sacred among Hindus, share the sidewalk with pedestrians in Calcutta. This port city—one of the world's most crowded—is the industrial and commercial center of eastern India.

Madras (Chennai), the major city of southern India, is a busy port on the southeastern coast. A center of music, dance, education, and the fine arts, Madras gives the visitor a colorful picture of Hindu life. Hindu temples built between A.D. 600 and 1600 are found throughout the area. For additional information, see the article on Madras (Chennai) in Volume M.

▶ **CULTURAL HERITAGE**

India's diverse cultural legacies date back thousands of years. One of the world's first civilizations developed in the Indus Valley about 2500 B.C. From the A.D. 300's to about 500, during the Gupta Dynasty, Indian art, literature, and the sciences flourished. Muslim influence reached its peak under the Mogul (or Mughal) emperors in the 1600's. Western culture, which took hold in the 1800's during the British colonial period, is much in evidence today, particularly in the cities. For more information on Indian culture, see the articles INDIA, ART AND ARCHITECTURE OF; INDIA, LITERATURE OF; and INDIA, MUSIC OF in this volume.

▶ **GOVERNMENT**

India's government is based on a constitution adopted in 1950. It has features similar to the U.S. government and the British parliamentary system. India consists of 28 states, Delhi (the National Capital Territory), and six federally administered territories. It has a national (or federal) government, and each state has its own elected legislature and a governor appointed by the president.

The national legislature, or parliament (Sansad), is made up of two houses. The People's Assembly (Lok Sabha) is elected directly by the people, except for a few members who may be appointed by the president. Its term is normally five years. Members of the Council of States (Rajya Sabha) are elected for 6-year terms by the state legislatures. Some members are also appointed by the president. The president and vice president are elected for 5-year terms by an electoral college made up of members of the national and state legislatures. The president serves primarily as a ceremonial head of state.

Real executive power rests with the Council of Ministers, headed by the prime minister. The prime minister is usually the leader of the political party that has the greatest number of seats in parliament.

▶ **HISTORY**

Indus Valley Civilization. The earliest civilization in the subcontinent developed in the valley of the Indus River, in what was formerly northwestern India (now part of Pakistan). Archaeologists have uncovered the remains of two great Indus Valley cities, Harappa and Mohenjo-Daro, both of which date from about 2500 B.C.

The Aryans. About 1500 B.C., Aryans from the northwest of the subcontinent settled in India and built a highly developed civilization. During the following centuries they gradually spread over all of northern India. In the 500's B.C. two great religions, Buddhism and Jainism, originated in eastern India. During the next 1,000 years Buddhism spread throughout Asia, and India became a "holy land" visited by pilgrims from far-off places. In the meantime, part of western India was conquered by Persia. Through the Persians, India came into contact with the Greek world. In 327–26 B.C., Alexander the Great of Macedonia invaded India but withdrew after his homesick army refused to go farther.

Hindu Kingdoms. Up until Alexander's invasion, the Aryan people had been divided into many small kingdoms. Inspired by Alexander, Candragupta Maurya, king of Magadha (modern Bihar), began to conquer the smaller kingdoms and build an empire in northern India. He unified the Aryan people under a single rule. Asoka, Candragupta's grandson, who reigned during the 200's B.C., was a great ruler who introduced a policy of religious and racial tolerance.

After Asoka's death, India again broke up into many small kingdoms. New waves of people from southwestern Asia brought foreign influences to northern India. In the same period several Dravidian kingdoms flourished in southern India. These kingdoms spread Indian influences to Southeast Asia.

Gupta Rulers. In the A.D. 300's the Guptas, a new dynasty (or ruling house), came to power in northern India. The best known of the Gupta rulers was Candra Gupta II, who extended his empire across northern India. The Gupta period was the golden age of Indian culture. Poets and artists flourished. Several great universities were established. It was during this era that the mathematical concept of zero was developed in India. Later the concept was carried by the Arabs to Europe.

The Gupta empire was destroyed at the end of the 400's by the Huns, a tribal people from Central Asia. Thereafter, for more than a century, northern India was under the control of a number of local kingdoms. Finally, early in the 600's, one of the kings, Harsa, was able to unify

The Moguls, Muslims from Central Asia, conquered northern India in 1526. Their leader, Babur (on center throne) proclaimed himself India's first Mogul emperor.

much of northern India. But Harsa died in 647, leaving no heir to his throne. As a result, northern India was again broken up into a number of small kingdoms.

During the post-Gupta period several Dravidian kingdoms flourished in southern India. Among these were Chola and Pallava, both seafaring states on the east coast.

Muslim Invasions. During the 1000's, Muslim invaders from Central Asia conquered northern India. They founded the sultanate (kingdom) of Delhi that dominated northern India for almost two centuries. In 1398 the Mongol conqueror Tamerlane invaded the Delhi Sultanate. As a result, northern India was again split into a number of kingdoms. However, in the south the Hindu empire of Vijayanagar was established, and it flourished until 1565.

The Mogul Conquest. The political disintegration of northern India led to an invasion by the Moguls, Muslims from Central Asia. Their leader, Babur, a descendant of Tamerlane and Genghis Khan, conquered northern India in 1526 and proclaimed himself India's first

Mogul emperor. His grandson Akbar, who reigned from 1556 to 1605, was one of India's most respected rulers. Unlike other Muslim rulers, Akbar allowed people of all religions to worship as they pleased. Akbar's son Jahangir ruled from 1605 to 1627. During his reign, an English ambassador sent by King James I became the first Englishman known to visit the subcontinent.

Mogul power reached its height during the reign of Emperor Shah Jahan (1628–58), who expanded the empire and moved its capital to Delhi. Shah Jahan's successor, Aurangzeb (or 'Ālamgīr), who ruled from 1658 to 1707, had neither the ability nor the tolerance of the former emperors. He destroyed many Hindu temples in northern India. The Mogul emperors who succeeded him were weak and unable to check invasions from the northwest. In 1739, Nadir Shah of Persia defeated Mogul armies and took most of the Moguls' wealth and treasures. The resulting political chaos paved the way for the spread of British power in India.

European Penetration of India. In 1498 the Portuguese navigator and explorer Vasco da Gama discovered the sea route to India. Soon afterward European traders—Portuguese, Dutch, French, and English—came to India to look for the fine cotton cloth, rare woods, jewels, silk, and spices they had heard about. The Portuguese were the first to establish colonies on the west coast of India. They later lost most of their Indian territories but remained in Goa until 1961.

In the early 1700's, the Dutch, French, and British set up trading settlements on the coast of India and became active rivals. In 1757 the British, under Robert Clive of the East India Company, won an important battle at Plassey by defeating the French and their local Indian allies. As a result, the rich Ganges Valley region came under the control of the British East India Company. For more information, see the article on the East India Company in Volume E.

The British Indian Empire. The Battle of Plassey laid the foundation of the East India Company's empire. The company, through war and diplomacy, continued to take over more and more Indian territory during the second half of the 1700's. Indian resentment of the British led to the Sepoy Mutiny of 1857, in which Indian troops (sepoys) serving under the British revolted. The mutiny was put down by the company. But in the following year, the British government took over the East India Company's Indian empire. In 1877, Queen Victoria was proclaimed empress of India. The political map of India remained basically the same from the time of the Sepoy Mutiny until the subcontinent was partitioned in 1947.

Below right: The Mogul emperor Shah Jahan, who ruled from 1628 to 1658, expanded his empire and moved India's capital to Delhi. *Below:* The British victory at the Battle of Plassey in 1757 laid the foundation of the British Raj (rule) in India.

Left: Jawaharlal Nehru (on left) and Mohandas K. Gandhi led the movement that won independence for India in 1947. Nehru was India's first prime minister. *Right:* Indira Gandhi, Nehru's daughter, also served as prime minister. She was assassinated in 1984.

The Indian National Movement. An Indian national movement began in the late 1800's because the Indians wanted a constitution that would permit greater self-government. When the British proved slow in granting reforms, the revolutionary movement grew. Soon the Indians were demanding freedom from British control. Important constitutional reforms were finally carried out by the British after World War I (1914–18), but they came too late to stop the tide of nationalism.

Mahatma Gandhi. Mohandas K. Gandhi, often called *Mahatma* (Great Soul), became the leader of the Indian national movement. Gandhi, a Hindu, was trained in law in England. He served twice as president of the Indian National Congress (later the Congress Party), which had been established in 1885 to work for the self-government of the Indian people.

In 1919, Gandhi began a policy of nonviolent protest to gain self-rule for India. He also sought to end discrimination against the Dalits. As part of his campaign of civil disobedience, he urged Indians not to buy British goods and to reject taxation without representation. Gandhi himself often fasted as a form of protest.

Partition and Independence. In 1935, under the Government of India Act, Britain gave India a new constitution. Muslim Indians, however, complained that the Hindu majority would gain control of the country and thereby place Muslim religion and culture in a disadvantageous position.

In 1940, Muslim leaders demanded a separate state of Pakistan to be formed from areas in the subcontinent that had a majority of Muslims. After all attempts failed to form a single unified government, it was agreed that Pakistan would be created.

On August 15, 1947, the Indian subcontinent achieved independence. It was partitioned into two nations, India and Pakistan (including what is now Bangladesh). After partition, about 9 million Hindus and Sikhs moved from Pakistan to India. The settling of these refugees was a major problem for India.

In January 1948, Gandhi was assassinated by an extremist Hindu who blamed Gandhi for the partition of the subcontinent. Gandhi's principal lieutenant, Jawaharlal Nehru, became India's first prime minister. For more information, see the biographies of Gandhi and Nehru in the appropriate volumes.

Relations between India and Pakistan were often hostile in the years that followed. In 1947 and again in 1965, the two nations went to war over the disputed territory of Kashmir. India's relations with China also were strained after Chinese troops attacked Indian border posts in 1962.

Recent History. Nehru died in 1964 and was succeeded by Lal Bahadur Shastri. When Shastri died in 1966, Indira Gandhi, Nehru's daughter, became prime minister. Clashes between India and Pakistan erupted once more in 1971, when civil war broke out in East Pakistan. Indian troops occupied East Pakistan and helped it become the independent nation of Bangladesh. In 1975 the Himalayan kingdom of Sikkim became India's 22nd state.

Indira Gandhi's electoral defeat in 1977 seemed to end her political rule and that of the Congress Party. The party, which had governed India since independence, split into rival factions. But in 1980, Gandhi returned as prime minister and as head of her branch of the party.

Although India is a relatively young nation, it is an ancient land, where the spiritual and the worldly have long existed side by side.

The 1980's were marred by conflicts among India's many ethnic and religious groups. The Sikhs were especially passionate in their demands for equal religious status and for greater self-rule for their state of Punjab. Some Sikhs resorted to violence. In 1984, government troops stormed the Golden Temple at Amritsar, where armed Sikh extremists had taken refuge. The attack on their holiest shrine angered the Sikhs, who denounced the Gandhi government. These events had tragic results. On October 31, 1984, Gandhi was assassinated by Sikhs. Her son Rajiv succeeded her as leader of the Congress Party and as prime minister.

Rajiv Gandhi headed the government until the 1989 elections, when the Congress Party lost its majority in Parliament. While campaigning for re-election in 1991, he was killed by a terrorist bomb. (See the biographies of Indira and Rajiv Gandhi in Volume G.)

The new head of the Congress Party, P.V. Narasimha Rao, became prime minister in 1991, but his party lost its majority in 1996. His successor was Atal Bihari Vajpayee, leader of the Hindu nationalist Bharatiya Janata Party. He was soon replaced by H.D. Deve Gowda of the left-center United Front coalition. Inder Kumar Gujral, also of the United Front, became prime minister in 1997. Vajpayee returned as prime minister follow-ing elections in 1998 and again in 1999. The states of Chhattisgarh, Jharkhand, and Uttaranchal were created in 2000.

Challenges. India, one of the world's top ten industrial nations, is self-sufficient in food. But economic gains have been undermined by population growth, and in 2001 a devastating earthquake in the industrial state of Gujurat further hurt the economy.

Meanwhile, tensions with Pakistan continued. In 1998 both countries tested nuclear weapons, raising fears of a nuclear confrontation over the disputed area of Kashmir. In 2001, Pakistani suicide bombers attacked India's parliament, killing 13 people. The attack strained relations even further, and troops were massed along their shared border. But in 2002, Prime Minister Vajpayee ruled out the possibility of another war. Later that year, A.P.J. Abdul Kalam, a missile scientist, was elected president. His priorities were to combat poverty and develop rural areas.

In 2003, Vajpayee initiated peace talks with Pakistan, the first since the attack on India's parliament. The discussions, which included talk of arms reduction, were met with enthusiasm by both sides.

The Congress Party—led by Rajiv Gandhi's widow, Sonia—swept the parliamentary elections in 2004. But Gandhi declined the office of prime minister. Manmohan Singh, India's former finance minister (1991–96), was selected to serve in her place.

On December 26, 2004, tidal waves resulting from an earthquake in the Indian Ocean devastated South Asia. More than 10,600 people in India alone were killed, primarily on the Andaman and Nicobar islands and in the mainland state of Tamil Nadu.

PRADYUMNA P. KARAN
Author, *The Himalayan Kingdoms*
Reviewed by BAKKRISHNA G. GOKHALE
Author, *The Making of the Indian Nation*

See also KASHMIR.

INDIA, ART AND ARCHITECTURE OF

From at least 3000 B.C. to the present day, many civilizations have flourished on the subcontinent of India (which includes today's countries of India, Pakistan, and Bangladesh). Each has made valuable contributions to India's rich artistic heritage.

Several of the world's major religions—including Buddhism and Jainism, Hinduism, and Islam—either began in India or flourished there. India has also been home to small communities of Jews, Christians, and Parsis (Iranian fire-worshipers who moved to India in the early A.D. 700's). Much Indian art, therefore, has a religious content.

▶SCULPTURE

The earliest examples of Indian art come from the Indus Valley, an area in present-day Pakistan. The Indus Valley civilization flourished from about 2500 to 1700 B.C. Many small sculptures of metal and clay survive from this period. They usually represent human or animal figures. Other objects include soapstone seals engraved with writing and animal forms. The seals may have been used to stamp trade goods or as a means of personal identification.

Four larger bronze statues—of a buffalo, rhinoceros, elephant, and bull with chariot driver—have been found near Bombay. They are thought to date from a slightly later period (about 1300 B.C.).

About 1500 B.C., nomads from the Russian steppes (plains) invaded India. The era that followed is known as the Vedic period, after the religious hymns called Vedas that were brought by the nomads to India. Except for some pottery and metal figures, few works of art remain from the Vedic period.

Buddhist Sculpture. Indian sculpture flourished during the Mauryan dynasty (about 321–184 B.C.). Much of the surviving art of this age is Buddhist. Among the most important monuments of the Mauryan period are large stone pillars that stood at crossroads and important sites. A pillar often had a lotus-shaped top bearing the figure of a lion, a symbol of imperial rule borrowed from Iranian art. Many pillars also featured important Indian symbols, including the elephant, the bull, and the lotus itself.

Asoka (Ashoka), the most famous Mauryan ruler, made Buddhism the state religion. But

Above: A bronze statue from the Chola period depicts the Hindu god Shiva in one of his characteristic forms, as Lord of the Dance. *Right:* A sculpture of a meditating Buddha is among the earliest images showing the god in human form.

he tolerated the worship of such traditional village gods as yakshas and yakshis, male and female nature spirits. Many larger-than-life stone images of these spirits were made during Asoka's reign, and smaller versions began to be placed on Buddhist monuments.

During the Mauryan period and the following Shunga dynasty, burial mounds (**stupas**) were built. Often, ornately carved gateways surrounded the stupas. Reliefs (raised carvings) on the gateways used symbols rather than a human image to represent Buddha.

During the Kushan dynasty (about A.D. 50–250), Buddhism spread to areas outside India. To teach new followers the story of Buddha's life on earth, relief carvings began to show Buddha in human form. Early images of Buddha had staring eyes and a tense smile. By the Gupta period (A.D. 320–475), images of Buddha had a more inward, meditative look, with downcast eyes and a graceful pose.

Hindu Sculpture. Small images of Hindu gods were also carved of stone. Although made in human form, the images were also meant to show the many different forms taken by Hindu gods. Some gods were given many arms or heads, and were always shown carrying certain emblems.

In northern India during the Gupta dynasty, images of Hindu gods were carved into the rock in man-made caves or housed in temples. Such temples appeared across India after A.D. 400. Elaborate relief carvings were made on the temple walls, representing a variety of gods and their attendants.

In southern India after 800, bronze figures of Hindu gods were made. It was believed that the spirit of a temple god could be transferred to the statue, which was then carried in a religious procession. Outstanding bronzes were made in the Chola period (800–1200).

During the period from 900 to 1500, Hindu sculpture in the north tended to emphasize rich decoration. Much of this sculpture was used to ornament religious buildings. Sculpture of figures decreased after 1200 when northern India was ruled by Islamic leaders, whose religion forbade the use of human images for worship. Figural sculpture was produced for Hindu rulers, however.

Traditional sculpture continues to be made in modern India, mainly for an international tourist market. Other sculptors have experimented with modern styles and techniques.

▶ **PAINTING**

The people of ancient India made little distinction between artists who made images in paint and those who carved in stone. Each brought reality into being through his art.

Wall Painting. In the first centuries A.D., large Buddhist temples and monasteries were cut into cliffs near Bombay. The walls of these cave-halls are decorated with both carved and painted images. Some of the paintings date from the first century and earlier, but most were made in the 400's, when support for the arts came mainly from the royal court of the Vakataka dynasty. The painting style used at one site, Ajanta, later spread from India into Afghanistan and Central Asia. Figures are realistically painted and firmly outlined. Color is used for shading and to suggest the body's solidity. The scenes seem to project out from the painted wall.

Manuscript Illustration. Illustrated manuscripts were made in India beginning in the 1000's. Early manuscripts had writing surfaces made from palm leaves. Some schools of manuscript illustration tried to imitate the complex colors and solidly modeled shapes of earlier wall paintings. In western India, however, a different style of manuscript painting developed. There, manuscripts that told the life stories of saints of the Jain religion were used as offerings in temples. Their illustrations had flattened shapes and areas of pure, bright color. Illustrations made in this style stand out from the text, and can be easily understood by the viewer.

Opposite page: A fragment of a wall painting from the Ajanta caves contains a realistic portrait of a princely couple. *Left:* An illustration from a Rajput manuscript shows the Hindu gods Krishna and Radha. *Below:* A painting by modern-day artist Amrita Sher-Gil depicts a scene from Indian life.

The Mogul (Mughal) dynasty came to power in the 1500's and ruled much of India until the British took control in the 1850's. Mogul rulers, who followed the Islamic faith, brought Islamic artists from Iran to train talented Indian painters. The literary works commonly illustrated in the Islamic world were very different from the religious texts illustrated by Indian artists. Many were myths or histories of kings. Akbar, one of the most famous Mogul rulers, encouraged painters to record the world around them. During his rule, Mogul painting combined Islamic, Hindu, and European elements into an original and expressive style.

Another style of manuscript painting developed in the courts of the Rajput rulers in northern India. These works continued to follow older Hindu themes but also adopted some Mogul traditions, such as portrait painting. Some Mogul court-painters went to Rajput kingdoms in the Pahari hills when Mogul power declined in the 1600's. A Pahari school of manuscript illustration developed in the 1800's that used pastel colors rather than the bright, intense colors of earlier Rajput paintings.

Modern Painting. The observation of nature encouraged by some Mogul rulers continued under the British, who first went to India as traders in the 1700's. Paintings made for the British East India Company include detailed studies of birds that resemble the works of the American painter and naturalist John James Audubon (who painted the birds of North America). European painters who worked in oils also went to India and painted for local Hindu rulers. In the late 1800's, art schools modeled on European institutions were established in Calcutta and Bombay. A number of talented Indian painters were trained at these schools.

Early in the 1900's, a South Indian artist, Ravi Varma, made large oil paintings of Hindu gods in the style of British portrait paintings of the 1800's. These works had a strong influence on modern images of Hindu gods. A painter from eastern India, Jamini Roy, used the simple lines of modern European painters such as Henri Matisse to cast traditional folk images in a new light.

The writer Rabindranath Tagore, who won the Nobel prize for literature in 1913, was also a painter. Tagore's nephew, Abanindranath, and his followers tried to combine Indian painting traditions with other Asian styles. Their work has had little influence on modern Indian art however.

The oil paintings of Amrita Sher-Gil, on the other hand, continue to influence many Indian painters. Sher-Gil, who was half Hungarian, studied in Europe, but her paintings have a well-observed Indian content.

Other modern painters have followed a variety of international models. Most seek in personal ways to find a means of expression that can be both modern and Indian.

Right: A Buddhist temple at Ellora is carved into the mountainside. *Below:* Clusters of curved towers characterize this Hindu temple at Khajuraho. *Below right:* A marble pillar inlaid with gemstones is from the Taj Mahal, an elaborate tomb built by a Mogul ruler.

▶ARCHITECTURE

During the Indus Valley period, cities were built according to a grid pattern of intersecting streets. Buildings were made of brick. Later Hindu cities seem less organized, although similar rules of planning were laid down in Hindu architectural manuals. In Buddhist India small trading towns formed as centers of commerce, linked by trade routes. Structures were built of brick or mud. They often had pillared halls, balconies, and vaulted roofs with dormer windows.

Cave Architecture. The design of Buddhist cave-halls carved into the mountainsides near

Bombay was based on the free-standing structures built in towns. Cave architecture continued at least into the 800's at such sites as Ajanta and Ellora. They were created by Hindus and Jains as well as Buddhists. In some cases, whole temples were carved out of the rock. The most famous rock-cut temple at Ellora is called the Kailasa temple, after the mountain on which the Hindu god Shiva was said to have his palace.

Temples. Large free-standing temples were built in India from the 500's onward, mainly by Hindus and Jains. In the north, these temples had curving towers. The architecture of the temple was used to symbolize many things: an altar, a residence for a god, a shelter for the worshiper seeking enlightenment. Many such temples were built in northern India. Outstanding examples are also found at Khajuraho in central India, Bhubaneswar on the eastern coast, and Somnath in the west.

In southern India, temples were more like palaces. Great walls with tall gateways were built to include much of the surrounding city within the temple grounds.

Islamic Architecture. Islamic rulers gained political control over northern India in the

The three marble domes of the Pearl Mosque rise above the massive sandstone walls of the Red Fort in Delhi. Mosques were built throughout India by Islamic rulers.

1190's. Long before this period, Islamic merchants along the coasts of India had hired local craftsmen to build structures for their use. One common type of Islamic building is the mosque, where the faithful gather for prayer. Most mosques have an open courtyard surrounded by a covered hallway and are oriented toward the sacred city of Mecca. (In India, this would be to the west-southwest.)

Under the patronage of sultans and emperors, a variety of Indo-Islamic architectural styles developed. Some were based on local styles, while others borrowed from Islamic traditions. Mosques, tombs, and palaces all survive from this era, known as the Sultanate period, and from the period of Mogul rule that followed it.

A masterpiece of Indo-Islamic architecture is the Taj Mahal. This large marble structure was built in the 1600's by Shah Jahan, a Mogul emperor, as a tomb for his wife. It combines architectural conventions from Central Asia with uniquely Indian craftsmanship and materials.

Modern Architecture. Architecture in modern India draws on a variety of contemporary styles. For example, buildings in the capital, New Delhi, were designed by the British architect Edwin Lutyens in the early to mid-1900's. They were built by Indian craftsmen, however, and are decorated with a variety of Indian designs.

After the creation of the nations of India and Pakistan in 1947, the Indian government asked the great French architect Le Corbusier to create a plan for the new capital of the Punjab State at Chandigarh. Le Corbusier also designed many buildings in the city of Ahmedabad in western India. One of his supervising architects, B.K. Doshi, founded India's premier school of architecture there in the early 1960's.

Doshi and other architects built major projects for the Indian government and for industrial housing. Their designs follow many of the conventions of the modern international style. Doshi also established a foundation for the study of India's traditional architecture. He and other modern Indian architects have sought to design buildings in a style based on India's past rather than on forms adopted from European traditions.

MICHAEL W. MEISTER
University of Pennsylvania

INDIA, LITERATURE OF

Much of what is called "Indian literature" refers to literature of the geographic area that includes today's countries of India, Pakistan, and Bangladesh. This entire region was known as India until 1947, when it was divided into two nations, India and Pakistan. Bangladesh separated from Pakistan in 1971.

The constitution of modern India recognizes 15 official languages, and many more are spoken throughout the country. (The major languages of India are covered under the section Languages in the article INDIA in this volume.) Sanskrit, the most ancient language of India, is spoken by relatively few people today. However, most modern Indian languages come from Sanskrit, just as the modern European languages French, Italian, and Spanish developed from Latin. The languages that developed from Sanskrit are spoken mainly in northern India. The languages spoken in the south belong to a different language family, called Dravidian.

Another language, Urdu, developed in the 1500's as a result of contact with Persian-speaking Muslims. Urdu is similar to Hindi, a language of northern India, but contains many Persian and Arabic words. English is spoken throughout India, mostly as a second language, by a small number of people.

Each of these languages and language groups has its own literary tradition. Much of what is considered classical Indian literature was written in Sanskrit or in Tamil, a Dravidian language. After A.D. 500, literature written in the modern languages of India began to emerge. Beginning in the 1800's, some Indian literature was written in English.

(All the literature of India has been influenced by its religions. To learn more, consult the articles BUDDHISM, HINDUISM, and ISLAM in the appropriate volumes.)

▶ VEDIC LITERATURE

The first period of Indian literature, from 1200 to 500 B.C., is known as the Vedic period. It was during this time that the Vedas, collections of hymns and other sacred lore, were composed. There are four Vedas. The oldest, the *Rig Veda*, contains more than 1,000 hymns. The Vedas were not written down but were passed on orally, so every word of the sacred texts had to be memorized accurately.

▶ SANSKRIT LITERATURE

The earliest examples of written Sanskrit are inscriptions that were carved on stone pillars in the early centuries A.D. Literature was probably first written down at about the same time. However, few manuscripts from before 1400 survive. Most of the texts were written on strips of palm leaves or birch bark, which soon decayed in India's hot, humid climate. People had to make new copies of literature they wanted to save. This process of copying and recopying preserved many works.

Epics. During the classical period (500 B.C.–A.D. 1200), two great Hindu epics were composed: the *Mahabharata* ("The Great Bharata"), by Vyasa, and the *Ramayana* ("The Wanderings of Rama"), by Valmiki. Scholars may never be able to determine exactly when these long narrative poems were completed. Although each text is attributed to one poet, they were most likely composed over several centuries, with later poets adding to the main story. The dates of composition for the epics are usually given as 400 B.C. to A.D. 400 for the *Mahabharata* and 200 B.C. to A.D. 200 for the *Ramayana*.

The *Mahabharata* tells of the war between two groups within one large family. It is one of the longest poems in the world, with about 100,000 verses. Part of the poem consists of a conversation between the warrior Arjuna and his chariot driver Krishna. Arjuna is counseled on the duties of a soldier by Krishna, who reveals himself to be the lord. This conversation, called the *Bhagavad Gita* ("The Song of the Lord"), is considered by many to express the basic beliefs of the Hindu faith.

The *Ramayana* is one of the most famous stories in Indian literature. It is the tale of Prince Rama and his wife Sita and of the adventures that follow Sita's capture by Ravana, a demon with ten heads. Sita is rescued with the help of Hanuman, a monkey general, and his army.

Puranas ("Old Lore") are another form of Sanskrit literature. These huge collections of knowledge contain myths and legends about Hindu gods and descriptions of the ways to worship them.

Kavya describes a type of written literature as well as a style of writing, either prose or verse. It was composed at India's royal courts. The language of kavya is very ornate and descriptive, with many puns and other kinds of wordplay. The standard of excellence for kavya was established by early works of literary criticism. These works stated that good literature must have a quality called *rasa*. The literal meaning of *rasa* is "juice." In literature, *rasa* is the essential part of the work, the "juices" that give the literature its distinctive flavor.

The most famous kavya poet was Kalidasa, who wrote during the 300's or 400's. His best-known work is the play *Sakuntala*. It tells the story of the marriage of a young girl, Sakuntala, to a king and the misadventures that result from a curse. Another work by Kalidasa, the narrative poem *Meghaduta* ("The Cloud Messenger"), recounts the thoughts of an exiled Yaksa, a semi-divine being. The Yaksa asks a passing cloud to carry a message to his beloved in the Himalaya Mountains.

A fine example of prose kavya is *Kadambari*, a long tale of love and reincarnation by Banabhatta, who wrote in the 600's. A song of devotion in the kavya style is the *Gitagovinda* ("The Cowherd's Song"), written in the 1100's by Jayadeva in praise of Lord Krishna.

Fables and Stories. Some Sanskrit prose concentrated on storytelling, both to educate and to entertain. Two examples are the *Pancatantra* ("The Five Books") and the *Kathasaritsagara* ("The Ocean of Story"). Other tales, called *Jatakas* ("Birth Tales"), were written in Pali, a language similar to Sanskrit that was used by Buddhists. The *Jatakas*, which contain moral lessons, tell of the earthly forms—both human and animal—assumed by the Buddha.

TAMIL LITERATURE

The Tamil language, although not as old as Sanskrit, has a rich literary tradition that has continued to the present day. One important

Sita is captured by the ten-headed demon Ravana in this scene from the *Ramayana*.

group of Tamil writings consists of more than 2,000 poems organized into eight collections. The poems are known as samgam literature because, according to legend, they were composed in academies called samgams. Thought to have been written during the first to the third centuries A.D., the poems are the oldest examples of non-Sanskrit literature in India.

One of the most famous Tamil epics is *Silappatikaram* ("The Jeweled Anklet"), by Ilanko Atikal. It tells the story of a man who is wrongly accused of stealing a jeweled anklet. The man is executed, and his faithful widow destroys the city in which he died. Another epic, a Tamil version of the *Ramayana*, was composed in the 1000's or 1100's by a writer named Kamban. In this version, Ravana is portrayed in a more positive fashion than in the Sanskrit version.

MEDIEVAL LITERATURE

During the first half of India's medieval period (500–1800), the modern languages of India began to emerge, although Sanskrit literature continued to be composed. At the beginning of this period, a religious movement known as *bhakti* ("devotion") occurred within the Hindu faith. It started in the south and soon swept across all of India. Followers of *bhakti* believed that worshipers could communicate directly with their chosen god or goddess, without the help of a Brahmin priest.

The *bhakti* revolution gave rise to poetry written in all the modern Indian languages— wonderful poems that speak directly to God. In the south, the Saiva poets addressed the god Shiva, and the Vaishnavas composed poems to Vishnu. In Hindi-speaking northern India, notable poet-saints included Surdas, who sang to Krishna, and Kabir, who sang passionately to his own personal god. Kabir's god was neither

Hindu nor Muslim but encompassed both faiths. Another poet, Miribai, lived in Rajasthan in western India. She composed her devotional lyrics to Krishna. Miribai was the best-known woman saint of the later Middle Ages. In Bengal, in the northeast, the poet Ramprasad composed emotion-filled songs to the mother goddess Kali.

From the Muslim poets of medieval India came the *ghazal*, a form of poetry written in Urdu. Poems written in this form consist of couplets, or pairs of lines, each containing a complete thought. The couplets can also be linked together; the last line of each couplet must rhyme. The subject matter of the poems concerns all aspects of life and love. Two of the finest *ghazal* poets were Mir and Ghalib.

▶ **MODERN LITERATURE**

The modern period began in the 1800's. During this period, India came increasingly under the control of the British, who ruled the region until India and Pakistan won their independence in 1947. The British presence greatly affected all aspects of Indian life, including literature. The sonnet form of poetry came into Indian literature as a result of contact with the British, as did two forms of prose fiction, the novel and the short story. Today, however, all of these literary forms are as much Indian as they are British.

Literature in all the modern languages of India blossomed during this period. The following discussion, however, focuses on the development of literature written in Bengali, a language of northern India.

Michael Madhusudan Dutt is considered the father of modern Bengali poetry. His most famous narrative poem is *Meghanadavadha Kavya* ("The Slaying of the Meghanada"; 1861). It is based on an episode in the *Ramayana* in which Rama slays Meghanada, the son of Ravana. In Dutt's version, Ravana, not Rama, is presented as the sympathetic hero. Dutt's many sonnets are the first examples of that form of poetry in Bengali literature. The sonnet continued to be a popular form among later Bengali poets.

The first novels in Bengali were written by Bankim Chandra Chatterjee. Before Chatterjee, most Indian literature had been written in verse. Chatterjee's novels were immensely popular in his day. Many, such as *Durgesnandini* ("The Chieftain's Daughter"; 1864),

were historical romances set in India. Others reflect his interest in social issues.

Rabindranath Tagore is without a doubt the best-known Indian author worldwide. Tagore wrote all kinds of literature: poetry, plays, novels, and short stories. He received the Nobel prize for literature in 1913. The award was based mainly on his collection of religious poems, *Gitanjali* ("Song Offerings"), which he translated into English in 1912. Tagore was knighted by the British crown in 1915 but gave back his knighthood four years later to protest an incident in which Indian demonstrators were killed by the British. Tagore was also an accomplished musician and composer. Two of his songs were chosen as the national anthems of India and Bangladesh.

The novels of Sarat Chandra Chatterjee depict life in the villages of Bengal, especially the social interactions of the villagers. One such work is *Pallir Samaj* ("Village Society"; 1916). Almost all his novels have been translated into other Indian languages, and many have been made into motion pictures.

Kazi Nazrul Islam is known as "the rebel poet," after his most famous poem, "Bidrohi" ("The Rebel"; 1922). He was a Muslim who lived in Calcutta, a city with a largely Hindu population. An important theme in his work is the need for brotherhood between Muslims and Hindus.

Jibanananda Das is best known for his collection of poems on rural Bengal, *Rupasi Bamla* ("Bengal the Beautiful"; 1957). The beauty of his language makes the Bengal countryside come alive for the reader. In his later works, Das focused on the problems of modern society. The novels and short stories of Mahasweta Devi are also concerned with social ills. Her writings forcefully and compassionately express the point of view of the poor and the tribal peoples of India.

Other Bengali writers have chosen English as their literary language. Bharati Mukherjee became a permanent resident of the United States in 1980. Her writings, including *Wife* (1975), concern the experience of living in a different culture. The works of R. K. Narayan, including *Talkative Man* (1986), are set in the fictional town of Malgudi.

CLINTON B. SEELY
Department of South Asian Languages
and Civilizations
The University of Chicago

INDIA, MUSIC OF

India is a large country of great variety, with many different peoples, languages, religions, and ways of life. Given its size and diversity, it is not surprising that India has two distinct but closely related musical systems—one in the south, known as **Karnatak** (or Carnatic) music, and another in the north, known as **Hindustani** music. This music is important not only in India but in all of South Asia, where it is comparable to the classical music of Europe and the Americas.

Two important elements of Indian music are *raga* and *tala*. *Raga* is a pattern of musical tones that gives a piece of music its distinctive character. *Tala* is meter, or the pattern of beats that organizes the rhythm.

A typical performance of Indian music features a solo singer or instrumentalist, who is accompanied by a drummer. Usually there is a second accompanist, who plays an instrument called a *tambura*. A *tambura* has four to six strings which, when plucked, produce two or three unchanging tones. This constant drone provides a background against which the soloist's melody is highlighted.

Karnatak Music. In Karnatak music, a solo instrumentalist usually plays the *vina*, an instrument somewhat similar to the guitar. A barrel-shaped drum called a *mridanga* provides the rhythm. An accompanying melody may also be played, most often on the violin. The violin was introduced into India about two centuries ago by the British, who ruled India at the time. Unlike European and American violinists, who usually stand and hold the violin between chin and shoulder, Indian violinists sit on the floor and prop the instrument between the chest and ankle. This position allows the fingers to slide easily up and down the strings, producing the smoothly connected sounds characteristic of Indian melody.

Most Karnatak melodies are songs called *kriti*, which have religious texts. Especially highly regarded are the *kritis* of three famous composers of the late 1700's and early 1800's: Tyagaraja, Muttuswami Dikshitar, and Syama Sastri. A performance of Karnatak music consists mainly of *kritis* by these composers.

However, a good performer is also expected to improvise, or make up on the spot, new music that may be inserted into the song. Often a completely improvised introduction, called an *alapanam*, is performed before the song. During the *alapanam* the performer explores the *raga* of the song that will follow it. This is done in a rhythmically free way, without any *tala* or rhythmic accompaniment.

Hindustani Music. Improvisation is even more important in Hindustani music. Here, the improvised introduction is called the *alap*. It usually comes before an instrumental piece. This piece, too, is largely improvised, as is the major Hindustani vocal form, called *khyal*.

The most common stringed instrument in Hindustani music is the *sitar* which, like the *vina*, is a distant relative of the guitar. Rhythm is provided by a small pair of drums called the *tabla*. Melodic accompaniment is used in *khyal* but not in instrumental performance. It is provided by the *sarangi*, a type of Indian violin, or by the harmonium, a keyboard instrument introduced in the 1800's.

Influence and Importance. Indian music of the Karnatak and Hindustani traditions has spread beyond Asia, influencing a variety of Western musicians. The country has many other kinds of music—more Indians listen to songs from popular films than to performers of *kritis* or *khyal*, just as more Americans listen to popular music than to works by Bach or Mozart. However, India's traditional music continues to be cherished.

CHARLES CAPWELL
University of Illinois

sitar   tambura

mridanga

INDIANA

Since at least the 1830's, the people of Indiana have been called Hoosiers, and the state nickname is the Hoosier State. The source of this name remains a mystery. Did the term come from the settlers' cry of "Who's here?" to visitors? Did it originate with the brawling Indiana rivermen, called "hushers" because they silenced opponents with their fists? Perhaps it stemmed from the English word "hoozer," meaning hill or hill people. Whatever the term's origin, few state nicknames are more distinctive or more proudly claimed.

Indiana is located in the east north central United States, in the region known as the Midwest. It is bordered by Ohio on the east, by Illinois on the west, and by Michigan on the north. The Ohio River forms the southern boundary of the state.

The mostly level and fertile land of central and northern Indiana encouraged the first settlers to farm, and farming has remained important to the state's economy. The hills and narrow valleys of the south, although poorly suited for agriculture, proved to be rich in mineral deposits. Later, the area became important for tourism. In the 1900's, Indiana emerged as a national leader in manufacturing. Industry blossomed in the northwest corner of the state, near the ports of Lake Michigan and the markets of Chicago, Illinois.

Although Indiana is one of the smaller of the fifty states in size, it ranks high in population. Most residents live and work in cities and towns. In the middle of the state, a large urban area is centered around Indianapolis, the capital and largest city. Elsewhere in the state, population centers have grown up near neighboring Chicago, Illinois; Louisville, Kentucky, and Cincinnati, Ohio. Yet this urban flavor can be misleading. A trip through Indiana reveals vast open spaces and thousands of farms surrounding rustic villages. This rural character is enhanced by a network of state and national recreational facilities, fish and wildlife areas, and nature preserves.

Indiana is many things in the popular mind. A common view is that of Hoosiers as down-to-earth, hard-working, church-going people, conservative and distrustful of authority. Yet the state has seen bold experiments in utopian (model) communities; wild speculation in land, canals, and railroads; and pacesetting innovations in manufacturing. It has nurtured national political leaders as well as great writers, artists, and musicians. The state also has an impressive tradition of amateur sports.

▶LAND

Indiana's average elevation is about 750 feet (230 meters) above sea level. The highest point, 1,257 feet (383 meters), is on a flat plateau in Wayne County, near the eastern border. The lowest point, 320 feet (98 meters), is at the junction of the Ohio and Wabash rivers in the southwest.

Land Regions

Indiana can be divided into three separate land regions, whose physical features were formed by three giant glaciers that moved across the area between 2 and 3 million years ago. Most parts of the state were smoothed by the vast sheets of moving ice, which leveled off hilltops and filled in low areas with soil. Only the south central area was not crossed by glaciers, remaining hilly and rugged.

The Northern Lake and Moraine Region covers the northern third of the state. Glaciers leveled this part of Indiana and dug out many small lakes. The region also has huge moraines (low ridges of earth and rock deposited by glaciers), bogs, marshes, and plains. The sand

Opposite page, clockwise from top left: Union Station is an Indianapolis landmark. A former railroad depot, it now contains shops and restaurants. The world-famous Indianapolis 500 auto race draws thousands of spectators. Indiana Dunes State Park preserves miles of scenic sand dunes along the shores of Lake Michigan.

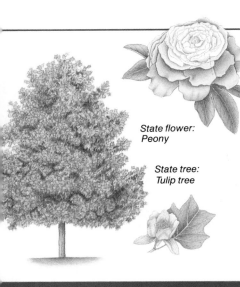

State flower:
Peony

State tree:
Tulip tree

FACTS AND FIGURES

Location: East north central United States; bordered on the north by Michigan, on the east by Ohio, on the south by Kentucky, and on the west by Illinois.

Area: 36,420 sq mi (94,328 km²); rank, 38th.

Population: 6,080,485 (2000 census); rank, 14th.

Elevation: *Highest*—1,257 ft (383 m), in Wayne County; *lowest*—320 ft (98 m), at the junction of the Ohio and Wabash rivers.

Capital: Indianapolis.

Statehood: December 11, 1816; 19th state.

State Motto: *The crossroads of America.*

State Song: "On the Banks of the Wabash Far Away."

Nickname: Hoosier State.

Abbreviations: IN; Ind.

State bird:
Cardinal

Left: Indiana is rich in fertile soils well-suited to agriculture. Most farms are in northwestern and central Indiana.

Below left: A covered bridge spans a quiet waterway in central Indiana. Rivers and lakes are abundant in the state.

Opposite page: Deep forests and rugged rock outcroppings are another facet of the state's varied landscape.

dunes along the shores of Lake Michigan are among the finest in North America.

The Central Till Plain stretches from border to border in central Indiana, covering almost one third of the state. In this area, glaciers deposited great amounts of earth material, or till. Most of the land is extremely flat. But here and there the melting ice left small hills and ridges with gentle slopes. Fertile soils have made this region a rich farming area.

The Southern Hills and Lowlands have a variety of surface features, including the rugged Norman Upland, the only part of the state that was not crossed by glaciers, and the flat Wabash Lowland. Much of the region has underlying deposits of limestone, with caves, underground streams, and thousands of sinkholes caused by the gradual erosion of the limestone. Wyandotte and Marengo caves, in Crawford County, are among the most beautiful in the United States.

Rivers and Lakes

Nearly all of Indiana's rivers flow into the Mississippi River. The longest is the Wabash, which flows for about 435 miles (700 kilometers) in Indiana, draining about two thirds of the state. The next longest river, the Ohio, follows the southern boundary for about 350 miles (563 kilometers).

About one thousand natural and artificial lakes dot Indiana, especially in the north. Lake Wawasee, in Kosciusko County, is the largest natural lake in the state. Artificial lakes are used as water reservoirs and for recreation, flood control, and electricity production. Monroe Lake, in Monroe County, is the largest artificial lake and the largest body of water in Indiana. Indiana also owns 143,000 acres (58,000 hectares) of Lake Michigan.

Climate

Indiana has relatively cold winters and hot, humid summers. Annual precipitation ranges from 36 inches (914 millimeters) in the north to 44 inches (1,118 millimeters) in the south. From March through June, tropical air from the Gulf of Mexico and cold air from the polar regions meet over Indiana, causing severe thunderstorms and tornadoes. Flooding commonly occurs in the winter or early spring. Annual snowfall amounts vary but generally range from 40 inches (102 centimeters) in the north to 10 inches (25 centimeters) in the south.

The average January temperature varies from 25°F (−4°C) in northern Indiana to 34°F (1°C) in the southern region. In July, the temperature averages 73°F (23°C) in the north and

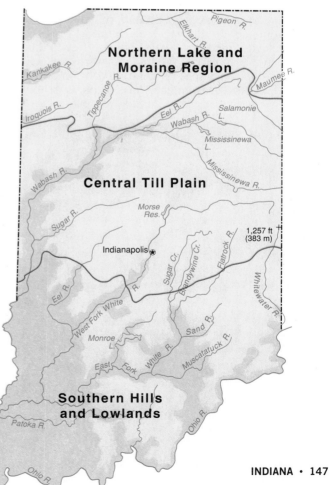

Among the animals native to the state are deer, raccoon, opossum, squirrel, cottontail rabbit, fox, and coyote. Game birds include ruffed grouse, pheasant, quail, and wild turkey. Each year some 15,000 sandhill cranes flock to the Jasper-Pulaski Fish and Wildlife Area in one of the nation's largest gatherings of this bird.

Natural Resources

In addition to water, forests, and wildlife, soils and minerals add to Indiana's natural wealth. Rich, loamy soil, deposited by glaciers in much of central and northern Indiana, forms the basis of the state's extensive agriculture. The least productive soils lie in the rugged south central area.

Limestone mined from the southern hills is an important resource. Bituminous (soft) coal, found mainly in the west and southwest, and petroleum and natural gas are the major fossil fuels. Other important minerals are crushed stone, sand, gravel, clay, peat, and gypsum.

79°F (26°C) in the south. The northeast has the shortest growing season with 150 frost-free days, while the southwest has a growing season of 190 days.

Plant and Animal Life

About one fifth of Indiana's land is covered by forests. Most of the trees are hardwood and include oak, hickory, maple beech, sycamore, ash, and poplar. Softwoods include pine, cypress, and red cedar.

Prairie grass is found on less than 5,000 acres (2,000 hectares) of protected prairie lands. Indiana's woodland wildflowers include the May apple, fire pink, bloodroot, toothwort, trillium, and the rare forked aster.

The state's lakes and streams are filled with sunfish, bluegill, bass, crappie, northern pike, and trout. The Indiana Department of Natural Resources maintains eight fish hatcheries.

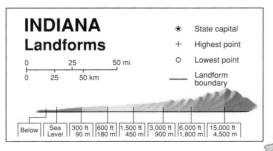

INDIANA Landforms

State capital
Highest point
Lowest point
Landform boundary

0   25   50 mi
0   25   50 km

| Below | Sea Level | 300 ft 90 m | 600 ft 180 m | 1,500 ft 450 m | 3,000 ft 900 m | 6,000 ft 1,800 m | 15,000 ft 4,500 m |

▶ PEOPLE

Of the more than 6 million people who live in Indiana, two thirds reside in urban areas, and half live in 11 of the state's 92 counties. More people live in central and northern Indiana than in the southern part of the state. The greatest recent population increases have occurred in the north central and northeast regions, in the Indianapolis metropolitan area, and in counties that contain major universities or corporations. In rural areas, only one out of five persons lives on a farm. The rest live in small towns.

Most of the people who settled Indiana in the 1800's came from other states. European immigrants came mainly from Germany, Great Britain, and Ireland. Today the state has a small number of foreign-born residents, who have come primarily from Germany, Mexico, Canada, England, Poland, and Korea. Most new arrivals in Indiana come from nearby states, particularly Illinois, Ohio, and Kentucky.

Education

Indiana's present system of education is founded on the state constitution of 1851, which called for tax-supported, free public schools. In early days, students were educated in one-room schools controlled by local authorities. Today, Indiana has 302 public school districts, run by professional corporations under the authority of a state board of education. The state education system also includes adult education programs and schools for the blind, deaf, and mentally handicapped.

Among Indiana's four-year public universities are Indiana University, with eight campuses; Purdue University, with five campuses; Ball State University in Muncie; the University of Southern Indiana in Evansville; and Indiana State University in Terre Haute. Ivy Tech State College is a two-year public college with 23 campuses.

Indiana has more than 30 private colleges, including the University of Notre Dame near South Bend, Butler University in Indianapolis, the University of Evansville in Evansville, Wabash College in Crawfordsville, and Earlham College in Richmond.

Libraries, Museums, and the Arts

Indiana has an extensive public library system, which reaches large numbers of people through its branches and bookmobiles. The state also has more than 300 academic, institutional, and special libraries. Rare and historic books are found in the Old Cathedral Library and Museum in Vincennes, Indiana University's Lily Library in Bloomington, the University of Notre Dame Library, and the library of the Indiana Historical Society in Indianapolis. The Indiana State Library in Indianapolis houses the largest collection of state-related materials, while the Calumet Regional Archives in Gary is a center for ethnic materials.

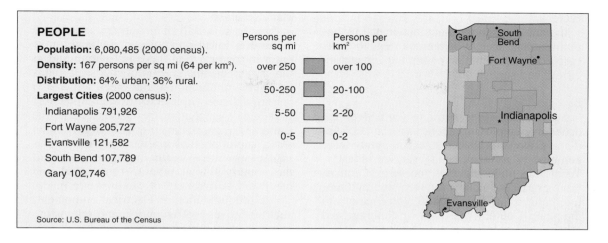

PEOPLE

Population: 6,080,485 (2000 census).

Density: 167 persons per sq mi (64 per km²).

Distribution: 64% urban; 36% rural.

Largest Cities (2000 census):

Indianapolis 791,926

Fort Wayne 205,727

Evansville 121,582

South Bend 107,789

Gary 102,746

Persons per sq mi	Persons per km²
over 250	over 100
50-250	20-100
5-50	2-20
0-5	0-2

Source: U.S. Bureau of the Census

Government plays an active role in the state's culture through its state museum and through commissions on the arts, humanities, and historic preservation. The state has a number of art museums, among them the Indianapolis Museum of Art. The Indianapolis Children's Museum is the largest children's museum in the world. Other notable museums include the Eiteljorg Museum of American Indian and Western Art in Indianapolis, the Howard Steamboat Museum in Jeffersonville, and the Louis A. Warren Lincoln Library and Museum in Fort Wayne.

Many art galleries, opera houses, and symphony orchestras are found in Indiana. Theaters and performing arts centers include the Verizon Wireless Music Center and the Indiana Repertory Theatre in Indianapolis and the Civic Theatre in Fort Wayne.

Sports

Professional sports in Indiana began in 1871, when the Fort Wayne Kekiongas joined the first professional baseball league formed in the United States. Today the top professional sports teams in the state are the Indiana Pacers and the Indiana Fever (basketball) and the Indianapolis Colts (football).

Amateur sporting events are huge attractions. Indiana University basketball and Notre Dame football have become part of sports history, spawning legendary players and coaches. But high school basketball reigns supreme. Games are already attended—Indiana has some of the country's largest high-school gymnasiums, built to accommodate large numbers of spectators. A championship game at the RCA Dome, in Indianapolis, can attract as many as 40,000 fans.

Far left: Students relax in a scenic spot on the campus of Purdue University, in West Lafayette. Purdue is one of several state-supported universities in Indiana.

Near left: A dinosaur exhibit at the Indianapolis Children's Museum attracts a group of interested spectators. The museum is designed especially for young people.

Right: High school basketball is followed enthusiastically in Indiana. Championship games played at the Hoosier Dome draw thousands of fans.

▶ECONOMY

Indiana's economy, once dominated by agriculture and later by manufacturing, today is based on a combination of farming, manufacturing, and service industries.

Services

Service industries are a major part of the economy, employing about two thirds of Indiana's workers. Wholesale and retail trade combine to form a leading service industry. Wholesale trade includes the distribution of farm products, metal products, and automotive equipment. Retail trade refers mainly to the sale of automobiles, food, clothing, and other products in stores and restaurants.

Finance, insurance, and real estate make up another important service industry. One of Indiana's largest public companies is the Lincoln National Corporation of Fort Wayne, an insurance and investment company. Other leading service industries include business, social, and personal services; transportation, communication, and utilities; and government services.

Manufacturing

About one fourth of Indiana's workers are employed in manufacturing. Indiana ranks ninth in the nation in industrial output and in the export of manufactured goods. It ranks first in the production of raw steel, radios and televisions, and engine electrical equipment.

Indiana's steel industry is centered in the Calumet region, in the northwestern part of the state. It produces 20 million tons of steel annually, which makes up almost one fourth of the country's total output. From steel and other metals a variety of products are made. These products include electrical equipment, such as stoves, refrigerators, and television, and transportation equipment, such as automotive and aircraft parts.

Among other leading manufactures are food products, plastics, and chemical products, including pharmaceuticals. Eli Lilly and Company, a leading maker of pharmaceuticals, is located in Indianapolis.

Agriculture

Indiana has more than 70,000 farms, which employ less than 5 percent of the work force. Most farms are smaller than 1,000 acres (405

Left: Prescription drugs are made at Eli Lilly, a large pharmaceutical company in Indianapolis. *Right:* Corn is harvested in an Indiana field. The state is a leading producer of corn and other farm products.

PRODUCTS AND INDUSTRIES

Manufacturing: Steel, transportation equipment, electrical equipment, pharmaceuticals, plastics, food products.

Agriculture: Corn, rye, winter wheat, soybeans, hogs, poultry.

Minerals: Coal, limestone, clay, crushed stone, sand and gravel.

Services: Wholesale and retail trade; finance, insurance, and real estate; business, social, and personal services; transportation, communication, and utilities; government.

Percentage of Gross State Product* by Industry

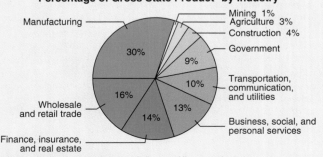

Manufacturing — 30%
Mining 1%
Agriculture 3%
Construction 4%
Government — 9%
Transportation, communication, and utilities — 10%
Business, social, and personal services — 13%
Finance, insurance, and real estate — 14%
Wholesale and retail trade — 16%

*Gross State Product is the total value of goods and services produced in a year. Source: U.S. Bureau of Economic Analysis

hectares) in size. Most are owned by individuals or families rather than by corporations. The major crops are corn, soybeans, wheat, and hay. Hogs are the main livestock product, followed by cattle and calves. Indiana ranks high in the production of popping corn, eggs, chickens and ducks, tomatoes for processing, and spearmint and peppermint.

Mining

More than 450 mining operations employ about 1 percent of Indiana's workers, mainly in coal, oil, and gas fields. Coal is mined in 20 counties in the southwest. Most coal is collected from the surface, not from underground. The state's electrical utility is the largest consumer of the coal. Indiana's petroleum reserves are also in the southwestern counties. Most of the state's nearly 1,000 gas and oil wells operate there.

The limestone deposits in south central Indiana have been quarried for more than 100 years. The famed Indiana limestone has been used in buildings throughout the country, including the Pentagon. Limestone is also used to make fertilizer and cement. Other mineral products include crushed stone, sand and gravel, aluminum, and clay.

Transportation

Indiana has a wide-ranging network of roads and highways. Several major highways, including interstates 70 and 65, cross the state from east to west and north to south. Five interstate routes converge on Indianapolis.

The state's rail system consists of nearly 5,000 miles (8,050 kilometers) of track. Coal and farm products account for half of all products shipped by rail. Amtrak trains provide passenger service to most major cities.

Ports on Lake Michigan provide access to the Atlantic Ocean by way of the St. Lawrence Seaway and enable ships to bring raw materials to the steel mills of the Calumet region. Lake Michigan ports include Burns International Harbor, operated by the Indiana Port Commission, and the Indiana Harbor. Ports on the Ohio River include the state-run Southwind and Clark maritime centers.

Indiana has more than 100 public-use aviation facilities. Indianapolis International Airport is the state's largest airport. Other large airports are in South Bend, Fort Wayne, and Evansville. The Indianapolis Downtown Heliport, which opened in 1985, was the nation's first full-service helicopter facility in a downtown area.

Communication

Indiana has more than 200 daily, weekly, and semi-weekly newspapers. Among the leading newspapers are the Indianapolis *Star*, the Fort Wayne *Journal-Gazette*, the South Bend *Tribune*, and the Evansville *Courier*. More than 30 television stations and nearly 200 radio stations operate in the state.

Indiana leads the nation in the production of raw steel. Sprawling steel mills dominate the landscape of East Chicago, Gary, and other industrial cities in northwestern Indiana.

Sand Lake, Chain O'Lakes State Park

Lincoln Boyhood National Memorial, Lincoln City

Whitewater Canal State Historic Site, Metamora

Angel Mounds State Historic Site, east of Evansville, was once the location of a prehistoric Indian village. The site contains large ceremonial and burial mounds built by the original inhabitants and a reconstructed Indian village of the 1300's.

Conner Prairie Pioneer Settlement, north of Indianapolis, is an open-air living-history museum depicting life in an Indiana prairie town of the 1800's. Costumed guides playing the roles of settlers demonstrate daily chores and customs amid authentically restored buildings.

Holiday World, in Santa Claus, is an amusement park with a holiday theme. Rides and other attractions relate to Christmas, Independence Day, and Halloween. Mail sent from the park receives a Santa Claus postmark.

Indiana Dunes National Lakeshore covers 13,000 acres (5,200 hectares) on the southern shore of Lake Michigan. The environment of dunes, marshes, ponds, and bogs supports a variety of plants and birds. Lakeshore activities include swimming, hiking, fishing, and horseback riding.

Indianapolis Motor Speedway, in Indianapolis, is the home of the world-famous Indianapolis 500 automobile race, held each May.

Levi Coffin House, in Fountain City, was known as the "Grand Central Station" of the Underground Railroad, the network that helped fugitive slaves escape to freedom in pre-Civil War days. The Quakers Levi and Catharine Coffin offered their home as a shelter to more than 2,000 slaves en route to Canada.

Lincoln Boyhood National Memorial, in Spencer County, contains a replica of the cabin that was the 16th president's boyhood home and the burial place of his mother, Nancy Hanks Lincoln. Lincoln State Park adjoins the Memorial.

New Harmony, in Posey County, was the site of a short-lived experimental community established in 1825. Many early buildings remain on the site.

Whitewater Canal State Historic Site, in Metamora, is a restored section of a canal built in the 1800's. The site features an old gristmill and an operating horse-drawn canal boat. Old Metamora, which adjoins the site, is a restored canal town.

Wyandotte Cave, near Leavenworth, is one of the largest cave complexes in the United States. It has five levels and 35 miles (56 kilometers) of underground rooms and passages.

State Recreation Areas. Indiana oversees numerous state parks, state forests, and nature preserves. A network of Hoosier Bikeway Routes guides bicyclists to many of the state's natural regions. For more information, write to the Indiana Department of Natural Resources, Division of State Parks, 616 State Office Building, Indianapolis, Indiana 46204.

▶CITIES

Indianapolis is the hub of activity in Indiana. Most of the other large cities are located in the north, especially around Lake Michigan. The two largest cities in the south are Evansville and Terre Haute.

Indianapolis, the capital and largest city in Indiana, is situated near the center of the state. It is often called the "Crossroads of America" (which is also the state motto) because of its importance as a transportation center. An article on Indianapolis follows this article on the state of Indiana.

Fort Wayne, Indiana's second largest city, was founded in 1824. Located at the junction of three rivers, it was occupied first by the Miami and Iroquois Indians and later was the site of a fort built by General Anthony Wayne. Known as the Summit City because it once stood at the highest point of the Wabash and Erie Canal, Fort Wayne now ranks high as an affordable and livable community. Among its assets are renovated downtown and riverside areas and a thriving economy based on automotive, high-technology, and service industries. The computerized gasoline pump was invented in Fort Wayne. Johnny Appleseed (John Chapman), the wandering planter of apple trees, and the Miami Indian Chief Little Turtle are buried there.

Evansville lies in what is called the "pocket" of Indiana, its southwest corner. The city dominates the economic and cultural life of southwestern Indiana, western Kentucky, and southeastern Illinois. Its physical layout on a horseshoe bend of the Ohio River has given it

Above: Indianapolis is Indiana's capital and largest city.
Top: Fort Wayne, the second largest city, is a center of economic activity in northeastern Indiana.

the nickname the Crescent City. Evansville made its mark with coal mining, mills, breweries, and lumber-related industries. Car, truck, and refrigerator production came later. The city has eleven historic districts and many other landmarks. Willard Library and the Evansville Museum of Arts and Sciences are distinguished cultural institutions.

Gary is the largest city in the heavily industrialized Calumet region, in northwestern Indiana. It was founded in 1906 by the United States Steel Corporation (now USX Corporation) and named for the corporation's chairman of the board, Elbert H. Gary. The city soon became a leading steel producer. The steel industry remains important despite a ten-year slump that occurred during the 1980's.

Indiana's domed state capitol, constructed of native limestone, stands in the heart of Indianapolis, the capital of the state since 1825.

Gary has many black residents and elected its first black mayor, Richard Hatcher, in 1967. Hatcher, who was re-elected four times, was one of the first black mayors of a major city.

▶ GOVERNMENT

The 1851 Indiana constitution contains the state's fundamental principles and laws. The legislative branch of state government is called the General Assembly. It is composed of a senate and a house of representatives. The governor, as head of the executive branch, sees that laws are enforced, appoints administrative and judicial officers, and is commander in chief of the state armed forces. The state supreme court, composed of five justices, is the top judicial body. Lower courts include the court of appeals, circuit courts, and superior courts.

Legislation enacted in 1980 gave local governments jurisdiction over their own operations, within constitutional limits. Counties, cities, and towns maintain roads, administer schools, collect taxes, and perform other duties that directly affect the lives of citizens.

GOVERNMENT
State Government
Governor: 4-year term
State senators: 50; 4-year terms
State representatives: 100; 2-year terms
Number of counties: 92

Federal Government
U.S. senators: 2
U.S. representatives: 9
Number of electoral votes: 11

For the name of the current governor, see State Governments in Volume S. For the names of current U.S. senators and representatives, see United States, Congress of the in Volume UV.

• County Seat   Counties in parentheses   ✱ State Capital

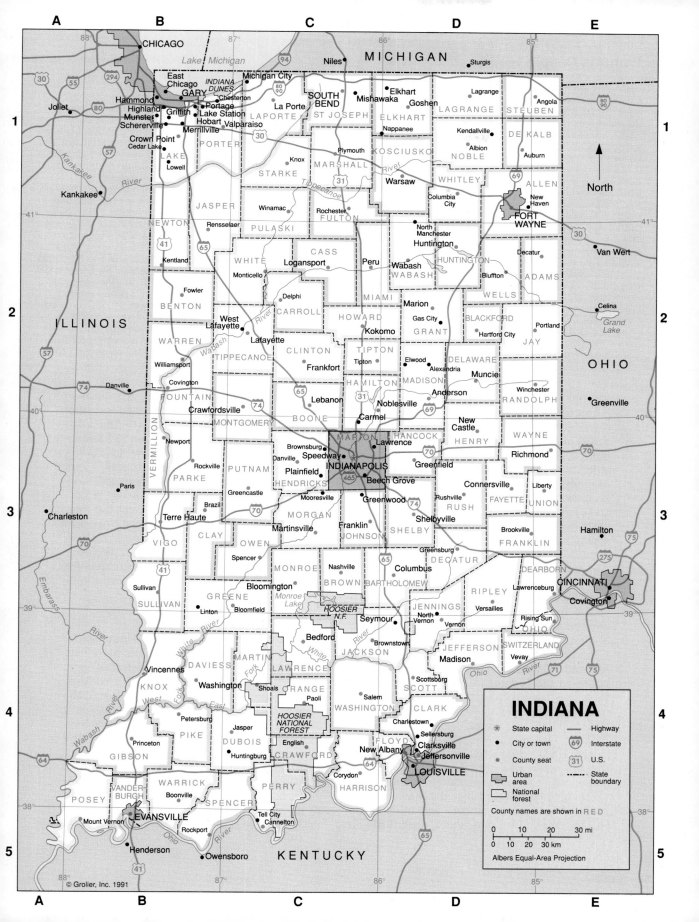

Famous People

Consult the Index to find more information in *The New Book of Knowledge* about the following people who were born in Indiana or are associated with the state: William Henry Harrison (1773–1841), the ninth president, and his grandson Benjamin Harrison (1833–1901), the 23rd president; labor and political leader Eugene V. Debs (1855–1926); authors Theodore Dreiser (1871–1945) and Kurt Vonnegut, Jr. (1922–); journalist Ernie Pyle (1900–45); astronauts Virgil (Gus) Grissom (1926–67) and Frank Borman (1928–); basketball players Oscar Robertson (1934–) and Larry Bird (1956–); and Vice President James Danforth (Dan) Quayle (1947–).

Joshua Bell (1967–), a violinist, was born in Bloomington. He received his first violin at age 4, made his orchestral debut

Joshua Bell

James Dean

with Riccardo Muti and the Philadelphia Orchestra at 14, and signed his first recording contract at 18. Famous for his moving performance on the soundtrack to the movie *The Red Violin* (1999), the Grammy Award-winning Bell is considered one the best violinists of this era.

James Dean (1931–55), an actor, was a native of Fairmont. He won wide popularity for his portrayals of rebellious ado-

lescents. Dean made only three movies, *East of Eden*, *Rebel Without a Cause*, and *Giant*, before his death in an automobile accident in 1955. He remained a cult hero, and his gravesite at Fairmont is still visited by hundreds of fans each year.

John Dillinger (1903–34), a bank robber, was born in Indianapolis. He gained notoriety in the 1930's when he became the leader of a gang that held up banks in the Midwest. Dillinger escaped jail twice and fought his way out of a police trap. He was gunned down by the FBI in Chicago after a woman acquaintance betrayed him.

David Letterman (1947–), a talk show host, was born in Indianapolis. Known for his sarcastic humor, Letterman began his career as a stand-up comedian. After a 1978 appearance on the *Tonight*

▶ **HISTORY**

Indiana's first inhabitants arrived more than 10,000 years ago to a land covered in forest and prairie. With handmade tools, they hunted, fished, and farmed. They established cities and built large burial and ceremonial mounds. Some of the mounds can still be seen, at Mounds State Park, near Anderson, and at Angel Mounds, near Evansville. These early peoples left the area for unknown reasons about 400 years ago. The next residents were Miami, Piankashaw, and Wea Indians, who settled along Indiana's large rivers.

Early Exploration and Settlement

The first known European to reach Indiana was the French explorer Robert Cavelier, Sieur de la Salle, who traveled south from Canada in 1679. He was followed by French fur traders, who gave cloth, beads, and other goods to the Indians in exchange for animal furs. The French built trading posts at sites near present-day Fort Wayne and Lafayette and founded Vincennes, Indiana's first permanent settlement.

The British competed with the French for the fur trade, and this rivalry was a major cause of the French and Indian War (1754–63). The French lost the war and surrendered control of Indiana and other lands to the British. At first, the British forbade

white settlement west of the Appalachian Mountains. Settlers soon disregarded that policy, however, and poured into the Ohio Valley, outraging the area's Indian residents.

During the Revolutionary War (1775–83), American General George Rogers Clark captured the British fort at Vincennes, helping to give Americans control of the region. At the close of the Revolution, the new United States extended west to the Mississippi River. Under the Ordinance of 1787, Indiana became part of the Northwest Territory. The Ordinance provided a government for the territory and made rules for partitioning it into states.

Territorial Years

Indians continued to resist white settlement. A union of tribes, led by the Miami Indian Chief Little Turtle, twice defeated large American armies in 1790 and 1791. An army led by General Anthony Wayne defeated the Indians at Fallen Timbers, near Toledo, Ohio, in 1794. Under the resulting treaty, the Indians gave up most of present-day Ohio and portions of the future state of Indiana.

In 1800, Congress divided the Northwest Territory. The western portion became the Indiana Territory, with William Henry Harrison as its governor and Vincennes as its capital. Although it was much larger than the present

Show, he began filling in for host Johnny Carson. He went on to host *Late Night with David Letterman* and the Emmy-award winning *Late Show with David Letterman*.

Cole Porter (1891–1964), a composer, was born in Peru. Educated at Yale University and Harvard Law School, Porter turned to composing and wrote his first musical comedy, *See America First*, in 1916. He went on to write more than thirty musical comedies, including *Anything Goes*; *Kiss Me, Kate*; *Can-Can*; and *Silk Stockings*.

James Whitcomb Riley (1849–1916), the "Hoosier poet," was born in Greenfield. His sentimental verse written in the dialect of his home state captured the public's imagination. Works such as "Little Orphan Annie" and "When the Frost Is on the Pumpkin" remain well known.

Knute Rockne

Knute Rockne (1888–1931), a football player and coach, was born in Voss, Norway. In 1910, Rockne enrolled at Notre Dame University near South Bend and became captain of the football team. From 1918 to 1930, Rockne was head coach at Notre Dame; he coached five undefeated seasons, won three national championships, and set the all-time highest winning percentage for college football.

Madam C. J. Walker

Madam C. J. Walker (1867–1919), a businesswoman, was born Sarah Breedlove in Delta, Louisiana. The daughter of former slaves, she was orphaned at age 7. Walker earned her fortune with the invention of hair-care products for African-American women. Building her business by selling door-to-door, she eventually opened a factory, salon, and training center in Indianapolis. She was the first African-American woman to become a self-made millionaire.

Jessamyn West (1902–84), a writer, was born near Butlerville. Many of her works are set in Indiana and reflect her Quaker beliefs. West's best-known work, *The Friendly Persuasion*, is a collection of stories about Quaker settlers in Indiana during the 1800's. It was later made into a successful film.

state of Indiana, the territory in 1800 had fewer than 6,000 residents. By 1809, the Indiana Territory had been reduced in size by the creation of Ohio (1803) and the territories of Michigan (1805) and Illinois (1809).

In 1809 the U.S. government bought large tracts of Indian lands in southern Indiana, opening up the region to white settlement. Some Indians felt cheated by the purchase agreement. They organized under the Shawnee leader Tecumseh and his brother, known as the Prophet, and fought to recover their lands. American forces, led by William Henry Harrison, defeated the Indians at the Battle of Tippecanoe in 1811. (This and other military successes helped Harrison win election as the ninth U.S. president in 1840.)

Hostilities with the Indians continued after the Battle of Tippecanoe, but by 1815 Indians no longer posed a threat to white settlement. Some Indians were moved from the area against their will. The tribes that remained gave up their hunting grounds in a series of agreements between 1818 and 1840.

Statehood

By 1816 the Indiana Territory had more than the 60,000 residents required for statehood by the Ordinance of 1787. In June, delegates gathered at Corydon, in southern Indiana, to write a constitution. Indiana joined the Union on December 11, 1816, as the 19th state. Corydon was the first state capital. Indianapolis became the capital in 1825.

Indiana's population soared after 1816. Pioneers came to upper Indiana from New England and to lower Indiana from the southern states. One of the new arrivals was future president Abraham Lincoln, who moved with his family from Kentucky at age 7 in 1816.

In 1825 the town of New Harmony was founded on the Wabash River by Robert Owen, a wealthy reformer. Owen wanted to establish a new kind of community in which all property would be shared equally among residents. The community was short-lived, but it drew many scientists, educators, and other intellectuals to Indiana.

Religious communities were founded by Quakers, who moved to Wayne County, and by Shakers, who settled near Oaktown. Black families formed communities, and Irish and Germans moved to the state in great numbers.

The new Hoosiers cleared the land and laid out towns. They built highways that spanned the state from north to south and east to west. A program to build canals linking Indiana's river systems to the Great Lakes was begun in the 1830's. By the 1850's, railroad lines

The National Road, the country's first federal road, was completed across Indiana in 1827. It became the main route for settlers traveling west to Indiana.

ran from New Albany, in the south, to the shores of Lake Michigan, in the northwest. The ambitious building program plunged the state into debt, but the improvements in transportation hastened Indiana's development.

By the Civil War (1861–65), Indiana's population had grown beyond 1 million. The state contributed nearly 200,000 men to the Union cause. After the war, the state's rail system continued to grow: By 1880, 46 railroad lines crisscrossed the state. Natural gas was discovered in east-central Indiana during the 1880's. The new energy source soon powered industries and illuminated homes and streets in Indiana's rapidly growing cities.

Early to Mid-1900's

As a new century dawned, traditional industries such as meat packing and grain milling were joined by a host of new enterprises. Medical drugs from the Eli Lilly company in Indianapolis, glass jars from the Ball glassworks plant in Muncie, and steel from the factories of Gary were transported by train throughout the country. Indiana was an early leader in the automobile industry. Between 1900 and 1920, more than 200 different makes of cars were produced in the state.

Hoosiers read works by famed native authors James Whitcomb Riley, George Ade, Theodore Dreiser, Booth Tarkington, and Lew Wallace. They enjoyed paintings by the artists of the Hoosier Group. "Hoosier Hysteria" over amateur sports began in 1911 with Indiana's first high school basketball tournament. In the same year, Ray Harroun won the first Indianapolis 500 auto race, held at the Indianapolis Motor Speedway.

The years following World War I (1914–18) brought more industrialization. As people moved to the cities, the state's population gradually became more urban than rural. Thousands lost their jobs in the Great Depression of the 1930's. Hoosiers supported many federal relief policies and adopted similar measures within the state.

World War II (1939–45) ended the Depression, as factories shifted to producing war materials and jobs again became plentiful. Hoosiers at first opposed the war, but sent 300,000 men and women to serve in the armed forces. The returning soldiers, taking advantage of financial benefits for veterans, crowded the state's universities.

Continued migration to the cities led to the creation of housing developments in outlying areas, called suburbs. People lived in the suburbs and commuted to the cities to work. Inner cities were deserted by businesses, which moved to the suburban areas. The state built miles of four-lane highways to serve the commuters. The new roads spurred the trucking industry but led to a decline in railroads.

Recent History

During the last decades of the 1900's, Indiana's economic base shifted from manufacturing to service industries. As steelmaking declined, state government policies encouraged the development of new businesses and welcomed foreign investors. Water transportation was revived with the building of ports on Lake Michigan and locks, dams, and maritime centers along the Ohio River.

After 1960 many Indiana cities began urban renewal projects to attract new life to their downtown areas. Indianapolis, in particular, enjoyed a building boom, constructing offices, hotels, convention centers, and sports facilities. The state continued to respond to social problems, especially issues of health, the environment, and civil rights.

ROBERT M. TAYLOR, JR.
Indiana Historical Society

INDIANAPOLIS

Indianapolis is the capital and largest city of Indiana. Located on the White River near the center of the state, Indianapolis makes up most of Marion County. About 790,000 people live within the city limits, but the population of the entire metropolitan area is more than 1.5 million. It is the third most populous city in the Midwest, behind Chicago and Detroit.

Numerous highways and railroad lines pass through Indianapolis, which is why it is often called the Crossroads of America.

Services, including wholesale and retail trade, banking, insurance, real estate, and government, make up the largest segment of the city's economy. Among its most important manufactured products are chemicals (including pharmaceuticals and paints), processed foods, electric and electronic equipment, automobile parts, industrial machinery, and fabricated metals.

Indianapolis is the site of several institutions of higher learning. Among the best known are Butler University, the University of Indianapolis, Marian College, and the combined Indiana University–Purdue University at Indianapolis.

Half a dozen television stations and more than two dozen radio stations broadcast throughout the area. The city also supports the state's leading daily newspaper, the *Star*.

For cultural entertainment, the city has a ballet company, a symphony orchestra, a repertory theater, and several museums. Among the latter are the Children's Museum, the Indianapolis Museum of Art, the Eiteljorg Museum of American Indian and Western Art, and the National Art Museum of Sport.

Indianapolis has many other interesting sites to visit. The Indiana Historical Society and the historic homes of President Benjamin Harrison and poet James Whitcomb Riley are open to the public. There are also the Indianapolis Zoo and the Soldiers and Sailors Monument, a famous landmark located in the center of the city.

Several professional sports teams have made their home in Indianapolis. The National Football League's Indianapolis Colts play at the RCA Dome; the National Basketball Association's Indiana Pacers and the Indiana Fever of the Women's National Basketball Association play at Conseco Fieldhouse; and the Indianapolis Ice, a hockey team, plays at the Fairgrounds Coliseum. In addition, Indianapolis hosted the 10th Pan American Games in 1987.

Perhaps the city's best-known attraction, however, is the Indianapolis 500 auto race, which takes place each May during the Memorial Day weekend at the Indianapolis Motor Speedway. The race is named for the distance the cars travel—a total of 500 miles (805 kilometers).

Indianapolis was founded in 1820 and became the state capital in 1825. The city grew as settlers arrived from the east and from Europe. In 1847 the first railroad to the city was completed. That same year, Indianapolis was incorporated as a city.

GEORGE W. GEIB
Butler University

Indianapolis, the third largest city in the Midwest, is an important distribution center. Its vast transportation network earned it the nickname Crossroads of America.

INDIAN OCEAN

The Indian Ocean is the third largest body of water in the world. With an area of some 28,356,300 square miles (73,442,477 square kilometers), it is smaller than the Atlantic Ocean and less than half the size of the Pacific Ocean, the world's largest ocean. Nevertheless, the Indian Ocean covers approximately water is generally accepted to be a line extending from the Cape of Good Hope (off the southern tip of Africa) to Antarctica. The boundary between the Indian Ocean and the Pacific Ocean on the east extends southward from the Malay Peninsula (part of Malaysia) along the western coasts of the islands of Sumatra and Java (parts of Indonesia) to western Australia and Antarctica.

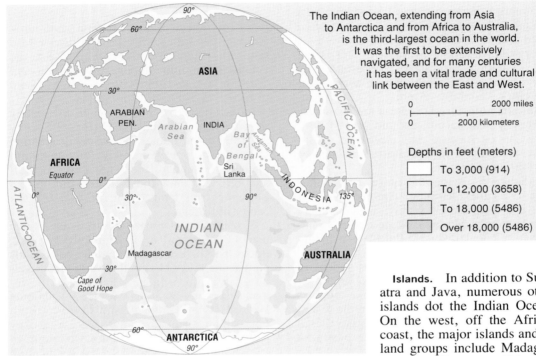

The Indian Ocean, extending from Asia to Antarctica and from Africa to Australia, is the third-largest ocean in the world. It was the first to be extensively navigated, and for many centuries it has been a vital trade and cultural link between the East and West.

0	2000 miles
0	2000 kilometers

Depths in feet (meters)

☐ To 3,000 (914)
☐ To 12,000 (3658)
☐ To 18,000 (5486)
☐ Over 18,000 (5486)

one fifth of the world's total ocean area and has played an important role in the history of world trade.

Location. The Indian Ocean is bounded on the west by Africa and on the east by Indonesia and Australia. Asia lies on the north, and Antarctica on the south. At its widest point, between southern Africa and southern Australia, the Indian Ocean measures 6,200 miles (9,980 kilometers) across. The ocean narrows in the north and is subdivided into the Arabian Sea and the Bay of Bengal by the southward jutting peninsula of India.

No natural landform separates the Indian Ocean from the Atlantic Ocean to the west. The boundary between these two bodies of water is generally accepted to be a line extending from the Cape of Good Hope (off the southern tip of Africa) to Antarctica. The boundary between the Indian Ocean and the Pacific Ocean on the east extends southward from the Malay Peninsula (part of Malaysia) along the western coasts of the islands of Sumatra and Java (parts of Indonesia) to western Australia and Antarctica.

Islands. In addition to Sumatra and Java, numerous other islands dot the Indian Ocean. On the west, off the African coast, the major islands and island groups include Madagascar, the Comoros, Réunion, Mauritius, the Seychelles, and Zanzibar. Madagascar (the world's fourth largest island), Comoros, Seychelles, and Mauritius are independent nations. Zanzibar is part of the African country of Tanzania.

To the north, lying west of India, are the Maldives, an independent state, and the Laccadive and other islands, belonging to India. The island nation of Sri Lanka lies off India's southern tip. The Andaman and Nicobar islands, additional territories of India, are situated east of the Indian peninsula. Many small islands are found in the Red Sea and the Persian Gulf. These associated seas of the Indian Ocean deeply indent the coastlines of the Arabian Peninsula and other parts of Southwest Asia.

The Land Beneath the Sea. Information obtained by the International Indian Ocean Expedition of the 1960's unlocked many of the secrets of the Indian Ocean. Before these marine studies, the underwater (or submarine) landforms of the Indian Ocean had been relatively unknown to oceanographers. The Indian Ocean's continental shelf (the underwater plain bordering most continents) was discovered to be fairly narrow and flat. In most areas, the continental shelf extends only 60 miles (98 kilometers) into the ocean. It broadens to 600 miles (980 kilometers) in the southeast, off the coast of Australia. Except where it is cut by the underwater canyons of rivers, the continental shelf of the Indian Ocean is made up of steep slopes that drop swiftly to the ocean floor.

The most important submarine landform in the Indian Ocean is the Mid-Oceanic (or Mid-Indian Ocean) Ridge. The ridge is an underwater mountain range, averaging 10,000 feet (3,281 meters) in elevation. It extends southward from the Arabian Peninsula and branches out into two separate ranges near Madagascar. The entire ridge takes the shape of an enormous upside down "Y," with the arms of the "Y" stretching nearly the ocean's width.

Volcanic activity is common on the ocean floor. The most active volcanic region is in the southeast, near the Java Trench. Here the Indian Ocean reaches its greatest depth—24,390 feet (7,434 meters) below sea level.

Climate. Most of the Indian Ocean lies within areas of tropical or subtropical climate. North of the equator, the climate over the Arabian Sea and the Bay of Bengal is dominated by the seasonal flow of the monsoon, a wind system that affects life in much of South and Southeast Asia.

During the summer, the southwest monsoon carries warm, wet air across the Arabian Sea and the Bay of Bengal inland toward the landmass of Asia. The southwest monsoon drenches the region with rain between the months of May and September. In the winter, the monsoon flow is reversed. During this season, the dry northeast monsoon winds blow outward from Central Asia across the Indian Ocean. This winter monsoon produces little rain as it moves south and west from October to April.

South of the equator, the southeast trade winds blow warm, moist air steadily to the north and west. The name "trade winds" dates from the days of sailing ships, when regular winds were vital to sea-going trade. (See the article TRADE WINDS in Volume T.)

Further south is the region of the strong winds known as the westerlies, which can bring stormy gales to the Southern Hemisphere. Changes in the monsoon winds may cause cyclones to develop, often devastating the shores of the Bay of Bengal and the Arabian Sea.

Economic and Strategic Importance. The Indian Ocean lies astride the sea-lanes connecting Europe and Asia. Historically, Portuguese, Dutch, and British merchants established trading posts and colonies along the coasts of the Indian Ocean to make easier the commerce in silks, spices, and other much-sought-after products from the East. Indian Ocean traffic expanded with the completion, in 1869, of the Suez Canal. This waterway, which linked the Mediterranean and Red seas, drastically cut the travel time between western Europe and Asia. Trade contributed to the growth of large coastal cities like Dar es Salaam (in Tanzania), Karachi (in Pakistan), Madras and Bombay (in India), and Singapore (the port of the island nation of Singapore). Other cities, such as Aden (in Yemen), with its close access to the Red Sea, grew because of its strategic location.

Today, most trade is centered on the two ports of Durban, in South Africa, and Singapore, because they are located on the major shipping lanes entering the Indian Ocean. Cargoes of oil move from terminals in the Persian Gulf through the Suez Canal to Europe, as well as across the Indian Ocean and through the Straits of Malacca to Southwest and East Asia. However, many of the most modern oil tankers are too large to pass through the Suez Canal. These supertankers must take the longer sea route around the Cape of Good Hope into the Atlantic Ocean.

In addition to its importance in trade, the Indian Ocean is rich in mineral and energy resources. Petroleum is found in several regions of the Indian Ocean, but particularly in the Persian Gulf. Huge deposits of chrome, manganese, iron, nickel, cobalt, and copper have been found on the ocean floor.

PAUL W. ENGLISH
Chairman, Department of Geography
University of Texas at Austin

INDIANS, AMERICAN

The people who discovered and first lived in the Americas are called American Indians or Native Americans.

Where Did They Come From?

Many thousands of years ago, late in the Ice Age, the Indians journeyed across the Bering land bridge, from Asia into Alaska. Their descendants explored along the west coast of North America, and as early as 13,000 years ago, they had covered both continents, reaching all the way to the southern tip of South America. It is not exactly known when the first Americans arrived, but some archaeologists (scientists who study the remains of past human lives) believe it might have been as long as 40,000 years ago.

American Indians, like the peoples of Asia from whom they are descended, usually have dark hair, dark eyes, and light brown skin. However, over thousands of years, they have developed a wide range of characteristics, appearances, languages, and customs. There are as many different Indian nations, or communities, in the Americas as there are nations in Europe, Asia, or Africa, and there is as much variety among them.

Ten thousand years ago, when the Ice Age ended, changes in climate and increasing populations inspired the Indians to experiment with growing different crops. Some became highly skilled farmers. As early as 7000 B.C. in Mexico, they cultivated corn and squash. Indians also raised turkeys, llamas, and guinea pigs for food. They also hunted deer and bison and regularly burned off patches of land to keep it in pasture, so the animals would come to graze. On the coasts, they hunted sea mammals from boats and caught fish, using a variety of efficient methods.

After 2000 B.C., the Indians developed states, each governing thousands of people. They established extensive trade routes across the continents and used cargo rafts and other boats to ship their goods from one trading point to another. In South America, llamas provided transportation on land.

From the present-day region of the midwestern United States to southern Peru in South America, centers of government were marked by enormous mounds of earth. Most of these mounds were flat on top, with palaces and temples built on them. Some were burial sites of honored leaders. American Indian cities were as big as the cities in Europe and Asia at that time, and their fine architecture is still greatly admired.

European invasions of the Americas began shortly after Columbus' discovery of the "New World" in 1492. The Europeans brought diseases with them, including smallpox and measles. These unfamiliar diseases spread quickly among the Indians, wiping

For additional information on ancient Indian empires and civilizations, consult the articles AZTECS, INCAS, and MAYA in the appropriate volumes. Also refer to the article INDIAN WARS of NORTH AMERICA in this volume and the history sections of individual state and country articles throughout *The New Book of Knowledge*.

out the populations of many Indian cities before the Europeans even saw them.

The Europeans started colonizing the Americas in order to cultivate new farmlands and create new jobs for the growing populations of Europe. To do so, they often had to fight the Native Americans for the land. Several factors gave the Europeans the advantage in these conflicts. First, they had some immunities to their own diseases and thus were not as completely devastated by them as the Indians

Left: The Bannock Indians of Idaho occasionally dress in native costumes to honor their heritage and preserve their ancient customs.

Below left: The Crow of Montana and many other North American tribes live on reservations, which were set aside by governments for the Indians to live on.

Below: Some Indians of Peru are descended from the ancient Incas. Indians make up a much larger percentage of the population in South America than they do in North America.

were. Second, the Europeans had horses and guns, which overpowered the Indians' hand weapons and arrows in battle. Third, European settlements in the Americas grew at such a rate that the Europeans' descendants eventually simply outnumbered the Indians.

One by one, the Indian nations were defeated. In the regions of present-day southern Canada, the United States, and southern South America, survivors were gathered up and moved to specific areas, called reservations.

In Mexico, Central America, and northern South America, the Indians of former great empires and small kingdoms remained as peasants and laborers, under Spanish rule. In the last few decades, developments in transportation and earth-moving machinery have made it profitable for outsiders to colonize the tropical lowland forests. Now the way of life for those Indians, too, is threatened.

Today Indian populations across both continents are once again on the rise. Indian leaders are beginning to achieve greater political success in fighting for the rights of their peoples. In addition, recent widespread concern over human rights has prompted governments and others to respect Indian cultures and traditions when responding to their needs.

►EARLY INHABITANTS: THE PALEO-INDIANS

America was first discovered during the Ice Age (the **Pleistocene** period), when huge glaciers covered most of Canada, the northern United States, and the Andes mountains of South America. So much water was frozen in the glaciers that there was less water in the oceans. As a result, land that is now below the sea then was above water. Alaska was connected to Siberia, in Asia, by a wide plain the geologists (scientists who study the physical history of the earth) now call Beringia. Today Beringia is under the Bering Strait, a narrow waterway that separates Asia from Alaska.

Beringia was covered with low bushes and grasses that served as pastures for mammoths (a kind of elephant), wild horses, small camels, and enormous buffalo. The earliest Indians must have lived by hunting these animals and by fishing. While looking for fish and game to hunt, some of these Native Americans moved out of Beringia and down the Pacific coast. When their descendants reached what is now California (south of the huge glaciers), the Indians spread inland.

Other groups traveled much farther south. For example, the people who lived 13,000 years ago at the site of Monte Verde in Chile in southern South America built small wooden cabins, hunted mastodons (similar to mammoths), and harvested potatoes and medicinal plants. Archaeologists call the early Americans "Paleo-Indians" (*paleo* is from the Greek word for "ancient").

About 12,000 years ago—over the thousands of miles from the Rocky Mountains to the Atlantic coasts of North and Central America—hunters were making handsome stone knives and spearheads called **Clovis points** and using them to kill and butcher mammoths. The families of these hunters no doubt harvested plants for food as well, although archaeologists cannot be certain of this. Unlike bones and stone tools, plants seldom are preserved in the Paleo-Indian campsites for scientists to uncover.

As the glaciers melted at the end of the Ice Age, Clovis toolmakers moved farther north. About 10,000 years ago, a smaller version of the Clovis point, called the **Folsom point**, replaced the Clovis type and was used for hunting and butchering bison. Mammoths and other Pleistocene North American animals including horses, the llama-like camels, bearlike sloths, and finally mastodons became extinct, possibly due to overhunting.

The Indians Adapt to Many Regions

As the people moved south below the ice-covered Canadian landscape, they spread inland through grasslands and oak forests. There they hunted the now-extinct small camels and the sloth as well as deer and antelope. They also discovered edible plants. Ferocious lions and cheetahs roamed the land. This kind of country extended throughout the western half of the United States, most of Mexico, and into

Left: Burial urns containing Indian remains have been found in the Atacama Desert in northern Chile. *Below:* To kill their prey, Paleo-Indians made spearheads, called Clovis points, out of stone.

Central America, where it merged into similar grasslands and oak forests that covered most of South America.

In South America, people hunted much the same type of game, plus mastodon, horses, tapirs, birds, and rabbits and other small animals, including large rodents called capybaras. On the coasts they could find fish and shellfish and hunt sea lions. They also ate potatoes and other native plants.

During the Ice Age, what is now the northeastern United States was covered with pine forests. Moose, deer, and giant beaver lived in these forests. The wide southeastern coastal plains were covered with tropical forests, where sloths and giant armadillos lived. Each of these environments prompted the Native Americans to invent tools that would enable them to catch and prepare its variety of game, fish, and plants.

▶ AFTER THE ICE AGE: THE ARCHAIC PERIOD

The Ice Age ended around 10,000 years ago. As the world's climate warmed, the enormous glaciers melted, flooding into river valleys and oceans and slowly raising sea levels. This period, which began about 8000 B.C. and continues today, is called the **Holocene**. For the past 10,000 years, the climate has been more or less the way it is today, but not always. About 5,000 years ago (or 3000 B.C.), many regions were warmer and drier than they are today. And from A.D. 400–700 and again from 1200–1800, some were colder.

Archaeologists divide the Holocene into periods according to cultural changes. Because cultures are shaped by the way people adapt to their resources, they vary from region to region. It took centuries before the effects of adaptation in the Holocene made substantial differences in Indian cultures. The earlier part of the Holocene is called the Archaic (or ancient) period.

The Climate Changes

Warming climate changed the American landscape. Increased rainfall made forests grow where there had been mostly grasslands. The big game animals either died, as did mammoths and American camels, or evolved into smaller animals, as did buffalo. Some species, including horses and yaks, disappeared from the Americas but survived in Asia. Others, such as sloths, disappeared from

North America but survived in South America. Small game, fish, shellfish, and edible plants also changed locations as climate changed. These changes occurred slowly, but over time they greatly affected all of the human communities.

New Foods Are Found and Cultivated

The Archaic period was a time of much experimentation, especially with edible plants. Around 7000 B.C., Indians in Mexico tried planting corn (maize) and squash. Seeds were traded to people in other regions. Knowing that the plants needed water, people cleared fields for them along riverbanks. It is possible that the first plantings of corn and squash may not have been for food. The squash shells may have been used as containers, and the bright yellow corn pollen may have been used for decorating. Corncobs were very small then, and the kernels were like today's popcorn. Other plants, including wild beans and mesquite pods, were collected for food and may have been planted.

Corn was soon carried south from Mexico. South American Indians grew corn in many environments. Indians developed a great number of varieties—popcorn, corn on the cob, and hard types for grinding into cornmeal. Some varieties grew well in tropical lowlands, others in tropical mountain valleys, and still others in temperate climates. In addition to corn, South American Indians in the lowland tropics grew manioc, a root that looks like a giant yam. They also domesticated beans, chili peppers, tomatoes, potatoes, sweet potatoes, peanuts, a grain called quinoa, peach palms and other fruit trees, cacao (chocolate) beans, cotton, tobacco, and a variety of plants used for medicines.

In eastern North America, hickory nuts were popular among the Indians around 3000 B.C. Several kinds of squash and native seed grains were cultivated. By 1500 B.C., sunflowers were grown for their seeds. Amaranth, a grain that now is usually considered a weed, was domesticated in Mexico and carried north for cultivation in the United States.

Throughout the Americas, Indians ate fish, shellfish, birds, and game animals. In the eastern United States and along both ocean coasts of North and South America, discarded shells of mussels, clams, oysters, and other shellfish were heaped in large mounds that can still be seen today along rivers and beaches. Fish were taken with hook and line, trapped, or speared. Even swordfish were speared in the Atlantic Ocean as early as 2000 B.C. Off the California coast, seals, dolphins, porpoises, and whales were killed from canoes. Ducks, geese, and deer were hunted with light spears thrown from a leverlike device (called an atlatl) that gave the hunter more power than the human arm alone could provide.

Settlement Patterns Change

Up until about 2000 B.C., people in the Americas lived in villages of small houses. In many areas, families left the villages for weeks or months, camping in light shelters or tents, to fish, hunt, or harvest wild plants. It seemed more sensible for the people to move to where the food was, rather than carry loads of food to the people. Gradually the populations increased.

To feed so many people, resources had to be used efficiently. Foods that could be stored for months, such as corn and seed grains, were carefully bred to yield bigger harvests. And food preparation and storage methods were developed and improved.

One invention that proved useful was pottery. The earliest pottery in the Americas has been found in northern South America; it is more than 5,000 years old. Archaeologists do not know whether South American Indians invented pottery or whether knowledge of the craft came from Asia. Pottery jars and bowls were used to store and cook grains and to make chicha (a beer made from corn). American Indians developed many distinctive styles of pottery. Some of this pottery was painted, and some was decorated with engravings or modeled into figurines.

After 2000 B.C., towns grew up in the southeastern United States; in Mexico; along the west coast and in the Andes mountain valleys of South America; and along river valleys in northeastern South America. In addition to houses, these towns had public plazas and temples. The plazas may have been used for ceremonies and as marketplaces. Merchants traveled hundreds of miles to trade valuable materials, including copper, ocean conch shells (used as trumpets), and stone (to make sharp knife blades). Through these merchants, religious beliefs and technical knowledge also were exchanged between the different groups of people.

► EARLY CIVILIZATIONS

After 2000 B.C., large and well-organized groups of people in several regions of Mexico and Peru developed the way of life we call "civilized," which means they lived in cities. Cities appeared elsewhere in the Americas later on. They never developed at all in some places, where food resources were poor.

The absence of cities in certain areas does not mean the local people lacked the intelligence to build them. It means the resources of the land could not support large numbers of people permanently living close together. Where climate made farming difficult, such as in the Canadian forests, on the western plains, in the jungles along the Amazon River in Brazil, or at the cold tip of South America, Indians were forced to spend most of each year

---

CONTRIBUTIONS INDIANS HAVE MADE TO WORLD CULTURES

Foods: Edible plants domesticated by Indians have become major staples in the diets of peoples all around the world. Such foods include corn (maize), manioc, potatoes, sweet potatoes, peanuts, squashes and pumpkins, tomatoes, papayas, avocados, pineapples, guavas, chili peppers, chocolate (cacao), and many species of beans.

Animals: Indians were the first to raise turkeys, llamas, guinea pigs, and honeybees for food.

Non-edible plants: Other plants of great importance developed by Indians include cotton, rubber, and tobacco.

Medicines: Indians discovered the medicinal use for quinine. Also, Canadian Indians knew how to prevent scurvy by eating plants rich in vitamin C, and they passed this information along to the Europeans.

Mathematics: The Maya of Mexico appear to have been the first to use the zero in mathematics. Scholars believe that Asians traveled across the Pacific Ocean and learned about the zero from the Maya.

Government: Indian governments in eastern North America, particularly the League of the Iroquois, served as models of federated representative democracy to the Europeans and the American colonists. The United States government is based on such a system, whereby power is distributed between a central authority (the federal government) and smaller political units (the states).

Economy: Indian contributions to the modern world's economy have been enormous. In the 1500's, Indian labor produced the gold and other valuable metals that helped bring the Spanish Empire to the height of its power. In the following centuries, Indian labor in the North American fur trade contributed significantly to the wealth of England, France, the Netherlands, and Russia. In addition, for hundreds of years the agrarian economies of the Latin American nations have been based on Indian labor on plantations.

in small family groups, collecting the few food resources available. These hunting families often traded meat and furs to towns at the edges of their regions and knew civilized customs, although they could not maintain cities in their own lands.

The Olmec Develop a Sophisticated Civilization in Mexico

The earliest civilization in Mexico is called the Olmec. It appeared at the narrowest part of Mexico (the Isthmus of Tehuantepec), where the Pacific and Atlantic oceans are only a few days' walk apart. The Olmec built houses and public buildings on huge platforms.

The Olmec created hundreds of statues and other monuments, of which the most famous are realistic heads carved from 6-foot (1.8-meter) boulders. These enormous men's heads may be portraits of Olmec kings. The Olmec seemed to believe in a god or legendary king that had the body of a human but the spirit of a jaguar. This god and a rattlesnake, which seems to have symbolized the earth, were often shown in carvings.

Ordinary Olmec citizens lived on farms below the platform cities. To grow their corn, squash, and other crops, they built water-storage tanks and piled the soil from the drainage ditches up in ridges. The raised fields were very practical because the Olmec had no tractors or animals to pull plows. Harvests were transported from fields to houses and storehouses in dugout canoes.

Canoes and rafts also carried goods between Olmec settlements and other nations in Mexico and Central America. Archaeologists believe Olmec goods possibly may have been transported across the Gulf of Mexico to Mississippi, where there is a platform city called Poverty Point. Olmec-style beads have been found at this site. Poverty Point may have been a trading port through which the Olmec could buy stone suitable for making knives and spear points.

Within Mexico, Olmec traders traveled overland hundreds of miles to what is now Mexico City and to Oaxaca in southwest Mexico. Craftspeople in Oaxaca made unusual round polished stone mirrors that could reflect and focus sunlight on tinder to spark a fire. Olmec priests may have kindled temple fires with these wonderful mirrors.

Other Cultures Thrive in Central America

After about a thousand years, the Olmec kingdoms seem to have lost their power. The platform cities were abandoned, and the fearsome jaguar-man was no longer portrayed. Other nations became important: **Oaxaca**, with its capital **Monte Albán**, a city built on a high mesa (plateau); **Maya**, which included several independent nations in southeastern Mexico, on the Yucatán Peninsula, and in Guatemala; and **Teotihuacán**, in the Valley of Mexico near present-day Mexico City. Like the Olmec, each of these nations flourished for about one thousand years. Teotihuacán lasted from about 200 B.C. to A.D. 750 or a few centuries later. The Maya abandoned cities in southern Yucatán around A.D. 950, but Maya kingdoms elsewhere continued as late as 1697. Today, Maya people make up the largest part of the population of Guatemala. (For more information, see the article MAYA in Volume M.)

Left: This ancient Maya burial site that archaeologists uncovered in Guatemala shows how some of the wealthier families prepared their dead for the journey to the underworld.
Right: The Olmec of Mexico sculpted gigantic stone heads, perhaps to honor their kings.

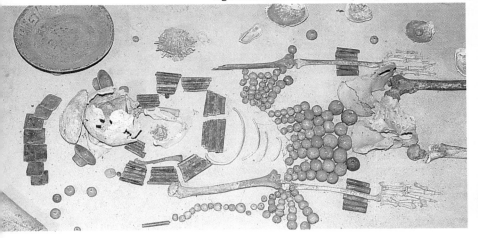

The First Cities of Peru

After 3000 B.C., huge earth platforms were built in South America, in the region of present-day Peru. Along Peru's Pacific coast, archaeologists have found what appear to be temples and other public buildings as well as plazas. Eagles, condors, and jaguars were carved and painted on the walls of the monumental buildings and seemed to have symbolized power. The people farmed in the river valleys from the steep Andes mountains to the sea. They relied on fish, seabirds, and sea mammals, including seals, for protein. They raised cotton, and at first they made cloth by twining, rather than weaving, the threads. For houses, people may have hung mats on pole frames, just as poor people do today in the Peruvian desert valleys.

A few centuries after earth platforms were first built in the coastal valleys, towns were begun in the mountain valleys of the Andes. Because buildings in these towns were often made from local stone, they are better preserved today than the wood, mat, or adobe buildings in the desert valleys.

By 1000 B.C., Andean towns included the temple center of **Chavín**. Powerful creatures were carved in the walls of these temples— alligators, jaguars, eagles, snakes, and bats— as well as a stern man (or god) holding up a staff, representing authority. Corn, manioc, and other useful plants are shown with these powerful beings as if good harvests depended on their blessings.

It is interesting that the animals and plants shown in the carvings come from different regions, including the Andes highlands, the Amazon Valley jungles, and the Pacific Ocean. This proves that there was regular trade between these areas. Mind-altering plant drugs from the jungles also were traded. These drugs seem to have been used by religious leaders, as they were trying to learn about a spiritual world.

▶ EMPIRES AND OTHER EXTENDED GROUPS

In the **Early Woodland** period (about 1000– 100 B.C.), the **Adena** built conical (cone- shaped) earth mounds in what is now the Ohio River region of the United States. The mounds covered tombs that were built like small log cabins. The Adena also built earth circles, probably to mark plazas for ceremonies. They lived in groups of wood and thatch houses and ate fish, deer, birds, nuts, squash, sunflower seeds, and native grains.

The Hopewell Build Centers in the Midwest

Archaeologists call the first large United States–centered political group "Hopewell." Hopewell, it seems, was made up of several tribes or kingdoms.

Hopewell thrived in the **Middle Woodland** period, from about 100 B.C. to A.D. 400. One of its centers was in present-day Illinois, another in Ohio. Smaller centers were located at Kansas City and other major river sites in the Midwest. Hopewell earth mounds can still be seen throughout the Midwest. Like the Adena before them, the Hopewell buried their leaders in log tombs under these mounds. With the bodies, clay pots were buried, which probably contained food and drink for the soul to take on its journey to the Land of the Dead.

Along with the pots, archaeologists also have found tobacco pipes with bowls in the shape of birds and animals, and ornaments cut out of sheet copper and delicate, shiny mica. Bits of cloth have been preserved because they were wrapped around copper ax heads. These indicate that the Hopewell were expert weavers, able to make everyday cloth and fine gauze from midwestern plant fibers.

To satisfy rich Hopewell leaders, traders imported unusual materials from as far away as Florida (conch shells), Canada (copper), and Montana (obsidian, a volcanic glass that is usually black).

Opposite page: Mounds of earth cover the tombs of Hopewell leaders who were buried about 2,000 years ago. These earth mounds still can be seen in many places throughout the midwestern United States.

Right: In the ancient city of Copán in Honduras, the Maya built ball courts, complete with bleachers for spectators. They played a game called *lachtli*, which is similar to today's soccer.

The Hohokam Establish Towns in the Southwest

Towns first appeared in the American Southwest (Arizona and New Mexico) about 2,000 years ago. The people lived in square wood-and-adobe houses built around public plazas. Most of these towns had a ball court, with bleachers and a playing floor. On these courts, a popular game was played. A hard rubber ball had to be knocked through a round goal about as high as a basketball hoop. Players could not use their hands, only their hips and knees (which were padded). The game was somewhat like basketball, played by soccer rules.

Archaeologists call the people in these towns the Hohokam; they are believed to be the ancestors of the present-day O'odham (also known as Pima and Papago). The Hohokam traded turquoise mined in New Mexico to peoples far south into Mexico, to what is now the Mexico City region.

Teotihuacán: Capital for a Vast Mexican Empire

From about 200 B.C. to A.D. 750, there existed an empire whose soldiers and merchants were seen throughout much of Mexico. Its capital city was Teotihuacán, which is now a spectacular ruined city outside Mexico City. Visitors today can see the ancient city's two gigantic pyramid platforms, once crowned with temples; the broad straight avenue with a series of stairs; and the courtyards, palaces, temples, market plazas, and apartment-house blocks. A little river flowed through the valley of Teotihuacán, which the people diverted and straightened, perhaps to make a park in the center of the city.

Archaeologists have uncovered crafts workshops and areas where foreign merchants lived and stored their goods. It seems that much of Teotihuacán's prosperity depended on obsidian mining and the manufacture of obsidian knife and sword blades. Inside and outside palaces, temples, and many apartment houses, walls were painted with bright murals of processions, goddesses, birds, jaguars, and a dragonlike rattlesnake that probably symbolized power.

Central American Kingdoms

During the era archaeologists call the **Classic** period (about A.D. 300–950), Central America had a number of small kingdoms or tribes. The people were familiar with the Maya to the north and the South American nations to the south. Although there was some overland trade through the mountains and jungles, sea travel was easier. Large cargo rafts and boats, carved out of big jungle trees, traveled across the Gulf of Ecuador, in the Caribbean, and in the Atlantic and Pacific oceans. People from Venezuela voyaged to the Caribbean islands and probably to Florida. In the west, Peruvian merchants made Ecuador a port of call on their voyages to and from western Mexico.

Ancient artifacts, including this Maya terra cotta figurine (*left*) and Moche funeral vessel (*above*), illustrate the skilled artistry of the pre-Columbian Indians (before Columbus).

South Americans Thrive in Different Regions

From about 200 B.C. to A.D. 1200, South America had two great centers in Peru (**Moche** and **Nazca**), one in Bolivia (**Tiwanaku**), and one in Brazil (**Marajoara**). Each of these centers had towns with plazas and temples, artists, highly skilled craftspeople, and large populations of farmers.

Tiwanaku was located in the high Andes Valley beside Lake Titicaca, one of the world's largest lakes. The capital city had a vast pyramid platform, surrounded by palaces and impressive courts. Underneath lay a carefully engineered system of stone drains. Other impressive sets of platforms and buildings were separated from the largest set by blocks of houses. A wide boat canal went from the capital city toward Lake Titicaca, several miles away.

On the flat, swampy lands beside the lake, Tiwanaku farmers built drainage ditches and raised crops of potatoes and quinoa grain. To keep potatoes edible after the harvest, the farmers freeze-dried them, laying them out on the raised fields to freeze at night and to dry under the daytime sun. Indian farmers still use this method to preserve potatoes. Some even are once again using the ditch-and-raised-field agricultural methods of ancient Tiwanaku. These were forgotten for centuries until archaeologists figured out the purpose of the thousands of small ridges alongside Lake Titicaca.

Moche and Nazca are located on the dry Pacific coastal plain of Peru. Communities in this region irrigated their farms from the rivers that run from the Andes to the coast. They built their villages and towns in the valleys. Seabirds, fish, and sea mammals always were important to the coastal Peruvians. Trade was conducted up into the highland valleys, over the Andes, and down into the jungles of the Amazon. Through trade, the Peruvians got food, drugs, raw materials, and manufactured goods for their own use. They also sold these goods up and down the Pacific coast.

Both Moche and Nazca are famous for their beautiful pottery. Moche produced jars in the shapes of animals, fruits, and vegetables, portraits of people, and miniature scenes of everyday life. In addition, the dry desert has preserved beautiful cloth made in Nazca, providing evidence of the extraordinary weaving skills of Peruvian Indians.

Marajoara lived on a large island in the Atlantic Ocean at the mouth of the Amazon River in Brazil. They built earth platforms to protect their homes and cemeteries from the floods that came down from the Amazon every year. The Marajoara made fine pottery. It was painted with fancy designs in black and red on a white background.

Archaeologists have found small weights that were used for spinning rods (spindles). These show that the Marajoara made cloth. However, because the climate is so wet, none has been preserved. Nor have any of their foodstuffs survived, although it is believed the Marajoara grew corn and manioc.

Along the rivers of the Amazon jungles lived villagers with a culture similar to the Marajoara. They could not build cities, however, because of the yearly floods, poor soil, and lack of stone. The villagers also made pottery that was delicately painted with designs. They painted similar designs on their own bodies. The climate there is too hot and humid for clothing.

The period between A.D. 1000 and the European invasions beginning about 1500 is called the Late Prehistoric period. It is the last segment of the American Indian past where we get our information mainly from archaeologists rather than from written sources. In the Late Prehistoric period, hundreds of American Indian nations had cities, towns, farms, roads, and canals similar to those in Asia and Europe at the time. The total population of the Americas may have been about 90 million people, with 30 million each in the empires of Mexico and Peru and close to 10 million in North America. Another 20 million were scattered throughout Central and South America.

The Mississippians

In the central United States region, a kingdom developed about A.D. 800. Its capital lay at the junction of the Missouri and Mississippi rivers, on the east side of the Mississippi just across from present-day St. Louis. Archaeologists call the Mississippian capital **Cahokia**. It is now a state park that is within easy visiting distance from St. Louis.

The Pyramid of the Magician at Uxmal in the Yucatán shows a platform structure that was typical of Maya architecture during the Classic period.

Cahokia was centered on a huge earth platform the size of a football field, 100 feet (30 meters) above the ground. In front of this platform, where temples and perhaps the ruler's palace once stood, was a grand plaza with additional platforms and conical mounds along the sides. At the far end of the plaza, a ruler was buried, his body covered with thousands of shell beads and pearls making up the shape of a glittering hawk.

Smaller, but still imposing, mounds with plazas were built next to the grand mound and plaza. Great posts marked the direction in which to watch the sun rise over the grand mound on the shortest day of the year (winter solstice). Scholars think that a public ceremony was held to celebrate the beginning of the new year, or sun cycle.

The people of Cahokia lived in square wood-framed, adobe-plastered houses. Most of these had kitchen gardens and storage sheds. Ridged cornfields covered the flat valley around Cahokia. For meat, the people ate fish, ducks, geese, and deer.

Trade routes ran hundreds of miles in all directions out of Cahokia, mostly along the rivers. Copper came from mines along Lake Superior on the Canadian border. Fine flint for arrowheads and knives came from Indiana and North Dakota. Ocean shells, used for pendants, came from Florida. Food products, such as dried buffalo meat, and leather from the west probably were shipped down the Missouri River. Decorated pottery bowls found in villages along the trade routes may have contained food or small objects traded out of Cahokia. Symbols such as the hawk or eagle, the spear thrower, and a hand with an eye in the palm were familiar to Mississippians, but their meaning is unclear. They may have been symbols of power or religious ideas.

By the time Europeans arrived in Mississippian territory, Cahokia had been abandoned. The Indians were living in smaller towns and were no longer building impressive mounds. For this reason, the Europeans thought the "Mound Builders" must have been a different people from the Indians they saw.

Hernando de Soto and his army were the first Europeans to travel through the southeastern United States from 1539 to 1543. They infected the Mississippians with diseases that killed whole communities, and the mounds fell into disrepair.

The Anasazi Build the First Pueblos

About the same time that Mississippian culture developed in the eastern United States, the Anasazi, the ancestors of today's Pueblo Indians of the Southwest, were building their first towns. These villages and towns, now in ruins, also are called Anasazi.

Beginning about A.D. 700, the Anasazi began building houses out of adobe, stone, and timber. The houses were all attached in a row, like a small motel. Plazas outside the rooms had meeting rooms for religious services. Later, the homes were built as large apartment blocks. Roads connected many Pueblo towns, and trade routes continued on south to Mexico, west to California, and east to the plains.

The Anasazi prospered in A.D. 1100, but in the 1200's, due to a very long drought, Pueblos in southern Colorado had to move downstream to the Rio Grande valley in New Mexico, where they could irrigate their farms from the river. A few Pueblos—the **Hopi**, **Zuni**, and **Acoma**—remained in their old homes and relied on rainwater dams to water their fields.

The Toltecs, Then the Aztecs, Rule the Valley of Mexico

About A.D. 850, one hundred years after the fall of the Teotihuacán empire in Mexico, a new empire appeared, centered just north of the Valley of Mexico. This empire was that of the Toltecs. Prince Ce Acatl Topiltzin Quet-zalcóatl, an enlightened ruler of the Toltecs, urged his people to produce food, useful goods, and art to please the god Quetzalcóatl. (Quetzalcóatl was portrayed as a serpent, shining with brilliant feathers, like the quetzal bird of the jungle.)

At this time, Toltecs appeared in the Yucatán, perhaps as conquerors, and built a city on the edge of the Maya city of **Chichén Itzá**. But Toltec power declined after 1200, and the Valley of Mexico was invaded by peoples from the north, led in 1224 by a man named Xolotl —a name that means "Monster." Xolotl settled in Tenayuca, in what is now northern Mexico City. He allowed another northern people, the **Aztecs** (or **Mexica**), to occupy an island in the marshy lake south of Tenayuca.

By 1440, several kingdoms governed the Valley of Mexico. One of these, **Texcoco**, was ruled by Netzahualcóyotl, a poet and philosopher who built gardens, aqueducts, and fine public buildings. The Aztecs were ruled by Montezuma I (or Motecuhzoma I), who gloried in war but invited his neighbor king to advise him how to beautify Tenochtitlán. One remarkable result was a botanical garden where rare plants from all over Mexico could be studied and admired.

Montezuma I's son, Ahuizotl, overcame rivals and made the Aztecs the dominant nation in Mexico. His successor, in 1502, was Montezuma II, who lived in splendor in a city like Venice with canals used to carry traffic to the temples, palaces, or markets.

The Anasazi of the American Southwest created distinctive black-on-white ceramic pottery (*below*). Some Anasazi lived in cliff dwellings, the most famous of which is Cliff Palace in southwestern Colorado (*right*).

The Aztecs once ruled a highly civilized empire in the Valley of Mexico. But in 1521, Tenochtitlán, the Aztec capital, was conquered by Spanish forces led by Cortés.

In 1519 the Spanish explorer Hernando Cortés landed on the east coast of Mexico, intending to conquer that land. Cortés enlisted the help of armies from the eastern Mexican nations, who had been fighting the Aztecs for many years. Principal among these nations was the **Mixtecs' Cholula**. After two years, Cortés conquered Tenochtitlán. He took Montezuma II prisoner by a trick, killed him, and claimed Mexico for the faraway Spanish king. Cortés was established there as the new governor. (For more information, see the article AZTECS in Volume A.)

The Incas Establish a Powerful Empire in Peru

The history of the Inca empire in Peru is similar to that of the Aztecs in Mexico. After the decline of Tiwanaku in the 1200's, there was a century of rivalry until one small nation, the **Quechua**, led by their king (called the Inca) Pachacuti Inca Yupanqui, began in 1438 to overcome neighboring kingdoms. By 1476, Pachacuti's successor, Topa Inca Yupanqui, completed the conquest of a huge empire stretching from Ecuador in the north into Chile and Argentina in the south, with its capital at Cuzco in the Peruvian highlands. The Quechua called their empire **Tawantinsuyu**, "Land of the Four Quarters." (Tawantinsuyu was the real name of the Inca empire.) Among its sections were the former **Chimu** kingdom

on the north coast of Peru and the **Aymara** lands around Lake Titicaca.

In 1532 the Spanish explorer Francisco Pizarro landed in Peru with his soldiers. Like Cortés, who had sought the help of rivals of the Aztecs, Pizarro was aided by Indian armies from kingdoms the Incas had conquered. The allied forces marched against the Inca, Atahualpa, who had just won a civil war against his brother, who was a rival to his throne. Atahualpa's exhausted soldiers fell to Pizarro's combined forces, and the Inca was made a prisoner and murdered by Pizarro. Pizarro declared the Indians' empire to belong to the king of Spain, and he named himself as the king's governor over the Indians. (For more information, see the article INCAS in this volume.)

This masterfully crafted gold ceremonial knife decorated with turquoise dates from about the 1400's. At this time, the Inca Empire was emerging in the highlands of the Andes Mountains in South America.

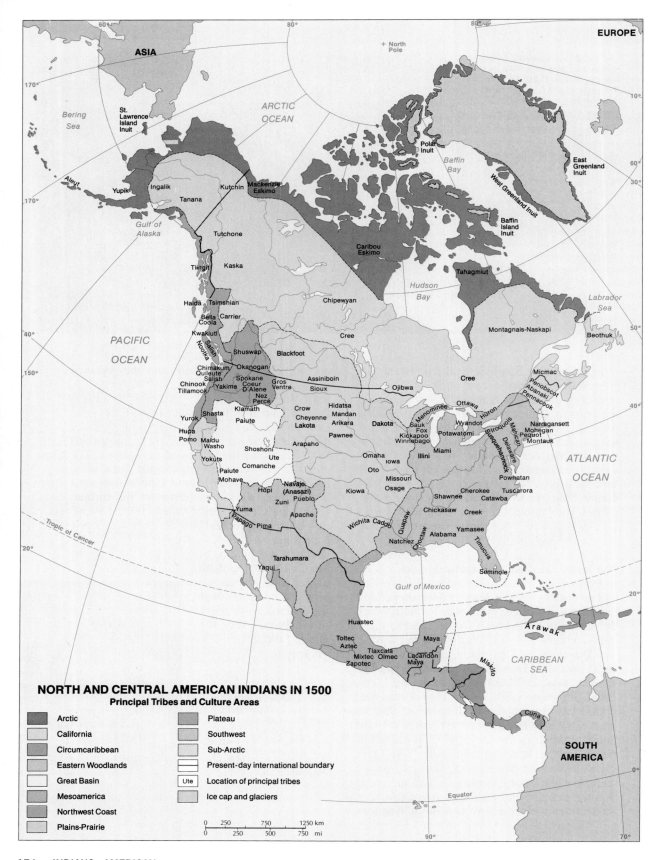

NORTH AND CENTRAL AMERICAN INDIANS IN 1500
Principal Tribes and Culture Areas

Arctic
California
Circumcaribbean
Eastern Woodlands
Great Basin
Mesoamerica
Northwest Coast
Plains-Prairie
Plateau
Southwest
Sub-Arctic
Present-day international boundary
Ute   Location of principal tribes
Ice cap and glaciers

0   250   750   1250 km
0   250   500   750 mi

Hundreds of different Indian tribes live in North America. Shoshoni Indians (*left*) from the Great Basin and southern plains were among the first to acquire horses from the Spanish in the 1600's.

Indians who lived on the plains (*below*) were farmers and hunters. They once depended on bison for their livelihood.

▶NORTH AMERICAN INDIANS SINCE 1500

Soon after Columbus' discovery of the "New World" in 1492, many European nations sent expeditions to explore the unfamiliar lands.

In the East

After 1501, every year hundreds of boats sailed across the Atlantic Ocean to North America from western Europe to fish and to hunt whales off Newfoundland in eastern Canada. These boats would stop at Newfoundland and at the mouth of the St. Lawrence River on the Canadian mainland, where they would dry the fish and process the whales before sailing back home. Indians would come down to the coast to trade furs to the fishermen for steel knives and axes and colored glass beads.

In 1581, French merchants sent out ships to trade for furs. The French set up a trading post at Tadoussac in Quebec, on the lower St. Lawrence. The Dutch began regular trade in 1606, and the English followed in 1607. Trading furs for tools, ornaments, cloth, and guns became a big business for the Indians in eastern Canada.

The Iroquois. Most of the St. Lawrence Valley (along the present-day U.S.-Canadian border and in upstate New York) was occupied by the Five Nations of the Iroquois. They included the **Mohawk**, **Oneida**, **Onondaga**, **Cayuga**, and **Seneca**. The area also was occupied by similar tribes, who were often hostile

to the Iroquois. These tribes included the **Huron**, **Erie**, **Tionontati**, **Neutral**, and **Susquehannock**.

The Iroquois lived in wooden houses that had sheets of bark for roofs. Their villages were protected by log palisades (fences made of pointed stakes), and cornfields lay near the villages. It was customary for groups of related women to live with their families in lines of apartments within the houses, which could be several hundred feet long. Most of the women in a house farmed together, while a few went off on hunting or trading trips with the men.

The Iroquois traded with Indians farther west in the Great Lakes region, where copper and stone suited for knife blades and arrowheads could be mined. They also traded with Indians farther north in Canada, whose territory was too cold for farming.

By the late 1500's, the Five Nations had formed an alliance they called the **League of the Iroquois**, or, in their language, the **Haudenosaune**. This alliance was intended to maintain peace between the Iroquois nations south of the St. Lawrence River.

In the 1600's, competition among northeastern Indians to do business with the French,

Dutch, and English traders caused much ill will and fighting. In 1649, for example, an army from the League of the Five Nations wiped out all of the Huron Indian towns along the St. Lawrence River.

The conflicts were worsened by the diseases that hit the region. As in the Caribbean, Mexico, and Peru, epidemics of smallpox, measles, and influenza wiped out Indians by the thousands. Whole villages of people died, and their farms were left untended.

In the 1700's the Iroquois were important allies to the British in their wars against the French. Alliances were marked with **wampum** belts. These belts were made from wide leather strips covered with beads (the wampum). Designs symbolized the terms of the agreements. Unhappily for the Iroquois, they lost the last war they helped the British fight —the American Revolutionary War (1775–81). The new country, the United States, took most of the Iroquois land as part of its victory over England.

After the war, some of the Iroquois became refugees in Canada, where the British set up small reservations for them. Other Iroquois refused to leave their homeland and agreed to stay on reservations set up by the United States government. In the 1800's the Iroquois improved their reservation farms, and many attended schools to learn new skills and professions. Mohawk men learned ironworking, and today, they are famed for their skilled construction work on skyscrapers and bridges.

The Iroquois built bark-covered longhouses to shelter their clan members. Each tribal unit contained a minimum of three clans —Bear, Wolf, and Turtle. A child's parents belonged to different clans; a child belonged to the clan of its mother.

Left: In the early days of exploration and settlement, Europeans traded colored glass beads to the Indians for furs.

Profiles

Brant, Joseph (1742–1807) (Indian name: Thayendanegea, meaning "he places two bets") was a leader of the Mohawks and the League of the Iroquois. Born in Ohio, he fought for the British against the French in a French

Joseph Brant

and Indian War campaign. Later, as a captain in the British Army during the American Revolutionary War (1775–81), he led the Iroquois in battle against American colonists in New York. Brant, who had converted to Christianity, became a missionary. After the war, he

led members of the Mohawk tribe to Ontario, where the British-Canadian government granted them a large tract of land. (For more information, see the article BRANT, JOSEPH in Volume B.)

Hiawatha (hi-a-WA-tha, meaning "maker of the rivers") (lived in the 1500's) was a Mohawk chief. According to legend, he helped found the League of the Iroquois at the urging of **Dekanawida**, a holy man. The members of the league pledged to abolish war and maintain law and order. The name Hiawatha later became the title of hereditary Mohawk leaders. Today the name sometimes is confused with the fictional Iroquois hero celebrated in "The Song of Hiawatha" by Henry Wadsworth Longfellow.

Parker, Ely S. (1829–95) (Indian name: Donehogawa, meaning "keeper of the western door of the long house of the Iroquois") was a Seneca Iroquois. In 1869, President Ulysses S. Grant named him commissioner of Indian Affairs, the first Indian to hold that post. Parker had been Grant's military secretary during the Civil War (1861–65), and in 1867 he became a brigadier general.

Tekakwitha, Kateri (1656?–80), daughter of a Mohawk chief, was the first North American Indian to be beatified (the first step toward sainthood). She was baptized by missionaries in 1676 and given the name Kateri (Katherine). Her conversion was so opposed in her native village, she was forced to flee in 1677 to the Christian Indian village of Sault St. Louis, near Montreal. There she devoted herself completely to religious life. Known as "the lily of the Mohawks," she was beatified by Pope John Paul II in 1980.

The Algonkians. Located north and south of the Iroquois were a number of smaller Indian nations speaking languages classified as Algonkian. These nations included the **Cree, Naskapi, Micmac, Passamaquoddy, Abnaki, Mahican, Munsee, Massachuset, Wampanoag, Narragansett, Mohegan, Pequot,** and **Montauk.** Except for the Cree and Naskapi, who lived too far north to grow corn, these peoples farmed and lived in villages of wooden houses with bark roofs, similar to the Iroquois' houses but smaller.

Algonkian-speaking Indians were the first to meet up with the English colonists. Several of the "Indian" words we know come from the Algonkian language: *squaw, papoose, wigwam* (a rounded, bark-covered house), *squash,* and *powwow* (which really meant "doctor" or "healer").

But in 1637, Massachusetts colonists turned on neighboring Indians in the Pequot War. The colonists wiped out a village of women and children before the Indian men could come to their aid. The colonists shot the Indians, whose bows and arrows were no match against the Englishmen's guns.

A second disastrous war between Massachusetts colonists and Algonkian Indians is known as King Philip's War (1675–76). "King Philip" was the Wampanoag sachem (chief) Metacomet. He tried to defend his people's territory against the Puritans, but Metacomet was defeated by the combined forces of the English colonists and Mohawk Indians from

A painting of an Algonkian village by an early English colonist in Virginia shows houses and fields of corn (maize) that were typical of the eastern Indian groups.

Pocahontas (po-ca-HON-tis) (1595?–1617) was the daughter of **Powhatan** (pow-ha-TAN) (1547?–1618) (Indian name: Wahunsonacook), who founded the Powhatan confederacy of Algonkian tribes in Virginia. According to legend, Pocahontas begged her father to spare the life of Captain John Smith, an English colonist from Jamestown, throwing herself over his body to protect him. In 1614, Pocahontas married Englishman John Rolfe. She converted to Christianity and was baptized Rebecca. Pocahontas died of smallpox while visiting England.

Samoset (SAM-o-set) (1590?–1653?), a Pemaquid chief, greeted the Pilgrims at Plymouth in 1621 with the words "Welcome Englishmen!" Samoset introduced the Pilgrims to **Massasoit** (MASS-a-soit) (1580?–1661), chief of the Wampanoag, and **Squanto** (?–1622) (Indian name: Tisquantum), a Patuxet, who had been

Pocahontas

Tecumseh

captured by explorers and sold as a slave in Spain. Squanto escaped and worked his way back home. When the Pilgrims arrived, he stayed with them, acting as their guide and interpreter. (For more information, see the article PLYMOUTH COLONY in Volume P.)

Tecumseh (te-CUM-seh) (1768?–1813) was the son of a Shawnee chief. With his brother, the **Shawnee Prophet** (1775?–1837?) (Indian name: Tenskwatawa), Tecumseh organized tribes from Florida to the Great Lakes to fight the white settlers. However, their forces were defeated by William Henry Harrison at the Battle of Tippecanoe in 1811. During the War of 1812, he was killed by U.S. forces in the Battle of the Thames. (For more information, see the article TECUMSEH in Volume T.)

New York. (For more information, see the article INDIAN WARS OF NORTH AMERICA in this volume.)

For the next three hundred years, Algonkians in the northeast lived quietly in the countryside, most of them in poverty. Modern Wampanoag made news in 1976 by trying to block the takeover of their few remaining landholdings on Cape Cod on which developers wanted to build vacation homes.

In the Southeast

Algonkian peoples occupied the Middle Atlantic states and parts of the Southeast, as well. They included the **Pamunkey** of Virginia and the towns of the **Powhatan** league (met by the Jamestown colonists in 1607); the **Shawnee** of Kentucky and Ohio; and the **Natchez** in the lower Mississippi Valley.

Other groups in this region spoke **Muskogean** languages. The tribes of this language group included the **Muskogee (Creek** and **Seminole), Choctaw, Chickasaw, Alabama,** and **Apalachee.**

A number of other Indian peoples in the southeast spoke a variety of **Siouan** languages. They included the **Cherokee, Catawba,** and **Yuchi.** The **Caddo** of this region spoke a **Caddoan** language.

During the 1500's and 1600's, Spain, France, and England tried to dominate the southeastern United States. Spain built forts along the Atlantic coast, where some of the Indians were forced to work for the soldiers and listen to Christian missionaries. Thousands died in the forts of diseases caused by crowded and unsanitary conditions.

Often the English killed the Indians to seize their harvested crops and remove them from desired lands. This kind of violence occurred in 1622 between the Virginia colonists and the Powhatan and other Virginia tribes. The French, concentrating on the northeastern section of the continent, never sent enough men to the Southeast to compete with Spanish and English colonization.

By the beginning of the 1700's, southeastern Indians had developed a profitable trade with the English. More than one hundred thousand expertly tanned deer hides and hundreds of captured Indians were sold through Charleston, South Carolina, in one year. (The slave trade encouraged Indian nations to war against each other to take one another captive to sell into slavery.)

Later in the century, Indians trading Indians into slavery ended (although the Indians continued to trade black slaves). Southeastern Indians focused their efforts on making their farms and businesses the equal of, or better than, those of the colonists. Besides corn, they cultivated wheat seed and peach trees and raised pigs, which they had gotten from the Spaniards. And by the early 1800's, some Creek and Cherokee owned plantations with fine homes for the master and mistress, slaves' cabins, orchards, vegetable gardens, and wheat, corn, and cotton fields. The prosperity

---

Profiles

Osceola

Sequoya

Macintosh, William (1775?–1825) was a chief of the Creek Indians. He fought on the American side during the War of 1812 and later was commissioned brigadier general in the U.S. Army. He served with Andrew Jackson in the First Seminole War against the Seminole Indians (1817–18). In 1825 he signed a treaty that gave Creek lands to white people. Because tribal law prescribed death for giving over Indian lands in such a manner, Macintosh was executed by a band of Indian warriors.

Osceola (os-ce-O-la) (1800?–1838), a Seminole warrior, led his followers in the Second Seminole War to prevent the removal of Indians to reservations. He was seized by U.S. troops and imprisoned. (For more information, see the article OSCEOLA in Volume O.)

Ross, John (1790–1866) (Indian name: Cooweescoowe, meaning "large white bird") was a Cherokee chief. Ross fought under Andrew Jackson against the Creek Indians in 1812. Later, after he failed to prevent the removal of the Cherokee from Georgia to Indian Territory, he led their journey to Oklahoma (1838–39). He then served as chief of the united Cherokee nation (1839–66).

Sequoya (se-QUOI-a) (1770?–1843) (also known as George Gist, or George Guess) was a Cherokee leader who developed a system of writing, which he taught to thousands of Cherokee, from Tennessee to Oklahoma. By 1827, the Cherokee were among the most literate peoples in the world. (For more information, see the article SEQUOYA in Volume S.)

of the Cherokee, Creek, Seminole, Choctaw, and Chickasaw earned them the title "The Five Civilized Tribes."

In 1830, U.S. President Andrew Jackson signed the Removal Act. This empowered the U.S. government to exchange Indian lands within the settled states for land in territories not yet settled by whites. The majority of the Five Civilized Tribes and members of other nations were forced to vacate their land and march hundreds of miles to "Indian Territory" in Oklahoma. Among the many thousands of immigrant Indians were **Delaware**, **Shawnee**, and **Miami** of the Ohio Valley; **Ottawa** from the Great Lakes region; and **Kickapoo**, **Sauk**, **Mesquakie** (**Fox**), **Potawatomi**, and **Illini** from the Illinois-Michigan region. So many of them died from the hardships of this march, the route they traveled is called the Trail of Tears. Once in Oklahoma, the people had to clear land for new farms and build new towns.

In the 1900's large oil deposits were discovered under the Cherokee section of the Oklahoma reservations. The income from this oil has given the Cherokee nation a better economic base than most other Indians.

One of the most populous Indian groups is the **Lumbee** of North Carolina. The Lumbee include Carolina Indians who refused to move west to Oklahoma. Among the Lumbee today are men and women who have studied at the top law and business schools and are devoting their abilities to strengthening the position of the Lumbee and other Indian communities.

On the Prairies and Plains

For centuries, the native Plains Indians maintained huge sections of prairie land as bison pasture and farmed in the valleys of the Missouri and other large rivers. On the plains, where there was not enough rain to grow corn, the Indians cultivated edible roots—prairie turnips, wild carrots, and camas—and traded dried bison meat and hides for corn in the farming towns.

Native to the lower Missouri River valley were the Siouan-speaking **Iowa**, **Missouri**, **Oto**, **Omaha**, **Osage**, **Ponca**, **Kansa**, and

In 1884, the Cheyenne of the northern plains were moved to a reservation in southeastern Montana. This photograph of "Scalp Cane and his Clan" was taken a few years later.

Keokuk

Keokuk (KE-o-kuk, meaning "watchful fox") (1783?–1848), was a Sauk leader with great ambition. He recognized the superior strength of the U.S. military and was thus opposed to the policies of Black Hawk, the Sauk chief, who resisted the whites' expansion into Indian lands in the area around Illinois. After Black Hawk was defeated in the Black Hawk War in 1832, Keokuk became chief of the united Sauk and Fox Indians. White settlement of Sauk and Fox lands eventually forced Keokuk and his followers to move to a reservation in Kansas.

Little Turtle (1752–1812) (Indian name: Michikinikwa), the son of a Miami chief, was a prominent figure in the Indian Wars in the Midwest. His forces decisively defeated U.S. troops commanded by General Josiah Harmar in 1790 and General Arthur St. Clair in 1791. Hoping for peace, Little Turtle later refused to lead the Indians when General "Mad Anthony" Wayne moved his troops against them in 1794. His people fought without him and later were defeated by Wayne at the Battle of Fallen Timbers. Little Turtle signed the Treaty of Greenville, turning over large tracts of land to the U.S. government. He later also refused to join Tecumseh's confederation.

Pontiac (1720?–1769) (Indian name: Obwendiyag) was a chief of the Ottawa, who fought on the side of the French against the British during the French and Indian War (1754–63). After the war, in response to British injustices against the Indians, Pontiac launched a series of attacks against British forts that is known as Pontiac's Rebellion. His sieges continued until the British signed a peace treaty in 1765. (For more information, see the article PONTIAC in Volume P.)

Profiles

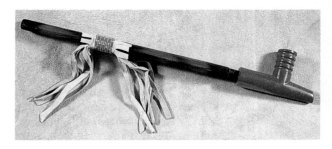

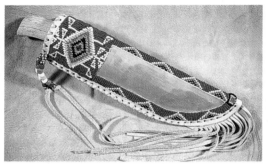

Quapaw. In the 1800's they were joined by the **Winnebago** from Wisconsin. Along the upper Missouri were other Siouan speakers, the **Mandan** and **Hidatsa**, whose farming towns served as trading centers for hundreds of years. Related to the Hidatsa were the **Crow** at the Montana headwaters of the Missouri River. Crow Indians typically spent the entire year hunting.

In the central plains were farming peoples speaking **Caddoan** languages. They included the **Caddo**, **Wichita**, **Pawnee**, and **Arikara**. Around Lake Superior, the upper Mississippi, and the northern prairies was **Sioux** territory, the lands of the **Dakota**, **Lakota**, **Teton Oglala**, and **Assiniboin**; the Algonkian-speaking **Cheyenne** and **Arapaho** also lived here. All of these peoples were farmers. They lived in villages but regularly went on long trips to hunt for bison.

As non-Indian Americans settled the upper Midwest region, the Sioux, Cheyenne, and Arapaho abandoned their homeland fields and villages to live year-round in bison-hide **tipis** (or tepees). They hunted and cultivated only small plots of land beside streams.

Out on the plains lived Indians who had preferred that way of life since prehistoric times. They included the Algonkian-speaking **Blackfoot** and **Gros Ventres** in the north; the **Numic**-speaking **Shoshoni** and **Comanche** in the middle and southern plains; and the **Kiowa**, whose distant relatives now live in the southwestern Pueblo towns.

Among the artifacts made by the Sioux were tobacco pipes (*top*) made from the hardened red clay of the upper Missouri region, and elaborately beaded knife sheaths (*bottom*).

The southern Plains Indians were the first to ride horses. In the 1600's, when many Indians were slaves to the Spanish, they stole horses from Spanish ranches in New Mexico. By the middle of the 1700's, all of the Plains and prairie peoples used horses in battle, as pack animals, for hunting, and as items for trade. Horses enabled them to transport easily large tipi covers and poles, extra food, clothes, and tools on V-shaped wooden-framed sledges, called travois.

Profiles

Black Kettle (1803?–68) (Indian name: Moke-ta-ra-to) was a Cheyenne chief who tried to keep peace with the whites by obeying U.S. orders to move his village to Sand Creek, Colorado. But in 1864, troops attacked the Indians anyway, killing more than 300. Four years later, Lieutenant Colonel George A. Custer led yet another attack on Black Kettle's new village in Oklahoma. Black Kettle was killed and about 100 other Indians were killed or wounded.

Crazy Horse (1849?–77) (Indian name: Tashunca-Uitco) was a chief of the Oglala Sioux who, along with Gall and Sitting Bull, steadfastly resisted white occupation of the northern Plains. In 1854 he was present at the Grattan massacre near Fort Laramie, Wyoming, which was the first clash between U.S. troops and the Sioux. In 1873 he participated in two skirmishes with Lieutenant Colonel George Custer's troops on the Yellowstone River. His followers developed into the great Sioux confederation that later defeated Custer and the Seventh Cavalry at the Battle of the Little Bighorn in 1876. In this battle, Crazy Horse served as a field leader. He surrendered in 1877, but was fatally wounded by a guard while resisting imprisonment.

Gall (1840?–94) (Indian name: Pizi), a Lakota Sioux warrior, fought with Crazy Horse against Lieutenant Colonel George Custer at the Battle of the Little Bighorn in 1876. He was chief of the Hunkpapa section of the Sioux encampment, the target of Custer's attack. After the battle, Gall escaped to Canada with Sitting Bull, but he returned in 1881. After a brief battle with General Nelson A. Miles, he was taken prisoner, but was later released.

Sitting Bull

Indians from the Mississippi River to the Rocky Mountains hunted bison for their meat and hides. By the late 1800's the bison had been killed almost to the point of extinction.

During much of the 1800's, the native Plains Indians and the immigrant Indians fought each other for territory. After the Civil War, the U.S. government sent the army west to force the Plains Indians off large sections of land and onto reservations. The government wanted the land to offer homesteads to war veterans, a policy that was begun at the end of the Revolutionary War.

The government wanted the Plains Indians to start farming in the Euro-American style. The Indians could keep cattle and continue to hunt bison on their reservations for additional meat. Unfortunately, droughts in the plains in the 1870's caused the Indians' new crops to fail, and most of their cattle died in the hard winters.

Breaking up the grasslands and neglecting to burn them off regularly reduced the bison's grazing pastures to the point that the over-hunted herds disappeared, leaving the Indians without food. The U.S. government sent flour, bacon, and some replacement cattle to the reservations, but without fresh foods Indians suffered from vitamin deficiencies, hunger, and disease.

Red Cloud (1822–1909) (Indian name: Makhpiya Luta), a chief of the Oglala Lakota, for years blocked the U.S. government from taking over Indian lands in Wyoming, Montana, and South Dakota. U.S. troops had built posts along the Bozeman Trail to protect whites passing through Lakota bison country on their way to the Montana gold fields. Red Cloud's attacks on these posts led to the abandonment of the trail in 1868. When this happened, Red Cloud signed a peace treaty with the government. Some of his contemporaries, including Sitting Bull and Crazy Horse, disapproved of Red Cloud's submission to the

Red Cloud

whites, and he lost his status as head chief in 1881. He later retired quietly to the Pine Ridge Reservation in South Dakota.

Sitting Bull (1831–90) (Indian name: Tantanka Iyotake) was a great Sioux leader of the Hunkpapa Lakota group. With chiefs Crazy Horse and Gall, he tried to prevent the whites from mining gold in the Black Hills after it was discovered in 1873. He planned the fighting strategy that allowed the Indians to defeat Lieutenant Colonel George Custer and his troops at the Battle of the Little Bighorn in 1876. After the battle, he and other Sioux fled to Canada. When he returned to the Dakota lands in 1881, he was imprisoned for two years. He later traveled with Buffalo Bill and his Wild West Show. Sitting Bull was shot and killed in 1890 while resisting arrest for encouraging the Ghost Dance religion.

Spotted Tail (1826?–81) (Indian name: Sinte Gleska) was a Brule Sioux of the Teton Dakota group, who defended the territory, rights, and customs of his people. After gold was discovered in the Black Hills in 1873, Spotted Tail went there to negotiate a treaty with U.S. commissioners. He strongly opposed the removal of the Dakota to "Indian Territory" in Oklahoma, but signed a treaty nevertheless, for which the government named him head chief of the Brule Sioux. He and his people were relocated to the Rosebud Reservation in 1877.

During these hard times, an Indian religion developed based on the hope that if enough people prayed together, God might make the non-Indian settlers disappear and the Indians' dead loved ones and the bison herds come back. This belief, which became known as the Ghost Dance religion, was taught by a Paiute doctor, Wovoka, who was also called Jack Wilson. In 1889, hundreds of Indians from all over the plains took the train to Nevada to hear Jack Wilson and pray with him.

The Massacre at Wounded Knee. The Ghost Dance religion quickly spread among the Lakota Sioux. U.S. government agents were afraid that this meant that the Lakota were going to try to recapture their lost territories. On December 15, 1890, Sitting Bull, a respected Sioux leader who had defended his people's right to follow the Ghost Dance religion, was shot to death at his home when people in his village tried to stop the police from taking him away to jail. Soon after, another leader, Big Foot, who was known for his skill in smoothing away conflicts, traveled with most of his fellow villagers to the Pine Ridge Agency in South Dakota. Hundreds of Lakota were meeting there to air their grievances.

On the morning of December 29, 1890, the soldiers went into the Indians' encampment at Wounded Knee Creek, demanding that the Indians surrender their guns. According to one account, one deaf young man could not under-stand what was happening and tried to hold on to his rifle. During a scuffle with the soldiers, the rifle went off, and both the Indians and soldiers began firing at one another.

The Battle of Wounded Knee was over in a few hours. Lakota men from Pine Ridge soon rode in to rescue whomever they could, but many already had been killed. The bloody bodies of mothers and children lay scattered over the snowy ground. Elderly Chief Big Foot was found shot dead in his tent. This massacre of over two hundred Lakota was written up in newspapers in the East, prompting non-Indian Americans to demand an end to military campaigns against the Indians.

Problems continued, however, for the Plains Indians. In 1887, Congress decided to cut up the reservations into individual family farms, instead of leaving them whole for Indians to cultivate together, as was their custom. Once each Indian family had been allotted a small farm (which was too small for a family to make a living from), the rest of the reservation land was made available to non-Indian homesteaders. No provisions were made for the Indian children to obtain farms when they grew up.

Other problems also developed. Reservation agents from the federal government would not allow the Indians to manage their own cattle herds, and they insisted that many animals be sold. The agents also allowed white farmers and ranchers to lease Indian land cheaply, and sometimes the Indians' water rights were given away.

Indian communities had little success attracting industries because the reservations were so far from cities, railways, and main highways. Many of these communities remained undeveloped. In the 1950's, Indians were urged to move into major cities to find work, but they seldom had sufficient skills for urban employment. In addition, many found they could only afford housing in slums, and hundreds of families returned to their reservations. Thousands, however, did remain in cities, and today there are more Indians in cities than on reservations.

Followers of the Ghost Dance religion believed that if Indians prayed together, the white settlers would disappear and the bison herds would return.

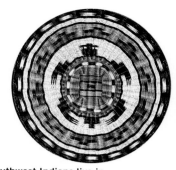

Many Southwest Indians live in stacked adobe houses, such as these in Taos, New Mexico (*left*). Pueblo Indians are famous for their functional and decorative artwork. The Hopi create fine baskets (*above*). The drums (*below*) are from Taos.

In the Southwest

In 1540 the Spanish began to organize Indian communities, from northern Mexico to New Mexico. The Indians of this region spoke various **Uto-Aztecan** languages and included the **Ute** and **Paiute** in Utah and Nevada; the **O'odham** (**Pima** and **Papago**), **Hopi**, and perhaps **Tanoan Pueblos** in Arizona; and the **Yaqui**, **Huichols**, **Tarahumara** (**Ramámuri**), **Tepehuan**, **Cora**, and **Mayo** in Mexico.

Another group of Indian nations that inhabited the Southwest were the **Yumans**. They lived along the lower Colorado River, including the Grand Canyon region, where the **Havasupai** had their village and farms. The Yumans included the **Quechan** (not the same as the South American Quechua), **Mohave**, **Cocopa**, **Maricopa**, and the **Yavapai** and **Walapai**. These nations spoke languages related to the **Hokan** languages of California. Under the hot, dry conditions of the desert, the Yumans needed little shelter or clothing. They could raise and gather enough food for themselves, but they could not produce products for trade.

Except for the Ute and Paiute, who lived too far north to grow corn, all of the Uto-Aztecan nations farmed. They grew corn, beans, and squash along the rivers. In the mountains and the desert, families lived wherever they could find water or a bit of land suitable for crops. In the larger river valleys, families lived in towns.

The Pueblos. Some southwestern nations were known as the Pueblos (which is Spanish for "people" or "community"). Their language groups included **Tewa** (**Santa Clara**, **San Juan**, **San Ildefonso**, and **Hano** on the Hopi reservation); **Tiwa** (**Taos**, **Sandia**, and

Isleta); and **Towa** (**Jemez** and **Pecos**). Tribes who speak the **Keres** languages include the **Santo Domingo**, **Zia**, **Cochiti**, **Laguna**, and **Acoma**. The **Zuñi** speak a unique language.

During the 1600's, Spanish domination of the Pueblos and the growing slave trade caused much hardship. In 1680 a San Juan leader named Popé organized a rebellion to drive the Spanish out of New Mexico. The Indians succeeded, but the Spanish returned in 1692 with more troops and guns and defeated the Pueblos town by town. Again, the Spanish imposed taxes and forced the Indians to attend Christian churches (anyone who did not come to Mass was whipped). The Pueblos adjusted by pretending to go along with Spanish rule, but, in fact, each town secretly continued its own religious ceremonies and traditional government practices.

Mexico took over the region after gaining its independence from Spain in 1821. Then the United States took it over after winning the Mexican War in 1848. The Pueblos carried on as always. One foreign ruler or another made little difference.

In 1924 the U.S. Congress passed a resolution to protect Pueblo lands. Ten years later, it passed the Indian Reorganization Act, which encouraged Indian groups to adopt written constitutions that would provide for limited self-government. But some Indians charged that the new constitutions actually restricted tribal sovereignty.

Today, tourists eager for Pueblo pottery and jewelry contribute to the economy of Pueblo villages. The Indians continue to farm and work at a variety of jobs in neighboring towns. As in other regions, more and more Indians are pursuing higher education and returning to their villages as teachers, lawyers, doctors, and agency workers.

The Apache and Navajo. Another major group of southwestern Indians is the Apache, to which the Navajo belong. Back in the Late Prehistoric period, a group of **Athabascan**-speaking (**Dené**) families in western Canada migrated south through the western plains. They learned corn farming and pottery making in Colorado and moved in between Pueblo villages in Arizona and New Mexico.

Wood-carved *kachina* dolls represent spirits of the dead. The Hopi use *kachinas* in religious ceremonies.

During the Spanish occupation, these small bands earned part of their living by capturing and selling other Indians as slaves. When the United States ended the slave trade in the 1860's, some Apache and Navajo began rustling (stealing) cattle and crops. In 1863, in order to stop this nuisance (and also to secure a route to California for the Union), U.S. troops destroyed Navajo fields and homes. Then they imprisoned the Navajo in a concentration camp where they were held until 1868.

In 1872, Apache similarly were forced into concentration camps. Many were transported all the way to Florida, and later to Oklahoma. Some were not permitted to return home until 1913. As late as 1930, some Apache hung on to freedom in the mountains across the Mexican border, where army troops continued to pursue them.

Eventually the Navajo were given a large reservation on the New Mexico–Arizona border and sheep and goats to replace those taken from them in 1863. They raised corn and other

Profiles

Geronimo

Maria Martinez

Geronimo (ge-RON-im-o) (1829–1909) (Indian name: Goyathlay, meaning "one who yawns") was a Chiricahua Apache warrior noted for his raids against Mexican, and later U.S., troops in the American southwest. His vengeance against non-Indians resulted from the ambush killings of his family in 1850. When the Chiricahua were removed to a reservation in eastern Arizona in the 1870's, Geronimo escaped to Mexico. There he was arrested and returned to the reservation. In 1881, after an Apache prophet was murdered, Geronimo resumed full-time raiding activities from a hide-out camp in the Sierra Madre. He eventually surrendered for the last time in 1886. He

was confined in Florida and later removed to Fort Sill in Oklahoma. (For more information, see the article GERONIMO in Volume G.)

Cochise (co-CHEES, meaning "firewood") (?–1874) was a chief of the Chiricahua Apaches, who kept the peace with the whites until 1861. In that year, he and several of his relatives were held hostage

by U.S. Lieutenant George Bascom, who falsely accused them of kidnapping a white child. The embittered Cochise escaped, but his fellow hostages were hanged. Cochise then joined forces with **Mangas Coloradas** (meaning "red sleeves") (1791?–1863), the leader of another Apache band. For the next ten years, they harassed whites by raiding isolated ranches and attacking stagecoaches and miners. Cochise finally surrendered to U.S. troops in 1871. Mangas Coloradas was killed at Fort McLane, it was said, while "trying to escape." Because of its large size, his head was cut off, boiled, and sent back east to be exhibited at lectures.

Martinez, Maria (1884?–1980), of the San Ildefonso Pueblo, was an artist renowned for her fine pottery. About 1919, she and her husband Julian created their now-famous black-on-black style, which became the most popular pottery style in the Rio Grande region.

The Navajo reservation that lies on the border of New Mexico and Arizona is the largest in the United States. Navajo children go to school and play games (*above*) while the adults earn a living. Many are sheep ranchers (*right*). Others work as miners, engineers, teachers, and artists.

crops where water was available and carefully grazed their animals wherever they could in the desert, and Navajo women turned the sheep's wool into handsome rugs and blankets. Men made beautiful turquoise and silver jewelry, for which they are now famous. Developers encouraged and marketed these crafts, providing another source of income.

During the drought of the 1930's, the U.S. government decided to build the enormous Hoover Dam on the Colorado River. Engineers claimed that the hundreds of thousands of Navajo sheep and goats that ate the vegetation above the dam would cause soil erosion and silt up the dam reservoir. Nearly half of the Navajo herds were destroyed by government order, throwing many families into poverty and causing much bitterness.

In spite of these hardships, several thousand Navajo men and women patriotically joined the armed forces in 1941 when the United States entered World War II. One group in particular proved to be of critical importance. They translated vital secret information into the Navajo language and transmitted it by radio to their allies. The enemy was unable to break this "code."

In the 1950's the Navajo reservation was explored for uranium, oil, gas, and coal. The Navajo mined uranium, where the danger from radiation led to increased risks of cancer.

Coal was located, and open strip-mining was begun, a practice that leaves giant, ugly pits in the landscape. These businesses, which also affected Hopi Pueblo land and Indian reservations in other western states, brought little to the Indian communities except pollution. Indians have organized to try to stop mining, or at least bring it partly under their control. They want to be among those making the decisions, regarding where and how the mining will be done. They also want a larger share of the profits.

The Navajo are recognized for their expert weaving techniques. Their brightly colored handwoven rugs and blankets are particularly popular.

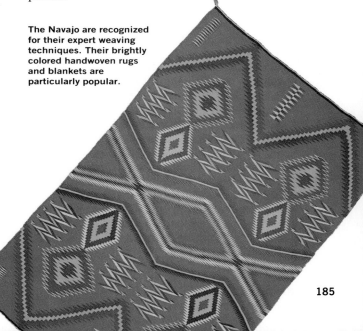

Left: Several groups of Great Basin Indians moved to the southern plains to pursue the bison herds. This 1834 painting by George Catlin shows the women of a Comanche village preparing bison hides, which they used for clothing and shelter.

Below: Hundreds of years ago in southeastern Utah, Indians carved these drawings, called petroglyphs, into the rocks along canyon walls.

In the Far West

West of the Rocky Mountains lived Indians who also spoke Uto-Aztecan languages. These Indians of the Far West occasionally camped in rock shelters, but they usually lived in **wickiups,** or crude shelters, expertly thatched with reeds or brushwood. The women also were accomplished basket weavers, making many different kinds of baskets, each designed for a particular use. Today, basketry is still an art form among the Indians of the Far West, and their best works appear in museums.

The Great Basin. Native Indians of the large desert region known as the Great Basin include the western **Shoshoni**, **Utes**, and **Paiutes** of Utah, Nevada, eastern California, and parts of Oregon and Idaho. They once lived along streams and lakes, where they fished, cultivated edible roots and other plants, gathered quantities of pine nuts, snared birds and rabbits in long nets, and hunted pronghorn antelope and mountain sheep. Rather than settle permanently in villages, these Indians moved to various camps near each different food source as it became ready to harvest.

Beginning in the 1840's, the Mormons, a religious group, moved west to build settlements. Miners and ranchers soon followed. The settlers pushed the small Indian communities out to the edge of the desert and took over all the land that was suitable for farming. Many Indians found jobs as laborers and household help, but some became so impoverished, they had to beg for food.

In 1883, Sarah Winnemucca Hopkins, the daughter of the northern Paiute leader Winnemucca and the granddaughter of Chief

Truckee, wrote a book called *Life Among the Piutes, Their Wrongs and Claims.* She went on lecture tours to eastern cities to persuade the government to restore land to her people so they could live decently.

Reservations were later set aside for some bands of Indians, but the best-watered areas had already been claimed by non-Indian settlers. This prevented the Indians from developing profitable farms or cattle herds. Furthermore, their reservations were placed so far away from major transportation networks, it was almost impossible to attract industries to their regions.

California. California Indians represented all of the major language groups except Siouan. Among the Hokan-speaking tribes were the **Washo**, around Lake Tahoe; **Chumash**, on the central coast; **Pomo**, north of San Francisco; and **Shasta**, around the mountain named after them. **Penutian**-speaking Indians included the **Klamath** and **Modoc** in the north and **Yokuts, Maidu, Wintun,** and **Patwin** in the Central Valley and San Francisco area. Uto-Aztecan peoples included the **Kumayaay** and the **Cahuilla** at Palm Springs. The **Yurok** and **Wiyot** in the north were distantly related to Algonkian-speaking Indians. Also in the north lived the **Hupa** and **Tolowa,** who spoke Athabascan languages.

Whatever their language, all of the California Indians lived in villages. Oak trees were grown for their acorns, which were ground into flour and used in porridges and breads. Because acorns are poisonous, the flour was specially treated to wash out the poison.

Besides acorns, the Indians harvested grain from native grass seeds. Because the Indians grew native plants rather than corn, explorers and colonists thought that the Indians' orchards and fields were uncultivated, and they thought the Indians were poor.

Throughout the 1800's, under both Mexican and U.S. rule, California Indians were enslaved or killed by the thousands. Miners and ranchers shot Indian parents and took their children for slaves. The enslaved Indians lacked proper food, housing, and sanitation, and many became sick.

In the 1900's California Indians were permitted to stay on small reservations. There they tried to earn a living by farming, although working on non-Indian commercial farms was generally necessary. Their land was taken for projects, such as building dams.

Acorns gathered from oak trees were an important source of food for the Cahuilla and other California tribes. They would grind them into flour to make bread and porridges.

During and after World War II, Indians from the plains and the Southwest moved to California cities to work in factories. Now, as a result, most of the Indians living in California do not come from native California tribes. Nevertheless, the native California Indians, including a number of well-educated professionals, work to maintain their cultural heritages and traditions.

Chief Joseph (1840–1904), a chief of the Nez Percé, was a brilliant military leader. In 1863 the U.S. government instructed the Nez Percé to move from their homeland in Oregon to the Lapwai Reservation in Idaho. But Chief Joseph and his followers ignored the order. In 1877, the government sent agents to enforce the relocation, and Chief Joseph decided to escape with his people to Canada. He led them on a 1,000-mile (1,600-kilometer) journey that is now considered a marvel of military history. On the way he eluded and outwitted some of the best officers in the U.S. Army. Finally, about 30 miles (50 kilometers) from the Canadian border, he was defeated by General Nelson A. Miles.

Washakie (WASH-u-kie) (1804?–1900) was a chief of an eastern band of Shoshoni in Wyoming. He fought the Blackfoot and Crow Indians and was noted for his cooperation with white pio-

Chief Joseph

Washakie

neers, helping many of them as they journeyed along the Oregon Trail. He aided hunters and trappers for various fur companies and served as a scout for the U.S. Army during its campaigns against the Cheyenne and other tribes. He was buried

with military honors at Fort Washakie, Wyoming.

Sacagawea (sac-a-ja-WE-a, meaning "Bird Woman") (1786?–1812), a Shoshoni, guided Lewis and Clark through the Pacific Northwest (1804–05). The presence of Sacagawea and her baby probably helped avoid hostilities with other Indians, because a woman and child would not have been part of a war party. (For more information, see the article IDAHO in Volume I.)

In the Far North and Northwest

The North Pacific coastal region, from Alaska down to northern California, once was part of a trade route that continued westward into northern Asia. In the 1600's, Russia extended a fur trade into Siberia, just as France and Britain were building their fur trade in North America. The Russians' headquarters in America was located at Sitka, in southeastern Alaska, where they built a fort in 1804. But their outposts reached as far as the Russian River in northern California.

Long before the Russians came, the northern Indian nations regularly traded among themselves and beyond. In the 1770's, Spanish, then British, ships sailed into the bays of British Columbia. The ships' captains, intending to claim the "new" land for their countries, were welcomed by flotillas (fleets) of long wooden boats carrying Indian chiefs dressed in sea-otter cloaks. Elaborately costumed dancers formally welcomed the new traders into well-established systems.

The Columbia River was a main artery, or branch, of the Pacific trade route (which linked up with the Southwest-Mexican routes in California). At the mouth of the Columbia, on the present-day Washington-Oregon border, lived a people known as the **Chinook**, who commanded the upriver and coastal routes. Their **Penutian** language was used in simplified form by traders and travelers all over the Northwest.

Upriver lived Indians who spoke **Sahaptian** languages (which are related to Penutian). They included the **Yakima**, **Walla Walla**, **Umatilla**, and **Nez Percé**. Just north of the Sahaptians and extending through the Rocky Mountains were the **Salish**-language speakers, including the **Shuswap**, **Okanagon**, **Coeur d'Alene**, **Kalispel**, **Spokan**, and **Flathead**. The language of the **Kutenai**, a small nation in the Montana Rockies, was unique.

Puget Sound and British Columbia make up another section of the Northwest. A number of Salish-speaking groups lived there, including the **Bella Coola**, **Squamish**, **Saanich**, **Snoqualmi**, **Skagit**, **Puyallup**, and **Quileute**. **Wakashan** speakers live mostly north of Puget Sound. They included the **Makah** on the northwest tip of Washington and the **Nootka (Nuu-cha-nulth)**, **Heiltsuk**, **Bella Bella**, and **Kwakiutl**, all from British Columbia.

The northern Northwest Coast, which stretches into Alaska, was home to the **Haida** (whose language is unique); the Penutian **Tsimshian**; and the **Tlingit**, who speak an Athabascan language. The interior forests of Alaska and western Canada are occupied by many small Athabascan groups, including the **Kutchin**, **Tanana**, **Sekani**, **Chilcotin**, **Ingalik**, **Koyokon**, **Dogrib**, **Yellowknives**, and **Chipewyan** (not the same as Chippewa).

For centuries, the major food resource for the Northwest Indians was salmon. Thousands were caught when the fish swam upstream to

The Indians of the Northwest Coast, from northern California to Alaska, became expert woodworkers. This Haida eagle mask (*left*) and Tlingit house (*above*) are carved and painted in the images of spirits and ancient heroes.

Roman Catholic missionaries throughout the Americas disregarded the Indians' native religions and tried to teach them Christianity. At the turn of the century these Nootka (Nuu-cha-nulth) children were enrolled in a Catholic boarding school in British Columbia.

spawn, and the Indians would slice and dry the meat to preserve it. They hunted sea mammals, mountain sheep, and goats, gathered large amounts of berries, and cultivated edible roots. When potatoes were introduced by European fur traders about 1820, the Northwest Indians quickly began planting them.

Weaving was an important craft. A specific breed of dog was kept for its woolly hair, and the wool of wild mountain goats was also used. Cloaks woven by these natives are called Chilkat blankets. They also made raincoats out of shredded cedar bark and wove rain hats like baskets. Northwest Indians created a variety of exceptionally fine baskets.

A famous custom of the Northwest was the **potlatch**, a feast hosted by one community for another to celebrate important events, such as weddings or reaching adulthood. Everyone in the host community worked to prepare lavish foods and gifts to demonstrate their generosity and the riches of the Creator of the world.

Northwest Coast houses were as long as the Iroquois longhouses, but they were higher, because they were made from the enormous logs of the Pacific rain forest. Several related families would share a house, food, and equipment. Each family had its own private section and cooking fire. Work was divided among the men and women of the house for greater efficiency, however, and the overall planning of the work was managed by their chief.

Paintings of spirits and heroes covered the house fronts and the tall screens inside. The entrances of some houses were painted to look like the mouth of a monster. Outside the houses stood **totem poles**, which are tall logs carved and painted with the likenesses of a family's ancient heroes. These totem poles mark the history and importance of the families of a particular house.

During the winters, the villagers held dramatic performances, dances, and celebrations. They used costumes and carved masks that are exhibited today in many art museums. Stage tricks, such as lowering actors from the roof with hidden ropes or jumping out of trapdoors, made the dramas truly exciting. These dramas are still performed today for visitors in cultural heritage centers, such as 'Ksan, near Hazelton, British Columbia. Young Indian artists study at these centers and produce excellent contemporary art in the traditional styles.

Like most other American Indian groups, those in the Northwest lost thousands of people to smallpox epidemics and other foreign diseases. Once non-Indian settlement began in the West in the mid-1800's, Northwest Coast villages developed commercial fishing with canneries, and lumbering. Income was good, and the Indians used their cash to buy food, household goods, and blankets to give away in potlatches. This practice, however, upset the missionaries and agents sent by the Canadian government to "civilize" the Indians. They considered it a waste to spend money on feasts instead of using it to buy private houses and furniture.

As a result, in 1884, the Canadian government banned potlatches. Those who ignored the law were imprisoned. In 1912 and 1915, Indians in southern Alaska and British Columbia organized to fight the law in the courts, but they were unsuccessful. The law was not revoked until 1951.

For more than one hundred years, the livelihood of the coast peoples has been tied to commercial fishing and lumbering. Both of these industries did poorly in the Depression years of the 1930's. Today the Indians find it hard to compete with foreign enterprises.

The Fur Trade. Indians in the Canadian forests lived by fishing and hunting moose, caribou, beaver, and waterfowl. Few edible plants, other than berries, grow in the north. Summers there are so short, there is not enough time for farm crops to ripen. However, the long, cold winters produce fine fur coats on the forest animals, providing the northern communities with a product to trade for goods from the south.

When Europeans (first the Norse, about A.D. 1000, and then the British, French, Portuguese, and Basques, beginning about 1500) came to eastern Canada, the Indians offered to sell them furs. Beginning in 1581, the Europeans organized expeditions to Canada, primarily to buy furs. By 1670, British investors had founded the Hudson's Bay Company to collect furs to sell in Europe. This tied the northern Indians into an international fur business that eventually circled the entire Northern Hemisphere.

American Indians exchanged furs for European metal goods, such as kettles, knives, axes, and small tools. These metal implements were less fragile than the Indians' pottery, stone, and bone objects. Indians also liked the Europeans' wool cloth, colored glass beads, guns, and liquor. Such goods were traded by Indian merchants along native trade routes that reached far beyond the trading posts managed by Europeans.

In the 1700's and 1800's, the European traders' needs increased the demand for food, which created another widespread business opportunity for Indians. They increased production of **pemmican** (chopped, dried bison meat, mixed with berries and fat) and other foods to sell to the trading posts, as well as to their regular Indian customers in the Midwest and in the prairie towns.

As European and American nations industrialized, the fur trade became less important.

Even today, however, furs provide the main source of income for thousands of Indian families in the Canadian north. Some of these communities must now compete for business with mink farms in the United States. This income is further jeopardized by the growing movement against killing animals for their fur.

Other Indian groups of the Far North included the Algonkian-speaking **Cree, Naskapi, Montagnais,** and **Ojibwa** (or **Chippewa**) and the Siouan-speaking **Assiniboin** and **Iroquois.** In the 1700's they worked in the fur trade as trappers, processors, transport laborers, and traders. They contacted, and sometimes settled among, Indians of the Far West, bringing European goods with them.

In the 1880's the trade in bison hides and pemmican ended when the bison herds disappeared. When southern Canadian prairie Indians lost that income, many became farm laborers to earn a living.

Today, commercial fishing is the most profitable business for Indians in the north. Local industries freeze the fish so it can be sold to supermarkets in the south. Another business is uranium mining, but many northern Indians oppose it because it exposes them to dangerous radiation. Some also object because uranium is used to make atomic weapons.

The Inuit (Eskimos). Inuit communities stretch all the way across the Far North, from Greenland westward to Siberia. (Inuit prefer to be called Inuit rather than Eskimo, the name given to them by foreigners.) The **Yupik** of southern Alaska speak a language related to the Inuit farther north. Technically speaking, the Inuit and Yupik are not Indians.

The Inuit and Yupik developed great hunting skills. They built big rowboats, called **umiaks**, from which crews hunted whales, and invented the fast, light **kayak** to hunt seals, walruses, and sea otters. On land they hunted caribou (reindeer). Hunting these animals provided the basis for their living.

Above left: In the wintertime the Inuit in central Canada live in domed snowblock shelters called *iglus*, which is simply their word for "house." *Above right:* The Inuit are skilled at fishing. After they have cleaned the fish, they preserve it by setting it out to dry on racks.

Left: Inuit clothing is carefully constructed to protect the natives from the extreme cold of the Arctic region. This fur-trimmed parka, made out of caribou hides, also shows the beauty of Inuit embroidery.

Opposite page: Throughout the Canadian Northwest were trading posts owned by the British Hudson's Bay Company. Indians exchanged beaver pelts for all kinds of European goods, including woolen cloth, guns, liquor, glass beads, knives, and kettles.

During the long frozen winters, Inuit lived in **iglus** (igloos) in small villages on the coast where the men could spear seals from the ice. Iglus are round, well-insulated houses, usually built of sod blocks over a frame, but sometimes they are made of ice blocks. In the summer, families camped inland in tents to fish, hunt caribou, and gather berries.

Inuit women are expert seamstresses. Long ago they developed a way to tailor clothing to protect people from the cold. The U.S. Army tested different forms of clothing for soldiers to wear in the extreme cold and found they could not improve on Inuit design. Inuit women also embroider garments expertly. Both Inuit and **Aleut** women (from the Aleutian Islands) make wet suits from fish skins for men to wear in kayaks, and they make delicate baskets from grass. In recent years, Inuit artwork has been sold by art dealers in cities, providing a source of income.

Today, Alaskan Indians and Inuit face problems similar to those of Canada's northern Indians. The development of Alaskan oil production has not provided many jobs for the native peoples, yet it has spoiled many of their hunting grounds. Alaska's growing population has also reduced the land resources. In 1971 the U.S. government arranged for one tenth of Alaska to be managed by Native American corporations. A few of these corporations have shown a profit, but others have too few resources to generate much income.

SOUTH AMERICAN INDIANS IN 1500
Principal Tribes and Culture Areas

- Tropical Forest
- Central and Southern Andes
- Tierra del Fuego
- Caribbean and Northern Andes
- Marginal Forest Areas
- Patagonia/Pampas
- Tropical Aquatic
- Mura — Principal Indian tribes
- Present-day international boundary

▶LATIN AMERICAN INDIANS SINCE 1500

From the 1500's until the 1800's, Spain ruled Central America and Mexico. South America was divided between Spain and Portugal. Both nations wanted the wealth of America's gold and other metals, as well as its agricultural products. Indians were enslaved to work in mines and on plantations (**haciendas**), which they were forbidden to leave. They had to labor for their owners as well as on their own plots of land, and they were ordered to use European-style agricultural methods.

Native religions officially were banned, although nearly everywhere, native beliefs became mixed with the Roman Catholic beliefs of the Spanish and Portuguese. Spanish leaders married native royalty, and their sons and other privileged Indian boys were schooled in European languages. Writing in Indian languages was virtually ignored and eventually forgotten. Indian customs came to be seen as backward and common.

The tremendous devastation to Indian populations by European diseases and conquests put European rulers in solid control in Latin America. They claimed all of the valuable land and resources for themselves. European colonization pushed Indian families and communities to lands beyond colonial control or forced them to move through government relocation policies.

In the 1800's, Latin American nations gained political independence from Spain and Portugal, but they did not reject European culture. Nearly five hundred years of European and other development has secured the dominant position of non-Indians in South America. The one major difference between North and South America, however, is that in several Latin American nations, Indians make up the majority of the population.

Mexico During and After Spanish Rule

Although the Indian nations of Mexico had allied themselves with Cortés to defeat the Aztecs, they later found the Spaniards unwilling to recognize their contributions to the conquest. Spain claimed that it alone had won the right to govern all of Mexico.

By about 1630, a century after Cortés took power, the population of Mexico had been greatly reduced by disease and famine. The majority of Indians were living in villages attached to Spanish-owned estates.

The Indians of Sibundoy live in an agricultural community on the Putumayo River in Colombia. The region once was part of the Inca Empire, and the people there still call themselves "Ingas."

The position of Indian communities in Mexico changed little during the 1600's and 1700's. Even when Mexico won its independence from Spain in 1821, patterns did not change. The great estates continued to be worked by poor farmers, forming a lower class that was distinct in language, dress, and customs from the ruling class. Persons of mixed parentage and Indians who did not have village homes formed a **mestizo** (or mixed) class. They spoke Spanish and dressed in the European style but usually worked as laborers or had only small businesses.

Non-Indians of the 1800's believed that Indian village cooperatives were "backward," and that owning individual family farms and businesses was the best way to live. Reform movements, intended to help the Indians, broke up their villages and taught the children to speak Spanish instead of their own languages. The Indians also were encouraged to give up their festivals and other customs.

In the 1800's the Latin-American wars for independence from Spain and Portugal inspired many Mexicans and South Americans to study the history of the U.S. Revolutionary War and the Constitution. In 1855, Benito Juárez, a **Zapotec** Indian from Oaxaca, led a revolt that gave Mexico a constitution similar to that of the United States. Then in 1862, France invaded Mexico and put a puppet em-

Above: The Indians of Guatemala make up about half of that country's population. They are descended from the peoples of the ancient Maya kingdoms. These girls live in the southern highlands.

Left: This Cofan Indian from Colombia is dressed in his native finery. The Indians of Colombia make up only 1 percent of the population. However, more than 50 percent are *mestizos*, people of mixed Indian and Spanish descent.

peror, Maximilian, in a palace on Chapultepec Hill. Juárez' forces defeated France in 1867, and Juárez served as president until he died in 1872. Four years later, the dictator Porfirio Díaz took over the presidency, and he ruled Mexico for the next 35 years. Díaz ruthlessly enslaved Indians, transporting thousands from their homes to work in mines and on commercial plantations.

Emiliano Zapata, a mestizo from Morelos, helped engineer a revolt that overthrew Díaz

in 1911. Zapata wanted plantation lands restored to the peasants, under the Indian system of communal ownership.

It took until 1934, under the presidency of Lázaro Cárdenas, who was part **Tarascan** Indian, for Mexico to open a government Department of Indigenous (native) Affairs to work on the problems of the poor Indian families, who make up the majority of Mexicans. In 1940 the first of a continuing series of Inter-American Indigenist Congresses met in Patzcuaro, Mexico, to discuss Indian problems throughout Latin America. But Mexico's Department of Indigenous Affairs lasted only until 1946. Two years later, some of its activities were placed in a National Indigenist Institute, which divided Mexico into 18 "indigenous zones," marking the country's major Indian nations or groups. The institute developed native-language books and teaching in village schools.

The problems of the poor, however, most of whom are Indian, have continued throughout the 1900's. Mexico's population continues to increase rapidly, and the country has difficulty developing industries to employ the millions who lack farmland.

Central America

In the 1500's, Central America, as well as northernmost South America, was a region of small kingdoms. Maya kingdoms held what is now Guatemala and adjacent Honduras as well as eastern Mexico. In the middle of the century, Spain invaded and conquered many of these kingdoms, and the common people were forced to worship in Christian churches and labor in mines and plantations. The Maya usually were allowed to remain in their villages and farm little plots of corn and beans, so long as they paid taxes in money or labor. However, this changed in the 1870's, when foreign businessmen turned much of Guatemala, including thousands of acres of Indian community lands, into coffee plantations.

In 1821, Guatemala and other Central American states declared their independence from Spain. Guatemala's government was taken over by a succession of dictators who cared nothing for the human rights of the Indian people. Revolution in 1944 replaced Jorge Ubico with Juan José Arévalo, whose government concerned itself with its Indian majority. The government instituted land reform, schools, health clinics, and labor and peasant organizations.

However, this government lasted only until 1954; governments that followed, once again, scorned the Maya. Throughout the civil war that began in the 1970's and escalated in the 1980's, whole villages of Indians were massacred. Hundreds of thousands of Maya escaped to Mexico and the United States.

The jungle lowlands of the southern Yucatán in Mexico, adjacent to Guatemala and Honduras, which at first were not attractive to the Spanish, became early refuges for Maya rebelling against Spanish rule. The last areas of the central Yucatán jungle were not completely penetrated by the Spanish until the end of the 1600's.

In 1847, **Lacandon** Mayas of the lowlands led the War of the Castes against the government of Mexico. The Indians took over most of the Yucatán and held sections of it for a generation. Then U.S. businessmen joined up with the Mexican dictator Díaz to rebuild plantations there. These plantations supplied twine and other products wanted in the United States, and Díaz' army backed up the businessmen's demand for cheap labor.

The same situation—corrupt dictators and foreign businessmen getting rich by forcing Indians to work like slaves—occurred on across the border, not only in Guatemala but in south Central America. On occasion throughout the 1900's, U.S. troops have been sent to Central American republics to help put down Indian rebellions.

The **Miskito** live in the part of the southeastern Caribbean mainland that was colonized by the British (Belize and the Caribbean coast of Nicaragua). The British encouraged the Miskito to take other Indians for slaves, giving the Miskito a reputation for being aggressive. In the 1980's, the Miskito opposed Nicaraguan plans to make national parks and forest preserves of much of the uncultivated land surrounding their villages. They protested, saying that the forests, where they hunt, are necessary to their food supply and should be managed by Miskito.

The **Cuna** of eastern Panama, south of the Miskito, have been somewhat more successful in preserving their independence. During the 1800's, many of their men worked as sailors on British and U.S. ships, and Cuna families developed coconut plantations. In the 1900's

they organized into villages represented by chiefs. The Cuna used their knowledge of non-Indian laws and practices to persuade the Panamanian government to make Cuna community lands into reservations and to help the villages maintain schools and health clinics.

Cuna make their living from farming, fishing, hunting, and working as laborers in Panama's cities. They also sell their crafts. Their organization has become a model for other Panamanian Indian groups.

Colombia

The best-known Indian group south of the Maya was the **Chibcha**, in what is now Colombia. The **Quimbaya** (who were famous for their skill with gold ornaments) lived to the west of them, and the **Chocó** lived farther west on the Pacific coast. The Chibcha kingdoms, aware of the might of the Incas' Tawantinsuyu to the south, were in the process of forming an alliance when the Spanish invaded in the 1500's. The Spanish were eager to help themselves to the gold that the nobles wore and that adorned the temples.

The Chibchan kingdoms could not resist the foreign conquest. Because the valleys of western Colombia enjoy a temperate climate, the Spanish settled in Chibcha lands, replacing native towns and farms with their own and forcing the Indians into labor. The language and culture of the Chibchan kingdoms was lost, although related languages are still spoken today by smaller Indian groups in western Colombia.

The Andean Nations (Tawantinsuyu)

The Inca's nation, Tawantinsuyu, suffered forty more years of fighting after Pizarro murdered Atahualpa in 1533. It was not until 1572 (when the last Inca, Tupac Amaru, was captured and executed) that the Spanish could claim they had conquered Peru. The Spanish viceroy then reorganized Indian communities into planned towns that were supervised by Spanish governors.

In Peru, as elsewhere in the Spanish American colonies, Indian royalty married Spanish leaders (for example, Pizarro married Inca Huayna Capac's daughter). Local Indian nobility became village headmen and dealt with the Spanish plantation owners. Taxes were collected from the Indian farmers and handed over by the village headmen, and the Indian

In Cuzco, Peru, Indians sell their goods and fresh produce from nearby farms in open-air marketplaces. Cuzco once was the capital of the Inca Empire.

communities had to provide workers for the Spanish estates and public projects.

Many Indian farmers could not afford to pay the taxes or to give as much time to the Spanish overlords as was demanded. Thus, many lost their land and became wage laborers or were drafted to work in mines. Mining was hard and dangerous work, and living conditions were poor. Millions of Indians died.

In 1780 a Quechua named José Gabriel Condorcanqui, who called himself Tupac Amaru II, led a rebellion against Spanish rule in Peru. Said to be a descendant of the last Inca, Tupac Amaru II was a respected Indian community leader and a successful businessman, who promised to restore the glory of Tawantinsuyu. His rebellion won the sympathy of some of the Catholic clergy, who agreed that the human rights of the Indians should be upheld.

Tupac Amaru II was executed in 1781, but in 1784, Spain ordered the worst abuses ended. Life for the Quechua, the Aymara on the eastern side of Lake Titicaca, and Indians of other regions eased somewhat. However, the fact that the mines were exhausted may have had something to do with this. The South American wars of independence around 1821 did not affect the Indians greatly. The leaders of the new republics were of Spanish descent, too, and the Spanish social system continued.

Foreign investors with improved machinery reopened mines toward the end of the 1800's. They demanded Indian labor and were supported by the armies of Peru and Bolivia. Estate owners continued to require labor and payments from the Indian communities.

Revolutions and Indian rebellions occurred periodically throughout the 1900's. None of these changed Indian life in Peru, Ecuador, Colombia, or Bolivia. The only exception was the 1952 revolution in Bolivia that led to land reform in the Lake Titicaca region. There, estates were broken up and control over the land was given to the Aymara and Quechua communities. Twenty years after the Bolivian reforms, Peru began a similar program, although the government attempted to turn the village communities into organized cooperatives. However, a major problem with such land reforms is that farmland does not expand as village populations grow, and it soon becomes scarce again.

An important part of social reform in Latin America has been providing schools for the Indian children. In 1931 an Indian school was opened in the Bolivian capital city, La Paz. Its opening day, August 2, is celebrated as "Indian Day" in Bolivia. A great debate centers on whether to teach Quechua and Aymara children in their native languages or exclusively in Spanish, the country's official language. Few schoolbooks are available in the native languages, and Spanish is used in the village schools.

Children are usually only taught through the primary grades, as most parents cannot afford to send them to high schools. Without electricity or money even to buy candles, Indian children study by the dim light of kerosene-soaked rags burning in tin cans. Young men look for work on construction projects and commercial plantations, and young women try to find work as servants in the cities. Their lack of education makes it difficult for them to find jobs or earn much money.

Around each of the major cities in what was Tawantinsuyu—Peru, Bolivia, Colombia, and Ecuador—are slums of shacks put up by thousands and thousands of Indians who cannot build a future for themselves in the stony fields of the high Andes. Many young people migrate to the jungle lowlands to clear land for homesteads, but this displaces the Indians who are native to that region.

The Tropical Lowlands

Tropical lowlands cover most of eastern South America. This region is home to a large number of independent Indian groups and small nations.

The greatest number of people in the lowlands belong to one of the three language families: the **Carib**, **Arawakan**, or **Tupí-Guaraní**.

Arawaks were said to be the original inhabitants of the Caribbean islands. They claimed that Caribs from Guyana and Venezuela invaded the islands, murdered the Arawak men, and married the women. The Caribs may have tried to defend their territories against the Spanish invaders by telling the Spanish tales of Carib cruelty and cannibal feasts, although no one can be sure of this now. But it is known that both Arawaks and Caribs lived in the islands and along the northeastern South American coast in 1500.

Both groups lived in villages. They farmed, fished, and traded with other islands and the mainland. When Columbus and the Spanish landed in the Caribbean islands, they were at first welcomed as new traders. But soon they took over the villages, and the Indians were enslaved and many died of disease. Within a century, the native communities of the islands had disappeared. Individual survivors mingled with the African slaves that were brought in to carry on the plantation labor.

Among other Carib-family languages is that of the **Makiritare** in western Venezuela. Arawakan includes the **Mehinacú**, from northern to central Brazil; the **Mojo** in eastern Bolivia;

the **Campa** in eastern Peru; and the **Tereno** in northern Paraguay's Chaco region. Tupí-Guaraní languages are spoken from the Brazilian coast all the way up the Amazon basin to the edge of the Andes, for example by the **Mundurucú** and the **Sirionú**.

Panoan languages are spoken at the headwaters of the Amazon in Peru and Brazil. They include **Shipibo** and **Conibo**, **Tukano** (where Colombia, Peru, Ecuador, and Bolivia meet), and **Yanomamo** (in westernmost Venezuela). The **Ge** languages of Brazil include **Apinaye** (in northeastern Brazil); **Kayapó**, **Shavante**, **Sherente**, and **Botocudo** (in central Brazil); and **Kaingang** (south on the Paraguay border). Other languages not apparently related to the major families include **Bororo** (in Brazil), **Nambikwara** (in central Brazil), and **Chiquitanto** (in eastern Bolivia). **Jivaro** is spoken by the Jivaro and **Shuar** of the Ecuador-Peru border region, and the **Guahibo** of the Venezuelan-Colombian borderlands.

The **Guaraní** occupied most of southern Brazil and Paraguay. This area, called the Gran Chaco, is covered with grasslands. ("Chaco" meant "hunting ground" to the Quechua.) Spanish invaders marched through the area looking for gold and silver. They discovered that what the Guaraní had was mostly purchased from Tawantinsuyu traders, and they left the country to colonists who were willing to settle the grasslands with cattle ranches. Spanish ranchers married Guaraní women, and the language continued to be used by the thousands of mestizo cowboys and

Many different Indian groups live in the tropical lowlands of Brazil. Members of these tribes include this Bororo chieftain (*left*) and a Kamayura bowman hunting fish (*right*). Many of the tropical lowlands peoples decorate their bodies with vegetable dyes.

other workers, who gradually formed the bulk of the population on the grasslands. Today, the Guaraní language is unique in that it alone among Indian languages is (along with Spanish) an official language of a modern-day nation (Paraguay).

From 1610 to 1767 (when Spain expelled Jesuit missionaries from America), Jesuit priests ran Catholic missions in Paraguay. They organized the Indians into planned towns, where they saw to it that the Indians worked and worshiped in the Spanish manner. After the expulsion of the Jesuits, thousands of Guaraní succeeded in returning to an independent life in the forests.

Meanwhile, in the forested regions (which were of no interest to the Spanish or Portuguese), the Guaraní native culture never was eliminated. These communities came to be called **Kaingua** ("forest people"). In the 1900's, Guaraní and non-Guaraní Chaco peoples, such as the **Toba**, went to work on ranches and in cities.

Most of the tropical lowlands are covered by rain forests, and the rest by grasslands or marshes. The Chaco and southern pampas grasslands have always made good hunting grounds. The marshes and lakes (and especially the deltas of the Paraná and Río de la Plata) were occupied by Indians who fished from canoes and hunted deer, guanaco (a kind of llama), and rheas (ostrich-like birds). They also were the southernmost corn farmers. The Indian nations of the region (now Uruguay and adjacent Brazil) have not survived. They included the **Querendí**, the **Charrua**, and other smaller groups.

The rain forest of the steep eastern slopes of the Andes is similar to the lowland forests of the Amazon Basin below, and its peoples lead similar lives. However, these *montaña* peoples in the higher elevations had been well integrated into the economy of Tawantinsuyu. They produced food, tropical bird feathers for noblemen's cloaks, and medicinal and religious-ritual drugs.

One group, the Jivaro, maintained a custom that seems to have been part of northern Peruvian Moche culture long before the Inca conquest. They preserved the heads of enemy warriors by removing the skull and stuffing the dried skin. These were the famous "shrunken heads" that made the Jivaro seem so fearsome to invaders, both Inca and Spanish.

Nearly all of the tropical forest peoples of South America live in villages in jungle clearings. Some groups build one very large thatch house for all the families in the village. Others build several large houses for related families. Hammocks, woven by the people out of homegrown cotton, provide the main furnishing, with perhaps a few wooden stools carved in the shapes of animals.

Generally, no clothing is worn. People bathe several times a day and are proud of being carefully groomed. They paint delicate designs on their skin, like those on their pottery. Manioc and corn, and more recently plantains, are planted in fields cleared near the villages, with vegetables and herbs at their edges. Fishing and hunting bring in meat, traditionally killed with bows and arrows, spears, or blowgun darts tipped with curare poison made from a tropical forest plant. When a village clearing gets dusty, the garbage dumps pile up, and the fields for crops are worn out, the villagers pack up their hammocks and pots and move to a new area to build new houses and clear fresh fields.

Spanish and Portuguese colonists avoided the tropical forests, preferring the cooler, higher lands that were able to support larger populations. In fact, until recently, some tropical-forest Indian groups had never before seen non-Indians.

Once modern earth-moving machinery became available, the governments of Brazil, Peru, Ecuador, Colombia, Venezuela, and Bolivia invited foreign businesses to invest in oil development, mining, lumbering, and plantations in the tropical forests. They used the heavy machinery to build roads and dam up the rivers.

Results were often disastrous. The destruction of the rain forests erodes the land and threatens the climate of the whole world. Much of the land can never support successful commercial farms, and because heavy machinery does most of the work, few people are given jobs.

Several international movements are now concerned about the tropical-forest Indians and oppose the neglect of their welfare. Ecologists who see the destruction of the tropical rain forests also work with Indian groups. They have tried to organize political protests and find legal ways to both protect the Indians' right to the land and help save the rain forests.

The Mapuche of southern Chile successfully defended their independence against the same Spanish invaders who conquered the Inca Empire in the 1500's. However, in the late 1800's, the Chilean government forced the Mapuche onto reservations.

Southern South America

The land in Chile and Argentina, south of the Andes, is not suited to growing either corn or manioc, the basic crops of lowland South America. Most of the area is grassland similar to the plains of North America, only with guanaco and rheas instead of bison.

Before Spaniards brought in horses in the 1500's, the **Mapuche** of Chile and **Tehuelche** of Patagonia (southern Argentina), like the Guaraní, hunted guanacos and rheas with bows and arrows, slings, spears, and **bolas**. (Bolas are round stones that are tied together with a cord. When bolas are thrown, the cord wraps around the animal and brings it down.) The guanaco hunters would drive herds of the animals into corrals to help slaughter them more efficiently.

After Spanish horses became common in the early 1700's, the pampas hunters used them to hunt and transport household goods from camp to camp, much like the North American Plains Indians of the same period. And like the Plains Indians, the pampas hunters gained a reputation for being warlike because they fought as cavalry troops to defend their lands.

Chile defeated the Mapuche between 1880 and 1882 and put them on 2,000 small reservations. Argentina's army conquered its native peoples between 1879 and 1883 and sent them into the drier sections of the pampas in the south and west. Today it is estimated that there are several hundred thousand Mapuche left. Many of them live by herding sheep and goats, some by fishing along the Pacific coast, and some by gathering pine nuts along the slopes of the Andes. A good number of others farm in the fertile central plain of Chile.

In Tierra del Fuego, in southernmost South America, the climate is cold and cloudy. Magellan stopped there in 1520, but Europeans considered it so poor and gloomy that few ever came back. Charles Darwin, the great naturalist, visited Tierra del Fuego in 1832. He wrote in his journal that the native people seemed very strange, wearing only short fur cloaks in spite of the chill and speaking a language he could not begin to understand. The Fuegians wore little clothing because they were often in the water, collecting shellfish, fishing, hunting seals, sea lions, and ocean birds, or moving camp by canoe.

The land there is so rugged and so densely forested in places that overland travel is almost impossible. Along the southwesternmost coast of Chile live the **Alakaluf** (today called the **Qawasqar**). On the southern tip of the continent lived the **Yahgan**—the world's southernmost people. To the north and east are the **Selknam** (also called **Ona**), who are related to the Tehuelche on the pampas.

In the 1900's, non-Indians took over southern Patagonia and Tierra del Fuego for sheep ranches. They employed some Indians on the ranches but made it difficult for the Mapuche and Tehuelche to succeed with their own small farms and herds. On the coast, commercial fishermen in motorboats displaced the Alakaluf, who could not afford more than their dugout canoes. In 1850 there were 4,000 Alakaluf. By 1985 only 40 remained, and they live in poverty, without any form of economic opportunity.

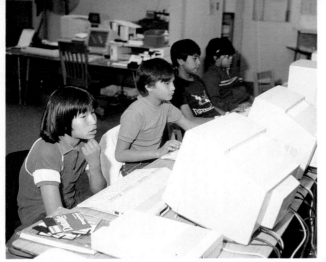

Sixth graders learn computer science at the Oglala Sioux Loneman school, which is located on the Pine Ridge Reservation in South Dakota.

▶ PRESENT-DAY ISSUES

Today, Native American populations are increasing, and attitudes toward them are slowly changing. People are learning a new respect for their ways of life, and appreciation of Native American culture is on the rise. More and more Native American authors are publishing works about themselves and their peoples, in their own languages, as well as in English and Spanish. Bilingual schools also are becoming more common, giving Native American children the opportunity to learn more about their own cultures.

Nevertheless, much prejudice still exists. For many years, textbooks failed to devote more than a few pages to Native American history, and they repeated familiar stereotypes, giving the impression that all Native Americans are alike. Instead of referring to Indian nations by their correct names—the names they call themselves—the books tended to describe the Native Americans in terms of how they obtained food—"the Bison Hunters," "the Southwest Corn Growers"—as if food were the most significant indicator of Indian life. Can you imagine a history textbook of Europe calling the British "the Sheep Herders" or the French and Germans "the Wheat Growers?" Even today, few people realize that there were hundreds of independent Indian nations in America, and most of them still exist, each with its own community, customs, language, and history.

The Question of Home Rule

The main issue challenging today's Native Americans is that of sovereignty (who is to govern them). Many North American Indian nations want home rule—which means they want the right to govern themselves. In order to achieve home rule, they are willing to adjust their laws and practices to avoid conflicts with the national governments of the United States, Canada, and Mexico.

Since the 1950's, Indian nations have pressed for independence. They formed the World Council of Indigenous Peoples, which includes leaders from all over the Americas, Australian Aborigines, and Sami (Lapps) from Norway and Sweden.

The United Nations recognizes the natives' right to maintain their own cultures as a basic human right. In 1982 the United Nations set up a Working Group on Indigenous Popula-

The remains of 24 Cheyenne, killed at Fort Robinson, Nebraska, in 1878, were recovered from a museum and returned to their Montana homeland for a proper Indian burial. Many Native Americans have made such efforts to reclaim their cultural rights and integrity.

The Ten Largest Indian Tribes in the United States[1]	
Tribe	**Population**
1. Cherokee	729,533
2. Navajo	298,197
3. Choctaw	158,374
4. Sioux	153,360
5. Chippewa	99,704
6. Apache	96,833
7. Blackfeet	85,750
8. Iroquois	80,822
9. Pueblo	74,085
10. Creek	71,310

[1]Indians living in the United States who are of Central and South American origin number 180,940. Source: U.S. Bureau of the Census (2000 census).

tions as part of the U.N. Commission on Human Rights. It recognizes Indian nations as nongovernmental organizations (NGO's) and Indian leaders are allowed to meet at the U.N. commission's headquarters in Geneva, Switzerland, to link with each other and to bring their problems to world attention.

A number of U.S. Indian groups lack reservations, either because their nations were absorbed before the policy of reservations came into effect in the 1800's, or because they accommodated colonization without conflict. In the United States, these groups have demanded that they be recognized as "Indian tribes" so they can receive economic, educational, and health assistance as do the "tribes" on reservations, who have treaties with the United States. This type of recognition by the U.S. government is seen as a step toward sovereignty. There seems to be increasing public support for the Indians' desire for more democratic and cooperative economic and political organizations, and U.S. and Canadian judges have ruled that the Indians should share the management of natural resources on treaty lands outside their reservations.

Reservations are not simply part of states or provinces. Residents do not pay state or provincial taxes and do not need to follow all state or provincial laws. For example, Indians can operate gambling casinos if they wish. Gambling has become a big business on many reservations. It provides employment opportunities, and profits are used to improve housing, roads, community centers, and to develop other businesses. However, the casinos unfortunately have caused a lot of conflict among the Indians themselves. Many Indians object to them because they tend to attract drug smuggling and other illegal activities. For example, in 1990, conflicts between opposing Indian groups erupted in violent riots on the St. Regis Mohawk Reservation on the U.S.-Canadian border.

Home rule, or self-government, will not provide a simple solution to the Indians' problems. Most of their problems stem from the prejudice of non-Indians and a general lack of economic opportunities. Unfortunately, home rule would not change this. The majority of Indian communities, for example, are far from centers of employment. The Indian reservations were set up on lands that the settlers did not want, and they are not suited to support businesses. Because of this, probably half of all the Indians in North and Latin America have moved to the cities, where they have faced discrimination in schools and in the work force.

There is one great difference between American Indians and everyone else in the Americas. They are the only people whose ancestors actually originated in the Americas, and not from overseas lands. America is their true homeland, the place where the American Indians' cultures must be preserved if their heritages are not to disappear altogether.

ALICE BECK KEHOE
Professor of Anthropology, Marquette University

Reviewed by ANN PHILLIPS BAY
Director, Office of Elementary and Secondary
Education, Smithsonian Institution

See also AZTECS; BRANT, JOSEPH; GERONIMO; INCAS; INDIAN WARS OF NORTH AMERICA; INUIT; MAYA; OSCEOLA; PONTIAC; SEQUOYA; TECUMSEH; and individual country, state, and province articles.

At the Tulsa Indian Actors Theater in Oklahoma, actors from many tribes perform stories that have been passed down from their ancestors.

Where are the Indians now?

When Europeans arrived in the New World, they brought devastation to many Native Americans. Over the centuries, millions of Indians died from European diseases, and countless thousands of others were killed in battles against the foreign intruders.

Today in the United States, Native Americans make up less than 1 percent of the total population. Many live on reservations, where they strive to preserve their native cultures. (Reservations are parcels of land that governments set aside for the Indians to live on.) A large number, however, have left the Indian reservations for towns and cities, where they live and work in non-Indian communities.

INDIAN WARS OF NORTH AMERICA

When Europeans first arrived in North America, they met what seemed to them strange and different human beings. Christopher Columbus (1451?–1506)—the first explorer of his time to discover the New World —had called these people "Indians" believing he had reached islands in the Sea of India.

As the Europeans explored North America, they encountered a wide variety of Native American settlements and civilizations. Often the two groups lived in peace and friendship. The Europeans had guns, iron kettles, glass beads, woven blankets, and other goods, which they eagerly exchanged for the Indians' furs, foodstuffs, and other supplies. In the early days, the Europeans also needed the Indians to teach them how to live and survive in the unfamiliar wilderness areas.

As the Europeans' presence grew, however, so did the Indians' resistance to their expansion. This gave rise to a series of wars that took place over the course of three centuries. These so-called Indian Wars usually resulted from cultural misunderstandings and from the Indians' resentment of and retaliation against the Europeans' oppressive treatment.

▶ **CONFLICT IN THE AGE OF EXPLORATION**

Conflict accompanied virtually all of the early European explorations of North America. Hernando de Soto's three-year journey through the Southeast (1539–42) was marked by raids on Indian villages and at least one major battle near present-day Mobile, Alabama. Francisco de Coronado's expedition into the Southwest (1540–42) was met with resistance by the Pueblo Indians.

The arrival of Europeans also affected relations among the Indians themselves. Horses, rifles, and armor were appealing tools of war, and observant chiefs were quick to enlist the Europeans' aid in their struggles to maintain and expand their tribe's territory.

As Europeans brought more weapons to North America, the number and intensity of conflicts increased. For example, in the Northeast, Dutch rifles and iron knives fueled the expansion of the Iroquois Confederacy and figured in countless battles between tribes trying to gain the advantage in the profitable fur trade.

▶ **WARFARE AND COLONIAL SETTLEMENT IN THE EAST**

The first European settlement to survive in North America was Jamestown, founded by the English in 1607. From the beginning, the settlers' relations with the Indians were strained but basically peaceful. However, by 1622 excessive demands by the English for land and corn eventually led the Algonquian chief, Opechancanough, to attack, killing 350 colonists. The English responded by conducting perpetual war against the Indians. They burned the Indians' corn, attacked their villages, and captured and sold some Indians as slaves. In 1644, Opechancanough attacked the English again, but this only led to the final defeat of the tidewater Virginia tribes.

The Pequot War (1637)

The first major Indian war in New England occurred in 1637. On May 1, Massachusetts militiamen, aided by Narragansett Indians, attacked a Pequot village in retaliation for the murder of a colonist. About 600 Indians— men, women, and children—were killed, and many others were taken into slavery.

King Philip's War (1675–76)

The most destructive war with the Indians in New England, however, was King Philip's War of 1675–76. King Philip, whose proper name was Metacomet, was chief of the Wampanoag Indians. He was the son of Massasoit, who had been a great friend to the Plymouth colonists. Metacomet deeply resented the domination of the colonists. Indian raiding parties burned many New England towns and killed and captured hundreds of colonists. But colonial forces finally crushed the Wampanoag and nearly exterminated the tribe altogether.

Bacon's Rebellion (1676)

While King Philip's War was being fought in New England, an Indian war raged on Virginia's borders. Virginia's Indian war was fueled by councillor Nathaniel Bacon and his followers, who revolted against Sir William Berkeley, Virginia's governor. They claimed Berkeley had unjustly protected some Indians who had come into conflict with some of Virginia's frontiersmen, and demanded that the Indians be removed from the path of white settlement.

The Pueblo Revolt (1680–92)

In 1598, Juan de Oñate expanded the empire of New Spain into the Rio Grande Valley in the Southwest. He established his headquarters at Santa Fe and dispatched Franciscan friars to occupy the surrounding Pueblo Indian settlements. The Spanish were able to conquer these villages in part because the tribes were isolated and divided. Common suffering among the Indians, however, inspired united action. In 1680, they attacked Spanish settlements and drove the invaders out of New Mexico. But in 1692, the Spanish reconquered the land and re-established control.

The French and Indian Wars (1689–1763)

The series of French and Indian wars that took place in colonial America were largely caused by the great struggle between the French and the British for control of North America. The rivalry resulted from the ongoing competition for control of the fur trade.

Between 1689 and 1763, four wars, each more violent than the last, were fought between the English and French and each side's Indian allies. These included **King William's War (1689–97)**, in which an expedition of Seneca Indians threatened Montreal; **Queen Anne's War (1702–13)**, which led to the Brit-

ish conquest of French Acadia (now Nova Scotia); **King George's War (1744–48)**, in which the French tried unsuccessfully to recapture Acadia; and the **Seven Years' War (1754–63)**, which ended French domination in Canada altogether. (The Seven Years' War is known in North America as the French and Indian War. For more information, see the article FRENCH AND INDIAN WAR in Volume F.)

With the surrender of French Canada to the British in 1760, British troops began to occupy former French forts in the interior while negotiators hammered out a formal treaty of peace. One of the many differences between the French and English in their relations with Indians was that the French more fully observed Indian customs that required a lavish exchange of gifts to show friendship. The British commander in America, Lord Jeffrey Amherst, was in no mood to indulge Indians in this fashion. He ordered that gifts of European goods no longer be given to Indians to cut costs. Amherst believed that Indians, as well as the English, should be "punished but not bribed" to influence their behavior.

Amherst's hard-nosed attitude stimulated what is known as Pontiac's rebellion. Pontiac, an Ottawa chief, called upon Indians to regain their earlier customs, cast off European ways,

A Sioux artist painted a scene of the Battle of the Little Bighorn, where Custer's troops were massacred in 1876. This was the Indians' last major victory in North America.

and oppose English claims to the interior. Pontiac's plan for a surprise attack on Fort Detroit in 1763 was partly frustrated by the watchfulness of the military. But other English forts fell under Indian control. After much hard fighting, Pontiac's forces were defeated and English control of the area re-established.

The defeat of the French left many Indians at the mercy of ambitious and aggressive English frontiersmen. To quiet the Indians' fears and to check uncontrolled colonial expansion, King George III of England issued the Proclamation of 1763 that "reserved" lands west of the Appalachian Mountains for the Indians and declared them temporarily off-limits to English settlers.

▶THE REVOLUTIONARY WAR (1775–81)

Growing differences between the royal government and the American colonists soon erupted into rebellion and war. Both sides saw the quarrel as a family affair and at first attempted to keep Indians out of the struggle. But as time went on, each side saw advantages in recruiting Indian allies. Ethan Allen of Vermont sent a message to the Iroquois urging them to help him fight—Indian style—against the British regulars, who "stand all along close together rank and file." Meanwhile the British were inviting the Iroquois to "feast on a Bostonian and drink his Blood."

Soon, Indian nations and confederacies were involved. Most significant among them were the Mohawks, led by Joseph Brant, who fought in New York and Ohio, and the Cherokees, who attacked colonial troops in the south. The war divided many Indian groups, including the tribes of the powerful Iroquois Confederacy. It also caused future conflicts between the Indians and the Americans, because the Indians had largely supported the British during the war.

Despite the valuable assistance of many Indian nations to the British during the American Revolution, Indian rights were ignored in the peace treaty that followed. Spanish allies of the American colonists worried about American expansion and asserted that lands between the Appalachians and the Mississippi River belonged to the Indians. But American negotiators successfully insisted that these lands were part of the new American nation. The treaty recognized this claim and said nothing about tribal territories or boundaries.

▶WESTWARD EXPANSION

Following the formation of the United States, the new government attempted to enforce its control over the Ohio Valley. In 1790, General Josiah Harmar's expedition into the Maumee Valley was repulsed by the Indians, and in 1791, General Arthur St. Clair suffered a worse defeat near present-day Fort Wayne, Indiana. St. Clair's defeat was the greatest American loss in all the Indian wars. More than 2,000 soldiers and militiamen were routed by the combined force of several tribes, and more than one quarter of the soldiers were killed. American authority was not established in the area until 1794, when General Anthony Wayne was able to defeat the Indians at the Battle of Fallen Timbers, near present-day Toledo, Ohio.

In the early 1800's an extraordinary Indian leader—Tecumseh, a Shawnee—urged all Indian tribes of the interior to join together and refuse to sell any more land to the colonists. With his brother Tenskwatawa—called the Shawnee Prophet—he established a village on the Wabash River near Tippecanoe Creek. There Indians from many tribes listened to his message of reform. Governor William Henry Harrison of the Indiana Territory watched this growing community with concern. When an excuse to attack the town presented itself in November 1811, during Tecumseh's absence, Harrison acted. With heavy losses, Harrison destroyed "Prophetstown," killing hundreds of Indians.

Tecumseh sought revenge by aiding the British in the War of 1812. He helped capture the American fort at Detroit. But the tide turned at the Battle of the Thames River on October 5, 1813, when the British were overwhelmed by Harrison's attack and Tecumseh was killed. With his death, Indian hopes for unity against the American advance were crushed for the time.

▶THE END OF WARFARE IN THE EAST

For the most part, Indian warfare in the East ended after the War of 1812. Tecumseh's followers in Ohio and British-allied tribes, such as the Creeks in the Southeast, were defeated. Remaining conflicts were generally caused by government efforts to relocate tribes to new homes west of the Mississippi River. In Illinois, resistance of the Sauk and Fox Indians, led by Black Hawk, brought both state and federal troops into action. At the Battle of Bad Axe in 1832, 150 of Black Hawk's warriors were killed, and Indian resistance to resettlement ended. Also, in Florida it took 30,000 soldiers to march 4,000 Seminoles west to the newly created "Indian Territory" in present-day Oklahoma. In the process, 1,500 soldiers were killed.

▶ **WARFARE IN THE WEST**

Americans are most familiar with the warfare centering on the Great Plains and Rocky Mountains west of the Mississippi River. Many early conflicts in the West were caused by Indian acts of violence directed against missionaries, traders, trappers, and travelers, on the one hand, or by American settlers, trappers, and militiamen against Indians on the other. Each side mistrusted and misunderstood the other. Each side perceived actions by the other, such as passing through the other's territory (Americans) or demanding payment for doing so (Indians), as unjust or improper. In November 1847, for example, the missionary Marcus Whitman was murdered by Cayuse Indians at a mission station near present-day Walla Walla, Washington. The Cayuse feared Whitman was responsible for the increasing number of whites moving along the Oregon Trail to the Columbia River basin. Between 1855 and 1858, a series of battles were fought in Puget Sound (where one group of Indians nearly captured the village of Seattle).

Between 1850 and 1880, numerous treaties were negotiated between whites and Indians in all parts of the West, from Nebraska to California. As in Washington, the original purpose of these treaties was to separate the two groups and reduce the risk of war. But as the size of the settler population increased, the agreements were intended to clear broad paths across the continent for the white settlers.

The process by which Indian tribes were restricted to reservations, their lives controlled by unsympathetic government agents, and many of their cultural traditions forbidden, is a story of periodic warfare followed by tragic defeat. In the 1860's and 1870's, this process of "clearing" the West for white settlement led to conflicts with the Navajos, Kiowas, Blackfeet, Comanches, Sioux, and Cheyennes. It also touched off conflicts with smaller groups who resisted confinement on the reservations. Most notable of these groups

were the Nez Percé bands, led by Chief Joseph, who fought American troops in 1877. This "war" was caused by Chief Joseph's refusal to leave his native Wallowa Valley in Oregon, which the American government claimed had been sold to the United States under an 1863 treaty.

Occasionally the Indians got the upper hand. In 1868, Chief Red Cloud and the Sioux were able to force the United States to withdraw its troops from Wyoming and eastern Montana. Geronimo and other Apache chiefs kept the U.S. army at bay in the Southwest in the 1870's and 1880's. But such victories, even the successful massacre of Lieutenant Colonel George Custer's regiment at the Little Bighorn River in Montana in 1876, were merely temporary interludes. The Indians responsible for "Custer's Last Stand"—the Sioux and Cheyenne—were soon put on reservations or chased into Canada, where they sought refuge.

▶ **THE WARS END**

An expert has estimated that in the long history of Indian-white warfare, the whites lost more men in actual combat than did the Indians. But the Indians were unable to succeed in the end largely because of the disruption to their cultures and the effects of European diseases, such as smallpox, which wiped them out in vast numbers. Also, the whites had the technological advantages of firearms, railroads, telegraphs, and the like, which allowed them to organize their forces more efficiently than the Indians could.

As a result of the American's growing power, wars of the last half of the 1800's did not have the same character as those of previous centuries. Skirmishes, attacks, and local massacres continued to occur. But the ultimate outcome was never in doubt. By the end of the 1800's, formal "warfare" ceased; it became impossible to maintain against the overwhelming power of the U.S. Army.

WILCOMB E. WASHBURN
Director, Office of American Studies
Smithsonian Institution
Reviewed by FREDERICK E. HOXIE
Director, D'Arcy McNickle Center for the
History of the American Indian
The Newberry Library

See also FRENCH AND INDIAN WAR; BRANT, JOSEPH; GERONIMO; OSCEOLA; PONTIAC; TECUMSEH.

INDOCHINA. See SOUTHEAST ASIA.

INDONESIA

Indonesia is a nation made up of thousands of islands that stretch in a long arc between the mainland of Southeast Asia and Australia. Indonesia is the largest country of Southeast Asia in both area and population. It ranks fourth among the nations of the world in population, after China, India, and the United States. Formerly a Dutch colony known as the Netherlands East Indies, Indonesia proclaimed its independence in 1945. It officially became an independent nation in 1949. Since that time, Jakarta has served as Indonesia's capital.

▶ PEOPLE

Most Indonesians are descended from Malay peoples who came to the islands from the Asian mainland thousands of years ago. Other ethnic groups include Chinese, Arabs, and people from India. Descendants of the earliest inhabitants of the islands live mainly in Papua (the western portion of the island of New Guinea). The native people of the island of Borneo are known as Dayaks.

Indonesia's large population is unevenly distributed among the islands. More than half the people live on the fertile island of Java. Since 1969, more than 5 million Javanese have been resettled on less populated islands in an effort to ease the overcrowding on Java, one of the most densely populated areas in the world.

Language. Bahasa Indonesia was adopted as the national language when Indonesia declared its independence. A version of Malay, it is spoken throughout the islands. About 250 other languages and dialects are spoken in various parts of the country, including English, Dutch, and Javanese.

Religion. About 90 percent of all Indonesians follow the religion of Islam, making Indonesia the world's most populous Muslim nation. Most of the people on the island of Bali are Hindus. Many of the ethnic Chinese are Buddhists. Christians are found on several of the islands, especially the Moluccas.

Left: Jakarta is the capital and largest city of Indonesia. *Above left:* A young dancer on the island of Bali preserves ancient Hindu traditions. *Above:* The Malays of Indonesia are mostly Muslims. Their language, known as Bahasa Indonesia, is the country's official language.

Large, powerful water buffalo are still used in Indonesia for plowing and other kinds of heavy work, although tractors are becoming increasingly common.

Some Indonesians, especially on Borneo and New Guinea, follow traditional native religions. Freedom of religion is guaranteed to all Indonesians under the constitution.

Education. Indonesian children are required to complete six years of primary school education. Increasing numbers of children are attending secondary school, which consists of three years of junior high school and three years of senior high school. Indonesia has many colleges and universities. The largest include Gadjah Mada University in the city of Yogyakarta, the University of Indonesia in Jakarta, and the Institute of Technology in Bandung.

Way of Life. In the cities, Indonesian men wear Western-style clothing. Native influence is seen only in the black velvet caps some of them wear. Indonesian women often wear wraparound skirts of hand-printed batik cloth, long-sleeved jackets, and scarves called *selendang* over their shoulders.

More than 40 percent of all Indonesians are farmers who till small plots of land. In much of the country, rice is the main crop. But on the drier eastern islands, corn or cassava (a starchy root) is the staple crop. In addition to these crops, vegetables, fish, eggs, chickens, and spices make up the daily diet.

Farm families are generally larger than city families, and everyone must work. Young girls help their mothers sew and thresh rice in the afternoons, after they have finished school and religious training. Boys as young as 8 help their fathers weed and plow the rice paddies. On Muslim religious holidays, there are grand festivities in which all the families of a community can take part because normal work is suspended.

In the cities people may work in the construction industry or in factories making clothing, shoes, and textiles, such as the batik-styled fabric for which Indonesia is famous. Others have jobs in modern shopping centers, hotels, or office buildings, while many of the poor eke out a living driving taxicabs or selling food from small street stands. When economic times are good, people from rural areas often move to the cities in search of a better life. When times are hard, they may return home.

▶ LAND

The islands of Indonesia extend for about 3,500 miles (5,640 kilometers) from the northern tip of Sumatra to the middle of the island of New Guinea. Indonesia shares New Guinea, the world's second largest island, with the nation of Papua New Guinea.

The country is usually divided into several island groups. The four major islands, Java, Sumatra, Borneo, and Sulawesi, belong to the group known as the Greater Sunda Islands. To the east of Java lie the Lesser Sunda Islands, which include Bali, Lombok, Sumba, Sumbawa, Flores, and Timor. Located between Sulawesi and New Guinea are the Moluccas, which include Buru, Ceram,

Indonesian women are expert at carrying loads of goods on their heads. For everyday wear, they favor clothes made from batik cloth.

Mount Rindjani, on the island of Lombok in Indonesia's Lesser Sunda Islands, rises above palm trees and green fields.

eruption in 1883 that caused great destruction and loss of life.

Indonesia shares the island of **Borneo** with the nations of Malaysia and Brunei. Borneo is the third largest island in the world.

The Indonesian part of Borneo, known as **Kalimantan**, covers most of the island. Many people in Kalimantan live in the coastal areas. The interior is rugged, with mountains, swift rivers, and dense rain forests and jungles. For more information, see the article BORNEO in Volume B.

The island of **Sumatra (Sumatera)** covers more than 163,000 square miles (422,170 square kilometers). Along the eastern coast are high swamps. The Barisan Mountains, with many active volcanoes, stretch along the southwestern coast. Most of the rivers—including the Musi, Hari, Indragiri, and Kampar—begin in these mountains and flow eastward and northeastward.

Four peninsulas make up the island of **Sulawesi** (formerly Celebes). They branch out from a mountainous area in the center of the island and are separated by three gulfs—Bone, Tomini, and Tolo. Sulawesi covers about 69,000 square miles (179,000 square kilometers). Most of the people live on the southwestern peninsula.

Ambon, Halmahera, Morotai, the Aru Islands, and many other small islands. Papua, the easternmost part of Indonesia, occupies the western half of New Guinea.

The Greater Sunda Islands (Sunda Besar). Indonesia's most heavily developed and densely populated island is **Java (Jawa)**, which lies south of the equator. Java covers about 49,000 square miles (127,000 square kilometers). In the north is a low coastal plain. Inland there are volcanoes, mountain ranges, and plateaus. Some isolated plains are found in the south. The longest river in Java is the Solo. Other rivers are generally short and broken by many rapids.

Krakatau (Krakatoa), an island in the Sunda Strait between Java and Sumatra, was the site of a terrible volcanic

Rice is the main food crop for much of Indonesia. Young rice plants are transplanted by hand. The fields are kept flooded until harvest.

Indonesia

The Lesser Sunda Islands (Nusa Tenggera). To the east of Java stretches a chain of mountainous islands known as the Lesser Sunda Islands. Their total area is about 28,000 square miles (72,500 square kilometers).

Bali, the best known of these islands, is famous for its scenic beauty, temples, sculpture, and crafts. Hindu customs and the Hindu religion are widespread on the island.

Timor is the largest island of the group. In 1976 the eastern part of the island, formerly a Portuguese colony, was declared part of Indonesia. East Timor achieved full independence in 2002.

The Moluccas (Maluku). The Moluccas, also known as the Spice Islands, lie between Sulawesi and New Guinea. They consist of hundreds of islands, covering a total area of about 33,000 square miles (85,500 square kilometers). The largest one, Halmahera, covers 6,870 square miles (17,790 square miles). Spices from the Moluccas, such as cloves, nutmeg, and mace, have been valued throughout the world for hundreds of years.

Papua. Formerly known as Irian Jaya, this part of Indonesia is situated in the western half of New Guinea. It covers approximately 160,000 square miles (414,000 square kilometers). In the interior, the peaks of the Maoke (Snow) Mountains rise to great heights. Parts of Papua have never been explored. More information about Papua can be found in the article NEW GUINEA in Volume N.

Climate. In general, the climate of Indonesia is tropical, meaning high temperatures, much rainfall, and a year-round growing season. Indonesia's climate is determined by its location on and near the equator and by the two different seasonal winds known as monsoons—the dry monsoon and the wet monsoon. Throughout the year temperatures average about 27°C (80°F) in the lowlands, although some relief from the humidity can be found in the mountains. Western Indonesia receives the heaviest rainfall. Rainfall in the east is more moderate.

Natural Resources. The most agriculturally productive areas of Indonesia are generally found in regions with volcanic soil and in river valleys. These are found in Java and in parts of Sumatra and Sulawesi.

Many of the islands have valuable mineral deposits. Petroleum is found on Java, Sumatra, and Borneo and in Papua, and there are extensive natural gas fields in Sumatra and Borneo. Tin is found on Bangka and Beli-

Right: Indonesia is the world's leading exporter of liquefied natural gas. *Below:* Many international manufacturers have moved their factories to Indonesia, where wages are relatively low.

tung, and copper and nickel on Sulawesi. Diamonds, gold, and silver are found on Borneo and Sumatra. Coal is also found on Sumatra.

▶ ECONOMY

Indonesia is one of the world's leading producers of tin, natural rubber, palm oil, copra (dried coconut meat), and petroleum and natural gas. It is also a major source of nickel, coffee, and tea. Manufacturing has increased greatly since the 1980's, although agriculture (including forestry and fishing) remains the single most important economic activity. Tourism is a growing source of income.

Beginning in 1997, after a decade of rapid economic growth, Indonesia was affected by an economic crisis that began in Thailand and soon spread through much of Southeast Asia. Millions of workers lost their jobs, the value of the currency fell, and prices for basic goods such as sugar, cooking oil, and rice increased dramatically.

Manufacturing. Petroleum and natural gas, textiles, cement, chemical fertilizers, plywood, food products, and rubber are among the nation's most valuable products. Clothing, paper, shoes, and electrical and electronic products also are made there. Much of the manufacturing activity is centered in Java, although the government is encouraging industrial development on other islands.

Agriculture, Forestry, and Fishing. Besides growing crops such as rice, cassava, and corn for food, many Indonesians work on plantations specializing in products for export. These include rubber, copra, palm oil, spices, and sugarcane. Chickens are the most widely found livestock, but goats, cattle, and sheep are also raised.

Indonesia's forests yield many resins, medicines, fibers, and fruits. Bamboo is a plant with many uses, and rattan is made into wicker products, such as furniture. The waters surrounding the islands provide ample quantities of fish for local consumption.

Many illegal fires are set to clear thousands of acres of tropical rain forest for farming and logging. In 1997 and 1998, when the normal monsoon rains did not arrive, the fires raged out of control, causing severe air pollution and health problems.

FACTS and figures

REPUBLIC OF INDONESIA (Republik Indonesia) is the official name of the country.

LOCATION: Southeast Asia.

AREA: 735,269 sq mi (1,904,347 km²).

POPULATION: 242,000,000 (estimate).

CAPITAL AND LARGEST CITY: Jakarta.

MAJOR LANGUAGES: Bahasa Indonesia (official), other languages and dialects.

MAJOR RELIGIOUS GROUPS: Muslim, Christian, Hindu, Buddhist, traditional religions.

GOVERNMENT: Republic. **Head of state**—president. **Head of government**—president. **Legislature**—House of Representatives.

CHIEF PRODUCTS: Agricultural—rice, cassava, peanuts, rubber, cocoa, coffee, palm oil and kernels, copra (dried coconut meat), livestock, sugarcane, corn, bananas, tea, spices (including pepper, nutmeg, and mace), soybeans, tobacco. **Manufactured**—petroleum and natural gas, textiles, cement, chemical fertilizers, plywood, food products, rubber. **Mineral**—petroleum, natural gas, tin, nickel, coal, copper, silver, gold, diamonds.

MONETARY UNIT: Rupiah (1 rupiah = 100 sen).

Mining. Indonesia is the world's largest producer of liquefied natural gas and a leading producer of tin. Bauxite (aluminum ore), nickel, copper, gold, and coal are also mined.

Trade. Indonesia's leading exports include natural gas and petroleum, textiles and clothing, wood products, shoes, and electrical and electronic products. Leading imports include machinery, transportation and electrical equipment, chemicals, and foods. Indonesia's chief trading partners are the United States, Singapore, and Japan.

Transportation. A road and railway network connects cities in Java and Sumatra. Sea and air transportation services link the various islands. The nation's largest airport, the Sukarno-Hatta International Airport, is located outside Jakarta. Garuda Indonesia, the national airline, provides both domestic and international service.

▶ MAJOR CITIES

Jakarta (also known as Djakarta) in western Java, is the capital of Indonesia and the economic center of the nation. Home to approximately 7 million people, Jakarta is by far the most populous city in Indonesia. For more information, see the article JAKARTA in Volume JK.

Surabaya, Indonesia's second largest city, is located in eastern Java. A major port, Surabaya was the primary naval base of the Dutch East Indies before 1942. The city remains a major point of export for Indonesian sugar, coffee, and spices. Also a center of manufacturing, Surabaya's industries include fishing, shipbuilding, textile manufacturing, and petroleum refining.

▶ CULTURAL HERITAGE

Many of Indonesia's arts developed as a result of foreign contact. Hindu and Buddhist influences are seen in many temples, such as those found on the island of Bali and in the Borobudur shrine in central Java.

Drama is often in the form of puppet plays called *wayang*. In these plays, puppets are used to enact stories from such ancient Hindu epic literature as the *Mahabharata* and *Ramayana*. The *wayang* are accompanied by music played by a *gamelan*, an orchestra of mostly percussion instruments.

On the island of Bali, girls from the age of 5 learn dances that tell old Hindu stories.

▶ GOVERNMENT

Indonesia is governed under a constitution that was approved in 1945. A president serves as head of both state and government and is assisted by a cabinet of ministers. The president, formerly elected by a government assembly, has since 2004 been popularly elected for a 5-year term.

Indonesia's one-house legislature is called the Dewan Perwakilan Rakyat (House of Representatives). It consists of 550 members, who are also elected to 5-year terms. Supreme court justices are appointed by the president.

▶ HISTORY

For many decades scientists believed that the earliest human beings lived on Java. In 1891, skull and bone fragments of "Java Man," who lived about 1 million years ago, were found there. But fossil remains of humanlike beings found more recently in eastern Africa predate those in Indonesia.

The Hindu Era. Indian traders and priests from Asia began to settle in parts of Sumatra and Java around the A.D. 100's. They later introduced both the Buddhist and Hindu religions and founded several kingdoms. The most important of these were Sriwidjaya, which flourished on Sumatra from the 600's to the 1200's, and Majapahit, which was dominant on Java from the 1200's to the 1500's. Islam was first introduced to the islands around 1100. It eventually replaced Hinduism as the major religion.

The Arrival of Europeans. The Portuguese who captured Melaka, in Malaysia, in 1511 were the first Europeans to come to the islands. Dutch traders founded the Dutch East India Company in 1602. It lasted until 1798, when the government of the Netherlands took over its functions. Several other European countries, including the United Kingdom, France, and Spain, developed commercial interests on some of the islands. They were soon barred by the Dutch, who gradually established a full colony in the region called the Netherlands East Indies. From the 1600's to the 1800's, the Netherlands slowly spread its influence over the islands.

The Dutch Colonial Period. In the early 1800's, the United Kingdom temporarily occupied Java and some of the other islands. The Netherlands, previously interested only

General Suharto served as president of Indonesia from 1968 to 1998.

in trade, then moved to establish strict political control, which it maintained for the next century. In 1918, a limited voice in government was given to Indonesians with the formation of the Volksraad (People's Council).

The Road to Independence. During World War II (1939–45), Japan's early military successes inspired Indonesian nationalists to take action. Japan also encouraged self-government after it occupied the Indonesian islands. On August 17, 1945, after Japan surrendered to the Allies, a revolutionary government was set up by nationalist leader Sukarno to resist Dutch reoccupation. Indonesia was declared a republic, but the Dutch refused to recognize the self-proclaimed nation. Finally, on December 27, 1949, Indonesia officially gained its independence.

Since Independence. Sukarno served as president of Indonesia from 1949 to 1967. In 1960, he dissolved the legislature. In 1965, he withdrew Indonesia from the United Nations. Later that year, Indonesian Communists attempted a coup against the government. About 500,000 people died in the fighting before the revolt was put down by the army. A new government was formed, led by General Suharto. Sukarno was stripped of power, although he retained the title of president until 1967. Indonesia rejoined the United Nations in 1966. The former Dutch colony of West New Guinea remained under Dutch rule until 1962. In 1969, the United Nations officially gave Indonesia control of the vast territory, now known as Papua. When civil war broke out on Portuguese East Timor in 1975, Indonesians occupied the colony and declared it a province of Indonesia in 1976.

After officially becoming president in 1968, Suharto strengthened the central government, and the economy flourished. But by 1998, riots sparked by rising prices and widespread unemployment forced him to resign.

His successor, B.J. Habibie, proved unable to unify the country.

In 1999, in the first democratic transfer of power in Indonesia's history, Abdurrahman Wahid was elected president and Megawati Sukarnoputri, Sukarno's daughter, was elected vice president. Wahid was unable to end economic hardships or ethnic and religious violence and was impeached by the legislature in July 2001. Megawati then became president. East Timor achieved independence on May 20, 2002. For more information, see the article TIMOR, EAST (TIMOR-LESTE) in Volume T.

In 2002, the government took steps to control militant groups, but terrorists later killed more than 200 people in Bali. Changes in government included constitutional amendments that would allow for direct presidential elections by the people and the elimination of a reserved bloc of parliamentary seats for the military beginning in 2004.

In 2003, scientists made an exciting discovery of a new human species, *Homo floresiensis*, on the island of Flores.

In 2004, former general Susilo Bambang Yudhoyono won a landslide victory in Indonesia's first direct presidential election. Later that year, on December 26, tidal waves caused by an enormous earthquake in the Indian Ocean slammed into Sumatra. About 165,000 people in Indonesia alone were reported dead or missing. At least 800,000 people were left homeless. Another powerful earthquake struck on March 28, 2005, killing about 1,000 more people, mostly on the island of Nias.

In 2005, the government signed a peace agreement with rebels of the Free Aceh Movement (GAM), who had long sought independence. The event ended a civil war that had raged in the province for 30 years.

ANTHONY SAS
University of South Carolina

INDUS CIVILIZATION. See ANCIENT CIVILIZATIONS (Asia: Harappan Civilization).

INDUSTRIAL ARTS

Industrial arts—now known as technology education—is recognized by educators as an integral part of learning in all well-rounded school systems in the United States today.

Industrial arts courses may begin in elementary school with an introduction to basic tools and processes used to make useful products. In junior high and middle schools, students are introduced to various units of study, including electricity, electronics, graphic arts (printing of all types), photography, materials (wood, plastics, and metals), power, transportation, and drafting. These various units may be taught individually or together in a comprehensive classroom.

Although learning about tools and power equipment and developing the skills to use them are very important to industrial arts programs, students eventually learn about the entire process of manufacturing many consumer products. First-hand information is often provided by field trips to various plants and manufacturing locations.

Because industrial technology continues to change, courses are constantly added to present-day technology education programs. The organization of a company and how a business is run, from its finances to the sales and promotion of products and services, are all a part of technology education.

In high school, industrial arts education gives students an opportunity to concentrate on their chosen fields of interest and to develop marketable skills and knowledge. For many this provides entry-level training that employers are quick to recognize. Thus, the possibilities for employment are enhanced.

Postsecondary school students who seek further training in industrial arts technology grow in number each year and many technical schools, colleges, and universities actively recruit them.

The intrinsic value and benefits of industrial arts courses at any level become apparent when participants can say, "I built it. I fixed it. I did it myself."

Reviewed by JOHN L. SZEPESSY
Technology Education Educator

INDUSTRIAL DESIGN

Every human-made object has a design. Throughout history, people have learned that the design or shape of an object has much to do with its usefulness. As people discover new materials and learn to produce things more skillfully, designs change and objects become easier to use.

When people made objects only by hand, designs changed slowly. But with the increased use of machines during the 1600's, changes in design began to occur more rapidly. By the 1830's machines of all kinds were in use, which also allowed identical products to be made quickly and by the thousands.

Early machine-made products were copies of handmade objects, but the machines of that time were unable to reproduce many of the beautiful details of what had been designed as a handmade product. As a result, many early manufactured goods were clumsy. Also, the person who operated a machine was not able to change a product's design. If a product needed a new shape, someone else had to design it. The machine would then have to be

changed so it could make the redesigned product.

Today new product designs and design changes are created by **industrial designers**—people who are specially trained as planners and stylists of mass-produced, machine-made goods. In fact, the designs of almost all the manufactured objects we use, such as cars, bicycles, toasters, telephones, and pens, have been created by industrial designers.

Ansa Plastic Baby Bottle

▶WHAT DETERMINES DESIGN?

Many things affect the design of objects. Among these are the way people live, the materials available for making objects, and the current technology.

A well-designed product suits the age in which it is created. In England in the 1700's, a silver coffeepot was carefully made by hand to fit the very formal life of the upper classes. The practical value of such a product was less important than how it looked. An intricately decorated coffeepot took a long time to make, but the cost of the labor of people to make it was cheap. The silver needed frequent cleaning, but the people who owned silver objects often had servants who kept them polished. Today, such labor is expensive and scarce. A coffeepot manufactured out of stainless steel, aluminum, or Pyrex glass is more suited to modern life. It can be made quickly and inexpensively, is easy to keep clean, and is free of extraneous decoration. Today life is more casual. Machine-made objects are designed as much for use as for decoration. They are made to be practical as well as good looking.

Chemex Pyrex Coffee Maker

Science and New Materials

Science makes possible the use of new materials and new methods of producing objects. Materials developed in the 20th century, such as plastics and special metals, were un-

Trimline Telephone by Henry Dreyfuss, 1965

dreamed of in earlier centuries. Today's mass-production techniques could not have been developed without modern technology.

New materials sometimes also lead to new forms for objects. For example, plastic made it possible to manufacture objects out of a single, continuous piece of material. Such molded plastic eliminates the need for joints and for the assembling of individual parts. It can be molded quickly as one piece, with little finishing work required. As a result, plastic has changed the form of many household products and furniture.

The Principles of Design

Ideas of what is good design change with the times. The modern industrial age has developed its own principles for design. One principle states that the design of a product must contribute to its use or function. Equally important, the materials used to make the

product must be suitable. A third principle is that the method of production must be considered. The taste and skill of each industrial designer guides his or her use of each of these principles.

Functionalism. Functionalism means that the shape of an object is determined by its use. A drinking glass must be shaped so it can contain liquids, be held comfortably and securely, and be cleaned easily. A car must operate properly, and be comfortable and easy to drive. An airplane must be shaped a certain way or it will not rise and move through the air. The principle of functionalism was first summed up by Louis Sullivan (1856–1924), an American architect, who said that "form follows function." A center of modern functional style was the Bauhaus, an art school in Germany. Founded in 1919, the Bauhaus helped spread modern design principles all over the world.

Use of Materials. Industrial designers should be familiar with the physical properties of the materials they can use. For example, because plastic is lightweight and does not break as easily as glass, it is a good material for soft-drink or baby bottles. Plastic melts or burns when heated, however, so it does not make a good frying pan. Different products require materials of different weights and strengths.

Methods of Production. Designers also need to consider the technical problems involved in making a product. They must make sure that a machine is available or can be built that will produce the object correctly. Generally they must understand machine production and work closely with industrial engineers.

▶ HOW A DESIGNER WORKS

When industrial designers are hired by a manufacturer, they are told about the product to be designed or redesigned and are given information about its purpose and how and where it will be used.

Dining Chair by Charles Eames, 1946

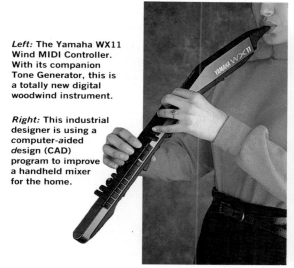

Left: The Yamaha WX11 Wind MIDI Controller. With its companion Tone Generator, this is a totally new digital woodwind instrument.

Right: This industrial designer is using a computer-*ai*ded *d*esign (CAD) program to improve a handheld mixer for the home.

They try to determine the needs and tastes of potential buyers, and they study similar products made by competing companies. The designers talk to the manufacturer's engineers about materials and construction, and learn what equipment is available in the factory.

On the basis of this information, a design is created and drawings are made of the product. Many changes may be made in these drawings before a design is finished. **Mock-ups**, or full-sized models, of the product are often made out of wood, plaster, or cardboard. When the manufacturer approves the design, a final model is made. Today computers are frequently used in the design process, often replacing hand-drawn plans and small-scale models. This technique is known as *c*omputer-*ai*ded *d*esign, or CAD.

Large design firms have a staff of specialists —draftspeople, illustrators, engineers, market researchers, and modelmakers—working under the direction of industrial designers. Some firms offer many specialized services as well as a total design service—designing everything connected with a business from the buildings to the stationery. Industrial design firms may also serve as consultants or advisors to those companies that have their own design departments.

▶INDUSTRIAL DESIGN SINCE THE BAUHAUS

In the late 1920's and early 1930's, many mass-produced appliances were redesigned because the pioneers of American industrial design, Raymond F. Loewy (1893–1986), Henry Dreyfuss (1904–1972), and Walter Dorwin Teague (1883–1960), convinced manufacturers that well-designed products could sell better than products that were badly designed.

Streamlining. American designer Norman Bel Geddes (1893–1958) was among the first to use **streamlining** in design—the technique of designing objects so that they have long, curving lines with no sharp angles. Streamlining allows air or water to flow easily over an object, and it is well suited to objects designed for speed, such as airplanes, boats, trains, and cars. But streamlining became a fad and was applied to all kinds of products, such as toasters and teapots, that did not need to be designed that way. In these instances, styling went against the principle of functionalism and in fact sometimes even interfered with the usefulness of the product. More often than not, however, industrial designers improve objects so that they are more efficient and better looking.

In recent years the miniaturization of electronic parts has had an impact on the design of products. The internal components of many machines are now so small that they no longer need to influence the outer form of the machine. As a result, designers are free to consider other factors, such as **ergonomics**—the study of how things such as machines and work situations can be adapted and used more effectively by people.

Reviewed by CARA MCCARTY
The Museum of Modern Art

See also COMMERCIAL ART; DECORATIVE ARTS; DESIGN; MANUFACTURING.

The factory system, which enabled a sharp increase in the production of goods, played a key role in the Industrial Revolution. This photo, taken in England in 1897, shows women working in a cotton mill.

INDUSTRIAL REVOLUTION

The Industrial Revolution began in England about 1760 and spread to the rest of Europe and the United States through the early 1800's. It is called a "revolution" because it caused great and sudden changes that dramatically affected the way people worked and lived. In many ways, the Industrial Revolution created the modern world.

The revolution began with the invention of new machines to manufacture cotton. These machines used new sources of energy: water and steam power. The machines brought great improvements by mass-producing cheaper products while creating new jobs for unskilled factory workers.

The Industrial Revolution led to new prosperity. Millions of people worldwide enjoyed a higher standard of living. But it also brought new problems. Low paid workers spent long hours in dangerous conditions. Child labor became common. Workers who had produced handmade goods at home lost their jobs because they could not compete with mass production by machines.

▶ FROM COTTAGES TO FACTORIES

By the mid-1700's, one particular industry in England had grown in importance: the production of cotton cloth. The first step was spinning cotton fibers into thread, or yarn, on a spinning wheel. Then the thread was woven into cloth on a hand loom. Because the spinners and weavers worked in their own houses, or cottages, spinning and weaving were known as **cottage industries**.

Usually, women did the spinning and men did the weaving. Agents collected the thread after it was spun and took it to the weavers, who then wove the cloth on their looms. The agents then collected the cloth and took it to market. Spinning took more time than weaving. As many as four spinners had to work to keep one weaver supplied with enough thread to stay busy.

Improvements in Spinning and Weaving

The Industrial Revolution in England led to improvements in both spinning machinery and the looms used to weave cloth. A loom has two sets of threads: the warp and the weft. The **warp** consists of strong threads that run lengthwise on the loom (from front to back). The **weft** is a single strand of thread. An instrument called a **shuttle** carries the weft thread across the loom, over and under the warp threads, weaving the two together.

Weavers moved the shuttle back and forth by hand until 1733, when an Englishman

Left: Before factories were built in the late 1700's, people made cloth and other goods by hand. Because they worked in their homes, or cottages, their businesses were called cottage industries.

Below: Arkwright's water frame sped the production of cotton thread. When he began operating several machines together under one roof, the factory system was born.

named John Kay patented an invention called the **flying shuttle**. This hollow wooden object, pointed at each end, contained the weft thread wound on a **bobbin**, or spool. A mechanical arm activated by a spring shot the flying shuttle across the warp. This process made weaving go faster than ever before.

The invention of the flying shuttle made it even more difficult for the spinners to keep the weavers supplied with thread. In 1764, an Englishman named James Hargreaves saw a better way to spin thread when he saw a spinning wheel fall over and its spindle continue to turn while in a vertical (upright) position. Hargreaves built a machine with eight vertical spindles in a row, linked together so that they all turned at once. His machine made it possible to spin half a dozen or more threads at the same time. He called the machine a **spinning jenny**. (Scholars are not sure but believe the jenny was named for Hargreaves' daughter.)

The first spinning jennies were operated by hand. But they spun thread so fast that weavers—working at hand looms—could not keep up with the tremendous supply.

Water Power and the Factory System

Before the Industrial Revolution, swift-flowing streams throughout Europe turned waterwheels, which were used to power machinery. In 1769, Richard Arkwright invented and patented a water-powered spinning machine called a **water frame**. Arkwright gathered many machines in one building, close to a river. He used shafts and belts to connect the machines to a waterwheel. The river's

current turned the waterwheel, which powered the machines.

In doing this, Arkwright began moving the English textile industry out of cottages and into **factories** (or mills, as they were called), where numerous workers and machines could operate under one roof. Arkwright's achievement earned him the title the father of the factory system. The development of the factories sped up production to an astonishing degree.

In 1779, Samuel Crompton used ideas from Hargreaves' and Arkwright's inventions to build an even better spinning machine called a **spinning mule**. Then in 1785, Edmund Cartwright built the first mechanical loom, which helped weavers keep up with spinners. These inventions encouraged the transfer of cloth production from cottages to factories.

Beginning in the 1790's, plantations in the southern United States began contributing to the growth of the English textile industry. They produced enough cotton to supply Eng-

The Watt steam engine, based on an invention of Thomas Newcomen's, was used to pump water out of flooded mine shafts. Steam engines made it possible for coal miners to dig deeper than ever before.

lish textile mills with all the raw material they needed. The invention of Eli Whitney's **cotton gin** (or engine) in 1793 (patented in 1794) sped up the processing of raw cotton. It efficiently removed seeds from cotton so that large amounts of fiber could be prepared for export.

▶ **A NEW WORLD OF POWER**

In addition to flowing water, England had two other key resources to power the Industrial Revolution: iron and coal. And coal mining led to the invention of the steam engine.

Iron and Coal

People had used iron for thousands of years. It came from a rocky ore that miners dug up from under the ground or found just below its surface. The iron had to be separated from the ore and impurities. The iron was then melted down, or smelted, and used to make many products such as tools, weapons, utensils, and axles.

About 1700 an English inventor, Abraham Darby, began experimenting with coal as a means of smelting iron. By removing some of the coal's impurities, he created a substance called **coke**, which burned even hotter than coal itself. This discovery opened the door to a new world of power.

For a while there was great activity in England's coal mines. After the coal near the surface of the ground was used up, the miners dug deeper to find underground deposits. It was then that they ran into trouble. England gets a lot of rain, which seeps deep into the ground. This water flooded the underground coal mines. The solution to this problem came from a new invention based on steam power.

The Steam Engine

About 1710, Thomas Newcomen invented an "atmospheric" engine that harnessed the power of steam. Although slow and inefficient, Newcomen's steam engine was a tremendous advance. It replaced human power in pumping out England's flooded coal mines, enabling miners to dig deeper than they ever had before. The engine used almost as much coal as it helped to mine. Still, because Newcomen's engine led to the practical use of steam power, he is hailed as one of the great inventors of all time.

The Pace of Change Quickens

James Watt experimented with Newcomen's invention, hoping to create a better steam engine. The Watt steam engine, patented in 1769, used less fuel and proved more efficient than Newcomen's. With a business partner, Matthew Boulton, Watt began producing his steam engines in the 1770's.

All across England, steam engines began to replace waterwheels. Since steam engines could operate anywhere, factories were soon being built in cities where the labor supply was more plentiful.

The development of steam power opened up a new world of technical possibilities. Changes in the manufacture of iron and steel kept up the pace of industrialization. In 1784, Henry Cort invented a new way to refine pig iron (crude iron) that caused the price of wrought iron to plunge. Cort's process produced most of the metal used to build the machinery associated with the Industrial Revolution. By 1750, Benjamin Huntsman had invented a method to manufacture cast steel. Before, steel had been too expensive and unreliable for widespread use. Huntsman's improved steel led to increased demand. Industrialists built huge ironworks and eventually steel mills to make machines, tools, and engines.

The use of machines in the cotton industry, Watt's steam engine, and improved iron and steel technologies built a solid economic platform. Many new industries were launched, while at the same time some older industries expanded in new ways.

▶ SOCIAL EFFECTS

The factory system introduced dramatic changes in how people lived and worked. Families moved to cities to find work. As a result, country villages became deserted and the cities grew by leaps and bounds, a process called **urbanization**.

At the factory, for the first time, workers were expected to work together in the same place, and their workday began and ended at specific times. Foremen closely supervised

---

WONDER QUESTION

How did the factory town of Lowell get its name?

Francis Cabot Lowell, a successful Massachusetts businessman, visited England about 1810 and toured its textile factories. The visit inspired Lowell to open a factory in the United States. In 1814, he joined with several other investors to open the Boston Manufacturing Company in Waltham, Massachusetts. The company's new factory purchased raw cotton and then performed all the steps necessary to turn it into finished cloth. Lowell furnished the factory with power looms copied from the ones he had seen in England. The successful factory was the first of its kind in the United States.

A few years after Lowell's death, his associates began buying riverfront land around East Chelmsford, Massachusetts, a former rural village. They created a town filled with water-powered cotton mills and named it Lowell in honor of their late partner. By the mid-1800's, the town of Lowell had more than fifty mills that employed about 13,000 workers and produced more than 2 million yards (1.8 million meters) of cotton cloth per year. It was the most productive industrial town in the nation. Girls and young women from the surrounding farms flocked to Lowell to become "mill girls." They lived in boarding houses where they were subject to strict rules of behavior and supervised by older women. As working conditions grew more harsh, the life of a Lowell mill girl lost its attraction for local women, and immigrants took their places at the mills.

---

their work. These changes caused conflicts between workers and employers.

In addition, the construction of new factories and the purchase of new equipment was expensive. To help earn back their investments, factory owners wanted to use the cheapest labor possible to increase their profits. It took very little strength or skill to operate the machines, so factory owners employed unskilled workers and children. Sometimes whole families went to work, often under very poor conditions. The factories were hot and dusty. Workers labored for up to 16 hours a day. There were no labor unions to protect workers. The poorly paid workers lived near the factories in the most crowded, dirty, and unsanitary districts of towns or cities. As a result, many factory workers became ill or died.

By the end of the 1700's, British reformers had already begun to expose the bad conditions in the industrial towns. Parliament introduced laws to limit working hours and forbid the employment of very young children. In the 1800's, writers such as Charles Dickens—once a child factory worker himself—wrote novels about the hardships endured by industrial workers. In response to public outcry, some British employers, including Robert Peel, Robert Owen, and John Fielden, tried to improve conditions in their factories. Yet in most factories, working conditions improved only after workers began organizing protests to demand change.

▶ THE TRANSPORTATION REVOLUTION

Industrialization and urbanization required supplies of heavy, bulky raw materials such as coal and iron. Transport costs were high. If a factory was close to a mine, coal was cheap. But coal quickly became expensive if it had to be moved long distances. The first solution was to use water to transport goods. This led to the widespread construction of canals, with goods transported on barges towed by mules or horses. But just as reliance on water power limited where factories could be built, so canals could not be built everywhere.

Steam engines and advances in metal manufacture led to a new solution: steam locomotives running along iron rails. By 1830 railroads proved themselves superior to horse-drawn transport, and a transportation revolution began. For the first time in history

In an 1872 engraving of London, French artist Gustave Doré showed the wretchedness of low-paid industrial workers who were forced to live in crowded slums blackened by the grime of nearby factories.

the water. In 1807, the American inventor Robert Fulton launched a steamboat on New York's Hudson River. Steamboats could move up or down rivers regardless of current and wind and linked inland settlements with ports on the coast. They allowed producers who lived far from the sea to sell their products to distant markets. Later, technical improvements brought steam power to the high seas. The combination of railroads and steamships opened up more possibilities for trade worldwide.

▶ THE INDUSTRIAL REVOLUTION SPREADS

About 1800, the Industrial Revolution spread to western continental Europe and across the Atlantic Ocean to the United States. Belgium was the first western European country to follow the British example of industrialization. It had long experience in the textile and metal trades. Just as in Great Britain, these industries were the first to change.

Two Englishmen, William Cockerill and his son John, brought the Industrial Revolution to Belgium. They set up wool-spinning mills in Verviers in 1799 and machine shops in

there was a means to travel over land that was hardly affected by the weather and could cheaply and quickly move large volumes of freight and passengers.

Meanwhile, a number of inventors turned to the challenge of using steam engines on

Profiles

Consult the Index to find more information in *The New Book of Knowledge* about the following people associated with the Industrial Revolution: Sir Henry Bessemer, John Deere, Oliver Evans, Robert Fulton, Elias Howe, Cyrus McCormick, Robert Owen, James Watt, and Eli Whitney.

Richard Arkwright

Samuel Crompton

industrial settings. He began as an apprentice in his father's business, a workshop that made metal products, and later took over management of the family business. In 1762, Boulton used his savings to open a large water-powered factory, the Soho (Iron) Works in Birmingham. The factory produced decorative metal objects, such as buckles, until Boulton went into business with James Watt in 1775. The Soho Works then began manufacturing steam engines and converted its own machinery from water to steam power.

Samuel Crompton (1753–1827), born in Lancashire, England, invented the spinning mule in 1779. A weaver by trade, Crompton spent his own money and five years working on the idea in his spare time. His machine revolutionized spinning, rapidly producing thread that was both finer and stronger than the thread

Sir Richard Arkwright (1732–92), born in Preston, Lancashire, England, established England's earliest water-powered textile mills. He was born into poverty and had little education. While working as a barber and wig-maker, Arkwright grew interested in textile machinery. He began experimenting with new designs and he developed a revolutionary spinning machine called a water frame. Arkwright became the leading textile manufacturer of

his time. His cotton mills, which employed about 5,000 workers, made him wealthy. Coincidentally, Arkwright's home town, Preston, became a major industrial town.

Matthew Boulton (1728–1809), born in Birmingham, England, became a leading manufacturer of metal products, including Watt steam engines, and promoted the use of steam engines in a variety of

Liège in 1807. Belgium had abundant coal and iron resources. It installed the newest British technologies for its iron smelting, pig iron production, and metal processing and fabrication. It was also the first country on the continent of Europe to build a blast furnace and later became the first to manufacture locomotives and iron ships. Belgium's ability to use copies of British inventions and innovations, combined with its iron and coal resources, allowed it to develop earlier and faster than other nations.

At the time the Industrial Revolution was sweeping through Great Britain, European nations were fighting one another in the Napoleonic Wars (1792–1815), which delayed the spread of invention and innovation. But in the 1820's, French scientists made many improvements in water power, including building the first version of the modern turbine. In Germany, the introduction and increased use of railroads provided the drive toward industrialization.

By 1850, Belgium, France, and Germany had made impressive industrial progress. However, they remained well behind Great Britain, the leader. But as inventions spread, they led to other changes. For example, deeper coal mines required the development of powerful steam pumps to drain water from the mine. A modified steam engine, placed on a frame with wheels, became a locomotive.

Improvements in heavy industry, particularly the development of the Bessemer steel-making process, accelerated the Industrial Revolution.

Locomotives required iron rails, which created a huge demand for mass-produced iron. Iron manufacture relied on coke, which in turn increased the demand for coal. This kind of rapid growth in several related industries had never before happened.

spun by earlier machines. Crompton failed to patent the spinning mule and was unable to profit from it, while many textile manufacturers used Crompton's mule in their factories and made fortunes. In 1812, Parliament gave Crompton a small cash reward for his invention, which by then had been installed in hundreds of spinning mills.

James Hargreaves (1722?–78), born in Lancashire, England, invented the spinning jenny about 1764. Poor and uneducated, Hargreaves worked as a spinner and weaver. He built and sold the spinning jennies to add to his income. Hand-spinners, fearing that Hargreaves' invention would make their jobs obsolete, raided his home and wrecked several machines. He fled with his family to Nottingham in 1768 and built a small, modestly successful spinning mill, where he worked for the rest of his life.

Thomas Newcomen (1663–1729), born in Dartmouth, England, was making and

Slater's Mill, Rhode Island

selling iron goods for a living when he decided to develop a machine to pump water out of mines. He spent ten years working on his idea for a steam engine. Another Englishman, Thomas Savery

(1650?–1715), held the patent (1698) for an inferior steam engine design, so Newcomen went into business with him to make and sell engines. The first Newcomen steam engine began pumping water out of an English mine in 1712.

Samuel Slater (1768–1835), born in Derbyshire, England, brought his knowledge of textile manufacturing to the United States and opened its first successful cotton spinning mill. Slater started out as an apprentice in an English textile factory under a partner of Richard Arkwright. While still in his teens, Slater demonstrated great skill with machinery. At the age of 21, he defied British law by going to the United States to use his skills. For his first mill in Pawtucket, Rhode Island, Slater had textile machinery built from designs he had memorized. He spent the rest of his life in New England and went on to build several successful cotton mills. (For more information, see RHODE ISLAND [Places of Interest].)

FROM FIELD TO FACTORY

In 1837, John Deere, whose name appears on the familiar green tractor seen on modern farms, changed the lives of farmers by improving the traditional horse-drawn plow. Deere started out as a New England blacksmith. He moved to Illinois, where farmers faced the backbreaking labor of plowing up prairie grass to create fields for their crops. Deere made their lives easier by adding steel strips to the plow, or "sodbuster." He began manufacturing farm equipment in 1868.

Farmers had always harvested grain by hand until Virginia farmer Cyrus McCormick invented a horse-drawn mechanical reaper in 1831. It was the first machine ever to harvest grain. The earliest model made so much noise that it frightened the horses. Like John Deere,

"OUR FIELD IS THE WORLD."

McCormick Harvesting Machine Co., Chicago.
ESTABLISHED 1831.

McCormick moved to Illinois to sell his machine to prairie farmers with huge fields to harvest. He patented his reaper in 1854 and began manufacturing reapers at his McCormick Harvesting Company. His reapers were sold around the world. McCormick's son merged the company with several others in 1902 to form International Harvester.

In the United States

The United States emerged from the Revolutionary War (1775–83) far behind in the race to industrialize. Great Britain wanted to protect its industrial power by preventing the export of machinery or skilled workers. Parliament outlawed the sale of English machinery to the United States. Laws even prohibited English inventors and skilled workers from emigrating there.

An English textile worker, Samuel Slater, realized that a fortune could be made by the person who introduced cotton manufacturing to the Americans. He outwitted British authorities and arrived in the United States in 1789 with the knowledge of English textile machinery in his head. A Rhode Island company provided the money for him to build spinning and carding machines like the ones he remembered.

Slater's mill used the force of flowing water to power the machinery. Since water power was widely available in New England, there was ample opportunity for industry to spread. The success of Slater's mill led to the construction of new mills throughout New England.

The Mill Village. At first, most textile manufacture took place in small mills located in villages that had reliable flowing water. The spinning mill became the economic center of these "mill villages." A mill employed up to 70 people. Often entire families worked at the mill or the adult men farmed nearby land owned by the mill owner.

Inside the mill adult men made up about 30 percent of the workforce. They performed the skilled jobs, including hand loom weaving and machine maintenance. Adult women made up about 40 percent of the workforce. They operated the spinning machines, and after the introduction of power looms, they ran them as well. Children, usually the offspring of the adult mill workers, completed the labor force. They performed many unskilled jobs and received low wages.

The small mill village was almost a self-contained world. There were social advantages to a work environment where everyone knew one another. Yet the mill owner dominated local economic life and enjoyed almost unchecked power. A bad or corrupt owner could financially ruin a family. However, most owners at this time treated their workers fairly. Ahead lay a much different future when textile production moved to large mills located in urban areas.

Railroads and Steelmaking. The railroad proved to be the driving force behind the Industrial Revolution in the United States.

Railroads linked different regions into a single national market, thus providing new opportunities for manufacturers. Producers found they could sell to distant markets, fueling more growth. Railroad construction led to the rapid expansion of the coal, iron, steel, and machine tool industries.

Steel mills began using an efficient new process to convert iron to steel. Henry Bessemer introduced his process in England in 1856. (In the United States, William Kelly developed a nearly identical process about the same time, but Bessemer patented his process first.) The Bessemer process produced steel that was well-suited for making rails for railroad tracks. The competing inventors eventually formed a business partnership and opened a steel mill in the United States.

The Industrial Revolution in Other Countries

Industrialization came to eastern and southern Europe and to Asia long after it had been firmly established in northern and western Europe and North America. Industrialization did not spread through Russia until the late 1800's. Japan began to industrialize toward the end of the 1800's and became a full-fledged industrial power by the 1920's. China did not become an industrial power until after World War II (1939–45).

Although each country followed its own path, industrialization usually first came to the textile industry. Later, the expansion of the railroads provided the force behind economic growth.

▶ THE DEVELOPMENT OF LABOR MOVEMENTS

As nations became more industrialized and the factory system grew, labor conditions worsened. Workers, particularly children, suffered from the eagerness of employers to make money at the expense of their employees' welfare.

The Industrial Revolution was both a revolution in technology and a revolution in the organization of production. The factory symbolized the Industrial Revolution. Inside the factory large groups of workers labored in new ways. They had to work faster and according to the schedule set by the owner. Much factory work was dirty and dangerous. Exposure to chemicals, dust, and waste by-products led to serious diseases. Unskilled workers knew that if they fell sick, got injured, or complained, they could easily be replaced.

Workers responded to harsh working conditions at first by protesting. Later they created organizations to promote change. Workers came to realize that they had to unite in order to negotiate with the owners, and so the labor movement was born. Every country experienced strikes, civil disorders, and violence between labor unions and business owners. Most, like Great Britain and the United States, eventually made necessary changes to improve workers' lives. But in other places, such as Russia, change came only as a result of a violent revolution.

JAMES R. ARNOLD
ROBERTA WIENER
Coauthors, *The Industrial Revolution*

See also CANALS; CHILD LABOR; CITIES (The History of Cities: The Industrial Age); INVENTIONS; LABOR MOVEMENT (How the Labor Movement Began); LOCOMOTIVES; MANUFACTURING; RAILROADS (History); STEAM ENGINES.

INDUSTRIAL WORKERS OF THE WORLD. See LABOR MOVEMENT.

WONDER QUESTION

Who were the Luddites?

Beginning in 1811, thousands of English handicraft workers protested violently against the use of industrial machinery. People who worked at such trades as knitting stockings and finishing woolen cloth feared that the new machines would take away their jobs. The protestors claimed that their leader was a man named Ned Ludd, but there was probably no such person. The Luddites organized into masked bands and conducted nighttime raids against factories and factory owners' homes. They smashed machines and set buildings on fire. Luddites murdered one factory owner who had ordered his men to gun down a band of protestors. By 1813, British authorities had squashed the Luddite movement, hanging the leaders and deporting many others to distant lands. The term "Luddite" is still used to describe someone who dislikes new technology.

INDUSTRY

The term "industry" is used to group companies that make the same kind of products or perform the same type of services. For example, companies that manufacture automobiles and other vehicles are part of the automotive industry. Those that process milk, butter, and cheese are included in the dairy industry. Banks and loan companies are part of the financial services industry.

Companies invest in countries that offer lower operating costs, including salaries. Here, factory workers in China produce shoes for a U.S. firm.

▶ KINDS OF INDUSTRY

Industries mainly produce goods or services, but some produce both. Manufacturing is an example of a goods-producing industry. Health care, insurance, and real estate are examples of service industries. The information industry offers both goods, such as printed magazines, and services, such as on-line news. (For a list of industries, see the feature accompanying this article.)

▶ WHAT INDUSTRY NEEDS

Industries require many inputs, including raw materials, labor, capital, and technology. There are two types of capital: finance capital, which is money, and physical capital, which includes buildings, machinery, and equipment. The mix of these inputs depends on the type of industry using them.

Raw Materials. Raw materials are natural or partially manufactured products that are used to make a new product. For example, manufacturing a pair of shoes requires leather for the uppers, rubber or leather for the soles, and rubber or wood for the heels.

Labor. Labor consists of the people employed by industry. A shoe company may employ people who make shoes, as well as those who sell them, along with support staff who maintain the company's computer network.

Capital. All industries require finance capital. A shoe company may use its capital to buy raw materials, pay its workers, and invest in researching and developing future products. It may also purchase physical capital, such as the machinery needed to make shoes.

Technology. All industries use technology. In recent decades, companies have benefited greatly from advances in communications technology. For example, a shoe company may use the Internet to advertise and sell its shoes. Or it may employ new production technologies to make its shoes faster and cheaper.

Management. Management plans, organizes, and oversees the work of the company. It sets out the work to be done, hires people, and coordinates all activities to meet production, marketing, and profit goals. It also works to keep production costs low so the company can sell its shoes at competitive prices.

Other Requirements. Industries require marketing strategies that inform their customers about their products and persuade them to buy them. They also need distribution networks that place their products in the markets where customers will buy them.

▶ DEVELOPMENTS AND TRENDS

By World War II (1939–45), the world's high-income countries, including England, France, Germany, and the United States, had strong manufacturing sectors. In contrast, the majority of people in most lower-income, or developing, countries worked in agriculture. But that changed in the 1970's and 1980's, as developing countries invested more in manufacturing and the number of manufacturing jobs grew.

By the late 1980's, some types of manufacturing began to shift from the high-income countries to the developing ones. For example, clothing output fell over time in the United States and rose in the developing countries of Brazil, China, India, and Mexico. This was partly because the developing countries were increasingly able to manufacture and export the type and quality of clothing that high-income countries wanted. It was also because U.S. clothing manufacturers moved their operations to developing countries, where costs, including salaries, were lower. **Offshoring** is the process of transferring business from one location to another to take advantage of lower costs.

Many companies from high-income countries now manufacture in China because it is cheaper to manufacture there than in their own countries. They export the goods they produce to their own and other countries. They also sell them in China's rapidly growing market of more than one billion people.

A number of developing countries are now major exporters of manufactured goods. Low-cost producers in Southeast Asia; South Asia, specifically China and India; Latin America; and Eastern Europe now provide more than 70 percent of footwear, 60 percent of audio and video equipment, and 45 percent of clothing sold in the United States.

The Shift to Services. For much of the 1900's, service industries grew alongside and supported those producing goods. Then, in the late 1960's, some services began to grow rapidly, helped by advances in computer and communications technologies. These advances enabled many service firms to process, package, and distribute their information faster, creating new services. They also made it easier to reach and serve more customers, even those in distant countries. The growth in service industries created jobs and income for people to buy more services as well as goods.

The world's high-income countries now devote more than half their economies to producing services. The same is true of some of the more advanced developing countries, such as Brazil and Mexico.

Over the next decade, continuing advances in communications, worker skills, transportation, and computing will make it easier for companies in many industries to operate and sell all over the world. More and more, companies will look outside their own countries for customers. They will also locate their operations wherever raw materials, lower cost labor, and technology enable them to produce cheaper and better products. In the process, manufacturing industries will continue to shift from high-income countries to lower income ones. And the high-income countries will concentrate on industries in which they are competitive.

Those trends are part of a process known as **globalization**—an increasing interaction among the people, companies, organizations, and countries of the world. Globalization is providing opportunities for companies in many industries to cut costs, find talented employees, and serve new customers. It is also presenting many challenges, as the number of world-class industry competitors rise.

DAVID YOUNG
The Boston Consulting Group

See also GLOBALIZATION; INDUSTRIAL REVOLUTION; INVENTIONS; TRANSPORTATION; articles on individual industries, such as IRON AND STEEL.

INERTIA. See MOTION.
INFECTION. See DISEASES.
INFINITY. See NUMBERS AND NUMBER SYSTEMS.

THE NORTH AMERICAN INDUSTRY CLASSIFICATION SYSTEM

The North American Industry Classification System (NAICS) was developed jointly by Canada, Mexico, and the United States. It replaced the U.S. Standard Industrial Classification (SIC) system. NAICS classifies the major divisions of industry as follows:

1. Agriculture, forestry, fishing, and hunting.
2. Mining, including extracting oil.
3. Utilities, including electric power.
4. Construction.
5. Manufacturing.
6. Wholesale trade.
7. Retail trade.
8. Transportation and warehousing.
9. Information, including print and online publishing.
10. Finance and insurance.
11. Real estate, rental and leasing.
12. Professional, scientific, and technical services.
13. Management of companies.
14. Administrative services.
15. Educational services, including colleges.
16. Health care and social assistance.
17. Arts, entertainment, and recreation.
18. Accommodation and food services.
19. Other services.
20. Public or government administration.

INFLATION AND DEFLATION

Inflation and deflation are movements in the average level of prices. Inflation is an upward movement; deflation is a downward movement.

With inflation, too much money chases too few goods, and prices rise—or costs rise and businesses pass them along to buyers in the form of higher prices. During a deflation, people have less money to spend and do not buy goods and services fast enough to use up those available. They spend so slowly that prices drop.

▶ WHAT CAUSES INFLATION?

An economy is working best when everyone who needs a job has one and when many goods and services are being produced. A slight upward shift in prices can help the economy grow. But a steady rise in the level of prices—or inflation—causes the real value of money to fall and thus reduces the number of things it will buy.

For example, a dollar is always worth 100 cents, but if the price of a candy bar increases from 50 cents to 100 cents, a dollar will buy only one candy bar instead of two.

When people realize their money is losing value, they hurry to buy before prices get any higher. Businesses perceive this as a growing demand for their products. They put money into new products, machinery, and factories. With their goods selling well, they may borrow money to expand their businesses. With businesses growing, there is a greater demand for workers. As a result, people get bigger salaries, spend their extra money, and may even borrow money to spend on goods. All of this can contribute to an upward pressure on prices.

Increases in prices may then cause workers to ask for higher salaries. This pushes up the cost of running a business, which, in turn, puts pressure on the business to raise prices again, and the whole process of inflation starts anew.

▶ WHAT CAUSES DEFLATION?

Deflation has been very rare in the past. A deflation may start when businesses find that their products are not selling well. This might be because they expected a bigger market. Soon they are not making enough money to repay money they borrowed from banks. They have to close down and lay off their workers, who then have less or no money to live on or to pay their debts. Other businesses also fail, and jobs become more difficult to get.

A **depression** is a period when many businesses are no longer active and many people are out of work. During the Great Depression of the 1930's, deflation occurred and many people were out of work.

▶ WHO BENEFITS FROM INFLATION?

Some people benefit during a period of inflation. People tend to buy real estate rather

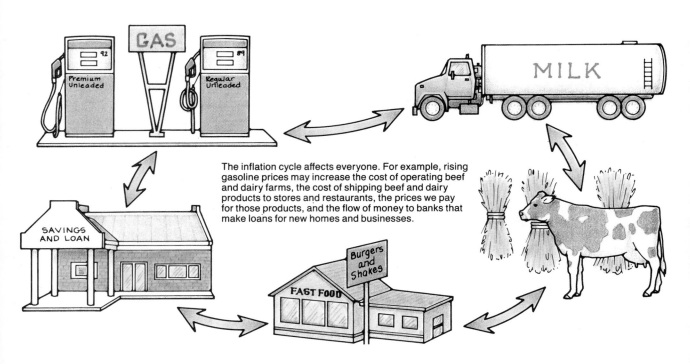

The inflation cycle affects everyone. For example, rising gasoline prices may increase the cost of operating beef and dairy farms, the cost of shipping beef and dairy products to stores and restaurants, the prices we pay for those products, and the flow of money to banks that make loans for new homes and businesses.

than to hold on to their dollars during an inflation because they believe that real estate will maintain its value or rise in value. This creates more demand for real estate and helps push up real estate prices. People who own real estate at the start of inflation can benefit from these price increases when they sell their property. People who have debts also benefit from inflation because their incomes rise while the value of their debt remains fixed.

The people who suffer during inflation are savers, people on pensions, those who earn a fixed salary, and creditors (people who lend money).

For example, a person lends $100 to a friend, who pays the money back a year later. During the year, prices double. So the lender receives the $100 back but can only buy the same amount of goods that $50 would have bought at the time when the loan was made.

There was a "galloping" inflation in Germany from 1920 to 1923. Prices rose a trillion times and completely wiped out Germany's savers and creditors, as money became worthless.

▶ WHO BENEFITS FROM DEFLATION?

During deflations, prices fall, and creditors, savers, and people on fixed incomes get greater value for their money.

For example, a person lends $100 to a friend, who pays the money back a year later. During the year, prices fall by half. So, the lender receives $100 back and can buy twice the amount of goods. Other people also take a loss—for example, when businesses sell goods at lower prices than they paid for them.

Nobody benefits from inflation or deflation for long. For example, Social Security payments in the United States and the United Kingdom go up automatically during an inflation. But as incomes become greater, the prices of goods are also rising.

▶ HOW GOVERNMENTS HELP MANAGE INFLATION AND DEFLATION

Before a government tries to manage inflation, it attempts to understand what is causing it. If the wrong policies are used, they may have the opposite effect from what was intended. Many different tools may be used, including directly controlling wages and prices. But the most important tools used by government economists are monetary and fiscal policies.

Monetary policy influences how an economy performs with respect to inflation, production, employment, and other factors. It works by influencing demand across the economy—that is, people's and firms' willingness to spend on goods and services.

In the United States, the Federal Reserve System, the country's central bank, is responsible for devising monetary policy. The Federal Reserve influences demand mainly by raising and lowering short-term interest rates (the percentage charged for the use of borrowed money). When short-term interest rates rise, there is usually a drop in money and credit. When short-term interest rates fall, the amount of money and credit in the economy usually increase.

The Federal Reserve's interest rate policies affect all kinds of economic and financial decisions people make—whether to get a loan to buy a new house or car or to start up a company; whether to expand a business by investing in a new plant or equipment; or whether to put savings in a bank, in bonds, or in the stock market.

The Federal Reserve tries to expand money and credit when businesses are failing and unemployment is rising. When inflation threatens, it tries to put on the brakes and reduce money and credit.

Fiscal policy influences the economy by changing how people are taxed and how the government spends its money.

In an inflationary period, the government may try to spend less than it receives in taxes. When it does this, the total amount of money being spent in the country goes down.

During deflations the government may spend more money than it receives in taxes. With more money being spent, business becomes livelier.

At present, many governments are trying out various ways to moderate their countries' economic ups and downs. Gradually they are learning how to avoid the extreme inflations and deflations of the past.

Reviewed by CHARLES STEINDEL, PH.D.
Economist

See also BANKS AND BANKING; DEPRESSIONS AND RECESSIONS.

INFLUENZA

Influenza, also known as flu or grippe, is a highly contagious respiratory disease. Each year it causes an estimated 100,000 hospitalizations and 36,000 deaths in the United States alone. Influenza-type illnesses have been reported throughout history, but it was not known until 1933 that influenza is caused by a virus.

Symptoms. Influenza provokes an immune reaction, causing symptoms throughout the body. But the virus itself does not spread beyond the nose, throat, and lungs. One to four days after infection, fever, headache, chills, body aches, and a dry cough begin. The fever fades after a few days, but other symptoms may develop, including sore throat, stuffy nose, and fatigue. (Influenza is not "stomach flu"; it rarely causes upset stomach or diarrhea.) Severe cases of influenza can result in life-threatening complications. For example, the virus can weaken the immune system, allowing bacterial infections, including pneumonia, to occur.

The Virus. Surface proteins on the virus enable it to infect cells, but the immune system recognizes these proteins and fights the infection. Influenza viruses are categorized based on the differences in their surface proteins. The three major types are A, B, and C. Type A usually causes the most severe form of the disease.

The virus continuously makes small changes in the surface proteins. These changes, called **drift**, lead to new strains of the virus, and these strains are less noticeable to the immune system. The type A virus sometimes makes a sudden large change, called a **shift**. This leads to a new subtype, which makes the virus all but unrecognizable, risking a **pandemic** (a worldwide epidemic). In 1918 and 1919, a shift caused the world's worst pandemic, the Spanish Flu, which killed 20 to 40 million people.

Deadly forms of influenza sometimes jump from animals to humans. Alert to the danger, scientists monitor likely transmission sites, such as Asian poultry markets.

Avoiding the Flu. Influenza spreads through the air or by touching the virus on a surface and then touching the eyes, nose, or mouth. Cases of influenza are more common in winter because people tend to stay indoors and are more likely to breathe the same air as an infected person. Also, in the dry air, the virus lives longer on surfaces.

Frequent hand washing and avoiding close contact with sick people are simple ways to avoid infection, but the best way is to be vaccinated. The virus is different every year, so the vaccine changes every year. The vaccine must be designed several months before flu season begins. During this time, the virus can change, making the vaccine less effective. If vaccine is scarce, the first to receive it should be those most at risk for complications: young children, people with asthma or other serious diseases, the elderly, and people with weak immune systems.

Treatment. Medications are available, but the best treatment is to rest and drink plenty of fluids. Antibiotics do not stop the virus but may be used to treat bacterial infections that are complications from the virus. Aspirin should not be given to children or teenagers with the flu, because it can cause Reye's syndrome, a serious disease.

New Outbreaks. The deadliest forms of influenza are often animal viruses that suddenly infect humans. Scientists monitor flu outbreaks and contain the spread of the virus. In 1997 in China, avian influenza spread from chickens to humans. To contain the disease, thousands of chickens were killed. Countries will have to share information and coordinate efforts to stop future outbreaks.

KAREN A. LACOURCIERE, PH.D.
Program Officer, Influenza Basic Research
National Institutes of Health, National Institute of
Allergy and Infectious Diseases

INFRARED RAYS. See LIGHT.

INK

Ink is the material used to record the words of history. It is also used for drawing, marking, and copying. But no matter how they are used, all inks consist of a **colorant** (the substance that provides the ink with color) and a **vehicle** (the liquid or paste that carries and binds the ink to a surface).

The colorants in ink are dyes or pigments. Dyes are absorbed by the medium being printed, such as paper, and are more permanent than pigments, which dry on top of the medium. The vehicle used also determines what qualities the ink will have. Vehicles are made up of a solvent, such as water or oil, that keeps the mixture smooth and flowing freely. Resins may also be added to the vehicle to create a varnish so the ink will dry quickly with a shiny surface.

Different Kinds of Ink. Ink is made up of different chemicals depending on how it will be used. Ballpoint pen ink is transferred from the inside holder to paper by a rotating ball, so the ink must flow slowly. The ink used in a ballpoint pen must be thicker than other writing inks to maintain the slow flow. Permanent blue-black writing ink is designed for legal documents so it must have a long life and dry quickly so it does not smear. It is often made up of iron, salt, water, and a natural dye. It is originally blue but becomes black when it dries. On the other hand, newspaper ink is designed for a short life and fast printing. News ink is often made up of a mineral oil vehicle and a carbon black pigment. The mineral oil soaks into the paper leaving a fairly dry surface, but the pigment dries on top of the newsprint and so is easily smeared. Different formulas are made for specialty jobs like decorating glass bottles, wallpaper, plastic, aluminum foil, textiles, and metals.

The History of Ink. The oldest of all inks are the Egyptian writing inks. Mummies dating as far back as 2500 B.C. were found wrapped in linen marked with an ink made of iron oxide. Early hieroglyphics (picture symbols) were written with inks made of soot, water, and vegetable gums.

One of the oldest inks still in use is India ink, a heavy black ink used in drawing and lettering. It was actually made in China in 2000 B.C. and was mistakenly called India ink years ago, and the name stuck. Carbon gives

Secret Messages
Throughout written history, hidden communications have been sent using invisible ink. One of the earliest methods used milk to write messages on paper. When the paper was dusted with soot and the soot blown off, the message could be read.

India ink its deep black color and gum arabic or glue keeps it from spreading too easily. It is very hard to remove. In central Asia, pages printed with this ink have been found that were under water so long they turned to rock; yet the printing was still legible!

By the A.D. 100's, the Romans were making a variety of inks, using soot and sepia. Sepia is the black fluid thrown off by cuttlefish when they are frightened. Sepia ink dries dark brown.

Medieval monks invented a kind of ink much like our present blue-black ink. They used crushed galls (a lumpy growth found on the trunks of some trees) mixed with iron salts such as copperas or green vitriol.

In families that could read and write during the 1500's and 1600's, making ink was the task of the housewife. In early America, women kept ink-making recipes along with their cooking recipes.

The development of Johann Gutenberg's press in the 1400's brought a need for printing ink. At first printers used water-based writing inks. But these flowed too freely and would not stay on the type. Very quickly the printers learned that inks mixed with boiled linseed oil worked much better. This type of ink became the standard printer's ink and remained so for over 400 years.

Since the 1940's the development of inks has accelerated because of new products such as ballpoint pens and marking pens. New processes, such as the replacement of linseed oil in printer's ink with petroleum products and glycerin, have provided inks that reproduce color better and dry faster. Even in today's computer age, ink remains an important tool in communication and the preservation of information and knowledge.

Reviewed by WILLIAM G. BEYER
The Parker Pen Company

See also PENS AND PENCILS; PRINTING.

INNOCENT III. See MIDDLE AGES (Profiles).

INOUYE, DANIEL K. See HAWAII (Famous People).

INSECTS

Insects are the largest single group of animals in the world. About 750,000 different kinds of insects are known, and more are being discovered every year.

Insects are found almost everywhere on earth. Some live deep in underground caves, and some on the tops of the world's highest mountains. There are insects that live on the surface of the ocean, far from land. Some live in dry deserts. Some live in hot springs whose water temperature is 120 degrees Fahrenheit. Many different insects have been found in cold barren Antarctica. One insect is able to live in vinegar. The young of another insect live in salty lakes. Insects can live in a great many different kinds of places. This is one of the reasons they have remained on earth for over 350 million years.

Many insects are very small. Only a few kinds grow to more than 1 or 2 inches. Some are so tiny they can hardly be seen. But the largest ones are bigger than some mice.

The small size of insects makes it possible

Insect fossils, such as those of the mosquito, provide a history of insects from their wingless beginnings to their development as the first flying animals.

for them to escape their enemies by crawling into cracks or other hiding places. And because they are so small, they need very little food and water to live. Thus their small size is a very great advantage.

▶ WHAT IS AN INSECT?

All adult insects have six legs, three on each side of their bodies. This is the one sure way to tell an insect. Each insect's body has three main parts—a **head**, a **thorax**, and an **abdomen**. Insects also have one pair of feelers, or

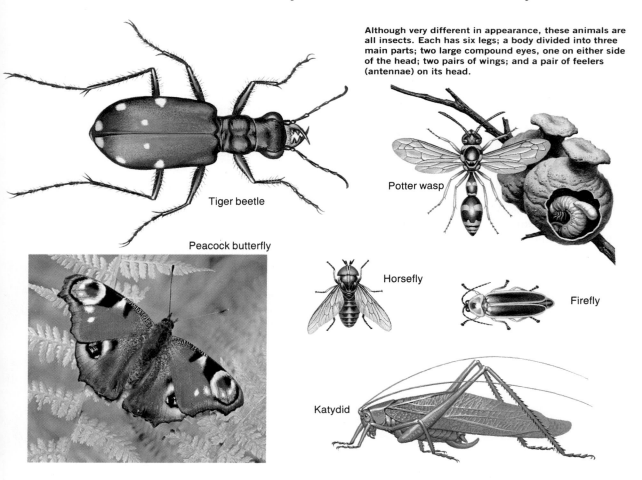

Although very different in appearance, these animals are all insects. Each has six legs; a body divided into three main parts; two large compound eyes, one on either side of the head; two pairs of wings; and a pair of feelers (antennae) on its head.

Tiger beetle

Peacock butterfly

Potter wasp

Horsefly

Firefly

Katydid

antennae, at the front of the head. Most insects have one or two pairs of wings.

Look carefully at a spider and count its legs. There are eight of them. Its body has two parts instead of three. A spider, therefore, is not an insect. The close relative of the spider, the scorpion, also has eight legs. It is not an insect either. Neither are the many-legged centipede and millipede.

▶ THE INSECT'S OUTSIDE APPEARANCE

If you can do so, catch a grasshopper and examine it. The grasshopper is a typical insect. See if you can find the three sections of the body.

The antennae at the front of the head are easy to see. Although the head is small, you should be able to see the eyes. You will have to look closely to see the mouth unless the grasshopper is chewing.

The thorax is next to the head. The wings and the three pairs of legs are attached to it. There are powerful muscles in the thorax, which you cannot see without cutting the insect open. These muscles control the movements of the legs and wings.

The hind portion of the insect's body is the abdomen. It is the biggest part of the body. The abdomen is in sections, or segments, that look like rings attached together at the rims. This makes the insect's body flexible—that is, it can bend and twist easily.

The mating and egg-laying organs are at the tip of the abdomen. Some insects also have another set of feelers, called **cerci**, at the end

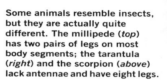

Some animals resemble insects, but they are actually quite different. The millipede (*top*) has two pairs of legs on most body segments; the tarantula (*right*) and the scorpion (*above*) lack antennae and have eight legs.

of the abdomen. Silverfish and many water insects have large cerci.

The Outside Skeleton

A tough outer coat covers the grasshopper's body. Most insects have such a coat. This is the insect's skeleton. It is like a shell enclosing the insect. It covers the soft parts of the body

Some insects, such as the silverfish below, have an extra set of feelers, called cerci, at the end of their bodies.

Cerci

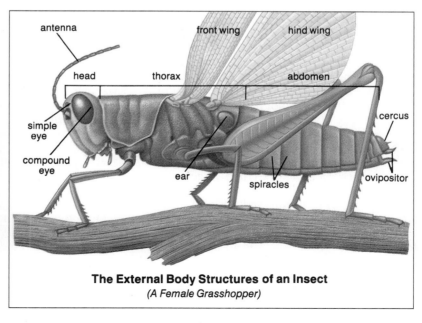

The External Body Structures of an Insect
(A Female Grasshopper)

antenna, front wing, hind wing, head, thorax, abdomen, simple eye, compound eye, ear, spiracles, cercus, ovipositor

Insect Life Cycles

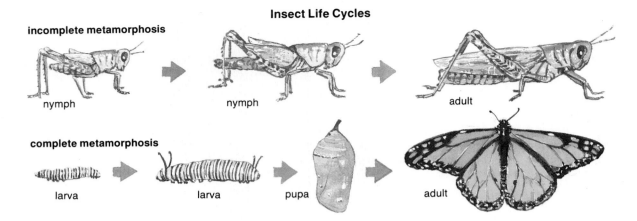

incomplete metamorphosis

nymph → nymph → adult

complete metamorphosis

larva → larva → pupa → adult

and supports them. Did you ever see an insect collection? What you saw were the outside skeletons of the insects with the wings attached.

Most insects have tiny hairs, or spines, growing out from the skeleton. Such hairs are often also found on the legs, the antennae, and the mouthparts. The skeleton is firm but lightweight, and so does not hamper the insect's flight.

The skeleton is made of a waterproof substance. This is a great help to the insect because it prevents water from soaking into its body. It also keeps the body from drying out. This outside skeleton, therefore, makes it possible for insects to live through long periods of wet or dry weather.

The hard outer shell protects the insect in other ways as well. It helps keep out germs and harmful chemicals. The shell acts as a shock absorber and as a shield against too much heat or cold. It also protects the insect from some of its enemies.

▶ HOW INSECTS DEVELOP

Some insects give birth to live young; however, most insects produce eggs and the young hatch from the eggs. Insect eggs are of many shapes. Some are long and oval; others are round like a ball. They often show beautiful surface markings and color patterns when seen through a magnifying glass.

Some insects lay only one egg at a time. Others, like termites, lay 10,000 or more in a day. They may lay this large number of eggs several times each year. Certain insects deposit large clusters of eggs in a protective case. The praying mantis and the cockroach are such insects.

Most insects go through several distinct forms as they grow from egg to adult. This method of growth is called metamorphosis. The word "metamorphosis" means "change in shape."

The Insect Larva

The young that hatch out of most insect eggs are called **larvae** (singular: larva). They look like worms and are sometimes incorrectly called worms. The "worm" in an apple or a tomato is really a larva.

You have probably seen caterpillars. They are the larvae of moths and butterflies. You may find it hard to think of a crawling caterpillar as the young of a butterfly. It does not look at all like the adult. The same thing is true of most insects. Their larvae sometimes have more than three pairs of legs. They have no wings. And their mouths and other body parts are different from those of the adult.

As soon as a larva hatches out of the egg, it begins to eat. It eats constantly, biting and chewing its food with powerful jaws, called mandibles. Its appetite never seems to be satisfied. It grows very rapidly, but its outer skin does not grow with it. Instead, the larva molts, or sheds its skin when it becomes too tight. Each time a new and bigger skin grows in place of the old one.

The Pupa

When a larva is full-grown, it stops eating. It buries itself under the ground, or it attaches itself to a leaf, the bark of a tree, or some other suitable place, and goes through a resting stage. This is called the pupal stage or **pupa**. A moth larva spins a **cocoon** around itself before becoming a pupa. A butterfly develops a shiny covering through which you can often see the body parts. The butterfly pupa is called a **chrysalis**. Other larvae develop a hard coat, or pupal case, as protection.

Left: A gypsy moth covers its eggs with scales from its own body. Center: The Spittlebug produces a mass of bubbles to cover its eggs. Right: The praying mantis deposits its eggs in the delicate, papery egg case it has made.

The Adult

An insect may remain in the pupal stage for several weeks. Many kinds remain in this stage all winter. Meanwhile great changes take place within the insect's body. The parts of the body develop and fit it for life as an **adult**. When these changes are complete, the pupal case splits and the adult insect crawls forth. In a few hours its body dries out. If it is a winged insect, it is ready for flight.

Butterflies, moths, bees, ants, wasps, and beetles all develop in this way. All go through the egg, larval, pupal, and adult stages. At each stage, the insect changes greatly in appearance and behavior. Scientists say these insects go through a **complete metamorphosis**. But many insects skip some of these stages. Those that do are said to go through an **incomplete**, or **gradual**, **metamorphosis**.

Incomplete Metamorphosis

Grasshoppers, crickets, cicadas, and dragonflies are among the insects that go through an incomplete metamorphosis. When the young hatches from the egg, it looks like the adult except that it is smaller and has no wings. It is called a **nymph**.

The larva of the swallowtail butterfly spins a chrysalis around itself. The larva lacks the compound eyes and the wings of the adult.

As the nymph grows, it molts when its skin becomes too tight. Tiny wings appear, which grow larger with each molt. With the last molt the wings become full size, and the insect is now an adult. Some insects with incomplete metamorphosis never develop wings. Lice and some crickets are examples of these.

How Long Do Insects Live?

There is no average length of life for adult insects as a group. The life of one kind of

Left: The cecropia moth larva spins its silken cocoon on a twig. Center: The chrysalis of the monarch butterfly hangs by a thread from a leaf. Right: A goldenrod gall fly emerges from its pupal case.

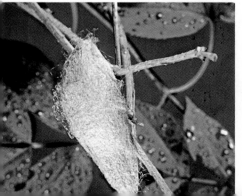

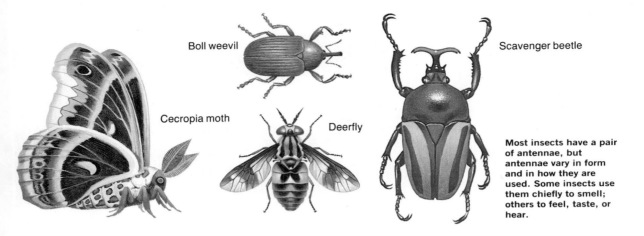

Boll weevil

Cecropia moth

Deerfly

Scavenger beetle

Most insects have a pair of antennae, but antennae vary in form and in how they are used. Some insects use them chiefly to smell; others to feel, taste, or hear.

insect may be very short. Mayflies, for example, live for less than a day. During that time they do not eat. They mate, lay their eggs, and die. Most adult moths and butterflies live for only a few days or weeks.

Some insects live for one summer; some live for several years. Probably the insect with the longest life is the queen of one kind of termite that lives in the tropics. Some scientists think this queen termite may live for as long as 50 years.

▶ THE INSECT'S SENSES

Insects have special organs for sensing the world around them, just as you have. Each sense organ usually responds to only one kind of sensation. The parts of an insect that receive sensation are called **receptors**. Insects' receptors are very different from our sense organs. For example, insects' "ears" are not found on their heads. Insects have no nostrils for smelling, yet their sense of smell is much stronger than that of a human being.

The Antennae

The antennae are remarkable sensation receptors. There are many different sizes and shapes of antennae among insects. All insect antennae are jointed, but some look like little knobs on the head of the insect. Others, such as those of the grasshopper, look like tiny strings of beads. The antennae of many moths are like waving feathers; butterfly antennae have clubbed tips.

Watch an insect as its antennae wave about in the air or feel the surface on which it is standing. The insect can feel, smell, and taste with its antennae. Some insects, such as the male mosquito, can hear with them. Insects use their antennae to feel whether a surface is wet or dry, smooth or rough, hot or cold. They also use them to sense the outside temperature and the humidity. Bloodsucking insects can sense the difference in temperature between an animal's body and the surrounding air with their antennae. This is how these insects find their victims.

Insects see with three simple eyes on top of head (*left*) and two compound eyes, made up of many tiny lenses (*center*). Complete image of object—such as flower (*right*)—is formed in brain, which combines separate images sent to it from lenses.

The antennae contain most of the insect's smell receptors. Thousands of tiny cells on the antennae receive odors that inform the insect of a food supply. For example, flies smell the odors given off by decaying plants and animals. Cabbage butterflies smell the odor given off by cabbage leaves. Ants find their way to a source of food supply by scent trails left by other ants in their colony.

Smell helps insects find the right kind of plant or animal on which to lay their eggs. It also helps them spot a natural enemy. The antennae of male insects can detect the scent of a female of the same kind, sometimes at a distance of more than a mile. The female insect gives off the chemical scent, called a **pheromone**, to attract male insects. In some insects the feet, mouthparts, and hairs on the skeleton are also sensitive to smell.

How an Insect Sees

Adult insects have **compound eyes**, made of many individual lenses called facets. You can see these if you examine a grasshopper's eye with a magnifying glass. The eyes of some insects have as few as nine facets each; the housefly's have 4,000; some dragonflies' eyes have 28,000.

Scientists have found a way of taking photographs through the lenses of the insect's compound eye. These photographs picture what an insect probably sees. They show that each facet sees a separate image of only a part of the object. Nerves going from each facet carry these separate images to the brain, where they are combined into one complete image. The more facets there are in the eye, the sharper is the complete image. But all insects are nearsighted. They cannot see an object clearly if it is farther than 2 or 3 feet away.

Each insect has two compound eyes. In most insects the eyes are on the sides of the head. This position of the eyes makes it possible for these insects to see in most directions. They are particularly able to detect moving objects.

Insects can see some colors. Plant-eating insects are especially sensitive to green. Butterflies that gather nectar from red and yellow flowers are more sensitive to these colors. Some insects, such as the honeybee, are able to see certain colors that the human eye cannot see. But the honeybee cannot see some colors that we can.

Most adult insects have another set of eyes. These are two or three simple eyes, each with one lens. They are called **ocelli**. The ocelli are located at the top of the insect's head. Unlike other animals, insects cannot turn, move, or focus either set of eyes. Although it is not known what insects actually see, scientists think that these simple eyes can only detect light and dark. The ocelli probably help make the insect more sensitive to light, so it can detect a broader range of light rays.

Taste and Feel

Tiny hairs on the mouthparts and the antennae contain most of the insect's taste receptors. Many insects taste with their feet as well —these insects can taste food by walking on it.

The hairs on the insect's skeleton, feet, and antennae are very sensitive feelers. Many insects have hairs on their abdomen that are also feel receptors. The receptors on the abdomen can sense vibrations in the earth when an insect is on the ground. They sense air currents when the insect is in flight.

Some insects have feel receptors on their wings. The receptors can sense that a solid object is approaching by the way air is displaced as the object moves. This is how a fly can sense that you are trying to swat it and why it darts away.

The Insect's Ears

Some insects locate the opposite sex for mating by means of sound. The organs for hearing, or "ears," are never found on an insect's head. The head is too small to contain organs of hearing.

Ears are found on different parts of the body in many different insects. For example, a grasshopper's ears are on the sides of the abdomen, underneath the wings. The ears are small, round disks that pick up sound vibrations and send them to nerves inside the body. Some moths also have this type of ear. There are simple ears near the tips of the antennae of many other insects. In many insects some of the hairs on the body are also sensitive to sound.

Some butterflies and moths are deaf. The insects with the most developed sense of hearing are the insects that produce sound, such as the katydid. The katydid can hear sounds that the human ear cannot.

▶ HOW INSECTS MAKE SOUNDS

Insects make sounds that carry messages to other insects of the same kind. The ears of each kind of insect can pick out the sound intended for it. The sounds are usually mating calls made by the male to attract the female. But with mosquitoes the female makes the sound to attract the male. Sometimes males make sounds to drive off rival males or to frighten away enemies.

A beekeeper can tell by the way the bees buzz whether they are angry or contented. Some ants, also, make sounds, probably as danger warnings to other ants in the colony.

Insects do not have voices, as we do. Most insect calls, or "songs," are made by the rubbing of one part of the insect's body against another. The katydid is a good example of an insect that "sings" in this way. This insect's sound-making apparatus is located on the two front wings. A series of notches, called the **file**, is on the left wing. A part of the right wing is hardened to form a **scraper**.

When ready to sing, the katydid raises its front wings and moves them rapidly in and out. This causes the scraper to saw back and forth across the file, something like the way a violin bow scrapes across the strings. The sounds produced by the katydid's wings are carried through the air to the ears of any female katydid that may be nearby.

Some grasshoppers have little knobs on the inner surface of their hind legs. The insect makes sounds by rubbing these hard knobs against the hard edge of the front wings.

Cicadas have a different way of making sounds. Their songs are made with drums.

The drum is in the abdomen of the male. Muscles attached to the drumhead pull it in and then let it snap back. This is done very quickly—sometimes as fast as 480 times a second. The shrill buzzing song of cicadas fills the air on a summer evening and can be heard a long way.

▶ WHAT INSECTS EAT

Insects eat many different kinds of material. Wood, paintbrushes, pepper, vinegar, wine-bottle corks, wool, paper, flour, mushrooms, bits of meat, and decayed matter are only a few of them. Some bore into plants and suck their juice. Some bite off pieces of leaves and can strip a plant bare. Bees and most butterflies and moths sip nectar from flowers and eat pollen, without harming the plant.

Many insects hunt other insects for food. The little orange and black ladybird beetle is one of these. It eats tremendous numbers of aphids, which it finds on plants. The praying mantis is another. Almost any insect is food for the mantis. Often, after mating, the female even eats the male. And as the young hatch out of the case, some of them devour the others. But the praying mantis is harmless to humans. In fact, it is useful because it destroys many garden pests.

You may have seen dragonflies darting about over ponds, catching small gnats and mosquitoes. The giant waterbugs, which may be up to 4 inches long, kill tadpoles, minnows, and small frogs, as well as other insects, for food. Hunting wasps capture insects of various kinds and store them in their nests. These serve as food for the wasps' larvae.

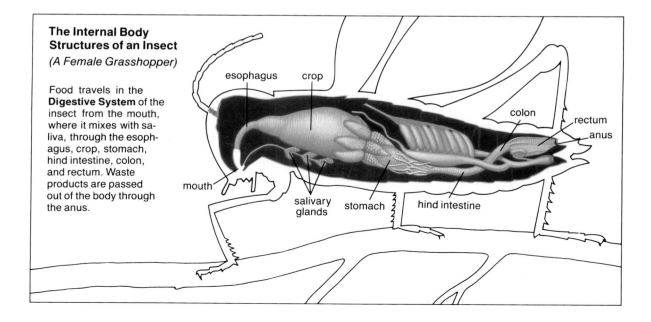

The Internal Body Structures of an Insect
(A Female Grasshopper)

Food travels in the **Digestive System** of the insect from the mouth, where it mixes with saliva, through the esophagus, crop, stomach, hind intestine, colon, and rectum. Waste products are passed out of the body through the anus.

esophagus   crop   colon   rectum   anus   mouth   salivary glands   stomach   hind intestine

There are insects, such as the female mosquito, that pierce the skin of other animals and suck drops of their blood for food. There are others, such as the cattle grub, that live inside another animal's body. A number of insects lay their eggs right on the body of other insects. When the eggs hatch, the larvae start eating the insect.

Some insects, like the cockroach, eat almost anything. But most insects will eat only one kind of food. The caterpillar of the monarch butterfly, for example, eats only milkweed leaves. It will starve to death if it cannot get these leaves. The caterpillar of a cabbage butterfly eats the leaves of plants in the cabbage family. It will also eat nasturtium leaves, because these contain an oil like that in the leaves of the cabbage family.

Termites are destructive wood-eaters. They get into damp wood through the ground. As they eat they bore tunnels inside the wood. They cannot live in daylight, so they never bore through to the surface.

How Insects Are Able to Get Their Food

The feeding habits of an insect depend upon its mouthparts. Over time, each kind of insect has developed specialized mouthparts that determine how it will feed. Insects that have powerful jaws bite and chew their food. Grasshoppers, beetles, cockroaches, and ants are examples of such insects. The mouthparts of some insects are developed into a hollow tube like a soda straw. These insects suck plant juices. Butterflies and moths have very long sucking tubes. When not in use the tubes are coiled beneath the insect's head.

Many insects have different mouthparts at different stages in their lives. For example, the caterpillar of the monarch butterfly has biting and chewing jaws, with which it eats milkweed leaves. During the pupal stage the mouthparts change to the sucking tube of the adult.

The hollow tubes of bloodsucking insects are like sharp, hollow needles. When a bloodsucking insect bites, saliva from glands in the

Insects eat a wide variety of substances and materials: The praying mantis devouring the grasshopper (*below*) dines mainly on other insects; the granary weevils boring into stored wheat (*top right*) eat plants; the waterbug feasting on a minnow (*bottom right*) attacks insects and other small animals.

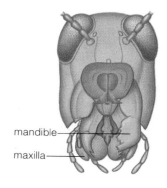

mandible

maxilla

Insect Mouthparts

Chewing
(Grasshopper)

The grasshopper's powerful jaws, called **mandibles**, move sideways to grind food. A second set of jaws, the **maxillae**, also move sideways and are used to push the food down the throat.

Piercing-Sucking
(Cicada)

The cicada uses the long needlelike structures, called **stylets**, to pierce plant tissue and suck up their juices.

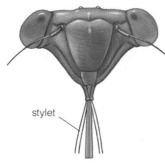

stylet

Sucking
(Butterfly)

The butterfly uses the long slender drinking tube, called a **proboscis**, to suck liquids, such as the nectar from flowers. The proboscis is coiled when it is not being used.

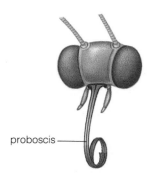

proboscis

Chewing-Lapping
(Honey Bee)

The bee uses its two sets of jaws, the **mandibles** and **maxillae**, to bite into a flower and chew. It sucks up the nectar from a flower with its long tonguelike **glossa**.

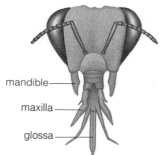

mandible

maxilla

glossa

Sponging
(Housefly)

The mouthparts of a housefly end in soft grooved lobes, called **labellum**, used to lap up liquid.

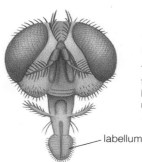

labellum

mouthparts is injected under the victim's skin. The saliva prevents blood from clotting at the puncture until the insect has finished its meal. A chemical in the saliva causes the sting and the swelling of a mosquito bite.

Some kinds of flies and mosquitoes carry disease germs, such as viruses or parasites, in their saliva. When these insects bite, they inject the disease germs into a person's body. When an insect carries and spreads a disease but does not develop the disease itself, the insect is called a **vector**. Malaria and yellow fever are spread in this way.

The fact that the larva seldom eats the same food as the adult is a great help in insect survival. The adult does not eat the larva's food supply. The larva does not have to compete with the adult for food.

Digesting the Food

An insect's body cannot use food as it is eaten. The food must first be changed in order for the body to be able to absorb and use it. The process by which this is done is called digestion. Insects, like most animals, have a special digestive system for this purpose.

The insect's digestive system is a hollow tube that goes from the mouth to an opening in the tip of the abdomen. Near the head of the tube are little saclike projections; these are the salivary glands. The glands pour saliva into the mouth. Saliva contains a chemical, called an **enzyme**, that starts to digest the food.

The tube is widened out in several places to form digestive organs. One of these is the stomach. A number of glands pour digestive juices into the stomach. This is where most of the food is digested. The last part of the digestive tube is called the hind intestine. Digested food passes from the stomach into the hind intestine and is absorbed into the blood.

Slender tubes are attached to the hind intestine. These tubes remove waste material from the blood and empty it into the hind intestine. From there the waste is carried out of the insect's body along with other wastes from the digestive system.

▶THE INSECT'S NERVOUS SYSTEM

An insect has nerves and a brain to switch sensations it receives into action. But an insect's actions are automatic. For example, an insect cannot think, "Danger is approaching; I must fly away." Instead it feels a certain kind of air current on its body. Feel receptors send the sensation to nerve centers. The nerve centers automatically cause certain muscles to contract. This contraction makes the wings move, and the insect flies away.

A large nerve center in the head is the insect's brain. The more intelligent the insect is, the larger the brain. A honeybee, for example, has a larger brain than a beetle of the same size. Nerve branches go from the brain to the eyes and the antennae. When an insect smells suitable food with its antennae, nerves from the receptors send the message to the brain. The brain in turn sends a message through nerves to the legs or wings, and the insect moves toward the food.

▶THE INSECT'S BLOOD SYSTEM

An insect's blood is not red like ours. Our blood contains a red chemical, hemoglobin, that carries oxygen throughout the body. The oxygen-hemoglobin combination gives our blood its bright-red color. An insect's blood does not carry oxygen; therefore it does not need hemoglobin. Its blood is usually clear instead of red. Sometimes it is a yellowish or greenish color.

The insect's heart is part of a long tube running along the top of the body, right under the skin. The tube opens just under the brain. There are tiny openings with valves along this tubelike heart. Blood is sucked into the heart through these openings. The heart contracts and forces blood to flow toward the head.

In the head the blood pours out over the brain and then flows backward through the body. As it flows backward it bathes the body organs, muscles, and nervous system. It brings them digested food and takes away waste material.

You can see an insect's heart in some living specimens. If you look carefully at a cutworm, a mosquito larva, or some caterpillars, you can see the tubelike heart along the back. Watch it beat. You may be able to notice that the heart beats faster when the insect is warm than when it is cold. The changes occur because insects are cold-blooded; their body temperature changes along with the changes in the temperature of their environment. When the outside temperature drops, an insect's body temperature also drops and its body processes slow down.

▶HOW AN INSECT BREATHES

Like all animals, insects must breathe. They need oxygen from the air to burn digested food. When the food burns, it gives the body energy. A waste product of this burning is a gas called carbon dioxide. The body breathes out the carbon dioxide together with the parts of the breathed-in air it did not use.

You breathe in and out through your mouth and the two nostrils in your nose. Insects have about 10 pairs of "nostrils" along the thorax and abdomen. Each segment of the insect's body has a pair of nostrils. They are little holes, called **spiracles**, which lead into a system of tubes that carry oxygen throughout the insect's body. If you look at a grasshopper through a magnifying glass, you can see the spiracles along the side of the abdomen.

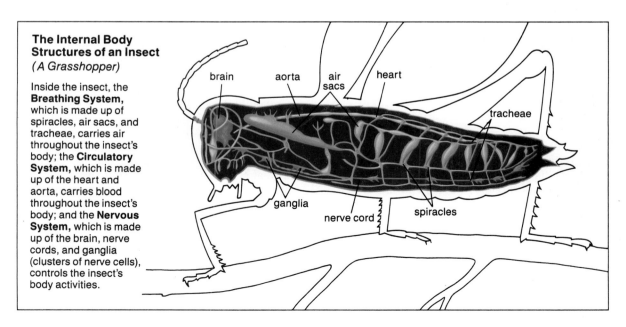

The Internal Body Structures of an Insect
(A Grasshopper)

Inside the insect, the **Breathing System,** which is made up of spiracles, air sacs, and tracheae, carries air throughout the insect's body; the **Circulatory System,** which is made up of the heart and aorta, carries blood throughout the insect's body; and the **Nervous System,** which is made up of the brain, nerve cords, and ganglia (clusters of nerve cells), controls the insect's body activities.

brain   aorta   air sacs   heart   tracheae

ganglia   nerve cord   spiracles

Halteres

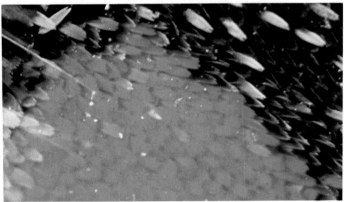

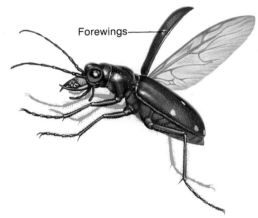

Forewings

The wings of the dragonfly (*top left*) have ribs, or veins, which help stiffen wings. The crane fly (*top right*) has knobbed stalks, called halteres, in place of hind wings. The forewings of beetles (*above right*) are hard, like shell. Butterflies and moths (*above left*) have wings covered with tiny scales.

Most insects breathe through their spiracles, but there are some exceptions. The water scorpion has a long breathing tube attached to the tip of its abdomen. It pushes the tip of this tube up through the surface of the water to get air. Many insects that live in water have gills instead of spiracles for breathing. The gills are special organs for taking in air that is dissolved in the water.

▶ INSECT FLIGHT

Insects were probably the first animals to fly. They developed wings many millions of years before there were birds or bats. Many insects have well-developed flying abilities; they steer accurately, hover, and are able to move sideways or backward in flight. The ability to fly has helped insects to survive. If conditions for life were not favorable, the insects could fly off to a different place.

Insect wings are very thin, like cellophane. They have many ribs, called veins. The veins help stiffen the wings. While all insect wings are alike in this way, they may be very different in other ways. The wings of butterflies and moths are covered with scales, which may be brightly colored. The forewings of beetles, called **elytra**, are hardened and shell-like. They fit like shields over the folded hind wings and protect them.

Some insects, such as flies and mosquitoes, have only one pair of wings. The hind wings have developed into stumps that help the insect balance itself when flying. These stumps are called **halteres**. Insects such as fleas, lice, bedbugs, and silverfish have no wings. Cockroaches have wings but do not often use them to fly. Among the ants the workers never have wings. Only the males and the queens have wings, at mating time. After the ants mate, the wings drop off and the insect remains wingless.

The wings of many insects move at great speeds. The wings of the housefly beat about 345 times a second. The wings of butterflies move much more slowly. They move only about 12 times a second.

Insects fly at different speeds. The housefly's speed is about 5 miles an hour. The butterfly's speed is about 12 miles an hour. Hawkmoths have been clocked flying at 30 miles an hour, and some scientists say that dragonflies can fly even faster than that. These are average "cruising" speeds of the insects. They can fly faster if they are escaping from an enemy.

▶ HOW INSECTS MOVE

Watch a fly as it walks. At each step it moves three legs forward at almost the same time. These are the front and hind legs on one side and the middle leg on the other. At the next step the other three legs move. In this way the insect is always resting solidly on three legs as it moves forward.

Most insect legs end in a pair of claws with a pad in between. In walking, the claws hook onto objects and help pull the insect along. This makes it possible for an insect to run very quickly. The pads between the claws have many tiny hairs with a sticky substance on them. They grip surfaces that are slippery, such as walls and ceilings, so that an insect can walk on them.

The legs of some insects are fitted for special purposes. For example, the hind legs of grasshoppers are long and have powerful muscles for jumping. This enables the grasshoppers to escape their enemies. The hind legs of some water beetles are very long and are set with stiff bristles. These legs work like oars in propelling the insect through the water. If you watch one of them swimming, you can see that it swims with a jerky motion, like a person rowing a boat.

An insect's legs, like the rest of its body, have skeletons on the outside. Muscles that control the leg movements are inside the skeleton. This protects the muscles and helps them work more efficiently.

▶ INSECT STRENGTH

Have you ever seen ants carrying sticks or pebbles? A scientist once saw an ant lifting a stone out of its nest entrance. He took both the ant and the stone back to his laboratory and weighed them. He found that the stone weighed 52 times as much as the ant. If a man of average weight were as strong as the ant is for its weight, he would be able to lift nearly 4 tons.

Other insects are even stronger than the ant. A bee can pick up things 300 times its own weight. Beetles are probably the strongest living things in relation to their size. If you had as much strength for your size as a beetle has for its size, you could easily lift almost 10,000 pounds.

Considering their size, insects are remarkably strong. One reason for their strength is the thickness of their muscles. The strength of a muscle depends on its thickness, not on its length. Another reason for the strength of insects is that they have more muscles than many animals. A person has about 800 mus-

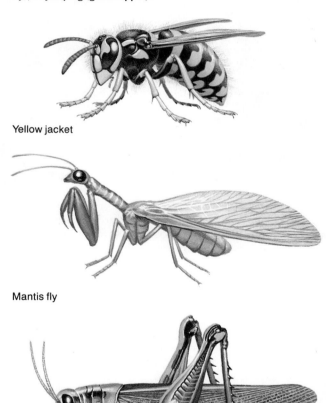

Many kinds of insects have legs that are adapted to special tasks, such as preparing their home (yellow jacket, a type of paper wasp), holding their food (mantis fly), or jumping (grasshopper).

Yellow jacket

Mantis fly

Short-horned grasshopper

To defend themselves against enemies, some insects blend into their surroundings, such as the walking stick (*left*). Others, such as the royal walnut moth caterpillar (*top left*), have spines that keep enemies at a distance. Still others mimic dangerous animals, such as the caterpillar (*top right*) that mimics a viper.

cles. A grasshopper has about 900, and some caterpillars have about 4,000. The muscles of insects also work better because of the way they are attached to the outside skeleton.

The strength of an animal does not depend entirely on its size. An animal may be 10 times larger than an insect, but it does not have 10 times the strength. This is because the ability of animals to lift things does not increase at the same rate as their size. The long muscle of a large animal, if it is no thicker than an insect's, is no stronger.

Some insects are able to jump great distances. Grasshoppers can jump 20 times the length of their bodies. At that rate a person would be able to jump one third the length of a football field. Fleas are probably the champion jumpers among insects. A tiny flea can make a jump 8 inches high and can go a distance of 13 inches. A person that could do as well could jump over a tall building.

The chief reason insects are such good jumpers is that they are so small. Large animals are heavier for their size than smaller animals are for theirs. For example, a 6-foot man may be about five times as long as the largest insect, which is about 15 inches long. But the man weighs hundreds of times more than the insect does. The insect can jump better because it carries less weight on its body for its size.

Considering the muscles, body structure, and weight of insects, scientists have come to this conclusion: If insects were to grow as large as humans, they would be little, if any, stronger.

▶HOW INSECTS PROTECT THEMSELVES

Insects have many natural enemies. They are captured and eaten by birds, bats, moles, frogs, and other animals. They also prey on each other. Yet in spite of their enemies, insects remain the most abundant of all animals. Most insects lay a great many eggs at one time. Often the young that hatch from these eggs become adults in a few weeks and are able to lay eggs in turn. Their ability to reproduce rapidly in such large numbers is one reason they are so numerous.

Protection by Disguise

Insects protect themselves from their enemies in many ways. One of these is by disguising themselves so that they blend into their surroundings. This is called **camouflage**. Many caterpillars and walkingstick insects are camouflaged to look like twigs. Many insects are colored and marked with different patterns that make them look like the background upon which they rest, such as tree bark or leaves. When some beetles fold up their legs and fall to the ground, they look like clumps of dirt.

Some harmless insects look ferocious and thus frighten off their enemies. For example, the hickory horned devil is a large caterpillar with vicious-looking spines. It scares its enemies away by its appearance.

Insect Mimicry

Some moths and butterflies fool their enemies by looking like an insect that is bad-tasting or has a poisonous sting. This is called **mimicry**. For example, the viceroy butterfly looks almost like the monarch butterfly, which has a bad taste to animals that try to eat it. These animals leave both butterflies alone after having tasted a few monarch butterflies.

The swallowtail caterpillar frightens enemies with the false eye spots on the back of its head.

Another insect that protects itself by mimicry is the hornet fly. It has markings like those of a hornet but has no stinger. Insects, toads, and other small animals whose mouths have been stung by hornets do not try to eat hornets again. Neither do they try to catch the hornet fly.

Protection by Chemical Warfare

Many insects defend themselves by "chemical warfare." If you have ever been stung by a bee, you know how effective this kind of protection is. Poison stings are used by many bees, wasps, hornets, and some ants. The stinger is a modified egg-laying organ, so only females sting. Some caterpillars protect themselves in the same way.

Many stinging insects are brightly colored. This is how such an insect warns its enemies that it is poisonous and to stay away.

Some insects give off a bad-smelling chemical to drive enemies away. Stink bugs, broad-headed bugs, and lacewings are often called the "skunks" of the insect world. Perhaps the most unusual kind of chemical warfare is that used by the bombardier beetle. When disturbed, this beetle ejects a puff of gas from the rear of its body. The gas has an irritating effect on the enemy.

The viceroy butterfly (*left*) is rarely attacked because its colors are so much like those of the monarch butterfly (*right*) which has an unpleasant taste.

Insect Matchup

Can you tell how an insect larva will look when it becomes an adult? Try to match the larvae below with the adult insects on the following page. Check your answers with the answer key.

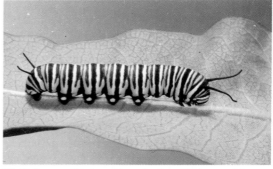

(4) As it grows, this insect larva feeds on the leaves of the milkweed plant.

(1) This insect larva breathes through a tube at the end of its body.

(5) The larva of this insect is highly prized as fish bait.

(2) More than 500 kinds of plants are food for this hungry insect larva.

(6) When it is disturbed, this insect larva curls into twiglike shapes.

(3) Because it eats insects that are harmful to plants, this insect larva is a gardener's friend.

(7) This insect larva hatches from its egg in less than 24 hours.

(a) The adult Dobsonfly lacks the gills of its larva.

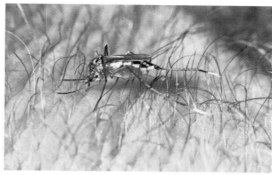

(e) The adult mosquito can be a carrier of many serious diseases.

(b) The adult gypsy moth is a very weak flyer that lays its eggs on tree trunks.

(f) The adult bluebottle fly scavenges for its food in decayed matter.

(c) The adult monarch butterfly flies long distances to winter along the Gulf of Mexico.

(g) The adult ladybird beetle develops from a larva in two to four weeks.

How well were you able to predict how an insect will look as an adult from the way it looks when it is young? Check your answers with the answer key below.

(d) The adult sphinx moth feeds while hovering like a hummingbird in front of a plant.

ANSWERS: 1, e; 2, b; 3, g; 4, c; 5, a; 6, d; 7, f.

▶INSECT SHELTERS

Most adult insects live by themselves in crevices, in soil, under rocks, or under loose bark. They are called solitary insects. Certain insects live together in colonies. These are called social insects. Ants, termites, most bees, hornets, and some wasps are examples of social insects.

Clockwise from right: **A many-chambered termite mound. The bald-faced hornets' paper nest hangs from trees or tall shrubs. The inside of the bald-faced hornets' nest shows the floors and cells in which eggs are laid. The paper wasp chews wood to make the cell nest that holds its larva. The female organ-pipe wasp builds a nest of tubes, with each tube containing an egg. The female potter wasp lays its eggs inside a jar-shaped nest, then seals the top.**

Shelters of Social Insects

Social insects build elaborate homes to shelter the colony. Bees build honeycombs and beehives. Hornets and wasps build paper nests. They make the paper by chewing bits of rotten wood and stems of plants. The material is mixed with saliva and becomes a pulpy mass. When it dries, the pulp stiffens into a

gray, paperlike material.

Most ants build nests in the ground. The nests are honeycombed with tunnels. The activities of the colony are conducted in the tunnels. Termites nest in darkness. Their nests are made of chewed-up wood. Some termites that live in tropical regions build tall mounds in which the colony lives.

Top: A gall cut in half shows the insect inside that caused the unusual growth. *Center:* The leaf roller wraps itself in a leaf every morning and comes out at night to search for food. *Bottom:* Eastern tent caterpillars live in tents spun from silk that they secrete.

Shelters of Solitary Insects

Only a few solitary insects build shelters. One of these is the leaf roller, a type of moth. Each morning the leaf-roller larva rolls a leaf around itself. It seals the ends with silk thread from glands in its mouth. At night it breaks out of its shelter to hunt for food.

Some females build shelters for their eggs. Most common of these are the solitary bees and wasps. One kind of wasp digs a small tunnel in the ground. She stocks the tunnel with food for the larva that will hatch from the egg. She does this by paralyzing a caterpillar with her sting and dragging the still-alive insect into the hole. Then she lays an egg in the "nursery" and seals the opening.

Solitary wasps called mud daubers build mud nests, in which they lay their eggs. They lay in a stock of paralyzed spiders as food for the young and then deposit their eggs in the nest. The potter wasp builds a jar-shaped nest of mud on a twig. Another, the organ-pipe wasp, builds a nest in the shape of long tubes cemented together like an organ pipe. Each tube is a cell in which she lays an egg.

Shelters Built by Larvae

Some adult insects do not build nests for their young but make it possible for the larvae to build shelters. Certain wasps, aphids, and flies pierce leaves or stems of plants and lay eggs inside the plant tissue. When the larvae emerge, they cause that part of the plant to swell—that is, they produce a **gall**. Some galls have only one larva in them, and some have many. The soft plant tissue inside the gall supplies food for the larva, and the hard outside covering gives the insect shelter.

The larvae of some insects build shelters without any help from the adults. You may have seen the gray "tents" of tent caterpillars fastened in the forks of tree branches. The tent caterpillars build the tent from silk that they secrete.

Caddis-fly larvae also build shelters. Caddis flies are a group of insects that live near the shores of ponds and streams. The eggs are laid in the water. The larvae that hatch out are called caddisworms. The "worm" builds a case around itself of small pebbles or sticks, glued together or bound with silk. It moves by pushing the front part of its body and its legs out of its case and pulling the rest of its "house" along with it.

Classification of Some Common Insects

Black carpenter ant
Order Name: Hymenoptera
Meaning of Name: ''Membrane wings''
Common Examples: Bees, ants, wasps
Distinctive Characteristics: Thin, filmy wings; chewing mouthparts

Dragonfly
Order Name: Odonata
Meaning of Name: ''Toothed''
Common Examples: Dragonflies, damselflies
Distinctive Characteristics: Mouth with beak resembling tooth; chewing mouthparts

Greenbottle fly
Order Name: Diptera
Meaning of Name: ''Two wings''
Common Examples: Flies, gnats, mosquitoes
Distinctive Characteristics: One pair of wings; piercing and sucking mouthparts

Beetle
Order Name: Coleoptera
Meaning of Name: ''Sheath wings''
Common Examples: Beetles
Distinctive Characteristics: Shieldlike front wings; chewing mouthparts

Grasshopper
Order Name: Orthoptera
Meaning of Name: ''Straight wings''
Common Examples: Grasshoppers, roaches, crickets
Distinctive Characteristics: Straight-edged wings (when present); chewing mouthparts

Leaf-legged bug
Order Name: Hemiptera
Meaning of Name: ''Half wings''
Common Examples: True bugs (water bugs, squash bugs)
Distinctive Characteristics: Partly leathery, partly clear wings; piercing and sucking mouthparts

Butterfly
Order Name: Lepidoptera
Meaning of Name: ''Scale wings''
Common Examples: Butterflies, moths
Distinctive Characteristics: Scale-covered wings; sucking mouthparts

Cicada
Order Name: Homoptera
Meaning of Name: ''Similar wings''
Common Examples: Aphids, cicadas
Distinctive Characteristics: Filmy wings of similar size; sucking mouthparts

Mayfly
Order Name: Ephemeroptera
Meaning of Name: ''Living for a day''
Common Examples: Mayflies
Distinctive Characteristics: Brief life span; chewing mouthparts

Protection for the Pupa

When it is in the pupal, or resting, stage, an insect is helpless. It needs complete protection. Cocoons spun by moth caterpillars give the pupae this protection. The cocoons are made of silk spun out from the salivary glands.

Cocoons are usually white, gray, or brown. They are easy to find in the winter, when trees are bare. You can see some kinds of cocoons hanging down from the branches, like tiny dull Christmas-tree decorations. If you try to tear one open, you will see why a cocoon is such a fine shelter for the pupa. The cocoon is so tough it will not tear easily.

Other insect larvae do not spin cocoons. Instead they develop a hard coat that serves as a shelter for the pupa.

▶THE IMPORTANCE OF INSECTS

Many insects are very useful to humans. Honeybees give us honey and wax. Silk comes from the cocoon built by the silkworm, the larva of a moth. Shellac is made from a substance given off by the lac insect.

Insects carry pollen from flower to flower as they flit about to gather nectar. This transfer of pollen helps plants produce fruit and seeds. Insects also serve as food for many birds.

But insects are humanity's chief competitors for shelter, clothing, and food. Termites eat the wood of homes; carpet beetles eat carpets; and the larvae of clothes moths eat holes in woolen clothing. The cotton-boll weevil destroys cotton crops. These are only some of the destructive insects. Even more important, insects do tremendous damage to food crops. A swarm of locusts can eat a field bare in a few hours. The larvae of certain moths spoil apples, pears, and other fruits.

Some insects spread disease germs. The germs of encephalitis, or sleeping sickness, as well as those of yellow fever and malaria, are carried by insects. Flies live on filth and carry germs on their feet and antennae.

▶CONTROLLING HARMFUL INSECTS

Humankind fights a constant battle against harmful insects. We do this in a number of ways.

One of these is by the use of insecticide sprays. (An insecticide is a chemical that kills insects.) For many years scientists have also been fighting harmful insects with other in-

Many insects are helpful to humans. The honeybee (*right*) produces honey and beeswax and also is an important crop pollinator. The silkworm (*below*) is the chief producer of silk.

sects—a method called biological control. The scientists have done this by bringing in natural enemies of insect pests, such as viruses and bacteria.

Insects are being studied for two main reasons. Scientists want to find ways to encourage the spread of useful insects and new ways to control insect pests. To destroy the pest without harming useful insects is one of the chief aims of scientists. They study an insect in all its life stages, to find when it is easiest to destroy the insect. Some insects are easier to attack as larvae and some as adults.

Spraying insects with insect-disease viruses or germs is being studied. In one experiment low-flying planes sprayed viruses on areas infested with tent caterpillars. After being sprayed once a year for 2 years, tent caterpillars in those areas were wiped out.

Each time scientists discover a disease that affects an insect, they look for a way to spread

Although there are over 750,000 species of insects, less than 1 percent are serious pests. However, the damage done by the 1 percent and the cost of fighting them adds up to billions of dollars each year. Methods used to control insect pests include spraying crops with pesticides (*right*) and using insects that prey on insects, such as the aphid-eating ladybird beetle (*below*).

that disease. One of these ways is to catch some of the insects in traps, infect them with the disease, and release them. The insects then spread the disease to others.

Modern entomologists—scientists who study insects—think that probably the best way to wipe out insect pests is to prevent the females from laying eggs. If no eggs are laid, in a few years that particular insect may be wiped out. To do this, research in methods of making insects sterile is being carried out. (Sterile means unable to reproduce.) The insects are treated with chemicals or are exposed to radiation.

Scientists are also studying certain special chemical sprays for plants. These chemicals are harmless to the plants. But they cause insects that eat them to become sterile.

Scientists have to be very careful when using this kind of technology that they do not cause a serious imbalance in nature. Eliminating one harmful insect may seriously alter the environment. If the mosquito population in one area is wiped out, the fish that feed on the mosquito may die out. If the fish die out, the birds that feed on the fish may also die out. Once this chain of events starts, it is very difficult to stop.

Baiting Traps for Males

It is often difficult to trap large numbers of insects in order to sterilize them. Entomologists have therefore experimented and found a way to trap the males.

Entomologists know that the females of many kinds of insects give off a scent to attract the male. The scent-producing chemicals of females are extracted and used to bait insect traps. Chemists have been able to make some scents artificially in the laboratory.

Males are attracted by the scent and flock to the traps in great numbers. Some kinds of male insects caught in this way are killed outright. Scientists have found it more effective to control other kinds by giving the males a disease or by sterilizing them. Then the males are released. Those infected with disease spread it to others. The sterile males mate with females, but the eggs never hatch out.

Entomologists hope that such techniques will lead to control of insect pests.

ROSS E. HUTCHINS
Author, *Insects and Their Young*

See also ANTS; BEES; BUTTERFLIES AND MOTHS; MOSQUITOES.

INSURANCE

No matter how careful people are, they may have losses that result from events that are beyond their control. Insurance protects people from these losses.

Insurance follows a rule called the "law of large numbers." When a large number of people face the same danger, the chances are that some will suffer losses but most will not. From experience it is possible to figure out how many will suffer a loss.

People buy insurance to share the risk of loss. They pay a fee, called a **premium**, which is based on the size of the risk. For example, an insurance company estimates that one $75,000 house out of every 1,000 such houses will burn down next year. It charges each of the 1,000 homeowners a premium of $75 ($75,000 divided by 1,000) plus an additional sum for expenses and profit. Until claims are paid, most of the money paid as premiums is invested, where it earns more money. If none of the houses burn down, the insurance company does not have to pay for any losses. It makes money. If more than one house burns down, the insurance company will have to pay for the extra losses from its reserve fund and from profits.

When people become insured, they take out policies. A **policy** states what losses are covered and how much the company will pay for these losses. When policy owners suffer losses, they fill out reports called **claims**. The company pays all or part of a claim, as called for in the policy. Most policies have a **deductible** of at least $200. That is, the policyholder must pay the first $200 of the loss.

▶ KINDS OF INSURANCE

There are many kinds of insurance, but they fall into three main groups—property and casualty insurance, life insurance, and health and accident insurance.

Property and Casualty Insurance

Property insurance pays all or part of the cost if people suffer losses of or damage to their homes, offices, furniture, clothing, cars, or other kinds of personal property. The damage may be caused by fire, robbery, storms, a car accident, or some other misfortune. In the United States the cost for damages caused by major floods, hurricanes, tornadoes, or earth-

Most homeowners buy insurance to protect themselves against loss or damage from fire. They can also purchase policies to cover losses from storms, theft, and riots.

quakes is shared by insurance companies and the federal government.

Casualty insurance includes what is sometimes called **liability** insurance. "Liability" means responsibility for damage. When cars collide, the driver at fault is liable and must pay for the damage done to the other cars and passengers. Many states will not license uninsured cars. In some parts of the United States, minor accidents are covered under "no fault" insurance. People who have been hurt receive payments for medical expenses no matter who was at fault.

Workers' compensation is a kind of casualty insurance that employers are required to buy. You can read more about it in the article WORKERS' COMPENSATION in Volume W.

Life Insurance

Owning life insurance is a way for a person to make sure his or her family will have money to live on after his or her death. Premiums are based on the amount of time the insurance company expects the person to live.

This impressive reception area serves Lloyd's of London, one of the largest insurance companies in the world. Lloyd's will insure extraordinary things such as the weather for a tennis match or a pianist's fingers.

Some policies let a person borrow money against the amount they have paid in while they are still living, to help pay for a youngster's college tuition, for example. Also, some policies pay a policyholder a sum of money every month after retirement. Many employers buy life insurance for their workers because group insurance costs less than if the workers bought policies on their own.

Health Insurance

Health insurance helps pay the expenses of illness or injury. A policy may include many kinds of health insurance or just one.

Hospitalization insurance pays part of the cost of being in a hospital. It usually includes the room, meals, laboratory tests, operating room, nurses, and medicines. **Surgical** insurance pays a set amount of a doctor's fee for performing an operation. **Regular medical** insurance helps pay a doctor's fee for treatment of an illness. **Major medical** insurance combines these and often covers long-term or expensive illnesses. The policyholder first pays a deductible for every year, and the insurance company usually pays a percentage of all medical bills after that.

Accident insurance provides special payments if a person is killed or injured in an accident. If a person becomes disabled and cannot work, **disability** insurance pays his or her lost income.

The United States government has a health insurance program for older people, called **Medicare**. It is discussed in the article SOCIAL SECURITY in Volume S. **Medicaid**, the government's health program for people with low incomes, is discussed in the articles OLD AGE (Volume O) and WELFARE, PUBLIC (Volume W-X-Y-Z). Some countries pay all medical expenses for every citizen.

▶ **INSURANCE COMPANIES AS BIG BUSINESS**

In the 1600's, shipowners, navigators, and merchants in London, England, began sharing the cost of losing ships to storms and pirates. These people met at Lloyd's coffeehouse because its owner collected all the latest shipping news for them. A person who wanted to protect a ship or its cargo would put a list of those items on one of the tables. Anyone who wanted to insure part of the cargo would write his or her name under the articles they were willing to cover. Lloyd's coffeehouse became Lloyd's of London, one of the world's largest insurance organizations.

Today insurance is big business. Many people work in the insurance industry. **Actuaries** figure out how much premiums should be. They also calculate such information as a person's average life expectancy, the number of car accidents that will occur in a year, and the likelihood of a flood destroying property.

People buy policies through an insurance company's local **agent**. Then **underwriters** decide whether the company can afford to take the risk of insuring them. For example, a person who has had several car accidents may have difficulty getting automobile insurance. Finally, should a policyholder submit a claim, a **claims adjuster** has to determine the amount the company must pay to cover the losses.

Reviewed by KENNETH W. KAUFMAN
Keevily Spero-Whitelaw, Inc.

INSURANCE, UNEMPLOYMENT. See UNEMPLOYMENT AND UNEMPLOYMENT INSURANCE.

INTEGERS. See NUMBERS AND NUMBER SYSTEMS.

INTEGRATED CIRCUITS. See TRANSISTORS, DIODES, AND INTEGRATED CIRCUITS.

INTELLIGENCE

Think about a hammer, a saw, a log, and a hatchet—which of these objects do you think belong in the same group? Your answer would tell a psychologist, a scientist who studies the mind and behavior, something about your intelligence. A psychologist who was curious about how people from different cultures think asked farmers in Central Asia the same question. After hearing the psychologist's question, the farmers thought: Why would anyone want to divide these things into groups? The psychologist explained that the hammer, the saw, and the hatchet were tools; the log was not. The farmers said all four objects belonged together because without tools and wood nothing could be built. Anyone who would do it differently was "stupid," in the farmers' words.

Everyone uses the words "smart" or "stupid" believing that these hold similar meanings for all of us. But what is considered intelligent varies from society to society. Even within the same society, ideas about intelligence change over time.

▶ **INTELLIGENCE: ONE ABILITY OR MANY?**

Many of our ideas about what elements, or abilities, make up intelligence have been influenced by the history of intelligence testing. In 1905, French psychologists, Alfred Binet and Theodore Simon devised the first intelligence test for schoolchildren. It was created to help the French government identify young people who would have difficulty with schoolwork. Although the Binet-Simon test results were reported as a single number, Binet did not think intelligence was simply one thing. The number was just a score on a test. He thought a person's abilities and test score could change with instruction—the more education a person got, the better the person would do on the test.

In 1916, the Binet-Simon test was translated into English and adapted for widespread use in schools by American psychologist Lewis Terman. Terman's test, the Stanford-Binet, has had a very large impact on Western society and schooling. Terman reported the test score as an intelligence quotient or IQ. Unlike Binet, he thought the score represented a person's intelligence and would not change much throughout a person's life, no matter how much schooling the person had.

Psychologists use a variety of methods to determine the areas of intelligence. Howard Gardner, a leading American psychologist, studied past research and also studied gifted people, brain-damaged people, people from different cultures, and young people's intellectual development. From his work, he determined that there are at least seven areas of intelligence: movement (which is important to people like dancers and athletes), music, mathematics, language, spatial abilities (which are important to people like artists and engineers), understanding oneself, and understanding others. Robert Sternberg, another American psychologist, studied the processes people use in solving test problems and also looked at the way they carried out work in their daily lives. He identified three areas of intelligence: planning, performance, and knowledge acquisition.

Psychologists are not only interested in what makes up intelligence, but also in how it grows and changes over time. Jean Piaget, a Swiss scholar, studied the development of intellectual abilities in young people. Piaget did not use paper-and-pencil tests. Instead, he observed young people and questioned them as they worked on tasks he had invented.

Piaget found that young people went through four stages of development. During the earliest stage (from birth to about 2 years of age), young people learned about the world through their senses and physical activity. In the two middle stages (from about 2 to 11 years of age), they learned through their experiences with objects or information in their immediate environment. By the last stage (from about 11 years of age and older), they could begin to make use of abstract-thinking skills, like those needed for algebra or physics. Piaget thought the four stages were universal—they applied to all forms of learning in all cultures.

While experts recognize the importance of Piaget's work, many no longer agree with his ideas. Later scholars found that Piaget's four stages did not apply to problems in language, music, and other subject areas Piaget did not study. Also, the stages were not as unchangeable as Piaget had proposed. Younger children often appear more capable than Piaget imagined. On the other hand, older children and adults may not reach the fourth stage, even with advanced schooling.

WHERE DOES INTELLIGENCE COME FROM?

Is intelligence the result of genetic inheritance (heredity) or the result of an individual's upbringing and experiences (environment)? This is one of the main questions about intelligence. If intelligence is due to heredity, then it is possible to believe that people are born with all the abilities they will ever have and can only be as intelligent as those abilities will allow. On the other hand, if intelligence is due to an individual's environment, it is possible to believe that most people would be pretty intelligent if they had the right learning opportunities.

Research suggests that both heredity and environment are important and that intelligence is not entirely determined by either factor by itself. The IQ scores of twins who were raised in separate homes are very similar. This indicates that intelligence, as measured by IQ tests, is largely determined by genetics. However, other studies reveal the importance of environment. The average IQ scores of many ethnic groups that have faced discrimination are lower than those of groups that have not historically faced discrimination. When members of these groups move to places that allow them equal opportunities, their children's average IQ scores are the same as those of other groups.

MEASURING INTELLIGENCE

Attempts to measure intelligence scientifically came about in the mid-1800's. During that time, some people thought that the size and shape of a person's skull revealed intelligence. Others measured intelligence by how fast or how well people could use their five senses. Someone who could quickly tell whether two rods were the same length might be considered smarter than someone who could not tell as quickly.

Binet and Simon's intelligence test was a breakthrough. The test asked young people questions geared to their age that relied not only on the use of the senses, but also on skills such as memory, reasoning, and comprehension. A young person's mental age was determined by the most difficult question completed on the test: If a 10-year-old completed all the questions suitable for a 10-year-old, the young person's mental age was 10; if a 10-year-old completed questions suitable for a 12-year-old, the young person's mental age was 12. The mental age was then used to establish an IQ score. To determine the IQ score, a person's mental age was divided by a person's real age, and the result was multiplied by 100. The average person's IQ score is 100. Measuring intelligence using tests that established an IQ score became popular with the Stanford-Binet test.

The Stanford-Binet and other IQ tests have been criticized for several reasons. Beginning with the earliest tests, IQ questions were said to have been created to reflect the ideas and attitudes of people from middle-class backgrounds. Because the tests are timed and require only short answers, they may not really show how well a person can think. Outside of test situations, people often work together or use other kinds of resources to solve problems. Since tests often do not ask people to solve problems important to them, it is difficult to connect IQ results to how well a person will function in the real world.

New tests have attempted to get rid of cultural bias. Other assessments include tasks that people use in their daily lives. There is also more of an effort to judge children over several performances and on other qualities such as persistence, interest, and motivation.

The new assessments are attempting to capture the complex nature of intelligence. They help us to learn about the different kinds of strengths we have. Perhaps the question we should be asking ourselves is not "Am I smart?" but "In what ways am I smart?"

MARA KRECHEVSKY
Harvard University
MINDY L. KORNHABER
Harvard University

See also TESTS AND TEST TAKING

Can you find the form that is identical to the target form? You will use spatial intelligence in making your choice. (The answer is "d.")

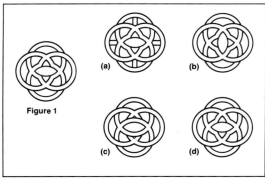

Figure 1

INTEREST

You have probably seen stores that rent everything from lawn mowers to baby chairs. But have you ever seen a store that rents money? Almost certainly you have. Banks, in effect, are "stores" that rent money.

If you were to rent a lawn mower, you would pay a rental charge—a certain amount of money for the use of the mower for a certain length of time. When you borrow money from a bank, you are "renting" the use of money for a certain period of time. The rental charge is called **interest.**

Banks also pay interest. Putting money in a savings account is like lending money to a bank. The bank pays to use your money.

Interest is determined by three things. The first is the amount borrowed, or the **principal.** The second is the unit rental charge, or **rate.** The third is the length of **time,** or **period,** the money is kept.

Banks generally state their lending charges in annual percentage rates. That is, they charge so many dollars a year for each $100. When the rate is 12 percent a year, it costs $12 to borrow $100 for one year. To borrow $300 at that rate for a year costs $3 \times 12, or $36. You can figure the cost by multiplying the amount of the principal by $\frac{12}{100}$ or 0.12, both of which mean 12 percent.

$$\frac{12}{100} \times 300 = 36 \text{ or } 0.12 \times 300 = 36$$

The time of a loan is often longer or shorter than a year. This must be taken into account in computing the interest charge. If you borrow $100 at 12 percent a year for two years, you will pay twice the yearly charge, or $24. If you borrow $100 at that rate for half a year, you will pay half the yearly charge, or $6. These calculations can be a formula in which I = interest, P = principal, r = rate, and t = time (in years or fractions of a year).

$$I = P \times r \times t$$

Here are some examples of the formula's use:

(1) **$375 at 10% for two years**

$$I = P \times r \times t$$
$$= 375 \times 0.10 \times 2 = 75$$
$$= \$75$$

(2) **$964 at 16% for three months ($\frac{1}{4}$ year)**

$$I = P \times r \times t$$
$$= 964 \times 0.16 \times \frac{1}{4} = 38.56$$
$$= \$38.56$$

Banks are not the only businesses that use interest rates. Many stores permit customers to charge merchandise—to buy it one day and pay for it later. The store charges interest on the amount the customer owes, as though it had loaned the customer that amount of money. It sets an annual rate for the interest, but it bills customers each month.

The kind of interest we have discussed is called **simple interest.** Another kind of interest is called **compound interest.** It is paid on the principal and on whatever interest has already been paid.

For example, suppose you keep $100 in a bank for 3 years. The bank pays 6 percent compound interest a year. At the end of a year, you have $106—your principal, plus $6 interest. The interest for the next year is figured on that amount. You earn 6 percent of $106, or $6.36. At the end of the year, you have $112.36 ($106 + $6.36). For the third year, the bank pays 6 percent of $112.36, or $6.74. At the end of 3 years, you will have $119.10.

Most banks pay interest that is compounded quarterly (that is, every three months) or even daily. It is complicated to figure such interest, so banks usually use computers. The table shows what your money would earn at various rates if interest were compounded annually, quarterly, or daily.

FRANCIS J. MUELLER
Author, *Intermediate Algebra*

See also PERCENTAGE.

Rate (%)	Compounded annually		Compounded quarterly		Compounded daily	
	1 year	5 years	1 year	5 years	1 year	5 years
5¼	$52.50	$291.55	$53.54	$297.96	$53.90	$300.15
8	80.00	469.33	82.43	485.95	83.28	491.76
10	100.00	610.51	103.81	638.62	105.16	648.61
12	120.00	762.34	125.51	806.11	127.47	821.94
14	140.00	925.41	147.52	989.79	150.24	1,013.48
16	160.00	1,100.34	169.86	1,191.12	173.47	1,225.15

TOTAL INTEREST EARNED ON A DEPOSIT OF $1,000

INTERIOR, UNITED STATES DEPARTMENT OF THE

The Department of the Interior (DOI) is the principal conservation agency of the United States government. It manages most of the nation's public lands and natural resources, protects fish and wildlife, and preserves the environmental and cultural values of national parks and historic sites. The DOI also oversees American Indian reservation communities and U.S.-administered island territories.

Office of the Secretary

The DOI is one of 15 departments within the executive branch of the U.S. government. It is headed by a secretary, who is a member of the president's cabinet. The secretary of the DOI is assisted by a deputy secretary, a solicitor (chief law officer), and five assistant secretaries, who coordinate the operations of the department's major bureaus and services.

The assistant secretary for **Policy, Management, and Budget** advises the secretary in all areas of administration. The assistant secretary also oversees the Office of Insular Affairs, which coordinates federal policy regarding the U.S.-administered territories of American Samoa, Guam, the U.S. Virgin Islands, the Commonwealth of the Northern Marianas, and other outlying Caribbean and Pacific territories.

The assistant secretary for **Fish and Wildlife and Parks** manages the National Park Service and the U.S. Fish and Wildlife Service (FWS). These services oversee some 380 national parks and 540 wildlife refuges. FWS also leads the effort to protect and restore endangered wildlife and plants.

The assistant secretary for **Water and Science** manages the U.S. Geological Survey, which conducts scientific studies (including mapping) of public lands, and the Bureau of Reclamation, which oversees and protects water and related resources.

The assistant secretary for **Land and Minerals Management** oversees the Bureau of Land Management, the Minerals Management Service, and the Office of Surface Mining, Reclamation, and Enforcement. These agencies operate leasing programs to develop energy and mineral resources and enforce the restoration of land that has been strip-mined.

The assistant secretary for **Indian Affairs** operates the Bureau of Indian Affairs, which administers federal programs for the Native Americans who live on or near national reservation lands.

In 1849, Congress created the Department of the Interior to administer the country's vast land holdings (notably the Louisiana Purchase and the Oregon Territory) and its Indian Affairs. DOI headquarters are located at 1849 C Street, N.W., Washington, D.C. 20240.

STEVEN GOLDSTEIN
Assistant to the Secretary and Director of Public Affairs, United States Department of the Interior

See also NATIONAL PARK SYSTEM.

Secretaries of the Interior		
Name	**Took Office**	**Under President**
Thomas Ewing	1849	Taylor
T. M. T. McKennan	1850	Fillmore
A. H. H. Stuart	1850	Fillmore
Robert McClelland	1853	Pierce
Jacob Thompson	1857	Buchanan
Caleb B. Smith	1861	Lincoln
John P. Usher	1863	Lincoln, A. Johnson
James Harlan	1865	A. Johnson
Orville H. Browning	1866	A. Johnson
Jacob D. Cox	1869	Grant
Columbus Delano	1870	Grant
Zachariah Chandler	1875	Grant
*Carl Schurz	1877	Hayes
Samuel J. Kirkwood	1881	Garfield, Arthur
Henry M. Teller	1882	Arthur
L. Q. C. Lamar	1885	Cleveland
William F. Vilas	1888	Cleveland
John W. Noble	1889	B. Harrison
Hoke Smith	1893	Cleveland
David R. Francis	1896	Cleveland
Cornelius N. Bliss	1897	McKinley
Ethan A. Hitchcock	1898	McKinley, T. Roosevelt
James R. Garfield	1907	T. Roosevelt
Richard A. Ballinger	1909	Taft
Walter L. Fisher	1911	Taft
Franklin K. Lane	1913	Wilson
John B. Payne	1920	Wilson
Albert B. Fall	1921	Harding
Hubert Work	1923	Harding, Coolidge
Roy O. West	1928	Coolidge
Ray L. Wilbur	1929	Hoover
Harold L. Ickes	1933	F. D. Roosevelt, Truman
Julius A. Krug	1946	Truman
Oscar L. Chapman	1949	Truman
Douglas McKay	1953	Eisenhower
Frederick A. Seaton	1956	Eisenhower
*Stewart L. Udall	1961	Kennedy, L. B. Johnson
Walter J. Hickel	1969	Nixon
Rogers C. B. Morton	1971	Nixon, Ford
Stanley K. Hathaway	1975	Ford
Thomas S. Kleppe	1975	Ford
Cecil D. Andrus	1977	Carter
James G. Watt	1981	Reagan
William P. Clark	1983	Reagan
Donald P. Hodel	1985	Reagan
Manuel Lujan, Jr.	1989	G. Bush
*Bruce Babbitt	1993	Clinton
Gale Norton	2001	G. W. Bush

*Subject of a separate profile. Consult the Index.

INTERIOR DESIGN

Interior design is the art of planning and carrying out the design for the inside of a room, a home, a business, or a public building. Interior design is also called **interior decorating**. Since we live and work mostly indoors, it is important that the interiors of our homes and other buildings please us and suit our needs. The best interior design makes people feel comfortable and happy. People who are not professional designers often decorate their own homes and businesses.

From the earliest times, people have decorated the places they live to make them as comfortable, convenient, functional, and beautiful as possible. The ancient Egyptians decorated their walls with murals, or large wall paintings. Their furniture was often inlaid with ebony and ivory. The ancient Romans also used wall paintings, as well as colorful mosaics on the floors.

In the Middle Ages (500–1500), the castles and manor houses of Europe were built more for defense than for beauty and comfort. Furniture was simple and useful. Interior design as we know it—with decorative furniture,

curtains, and rugs—emerged toward the end of the Middle Ages and during the Renaissance (1300–1600), a time when comfort and beauty became more important to people.

During the Renaissance, people traveled to distant lands and rediscovered the art of ancient Greece and Rome. As a result, new styles of interior design developed. There have been many decorating styles over the years. Some have been simple and elegant. Some have been rich and elaborate. Many things continue to affect styles of decora-

Top: A bedroom from ancient Rome is decorated with lavish murals. *Below:* Elegant furniture and lots of accessories distinguish this formal living room. *Right:* The contemporary feel of this living room comes from its clean, straight lines and large windows.

Above: A simple black-and-white color scheme and bright natural light give this kitchen a modern appearance. *Right:* In this kitchen, warm light, wood tones, and rustic furnishings create a country atmosphere.

tion—travel to other countries, scientific discoveries, lifestyle changes, and changes in architecture and building methods.

▶ **ELEMENTS OF DESIGN**

A well-designed room creates a mood that suits its use and the people who will use it. The designer uses various elements to create these moods. Among the most important elements of design are the style; the balance, scale, and placement of the furniture; color and light; and pattern and texture.

Style. Today people can choose from the styles of many periods, from the traditional designs of the past to modern, or contemporary, styles. They tend to choose styles that suit the way they live. For example, Early American furniture was sturdy and plain. The early settlers were too busy farming and clearing the wilderness to make anything but necessary and useful objects. Today this style is a favorite of people who want a "country" look.

Some people want a more formal look. They might choose elegant furniture in the Chippendale style, which was first popular in England in the 1700's. Or they might want a contemporary look, with clean lines and lots of glass. It is not necessary for all the furnishings to be from exactly the same style or period, but they should reflect the same mood.

Balance and Scale. "Balance" refers to the way the furnishings of a room are arranged.

Furniture should be arranged to take into account the natural traffic patterns of a room and what is pleasing to the eye. It would look odd if all the tall pieces were at one end of the room and all the low pieces at the other.

"Scale" refers to the size of the furniture in relation to the room, to other pieces of furniture in the room, and to the people who will use it. Large pieces of furniture may look crowded in a small room, and small furniture may seem lost in a large room. A delicate table might seem out of place next to a heavy, overstuffed sofa.

Color and Light. Color is important in creating the mood of a room. Yellow, orange, and red are warm, cheerful colors. Blue and green are cool, relaxing colors. Earth tones—brown, orange, rust, dark green, and gold—help create a cozy, country look. White and beige—perhaps with accents of bright red, blue, or fresh green—produce a crisper, more formal look.

The colors chosen for a room make up its color scheme. The designer may choose a monochromatic scheme (a scheme using variations of the same color). This often produces a restful mood. Or the scheme may include related colors, such as yellow and orange or blue and green. Contrasting colors—red and blue, for example—can create an exciting color scheme. If too many colors are used, they can be distracting. Color and light go hand in hand. Light colors will reflect light, while dark colors will absorb light and make a room darker. A room that gets little natural light will seem brighter if light colors are used.

Lighting should suit the mood and the use of the room. A busy kitchen will need more light than a study. Window curtains, shades, and shutters can be used to control the amount of daylight. At night most rooms need background lighting and area lighting. Background lighting, such as that from wall lamps or recessed lights, is reflected from the walls and ceiling to light the whole room softly. Area lighting provides more light for such tasks as reading, playing cards, or using a computer.

Pattern and Texture. Designers use fabrics, rugs, and wall coverings to add pattern and texture to a room. They try to choose patterns and textures that will blend well and will suit the style of the furnishings. Adding pattern and texture helps keep the room from being boring. And when the same pattern is used in several places it can help unify the room.

▶**HOW AN INTERIOR DESIGNER WORKS**

Suppose that an interior designer is asked to decorate a casual living room for a family of four. The first step is to meet with the family. The designer will measure the room and find out how the family wants to use it and how much money they can spend on decorating it. This will affect the kind of furniture they buy and the way it will be arranged. If they do a great deal of entertaining, for example, they will need more seating than they would otherwise. If they have books, a sound system, or video-game equipment they want to use in the room, the designer will have to devise shelves to hold these items.

Next the designer draws a plan of the room, putting in doors and windows, and marks the plan to show where the furniture will be placed. The plan is done to scale. That is, if the scale is 1 inch (2.54 centimeters) to 1 foot (30 centimeters), every foot (30 centimeters) of the room's dimensions will be shown as 1 inch (2.54 centimeters) on the plan. The furniture is shown in the same scale.

The plan reflects the room's traffic pattern—how people will probably move through the room—as well as its use. The furniture should be arranged so that the space in the room is used in an appealing way—so that pieces are not crowded together or spaced too far apart. Furniture placement must also be functional. For example, side ta-

A scale drawing (*right*) allows an interior designer to plan the layout of a room. Designers may also use computer-generated images (*below right*) to test different furniture styles and color schemes. The finished room (*below*) reflects the careful planning.

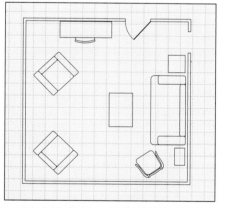

DECORATING YOUR ROOM

Your room is the one place in your home that belongs to you. Even if you share it with someone else, there are many ways to put your personal stamp on it.

Your Room Plan

Measure your room accurately, then make a scale drawing of it on graph paper. Remember to include the location of the windows, doors, and radiators. Doors should not hit anything, and no furniture should block a radiator. You want to use the natural light from the windows. On another piece of paper, draw the shapes of your bed and other furniture to scale, and cut them out. Place the furniture shapes on the drawing so that they represent how your furniture is arranged now. Move the shapes around until you get a new arrangement that you like.

Think about what you do in your room besides sleep. Do you do homework and work on hobbies there? Do you lie on your bed to talk on the telephone or listen to music? Do you entertain friends there? Now, think about what furniture accommodates those activities. A sturdy chair and a practical desk with a good light are important for doing homework. A bed placed along a wall can be used as a couch if you add cushions.

Next, with someone's help, try to arrange the actual furniture. Is the arrangement practical and appealing to you? If it is, you have done an excellent job. If it is not, rearrange it on paper and try again.

Your Color Scheme

The color of your room can reflect your interests and personality. Do you like sports? How about using your team's colors and logo as part of your color and design scheme? If you like the beach, try using the colors of shells for your walls and bedsheets.

Wallpaper, fabrics, posters, and pictures can all be used to add color to your room. Wallpaper borders and stenciling can enliven the ceiling or walls. Desk accessories can be covered with wrapping paper, and window shades can be decorated with fabric trim or painted scenes.

Storage Space and Organizers

If you have a convenient place to store your things, it will be easy to keep your room neat. You will also create more space for your possessions, and it will be easy to find what you need when you need it.

Begin with the closet. The top shelf may be hard to reach, so it is ideal for things that you do not use every day (such as seasonal sweaters and ice skates). Storage cubes can be stacked in your closet, and shoe bags that hold many pairs of shoes can be hung on the walls.

bles should be near chairs. The designer also determines the room's focal point. If it has a fireplace or a good view through a window, chairs and sofas will be placed so that people can enjoy these things. With a computer-aided design (CAD) program, a designer can use computer graphics to show a client a three-dimensional view of how the finished room might look.

When the family has approved the plan, the designer helps them decide on the style of furniture and the color scheme of the room. They may want a country look, a contemporary look, or an Asian look. Or they may prefer a mixture of styles. Then the designer helps the family choose pieces that fit the room's scale as well as its style.

The next step is to design a background—wall and floor coverings, fabrics, and window treatments—that works with the style chosen for the room. Wallpaper or wood paneling on the walls might suit a country look, for example. The designer may even add ceiling beams to complete the look. On the other hand, glossy painted walls and mirrors might go well in a contemporary room. The floor covering may be wood with area rugs in front of the sofas and chairs, or wall-to-wall carpeting. Formal draperies might suit one room and casual, wooden shutters another.

The designer will also devise the lighting for the room. There must be strong lamps near sofas and chairs for reading. Spotlights and track lights can be used to highlight a work of art or to wash a wall with light. If the lights are controlled by dimmers, they can be changed from soft to bright to meet the requirements of the moment.

In addition to having an area for schoolwork and plenty of play space, this child's bedroom is decorated with accessories that reflect an interest in transportation. The coordinated color scheme unifies the room.

Belts, ties, scarves, and even jewelry can hang on the inside of the closet door.

Three storage areas are often overlooked in bedrooms. One area is under the bed. Toys, games, or sports equipment can be kept there. Another area is above the door and below the windows. These are ideal places to hang shelves on brackets. The third area often ignored is the ceiling, from which you can hang plants or attractive lightweight baskets for storage of small items.

Your Accessories

Accessories are pictures and posters, flags, maps, mirrors, vases, and personal treasures. If you draw or take photographs you might want to frame some of your work and hang it on your walls or even your ceiling. Bulletin boards can be used to display items as well.

One last item is proper lighting. You will need a desk lamp; a floor, table, or wall lamp for wherever you read; and, if possible, an overhead light to illuminate the entire room.

Decorating your room can be fun and rewarding. If you begin with confidence and proceed carefully, you can create a pleasant and comfortable place to spend time and entertain friends.

BARBARA BROOKS
Family Circle magazine
Reviewed by KATHRYN GEORGE
Decorating Remodeling Magazine

The final step is to add accessories to the room. Accessories include paintings, vases, candlesticks, and other personal things.

▶ **CAREERS IN INTERIOR DESIGN**

Interior designers work in many areas. For instance, real-estate developers and furniture stores may employ designers to advise their customers. In addition to decorating homes, designers help make offices, restaurants, schools, and hospitals as comfortable and attractive as possible.

Most successful designers have had some formal study in preparation for their profession. There are schools that teach how to draw, how to measure rooms and make scale drawings, how to decide what furnishings are appropriate for what space, and how to design structural changes. Courses cover design for homes and businesses, as well as the history of interior decoration.

There are several organizations that can help students and professional interior designers. The largest of these, the American Society of Interior Designers (ASID), publishes a student newsletter and also sponsors scholarship competitions. Other organizations include the Interior Design Educators Council (IDEC) and the International Interior Design Association.

FRED LOWE VESTAL
Interior Designer
Reviewed by KATHRYN GEORGE
Decorating Remodeling Magazine

See also ANTIQUES AND ANTIQUE COLLECTING; COLOR; DECORATIVE ARTS; DESIGN; FURNITURE; RUGS AND CARPETS; TEXTILES.

INTERJECTION. See PARTS OF SPEECH.

INTERNAL-COMBUSTION ENGINES

An internal-combustion engine changes the heat energy of burning fuel into power and motion. This power can be harnessed to turn the wheels of an automobile or truck, the propeller of an airplane or ship, and the shaft of a generator, as well as run many other machines.

"Internal combustion" means that the fuel is burned inside the engine, where it does its work. Gasoline engines, diesel engines, and gas turbines are all internal-combustion engines. The steam engine is an external-combustion engine, because its fuel is burned in a separate firebox, away from its moving parts. When fuel is burned in an internal-combustion engine, it produces great quantities of rapidly expanding gases. These gases drive a piston or a rotor directly.

Internal-combustion engines are divided into two basic classes. These are reciprocating engines, in which the work is done by a piston moving back and forth in a cylinder, and rotary engines, in which the work is done by a turning rotor. Gasoline and diesel engines are reciprocating engines. Gas turbines and the Wankel engine are rotary engines.

This article focuses mainly on the gasoline engine. You can find out more about other types of engines in the articles DIESEL ENGINES in Volume D, ENGINES in Volume E, and TURBINES in Volume T.

▶ HOW THE GASOLINE ENGINE WORKS

In a gasoline engine, fuel is burned in a **cylinder**, which is a chamber closed at one end. As the fuel burns, the expanding gases press outward in all directions. They cannot escape through the sides or the closed end of the cylinder. But at the other end of the cylinder is a movable stopper, or **piston**, which slides back and forth. The pressure of the expanding gases drives the piston down with great force. As the piston travels down, it turns a **crankshaft**. In this way the straight-line motion of the piston is converted into rotary, or turning, motion. The turning crankshaft brings the piston back up in the cylinder again. A strong metal **connecting rod** links the piston to the crankshaft.

Early designers ran up against the problem of keeping the expanding gases from leaking past the piston and wasting power. The piston could not be made to fit too tightly, since heat from the burning fuel would cause the piston to expand and get stuck. The problem was solved by the use of **piston rings**. These are thin, springy metal rings that fit in grooves around the piston and project a short distance. The rings press tightly against the cylinder walls and keep gas from leaking past.

The Four-Stroke Cycle. Gasoline engines do not produce power on every stroke of the piston. Most are designed so that only one stroke out of every four produces power. The other three strokes get the engine ready for the next power stroke.

FOUR-STROKE CYCLE IN A GASOLINE ENGINE

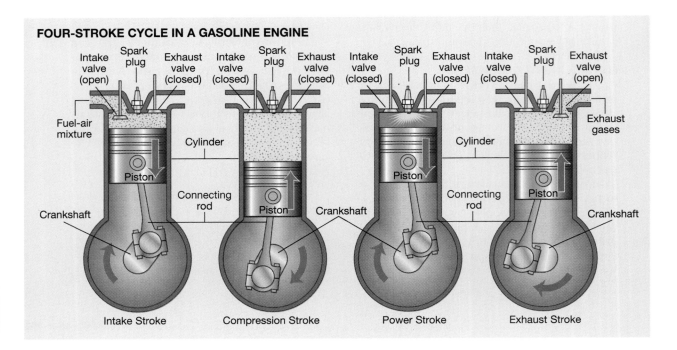

Intake Stroke | Compression Stroke | Power Stroke | Exhaust Stroke

On the first stroke the piston moves downward, sucking in a mixture of fuel and air through a small hole in the top of the cylinder called an **intake port**. This stroke is called the **intake stroke**. A valve in the intake port, called the **intake valve**, opens up to let in the fuel-air mixture and closes again at the end of the stroke.

During the **compression stroke**, the piston moves up toward the top of the cylinder. Since the intake valve is now closed, the fuel-air mixture cannot escape, and the rising piston squeezes it into a much smaller volume. The more tightly the piston compresses the fuel-air mixture, the faster it will burn and the more power it will produce. The amount that the piston compresses the fuel-air mixture is called the **compression ratio**. For example, a compression ratio of 8:1 means that the fuel-air mixture takes up eight times as much space at the beginning of the compression stroke as it does at the end.

When the piston reaches the top of the compression stroke, an electric spark ignites the fuel-air mixture. The gases produced by this rapid burning of the fuel expand with great force—about 60 to 70 times that of normal atmospheric pressure—and drive the piston down, in the **power stroke**.

Finally, in the **exhaust stroke**, the piston begins to rise again, and an exhaust valve in the top of the cylinder opens. The rising piston pushes the burned gases out. When the piston reaches the top of its stroke, the exhaust valve closes, and the engine is ready to begin a new cycle. This cycle is repeated as often as several thousand times a minute.

As anyone who has ever run a gasoline-powered lawn mower knows, a one-cylinder engine vibrates a great deal. The reason is that only one stroke out of every four is a power stroke. Engine designers learned that they could get around this problem by using a number of smaller cylinders instead of one large cylinder. With a number of cylinders attached to the same crankshaft, at least one cylinder is always giving a power stroke. The engine produces a steady flow of power.

The Two-Stroke Cycle. An engine that works on a two-stroke cycle produces power on every downstroke of the piston, or every second stroke. It does this by combining three operations—exhaust, intake, and compression—into one stroke.

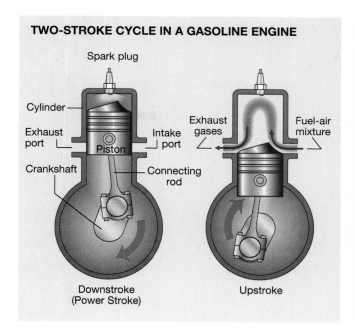

TWO-STROKE CYCLE IN A GASOLINE ENGINE

Spark plug

Cylinder

Exhaust port

Piston

Crankshaft

Intake port

Connecting rod

Exhaust gases

Fuel-air mixture

Downstroke (Power Stroke)

Upstroke

The two-stroke engine has no intake or exhaust valves. Instead, it has open ports in the sides of the cylinder. The piston covers and uncovers these ports as it rides up and down. The fuel-air mixture is compressed before it enters the cylinder, either by a piston or, in some engines, by a blower.

As the piston reaches the bottom of the stroke, it uncovers the intake and exhaust ports. The fuel-air mixture sweeps in through the intake port as the burned gases go out the exhaust port. Sometimes some of the fuel-air mixture passes out the exhaust port along with the burned gases. This wastes fuel. Sometimes part of the burned gas remains in the cylinder. This means that the fuel-air mixture does not burn as well as it should.

The two-stroke principle permits the use of smaller, lighter engines. Because two-stroke engines use more fuel than equally powerful four-stroke engines, they are chiefly used where small size and light weight are important, as in outboard motors for boats.

▶ **PARTS OF THE GASOLINE ENGINE**

The cylinder block and head, piston, connecting rod, and crankshaft are the basic parts of the engine. But there are many other parts, without which the engine will not run.

Fuel System. One of the most important parts mixes the fuel with air so that it will burn fast enough to create a push on the pis-

CROSS SECTION OF A GASOLINE ENGINE

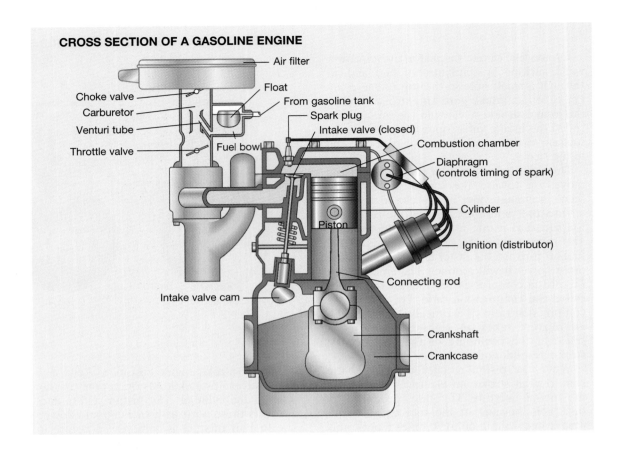

ton. In older engines, a device called a **carburetor** breaks up the liquid fuel into a fine mist of tiny droplets by means of a high-speed jet of air. The droplets of gasoline turn into a vapor, which burns very rapidly in air and expands with great force.

An engine needs a richer mixture (one that contains more gasoline) when it is just starting than it does when it has warmed up. In engines with carburetors, this is taken care of by a valve called the **choke**, which controls the proportions of gasoline and air in the fuel-air mixture. Another valve called the **throttle** controls the speed of the engine by regulating the amount of fuel-air mixture that can enter the cylinders.

Most newer gasoline engines use **fuel injection** instead of a carburetor. Fuel injection is the method of spraying a small amount of fuel into each cylinder. The piston compresses the mixture of air and fuel, and the mixture ignites. Fuel injection allows very carefully controlled amounts of fuel and air to enter each cylinder. This provides more power, and unburned fuel is not wasted.

The amount of power a particular engine can produce depends on the amounts of fuel and air that can enter the cylinders. Some engines are equipped with pumps called **turbochargers** or **superchargers**, which can force additional fuel and air into the cylinders. Turbochargers are driven by exhaust gases, while superchargers are driven by the engine. Both devices help make fuel burning more complete and thus deliver more power.

Ignition System. An electric spark is needed to ignite the fuel-air mixture in the cylinder. The electric current is provided by a battery. The current passes through the coil, which increases the voltage of the current. In older engines, the current then travels to the distributor, which sends the electricity to the spark plugs in an exactly timed sequence. There is a spark plug in the head of each cylinder. Electric sparks jump the gap between two electrodes on the spark plug and ignite the fuel-air mixture in the cylinder. Many newer engines use a computer-controlled electronic ignition system instead of a distributor to trigger the spark plugs.

Lubricating System. The engine must be kept lubricated so that its moving parts will slide smoothly over each other. Without lubrication the moving parts would soon become overheated and jam. They would also wear out very quickly. An oil pump forces oil from the crankcase through tiny openings in the cylinder block, the crankshaft, and the connecting rods, so that the oil reaches every moving part. The crankcase serves as a central oil reservoir. Most engines have an oil filter to strain dust and grit out of the oil.

Cooling System. It takes more than lubrication to keep the engine from becoming overheated. There must be some way of getting rid of the unused heat from the burning fuel. Large automobile or truck engines usually have a liquid cooling system. A water pump circulates a liquid coolant through passages in the cylinder block. The coolant takes up heat from the engine and gives it up to the air as the coolant passes through the radiator. The radiator is basically a set of thin-walled metal tubes through which heat can easily pass. These tubes are covered with metal fins to increase the area that gives off heat to the air. A fan driven by the engine pulls air through the radiator.

Exhaust System. The poisonous gases made by the burning fuel must be led away after they have done their work of driving the piston. A chamber called the exhaust manifold collects the burned gases from each cylinder. From the manifold the gases pass through an exhaust pipe and out into the air. A silencer called a muffler is usually added to the exhaust pipe.

▶ **HISTORY**

The first practical internal-combustion engine was built in 1859 by French engineer Étienne Lenoir. His engine operated very smoothly. But it was not very powerful, because the fuel-air mixture was not compressed and so did not burn fast enough.

The next step forward was the four-stroke cycle, including compression of the fuel-air mixture, patented in 1862 by another French engineer, Alphonse Beau de Rochas. However, it was not until 1876 that the first four-stroke engine was successfully built, by German inventor Nikolaus Otto. In 1885, another German engineer, Gottlieb Daimler, developed the first successful four-stroke engine to burn gasoline. The following year, Karl Benz, also of Germany, patented the first practical automobile powered by an internal-combustion engine. Other inventors added various improvements over the years, but today's internal-combustion engines are basically the same as those of the late 1800's.

In 1954, German engineer Felix Wankel patented a new type of rotary engine. Instead of pistons, the Wankel engine has a three-faced rotor sweeping around inside an oval combustion chamber. In one revolution of the rotor, a complete four-stage engine cycle takes place on each of the rotor's three faces. The Wankel engine runs more smoothly and has fewer moving parts than the piston engine. However, piston engines have so far remained more popular for automobiles, largely because of their greater efficiency.

▶ **NEWER DEVELOPMENTS**

Many technological advances have been applied to the internal-combustion engine since the 1950's. Along with fuel injection and turbocharging, mentioned above, are pollution controls and computerization.

Pollution Controls. In the 1960's, the first laws were passed in the United States to reduce pollution from internal-combustion engines. Pollution controls were introduced into automobiles. These included modifying the internal-combustion engine so that more complete burning of fuel takes place and lowering combustion temperatures.

Another pollution-control method has been to recirculate exhaust gas and fuel vapors back into the cylinders for further combustion. And perhaps the most important pollution-control device is the catalytic converter. This device uses a special chemical called a catalyst to convert some of the exhaust pollutants into harmless substances.

Computerization. Most new automobiles now have tiny computers that control many of the engine's functions, such as engine speed, pollution control, choke settings, and mixing fuel and air. The computer can analyze how the automobile's systems are operating and re-adjust the engine for greater efficiency. It can even alert the driver to any trouble developing in the engine.

Reviewed by Ford Motor Company

See also AUTOMOBILES; DIESEL ENGINES; ENGINES; JET PROPULSION; TURBINES.

INTERNATIONAL DATE LINE

The international date line is the imaginary line on the Earth where a calendar day ends and the next one begins. It extends from the North Pole to the South Pole along or close to the **180th meridian**, one of the longitudinal lines that are drawn on maps and globes. The date on the western side of the line is one full day ahead of the date on the eastern side of the line. For example, when it is 6 P.M. Friday on the western side of the line, it is 6 P.M. Thursday on the eastern side. Why is this so?

The Earth is divided into 24 standard time zones. Each zone covers 15 degrees longitude, extending 7½ degrees east and 7½ degrees west from its central meridian of longitude. This is a convenient measure, because the Earth rotates eastward at the rate of 15 degrees longitude an hour. Moving westward, therefore, each succeeding time zone is one hour earlier than the zone before it. Moving eastward, each succeeding zone is one hour later. The starting zone is labeled by the **prime meridian** (0 degrees longitude), which runs through Greenwich, England—the site of the world's first astronomical observatory.

Suppose it is 6 A.M. Friday at the prime meridian. What time is it in the standard time zones of the "later half" of the world, moving east from the prime meridian to the 180th meridian (zones +1 through +12)? The time in each eastward zone is 1 hour later than the time in the preceding zone (zones –1 through –12). Therefore, in this half of the world (representing the 12 hours from 6 A.M. Friday to 6 P.M. Friday), the latest time on the globe (6 P.M. Friday) is found at the 180th meridian. What time is it in the "earlier half" of the world, moving west from the prime meridian to the 180th meridian? Each westward zone is 1 hour earlier than the preceding one. Therefore, in this half of the world (representing the 12 hours from 6 A.M. Friday to 6 P.M. Thursday), the earliest time on the globe is also found at the 180th meridian.

Nations of the world selected the 180th meridian as the dividing line between the Earth's earliest and latest hours because it runs largely through ocean rather than land. And by zigzagging away from the 180th meridian in a few places, the international date line avoids land entirely. This prevents nearby villages and towns from having two different dates.

GERALD L. GREENBERG
Former Chief of Information Acquisitions
Earth Science Information Center
United States Geological Survey

See also TIME.

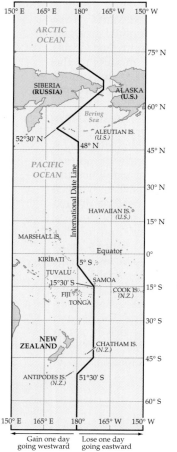

Gain one day going westward | Lose one day going eastward

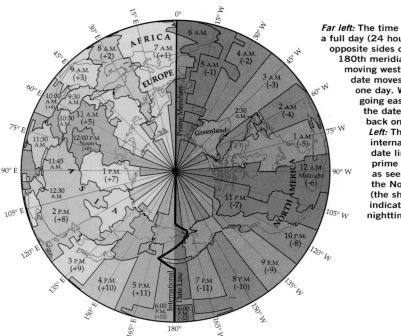

Far left: The time differs by a full day (24 hours) on opposite sides of the 180th meridian. When moving westward, the date moves forward one day. When going eastward, the date is set back one day. *Left:* The international date line and prime meridian as seen from the North Pole (the shaded half indicates nighttime).

The ratified Intermediate Range Nuclear Forces (INF) Treaty, banning production and use of some nuclear weapons, was signed by U.S. President Ronald Reagan (left) and Soviet leader Mikhail Gorbachev in 1988. Such treaties are a basis of international law.

INTERNATIONAL LAW

International law is the system of rules that nations have agreed to follow in their behavior toward each other. These rules arose from the need of countries to try to live in harmony with one another. International law developed gradually, over many centuries, and is still in the process of change.

Sources of International Law. The two main sources of international law are treaties and custom. Treaties (or conventions) are agreements signed by nations. They may be between two nations, as in a treaty to return criminals from one country to another; or among many nations, as in the charter that created the United Nations.

International custom includes rules that have developed through long usage. Rules protecting diplomats, for example, were long observed by nations, although they were not written into formal treaties until relatively recent times.

To a lesser extent, international law may also be derived from general principles of law, such as the right of a country to defend itself. Such basic principles of law become guidelines for the development of rules of international law. Other limited sources of international law include the decisions of national and international courts, and the writings of legal scholars. International organizations historically had little impact on international law. The United Nations has had greater influence than earlier organizations,

but resolutions of its General Assembly are not considered binding by many nations. In some instances, nations may agree on decisions by courts based on the concept of "fairness and justice," (*ex aequo et bono*).

A Law of Nations. International law is a law of nations. Unlike national (or domestic) law, the participants are countries, not people. In some areas, however, such as human rights, individuals may play an important role. They may, in some cases, take a nation before an international court, such as the European Court of Human Rights.

The rules of international law are more difficult to establish and to enforce than the laws of individual countries. There is no clearly established authority within the framework of international law that can make rules for all nations. There is no single court system to regularly interpret these rules, and no police or military establishment to enforce them. For these reasons, the question is sometimes raised of whether international law really is law.

The International System: International law *is* law, even though it lacks the clear, regular features of national law. Instead of one system of courts, for example, several are used. The most important is the International Court of Justice (at The Hague, in the Netherlands), which can and does rule on any aspects of law presented to it by nations. Nations do not have to use the International Court, but if they do, they are bound by its decisions.

Certain agencies, such as the International Civil Aviation Organization, also have the authority to act as courts in specific cases. In addition, special commissions often are established by nations to interpret and apply the rules of international law.

Agreement and Enforcement. One of the key elements in international law is agreement. Nations must first agree to accept rules of international law before they can be bound by them. A treaty between the United States and Russia on arms control, for example, is binding only on these two countries. Similarly, an agreement on ways to protect the environment signed by twelve nations would have to be observed by the twelve nations concerned, but not necessarily by others.

In general, the great majority of countries adhere to the important international conventions and to those rules that have been established by long usage.

The question of enforcement is one of the most difficult aspects of international law. Without an international police or military force, nations would appear to have little power to compel other nations to observe the rules of international law, aside from going to war. In fact, there are penalties that can be imposed on countries, although they are not as clearly defined or as regularly enforced as the penalties for violations of domestic law.

Sanctions. Countries that violate international law may have economic sanctions (penalties) applied against them. As one example, many nations imposed trade and other sanctions against South Africa because of its racial laws. In extreme cases, force may be used—either war or a single military action intended to deter further violations.

The main problem in enforcement is not in finding ways to penalize nations for violations of international law. Rather, it is getting nations to agree on the means to be used. As a result, sanctions, especially those involving military force, are often used by a single country or just a few countries. Countries acting alone in claiming to enforce international law, however, may themselves be subject to sanctions if they have violated international law.

Political Measures. Political measures are more commonly used than military action in enforcing international law. Public opinion plays an important part in forcing nations to abide by the rules. A country that has been

The surviving leaders of the Nazi German government were tried for war crimes after World War II by an international tribunal in Nuremberg, Germany.

criticized for violations of international law may find it difficult to conclude treaties and similar political and economic arrangements with other countries. Political leaders in democratic countries may even be forced out of office because of charges that they violated international law.

Mutual Benefit. The threat of penalties, however, is far outweighed by the idea of mutual benefit in leading countries to obey the rules of international law. International law developed, after all, because countries found it to be in their best interests to agree on certain rules to govern their relations with each other.

Rules on private property, for example, are intended to protect people from having their property in another country taken away without just compensation. Rules on the law of the sea and of airspace allow ships and airplanes to travel the world in an orderly fashion. Prohibitions against the illegal use of force not only protect small nations from large nations, but also help to keep large nations from conflicts with each other.

A last, but especially important, mutual benefit is predictability. The rules of international law permit a country to know what to expect in its relations with other countries. It is the unexpected that has often led to conflicts among nations.

GARY L. MARIS
Stetson University
Author, *International Law: An Introduction*

See also INTERNATIONAL RELATIONS; TREATIES.

INTERNATIONAL RELATIONS

International relations is a branch of political science that deals with the way nations get along, or manage their relations, with one another. When all goes well, relations among nations are peaceful. But countries, like human beings, do not always agree. When trouble arises, there is no worldwide police force that can step in to keep order among nations. Nor is there a single government or body of laws that all countries have agreed to obey.

Foreign Policy. Instead, each country draws up its own foreign policy—the general course it tries to follow in dealing with other nations. A country's foreign policy is designed to protect its security and advance its interests. This policy may be influenced by history, tradition, and public opinion—and by the power the country has to carry out its aims.

Even if countries try to get along, they are bound to differ on some of their foreign policy goals. When these differences become serious, countries usually try to settle them by peaceful means. But they may go to war to achieve their goals if peaceful negotiations fail. Thus a main task of those involved in international relations is to avoid conflict by building peaceful relations among nations. This is the function of diplomats and other foreign policy experts of government.

Diplomacy. Diplomacy has been described as the art and practice of achieving national goals by peaceful means. Diplomats—those who engage in diplomacy—represent their countries abroad. They may do so at international conferences, held for the purpose of regulating trade, making disarmament agreements, arranging peace treaties, or settling other international issues. Or they may reside in a country as official representatives of their governments. Such diplomats are usually referred to as ambassadors.

Alliances. Nations traditionally sought alliances as one way of protecting themselves and their interests. Alliances are formal agreements between two or more countries, in which they promise to support one another in a common policy toward other countries. Members of an alliance are called allies. Alliances are usually formed by countries that have a common interest or, more importantly, a common enemy. One aim of alliances was to maintain a balance of power, preventing one nation from becoming so powerful as to dominate all others.

In 1999, member nations of the North Atlantic Treaty Organization (NATO) met at the World Court in the Netherlands to discuss the ongoing civil war in Yugoslavia.

Nations that refuse to take an active part in international affairs in this way in peacetime are said to be following a policy of isolation. Nations that refuse to ally themselves with any nations in a war or other conflict are said to be neutral or following a policy of neutrality. But it is difficult today for a nation to maintain a policy of isolation. International trade, for example, has made all nations increasingly interdependent.

Arbitration and Mediation. If diplomacy fails, countries may choose arbitration as a way to avoid the use of force. If the parties agree, their dispute can be submitted to the International Court of Justice at The Hague, in the Netherlands. (This body is sometimes called the World Court.) The Court was created to settle disputes between countries, just as disagreements among individuals are settled in national (or domestic) courts. It has judges drawn from many countries. As an alternative, a neutral country may be asked to arbitrate a dispute. Since the decisions made in arbitration must be accepted, countries often prefer the process of mediation instead. A mediator offers suggestions, not binding on the parties concerned, which may point a way out of the disagreement.

International Organizations. Statesmen long sought the creation of a world organization that would enforce peace and help settle disputes among nations. The first such organization, the League of Nations, was conceived by U.S. president Woodrow Wilson and established under the Treaty of Versailles (1919), at the end of World War I. (The treaty also created the International Court of Justice.) The United Nations, which replaced the League in 1945, is today the primary international organization dedicated to helping nations resolve conflicts.

SAMUEL FLAGG BEMIS
Yale University
FRED HARVEY HARRINGTON
University of Wisconsin

See also DISARMAMENT; INTERNATIONAL LAW; LEAGUE OF NATIONS; NORTH ATLANTIC TREATY ORGANIZATION (NATO); PEACE MOVEMENTS; UNITED NATIONS.

INTERNATIONAL TRADE

International trade is the exchange of goods and services among countries. In most cases, countries do not trade the actual goods and services. Rather, they use the income received from the sale of their products to buy the products of other countries.

Why Nations Trade. Nations trade for several reasons. Most important, they must trade because natural resources vary from country to country. For example, Canada is rich in deposits of the mineral nickel, but its climate is too cold for oranges to be grown. The United States has little nickel, but it produces, among other things, large crops of oranges. Therefore, it makes sense for the United States to export (sell) oranges to Canada and import (buy) Canadian nickel.

Most international trade is carried out between industrialized nations that have relatively high standards of living. One reason for this is that people in such countries usually have enough income to buy foreign products. Another is that industrialized countries generally produce a greater variety of goods.

Primary Products. Many countries with little industry get much of their income from the export of one or two primary products. Primary products are the raw materials from which manufactured goods are made. They may be agricultural products; minerals; or forest products. The African nation of Ivory Coast, for example, is the world's chief producer of cacao, from which chocolate is made. Saudi Arabia and other oil-rich countries of the Middle East rely on petroleum exports for much of their income. Malaysia in Southeast Asia is a major exporter of rubber.

WONDER QUESTION

What are free ports and foreign-trade zones?

Most trading nations have customs-free zones set aside in or near their ports. The purpose of these zones is to encourage the use of the host country's materials, products, facilities, and services by companies involved in international trade. Merchants who send goods to a foreign country usually have to pay a tariff on the goods as soon as the goods arrive. Imports also may be subject to quotas. This is not true in a free port or customs-free zone. Foreign goods can be brought into these zones without being immediately subject to tariffs and most other restrictions. As long as the goods remain in the zones, they are not taxed.

Within a zone, the goods can be stored, processed, or combined with domestic items. If they are exported again, no tariffs are paid. Merchandise entering the host country from a zone is subject to customs taxes when it leaves the zone. At that time other restrictions, such as quotas, also apply.

JOHN J. DA PONTE, JR.
Foreign-Trade Zones Board
U.S. Department of Commerce

International shipping is the primary means of exchanging goods among nations. This Korean freighter in the port of Seattle, Washington, is loaded with American products for export.

The economies of such countries are heavily dependent on world prices for their products. If prices fall, the living standard of their people may suffer. To offset this, many countries try to diversify their economies, so that they can offer a greater variety of goods and services.

Balance of Payments. The record of all of a country's transactions with other countries is called its balance of payments. The difference between what a country exports and what it imports in a given year is called its balance of trade. If the monetary value of its exports is greater than the costs of its imports, a country is said to have a surplus in its balance of payments. If a country pays more for its imports than it receives for its exports, it has a deficit. A country that has a deficit must borrow or otherwise make up the difference in its balance of payments.

Tariffs and Other Trade Barriers. Governments sometimes set up barriers to international trade. One of these is the import duty, a tax on foreign goods that makes them more expensive to buy. All of one country's import duties are known as its tariff. Some countries also charge a duty on goods that are exported. Import and export duties are sometimes called customs duties. A country may also place a quota on other countries' products. A quota limits the quantity of a particular product that can be brought into a country in one year.

Setting up trade barriers is called protectionism. Countries usually impose tariffs and other barriers to trade to protect their own industries, particularly if they are new and as yet unable to compete with foreign industries. Protectionism and other restrictions on trade have long been in use. Since the end of World War II, however, the emphasis has been toward free trade, or the lowering of such restrictions.

Trade Organizations. In 1947 a group of 23 leading trading nations, including the United States, Canada, and many of the countries of Western Europe, formed the General Agreement on Tariffs and Trade (GATT). Renamed the World Trade Organization (WTO) in 1995, it now has more than 130 member countries that have agreed to abide by certain rules of international trade. These include nondiscrimination in trading patterns, reduction of tariffs through negotiations, and consultation by members on trade problems. The North American Free Trade Agreement (NAFTA), which was signed by Canada, the United States, and Mexico in 1992, created the largest free trade group in the Western Hemisphere. Other such regional organizations include the European Union (EU); the Organization of Petroleum Exporting Countries (OPEC); the Caribbean Community (CARICOM); the Central American Common Market (CACM); the Asia-Pacific Economic Co-Operation (APEC) group; and the Association of Southeast Asian Nations (ASEAN).

JOHN M. SUMANSKY
Director, Center for Economic Education
Bradley University

See also EUROPEAN UNION; GENERAL AGREEMENT ON TARIFFS AND TRADE (GATT); NORTH AMERICAN FREE TRADE AGREEMENT (NAFTA); TARIFF.

INTERNET. See COMPUTERS (Computers and the Internet).

INTESTINES. See DIGESTIVE SYSTEM.

The *nalukatak*, or "blanket toss," is a ceremonial custom of the Inupiat of Alaska (*top left*), an Inuit group that is closely related to the Inuit of Siberia, Russia (*top right*). A father and son kayak in the Canadian territory of Nunavut (*above*). Two Inuit women in Canada's Northwest Territories leave church on a snowmobile (*right*).

INUIT

The word "Inuit" means "the people" or "the real people." It refers to several groups of people living in the Arctic who share a common origin and similar cultural traditions. Among these groups are the Inupiat and Yupik of Alaska, the Inuit and Inuvialuit of Canada, the Kalaallit of Greenland, and the Yupik of Siberia.

At one time the word "Eskimo" was commonly used to describe the Inuit people. In some parts of the Inuit homeland, such as certain areas of Canada, people prefer to call themselves Inuit, as in their experience "Eskimo" has taken on a bad meaning. This is not the case in Alaska, where the term is still acceptable and used.

▶ ORIGINS

The Inuit people first entered North America about 5,500 years ago, crossing the Bering Strait from Asia. They moved rapidly across northern Canada to Greenland. Some Inuit groups then moved westward again, back to the Bering Sea area. For thousands of years, they lived in the Arctic, a region of vast, treeless plains, icy seas, and barren, rocky islands.

Isolated from other peoples, they developed a lifestyle suited to the harsh environment.

As a racial and cultural group, the Inuit are quite distinct from North American Indians. The Inuit are descended from an ancient Mongoloid people of Siberia in northern Asia. The Aleuts, who live in the Aleutian Islands and other islands in the North Pacific Ocean, are closely related.

Today the Inuit are no longer cut off from the outside world, and their way of life has changed. The Inuit population is not large, but it is growing. About 155,000 Inuit live in Alaska, Canada, Greenland, and Russia. Most Inuit now blend the old ways with the new. If you were to visit an Inuit community, you would find most of them living in modern houses, going to work or to school, and taking part in activities not too different from your own. But even with these changes, they still share common cultural traditions.

Language. Inuit languages have been spoken for thousands of years, but they were not written down until modern times. They form the Inuit-Inupiaq language family, which has no known connections with other language groups. Differences among the Inuit-Inupiaq dialects are small.

▶ **TRADITIONAL WAY OF LIFE**

This section describes the Inuit's traditional way of life, which they followed until modern technology and other advancements became available.

Group Life. The Inuit lived in fairly small groups. There were villages of over 500 people on the northern Alaska coast, but in the eastern regions (Greenland, Baffin Island, and Labrador), typical groups had only 25 to 45 people. Eastern groups moved from place to place through the year. They would spend winter near the coast, hunting seals and fishing. In summer, they would move inland to hunt caribou and gather berries. They crossed snow and ice in sleds pulled by dogs, and they traveled on water in open boats called umiaks.

Close cooperation was important if the members of a group were to survive. For example, in eastern groups ten to twelve hunters would be needed to harpoon seals at their breathing holes in the winter sea ice.

For thousands of years, the Inuit have survived by hunting and fishing in their frozen habitats (*above*). Fish (*left*) is a mainstay of the Inuit diet. It is cleaned, then dried on racks to preserve freshness.

Much larger groups—more than 100 people—would work together to hunt caribou and large sea mammals such as whales. A few activities could be carried on by individuals and small family groups—tracking bears, fishing with nets, and gathering berries.

Food Preparation. Meat, fat, and fish made up a large part of the Inuit diet. Vegetables were scarce. Very little food was wasted. But because the Inuit depended on hunting and fishing, hunger and even starvation were common when fish and game were not plentiful. Meat and fish caught in summer were stored in shallow pits that were dug down to permafrost and covered with piles of stones to keep out hungry animals.

Wood to make fires for roasting or baking was scarce in most areas. Meat and fish were often eaten raw. Raw meat or fish was frozen and cut into thin strips, which were dipped in whale or seal oil. Some meat, especially meat from large sea mammals, was eaten in a partly decayed state. The decay made tough

meat more tender and easier to digest. If food was cooked, it was almost always boiled, using the heat from oil lamps.

Shelter. The Inuit word "igloo" means "shelter." It can refer to any kind of house, not only the dome-shaped snow houses that many people associate with the word.

In summer, most Inuit lived in tents made of animal skins. In western Alaska, very large winter tents were made by placing heavy walrus skins over wood frames. On the northern coast of Alaska, dome-shaped houses were built of logs and whale ribs. The dome was raised over a depression in the ground and was covered with frozen turf. In Greenland, houses were built of stone slabs.

Snow houses were used only in the eastern and central regions. They were made from blocks of packed snow (not ice), built into a dome. Small snow houses with short tunnel entrances were used while traveling. Larger snow houses were used as winter residences. Long tunnel entrances provided storage

How to Build a Snow House

Snow houses were once built in parts of Canada and Greenland as winter homes. Today they are sometimes built for temporary shelter.

The house begins with a circle of blocks of snow (not ice). The blocks are set on edge, slanting inward, and shaped as shown in the picture.

More blocks are added, spiraling upward and inward to form a dome.

A small air hole is left at the top of the dome. The original entrance is closed, and an entrance tunnel is dug below floor level, as shown in the photograph at the left.

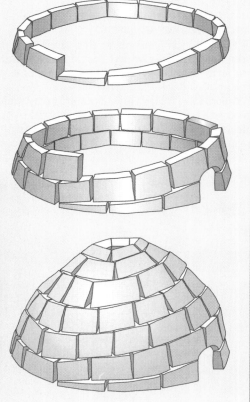

space; the entrance tunnel opened into the house below floor level.

Clothing and Crafts. The Inuit wore boots called mukluks, trousers, and hooded jackets called parkas—all made of animal skins. In winter, they wore two layers of clothing. Caribou fawn skin was preferred in winter because it was soft and warm. Coastal groups preferred sealskin in late spring and summer because it was waterproof. Clothing was often embroidered and had decorative fringes.

The Inuit decorated tools and objects for everyday use. Bone, ivory, wood, and a soft stone called soapstone were used to make small figures of people and animals, as well as weapons and tools. Tools were carefully carved to fit the hand of the user. In the Pacific and far western areas, masks were carved of wood, painted, and decorated with feathers and animal skins.

Religious Beliefs. The Inuit religion showed a deep concern with life, health, sickness, starvation, and death. All Inuit groups believed in a supernatural power called Sila. They shared belief in a small number of spirits (such as Sedna, the goddess of life, health, and food), and they believed that people and animals had souls that lived on after death. But each group had certain beliefs, rituals, and taboos of its own. Shamans (religious leaders), using trances, drama, and magic tricks, were believed to help establish and keep contacts with the spirit world.

Games of skill, such as wrestling, racing, and harpoon-throwing, were sometimes essential parts of religious rituals, as were storytelling, singing, drumming, and dancing. These activities were major sources of entertainment as well.

▶ CONTACTS WITH THE OUTSIDE WORLD

The first Europeans to encounter the Inuit were Vikings from Iceland, who established a settlement in Greenland. Contact between them began about A.D. 1200 and continued until about 1400. But some Inuit groups in the northern Arctic islands did not have much contact with outsiders until the late 1800's.

The Inuit are known for sculptures carved from soapstone (*above*) and other natural materials, such as ivory, wood, and bone.

After 1850, the arrival of European and American whalers and fur traders brought many changes. The Inuit worked for the whalers and sold furs to the traders. The outsiders, in turn, provided a steady source of metal tools and rifles. Because of the new tools and weapons and the new demand for furs, animals were hunted and killed in greater numbers. In some areas, animals such as caribou and seals were hunted almost to extinction.

The outsiders also brought new diseases to which the Inuit had no natural resistance. Smallpox, tuberculosis, influenza, whooping cough, pneumonia, mumps, scarlet fever, and diphtheria were the most dangerous of these diseases. After the late 1800's, when larger numbers of Europeans began to live year-round in the Arctic, these diseases became more widespread, and many Inuit died.

▶ THE INUIT TODAY

Today none of the Inuit live as their ancestors did. The once isolated northlands have been opened up by air travel, highways, powerful modern ships, and satellite communications. Few—perhaps 10 percent—still live off the land, following a way of life based on hunting, fishing, and trapping. Another 10 to 15 percent have full-time, year-round jobs. Most, however, work and live in settlements for part of the year and hunt, trap, and fish the rest of the time.

In the settlements, most houses are simple wood-frame buildings. But they have heat, electricity, radios, telephones, color television sets, and other modern conveniences. In Greenland, many Inuit live in modern high-rise apartment buildings. Most settlements have schools providing instruction up to the eighth grade. Many have adopted Christianity, and most settlements have a church. Other public buildings include general stores, health care facilities, and a post office. Only a few communities do not have an airstrip.

Apart from traditional-style parkas and mukluks—now made of factory-produced materials—the people have adopted European and American dress. They buy some meat from stores. But caribou, seals, whales, and fish are still widely hunted.

Economic and Political Issues. As more and more Inuit have changed their way of life, they have been drawn into mostly low-level, low-paying jobs. Many are unemployed or do not earn enough money to buy what they need. About half the population is considered poor by Western standards.

Although modern technology and conveniences are increasingly available, many Inuit continue to depend on traditional ways of life. Dogsleds, for example, remain a popular and practical mode of transportation.

Many Inuit believe that the routines of employment are an invasion of their dignity, independence, and self-reliance, which may account for relatively high rates of violence, crime, alcoholism, and mental stress in Inuit communities.

In addition, disease and malnutrition contribute to their difficulties. Infant deaths are more than ten times higher among the Inuit than among other North Americans.

Since the 1960's, the Inuit have fought to reclaim their rights to Arctic lands and to preserve their culture. In the eastern Canadian Arctic, the Inuit have formed several cooperative economic associations. These associations provide them with a way to market valuable soapstone carvings and other arts and crafts, which are in great demand. The Inuit have also worked to preserve their

language. In Greenland, the Inuit language has been declared an official language equal in status to Danish. The Inuit language is taught in schools in Alaska and Canada.

The Inuit also have formed a number of political groups. The Alaska Federation of Natives is one of these. In Canada, several groups have been active. These include the Inuit Tapirisat (or Brotherhood), the Committee for Original Peoples Entitlement, and the Northern Quebec Inuit Association. Each of these associations has been successful in reaching agreements on land issues with the governments concerned. The first agreement, the Alaska Native Claims Settlement Act (1971), awarded land and cash settlements to 200 Inuit, Aleut, and Indian villages. There were similar agreements in Canada. The Northern Quebec Inuit Association signed the James Bay Agreement in 1975, and the Committee for Original Peoples Entitlement signed an agreement regarding the Mackenzie River Delta.

However, the most significant political achievement for the Inuit community came in 1992, when a plebiscite in the Canadian Northwest Territories authorized the creation of a new territory called Nunavut, meaning "our land." Nunavut, which was created out of the eastern half of the Northwest Territories (and covers one-fifth of Canada's total area), came under the administration of the Inuit people within the Canadian confederation on April 1, 1999.

A long-standing Inuit land claim was settled in January 2005, when the Labrador Inuit Association, the government of Canada, and the government of Newfoundland and Labrador signed an agreement creating a region of self-government in northern Labrador. Covering 28,000 square miles (72,500 square kilometers), the region is known as Nunatsiavut ("our beautiful land").

DEREK G. SMITH
Carleton University

See also NUNAVUT.

INVENTIONS

Lightbulbs. Telephones. Computers. Microwave ovens. Televisions. CD/DVD players. Cars. Space shuttles. Everywhere we look in our world, we see inventions. Some, such as those mentioned above, are complex combinations of technology. Others are less obvious. For example, people invented the saws and lathes used to cut and shape the wood for the furniture in our homes. Inventors created the plastics used to form containers for leftover food and cases for cellular telephones. And they came up with ideas for showers and toilets and washing machines and garbage disposals. Our lives are so full of inventions that we tend to take them—and the people who created them—for granted.

▶ WHAT DEFINES AN INVENTION?

Inventions are new and unique technical or scientific solutions to specific problems. When someone looks at something and thinks, "I can do that better," or "I can think of another way to use that," that person is taking the first step toward invention.

Some inventions are protected by patents. A **patent** is a document that gives an inventor the rights to make and sell an invention and recognizes that that invention is unique. Patents help inventors benefit financially from their ideas, but not all inventions are patented. Some—such as the formula for Coca-Cola—are kept as trade secrets. Others are not patented because the creators do not wish to patent them. For example, the inventors of the transistor did not seek a patent because they wanted as many people as possible to have access to the new technology. In other cases the inventor does not have the financial resources to take the invention through the patent process.

▶ WHO INVENTS AND WHY?

The word "inventor" may bring to mind Thomas Edison or Alexander Graham Bell. We often think of inventors as legendary

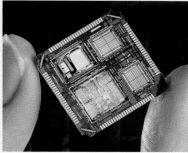

Invention occurs in all branches of science and technology. From the space shuttle (*top*), an all-purpose, reusable space vehicle, to the computer chip (*above*), which dramatically decreased the size of computers, to Dolly (*left*), the first animal cloned from an adult cell, inventions shape the way we live.

people from the past or geniuses working in well-equipped laboratories. But people are creating inventions all the time.

Most inventors share common traits. They tend to be bright, persistent, competitive, and comfortable taking risks. Inventors can solve problems creatively, learn from failure, see new possibilities in familiar materials, and be open to unexpected results. They can visualize solutions to problems in their minds and are good at seeing how one thing is similar to another. And inventors enjoy what they do. As American inventor Beulah Henry once remarked, "I invent because I cannot help it."

THE PROCESS OF INVENTION

Invention is seldom a straightforward process. There is no single recipe to follow to create something new. But inventors often start by doing their homework—learning what has previously been done in their fields and, sometimes, developing new skills needed to bring their ideas to fulfillment.

Even good initial ideas must be refined. Inventors may work out the potential problems with their ideas by sketching designs or building models. Testing an idea can lead to improvements in the original design.

Invention is also a communal process. Each invention represents input from a variety of people, including the inventor's family and friends, assistants and colleagues, inventors who have worked on similar inventions, lawyers, bankers, draftspeople, researchers, prospective buyers, and others. Inventors work within their societies, and their inventions reflect the time, place, and people with whom they interact.

Innovation continues even after an invention is on the market. For example, people are still submitting patent applications for paper clips, clothespins, and corkscrews. Gradual improvements are a key part of the invention process.

WHERE DOES INVENTION TAKE PLACE?

History shows that invention can happen anywhere, from high-tech laboratories to basement workshops. Kevlar, the material in bullet-resistant vests, was developed in a large, corporate research laboratory. Early computing pioneers William Hewlett and David Packard started their electronics company in a garage. Inspiration for inventions may also come from nature. Swiss inventor George de Mestral thought of the idea for Velcro after noticing how burrs stuck to his dog's fur after a walk in the fields. An inventor's physical surroundings seem to be less important than living in a society that values change and new ideas.

INVENTION THROUGH THE AGES

In the 1800's the profession of inventor arose, but people had been inventing long before this title came about. New inventions build on older technologies.

The Stone Ages. Our ancestors began making stone tools—perhaps the earliest inventions—about 2 million years ago. These early humans were nomadic hunters and gatherers. They used stone tools to kill and butcher game and supplemented their diets by foraging for seeds, roots, vegetables, and fruits.

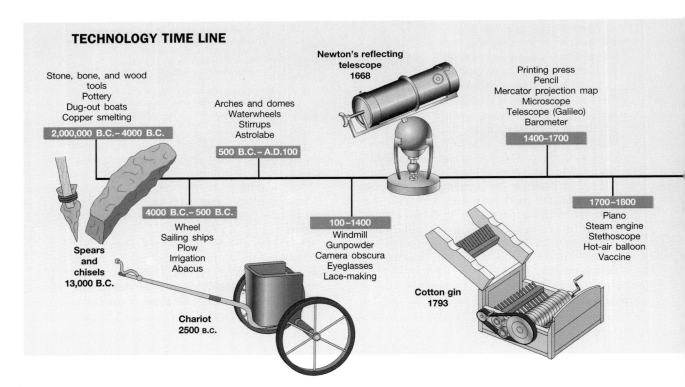

TECHNOLOGY TIME LINE

Stone, bone, and wood tools
Pottery
Dug-out boats
Copper smelting

2,000,000 B.C.–4000 B.C.

Spears and chisels
13,000 B.C.

4000 B.C.–500 B.C.
Wheel
Sailing ships
Plow
Irrigation
Abacus

Chariot
2500 B.C.

Arches and domes
Waterwheels
Stirrups
Astrolabe

500 B.C.–A.D.100

100–1400
Windmill
Gunpowder
Camera obscura
Eyeglasses
Lace-making

Cotton gin
1793

Newton's reflecting telescope
1668

Printing press
Pencil
Mercator projection map
Microscope
Telescope (Galileo)
Barometer

1400–1700

1700–1800
Piano
Steam engine
Stethoscope
Hot-air balloon
Vaccine

About 500,000 years later they discovered ways to make fire. Fire allowed them to cook their meat and also served to protect them from wild animals and keep them warm in colder climates.

Agriculture and Early Civilizations. Eventually people began growing crops, rather than just collecting whatever was in season. Farming provided a dependable food source, which allowed groups of people to band together and settle down. By about 8000 B.C., farm villages of 200 people or more had formed in the Near East. Archaeological findings suggest that agriculture was established in Southeast Asia, China, and parts of Africa about the same time. Some villages grew into cities, with civilizations taking form in the fertile valleys of the Nile, Tigris-Euphrates, and Yangtze rivers.

Life became more complex, and the inventions from this period reflect the increasing technological and social sophistication of the people. Innovations in agriculture took place. About 5000 B.C. people built irrigation channels that brought water from the Nile and Tigris-Euphrates river basins to crops in the fields. And the plow was first used in Mesopotamia about 3000 B.C.

Metal replaced stone for many uses. Advances in metallurgy included the invention of bronze, an alloy of copper and tin. Tools and weapons made of bronze were lighter and could be made sharper than stone tools. Bronze was also used for personal items. Mirrors and decorative pins dating from about 4000 to 3000 B.C. have been found in Egypt.

The ancient Egyptians learned to use livestock to pull their plows, an advancement that increased their crop yields.

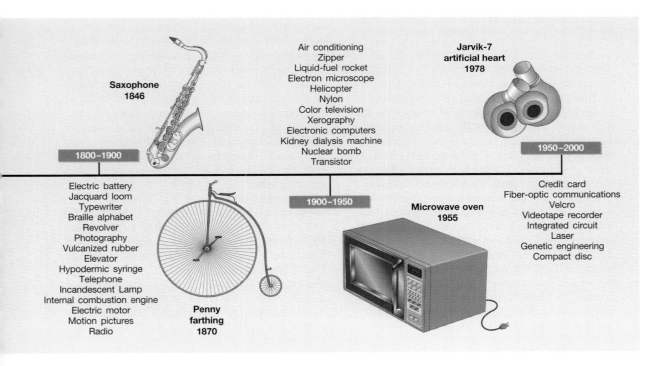

Saxophone
1846

1800–1900

Electric battery
Jacquard loom
Typewriter
Braille alphabet
Revolver
Photography
Vulcanized rubber
Elevator
Hypodermic syringe
Telephone
Incandescent Lamp
Internal combustion engine
Electric motor
Motion pictures
Radio

Penny farthing
1870

Air conditioning
Zipper
Liquid-fuel rocket
Electron microscope
Helicopter
Nylon
Color television
Xerography
Electronic computers
Kidney dialysis machine
Nuclear bomb
Transistor

1900–1950

Microwave oven
1955

Jarvik-7
artificial heart
1978

1950–2000

Credit card
Fiber-optic communications
Velcro
Videotape recorder
Integrated circuit
Laser
Genetic engineering
Compact disc

The invention of writing systems was one of the most important innovations of this era. Writing allowed people to create permanent records of events. An early form of writing on stone tablets was invented in Sumeria. It was called **cuneiform**, from the Latin for "wedge-shaped." Cuneiform writing was used and adapted by other groups. The Egyptians invented papyrus, an early form of paper, about

Cuneiform is one of the earliest known forms of writing. Its wedge-shaped characters were carved or pressed into stone or clay tablets or wooden boards covered with wax.

3500 B.C. It was followed by the invention of ink made from soot, water, and plant gum.

The earliest known wheels were invented in Mesopotamia between 3500 and 3000 B.C. The wheel was used both horizontally, as a potter's wheel, and vertically for a variety of transportation uses. Chariots, for example, were a common form of transportation for the ancient Egyptians, Greeks, and Romans.

Progress in Communications. Technology developed by building on earlier innovations. Written communication became increasingly more sophisticated. An alphabet consisting of 22 letters was created by the Phoenicians. It was based on the cuneiform style of writing, in which characters represented particular sounds. In Asia Minor an alternative to papyrus, called parchment, was made from untanned animal skin about 190 B.C., and the Chinese invented the modern form of paper

in A.D. 105. Wood-block printing was invented in Japan and China about A.D. 740. The Chinese used this method to print the first book in A.D. 868. About 200 years later they invented an early form of movable type—some 400 years before Johannes Gutenberg invented his printing press.

Even an invention as basic as the wheel found new uses. In Greece about 85 B.C., horizontal wheels made of stone were used in water-powered mills for grinding grain into flour. Similar wheels were used in windmills to grind grain about A.D. 650 in Persia. Wheels began to be used in wheelbarrows in China between A.D. 200 and 300.

The Middle Ages and the Renaissance. During the Middle Ages (500–1500), new ideas about science and physics began to shape inventions. The development of lenses led to the invention of eyeglasses in Italy about 1280. Eventually lenses were also used to create telescopes and microscopes. These inventions marked significant changes in the way people viewed the world. People could see things they never could before, from moons circling a distant planet to micro-organisms in a drop of water.

Even as people were learning more about the sun and the stars, they were becoming less dependent on them for certain things. A significant invention of this period was the magnetic compass, which made navigation easier and more accurate. Prior to its development, sailors navigated using the stars. With the invention of the mechanical escapement clock in Europe about 1300, people began to measure time by means other than the sun. In the escapement clock, a bar caught and released the teeth of a rotating gear, marking equal periods of time. In 1656 Christiaan Huygens invented a more accurate clock, which used a swinging pendulum to mark time.

The Industrial Age. In the early 1700's, Europe was on the verge of large-scale industrialization. The steam engine helped drive the shift from agriculture to industry. Thomas Newcomen, an English blacksmith, designed the first steam engine in 1712. It was originally developed to suck water out of flooded mines. About 50 years later James Watt, a Scottish inventor, transformed the steam engine into a machine that could provide power for factories.

The textile industry was changed dramatically by the introduction of the steam engine. Prior to this period most cloth was made by hand at home. The steam engine provided the power to run machines that made spinning and weaving faster. Cloth-making factories offered jobs away from the home and farm.

Industrial technologies were transferred across the Atlantic to the United States in the early 1800's. They led to an American innovation with lasting effects: mass production. Mass production was based on the idea of interchangeable parts. Rather than crafting each product by hand, products were produced as a series of parts. Each part was produced in large quantities by a machine, and then the parts were assembled. If a part failed, it could quickly and easily be replaced with a new one. The gun-making industry was one of the first to use this new technique.

The 1800's were a significant time for invention. Many of the technologies that are part of our daily lives were invented then, including many related to transportation.

The modern bicycle developed gradually. A bicycle with no pedals was invented in the 1820's. The velocipede was a later model, with pedals attached to the front wheel axle. It was invented in 1839 by Kirkpatrick Macmillan. High-wheeled bicycles, or penny farthings, became popular in the 1870's, but they were difficult and dangerous to ride. John Starley introduced the safety bicycle in 1885. Like today's bicycles, the safety bicycle had two wheels of smaller, equal size, making it easier and safer to ride than the penny far-

Henry Ford was a pioneer of the modern automobile industry. Here, Ford stands between two versions of the Model T—one of his most popular cars.

things. Bicycling soon became popular with many people, including women and children. Bicycles gave them a freedom of movement they had not previously had.

Like the bicycle, the automobile was improved upon over time by a series of inventors. These included Etienne Lenoir, Nikolaus Otto, and Rudolf Diesel, who created and improved the internal combustion engine, and Karl Benz, who introduced the first gasoline-powered car for public sale in 1885.

Inventors began to explore electricity during this period as well. We take electricity for granted today, but 300 years ago it was a little-understood mystery. Benjamin Franklin studied lightning, a naturally occurring form of electricity. He invented the lightning rod to divert lightning away from buildings and prevent its dangerous effects. In Italy, Alessandro

At the end of the 1700's, steam engines became the power supply for factories and mills. Textile mills such as this one (*left*) provided employment opportunities for women outside the home.

Harold Edgerton

Gertrude Elion

Stephanie Kwolek

Biographies of the following inventors whose innovations and ideas shaped our world are included elsewhere in *The New Book of Knowledge*: BELL, ALEXANDER GRAHAM; BESSEMER, SIR HENRY; EASTMAN, GEORGE; EDISON, THOMAS ALVA; FRANKLIN, BENJAMIN; KETTERING, CHARLES FRANKLIN; MARCONI, GUGLIELMO; McCORMICK, CYRUS; MORSE, SAMUEL F. B.; WATT, JAMES; WHITNEY, ELI; and WRIGHT, WILBUR AND ORVILLE.

Harold Edgerton (1903–90) was born in Fremont, Nebraska. He received a bachelor's degree in electrical engineering from the University of Nebraska. Summer jobs at Nebraska Power and Light and a year working at General Electric convinced him that he wanted to run an electrical power plant for a living. He went to graduate school at the Massachusetts Institute of Technology in 1926 to study the large electric motors found in power plants. While conducting his studies, he noticed that a mercury tube he was using to send power surges to electric motors flashed brightly as the power peaked. During the flash of light, the motor's turning parts appeared to be standing still. By 1932, Edgerton had turned his experiments with motors and mercury tubes into a commercial product he called the stroboscope. The flash of the stroboscope was renewable, so it had an advantage over flashbulbs. Also, the flash was so fast that it allowed stop-action photography, an enormous benefit to photojournalism. Today most 35-millimeter cameras have small strobes built into them.

Gertrude Elion (1918–99), born in New York City, was very close to her grandfather while growing up. When she was only 15, he died of cancer. The experience influenced her to make a career of fighting disease. Elion graduated from Hunter College with a degree in chemistry while the United States was in the midst of the Great Depression. At this time the few positions that existed in laboratories were not available to women. However, she eventually got a job at the Burroughs Wellcome pharmaceutical company and began researching new ways of developing effective drugs. With her colleague, George Hitchings, Elion identified differences in the way normal and disease-causing cells grow. Once they understood the cells' metabolisms, they could stop the growth of one kind of cell, while leaving another untouched. This led to the development of highly successful drugs for treating leukemia, malaria, gout, and herpes virus infections and for preventing rejection of transplanted organs. Later scientists used the same methodology to develop AZT (azidothymidine), the first drug used to fight AIDS. Gertrude Elion and George Hitchings' work was honored with the 1988 Nobel Prize in physiology or medicine.

Douglas Engelbart (1925–), born in Portland, Oregon, was instrumental in the personal computer revolution. Before computers could become the tools we take for granted today, they had to be made so easy to use that the nonspecialist would embrace them. Engelbart was studying electrical engineering at Oregon State University when he was drafted in 1944. He chose the navy's training course in electronics, where he learned to service radar, sonar, and communications equipment. After the war, he finished his education and went on to a job at the Stanford Research Institute. Engelbart had a vision of people sharing information on different computers and using graphic representations to convey information. In 1968, he presented a demonstration of his dream, including networked computers, multiple windows, help menus, icons, and a new method of moving around the computer display—the mouse (for which he received a patent in 1970). It took another 16 years for some of these now-familiar tools to make their way into the consumer market in the first Apple Macintosh computer. Engelbart also pioneered linked hypertext documents, which allow us to follow links between sites on the World Wide Web.

Beulah Henry (1887–1973?) was born in Raleigh, North Carolina. She began sketching out inventions when she was a young girl. In 1912 at age 25, she received her first patent, for an ice cream freezer. A year later she patented a handbag and a parasol (small umbrella). The latter featured changeable snap-on covers that allowed a woman to coordinate her parasol with her outfit. Another invention was the Latho—a sponge that opened to hold a bar of soap and then snapped closed to keep it inside. Henry also created a number of educational inventions for children. By 1924 she had inventions patented in four different countries and was the president of two newly incorporated companies. In all, Henry had about 110 inventions and received 49 patents. The last one was issued in 1970. Her many inventions earned her the nickname, the Lady Edison.

Volta invented the first chemical battery in 1800. Michael Faraday demonstrated the principle of the electric motor in 1821, and Joseph Henry invented the first practical electric motor a decade later. These developments eventually allowed machinery to be run by electricity as well as steam. Electric motors became a part of daily life.

In 1835, Samuel F. B. Morse began to work determinedly on a new electrical technology—the telegraph. He developed a code of long and short electric impulses that could be sent through a length of wire to activate an electromagnet and be recorded on a moving sheet of paper. The first public demonstration of the telegraph took place on January 11,

Lewis Latimer

Charles Townes

Vladimir Zworykin

Stephanie Kwolek (1923–　) was born in New Kensington, Pennsylvania. As a child she explored the natural world with her father, collecting wildflowers and seeds for her scrapbook. After studying chemistry and biology at the Carnegie Institute for Technology, Kwolek joined the DuPont company. Her work focused on polymers, the long, chainlike molecules that make up synthetic materials such as nylon. In 1964 she began to work with liquid crystal solutions, and her experiments produced an unusual polymer. When the polymer was put into a spinneret machine that spins polymers into fibers, the resulting fibers were exceptionally strong—more strong by weight than steel. The polymer was Kevlar. Today Kevlar is found in a wide range of products, such as ropes, skis, and bullet-resistant vests. Stephanie Kwolek retired in 1986 with 17 patents to her name. She was inducted into the National Inventors Hall of Fame in 1995.

Lewis Latimer (1848–1928), the son of former slaves, was born in Chelsea, Massachusetts. He served in the U.S. Navy during the Civil War and then took a job as an office assistant in a Boston law firm that specialized in working with inventors. By studying and practicing on his own, Latimer became an accomplished draftsman. This earned him a substantial promotion at the law firm and put him in direct contact with inventors. In 1880, Latimer was hired by electrical inventor Hiram Maxim. This gave Latimer a chance to learn about incandescent lighting.

Because of the expertise Latimer had gained working for Maxim, Thomas Edison (Maxim's rival) hired Latimer to handle patent matters for Edison's inventions. Latimer wrote *Incandescent Electric Lighting: A Practical Description of the Edison System* in 1890 and earned a number of patents for incandescent lamp filaments in his own name.

Charles Townes (1915–　) was born in Greenville, South Carolina. After receiving a Ph.D. in physics from the California Institute of Technology in 1936, he joined Bell Laboratories. During World War II he was involved in the design of radar defense systems, which led to an interest in microwave spectroscopy. After the war, as a professor at Columbia University, he and his graduate students designed the maser (for *m*icrowave *a*mplification by *s*timulated *e*mission of *r*adiation)—a device that amplified radio waves. It was the forerunner to the laser, which amplified visible light—a more intense form of energy. Townes and his brother-in-law, physicist Arthur Schawlow, worked together to come up with the idea for a laser (the name stood for *l*ight amplification by *s*timulated *e*mission of *r*adiation). They described a way to bounce light back and forth between two thinly silvered mirrors in order to create a highly concentrated beam of light of a single wavelength. The first functional laser was built by Theodore Maiman in 1960. Townes won the Nobel Prize in physics in 1964.

Earl Tupper (1907–83) was born in rural Berlin, New Hampshire. After high school he studied chemistry through a correspondence course, and in 1937 he was hired by the DuPont company. Tupper left DuPont after a year to start his own company, Tupper Plastics. Tupper Plastics prospered during World War II making military products. After the war, Tupper switched to making consumer goods, such as soap dishes and tumblers, that were made from an improved type of polyethylene he had developed. In 1946, Tupper introduced Tupperware, a line of kitchen containers made of molded polyethylene. The containers had a unique airtight, water-tight seal that he had invented to keep food fresh and prevent spills.

Vladimir Zworykin (1889–1982), was born in the town of Murom, Russia. His father ran both a grain business and a steamship line. The family lived a comfortable existence, offering Vladimir his first experiences with electrical gadgets—fixing the doorbells in the house and making repairs on the steamships. Zworykin attended the St. Petersburg Institute of Technology where he began working with Professor Boris L'Vovich Rozing, who introduced Zworykin to the concept of television. After receiving his degree in engineering, Zworykin moved to Pittsburgh, Pennsylvania, to take a job with Westinghouse Electrical Corporation. He moved from assembling radio tubes to television research. A competition came about as two companies were working on electronic television technology at the same time. By 1923 Zworykin had developed a working cathode ray camera tube (CRT). His competitor, Philo Farnsworth, developed an image dissector tube and a CRT receiver. Eventually the best qualities of Zworykin's and Farnsworth's tubes were combined in the image iconoscope. A later tube, the image orthicon, became the unquestioned standard in television tubes for two decades.

1838. Construction of an actual line from the Capitol building to Baltimore began in March 1843. By the summer of 1846, telegraph wire connected the northeast United States.

Thirty years later, on March 10, 1876, the words, "Mr. Watson, come here. I want you!" traveled through a wire strung between two rooms of Alexander Graham Bell's Boston laboratory. Bell had spent several years working on improvements to the telegraph when he had the idea of transmitting speech by wire. He was not alone in his quest. We recognize Bell as the inventor of the telephone, but he filed his patent just a few hours before his closest competitor, Elisha Gray.

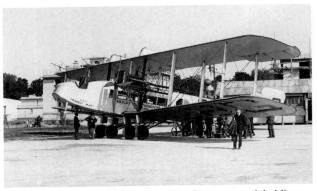

The *Princess Mary*, one of the first commercial airliners, was used by a British aviation company to fly passengers between London and Paris.

Thomas Edison improved upon Bell's work by inventing a way to make a voice on the telephone sound clearer and louder. While working with the telephone, he began to think about ways to record sound. In 1877, he succeeded in designing a device he called the phonograph, which could record and play back sound.

Soon after his success with the phonograph, Edison began work on his most famous invention, the lightbulb. Edison did not invent electric lights—arc lights had been invented by Humphry Davy in England in 1809. In Davy's lamp, an electric current jumped the empty space between two rods of carbon and produced a bright arc. Arc lamps were used as streetlights and in large public spaces, but people used gas lights in their houses. Gas lighting was dependable and gave a soft warm light, but the open flames were dangerous and they flickered a lot.

The lightbulb that Edison invented was called an incandescent lamp because it used a filament material that could get hot enough to glow (become incandescent) but did not burn up in the process. But Edison did more than invent a lightbulb. He used his knowledge of electricity and gas lights to invent an entire system of electric lighting, including sockets, switches, and insulated wires.

Everyday life in the 1800's was much changed by these inventions. And the pace of life sped up. People did not have to wait for letters to travel back and forth in the mail because they could send a telegram or pick up a telephone instead. Workdays became longer because artificial light was provided by the electric light. And new methods of transportation helped create a workforce of commuters, who no longer needed to live within walking distance of work.

The pace of life continued to speed up after the Wright brothers' successful flight at Kitty Hawk, North Carolina, in 1903. With the development of the airplane, people would soon be crossing the continent in a matter of hours rather than days.

Entry into the Modern Era. In 1895, Guglielmo Marconi transmitted radio waves through the air to a device attached to a bell on the far side of the room, and the bell rang. Marconi continued to refine his "wireless" apparatus, gradually increasing the distance he could send a signal. At first, radio transmitted the dots and dashes of Morse code, not voices or music. Its most widespread use was for communication between ships at sea and from ships to shore. The importance of shipboard radio was underscored by the sinking of the *Titanic* on April 14, 1912. The distress call sent by the ship's wireless operator was credited with saving more than 700 lives that night.

Commercial radio broadcasting began with the experiments of gifted amateurs. One such operator, a Westinghouse Electric Company employee named Frank Conrad, gained a reputation among his fellow hobbyists for playing music on the air. Westinghouse thought radio sales would increase if such programs became commonplace. With Conrad at its head, Westinghouse's station KDKA in Pittsburgh went on the air on November 2, 1920, broadcasting the results of Warren Harding's success-

Listening to the radio became a favorite pastime during the 1920's when the new "wireless" technology arrived in many people's homes.

The invention of television changed people's knowledge of the world. They could now see other places without leaving their living rooms.

ful bid for the presidency. Radio's popularity soared as Americans enthusiastically embraced this new form of communication.

Television was a primary focus of research in the mid-1920's. Two different forms of television developed nearly side by side. One was the electronic method we know today. The other system was called mechanical television, because it combined electronics with spinning, perforated discs that scanned the images to be transmitted. After the mechanical television systems failed to achieve well-defined pictures, work on electronic systems intensified. Two main competitors were researching electronic television—Vladimir Zworykin and Philo T. Farnsworth.

In 1923, Zworykin invented a cathode ray camera tube. But it was Farnsworth who transmitted the first electronic television image—a horizontal line—in 1927. By early 1933, Zworykin had a complete television system in operation; however, commercial television broadcasting was delayed by the Great Depression and World War II. Television became popular in homes in the 1950's.

The Information Age. Advances made in electronics during World War II led to major improvements in computers. The first general purpose, all-electronic computer went into operation in 1945. It took up 1,000 square feet (92 square meters) and was run by several trained programmers. This machine, the ENIAC (Electrical Numerical Integrator and Computer), weighed 30 tons; contained about 18,000 vacuum tubes, 1,500 relays, and 6,000

switches; and used 174,000 watts of electricity. It was the fastest, most powerful computing device in existence. Today many personal computers are more powerful than the room-sized ENIAC. The invention of the transistor and the integrated circuit were key to this transformation.

In 1947, Bell Laboratories researchers William Shockley, John Bardeen, and Walter Brattain were looking for a way to improve the switching mechanisms that routed telephone calls. They decided to investigate semiconductors, which use less power than vacuum tubes and whose ability to conduct electricity can be controlled more precisely. The result of their work was the transistor, a semiconductor device that can act either as an amplifier of electrical signals or as an on-off switch.

The transistor quickly transformed the electronics industry, but it had its limitations. Complicated circuits were designed by connecting many transistors by wire, and if one connection failed, the entire circuit failed. So Jack Kilby, an engineer at Texas Instruments, decided to eliminate the wires. He came up with a way to put all the elements of the circuit on a single piece of germanium, a common semiconductor. About the same time, Robert Noyce described how the circuit could be set up on a piece of silicon, and the integrated circuit—or computer chip—was invented. Today integrated circuits are used in everything from cell phones and computers to the space shuttle.

Early computers such as the ENIAC (*below*) took up the space of an entire room. Even at this size, they could not store their own programs.

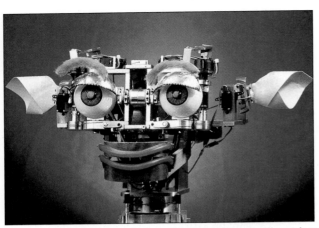

Scientists are exploring artificial intelligence. Kismet is a robot designed at MIT and programmed to "learn" different emotions. Here Kismet is expressing happiness.

The space shuttle was first launched in 1981. It is a reusable space vehicle that combines the technologies of both rockets and airplanes. Rocket pioneer Robert Goddard launched the first successful liquid-propellant rocket in 1926. His experiments were crucial to the future development of space travel.

The U.S. space program has been at the cutting edge of invention in many fields. Research for space travel has led to improvements in rocket fuel and design, new materials for spacesuits and rocket hulls, and methods of food preservation. Advances in robotics, heating and ventilating systems, and even medicine have also been driven in part by the space program.

Medical inventions that enhance our ability to prevent and treat disease are continually being developed. In the early 1970's, American scientists Herbert Boyer and Stanley Cohen invented a way to snip pieces of DNA in specific places, so that other pieces of DNA could be inserted. This was recombinant DNA technology, or genetic engineering. Genetic engineering has changed the way many drugs are produced, making them safer and less expensive.

Perhaps the most significant invention of the information age was the Internet, which dramatically changed the way we get our information. The idea for the Internet began in 1962 when J.C.R. Licklider of the Massachusetts Institute of Technology (MIT) wrote about something he called the Galactic Network. Later that year, as head of the com-

puter research program at the Advanced Research Projects Agency (ARPA) of the U.S. Department of Defense, Licklider started working on this idea of linking separate and distant computers. In 1965, two computers—one at MIT and the other at the University of California at Berkeley—were linked by telephone lines, and in 1967 the plan for the ARPA system of networked computers (ARPANET), the forerunner of the Internet, was initiated. The first two computers in ARPANET were connected in September 1969, and the first public demonstration of the system, which included electronic mail, came in 1972. The next major step was the creation of the World Wide Web. The WWW was the idea of Tim Berners-Lee, who was a researcher at the European Organization for Nuclear Research. He wanted to easily share documents with distant colleagues. Berners-Lee's 1989 proposal for the WWW included elements such as browsers and linked text that we know well today. By the end of the 1990's, millions of people were connected through the Internet.

▶ THE FUTURE OF INVENTION

The future of invention is limited only by inventors' imaginations. We can expect to see advances in a number of areas. For example, digital communication technologies are flourishing. The capabilities of cell phones, laptop computers, and PDA's (personal digital assistants) will probably continue to merge, and these devices will become smaller. Biotechnology is another area of substantial research. Inventions in the field of biotechnology carry important ethical issues with them. Therefore, inventions related to cloning, stem cell research, and genetically modified food will continue to be controversial for some time. Finally, artificial intelligence is an important area to watch. Industrial robots are now relatively common and may soon be "smarter" and capable of doing even more. Nanotechnology may lead to miniature robots that can be implanted in the human body to fight disease. The future of invention rests with the keenest minds of today—and tomorrow.

JOYCE E. BEDI
The Lemelson Center of the Smithsonian Institute

See also AUTOMATION; PATENTS; SCIENCE; TECHNOLOGY; and articles on individual inventions.

IODINE

Iodine is a member of a family of nonmetal chemical elements called the halogens. As a solid, iodine is a gray-black crystal with a shiny metallic appearance. But even at ordinary room temperatures, iodine can change from a solid directly into a purple vapor with a strong, irritating odor. The process of changing from a solid into a gas without first becoming a liquid is called **sublimation**.

Iodine is very active chemically. It combines easily with other substances by gaining or losing electrons to form chemical compounds. In fact, iodine is never found alone in nature. It is always combined with other elements.

A major source of iodine is Chile saltpeter, a mineral that is found in great quantities in Chile. It was during the processing of saltpeter that the French manufacturer Bernard Courtois found iodine in 1811. The salty water found underground near petroleum deposits, called oil-well brine, is another source of iodine.

Humans need iodine in order to stay healthy. Most people get enough iodine from

FACTS ABOUT IODINE	
Chemical Symbol	I
Atomic Number	53
Atomic Weight	126.904
Melting Point	236,3°F (113.5°C)
Boiling Point	363.83°F (184.35°C)

the food and water in their diet. Table salt with iodine added can be used in regions where the food and water do not contain enough iodine, such as the Alps of south central Europe and the Great Lakes area of the United States.

Light-sensitive iodine compounds are used in making photographic film. Other iodine compounds are used in making bread. For a long time, tincture of iodine—iodine dissolved in alcohol—was used as a disinfectant (germ killer) on cuts and scratches. Now other forms of iodine less irritating to the skin and tissues are used as first-aid antiseptics. Compounds of iodine are also used to treat cancer and other diseases of the thyroid gland, to locate a variety of tumors, and to trace chemical substances as they travel through the body.

JOHN PRICE
Chemical Week

See also ELEMENTS, CHEMICAL.

IONOSPHERE. See ATMOSPHERE.

IONS AND IONIZATION

Although they may not be readily seen, ions are all around us in our daily environment. Many familiar substances that we use every day contain ions, such as the salt used to flavor food. Without the ions in our bodies, we would not be able to function normally.

An ion is an atom or a group of atoms that carries an electric charge. An atom consists of a center, called a **nucleus**, containing one or more protons. Each **proton** is a particle with a positive electric charge. Most atomic nuclei also contain **neutrons**, which have no electric charge. Particles called electrons surround the nucleus. Each **electron** carries a negative electric charge. All the small particles making up an atom are called **subatomic particles**.

Ordinarily, atoms have exactly the same number of protons and electrons. The negative charges on the electrons cancel out the positive charges on the protons, so the atom is electrically neutral. But if an atom loses or gains one or more charged particles, the positive and negative charges will no longer balance. The atom now has an electric charge; it has become an **ion**. This process is called **ionization**.

Protons are heavy particles, and they are held in the nucleus of an atom by strong forces. Only powerful processes such as atomic fission or radioactive decay can move the protons away from the nucleus. Electrons, which are small, light particles outside the nucleus, are easy to remove. Ionization usually involves taking away electrons, although sometimes they can be added to an atom.

▶HOW ATOMS BECOME IONS

The electrons in an atom are arranged in layers around the nucleus in a series of shells. Each shell can hold only a certain number of electrons. The arrangement of electrons is less likely to change if all the shells have the full amount of electrons. If the outermost shell does not contain the full amount of electrons, the atom can easily lose those electrons that are on the outermost shell. However, the atom will now have more protons than electrons, so the charges will no longer cancel out. The

Long streams of glowing colored lights shoot across the night sky during a sighting of the aurora borealis, or northern lights, in Alaska.

atom has become a positive ion. It now carries a positive charge and is called a **cation**.

If the outermost shell is almost full, electrons are more easily added to the shell than lost from it. The atom, which will have more electrons than protons, will become a negative ion. An ion that carries a negative charge is called an **anion**.

How Ions Behave. The charge on an ion influences its behavior. If ions have the same electric charge (both positive or both negative), they repel each other. Ions with opposite electric charges attract each other.

▶**IONIC SUBSTANCES**

Many common substances are ionic, meaning they are made up of ions. Ionic substances, which contain a mixture of positive and negative particles, are formed by chemical reactions. When these reactions occur, electrons are transferred between atoms to form ions.

Ionic Solids. Table salt, or sodium chloride, is an ionic solid made up of a mixture of sodium cations and chloride anions. A sodium cation has a charge of +1, and a chloride anion has a charge of -1. Because salt contains equal numbers of sodium and chloride ions, the charges cancel out.

Ionic Solutions. Many ionic solids dissolve in water, forming a solution. When this happens, the positive and negative ions in the solid structure become separated and are free to move around in the water.

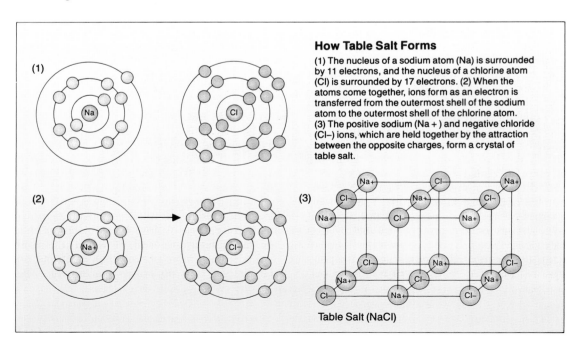

How Table Salt Forms

(1) The nucleus of a sodium atom (Na) is surrounded by 11 electrons, and the nucleus of a chlorine atom (Cl) is surrounded by 17 electrons. (2) When the atoms come together, ions form as an electron is transferred from the outermost shell of the sodium atom to the outermost shell of the chlorine atom. (3) The positive sodium (Na+) and negative chloride (Cl–) ions, which are held together by the attraction between the opposite charges, form a crystal of table salt.

Table Salt (NaCl)

If electrodes, two strips of metal with opposite charges, are placed in water containing dissolved ions, the positive ions (cations) move toward the negative electrode, and negative ions (anions) move toward the positive electrode. This process of separating ions is called electrolysis. As the ions travel, they carry charges with them, passing an electric current through the solution.

Electrolysis is used during a process called electroplating to cover metals with thin layers of other metals. Many familiar objects are electroplated. Jewelry is often electroplated using gold (gold-plated), and eating utensils are often electroplated using silver (silver-plated).

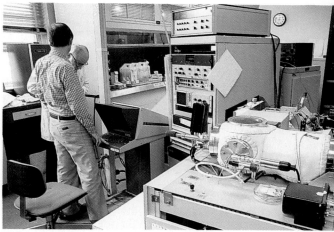

With an instrument called a mass spectrometer, scientists measure ions to identify tiny amounts of unknown substances, such as traces of air pollutants.

▶OTHER IONIC STATES

Atoms can also be ionized by heating them to extremely high temperatures or by bombarding them with charged particles.

Plasma. If a solid substance is heated, it melts into a liquid. If the heating continues, the liquid boils away and becomes a gas. The gas can be heated still further until the atoms start losing electrons. Then the gas becomes a plasma. Plasma is an extremely hot mixture of only charged particles—positively charged ions and negatively charged electrons.

The sun and stars are made of plasma that is so hot that all of the electrons, not just some, have been stripped from the atoms. Thus, the plasma consists of a mixture of bare atomic nuclei and electrons. At the temperature of a star, which can be millions of degrees, the bare atomic nuclei can collide with each other. Particles can pass from one nucleus to the other. The nuclei can even join to form the nucleus of a heavier atom. This process is called **nuclear fusion**. The energy of every star, including our sun, comes from nuclear fusion.

The Ionosphere. The sun constantly throws electrons and other charged particles off into space. Some of these particles are trapped by the earth's magnetic poles. Some of the trapped particles collide with atoms in the earth's atmosphere, at altitudes above about 50 miles (80 kilometers). The collision strips some of the electrons from the atoms, leaving positive ions. At such high altitudes, the atmosphere is thin, and the positive ions and electrons are too far apart to re-combine easily. As a result, this upper part of the atmosphere contains many charged particles and is called the ionosphere.

When an atom of the atmosphere is ionized by a collision with a charged particle, a tiny flash of light is released. The collisions usually occur so far above the surface of the earth that the flashes of light from these collisions are not visible. Above the north and south magnetic poles, however, the earth's magnetic field curves down toward the planet's surface. Charged particles trapped in the magnetic field can come much closer to the atmosphere. As a result, the night skies in the polar regions glow with dancing sheets of colored light. In the Arctic, these lights are called the northern lights, or aurora borealis. In the Antarctic, they are the southern lights, or aurora australis.

▶USES OF IONS AND IONIZATION

Because of their special properties, ions have many important uses in industry and research. One of the most familiar ion products is the battery. The electric current produced by a flashlight battery comes from a chemical reaction inside the battery that causes a flow of ions. Ionization processes are also used to detect radioactivity, study nuclear reactions, and remove salts from substances such as water to make water soft and raw sugar juices to refine sugar.

KRISTIN LANDON
Science Writer

See also ATOMS; BATTERIES; CHEMISTRY; ELEMENTS, CHEMICAL; NUCLEAR ENERGY.

IOWA

Iowa was named for the Ioway Indians, who once lived in the area. The Iowa River also was named after this tribe. The Indians called Iowa "the beautiful land." Iowa's nickname, the Hawkeye State, is believed to be in honor of Black Hawk, a Sauk Indian chief who led his people in a fight for their lands in the early 1830's. Another nickname, "the land where the tall corn grows," reflects Iowa's importance as a farming state.

Iowa is located in the north central United States, in the heart of the region known as the Midwest. The state lies between two of the nation's mightiest rivers, the Mississippi on the east and the Missouri on the west. For this reason, Iowa is often called the land between two rivers.

Signs of agriculture are evident throughout Iowa's gently rolling landscape. In summer lush green fields of corn and soybeans, evenly laid out in squares and rectangles, cover much of the land. Stands of trees shade farm buildings, and dairy cattle graze in pastures. In the fall, corn-picking machines and combines move through the fields harvesting crops.

The rolling contours of the land change in the northeast, where tree-covered hills rise along the Upper Iowa River. Because of its steep hills and narrow valleys, this area is known as the little Switzerland of America. It is a favorite recreation spot for Iowans. Another series of hills, formed by windblown soil, spans the state's western border.

Although farms cover more than 90 percent of Iowa's land, most state residents are employed in manufacturing and other nonagricultural jobs. More Iowans live in urban areas (cities and towns of more than 2,500 residents) than in rural areas. The state has several large cities with populations of more than 100,000, but it also has hundreds of medium and small towns. Small-town activities such as community fund-raisers are an important aspect of life in Iowa. One statewide event that attracts city- and town-dwellers alike is a bicycle ride sponsored by the *Des Moines Register*, Iowa's largest newspaper. RAGBRAI (The *Register*'s Annual Great Bike Ride Across Iowa) passes through many small communities, giving participants from all over the state a chance to sample Iowa's small-town hospitality.

▶LAND

The land surface of Iowa has been formed by glaciers, which left their marks thousands of years ago, and by rivers, rain, and wind, which are still causing changes.

Land Regions

Between 2 and 3 million years ago, glaciers began to move across the land that is now Iowa. The moving ice leveled off hilltops and filled in low areas with soil. As each glacier melted, it left a jumble of rocks, sand, and gravel, called till. In all, four different glaciers moved across Iowa, affecting different areas. As a result, three separate land regions were formed: the Young Drift Plains, the Dissected Till Plains, and the Driftless Area.

Young Drift Plains. This area, which makes up most of northern and central Iowa, was covered by the last glacier. The land was left somewhat level and poorly drained, with many lakes and swamps. A deep layer of fertile soil developed from deposits left by the glacier, making the area the best in the state for agriculture. Much of the swampy land has been drained for use as farmland.

Dissected Till Plains. This area stretches across southern Iowa and includes a strip of land along the western border. It was covered by the first two glaciers. Later, rivers carved

Farms cover much of Iowa's land, but most Iowans live and work in cities. An annual bike ride across the state attracts both urban and rural dwellers.

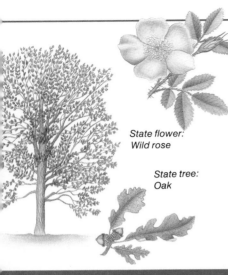

State flower:
Wild rose

State tree:
Oak

FACTS AND FIGURES

Location: North central United States; bordered on the north by Minnesota, on the east by Wisconsin and Illinois, on the south by Missouri, and on the west by Nebraska and South Dakota.

Area: 56,276 sq mi (145,754 km²); rank, 26th.

Population: 2,926,324 (2000 census); rank, 30th.

Elevation: *Highest*—1,670 ft (509 m), in Osceola County; *lowest*—480 ft (146 m), at the Mississippi River.

Capital: Des Moines.

Statehood: December 28, 1846; 29th state.

State Motto: *Our liberties we prize and our rights we will maintain.*

State Song: "The Song of Iowa."

Nicknames: Hawkeye State (official); Land Between Two Rivers.

Abbreviations: IA; Ia.

State bird:
Eastern goldfinch

out hills and ridges, and winds blew fine particles of soil great distances. In the west some of this windblown soil, called loess, piled up along the Missouri River, creating bluffs as high as 300 feet (91 meters). Although fertile, the region's soil is less suitable for farming than that of the north.

Driftless Area. Only one glacier moved across this area, which lies along the Mississippi River in northeastern Iowa. As a result, it received less leveling than Iowa's other regions. Parts of the Driftless Area are extremely hilly and rugged, especially along the Upper Iowa River. Most of the glacial deposits were washed or blown away, leaving the area with thin soil poorly suited for agriculture.

Rivers and Lakes

The Mississippi River forms all of Iowa's eastern boundary, and the Missouri, together with the Big Sioux River, bounds the state on the west. The rivers within Iowa are separated by a low divide in the western part of the state.

Rivers west of the divide flow southwestward to the Missouri. Those east of the divide flow southeastward to the Mississippi.

Most of the state's natural lakes are small and are located in the northwest. Iowa's lakes, both natural and artificial, are popular recreation areas, especially during the summer.

Climate

Iowa has four distinct seasons. Each brings delightful weather as well as some disagreeable days. The climate, with its dependable rainfall, warm summer months, and relatively long growing season, is good for farming.

Annual temperatures and precipitation vary greatly across the state. The average January temperature is 21°F (−6°C), and the average July temperature is 73°F (23°C). Most of the precipitation comes during the summer months in the form of rain from thunderstorms. Precipitation averages about 27 inches (686 millimeters) in the northwest and about 35 inches (890 millimeters) in the southeast.

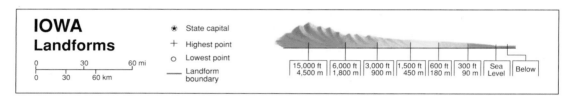

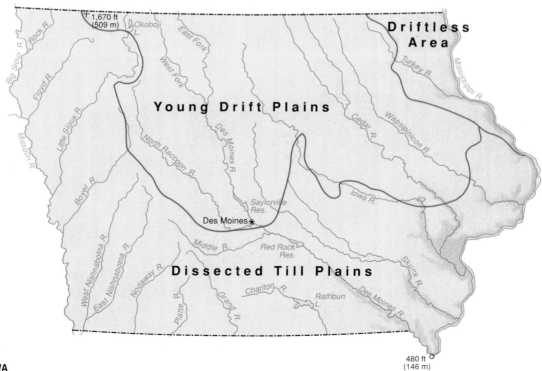

Above: The Mississippi River forms Iowa's eastern boundary. Barges on the river carry grain and other freight to and from Iowa ports.

Right: In the west, high bluffs rise along the Missouri River. They were formed centuries ago by windblown soil called loess.

The growing season begins in May and ends in October with the first killing frost. The length of the growing season varies from 170 days in extreme southeastern Iowa to 140 days in the northwest. Everywhere, the growing season is long enough to grow corn.

Plant and Animal Life

Iowa has a variety of trees, both hardwood and conifer. Hardwoods include maples, hickories, oaks, walnuts, and lindens. Conifers include balsam firs and white pines.

Native grasses covered Iowa in early days. This prairie grass, which reached the top of the pioneers' wagon wheels, is now found only in scattered patches and in prairie grass preserves maintained by the state. Iowa's abundant wildflowers are another legacy of the early prairie. Blue pasqueflowers, bloodroots, marsh marigolds, and violets bloom in spring. In summer, phlox, yellow coneflowers, and wood lilies can be seen, as well as the wild rose, the state flower. Autumn varieties include goldenrod, gentians, and prairie asters.

Many different kinds of fish live in Iowa's rivers and lakes. Catfish is the "king of fish" in the state's warm-water rivers. Several species of trout live in the colder northeastern streams. Walleye, northern pike, yellow perch, crappie, bluegill, and bass are among the varieties found in lakes.

A complete listing of Iowa's birds would total more than three hundred. Permanent residents include the goldfinch, the state bird, as well as blue jays, cardinals, and many varieties of owls, woodpeckers, and sparrows. Game birds include ring-necked pheasants, partridge, quail, and grouse. Passing over Iowa are the Mississippi and Missouri flyways, major routes for migrating waterfowl.

Iowa is home to white-tailed deer, as well as to many smaller animals, such as squirrels, raccoons, and cottontail rabbits.

Natural Resources

Iowa's most important natural resource is soil. Other resources include minerals and an abundance of water.

Soils. Prairie soil is the kind of soil most widespread throughout the state. It developed on top of deposits left by glaciers. Each year, the prairie grass that covered the land died and decayed into the soil. The decayed matter, called humus, helped make the soil fertile. Along the rivers, where forests grew, the soil is low in humus and more acid than the prairie soil. Loess (windblown soil) helped to form the soil of western Iowa.

Iowa devotes special effort to soil conservation. For years Iowa farmers have followed such conservation practices as contour plowing, strip-cropping, and terracing.

Minerals. Nearly all of southern Iowa contains beds of bituminous (soft) coal. Sand and gravel deposits are numerous in the north. Other important minerals are limestone, gypsum, and clay.

▶PEOPLE

Nearly 3 million people live in Iowa, and more than half of them reside in urban areas. Iowa has two cities with populations of 100,000 or more and eight metropolitan areas. Before 1960, most people lived on farms or in towns with populations below 2,500. Today, Iowa still has nearly 700 small towns spread throughout its 99 counties, but only a small percentage of Iowans live on farms.

Most of the people who settled in Iowa in the 1800's came from Pennsylvania, Indiana, Ohio, and other states to the northeast. Immigrants from Europe never made up more than 19 percent of Iowa's total population. European immigrants came mainly from Germany, Ireland, England, and the Scandinavian countries. After 1900, a small number came from southern and eastern Europe. Later immigrants came to Iowa from Southeast Asia in the 1970's.

Today descendants of European immigrants hold festivals and other events to celebrate their heritage. In the Amana colonies, a group of communities near Iowa City, German-Americans celebrate fall with an Oktoberfest. Iowans of Dutch descent sponsor tulip festivals in both Pella and Orange City.

Iowa is also home to the Mesquakie Indians, who live in Tama County. Their settlement is not on a reservation but on land they bought from the federal government in the 1850's. Each August, the Mesquakie hold a powwow, at which they display and interpret their culture for visitors.

Education

Iowa is known for its excellent schools. The state has one of the highest literacy rates in the nation: Almost 100 percent of its residents can read and write.

Iowa's first school was opened in Lee County in 1830. The present system of public education is based on a state law of 1858.

Below: Iowans of Dutch descent hold a tulip festival each year in Pella. *Bottom:* The Mesquakie Indians, a Native American tribe, display aspects of their traditional culture to visitors at an annual powwow.

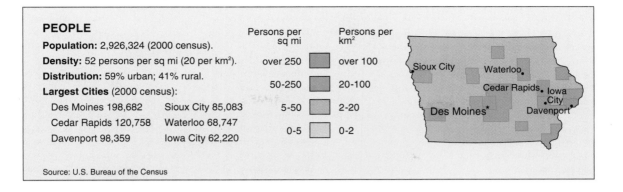

PEOPLE

Population: 2,926,324 (2000 census).

Density: 52 persons per sq mi (20 per km²).

Distribution: 59% urban; 41% rural.

Largest Cities (2000 census):

Des Moines 198,682	Sioux City 85,083
Cedar Rapids 120,758	Waterloo 68,747
Davenport 98,359	Iowa City 62,220

Persons per sq mi		Persons per km²
over 250		over 100
50-250		20-100
5-50		2-20
0-5		0-2

Source: U.S. Bureau of the Census

The elementary and secondary school system consists of 436 public school districts that are supervised by a state board of education. State-supported higher education includes 15 community colleges and vocational schools and three state universities.

The oldest state university is the University of Iowa. It was established by an act of the first General Assembly in 1847 and opened in 1855. Iowa State University of Science and Technology at Ames was established in 1858 and opened eleven years later. The University of Northern Iowa was started as a teacher-training school in 1876.

In addition to its public institutions, Iowa has more than 25 private colleges and universities. Iowa Wesleyan College in Mount Pleasant is the oldest college in the state. It was established in the early 1840's. Other private colleges and universities include Coe College in Cedar Rapids, Drake University in Des Moines, Grinnell College in Grinnell, Luther College in Decorah, Morningside College in Sioux City, Simpson College in Indianola, and the University of Dubuque in Dubuque.

Libraries, Museums, and the Arts

Iowa has more than five hundred public libraries. The state also sponsors a traveling service that loans books to local libraries. The State Historical Society maintains libraries in Des Moines and Iowa City that specialize in the history of Iowa and the Midwest. Iowans take special pride in the Herbert Hoover Library in West Branch.

Many cities and towns have museums devoted to history, natural history, science, or the fine arts. The largest is the Iowa Historical Museum in Des Moines. Others include the Putnam Museum in Davenport, the Museum of History and Science in Waterloo, the San-ford Museum and Planetarium in Cherokee, the Norwegian-American Museum in Decorah, and the Cedar Rapids Museum of Art. The Des Moines Art Center has important collections of paintings and sculpture, as does the Davenport Municipal Art Gallery.

The state has several large facilities for the performing arts. Hancher Auditorium in Iowa City, C. Y. Stephens Auditorium in Ames, and the Civic Center in Des Moines attract internationally known performers. A number of cities have symphony orchestras, including Des Moines and Cedar Rapids.

The Old State Capitol stands on the campus of the University of Iowa, in Iowa City. The school, which opened in 1855, is Iowa's oldest state university.

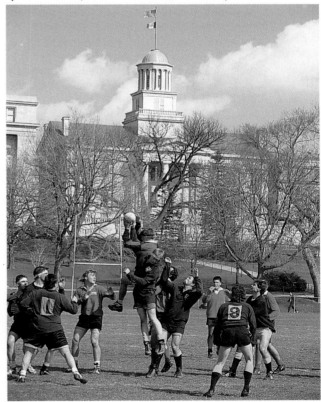

▶ ECONOMY

Iowa's economy, once dominated by farming, is now based on a combination of agriculture, manufacturing, and service industries. Although Iowa continues to be a leading agricultural state, most of its workers are employed in nonagricultural jobs.

Services

Service industries are a vital part of Iowa's economy and are expected to grow considerably in the future. They employ about 65 percent of all working Iowans.

Wholesale and retail trade combine to form a leading service industry in Iowa. Wholesale trade includes the distribution of automobiles, machinery, and food products. Retail trade refers mainly to the sale of food, clothing, automobiles, and other products in stores, restaurants, and shops. Financial services, including banking, insurance, and real estate, are another important type of service. Other leading service industries include business, social, and personal services; transportation and communication; and government services.

Manufacturing

About 20 percent of the labor force is employed in manufacturing. Two leading manufacturing activities are farm-related: the processing of foods from Iowa farm products and the manufacture of farm machinery.

The processing of foods and related products is Iowa's most important kind of manufacturing. Meat-packing plants prepare beef, pork, and lamb for market. Other plants produce flour, breakfast cereals, animal feeds, and other products made from grains.

Tractors, combines, and nearly every other kind of farm implement are made somewhere in the state. Factories in Iowa also turn out a large number of products not related to agriculture. These include household appliances, recreational vehicles, and chemical products.

PRODUCTS AND INDUSTRIES

Manufacturing: Food products, tractors and other farm machinery, washing machines and other household appliances, recreational vehicles, chemical products.

Agriculture: Corn, soybeans, hogs, beef cattle, oats, hay, dairy products, poultry, apples.

Minerals: Limestone, sand and gravel, gypsum, coal.

Services: Wholesale and retail trade; finance, insurance, and real estate; business, social, and personal services; transportation, communication, and utilities; government.

Percentage of Gross State Product* by Industry

- Manufacturing 22%
- Construction 3%
- Transportation, communication, and utilities 8%
- Government 9%
- Agriculture 12%
- Business, social, and personal services 13%
- Wholesale and retail trade 16%
- Finance, insurance, and real estate 17%

*Gross State Product is the total value of goods and services produced in a year. Source: U.S. Bureau of Economic Analysis

Agriculture

Iowa is a leading agricultural state mainly because of its productive soil, which is among the best in the country. Agriculture is important throughout the state, although it employs less than 15 percent of the labor force. Iowa is often ranked either first or second among the states in the production of hogs, corn, and soybeans. The state also produces about 10 percent of the country's grain-fed beef.

Northeastern Iowa is known for its dairy farming. Its hilly land is better suited to hay and pasture than to corn or other grains. The north central part of the state is known as the cash-grain area. Here grains are grown to be sold for cash. Corn, soybeans, and oats are the most important crops, with only a small amount of land used for hay and pasture.

In the rest of Iowa, most agriculture consists of a combination of crops and livestock. The river floodplains are used mainly for grain crops. The hilly slopes are used for pasture. But many of the slopes become good cropland when the right conservation methods are used.

The sale of livestock is an important source of income throughout the state. In several areas, calves are shipped in from western states and raised on grain from Iowa farms.

Mining

Mining employs less than one percent of Iowa's labor force. Limestone is the most valuable stone quarried in the state. Sand and gravel ranks second. Much of the limestone and the sand and gravel is used to make concrete. The poorer grades of limestone are powdered and used as fertilizer.

Iowa is one of the nation's leading producers of gypsum, which is used in making building materials and fertilizers. Most of the coal mined in the state is used for heating and as an energy source in plants that produce electric power. South central Iowa is the state's main coal-producing region.

Transportation

Iowa has an extensive network of roads and highways. Several major highways, including interstates 80 and 29, cross the state from east to west and from north to south.

Iowans began to build railroads across the state in the 1850's. Construction continued until every section of the state had rail service. Far fewer railroads operate in Iowa today than in the 1800's, but those that remain are important as carriers of freight.

Barges on the Mississippi River carry grain, coal, and other freight to and from Iowa. The major ports are Dubuque, Clinton, Davenport, Muscatine, Burlington, and Fort Madison. On the Missouri River, which has much less barge traffic, the major ports are Sioux City and Council Bluffs.

Approximately one hundred Iowa cities and towns have air service. The largest airports are in Des Moines, Cedar Rapids, Davenport, Sioux City, and Waterloo.

Communication

Iowa's first newspaper was the *Du Buque Visitor*, published in Dubuque in 1836–37. The *Burlington Hawk-Eye* is the oldest paper in continuous publication. It began as the *Territorial Gazette and Burlington Advertiser* in 1837. Today there are about 350 weekly newspapers and about 40 dailies. The *Des Moines Register* is Iowa's largest newspaper. There are more than 190 radio stations and 15 television stations throughout the state.

Opposite page: Iowa is famous for its corn crop, which is often the largest in the country. The raising of beef cattle is another important agricultural activity. *Below:* Much of Iowa's industry , such as the production of farm equipment, is tied to agriculture.

Places of Interest

Amana Colonies, seven small communities near Iowa City, were founded in the 1850's by members of a German religious group. Today, visitors can tour woodworking shops and woolen mills, visit museums and century-old homes, and sample traditional German food in local restaurants.

Effigy Mounds National Monument covers almost 1,500 acres (600 hectares) near McGregor. It contains prehistoric burial mounds in the shapes of birds and bears. Relics from the mounds are exhibited in a museum on the grounds.

Grotto of the Redemption, a religious shrine in West Bend, is an artificial cave built of rocks, fossils, shells, and other materials from many states and countries.

Herbert Hoover National Historic Site, in West Branch, includes the cottage in which the 31st president was born and the graves of President and Mrs. Hoover. The Herbert Hoover Presidential Library and Museum adjoins the site.

Little Brown Church in the Vale, near Nashua, was made famous by a hymn of the same name. The church is a popular place for weddings.

Living History Farms is a 600-acre (243-hectare) site near Des Moines. It features fully operating farms that show rural life in 1840, in 1900, and in the future. The site also includes an Ioway Indian village of 1700 and a replica of a town of the 1870's.

Old State Capitol, on the campus of the University of Iowa in Iowa City, was the last capitol of the Territory of Iowa and the first capitol of the state. The building has been restored to its original condition.

Old Shot Tower, in Dubuque, is a stone tower built in 1855 for the making of lead shot. Molten (melted) lead was dropped through a screen at the top of the tower. The lead pellets cooled as they fell, becoming solid when they dropped into water at the bottom of the tower.

State Historical Building, in Des Moines, houses the state historical museum, with displays portraying Iowa history and heritage. The building also contains the state archives and library.

State Parks. For information on Iowa's numerous state parks, contact the Department of Natural Resources, Wallace State Office Building, Des Moines, Iowa 50319.

Birthplace of Herbert Hoover, West Branch.

Furniture craftsman, Amana Colonies.

Living History Farms, near Des Moines.

Left: Dubuque, located on the west bank of the Mississippi River, is an industrial center and river port. It was named for Julien Dubuque, who began to mine lead near the site of the city in 1788.

Below: Iowa's capitol building, in Des Moines, stands on a hill overlooking the city. Des Moines was made the capital of the state in 1857.

▶ CITIES

Most of the largest cities are in the eastern part of the state. Exceptions are Des Moines and Ames in central Iowa and Sioux City and Council Bluffs on the western border.

Des Moines, Iowa's capital and largest city, is located on the Des Moines River. A fort built in 1843 was the forerunner of the present city. By 1851 there were five hundred settlers in the area. In 1857 the capital was moved from Iowa City to Des Moines.

The capitol stands on a hill overlooking much of the city. Nearby are state and federal office buildings. Besides being the center of state government, Des Moines is the industrial and financial center of Iowa. It is known especially as a convention city and as the home of many large insurance firms and publishing companies.

Cedar Rapids, Iowa's second largest city, is located on the Cedar River in the east central part of the state. It was named for the swift rapids in the river. Cedar Rapids is an important industrial center that is surrounded by a rich farming area. The many products manufactured in the city include oat cereals, corn products, machinery, and radio transmitters and receivers.

Davenport is part of a metropolitan area called the Quad-Cities. The Quad-Cities area also includes Bettendorf, Iowa, as well as the Illinois cities of Rock Island and Moline. Davenport is a center of industry and retail trade.

It is the site of many picturesque Victorian homes along the Mississippi River.

Sioux City is western Iowa's largest city, and it is more reminiscent of the West than any other city in the state. A large livestock market for a four-state area, the city is also a major port on the Missouri River and a transportation hub. It is notable for its fine parks and places of scenic and historical interest.

Waterloo, located on the Cedar River in northeastern Iowa, is a center of meat packing and farm machinery manufacturing. The National Dairy Cattle Congress is held in Waterloo each fall, attracting livestock producers from all over the world.

Iowa City, located on the Iowa River in the eastern part of the state, is the center of a rich agricultural area and the site of the University of Iowa.

Dubuque, located on the west bank of the Mississippi River, is one of Iowa's most picturesque cities. Its industries include the manufacture of tractors, plumbing supplies, and fertilizers.

▶ GOVERNMENT

The government of Iowa is based on a constitution adopted in 1857. The governor is the head of the executive branch of the state government. In 1972 the term of the governor and other high state officials was lengthened from two to four years. The governor appoints certain state officials. The governor must also take final action on bills passed by the legislature, either signing them into law or vetoing them. The governor can call special sessions

GOVERNMENT

State Government
Governor: 4-year term
State senators: 50; 4-year terms
State representatives: 100;
2-year terms
Number of counties: 99

Federal Government
U.S. senators: 2
U.S. representatives: 5
Number of electoral votes: 7

For the name of the current governor, see STATE GOVERNMENTS in Volume S. For the names of current U.S. senators and representatives, see UNITED STATES, CONGRESS OF THE in Volume U-V.

of the legislature and, under certain conditions, adjourn the legislature.

The legislative branch of the government is called the General Assembly. It is made up of a senate and a house of representatives. Legislative sessions are held yearly.

The highest state court is the supreme court. It is made up of nine justices. The major trial courts are called district courts. Justices and district judges are appointed by the governor, then run for re-election.

Iowa's cities are governed by city councils elected by local residents. The council is the policy-making body of municipal governments. Although the mayor works with the council, and some cities have city managers, only the city councils can pass ordinances.

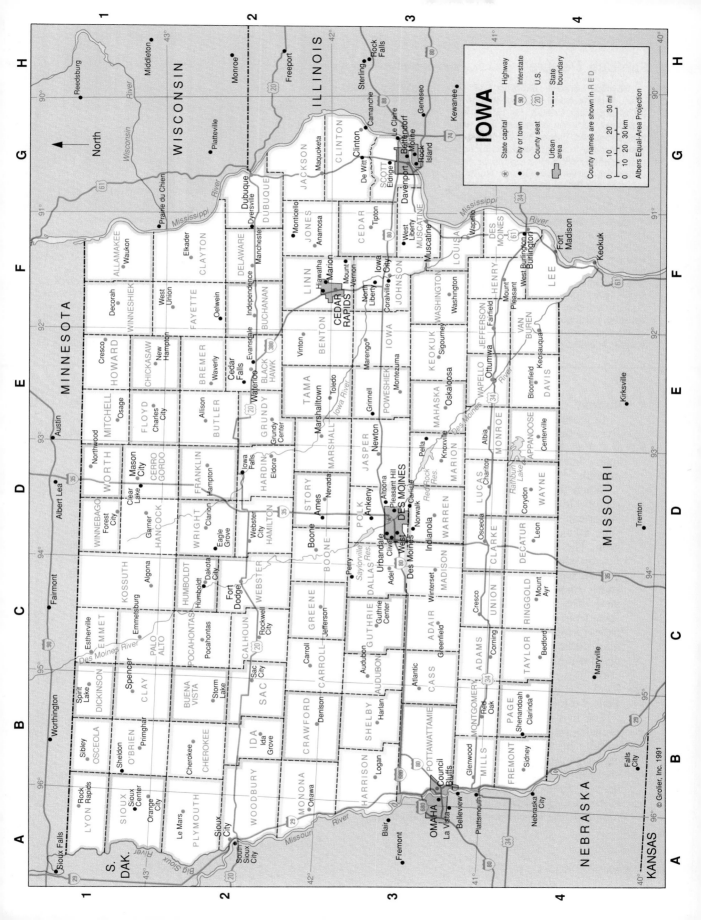

Famous People

Norman Ernest Borlaug (1914–), an agricultural scientist, was born on a farm near Cresco. He developed improved varieties of wheat and rice that produced higher yields of grain. The increase in world food production that resulted from such crop research is called the "green revolution." Borlaug received the Nobel peace prize in 1970 for his contribution to the fight against world hunger.

Carrie Lane Chapman Catt (1859–1947) was a leader in the campaign for women's suffrage (right to vote). She was born in Ripon, Wisconsin, and at age 7 moved with her family to Iowa. She graduated from Iowa State College (now Iowa State University) with top honors, the only woman in a class of seventeen students. Catt was president of the National American Woman Suffrage Association from 1900 to 1904 and from 1915 to 1920. In her second term, she organized the campaign that led to the ratification in 1920 of the 19th Amendment to the U.S. Constitution, giving women the right to vote. She also founded the League of Women Voters and was active in the world peace movement.

Carrie Lane Chapman Catt

Herbert Clark Hoover

Grenville Mellen Dodge (1831–1916), a railroad engineer, was born in Danvers, Massachusetts. He went to Iowa in the 1850's to survey for a railroad. During the Civil War, Dodge was an officer in the Union Army. After the war he supervised the construction of 9,000 miles (15,000 kilometers) of track for the Union Pacific and other western railroads. Later, Dodge helped build railroads in the South and in Cuba.

Paul Engle (1908–91), poet, novelist, and teacher, was born in Cedar Rapids. He taught at the University of Iowa and co-founded the International Writing Program there, which has trained many famous writers. Engle's books of

▶HISTORY

In prehistoric times, several Indian cultures lived in the area that is now Iowa. One group is called Mound Builders, because they left many burial mounds, some in the shape of animals.

When the first white explorers reached the region, Iowa was the home of many Native American tribes. The Ioway, from whom the state takes its name, lived throughout the region. The Sauk and the Mesquakie (called the Fox by white settlers) lived mainly in the south and the east, while the Omaha, Oto, and Missouri tribes lived in the west and the southwest. The Santee Sioux moved into northern Iowa from their main home in Minnesota. The tribes, which belonged to the Prairie-Plains Indian culture, engaged in hunting, trapping, and farming. Their most important crop was corn.

Early Exploration and Settlement

The first Europeans to reach Iowa were the French explorers Jacques Marquette and Louis Jolliet. In 1673 the two explorers and five crew members traveled by boat down the Mississippi River, landing on Iowa's eastern border on June 25. Another French explorer, Robert Cavelier, Sieur de la Salle, reached the mouth of the Mississippi in 1682 and claimed the whole Mississippi Valley for France. He named it Louisiana in honor of Louis XIV, king of France. In 1762 France gave control of the Louisiana region to Spain.

Julien Dubuque, a French-Canadian adventurer, was the region's first white settler. Dubuque, who had traveled to the area west of the Mississippi to seek his fortune, discovered that the Mesquakie Indians had valuable lead mines there. He gained the friendship of the Indians and in 1788 received their permission to work the mines. In 1796 the Spanish government granted Dubuque legal right to the land, the future site of the city of Dubuque.

In 1800, Spain returned the Louisiana region to France. France sold it to the United States in 1803, a transaction known as the Louisiana Purchase.

Territorial Years

Iowa became part of the United States in 1803 as part of the Louisiana Purchase. In 1805 it was included in the Territory of Louisiana. The year after the Louisiana Purchase, U.S. President Thomas Jefferson sent two army officers, Meriwether Lewis and William Clark, to explore the new territory. Lewis and Clark traveled up the Missouri River, exploring what is now the western border of Iowa. In 1805, Lieutenant Zebulon M. Pike headed poetry include *Worn Earth*, *Corn*, *West of Midnight*, and *A Prairie Christmas*.

Herbert Clark Hoover (1874–1964), 31st president of the United States, was born in the small Quaker village of West Branch. A biography of Hoover appears in Volume H.

John Llewellyn Lewis (1880–1969), a labor leader, was born in the coal-mining community of Lucas, Iowa. He became president of the United Mine Workers of America. A biography of Lewis can be found in Volume L.

Henry Agard Wallace (1888–1965), 33rd vice president of the United States, was born in Adair County. Wallace helped to develop high-yielding strains of hybrid corn and then sold the seed through his own company. He also was editor of *Wallaces' Farmer*, the Midwest's leading farm journal. As U.S. secretary of agriculture (1933–40) during the Great Depression, he devised a federal price support program to help farmers. Wallace served as vice president from 1941 to 1945 and as secretary of commerce in 1945–1946. He was the presidential candidate of the Progressive Party in 1948.

Grant Wood (1891–1942), a leading American artist, was born on a farm near Anamosa. He specialized in paint-

Grant Wood

John Llewellyn Lewis

ing people and scenes of rural midwestern America. A biography of Wood appears in Volume W.

an army expedition that traveled up the Missouri River looking for sites for military posts. Iowa's first fort, Fort Madison, was built in 1808. Other expeditions into the area were made during the 1820's and 1830's.

Throughout the period from 1804 until the early 1830's, the Iowa country remained Indian land and was not open to legal settlement. Many Sauk and Mesquakie Indians were forced to move there from neighboring Illinois to make room for white settlers. One band of Indians, led by Black Hawk, tried to return to their former lands in Illinois. They were defeated by U.S. troops in the Black Hawk War of 1832. As a result of the Black Hawk War, the Indians gave up a portion of Iowa land along the Mississippi River. The following year, many whites began to settle there, and communities sprang up along the river, including Davenport, Burlington, Ft. Madison, and Keokuk. Gradually, all the Indians who had once lived in Iowa were moved to Missouri, Oklahoma, Nebraska, and South Dakota.

Iowa had become part of the Territory of Missouri in 1812, when Louisiana gained statehood. Missouri became a state in 1821, and for 13 years Iowa had no legally authorized civil government. In 1834 it became part of the Territory of Michigan, and two years

An early engraving depicts the 1673 expedition of Jacques Marquette and Louis Jolliet. The French explorers were the first Europeans to reach Iowa.

later it was included in the Territory of Wisconsin. Finally, in 1838, the Territory of Iowa was established by Congress, and Robert Lucas was appointed territorial governor. The first territorial capital was at Burlington. The capital was moved to Iowa City in 1841.

Statehood

Almost immediately after Iowa became a territory, the governor and other officials began to work for statehood. In 1844, Iowans submitted a state constitution to the federal government in Washington, D.C. But it was rejected because of the state boundaries that it proposed. In 1846, Iowans held a second constitutional convention and drew up new boundaries. This constitution was accepted, and on December 28, 1846, President James K. Polk signed a bill making Iowa the 29th state.

In 1857, Iowa adopted a new constitution, which is still in effect today. Among other changes, the new constitution moved the state capital to Des Moines.

Iowa's population grew rapidly, from about 23,000 in 1838, to nearly 100,000 at statehood, to more than 650,000 by 1860. Settlers poured in as stories of Iowa's fertile land reached states to the east. Iowa continued to grow after the Civil War (1861–65). The first rail line across the state was completed in 1867; soon five railroads crossed Iowa from east to west. Steamboats traveling the Mississippi River brought many new settlers into the state and carried cargo from the upper Mississippi Valley to St. Louis and New Orleans.

Good times and high prices alternated with depressions, such as those of 1873 and 1893. Farm organizations, especially the Grange, were formed to help farmers. Industry grew after 1880, and the combination of farm and factory began to benefit the state.

Early 1900's

By 1900, Iowa was a major agricultural state, producing mainly corn, hogs, oats, barley, cattle, and hay. Iowa's industries were mostly farm-related and included the Quaker Oats Company in Cedar Rapids, meat packing plants in Sioux City and Ottumwa, and farm machinery manufacturing in Dubuque. The Maytag Company, founded in Newton in 1893, began producing electric washing machines in 1909. By 1900, every part of Iowa had train service, making it possible for manufacturers to ship their products all over the country.

Iowans were concerned about social issues. They worked hard to improve their public schools, achieving one of the highest literacy rates in the nation. Many Iowans supported state and national prohibition laws, which forbade the manufacture and sale of alcoholic drinks. Most people still preferred to live on farms and in small towns. Many Iowa towns formed booster clubs, which worked to improve life in their communities and attract new businesses.

Land prices continued to rise until the Great Depression of the 1930's. Many farmers who had borrowed money to buy additional land lost their farms when they could not pay off their debts. After World War II (1939–45), the value of agricultural products increased, and farmers again prospered. A variety of new industries moved into Iowa, and state leaders began a strong effort to balance agriculture with industry.

Later 1900's

Many new industries came to Iowa after 1950. The new manufactures often were not farm-related. Iowans increasingly moved from farms and towns to cities, drawn by the prospect of work in industry. The 1960 census reported that, for the first time in its history, Iowa had more urban residents than rural residents. Since that time, the percentage of urban residents has increased slowly but steadily.

Agriculture remains important in Iowa, but manufacturing now accounts for more of the Gross State Product. During the early 1980's, high interest rates on land and falling agricultural prices plunged many farmers into debt. As in the Great Depression, many families lost their farms. The farm slump also harmed makers of farm machinery, animal feeds, fertilizer, and other products associated with agriculture. State leaders continued their efforts to diversify Iowa's economy and reduce the state's dependence on agriculture and related industries.

Iowans today hold many of the same values as their parents and grandparents. They believe in the importance of good schools and spend more than half their state budget on education. They continue to be concerned about social problems, particularly environmental issues. Iowans' political opinions become a focus of national attention during each presidential election year: Iowa holds the first presidential caucus, in which representatives of a political party meet to select a candidate.

DOROTHY A. SCHWIEDER
Professor of History, Iowa State University

IRAN

Iran, once known as Persia, is a country in Southwest Asia located at a strategic crossroads between Europe and Asia. More than 2,500 years ago, Cyrus the Great united the country and founded the great Persian Empire. Iran was long ruled by shahs, or kings. In 1979 the country became an Islamic republic.

▶ **PEOPLE**

The Iranians are an Aryan people whose ancestors migrated to the area from Central Asia before 1000 B.C. Persian (Farsi), the official language, is written in an Arabic script but is related to the languages of Europe. The dominant culture is Persian. But Iran's many peoples include Azerbaijani Turks, Kurds, Lurs, Bakhtiaris, Arabs, Qashqais, Baluchis, and Turkomans.

Religion. The great majority of Iranians are Muslims, or followers of Islam. Most Iranians belong to the Shi'a branch of Islam, which is described in the article on Islam in this volume. Iran is the major Shi'ite country in the Muslim world. Large numbers of Christians, Baha'is, and Jews left Iran after the Islamic revolution in 1979.

Education. The revolution brought about many changes in the educational system. Today Islamic teachings and values are part of the course of study. Five years of primary education are required. Girls are taught separately from boys.

Iran is an Islamic republic, and most of its citizens are Muslims. Religion plays a major role in daily life and is centered around places of worship called mosques. Most Iranian women follow the Muslim tradition of wearing a body veil, called a chador. Some men wear turbans, not for religious reasons but to protect their heads from the hot sun.

Way of Life. Iran is a land made up of more than 40,000 villages. A typical small village has a mosque (a Muslim place of worship), a public bathhouse, and a bazaar, or market. For centuries most Iranians were farmers or nomads who grew food for themselves, herded animals, and made rugs or other handicrafts. In recent decades millions of poor Iranians have moved to the cities in search of a better way of life. But many still live much as their ancestors did.

▶ **LAND**

Land Regions. Iran is centered on a huge plateau surrounded by mountain ranges on all sides but the east. In the north, just below the Caspian Sea, are the Elburz Mountains. The Zagros Mountains extend along Iran's western and southern borders. The east central plateau is a vast desert region. It contains two of the most uninhabitable deserts in the world, the Dasht-i Kavir and the Dasht-i Lut.

Rivers, Lakes, and Coastal Waters. Iran is bordered on the south by the Persian Gulf and the Arabian Sea. The Caspian Sea forms part of its northern border. Iran has very few rivers, and most of its lakes are salty.

Climate. Iran's climate is generally dry. Almost all precipitation falls during the winter, much of it in the form of snow. Winters are mild in the north and warm in the south. Elsewhere, January temperatures average near or below freezing. Summers are usually very hot except in the mountains.

Natural Resources. The history of Iran has been deeply influenced by the presence or absence of water. Population centers have grown up where water is plentiful, and many struggles have taken place over water rights.

Iran has some of the world's largest reserves of oil and natural gas. Coal, iron ore, copper, manganese, and gypsum are also found there.

▶ **ECONOMY**

Historically, Iran was mainly an agricultural country, but today the production of petroleum and natural gas dominates the economy. Food processing and the making of textiles and metal goods are also important.

Trade. Oil and petrochemicals make up more than 90 percent of Iran's exports. Others include carpets, cotton, dried fruits, and pistachio nuts. Iran trades mainly with Japan and the nations of western Europe.

Below: Nomads in the south search for grazing lands for their livestock. Most of the land in Iran is too dry for human habitation. *Below right:* Production of oil and natural gas is Iran's chief industry.

Transportation. All of Iran's major cities are linked by highways and railroads. The two chief international airports are located near Tehran and at Abadan. Kharg Island in the Persian Gulf is the main terminus for oil exports.

▶ MAJOR CITIES

Tehran, the capital, is the center of the nation's political and commercial activities. An article on Tehran appears in Volume T.

Meshed, an important trade center, is located in a rich agricultural region in the northeast. It is surrounded by orchards, gardens, vineyards, and wheatfields. A holy shrine in Meshed is a destination of annual pilgrims, making the city a place of special significance to Shi'ite Muslims.

Isfahan was once the capital of the country. Its bazaar is considered one of the most magnificent marketplaces in the Middle East. The city also has many lovely tiled mosques and ancient palaces and stone bridges.

▶ CULTURAL HERITAGE

Iran's history is rich in artistic traditions. Many famous poets, architects, and skilled artisans have come from Iran.

Literature. From the A.D. 900's onward, Persian poets have left their imprint on world literature. Among the most famous are Omar Khayyam (1048–1131), Saadi (1213?–92), and Hafiz (1325–89?). Poetry is still a major means of literary expression in modern Iran.

Art and Architecture. The magnificence of Iranian architecture is seen in the beautiful mosques found everywhere in the country. Iranian artists are also known for their intricate calligraphy (fine handwriting), miniatures (paintings), and metalwork. Perhaps the

Isfahan, Iran's third largest city, is noted for its magnificent architecture. The Imam Mosque, with its beautiful blue dome, dates back to the 1600's.

Brilliantly colored Persian rugs are among Iran's most famous products. Such rugs may have as many as 2,400 hand-tied knots per square inch (372 per square centimeter).

country's most famous craft is the weaving of Persian rugs.

▶ GOVERNMENT

The present government of Iran, established under a new constitution approved in 1979, is unique in Iranian history. All branches of the government are subject to the *faqih*, Iran's spiritual leader, who is the highest political authority in the land. Ruhollah Khomeini, better known as Ayatollah

ISLAMIC REPUBLIC OF IRAN is the official name of
the country.
LOCATION: Southwest Asia.
AREA: 636,293 sq mi (1,648,000 km²).
POPULATION: 68,000,000 (estimate).
CAPITAL AND LARGEST CITY: Tehran.
MAJOR LANGUAGE: Persian (Farsi).
MAJOR RELIGIOUS GROUP: Muslim.
GOVERNMENT: Islamic republic. **Head of state—**
Supreme religious leader—*faqih.* **Head of
government**—president. **Legislature**—*Majles.*
CHIEF PRODUCTS: Agricultural—wheat, rice,
barley, sugar beets, sugarcane, fruits, livestock.
Manufactured—refined petroleum and petroleum
products, textiles, processed foods, transportation
equipment. **Mineral**—petroleum, natural gas,
metal ores, coal, manganese, gypsum.
MONETARY UNIT: Rial (1 rial = 100 dinars).

Khomeini, held this office until his death in
1989. ("Ayatollah" is a religious title meaning
"reflection of Allah"). Ayatollah Khomeini
was succeeded by Ali Hussein Khamenei.

Iran's chief executive is the president, who
is elected by the people for a 4-year term.
The legislature, known as the *Majles,* has 270
members elected to 4-year terms. All laws
passed by the *Majles* must be approved by
the Council of Guardians to ensure that they
agree with Islamic principles.

▶ **HISTORY**

Early Empires. The Iranians arrived
in the region from the north about
3,000 years ago. The first Iranian empire, that of the Medes, lasted until
the 500's B.C., when the Persian ruler
Cyrus, known as the Great, of the
Achaemenid dynasty, united the Iranians under his rule and created a
vast empire. Later Persian kings, notably Darius I, expanded this empire.

The Achaemenid dynasty eventually collapsed, in 330 B.C., under the
onslaught of Alexander the Great,

whose successors established the Greek-
speaking Seleucid Empire. They were succeeded by the Parthians, another Iranian
people, who ruled until about A.D. 224. The
last of the great Persian empires, that of the
Sassanians, lasted until A.D. 642. The Sassan-
ian Empire fell before the attacks of
mounted Arab warriors who carried with
them a new religion and way of life known as
Islam. For more information on this period,
see the article PERSIA, ANCIENT in Volume P.

Between the 600's and the 1400's, Persia
experienced political and social chaos. Beginning in the 1000's, outside invaders such as
the Seljuks, the Mongols, and the Timurids
conquered and devastated the Persian
plateau. Persia did not begin to reclaim its
national identity and power until 1501.

The Safavid Dynasty. In the year 1501, a 13-
year-old boy known as Shah Ismail Safavid
marched triumphantly into Tabriz. Shah Ismail made Shi'ite Islam the official religion of
Persia. The Safavid kings created a unified
nation that held off repeated challenges from
the Ottoman Turks to the west, the Uzbeks to
the northeast, and the Moguls to the east.

The greatest Safavid king was Shah Abbas
the Great, who ruled from 1587 to 1629. He
moved his capital to Isfahan, modernized the
government and the army, and established relations with various Western nations.

In 1736 a Turkic warrior known as Nadir deposed the last Safavid heir and crowned himself shah. Nadir Shah extended Persia's

Mohammed Reza Pahlavi, shown here at his
coronation, was the last shah (king) of Iran.
Despite the shah's attempts at social and
economic reform, the Iranian people rebelled
against his power and obvious wealth.

In 1979, religious leader Ayatollah Ruhollah Khomeini led a revolution that deposed the shah and declared Iran an Islamic republic.

boundaries significantly before he was assassinated in 1747. Between 1750 and 1779, most of Persia was ruled by the Zands, a local tribe, from their capital in Shiraz.

The Qajar Dynasty. Beginning in 1779, a warrior from the Turkish Qajar clan named Agha Mohammed Khan fought to establish a new ruling dynasty in Persia.

The Qajar family ruled Persia until 1925. During this time, Britain and Russia extended their influence into Persia, and Russia took over large areas of former Persian territory in the north.

A reform movement in 1905–06 led to the creation of a parliament and the adoption of a European-style constitution. During World War I (1914–18), neutral Persia was used as a battleground by the great powers, and Britain and Russia (later the Soviet Union) continued to intervene in its internal affairs.

In 1921 the last Qajar shah was overthrown. One of the leaders of this coup was an illiterate but strong-willed army officer named Reza Khan. In 1925 he became the shah of Iran.

The Pahlavi Dynasty. Reza Shah Pahlavi was a dictator who used his position to gather great wealth for himself and his family. But he was also a strong nationalist who built a powerful nation. Rebellious tribes were defeated; Western codes of law were adopted; and a modern educational system was set up. In 1935, Reza Shah officially changed the name of the country from Persia to Iran.

In 1941, Britain and the Soviet Union forced the shah to give up the throne because of his pro-German sympathies. His son, Mohammed Reza, succeeded him.

Mohammed Reza Pahlavi, the last shah of Iran, ruled for 37 years. He built a powerful military and police organization while introducing various reforms. But by the early 1970's, opposition to his rule mounted among Iranians from all walks of life. Students and professional people criticized the shah's absolute rule and the harsh treatment of his opponents by the secret police. Among the shah's most powerful critics were the Shi'ite religious leaders. Confrontation with the shah led to a year of violence (1978–79) in which more than 10,000 Iranians died.

The shah was driven from his country on January 16, 1979. The Constitution of 1906 was set aside, and Iran became an Islamic republic led by Ayatollah Khomeini.

The Islamic Republic of Iran. The first years of the republic were violent. Most of the people had opposed the shah, but they did not agree on the kind of society Iran should become. The new government faced opposition from leftist guerrillas, Westernized moderates, and right-wing supporters of the old regime. On November 4, 1979, after the shah was admitted to the United States for medical treatment, Iranian students seized the U.S. embassy in Tehran. They held Americans there as hostages and demanded the return of the shah and his fortune to Iran. Even after the shah died on July 27, 1980, the hostages were not released. They were finally freed on January 20, 1981, but Iran's relations with the United States remained strained.

In 1980, Iraq invaded Iran. The war cost Iran more than a million casualties before it ended in 1988. Ayatollah Khomeini died in 1989. He was succeeded as *faqih* by former president Ali Khamenei. Hashemi Rafsanjani was then elected president. Iran remained neutral in the 1991 Persian Gulf War.

In 1997, reformist Mohammad Khatami won the first free presidential election held since 1979. He was easily re-elected in 2001.

A political crisis erupted in 2004 when the conservative Guardian Council prevented thousands of reformists from running for election to parliament. Meanwhile, the international community raised concerns over Iran's nuclear program, suspecting that it was being used to produce illegal weapons. In 2005, Mahmoud Ahmadinejad, a conservative, succeeded Khatami as president, signaling an end to the reformists' ambitions. Iran then announced it would resume uranium conversion activities, prompting possible sanctions from the United Nations.

JAMES A. BILL
Coauthor, *Politics in the Middle East*

IRAN-CONTRA AFFAIR

The foreign-policy scandal known as the Iran-Contra Affair was revealed in 1986, when U.S. president Ronald Reagan confirmed reports that American weapons had been sold to Iran, a country then considered an enemy of the United States. The sale was allegedly made with the hope that Iran would help negotiate the release of seven American hostages held by terrorists in Lebanon, even though official U.S. policy did not support negotiating with terrorists.

Fuel was added to the scandal when it was discovered that some of the secret funds raised from the arms sale were given to the contras, a rebel band of guerrilla soldiers who were fighting to bring down the Sandinista government in Nicaragua. Reagan wanted to help the contras, claiming Nicaragua was in the hands of a Communist dictatorship. Nevertheless, Congress had voted to stop giving military aid to the contras.

When questioned by the press in 1987, Reagan claimed he did not intend arms to be swapped for hostages and denied knowing about funds going to the contras. He appointed a special commission, headed by former Texas senator John Tower, which criticized the president's management style. Later that year, Congressional investigators heard testimony confirming that illegal payments had been made to the contras.

In another investigation, Independent Counsel Lawrence E. Walsh won convictions against John Poindexter, Reagan's former national security adviser, and Oliver North, a national security staff member, on charges stemming from the scandal. But federal courts later reversed both convictions. Also convicted were Robert McFarlane, another former national security adviser, and Elliot Abrams, former assistant secretary of state. Caspar Weinberger, Reagan's secretary of defense, was also indicted on charges of trying to cover up the scandal. But in 1992, President George Bush pardoned them and several others who had been implicated. Walsh charged that the pardon was part of the cover-up.

ROBERT SHOGAN
The *Los Angeles Times*

Lieutenant Colonel Oliver North, a central figure in the Iran-Contra scandal, testified before Congress in 1987.

IRAQ

Iraq is a nation of Southwest Asia, situated at the center of the region known as the Middle East. Its neighbors are Saudi Arabia, Jordan, and Syria on the west; Turkey on the north; Iran on the east; and Saudi Arabia and Kuwait on the south. Iraq also has a short coastline on the Persian Gulf.

Nourished by the Tigris and Euphrates rivers, the area was once called Mesopotamia, meaning the "land between rivers." Although it was home to some of the world's earliest civilizations, the modern nation of Iraq has existed only since 1932, following a brief period of British administration after World War I (1914–18). Since then, Iraq has experienced several wars and political upheavals, most recently the overthrow of its dictator, Saddam Hussein, in the American-led Iraq War in 2003.

▸ **PEOPLE**

Nearly 80 percent of Iraqis are Arabs. This population is split between the two great branches of Islam—Sunni Islam and Shi'i Islam. (Most of the world's Muslims are Sunnis.) Shi'i Islam is dominant in Iran and in southern Iraq. While Shi'ites in general make up nearly two-thirds of Iraqi Muslims, in the past they have been less influential than the Sunnis, both politically and economically.

The Kurds, who live in the mountains of the northeast, are Iraq's largest minority group. Along with additional communities in Turkey and Iran, the Kurds have long sought their own independent state.

Language. Arabic is the national language of Iraq. The Kurds, who are non-Arabs, speak Kurdish. In some places, Assyrian and Armenian are also spoken.

Most Iraqis, such as these children dressed in traditional costume (*left*), are Muslims, who worship in temples called mosques (*above*). A large minority of Kurds (*top*) live in the mountains of the northeast.

Religion. Almost all Iraqis are Muslims, followers of the religion of Islam. About 4 percent of the population is Christian. There is also a small sect known as Yazidis whose religion combines Islam and earlier forms of worship. Thousands of Iraqi Jews immigrated to Israel after that country was founded in 1948.

Way of Life. Traditionally, most Iraqis earned their livelihood by farming or raising livestock. Farmers lived in villages, usually in houses made of sun-dried mud brick (much like the adobe used for buildings in the southwestern United States). Most produced only enough to meet their own families' needs. Wheat and other cereal grains, fruits and vegetables, and milk made up the typical diet. Meat, usually mutton (sheep) or lamb, was reserved for special occasions.

The nomadic Bedouin of Iraq's desert regions herded livestock, particularly camels and goats. Now relatively few in number, the nomads traveled well-known routes, seeking grazing land and water for their animals.

▶ LAND

Land Regions. Iraq is divided into four land regions: the lower Tigris-Euphrates Valley; the upper Tigris-Euphrates Valley; the mountains and hills of the northeast (inhabited by the Kurds); and the desert upland of the southwest and west.

The lower Tigris-Euphrates Valley is a poorly drained plain that begins just north of Baghdad, the capital, and reaches southward to the head of the Persian Gulf. There are several large, shallow lakes and a marsh area in the southern part of this region.

The upper Tigris-Euphrates Valley is made up of several fertile river valleys created by the Tigris River and its major tributaries. This steppe (grasslands) region is higher and much more hilly than the lower valley region.

The mountains of northeastern Iraq are a continuation of the Zagros Mountains of Iran. They are high and rugged, with peaks more than 10,000 feet (3,050 meters) high.

Wheat, barley, and other cereal grains are grown in the upper Tigris-Euphrates Valley, Iraq's primary agricultural region.

Mount Ebrāhīm, Iraq's highest point, rises 11,644 feet (3,549 meters) in this region.

The western desert upland—a rather level, hard-surfaced plain—is part of the much larger Syrian desert. The Euphrates River cuts through this desert in a deep and flat-floored, steep-sided valley. The surface of the desert is marked by many wadis (river beds that are dry except during the rainy season). The desert area is uninhabited apart from the nomadic Bedouin tribes.

Rivers. The Tigris and Euphrates rivers rise in the mountains of Turkey. The Euphrates is considerably longer than the Tigris and flows across eastern Syria before it reaches Iraq. Near Al Qurnah, in southern Iraq, they join to form the Shatt al Arab, which empties into the Persian Gulf. The Shatt al Arab marks part of the boundary between Iraq and Iran. Navigation rights on the river have sometimes been a cause of friction. The Euphrates is generally rather shallow. The Tigris is deeper and is normally navigable (allowing the passage of ships) as far upstream as Baghdad.

The waters of the Tigris-Euphrates system are the lifeblood of the country. But historically the rivers have at times caused great destruction. Their waters rise regularly in spring and early summer, flooding vast areas of the lower valley each year. Because the lower Tigris-Euphrates plain is so poorly drained, much potential farmland cannot be used. In addition, nearly half the land lies idle each year because of excessive salt in the soil.

Climate. Iraq receives little rainfall except in the high mountains of the northeast. The entire southwestern part of the country is tropical desert, receiving less than 10 inches (250 millimeters) of rain a year. The climate in the northeastern part, except in the mountains, is semiarid, with a rainfall of between 10 and 20 inches (250 and 500 millimeters). The summers (May through October) are dry. Winter (November through April) is the rainy season, when grains such as barley and wheat are grown on the steppe without irrigation. These crops are harvested in the spring or early summer. Crops grown in the desert and in the steppe during the summer must be irrigated.

Temperatures in summer are very high. The average temperature in July, the hottest month, is between 86 and 95°F (30 and 35°C). Nights are cooler but still hot. In the winter temperatures vary from about 45°F (7°C) in the north to about 55°F (13°C) in the south. Winter days are usually warm and pleasant, but winter night temperatures often come close to freezing.

Natural Resources. The natural vegetation of Iraq consists mainly of wild oak, hawthorn, willow, and pine trees. Iraq's only forests are in the mountains. Because of the overcutting of trees, these forests have been largely reduced to scrub growth of little value, although there has been some reforestation. Steppe grass and desert scrub provide food for livestock.

Iraq has some of the largest petroleum reserves in the world. Some of the richest deposits are found in the south in the Rumelia oil field, which Iraq shares with Kuwait. Iraq also has considerable amounts of phosphate rock (used in making chemical fertilizers), sulfur, and natural gas. Rivers provide water for irrigation and are a source of hydroelectric power. The country also has large thermal and natural-gas power plants.

▶ ECONOMY

Iraq is chiefly an agricultural country, but the development of its oil reserves in the latter half of the 1900's transformed the economy. In 1960, Iraq became a founding member of the Organization of Petroleum Exporting Countries (OPEC).

Oil is Iraq's chief export and source of income. After the Persian Gulf War of 1991,

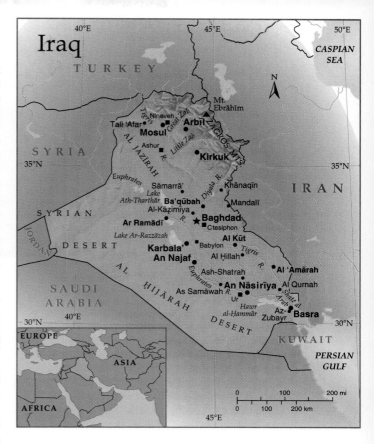

however, revenues were severely reduced due to economic sanctions imposed by the international community in response to Iraq's continued military aggression. Since the end of the Iraq War in 2003, great efforts have been made to revitalize Iraq's oil industry and all other aspects of the economy and the infrastructure, such as roads and bridges.

Services. Services account for more than half of Iraq's economy. The two strongest segments of the service industries are government and banking.

Manufacturing. The extraction and refining of oil is Iraq's chief industry. Others include the manufacture of chemicals, textiles, construction materials, and processed foods.

Agriculture. Modern farming methods have greatly increased Iraq's agricultural production. Barley and wheat are the chief cereal grains. Rice is grown in the south, where water for irrigation is abundant. Iraq is the world's largest producer of dates, the chief export crop. Cotton, sugarcane, and sugar beets also have significant commercial value.

Livestock are also an important part of Iraq's agricultural economy. Camels, sheep, and goats are raised in many parts of the country. Cattle are grazed in irrigated areas. Wool and animal hides are exported, and milk and meat are consumed locally.

Transportation. Roads, railways, and one airline connect Iraq's major cities. But many structures were destroyed during the Iraq War. Most people in rural areas rely on bicycles or animals for transportation. Oil and natural gas are transported by pipelines.

Communication. Six daily newspapers are published in Iraq—four in Arabic, one in Kurdish, and one in English. The country has limited television and radio networks.

Farm families sell locally grown produce in urban open-air markets. Agriculture employs about one-fifth of Iraq's total workforce.

▶ MAJOR CITIES

Baghdad is the capital and largest city of Iraq and the center of its commerce and industry. The city is situated in the east central part of the country, on both banks of the Tigris River. For more information, see the article BAGHDAD in Volume B.

Mosul, the capital of the Nineveh province, is the major center of administration and agricultural trade in northern Iraq. It is situated on the upper Tigris River, near the ruins of the ancient city of Nineveh, once a capital of the Assyrian Empire. It has been the chief city of northern Mesopotamia since the A.D. 900's.

Basra, the capital of the Basra province, was founded in A.D. 636 and is Iraq's chief port and primary outlet to the Persian Gulf. Much of the city was destroyed, first during the Iran-Iraq War and later during the Persian Gulf and Iraq wars.

▶ CULTURAL HERITAGE

Art and Architecture. Iraqi art and handicrafts are essentially Arabic. Miniatures painted on camel bone or ivory, mosaic inlay work, as well as rugs, textiles, and copper and brass utensils, are produced for both the local market and the tourist trade.

One distinctive type of artistic work associated with Iraq is the silverware produced by the Mandeans (a people also known as the Sabeans). The Mandeans are a small religious sect whose beliefs require that they live close to running water. Their silverware is

Baghdad was founded in A.D. 762 on the Tigris River. It became the capital of modern Iraq in 1958.

decorated with scenes or figures well known in Iraqi life and history. Iraq is also known for its distinctive embroidered rugs.

See the article ISLAMIC ART AND ARCHITECTURE in this volume.

Literature. Iraq was a center of Arab learning in the Middle Ages. Its literary achievements are part of the Arabic culture as a whole. See the article ARABIC LITERATURE in Volume A.

▶ GOVERNMENT

In April 2003, during the Iraq War, Iraqi president and dictator Saddam Hussein was overthrown by American and British forces and their allies. The United States set up a temporary governing council of Iraqi leaders, who transferred authority to a provisional Iraqi government in June 2004. The first democratic elections took place in 2005.

▶ HISTORY

The land now known as Iraq has been called the Cradle of Civilization. The ancient Sumerians, Babylonians, and Assyrians all developed great empires in the region between the Tigris and Euphrates rivers. At later times, it was ruled by the Greeks, the Romans, the Persians, and the Ottoman Turks.

Under the Abbasid rulers (750–1258), Baghdad became a center of learning for the entire Muslim world. But the Mon-

This ancient bas-relief sculpture was found in Calah (present-day Nimrud), a capital of the Assyrian Empire.

gols invaded the region in 1258, leading to its decline. The Ottoman Turks, after a long struggle, won Baghdad and the Tigris and Euphrates Valley from Persia in 1638. The region remained a part of the vast Ottoman Empire until the end of World War I, in 1918.

Creation of the Modern Nation. After World War I, Great Britain was given control of the region as a mandate of the League of Nations (the forerunner of today's United Nations, or UN). The mandate period lasted from 1920 to 1932, when Iraq became an independent constitutional monarchy, under King Faisal I.

From the 1930's to the 1950's, Iraqi politics were dominated by Prime Minister Nuri es-Said, a pro-Western leader who did much to modernize Iraq. In 1945, Iraq became a founding member of the Arab League. However, in 1958 the monarchy was overthrown in a military coup led by General Abdul Karim Kassem. Nuri es-Said, King Faisal II, and all the members of the royal family were murdered, and Iraq was declared a republic. Kassem himself was murdered in 1963.

Kurds, a non-Arab people who seek an independent state, have long been persecuted in Iraq. At the end of the Persian Gulf War in 1991, many fled to refugee camps to find protection among United Nations peacekeeping forces.

The Republic. In 1968 the Baath Party seized power. Its first leader was Ahmad Hassan al-Bakr. He was followed by Saddam Hussein, who came to power in 1979. Iraq's abundant oil revenues were used to develop the economy. But the government dealt harshly with its internal enemies and pursued an aggressive foreign policy.

Three Wars. In 1980, Iraq invaded Iran. Iraq's aim was to gain control of the Shatt al Arab waterway, and perhaps the Iranian oil fields as well. A long and costly war followed, ending in 1988 with no clear victor.

On August 2, 1990, Iraq invaded and quickly conquered its small but oil-rich neighbor Kuwait. The UN condemned the Iraqi action and imposed economic sanctions. When Iraq did not withdraw from Kuwait by the UN deadline of January 15, 1991, a coalition of nations, led by the United States, went to war against Iraq to liberate Kuwait. See the article PERSIAN GULF WAR in Volume P.

Saddam Hussein remained in power after the war, in spite of his defeat. But U.S. concerns about Iraq's failure to comply with the terms of the peace treaty steadily increased. In 2002, the United States persuaded the UN Security Council to pass a resolution ordering Iraq to abandon its supposed production of weapons of mass destruction or face "serious consequences." Iraq allowed UN weapons inspectors into the country. By early 2003, no such weapons had been found. Nevertheless, intelligence reports claimed they did exist.

On March 19, 2003 (March 20 in Iraq), the United States and its allies invaded Iraq. Saddam Hussein's regime fell when the troops seized Baghdad on April 9, and Hussein fled. See the article IRAQ WAR in Volume I.

The United States formally ended the military occupation of Iraq on June 28, 2004, by transferring sovereignty to an appointed interim government. U.S. and allied troops remained to help maintain order.

Elections. On January 30, 2005, Iraq held its first democratic election in more than 50 years to select members of provincial parliaments and a national assembly. Low voter turnout was recorded only among Sunni Muslims, a minority group that formed the core of the violent insurgency against the interim government.

On April 6, after weeks of hard bargaining among the different factions, Jalal Talabani, a Kurdish military leader, was chosen to serve as president—thus becoming the first Kurd to serve as president of an Arab country. Talabani then named Ibrahim al-Jaafari, a physician and a Shi'ite leader, as prime minister. Most cabinet posts eventually went to Shi'ites; however, Kurds and Sunnis were also represented. Women were chosen to head seven of the 31 ministries.

The assembly then drafted a constitution, which was approved in a national referendum on October 15 by nearly 80 percent of the voters, mostly Shi'ites and Kurds. A permanent national assembly was to be elected in December 2005. Meanwhile Saddam Hussein went on trial before a special Iraqi tribunal. The former dictator was charged with mass torture and killings after an attempt on his life in 1982. Hussein was defiant in the court room, refusing even to give his name. The trial was adjourned after one day.

JOHN R. RANDALL
Ohio State University

Reviewed by ARTHUR CAMPBELL TURNER
Coauthor, *Power and Ideology in the
Middle East*

See also BAGHDAD; HUSSEIN, SADDAM; KURDS.

A mural on a building in Baghdad once depicted Saddam Hussein as the supreme leader of his people. Hussein ruled Iraq from 1979 until he was overthrown in 2003.

IRAQ WAR

In the spring of 2003, the United States and its allies went to war against Iraq, an oil-rich country in the Middle East under the rule of a dictator, Saddam Hussein. Within weeks, coalition forces under the command of U.S. general Tommy R. Franks had driven Hussein from power. But groups of armed Iraqi insurgents opposed to the U.S. occupation mounted an armed campaign against U.S. forces and those Iraqis who cooperated with efforts to establish a new government.

Background. The war, which the United States called **Operation Iraqi Freedom**, had its roots in the Persian Gulf War of 1991 and the terrorist attacks of September 11, 2001. The Gulf War was triggered in July 1990 by Iraq's invasion and occupation of Kuwait, its neighbor to the south. When diplomatic efforts failed to persuade Iraq to withdraw from Kuwait, the United States and a broad international coalition launched the military campaign Operation Desert Storm against Iraq. Kuwait was soon liberated, and a cease-fire was signed. Hussein was allowed to remain in power but under certain conditions imposed by the United Nations (UN).

To prevent future aggression, the UN ordered Iraq to destroy any weapons of mass destruction (biological, chemical, and nuclear) and imposed severe economic sanctions until Iraq could prove the weapons had been eliminated.

Throughout the 1990's, Hussein consistently ignored the terms of the cease-fire agreement. He further outraged the international community with his brutal treatment of opponents within his own country, notably the Kurds and the Shi'ite Muslims. After terrorists attacked the United States on September 11, 2001, President George W. Bush and his advisers contended that Iraq possessed weapons of mass destruction and threatened U.S. security. Some U.S. officials also charged that the Iraqi government had ties to the Al Qaeda terrorists responsible for the attacks.

In his January 2002 State of the Union Address, President Bush branded Iraq as part of an "axis of evil." The following September, in a speech to the UN General Assembly, Bush accused Iraq of continuing to develop weapons of mass destruction and warned that a military response would be unavoidable if Iraq did not voluntarily disarm. Congress quickly passed a resolution supporting the president's position and approved the use of force against Iraq. Then in November, the UN Security Council unanimously adopted Resolution 1441, which imposed strict new arms inspections on Iraq. Iraq continued to deny it had weapons of mass destruction, and the UN inspectors did not find any. Bush remained unconvinced.

On February 24, 2003, the United States appealed to the United Nations for a second resolution that would approve taking action against Iraq. Britain fully supported the United States, but France, Germany, and Russia called for continued inspections. Bush finally abandoned the effort to gain UN support.

Right: On April 9, 2003, jubilant Iraqis in Baghdad tore down a statue of their fallen dictator, Saddam Hussein. *Below:* On April 14, U.S. marines seized Tikrit.

On March 17, Bush advised Hussein and his sons to leave Iraq within 48 hours or face war. There was no response. On March 19 (March 20 in Iraq), the United States launched an aerial attack on government targets in Baghdad, the Iraqi capital. Although the war was not endorsed by the UN, the United States claimed the support of at least 45 nations in addition to military backing from Great Britain, Australia, and Poland.

Course of the War. On April 9, 2003, U.S. troops seized Baghdad, ending Hussein's rule. U.S. Marines toppled a 40-foot (12-meter) statue of the dictator, while Hussein himself fled. On May 1, 2003, aboard the aircraft carrier USS *Abraham Lincoln*, President Bush declared that "the United States and our allies have prevailed," adding that "major combat operations in Iraq have ended."

Coalition forces had little time to celebrate their victory. They first had to suppress the widespread looting that swept Iraq. Shortages of water and medical supplies increased the danger of disease. A more serious and persistent threat came from armed insurgents, who attacked U.S. forces as they went about their duties. Some were Hussein loyalists, but others were believed to be staunch Muslims who resented the American presence.

Aftermath. In a step toward establishing democracy, the United States organized an interim governing council of 25 Iraqi leaders to run the country under the direction of the chief U.S. administrator, L. Paul Bremer III.

To help share its burden in Iraq, the United States persuaded the UN Security Council to approve a multinational armed force to operate in Iraq under U.S. leadership. The Security Council also appealed to member countries for troops and money to help stabilize Iraq. Although France, Russia, Germany, and Pakistan refused to make any contributions, other countries pledged more than $13 billion in loans and grants.

On December 13, 2003, Saddam Hussein was finally arrested. After months of questioning by U.S. officials, he was held for trial by the Iraqis. In the wake of Hussein's capture, the United States accelerated its plans to end its occupation of the country and turn over power to a provisional Iraqi government by June 30, 2004.

Despite continuing violence by insurgents opposed to the U.S. occupation, President Bush vowed there would be no delay in tranferring sovereignty. He agreed to allow the UN—in consultation with the United States—to appoint the new government. It was hoped that UN participation would boost international support in rebuilding Iraq and suppressing the violence. But American efforts to build good will among Iraqis were set back by the disclosure that Iraqi prisoners had been mistreated by their American captors at Abu Ghraib prison.

On June 28, 2004, two days ahead of schedule, the U.S.-led Coalition Provisional Authority transferred sovereignty over the country to an interim government. The transfer, which was endorsed by a UN resolution, was moved up two days to avoid possible attacks by insurgents. About 160,000 coalition troops, mostly Americans, remained in Iraq to help restore order.

But the violence persisted. Car bombings took many Iraqi lives. Insurgents also stepped up their strategy of kidnapping foreign civilians and soldiers and holding them as hostages to persuade foreign governments to pull their troops out of Iraq. UN Secretary General Kofi Annan, who declared the war "illegal," questioned whether Iraq's first postwar elections could take place because of the insurgency. Although they were threatened with violence, many Iraqis voted as scheduled on January 30, 2005. It was Iraq's first free election in more than 50 years.

Meanwhile, the U.S. Army investigated the abuse of prisoners at Abu Ghraib. The only senior officer punished for abuse was Brigadier General Janis Karpinski, who had commanded the military police unit at the prison. A small number of soldiers were court-martialed for their involvement.

Insurgent attacks declined after the election, but full-scale violence resumed in April. By November 2005, more than 2,000 U.S. soldiers had been killed and more than 14,000 wounded. Britain and other allies had suffered about 200 fatalities. Iraqi civilian deaths were estimated at about 25,000. Despite continued pressure to withdraw, President Bush vowed that the United States would "complete the job in Iraq."

ROBERT SHOGAN
Adjunct Professor, Johns Hopkins University

See also HUSSEIN, SADDAM; IRAQ; PERSIAN GULF WAR; TERRORISM, WAR ON.

IRELAND

Ireland is an island in the Atlantic Ocean, located just west of the larger island of Great Britain. Renowned for its lush green fields and hills, Ireland has long been known as the Emerald Isle.

Most of the island is occupied by the Republic of Ireland, an independent nation that is the focus of this article. The northwestern region, known as Northern Ireland, is part of the United Kingdom. A separate article on Northern Ireland appears in Volume N. This division of the island has caused great political turmoil and much bloodshed for hundreds of years.

The Republic of Ireland is a land of about 3.6 million people. Most Irish people are descended from the Gaels, a branch of Celtic peoples who migrated to the island from the European mainland more than 2,000 years ago.

▶ PEOPLE

Most of the people of the Republic of Ireland are descended from the Gaels, who were Celts. Other Celts from Scotland, Vikings from Scandinavia, Normans from France, and Anglo-Saxons from England also settled on the island. Because these early peoples intermarried, there is little ethnic division today.

Historically, many Irish people have left the island to seek their fortunes abroad. Today there are more Irish-descended men and women living outside Ireland than there are in the republic itself. And despite the nation's economic growth, especially since the late 1900's, many Irish people continue to immigrate to the United States, Great Britain, and elsewhere, seeking higher wages and wider choices of occupation.

Language. For many centuries the Gaelic language was spoken throughout the country. Gaelic, also known as Irish, is one of the oldest languages in Europe. Although it is still taught in schools and considered the nation's first official language (English is second), Gaelic has been replaced by English as the common language of almost the entire population. Today Gaelic is spoken by only a few people, mainly in areas along the western coast. The Gaelic name for Ireland is Éire.

Religion. The Irish are known to be a religious people, and the nation's constitution guarantees freedom of worship to all religions. More than 90 percent of the people are Roman Catholic.

Education. Religious and moral training is a basic goal of Irish education, which is free and compulsory for all children to the age of 16. Almost all primary education is run by religious groups and is supported by state funds. Teachers are paid by the state, but the management of the schools is mainly under local control. Secondary schools are privately run but are subject to state inspection because they receive

Millions of books are housed in the Long Room of the library at the University of Dublin, better known as Trinity College.

heartier cousins, ale and stout. Villagers and city folk alike often gather at their local pub, or tavern, to eat, drink, and listen to the music of local musicians.

Sports. The Irish are great sports lovers. Among the most popular games are Gaelic football and hurling, a game that resembles field hockey. Every year the 26 counties of Ireland take part in national football and hurling contests. The all-Ireland championship finals attract huge crowds.

Irish Thoroughbred horses have an outstanding reputation. They have won races all over the world, including Ireland's own Irish Derby, which takes place in Country Kildare at the Curragh Racecourse, which is just one of more than two dozen racecourses in the country.

▶ **LAND**

In area, Ireland is roughly one-tenth the size of the state of Texas. More than 100 small islands lie off the Irish coast. The most important of these are the Aran Islands, off Galway Bay in the west.

Land Regions. Ireland can be divided into two main physical regions—a large central lowland and a coastal rim of hills, plateaus, and mountains. The lowland is a fertile plain covered with farms, pastureland, and peat bogs. Ireland's highest point, Carrantuohill, is in the Macgillycuddy's Reeks range in the southwest.

some state funds. The majority of Catholic secondary schools are managed by religious orders.

Ireland's many universities include Dublin City University, the University of Limerick, the University of Dublin (better known as Trinity College), and the National University of Ireland. The National University has campuses in Dublin, Maynooth, Cork, and Galway.

Food and Drink. Many Irish specialties are made with locally produced ingredients. Irish stew, for example, is made with mutton, which comes from sheep, and potatoes, which have been the staple crop in Ireland for hundreds of years. The Irish also use homegrown barley to produce their famous Irish whiskey. Other popular drinks include beer and its

Rivers, Lakes, and Coastal Waters. The island of Ireland is surrounded by the Atlantic Ocean. The North Channel and the Irish Sea separate Ireland from Great Britain.

Ireland has many lakes and rivers. North of Macgillycuddy's Reeks are the Lakes of Killarney, which are among the most beautiful in all of Europe. Ireland's longest river, the Shannon, has been made navigable by a system of

Many pubs (taverns) in Ireland feature the music of local musicians. Over the centuries, the Irish have produced some of the world's loveliest folk songs.

Ireland's extraordinary natural beauty is displayed in the lush green farmlands in County Kerry (*above*) and the Cliffs of Moher on the Atlantic coast (*right*).

canals linking it with the Irish Sea. The Nore, Suir, and Barrow rivers in the southeast, known as the sister rivers, are wonderful for fishing. The Blackwater in the southwest is famous for its salmon. The River Liffey flows through Dublin. The Boyne, north of Dublin, was the site of a historic battle in 1690.

Climate. Abundant rainfall is what makes Ireland so green. In some parts of the country, it rains for brief periods on more than 200 days a year. Even during the driest months it rains for short periods almost every other day. On the west coast the annual rainfall varies from about 40 inches (1,020 millimeters) to almost 100 inches (2,540 millimeters). Rainfall in the eastern part of the country is somewhat less.

Ireland's climate is greatly affected by the sea. Because it is exposed to the prevailing westerly winds that cross the Gulf Stream, the climate is milder than that of many other countries in the same latitude. Winters are usually mild, and summers are pleasantly cool. Ireland's average annual temperature is 50°F (10°C).

Natural Resources. Many of Ireland's old lake basins are filled with peat bogs, which supply fuel in the form of turf, or peat. But the country has few mineral resources. Coal and oil must be imported. Small quantities of iron, zinc, copper, barites, lead, and silver are found. Gypsum, marble, limestone, flagstone, and slate are quarried for construction.

▶ ECONOMY

In the past, Ireland's economy was based on agriculture. Many new industries developed by the end of the 1900's, but in spite of economic growth, Ireland often has a relatively high rate of unemployment.

Services. Service industries account for more than 50 percent of Ireland's annual revenues. Tourism and the service establishments it supports, such as hotels and restaurants, contribute greatly to the economy.

Manufacturing. Manufacturing accounts for nearly 40 percent of Ireland's revenues. Ireland is famous for its cloth, particularly tweeds and linens. It is also known for its alcoholic beverages, namely beers, stouts, ales, and Irish whiskey. Other products include clothing, chemicals, pharmaceuticals, machinery, and transportation equipment. Glass and crystal, produced in the city of Waterford, are world-renowned.

Agriculture. The high rainfall and mild temperatures make Ireland one of the finest grass-producing areas in the world. As a result, the main rural occupation is raising cattle, sheep, pigs, and horses. Cattle and cattle products account for about 50 percent of the total agricultural output and are the most profitable agricultural export. Ireland's most important field crops are oats, potatoes, barley, wheat, turnips, and sugar beets.

Many shops sell traditional knit sweaters and other items of clothing made from Irish yarns and fabrics.

Trade. Exports from Ireland are sent mainly to the United Kingdom. They include chemicals, data processing equipment, industrial machinery, and farm animals. Goods imported into Ireland include food, animal feed, machinery, textiles, and petroleum. Ireland is a member of the European Union (EU) of nations that work together to maximize their economic interests in world markets.

Transportation. Córas Iompair Éireann (the Irish Transport System) manages all of Ireland's rail and bus lines. There is also a well-developed system of roads. The larger main roads lead to country roads that go through towns and villages. Major seaports are located in Dublin, Cork, and Limerick.

Ireland's main international airport is Shannon, near Limerick. Additional airports are located near Dublin and Cork. Aer Lingus, Ireland's national airline, flies to cities in Europe and North America.

Communication. Ireland's radio and television stations are controlled by the Radio and Television Authority, whose members are nominated by the government. Commercial firms, however, may sponsor television and radio programs and run advertisements.

Ireland has seven daily newspapers that circulate throughout the country. Five of them, including *The Irish Times*,

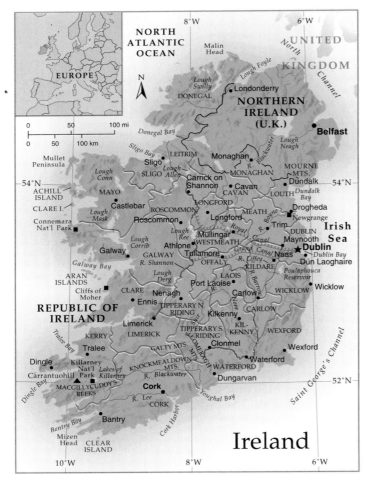

REPUBLIC OF IRELAND is the official name of the country.

LOCATION: Northwestern Europe.

AREA: 26,600 sq mi (68,894 km^2).

POPULATION: 3,800,000 (estimate).

CAPITAL: Dublin.

MAJOR LANGUAGES: Gaelic (Irish), English.

MAJOR RELIGIOUS GROUP: Christian (Roman Catholic).

GOVERNMENT: Republic. **Head of state**—president. **Head of government**—prime minister (*taoiseach*). **Legislature**—Oireachtas (national parliament), consisting of the Dáil Éireann (house of representatives) and the Seanad Éireann (senate).

CHIEF PRODUCTS: Agricultural—livestock and livestock products, milk and other dairy products, wheat, barley, potatoes, turnips, sugar beets, oats. **Manufactured**—food products, brewing, textiles, clothing, chemicals, pharmaceuticals, machinery, transportation equipment, glass and crystal. **Mineral**—zinc, copper, lead, iron, barites, silver, gypsum, marble, limestone, slate.

MONETARY UNIT: Euro (1 euro = 100 cents).

are published in Dublin. The other two are published in Cork. Many other cities and towns publish their own local newspapers.

▶ **MAJOR CITIES**

Dublin, the capital, is Ireland's largest city. Approximately 500,000 people live within the city limits. Nearly 1 million people live in the greater metropolitan area.

Located in eastern Ireland at the mouth of the River Liffey, Dublin is a seaport as well as the nation's cultural, political, and economic center. Chemicals, clothing, metal products, and stout are just a few of the goods produced there.

Dublin is home to the National Museum of Ireland, the National Library, and the Irish Museum of Modern Art. Additional landmarks include Christ Church and Saint Patrick's cathedrals, Trinity College, Dublin Castle, the Dublin Writers Museum, and the famous Abbey Theatre. O'Connell Street, named for Daniel O'Connell, a leader of the early nationalist movement, lies at the heart of the commercial district. Dublin hosts a variety of annual festivals and events, including the Dublin Theatre Festival and the international Dublin Horse Show.

Cork, Ireland's second largest city, is a major seaport, located at the mouth of the Lee River at the head of Cork Harbor in the southeast. Founded as a monastery in the 600's, Cork today is a center of manufacturing. Leather goods, beer, and whiskey are among the products made there. Cork also serves as a storage depot for imported petroleum. Every year the city hosts the Cork International Film Festival.

▶ **CULTURAL HERITAGE**

The arts have flourished in Ireland since ancient times. Many of history's greatest musicians, writers, and artists have come from Ireland.

Music. Irish music is arguably the country's greatest contribution to the performing arts. Some of the most popular Irish folk melodies have endured since ancient times

The O'Connell Bridge crosses the River Liffey in Dublin, the capital and largest city of the Republic of Ireland.

and rank with the most beautiful in the world. Irish music, played by immigrants in new lands, has widely influenced the music of other nations. In recent times, many Irish popular musicians and rock groups achieved world fame, among them Van Morrison, U2, Sinéad O'Connor, and Enya.

Art and Architecture. In the Middle Ages, the decoration of manuscripts in Ireland reached a degree of skill that has seldom been equaled. The most famous example is the *Book of Kells*, which was written about A.D. 800 and is now in Trinity College.

Also dating from the Middle Ages are the beautiful Celtic crosses that dot the Irish landscape. Lovely gold ornaments of great antiquity also can be seen in Dublin's National Museum. Fine architecture can be seen in the large cities, especially in Dublin, with its magnificent Georgian-style houses dating from the 1700's.

Literature and Theater. Irish writers have won fame in literature, poetry, and drama. Much has been written in Gaelic, but the best-known writers wrote in English. William Butler Yeats (1865–1939) is considered among the greatest poets of the 1900's. And the prose of James Joyce (1882–1941) has tremendously influenced modern writers.

The great names in drama from the 1800's on include Oscar Wilde (1854–1900), George Bernard Shaw (1856–1950), Lady Augusta Gregory (1852–1932), John Millington Synge (1871–1909), Sean O'Casey (1880–1964), and Samuel Beckett (1906–89). For more information, see the article IRELAND, LITERATURE OF in this volume.

Among Ireland's oldest artifacts are the famous Celtic crosses, carved during the Middle Ages for use as grave markers.

Sean O'Casey was one of Ireland's most celebrated playwrights.

Dance. Dancing is a popular form of recreation in Ireland. At musical entertainments, each called a *céilis*, lively step dances are performed to traditional jigs and reels. Irish step dancing was popularized in the late 1900's with the tour of the internationally acclaimed production *Riverdance*.

Film. Irish films have gained international recognition. Neil Jordan and Jim Sheridan are among the most widely acclaimed Irish directors. Notable actors include Liam Neeson, Brenda Fricker, Gabriel Byrne, Pierce Brosnan, and Colin Farrell.

▶**GOVERNMENT**

Ireland is a democratically governed republic. All citizens over the age of 18 may vote. The Oireachtas, or national parliament, is composed of the Dáil Éireann (house of representatives) and the Seanad Éireann (senate). Elections for both legislative bodies are held every five years. Ireland's two main political parties are Fianna Fáil and Fine Gael.

Dáil Éireann elects a *taoiseach*, or prime minister, who nominates the members of the cabinet. These ministers receive their seal of office from the president of Ireland, the head of state, who is elected to a 7-year term by the people. Supreme court justices are appointed by the president on the advice of the prime minister and other cabinet members.

▶**HISTORY**

Irish history may be said to date from the coming of the Celts about the middle of the 300's B.C. However, prehistoric peoples first inhabited the island. Beautiful gold jewelry and pottery that have been preserved reveal their artistic skills. Their religious beliefs and practices are indicated in the decoration of their burial places. The most famous of these can still be seen at Newgrange, in County Meath.

Early History. The Celts came from the region known as Gaul, now France. With their swords of iron, they soon dominated these early peoples. The Celts developed an exact code of laws and are said to have honored their poets as much as their kings.

In the A.D. 400's, St. Patrick (389?–461?) came to Ireland and converted the people to Christianity. As a result, many monasteries were built, and Irish monks brought the Christian faith and culture to Europe. Ireland became a center of learning and was known as the Island of Saints and Scholars. However, a series of weak rulers led to a series of foreign invasions.

The first invaders were Viking sailors who came from northern Europe in the 800's. They founded many of Ireland's coastal cities, including Dublin, Cork, and Limerick. They remained in control of the cities until the Irish king Brian Boru (926–1014) won the Battle of Clontarf, near Dublin, in 1014.

The English in Ireland. In 1171, the English king Henry II (1133–89) invaded Ireland and persuaded the Gaelic kings to submit to him. English colonists then settled in Ireland. They spoke English and Norman French rather than Gaelic. In time, they began to intermarry with the Irish and to adopt their customs. But in 1366 it became illegal for the English to intermarry with the Irish.

After the Protestant Reformation began in the 1500's, feelings of hostility and separateness developed into a religious war. King Henry VIII (1491–1547) of England and his Protestant successors wanted Irish Catholics to follow the teachings of the Protestant Church of England. The Irish resisted the English strongly. Hugh O'Neill (1550–1616) rallied Irish forces in Ulster in northern Ireland and won several victories during a nine-year war. But with the Battle of Kinsale in 1601, the Irish were decisively defeated.

When a Catholic king, James II (1633–1701), came to power in England in 1685, the Irish felt new hope. But the Protestant English nobles were opposed to James's Catholicism. And after James was overthrown in the Glorious Revolution of 1688, the nobles offered the throne to his daughter, Mary II (1662–94), and his son-in-law, the Protestant William III (1650–1702).

James fled to Ireland, but William pursued and defeated him at the Battle of the Boyne (River) in 1690. And to further subdue the Irish, the English Parliament passed the Penal Laws. By these laws Irish Catholics lost their legal and religious rights, and many were reduced to poverty.

In 1801, an Act of Union, championed by the English prime minister, William Pitt the Younger (1759–1806), declared Ireland part of the United Kingdom. The Irish were promised seats in the British Parliament, but in fact they did not gain representation until 1829, when the Penal Laws were repealed. This victory was brought about mainly through the efforts of the great Irish patriot Daniel O'Connell (1775–1847). O'Connell also tried but failed to get the Act of Union repealed.

Further calamities beset Ireland. From 1845 through 1848, a fungus attacked the potato crop and wiped out the food supply

In the 1840's a blight on Ireland's potato crop caused widespread famine. More than a million people left Ireland, immigrating to the United States and other countries.

for more than half of Ireland's people. About 1 million Irish died of hunger and disease during the famine. More than 1 million more fled to the United States and other countries. Many Irish blamed the English for not providing enough help during the famine, and their anger greatly increased the popular demand for home rule.

The Struggle for Independence. When World War I broke out in 1914, many Irish

Catholics and Irish Protestants alike joined the British Army to fight Germany and its allies. But many others instead joined the Irish Volunteers, a group formed in 1913 to defend the rights of the Irish people. The Irish Volunteers then joined forces with the Citizen Army, another group that was formed to defend Irish workers after the great Dublin strike in 1913. Led by Pádhraic Pearse (1879–1916) and James Connolly (1870–1916), the rebel force attempted to capture Dublin on Easter Monday, 1916. Proclaiming Ireland a republic, the force of about 1,000 held parts of the city for about a week. But British troops finally forced them to surrender, and 15 Irish leaders were executed.

Although the Easter Rising was a military failure, the soldiers' heroism excited the people. They flocked to support the Sinn Féin (Ourselves Alone) political party, which called for political and cultural independence for all of Ireland. Following a declaration of independence on January 21, 1919, fighting broke out between the newly formed Irish Republican Army (IRA) and British troops (who were called the Black and Tans for the colors of their uniforms). A bitter war continued until 1921, when Irish and British representatives signed a treaty declaring much of Ireland a self-governing country within the British Commonwealth of Nations. However, six of the nine counties in northern Ireland's Ulster region did not join the newly created Irish Free State. They remained a province of the United Kingdom and became known as Northern Ireland.

Although the treaty was accepted by the Irish house of representatives, many Irish people were opposed to it. Civil war followed between supporters and opponents of the treaty. Many people were killed, including Michael Collins (1890–1922), a leader of the IRA and a founder of the Irish Free State, who supported the treaty.

In 1926, Eamon de Valera (1882–1975), who led the Irish opposition to the treaty, formed the republican party Fianna Fáil. By

Eamon de Valera was a leader in Ireland's fight to free itself from British rule. Ireland was declared an independent republic in 1949.

1932 his party was in control of the government. A new constitution, drawn up in 1937, called for the country to be ruled by a president and a *taoiseach* (prime minister). In 1949, Ireland officially left the British Commonwealth and became an independent republic. In 1973 it joined what is now the European Union.

Efforts Toward Peace. Many Irish nationalists have always refused to recognize the partition of Ireland. Tensions caused by the division have led to years of civil violence. In an effort to ease the bitter dispute, representatives from the United Kingdom and the Republic of Ireland signed an accord in 1985, giving the Irish government an advisory role in setting policy for Northern Ireland. The accord provided for an intergovernmental conference, composed of Irish and British officials, to discuss issues affecting the province. But responsibility for Northern Ireland remained with the United Kingdom.

In 1995, Irish and British government leaders established a new framework for negotiations on Northern Ireland, with the provision that the province's future would be determined by the people themselves.

In 1998, a majority of people in both the Republic of Ireland and Northern Ireland voted in support of a historic peace agreement. Representatives of the Republic of Ireland agreed to participate with Britain, Scotland, and Wales in a new Council of the Isles. And in 1999 the Irish constitution was amended to formally revoke the Republic of Ireland's claim to Northern Ireland.

Mary McAleese, the current president of Ireland, was first elected in 1997. That same year, Bernie Ahern was appointed prime minister.

Reviewed by the Consulate General of Ireland
New York City

See also CELTS; IRELAND, LITERATURE OF; NORTHERN IRELAND; UNITED KINGDOM.

IRELAND, LITERATURE OF

The literature of Ireland includes works in both the Irish language and the English language. The Irish language is one of the Celtic languages, which belong to the Indo-European family. Celtic languages were spoken in many parts of Europe before those areas were conquered by the Romans. The Celts in Ireland, however, were left undisturbed. The Romans never reached them, and their language survived. Vikings invaded Ireland beginning in the A.D. 800's, but they were eventually driven out. When the Normans conquered Ireland in the 1100's and 1200's, they introduced the French and English languages, but Irish continued to be spoken and written. During the 1500's and 1600's, the English started plantations in Ireland and gradually became the country's landowners and aristocracy. Deaths during the Great Famine of 1846–48 and the widespread emigration of Irish-speaking people that followed caused English to become the dominant language in Ireland.

▶ EARLY IRISH LITERATURE

Early Irish literature is written in the oldest spoken language of western Europe. After Ireland accepted Christianity between A.D. 460–560, monasteries sprang up as centers of learning. The monks wrote in Latin but soon began to compose in Irish. Ancient history, myths, and tales, which until then had been passed on orally, were written down in the 600's–800's. Later they were recopied in great manuscripts that still survive.

The Hero Tales. Irish sagas, or hero tales, have been called a window on the Iron Age because they reflect civilization between the 100's B.C. and the A.D. 400's. They are about battles, cattle raids, feasts, voyages to the otherworld, visions, elopements, and deaths.

The adventures of Cuchulain in the Ulster Cycle of tales are examples of Irish sagas. Cuchulain earned his name, which means "the hound of Culann," as a boy, when he killed the famous watchdog of Culann the smith. He took the dog's place until another pup could be trained. Later, Cuchulain single-handedly defended Ulster province against Maeve, queen of a neighboring province, who organized a cattle raid to capture Ulster's prize brown bull. The Ulster Cycle also contains the oldest love story of Irish literature. Conchobar, king of Ulster, chose the beautiful Deirdre for his bride. Before the marriage, she fell in love with Naisi, whose three brothers helped the couple elope to Scotland. Conchobar was determined to get Deirdre back, so he cunningly urged them to return. When they did, he had the brothers killed, causing Deirdre to take her own life.

Tales of the Fenian Cycle are about the hero Finn MacCool and his band of warriors. They loved war and hunting. The most famous story of the cycle is "The Pursuit of Diarmuid and Grania," which is quite similar to the Deirdre story. Finn chose Grania to be his wife, but she eloped with Diarmuid. Finn pursued them and made peace. Later, however, when Diarmuid was wounded, Finn allowed him to die. In another tale of the Fenian Cycle, two of Finn's men tell 200 stories about Ireland's past to St. Patrick. This tale is called "The Colloquy of Ancients." It informed St. Patrick about heroes and great deeds of ancient times. The tale also explained the meanings of the names of different places and told of some adventures of the Fenians before St. Patrick came to Ireland.

Early Poetry. Nature was a common theme in Irish poems of this early period. One about winter is translated as follows:

Winter has come with scarcity,
Lakes have flooded on all sides,
Frost crumbles the leaves,
The merry wave mutters.

In another poem from the 700's the author is relieved that a storm will keep Viking invaders at home.

Fierce is the wind tonight,
It ploughs up the white hair of the sea.
I have no fear that the Viking hosts
Will come over the water to me.

An early example of personal poetry was written by a scholar about himself and his cat.

I and Pangur Ban my cat,
'Tis a like task we are at:
Hunting mice is his delight,
Hunting words I sit all night.
. . . So in peace our tasks we ply
Pangur Ban my cat and I;
In our arts we find our bliss,
I have mine and he has his.

Earlier Irish works were recopied and collected in large manuscripts during the 1400's and 1500's. Lives of saints, poetry, and tales of wonder and adventure were also written. Great books like *The Odyssey, The Aeneid, The Voyages of Marco Polo,* and *The Conquests of Charlemagne* were translated into Irish.

During the troubled political times of the 1600's, few literary works were written. Laws barred Catholics from the legal profession and public office and from attending universities. Ireland had become "two nations." In the 1700's, Irish-born writers such as Oliver Goldsmith and Richard Brinsley Sheridan went to England to pursue their literary

The Irish poet and dramatist William Butler Yeats was a leader in the development of a national Irish literature. He used Irish themes in his works and helped found the Abbey Theatre, Ireland's national theater.

careers. Jonathan Swift, who also lived in England for a time, returned to Dublin as Dean of St. Patrick's Cathedral. His works about Ireland called attention to the country's economic problems. *A Modest Proposal* (1729) is an example.

Another writer, Maria Edgeworth, moved from England to live on her father's estate in Ireland. She published a novel called *Castle Rackrent* (1800). In it, Thady Quirk, an old steward, tells the story of the decline and fall of a family of Irish landowners. Edgeworth's later novel, *The Absentee* (1812), described the sufferings of Irish peasants under powerful land agents in charge of estates whose landlords went to live in England. Both novels are portraits of how Irish land was managed.

▶ THE IRISH LITERARY REVIVAL

Seeds of a literary revival in Ireland were sown early in the 1800's. Daniel O'Connell, an Irishman, won the right to sit as a member of the English Parliament, and a new sense of nationhood was born. Thomas Davis, a poet, founded *The Nation,* a newspaper that made the Irish more aware of their traditions and history. Poets Thomas Moore and James Clarence Mangan popularized Irish legendary and historical themes in their works. When Standish James O'Grady published his study on Ireland's heroic period, both Irish and Anglo-Irish writers were inspired to draw on the rich materials of the ancient past. Douglas Hyde, who later became Ireland's first president, gave a lecture called "The Necessity of De-Anglicizing the Irish Nation." He also helped form The Gaelic League in 1893 to revive Irish as a spoken language.

Yeats. William Butler Yeats was closely identified with the literary revival movement. His aim was to write for an Irish audience about Ireland. He renewed both poetry and drama and made the spoken language the language of literature as well. Yeats's early poems drew inspiration from Irish fairy tales and folktales and events of the Ulster and Fenian cycles. Some later themes included the defense of art, the praise of aristocratic life, and Irish public and political figures. Among his well-known poems are "The Lake Isle of Innisfree," "The Wild Swans at Coole," "Easter, 1916," "The Second Coming," and "Sailing to Byzantium." Yeats also wrote 26 short-verse plays. He was awarded the Nobel prize for literature in 1923.

Lady Gregory. Isabella Augusta Persse, Lady Gregory, was an important figure of the literary revival in her own right. She translated ancient Irish epics into English, wrote more than 20 plays, and gathered folklore and folktales from peasants in western Ireland.

An Irish Theater. Several literary figures, including William Butler Yeats and Lady Gregory, whose interests centered around drama were drawn together to plan the establishment of an Irish literary theater. A dramatic company was formed in 1902, and Dublin actors staged Yeats's play *Cathleen ni Houlihan,* about the 1798 Irish uprising. In 1904, the company was given a building that became the Abbey Theatre. The opening performance featured Lady Gregory's folk com-

edy *Spreading the News* and Yeats's verse play *On Baile's Strand,* which was about the hero Cuchulain.

Synge. A chance meeting in Paris between Yeats and John Millington Synge sent Synge to live on the Aran Islands off the west coast of Ireland. Here he saw the stark lives of the fishermen's families and heard the lilt of their everyday speech. His powerful one-act play *Riders to the Sea* (1904) came out of this experience. Another work, *The Playboy of the Western World* (1907), is today considered to be his masterpiece. This satire's portrait of the hero Christy Mahon and the village peasants of the west caused riots at its first performance at the Abbey Theatre and, later, in Philadelphia.

O'Casey. Sean O'Casey is especially remembered for three plays about the Irish struggle for freedom from England in the 1900's. *The Plough and the Stars* (1926) is set during the 1916 Easter Uprising. *Shadow of a Gunman* (1923) takes place during the Black and Tan British raids against Irish Republican gunmen. *Juno and the Paycock* (1924) features a Dublin family during the civil war of 1922 when Irish republicans resisted the "compromise" of dominion status for Ireland. O'Casey is also remembered for a series of books, published between 1939 and 1956, about his life and times.

Above: The plays of John Millington Synge are set in the peasant villages of western Ireland. This scene is from *The Playboy of the Western World,* his best-known work.

Right: Lady Gregory was an important figure in the Irish literary revival. She wrote many plays on Irish subjects, collected folklore, and helped found the Abbey Theatre.

Joyce. James Joyce is one of the most challenging writers of the 1900's. He is credited with remaking the short story in *Dubliners* (1914), a collection of 15 stories that sketch childhood, adolescence, maturity, and public life in Dublin settings. Joyce's three experimental masterpieces, *Portrait of the Artist as a Young Man* (1916), *Ulysses* (1922), and *Finnegans Wake* (1939), changed the form of the modern novel. He pioneered a style of writing called stream of consciousness, in which the free flow of language reveals a person's thoughts, feelings, and memories. *Por-*

trait follows the life of Dubliner Stephen Dedalus who chooses a career as a writer/artist and later decides to leave Ireland. It is essentially Joyce's own story. *Ulysses* is the one-day quest of Dubliner Leopold Bloom. Modeled after Homer's *Odyssey,* its subject matter and writing style make it a challenging book for even the most sophisticated reader. Joyce's last work, *Finnegans Wake,* is perhaps the most difficult

James Joyce experimented with new literary techniques. He used a method called stream of consciousness to describe his characters' unspoken thoughts and feelings.

book in modern literature. Joyce described it as "an imitation of the dream state … a sleep book." He considered it his best work, but few readers succeed in mastering it.

Behan. Brendan Behan was an active Irish republican who turned to writing plays about IRA activity in *The Quare Fellow* (1954) and *The Hostage* (1958). His prose memoir *Borstal Boy* (1958) relates his experiences at age 16 in the Borstal, a British reformatory for minors. It has been called Behan's "Portrait of the Artist as a Young Delinquent."

Beckett. Irish-born Samuel Beckett settled permanently in Paris in 1937 and wrote his works in French. He reshaped modern drama in his theater-of-the-absurd plays *Waiting for Godot* (1952) and *Endgame* (1957). These plays lack plot, characters, and meaningful dialogue in the usual sense. They do, however, present basic human attitudes and situations. Beckett's novels are also considered masterpieces. The genius of Beckett was recognized in 1969 when he was awarded the Nobel prize for literature.

▶ MODERN POETRY AND FICTION

Ireland's foremost poet today is Seamus Heaney, who enjoys a worldwide reputation.

His poem "Digging" recalls how two generations of his family made their living with the spade—his grandfather in a peat bog and his father on a potato farm. Of himself, Heaney says:

> But I've no spade to follow men like them.
> Between my finger and my thumb
> The squat pen rests.
> I'll dig with it.

Austin Clarke, Patrick Kavanagh, and Thomas Kinsella are also significant Irish poets of the later 1900's.

Liam O'Flaherty, Seán O'Faoláin, and Kate O'Brien are important writers of modern Irish fiction. Frank O'Connor (1903–66) is the author of the delightful short stories "My Oedipus Complex," "The Drunkard," and "First Confession."

▶ FOLKTALES AND MEMOIRS

Village storytellers once recited Irish folktales about animals, birds, fairy people, witches, kings, and heroes to neighbors gathered around a peat fire. Informal collections of folktales were published in the 1800's, following the lead of the Grimm Brothers' collections of German folktales. In the 1900's, the Irish Folklore Commission taped versions of thousands of folktales, identified their types, and recorded the names of the storytellers and their towns. Two enjoyable Irish folktales are "Sean Palmer's Voyage to America with the Fairies" and "Daniel O'Connell Wears His Hat in Parliament."

Many Irish authors have written memoirs of their times and experiences. Maurice O'Sullivan gave the name *Twenty Years A-Growing* (1933) to the account of his childhood and adolescence on Great Blasket Island off the coast of Dingle. The title came from his grandfather, who told him that life is divided into twenty years a-growing, twenty years a-blossom, twenty years a-stooping, and twenty years declining. Great Blasket Island, once home to Irish-speaking fishermen's families, is no longer inhabited. O'Sullivan's record is important, for it chronicles a way of life that has all but disappeared.

PHILIP DRISCOLL
Brandeis University
Reviewed by M. TERESA BRADY
Pace University

IRELAND, NORTHERN. See NORTHERN IRELAND.

The Brooklyn Bridge, which crosses the East River to connect the New York boroughs of Manhattan and Brooklyn, was the first suspension bridge built using steel-wire cables.

IRON AND STEEL

Iron and steel affect our lives more than any other metals. Long ago prehistoric people used the iron from meteorites to make tools. Today most iron is used to make steel. Steel is one of the most versatile and inexpensive metals used by humans. People use steel to make many of the same tools prehistoric people used —eating utensils, cooking pots, and weapons. Yet steel is also used to make many tools of modern technology, such as automobiles, televisions, computers, jets, satellites, and surgical instruments. Centuries from now, an archaeologist studying the relics of our 20th-century civilization might call this the Age of Steel.

▶ **WHAT ARE IRON AND STEEL?**

Iron is the most useful of the metallic elements. It is one of the most common elements in the earth's crust, where it occurs widely in chemical compounds. It is rarely found in its pure form on the earth, except in meteorites.

Steel is an alloy, or mixture, of iron and carbon. An alloy that contains less than 50 percent iron is not considered to be a steel. The carbon content of steel ranges from 0.03 percent to about 2.25 percent. Steel sometimes has other elements that give it characteristics such as hardness or toughness. The kind of steel we usually see is a hard, silver-gray metal that has great strength and flexibility in proportion to its weight.

Kinds of Steel

Thousands of kinds of steel can be made, depending on the types of elements added to the steel alloy. There are roughly three types of steels: carbon steel, low-alloy steel, and high-alloy (or stainless) steel.

The carbon steels have up to 1.65 percent of **manganese** or small quantities of silicon, aluminum, copper, and other elements. Manganese helps to prevent the steel from being brittle and improves its strength, hardness, and flexibility. Carbon steels are used for automobile bodies, appliances, machinery, ships, and buildings.

The low-alloy steels have a total of 1 to 5 percent of common elements such as nickel, chromium, molybdenum, tungsten, or titanium. Low-alloy steels are used mostly in products such as aircraft parts, tools, and gears, which require steel with special characteristics.

The high-alloy steels contain over 5 percent of at least one element, such as chromium, nickel, manganese, molybdenum, or tungsten. A large proportion of high-alloy steels are stainless steels and are used in making jet engines, chemical equipment, tableware, cooking utensils, and cutting tools.

Mining and Processing the Raw Materials

Iron Ore. Iron ore was formed by a process that began more than 2 billion years ago, when the earth's surface was mostly covered by oceans. Iron compounds in the ocean water

After the iron ore is mined, it is loaded into ore cars and carried to a processing center where it is made into a form that can be used in ironmaking.

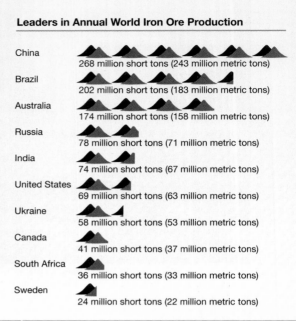

Leaders in Annual World Iron Ore Production

China	268 million short tons (243 million metric tons)
Brazil	202 million short tons (183 million metric tons)
Australia	174 million short tons (158 million metric tons)
Russia	78 million short tons (71 million metric tons)
India	74 million short tons (67 million metric tons)
United States	69 million short tons (63 million metric tons)
Ukraine	58 million short tons (53 million metric tons)
Canada	41 million short tons (37 million metric tons)
South Africa	36 million short tons (33 million metric tons)
Sweden	24 million short tons (22 million metric tons)

settled to the ocean floors. There the iron compounds combined with sand and silt (soil made up of fine rock particles) to gradually form rock. Other iron ores were formed when volcanoes deposited iron-rich lava on the earth's surface.

Iron ore is found throughout the world. In North America, the richest deposits are found near Lake Superior in Minnesota, in Michigan, and in parts of Canada near Lake Superior. California, Missouri, and Wyoming also have large deposits. There are also large quantities of iron ore in Russia, Brazil, Australia, and Venezuela.

Types of Iron Ore. Iron is almost always found in nature in combination with other elements—most commonly oxygen, carbon, sulfur, and silicon. These combinations form the iron ore that is the most important raw material for making iron and steel. The main types of iron ore are magnetite, hematite, limonite, siderite, and taconite. The highest percentages of iron—about 70 percent—are found in **magnetite** and **hematite**.

Mining the Ore. There are two main ways to mine iron ore: open-pit mining and shaft, or underground, mining. The open-pit method is used to mine ore deposits close to the surface of the earth. Power shovels dig away the earth cover, scoop out the ore, and load it into trucks or railroad cars. Most of the ore mined in open pits is high-grade ore. It usually contains about 52 percent iron.

Shaft mining is used to mine ore buried deep in the ground. Miners dig shafts and tunnels into the earth and bring up the ore. Then it is inspected for impurities and graded according to its quality. High-grade ore is sent directly to the furnaces to be melted into crude iron. Low-grade ore must first be processed to remove impurities.

Processing Ore. The first step in processing low-grade ore is blasting large chunks of ore out of the earth. The chunks are taken to mills and ground up. Magnets are used to draw out the iron-bearing minerals from the ground-up rock, and the waste rock is thrown away. The powdered ore is dried and formed into pellets containing about 60 percent iron. The pellets are then sent to the furnace.

▶**MAKING IRON**

To convert iron ore into iron products, the ore is refined to the point where it reaches 90 to 95 percent purity. This process requires great heat and a substance known as a reducing agent, which draws oxygen out of the iron ore.

Most iron is made in a **blast furnace**, a huge cylinder made of steel and lined with special fire-resistant bricks, called firebricks. Iron ore is combined with a reducing agent, then heated in the blast furnace to temperatures high enough to melt the iron.

Raw Materials

The most important reducing agent used in blast furnaces is **coke**. It is a grayish-black substance that gives off intense heat when burned. Coke is composed mostly of carbon. It is made by heating bituminous (soft) coal in closed containers called coke ovens.

Another important raw material used in blast furnaces is **limestone**. Limestone helps to remove impurities from iron ore. It acts as a cleaner—steel makers call it a flux—because it soaks up unwanted sulfur and phosphorus. Limestone, one of the most common rocks on the earth, is made up mostly of the shells and skeletons of prehistoric sea organisms.

The amount of raw materials that go into a blast furnace is enormous. To make 1 ton of crude iron, about 1.5 tons (1.37 metric tons) of iron ore are needed, plus 0.6 ton (.55 metric ton) of coke and 0.3 ton (0.3 metric ton) of limestone. During a 24-hour period, a blast furnace may consume nearly 150 railroad cars full of solid raw materials. It also consumes about 4 tons (3.64 metric tons) of air for every ton of iron produced. Air is used to cool the furnace and to clean waste gases.

Operating a Blast Furnace

Blast furnaces are essentially giant ovens lined with firebricks. They may be over 100 feet (30 meters) high and over 30 feet (9 meters) in diameter at the base. Facilities at the top of the furnace allow for the loading of raw materials into the furnace and for the cleaning of waste gases. Iron ore, coke, and limestone are loaded into the furnace in alternating layers.

Next to each blast furnace are tall stoves to heat the air blown into the furnace. The air, heated to about 1,600°F (870°C), burns the coke. The coke gives off intense heat and huge quantities of carbon monoxide gas. The gas combines with the oxygen in the iron ore and passes off as carbon dioxide, leaving molten (melted) iron in the bottom of the blast furnace.

The limestone, which melts in the intense heat, combines with the waste materials in the iron ore. It makes a fluid scum called **slag**, which is removed from the surface of the iron.

A blast furnace operates day and night, seven days per week. Raw materials are fed into it as fast as they are needed. This is the most efficient way to produce iron. If the furnace is shut down for repairs, several days are needed to make it operate smoothly again.

Every four or five hours the blast furnace is **tapped** to remove the molten iron. First the slag is removed through an outlet in the side of the furnace. Another hole, called a taphole, is then opened to allow the molten iron to run out, 100 to 300 tons (91 to 273 metric tons) at a time. The molten iron is poured into railroad tank cars and taken to steelmaking furnaces or

The raw materials needed to make iron are piled outside the blast furnace (*below*); inside, the movement of materials is monitored from the control room (*left*).

to molds where the iron is allowed to solidify for future use.

Iron Products

Today about 90 percent of the iron that is produced in blast furnaces is used in steelmaking. This was not always the case. Until 1870, very little steel was produced, and iron was the most important end product. Iron that is not used for steelmaking is used by **foundries**, which are plants that produce iron products.

Cast Iron. Melted iron that is poured into a mold is called **cast iron**. When the melted iron is cooled and hardened, it is called **pig iron**. It was given this name because at one time molten iron used to be poured into small sand molds surrounding the blast furnace. Ironworkers thought the molds looked like suckling pigs around their mother.

Pig iron is melted in foundries and processed into various types of cast iron. Cast-iron products include engine blocks for automobiles, water and drainage pipes, and fire hydrants.

Wrought Iron. Wrought iron is created by melting and refining pig iron. Molten pig iron is poured over a substance known as silicate slag, which is made from melted sand. The iron and silicate mixture is then compressed to form blocks of wrought iron. Wrought iron can be formed into many shapes, is easy to weld, and resists corrosion. It is most often used for furniture, decorative ironwork, and corrosion-resistant pipes.

▶ MAKING STEEL

Steel is essentially iron that has been refined so it contains less than 1.7 percent carbon. Iron produced in blast furnaces contains about 5 percent carbon, which makes it too brittle for most industrial uses. Steel attains great strength and flexibility through a process of removing carbon and other elements from pig iron. Sometimes small amounts of other elements such as manganese, molybdenum, chromium, and nickel are added as well.

Most steel is produced by one of four methods: basic oxygen process, electric furnace process, open-hearth process, and Bessemer process. In each method, the materials for steelmaking are placed in a furnace that produces a batch, or **heat**, of refined steel.

The Basic Oxygen Process

More steel is now produced by the basic oxygen process than by any other method.

Above: The molten iron glows with heat as it streams from the blast furnace into the insulated railroad car, called a torpedo. The torpedo keeps the iron hot and liquid while it is being taken to refining furnaces. *Right:* While some processes may require up to eight hours to produce a batch of steel, the basic oxygen process takes about 30 to 45 minutes. Its speed has made it the most used method of steelmaking.

Molten iron from the blast furnace is poured into a basic oxygen furnace. A long, water-cooled pipe, called an oxygen lance, is lowered through the mouth of the furnace until its end is just above the molten metal. Pure oxygen is blown through the pipe onto the metal. The oxygen combines with the impurities, which either form part of the slag or pass off as exhaust gases.

The exhaust gases are collected by a hood over the furnace and are cleaned before being released into the atmosphere. It takes about 45 minutes to produce a heat of steel in the basic oxygen process—much less time than is required by other methods of steelmaking. When the steel is ready, the furnace is tilted onto its side, and the molten metal is poured off.

The Electric Furnace

The electric furnace process uses tremendous charges of electricity to produce steel. The raw material used is almost always scrap iron. Scrap iron is loaded into the furnace, while large sticks of carbon, called electrodes, are lowered from the roof of the furnace to just above the surface of the metal. When the power is turned on, the current jumps the gap between the electrodes and the metal, making an electric arc. The arc generates terrific heat —6,000°F (3,312°C)—and melts the metal. When the heat (batch of steel) is finished, the furnace is tilted to pour the steel into a ladle.

High-quality steels, such as stainless and heat-resistant steels, are often made in electric furnaces. Electric furnaces also are used to make ordinary carbon steel, especially at small steel plants where a blast furnace would be too costly.

The Open-Hearth Furnace

For many years most of the world's steel was produced in open-hearth furnaces. An open-hearth furnace is like a huge, shallow tank lined with heat-resistant bricks. Gas, oil, powdered coal, or tar may be used as fuel. The fuel is mixed with hot air in burners located at each end of the furnace. Flames sweep down from the burners and across the open hearth just above the materials to be melted. The furnace is fed with limestone, steel scrap, and molten iron. The open-furnace method usually requires up to twelve hours to produce one heat of steel.

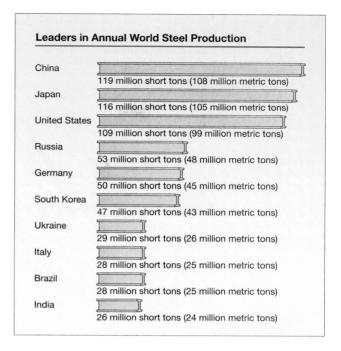

Leaders in Annual World Steel Production

China	119 million short tons (108 million metric tons)
Japan	116 million short tons (105 million metric tons)
United States	109 million short tons (99 million metric tons)
Russia	53 million short tons (48 million metric tons)
Germany	50 million short tons (45 million metric tons)
South Korea	47 million short tons (43 million metric tons)
Ukraine	29 million short tons (26 million metric tons)
Italy	28 million short tons (25 million metric tons)
Brazil	28 million short tons (25 million metric tons)
India	26 million short tons (24 million metric tons)

The Bessemer Process

The Bessemer process is the oldest method for producing large quantities of steel. It was invented in the 1850's by two men working independently of each other—Henry Bessemer, a British steel manufacturer, and William Kelly, a Kentucky ironmaker.

The Bessemer process produces steel by blowing air through molten iron at high pressure. The molten iron is placed in a pear-shaped container called a Bessemer converter. Air is blown in from the bottom through hundreds of small holes called **tuyeres**. The oxygen in the air burns away most of the unwanted materials mixed with the iron.

The drawback of the Bessemer process is that it does not efficiently remove some unwanted elements, such as nitrogen. As improved methods were developed, the Bessemer process gradually went out of use. It is no longer used in the United States, and it is used only to a limited extent elsewhere.

Processing Steel

After liquid steel has been created in the furnaces, it must be further processed and cast into a solid form before it can be used in manufacturing. The molten steel, which is poured at a temperature of about 3,000°F (1,647°C), is usually put through one of two processes, **ingot casting** or **strand casting**.

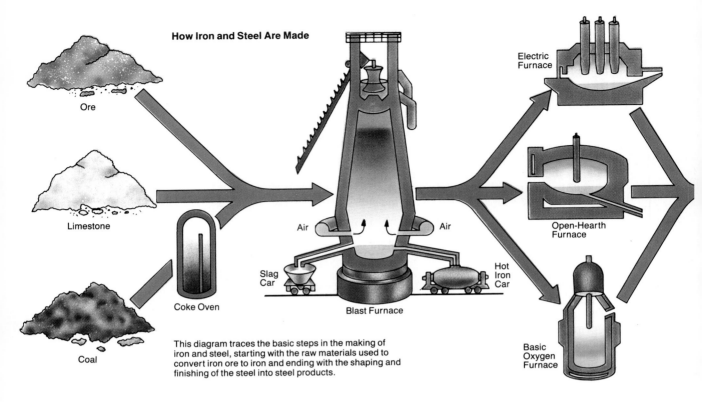

How Iron and Steel Are Made

Ore

Limestone

Coal

Coke Oven

Slag Car

Air

Air

Hot Iron Car

Blast Furnace

Electric Furnace

Open-Hearth Furnace

Basic Oxygen Furnace

This diagram traces the basic steps in the making of iron and steel, starting with the raw materials used to convert iron ore to iron and ending with the shaping and finishing of the steel into steel products.

Ingot Casting. Ingots are tall, triangular pieces of steel ranging in weight from less than a ton to several hundred tons. Liquid steel is poured from a ladle into molds and allowed to solidify. After the steel has solidified, the molds are stripped away by giant tongs. The ingots are then heated to a uniform temperature of about 2,200°F (1,203°C). Heating is necessary for the ingots to be shaped properly in the next stage of processing.

Steel mills generally form the heated ingots into three general shapes: **blooms, slabs,** and **billets.** Blooms and billets are squared pieces. Slabs are wide, flat, rectangular pieces. All are about 8 to 12 feet (2.4 to 3.7 meters) long. Blooms, slabs, and billets are known as semifinished steel.

Strand Casting. Strand casting, which used to be called continuous casting, got its name from the long strand of steel produced. The steel is then cut into blooms or slabs while it is still hot.

Molten steel is poured into the top of a casting machine, which cools the steel as it passes through molds. The steel is poured vertically at first, but as it cools, it is drawn out horizontally at a controlled rate into a long strand. Banks of rollers squeeze the steel into a thinner and thinner strand. At the end of the casting process, the steel may be traveling as fast as 3,000 feet (900 meters) per minute. Each bank of rollers is powered by several electric motors. Modern strand casting mills are oper-

As steel is tapped, it flows from the furnace into a large pot-shaped ladle. Elements such as copper, chromium, and nickel may be added to the molten steel at this stage to refine it further. After the liquid steel has cooled, it is ready for the next step of either ingot production or strand casting.

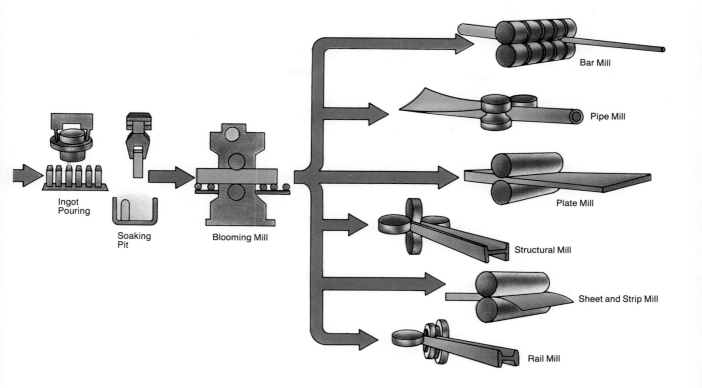

Ingot Pouring

Soaking Pit

Blooming Mill

Bar Mill

Pipe Mill

Plate Mill

Structural Mill

Sheet and Strip Mill

Rail Mill

ated by remote control from air-conditioned enclosures high above the mill.

Rolling Mills. Most semifinished steel, whether it is produced from ingots or from strand casting, undergoes additional processing. The most common method is **rolling**. In this process, steel is reheated and put through a series of giant rollers that squeeze the steel into shapes and sizes that are easier to use in manufacturing.

The rolling process is especially important because it improves the quality of the steel. Rolling or squeezing steel under tremendous pressure closes holes in the metal. It also breaks up impurities in the steel and refines the grain structure of the steel so that it becomes tougher and more flexible.

There are six main kinds of steel products created in rolling mills: sheet and strip, bars, rails and beams, plates, pipes and tubes, and rod and wire.

Sheet and **strip** steel account for over a third of the steel produced in the United States. Both sheet and strip are flat types of steel, usually less than ¼ inch (6.4 millimeters) thick. Sheet and strip steel are used for auto-

mobiles, kitchen appliances, furniture, tools, and many other products.

Most sheet and strip steel are produced in machines called hot-rolling mills. The steel is reheated and then fed through several sets of heavy rollers. Each set of rollers compresses the steel, so that it becomes thinner and thinner as it passes through the mill. Within just a few minutes, a hot-rolling mill can convert a steel slab 5 inches (13 centimeters) thick and 8 feet (2.4 meters) long to a sheet ¹⁄₁₆ inch (1.6 millimeters) thick.

Stripped of their molds, ingots are placed in the soaking pit. There, the ingots are heated through to a uniform temperature before they are rolled or shaped.

Left: Each time this piece of steel passes through the giant rollers of the finishing mill, it becomes smaller and closer to its eventual shape. *Below:* At the construction site, the finished product, an I-beam, is hoisted into place.

As the steel leaves the mill, it is wound into coils by machines. The coils of steel may be further treated by pickling and cold rolling. Pickling involves treating the steel with acid, which removes the oxide that forms during hot rolling. Cold rolling involves pressing the steel through several rollers. This process makes the steel thinner and more flexible.

Many hand tools and automobile parts are manufactured from **bars**—the second most widely used steel product. They are rolled from steel billets into many shapes including square, round, half-round, oval, hexagonal, and flat. Bars are formed in a bar mill, which is similar to a hot-rolling mill, except that the rollers have grooves pressing the steel into bars. A modern bar mill can produce up to 85 tons (77 metric tons) of finished bars an hour at the rate of about 3,300 feet (1,006 meters) a minute.

Rails and **beams** are hot-rolled in much the same way as bars. They are widely used in construction. Bridges, buildings, heavy machinery, railroad rails, and supporting towers for electric lines are built with steel rails and beams. Rails and beams are usually rolled from steel blooms into the various sizes and shapes. One of the most common types of beams is the I-beam, which is so named because it is shaped like the capital letter I. Skyscrapers could not be built without steel rails and beams.

The oldest steel products from the industrial age are probably **plates**. They are usually thicker than ¼ inch (6.4 millimeters) and are used where thick, strong pieces of steel are needed. The main uses for plates are in ships, bridges, oil and water tanks, and floors for buildings. Plates account for about 10 percent of all U.S. steel shipments each year. Plates are rolled from slabs of steel, then further processed on another rolling machine, and finally inspected before shipment.

Pipes and **tubes** are made from flat steel that is rolled from slabs. Pipes and tubes with seams are produced from steel that is formed into a cylinder by either hot or cold rolling processes and then welded along the seam. Seamless steel pipe is formed by either rolling steel slabs around a point or forcing hot steel through a mold with a solid center that cuts a core in the steel. Steel pipes and tubes are used in manufacturing furniture, bicycles, aircraft, and boilers.

Nuts and bolts, reinforcing rods for concrete, staples, nails, and needles are all manufactured using **rod** and **wire** steel. Wire is made by pulling hot-rolled steel rods through a series of dies. The rods are then dipped in lime, dried in ovens, and drawn through dies with smaller and smaller holes. As they are pulled through each die the rods get thinner and longer, until they reach the desired size.

Coated Steels. Many steels are manufactured with special coatings to protect the steel against corrosion or to make its finish more attractive. Some of the most important coating processes are **electroplating** and **galvanizing**. Electroplating makes tin-plated steel by placing a coating of tin on steel using an electric current. Galvanizing is a process that coats steel with a layer of zinc. These coatings protect the steel against rust.

Another useful coating placed on steel is porcelain-enamel. This coating, which provides an easily cleaned surface for kitchen appliances, is made by baking enamel onto steel at very high temperatures.

▶**IRON AND STEEL IN HISTORY**

Iron is one of the oldest metals known. Prehistoric peoples discovered that iron from meteorites could be fashioned into tools, weapons, and other useful objects. No one knows how or when humans first learned how to smelt (refine) iron from ore. It probably occurred accidentally, when people built fires with rock containing iron ore. The ore was left in the ashes of the fire, and people eventually learned how to melt and hammer it to create iron tools and weapons.

Using iron in tools and other objects led to a new age—the **Iron Age**. Archaeologists date the beginning of the Iron Age at about 1200

B.C. The first peoples to use iron were from the region now known as the Near East.

The ancient Hittites probably learned to make iron tools and weapons about 1200 B.C., although some iron artifacts have been found in Egypt dating back to about 2900 B.C. People in India and China also developed methods of making iron at about the same time. By about 1000 B.C., many civilizations in the ancient world were making iron tools. People in the Americas, however, did not know about iron until the arrival of the Italian explorer Christopher Columbus.

First Uses of Steel

Steel has also been known almost since the beginning of recorded history. Small amounts of steel were made during the early part of the Iron Age. When the troops of Alexander the Great marched into India in the 300's B.C., they fought warriors who used steel weapons. Steel went into the blades of the famed swords of Damascus and Toledo, and in China, craftsmen were making steel by about A.D. 400.

Early Ironworks

Europeans made some steel throughout the Middle Ages. Clock springs and other precision-made articles were made of steel. But steel was made only slowly and in small quantities, so it remained very expensive and rare for many centuries. Iron remained the backbone of the Western world's growing technology until the 1800's.

The first ironworks (a mill where iron is smelted) in the United States was built in Virginia in 1621, but it was destroyed in an Indian raid only a year later. In 1646 the first successful ironworks in North America was founded at Saugus, Massachusetts. This site, which has been rebuilt and is now preserved as a national historic site, is regarded as the birthplace of the American steel industry. The furnaces at Saugus primarily made cast-iron bars used by local iron workshops.

▶**THE NEW AGE OF STEEL**

Iron remained the chief industrial metal until the Industrial Revolution. Then the discovery of economical methods of making steel revolutionized the industry. In the mid-1800's, steel replaced iron as the basic material for the tools and equipment used in the growing mass-production industries.

The new age of steel can be said to have begun about 1860, when the Bessemer process became widely used. The Bessemer process created steel in large quantities at relatively low cost for the first time in history. By 1880, about 90 percent of American-made steel was made with the Bessemer process.

The first open-hearth furnace was used in Europe in about 1864, and in the United States in 1868. By 1908 the production of steel by open-hearth furnaces was greater than the output by the Bessemer process.

The Growth of the U.S. Steel Industry

The U.S. steel industry continued to grow through the late 1800's and early 1900's. Annual production of steel grew greatly between 1880 and 1910, rising from about 1.4 million tons (1.274 million metric tons) to more than 28 million tons (25.48 million metric tons). By 1889 the United States led the world in steel production. It continued to do so until the 1970's, when the Soviet Union became the world leader.

Through World War II, the United States steel industry continued to increase its output and to develop new methods of rolling and shaping steel and creating new alloys. The development in 1923 of the continuous hot-strip mill made it possible to create low-cost steel sheets and strips. This invention led to the tremendous growth of the automobile industry and other consumer-goods industries.

World War II caused great destruction to most of the world's steel industries. As a result, the U.S. industry, which was relatively undamaged, dominated steel production in the postwar years. Japan, Germany, and other European industries began to rebuild their steel industries using new, more efficient equipment than the older equipment American mills continued to use. As a result, the American steel industry began to lag behind the Japanese and European industries.

In the 1970's, U.S. production of steel began to drop while other nations increased their output. The decrease in production created widespread unemployment in the U.S. steel industry. By the 1980's, however, many U.S. steel companies had invested heavily in new techniques and equipment. The industry also began to increase production of specialized steels that are used to make components for electronic equipment, such as computers.

Today's Steel Industry

Modernization and Computer Technology. The steel industry has changed greatly during the past few decades. Steel continues to be used in traditional heavy industry and construction—for bridges, heavy machinery, buildings, and automobiles. Yet many industrial components previously made with steel are now created more cheaply with synthetic materials such as plastics and ceramics.

Ever since the early 1960's, computer technology has been transforming the steel industry. Today computers perform many routine tasks of steel production, often with greater speed and accuracy than humans can. Most modern steel factories are likely to have highly automated production equipment with computer-controlled systems and highly skilled workers. Metallurgists (scientists who study metals), computer programmers, machinists, electricians, engineers, and other skilled workers are all needed to build and maintain modern steel mills.

Environmental Protection. In addition to trying to discover new methods of producing steel, researchers in the steel industry are also concerned about the environment. Environmental pollution became a central public concern for nations throughout the world in the 1980's. The problems were most severe in Eastern European nations, where the extent of environmental damage caused by steel mills and other heavy industry became widely known for the first time in the late 1980's.

The steel industry in most developed nations has responded to the public's concerns about pollution by developing new techniques of controlling air and water pollution. Waste gases are no longer allowed to be released into the environment without treatment. A series of scrubbers, or filters, are used to clean waste gases of the impurities released in the production of steel.

Similarly, water used to cool steel during the production process is filtered and cleaned before it is released back into the environment. New techniques of controlling environmental pollution will continue to be an important part of the steelmaking processes of the future.

MARK DANIEL HOFF
Technical Writer

See also ALLOYS; INDUSTRY; INVENTIONS; METALS AND METALLURGY; MINES AND MINING.

IROQUOIS INDIANS. See INDIANS, AMERICAN.

Although modern irrigation methods (the portable sprinkler at left) are widely practiced, primitive methods (the waterwheel above) are also used.

IRRIGATION

All plants need water to grow. In some places, nature supplies all the water required. In other places, people must supplement (add to) nature's supply. The practice of supplying water to ensure proper growth of plants and to increase the yield of crops is called irrigation.

Only about 15 percent of the world's farmland is irrigated, but the irrigated land produces a much larger percentage of the world's food supply. The countries with the largest areas of irrigated land are China, India, Pakistan, Russia, and the United States. In the United States, most of the irrigated cropland is in the western part of the country.

In some places, there is so little rainfall that virtually all water needs must be met by irrigation. This is true of arid regions, such as parts of Egypt, India, Israel, and the western United States. In these places crops could not be grown without irrigation. In other places, there is enough rainfall but not at the times the crops need it. Even in high rainfall areas, irrigation is needed to grow certain crops. For example, rice fields must be flooded until harvest, and irrigation supplies all the water for plants in greenhouses.

▶ IRRIGATION MANAGEMENT

Irrigation management involves supplying water to the crop at the proper time and in the correct amount in order to minimize waste. Irrigation water is often lost by surface runoff, leaching, seepage, and evaporation.

Surface runoff occurs when water is applied faster than the soil can absorb it. Leaching is the downward movement of water to below the root zone where plants cannot get it. Some leaching may be beneficial since it can carry away harmful salts. However, excessive leaching is undesirable because it wastes irrigation water and can pollute groundwater (water within the earth that supplies wells and springs) with pesticides and fertilizers. Seepage is the leakage of water through the sides

The Grand Coulee Dam and the reservoir behind it, which are part of the Columbia River Basin Project, provide irrigation water for more than a million acres of land.

and bottoms of irrigation channels and reservoirs. Evaporation occurs when water exposed to the air changes to gas and is lost.

▶ IRRIGATION METHODS

Irrigation has been practiced in some form since the earliest recorded history of agriculture. Great rivers such as the Nile, Ganges, Hwang Ho (Yellow River), and the Tigris and the Euphrates flooded every spring. The flooding brought silt (fine soil particles) to the land and stored enough moisture to grow crops. People soon learned to build canals, storage reservoirs, and drainage ditches to control the flow of water.

Today, water for irrigating croplands is obtained either from surface water supplies, such as reservoirs and rivers, or from groundwater. The best method of applying water to the land depends on many factors. These include the surface features and slope of the land, the ability of the soil to absorb water, the amount of water needed by different crops, the soil's natural drainage, the wind, and the level of technology and energy available to move the water. There are four basic methods of irrigation—surface, sprinkler, subsurface (below the surface), and trickle.

Surface Methods. These are by far the most widely used methods because they use the simplest technology and are the least expensive. Water is applied directly to the soil, and it flows by gravity over the surface of the soil. The two chief types of surface irrigation are flood and furrow.

In flood irrigation the entire surface is covered by water, which then soaks into the soil. Small soil mounds or dikes around the edges of the field prevent runoff. Flood irrigation is usually used with close-growing crops such as alfalfa and small grains. Relatively level or gently sloping land is needed.

Furrow-irrigated crops are grown in rows, and water is applied in the small ditches, or furrows, between the rows. Typically corn, cotton, potatoes, and many vegetables are irrigated using the furrow method.

Sprinkler Method. In this method, water is pumped under pressure and forced out into the air through rotating sprinklers or perforated pipe. Then, like rain, it falls to the ground. Some sprinkler systems are set into the ground. Others are portable. In a properly designed system, there is little surface runoff, and the water is evenly distributed over the field, except when wind interrupts the sprinkler pattern. Other disadvantages of sprinkler irrigation include the high cost of sprinkler pipes and water pumps, and the need for energy to pump water.

In hot weather, sprinklers may improve plant growth because water evaporating from the plant surfaces removes heat and cools the plant. In cold weather, a sprinkler system can be used to prevent frost damage to crops. Water on a plant releases heat as it freezes and prevents the plant temperature from dropping to levels that can cause damage.

Subsurface Methods. Subsurface, or subirrigation, methods apply water from below or

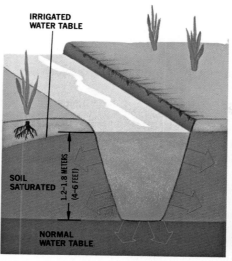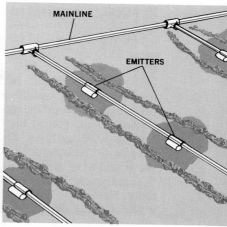

Left: In furrow irrigation, water seeps from narrow furrows into the ridges planted with crops. *Center:* In one method of subsurface irrigation, the surface of the ground remains dry as water applied through open ditches raises the water table nearer to the root zone. *Right:* In trickle irrigation, water slowly trickles through emitters, tiny holes in pipes, to water the soil near the plants.

within the root zone. One method raises the water table (the level below which the ground is normally saturated with water), bringing it nearer to the surface but below the root zone of the plants. Open ditches or underground perforated pipes bring water into the soil just below the root zone. The water then moves upward, into the root zone, by capillary action. Potted plants are often subirrigated by periodically flooding the bench or saucer they are sitting in. One disadvantage of subirrigation is that as the water moves upward into the root zone, salts may accumulate there and decrease plant growth.

Trickle Method. In trickle, or drip, irrigation, water is supplied through the small holes or valves (called emitters) in plastic pipes. The water is delivered very slowly to the surface of the soil near the plants being irrigated. Because it is expensive to install, trickle irrigation is generally used where high-value crops are grown, such as in greenhouses, orchards, vineyards, and ornamental gardens. Keeping the emitters unclogged and replacing tubes chewed by insects and rodents also add to the high cost of trickle irrigation.

Because it allows for the watering of all or only a specific part of the crop root zone, trickle is the most efficient method of irrigation. With only the crop root zone receiving irrigation water, the growth of weeds between crop rows is greatly reduced and there is little or no loss of water due to runoff, leaching, and evaporation.

▶ **PROBLEMS WITH IRRIGATION**

Irrigation can have undesirable effects on the environment in the form of water pollution. Irrigation runoff or leaching may carry salts, fertilizers, pesticides, and other chemicals into our water supplies. Proper irrigation management and choice of the right irrigation method can prevent such pollution.

Salt accumulation and waterlogging may also occur with long-term irrigation. Irrigation water contains small amounts of salt that may accumulate to toxic levels over many years. Waterlogging occurs when long-term irrigation raises the water table too close to the soil surface. Most plants cannot grow in waterlogged (water-saturated) soil.

The worldwide demand for water continues to increase, especially in the arid regions where irrigation is a chief user of water. As the groundwater that has accumulated over many centuries is rapidly used up, new sources of irrigation water will have to be developed. Seawater, icebergs, and purified water from sewage treatment plants may all be future water sources. Conservation methods, such as landscaping using native species as well as plants with low-water requirements instead of irrigated lawns, can also help save water. With good management and more efficient irrigation technologies, the ever-increasing needs for water can be met.

Reviewed by DAVID R. HERSHEY
Department of Horticulture
University of Maryland

IRVING, WASHINGTON (1783–1859)

One day in April 1789, an elderly Scottish nurse and a small boy followed George Washington into a shop on New York's Broad Way. "Please, your Honor, here's a bairn that's named after ye!" said the nurse. Washington, just inaugurated as the first president of the United States, placed his hand on the boy's head and blessed him. The boy's nurse was delighted. "Now he'll amount to something!" she is said to have declared.

Washington Irving did amount to something. He was the first American to succeed as a professional writer, achieving fame in Europe as well as in the United States. He is considered by many scholars to be the father of the American short story.

Washington Irving was born on April 3, 1783, in New York City. The American Revolution had just ended, and the new baby was named for the country's great war hero. Washington was the eleventh child in the Irving family. His father, a strict and pious man, was a merchant and a deacon in the Presbyterian Church. Washington started school at the age of 4, but he was never a serious scholar. He preferred reading travel and adventure books to studying.

In 1801 Irving became an apprentice in a law office. The following year he began to write for his brother Peter's newspaper, the *Morning Chronicle,* signing himself Jonathan Oldstyle. His humorous essays satirized the New York theater and poked fun at local fashions. A trip to Europe in 1804 helped satisfy his urge to travel.

In 1806 Irving passed the bar examination, allowing him to practice law. Soon after, he joined with his brother William and his friend James Kirke Paulding to produce a humor magazine called *Salmagundi.* It was received enthusiastically and was published for more than a year. In 1809 Irving published *A History of New York from the Beginning of the World to the End of the Dutch Dynasty,* a comic history. He again signed his work with a fictitious name, creating the character of Diedrich Knickerbocker as the book's author. The *History* was the first great book of humorous literature written by an American, and its success made Irving well known abroad.

In 1815 Irving again went to Europe. During 1819 and 1820, when he was living in

Washington Irving was the first American writer to achieve international fame. His well-known tales "Rip Van Winkle" and "The Legend of Sleepy Hollow" influenced the development of the American short story.

England, he published *The Sketch Book of Geoffrey Crayon, Gent.,* a collection of essays and stories. It included the tales "Rip Van Winkle" and "The Legend of Sleepy Hollow." These stories, which were based on old German folktales, are among the earliest examples of the short story. *The Sketch Book* was an immediate success, and Irving began his career as a professional writer.

Irving remained in Europe for twelve more years, writing two sequels to *The Sketch Book.* In 1826 he was appointed to a diplomatic post in Spain. There he turned to biography and history, writing *The Life and Voyages of Christopher Columbus* (1828) and *The Conquest of Granada* (1829). His three-year stay in Spain also inspired *The Alhambra* (1832), a collection of Spanish and Moorish legends.

After serving as a diplomat in England from 1829 to 1832, Irving finally went home to the United States, where he was greeted with acclaim. In 1834 he settled at Sunnyside, an estate on the Hudson River near Tarrytown, New York. There he began work on a long-planned biography of George Washington.

In 1842 Irving accepted the post of United States minister to Spain. He resigned after four years, returning home to complete his book on Washington. The work, which he considered his finest literary achievement, was published in five volumes between 1855 and 1857. Irving died in Tarrytown on November 28, 1859.

Reviewed by REGINALD L. COOK
Middlebury College

An excerpt from "Rip Van Winkle" appears on the following pages.

RIP VAN WINKLE

[Rip, a good-natured, somewhat lazy fellow, was hunting in the Kaatskill Mountains when he heard a distant voice calling his name.]

He looked around, but could see nothing but a crow winging its solitary flight across the mountain. He thought his fancy must have deceived him, and turned again to descend, when he heard the same cry ring through the still evening air: "Rip Van Winkle! Rip Van Winkle!" At the same time, Wolf bristled up his back and, giving a low growl, skulked to his master's side, looking fearfully down into the glen. Rip now felt a vague apprehension stealing over him; he looked anxiously in the same direction and perceived a strange figure slowly toiling up the rocks, and bending under the weight of something he carried on his back. He was surprised to see any human being in this lonely and unfrequented place, but supposing it to be some one of the neighborhood in need of his assistance, he hastened down to yield it.

On nearer approach he was still more surprised at the singularity of the stranger's appearance. He was a short, square-built old fellow, with thick, bushy hair and a grizzled beard. His dress was of the antique Dutch fashion: a cloth jerkin strapped around the waist and several pairs of breeches, the outer one of ample volume, decorated with rows of buttons down the sides and bunches at the knees. He bore on his shoulder a stout keg that seemed full of liquor, and made signs for Rip to approach and assist him with the load. Though rather shy and distrustful of this new acquaintance, Rip complied with his usual alacrity, and mutually relieving one another, they clambered up a narrow gully, apparently the dry bed of a mountain torrent. As they ascended, Rip every now and then heard long rolling peals, like distant thunder, that seemed to issue out of a deep ravine, or rather cleft, between lofty rocks, toward which their rugged path conducted. . . . Passing through the ravine, they came to a hollow, like a small amphitheater, surrounded by perpendicular precipices, over the brinks of which impending trees shot their branches, so that you only caught glimpses of the azure sky and the bright evening cloud. During the whole time, Rip and his companion had labored on in si-

Rip Van Winkle unwittingly drinks a magic potion.

lence, for though the former marveled greatly what could be the object of carrying a keg of liquor up this wild mountain, yet there was something strange and incomprehensible about the unknown that inspired awe and checked familiarity.

On entering the amphitheater, new objects of wonder were to be seen. On a level spot in the center was a company of odd-looking personages playing at ninepins. They were dressed in a quaint outlandish fashion; some wore short doublets, others jerkins, with long knives in their belts, and most of them had enormous breeches, of similar style with that of the guide's. Their visages, too, were peculiar; one had a large beard, broad face, and small piggish eyes, the face of another seemed to consist entirely of nose and was surmounted by a white sugar-loaf hat set off with a little red cock's tail. They all had beards, of various shapes and colors. There was one who seemed to be the commander. He was a stout old gentleman, with a weather-beaten countenance; he wore a laced doublet, broad belt and hanger, high-crowned hat and feather, red stockings, and high-heeled shoes, with roses in them. The whole group reminded Rip of the

Rip returns to his village after sleeping for 20 years.

figures in an old Flemish painting in the parlor of Dominie Van Shaick, the village parson, which had been brought over from Holland at the time of the settlement.

What seemed particularly odd to Rip was that though these folks were evidently amusing themselves, yet they maintained the gravest faces, the most mysterious silence, and were, withal, the most melancholy party of pleasure he had ever witnessed. Nothing interrupted the stillness of the scene but the noise of the balls, which, whenever they were rolled, echoed along the mountains like rumbling peals of thunder.

As Rip and his companion approached them, they suddenly desisted from their play and stared at him with such fixed, statue-like gaze, and such strange, uncouth, lackluster countenances, that his heart turned within him and his knees smote together. His companion now emptied the contents of the keg into large flagons and made signs for him to wait upon the company. He obeyed with fear and trembling; they quaffed the liquor in profound silence and then returned to their game.

By degrees Rip's awe and apprehension subsided. He even ventured, when no eye was fixed upon him, to taste the beverage, which he found had much of the flavor of excellent Hollands. He was naturally a thirsty soul and was soon tempted to repeat the draft. One taste provoked another; and he reiterated his visits to the flagon so often that at length his senses were overpowered, his eyes swam in his head, his head gradually declined, and he fell into a deep sleep.

On waking, he found himself on the green knoll whence he had first seen the old man of the glen. He rubbed his eyes—it was a bright, sunny morning. The birds were hopping and twittering among the bushes, and the eagle was wheeling aloft and breasting the pure mountain breeze. "Surely," thought Rip, "I have not slept here all night." He recalled the occurrences before he fell asleep. The strange man with a keg of liquor—the mountain ravine—the wild retreat among the rocks—the woebegone party at ninepins—the flagon—"Oh! That flagon! That wicked flagon!" thought Rip. "What excuse shall I make to Dame Van Winkle?"

. . . As he approached the village he met a number of people, but none whom he knew, which somewhat surprised him, for he had thought himself acquainted with every one in the country around. Their dress, too, was of a different fashion from that to which he was accustomed. They all stared at him with equal marks of surprise, and whenever they cast their eyes upon him invariably stroked their chins. The constant recurrence of this gesture induced Rip, involuntarily, to do the same, when, to his astonishment, he found his beard had grown a foot long!

He had now entered the skirts of the village. A troop of strange children ran at his heels, hooting after him and pointing at his gray beard. The dogs, too, not one of which he recognized for an old acquaintance, barked at him as he passed. The very village was altered; it was larger and more populous. There were rows of houses which he had never seen before, and those which had been his familiar haunts had disappeared. Strange names were over the doors—strange faces at the windows—everything was strange. His mind now misgave him; he began to doubt whether both he and the world around him were not bewitched. Surely this was his native village, which he had left but the day before. There stood the Kaatskill Mountains—there ran the silver Hudson at a distance—there was every hill and dale precisely as it had always been. Rip was sorely perplexed. "That flagon last night," thought he, "has addled my poor head sadly!"

ISAAC

Isaac, son of Abraham, was the second of the patriarchs, or fathers, of the Jewish people. Isaac was born to Abraham and Sarah in their old age, when they had almost given up hope of having a son. In Hebrew the name Isaac (Yitzhak) means "he laughs" or "laughter."

The wonderful faith of Abraham and the great loyalty of Isaac were shown when God commanded Abraham to offer Isaac up as a sacrifice. Abraham tied Isaac to the altar and was about to place the knife to his throat when God's angel stopped him.

Shortly after Sarah died, Abraham sent his faithful servant Eliezer back to Ur, the land of Abraham's kindred in the north Arabian desert, to find a proper wife for Isaac. (This was an ancient custom.) Eliezer decided to choose the first young woman who would offer water to him and his thirsty camels. This was the test of kindness. He discovered Rebekah at the well in this way. He made arrangements with her father and brother and brought her back to Canaan, home of Abraham and Isaac. Soon afterward, Isaac and Rebekah were married.

Isaac and Rebekah had twin sons, Esau and Jacob. From birth they were different. Esau, the firstborn, grew up to be "a cunning hunter, a man of the field." Jacob was "a plain man, dwelling in tents." Isaac seemed to prefer Esau; Rebekah loved Jacob.

Esau, in a moment of hunger, sold his birthright to Jacob for a pot of lentils. The birthright brought honor as head of the family and a double share of the inheritance. Later Esau regretted his deed. With Rebekah's help, Jacob then tricked Isaac into giving him a blessing intended for Esau. Esau found out and threatened to kill Jacob. Jacob, at Isaac's command, fled to Padanaram, his mother's former home, where he lived many years.

The Bible says Isaac "died, and was gathered unto his people, being old and full of days: and his sons Esau and Jacob buried him."

MORTIMER J. COHEN
Author, *Pathways Through the Bible*

ISABELLA. See FERDINAND AND ISABELLA.

ISAIAH

Isaiah was a prophet who lived in the southern kingdom of Judah in the 700's B.C. He has been called the prophet-statesman. He was a great preacher who explained to the people what God wanted of them. He was also a fine poet. His work is in the Book of Isaiah in the Bible.

Isaiah was a native of Jerusalem, and he was sad to see the evil that he believed would bring the city to ruin. Isaiah may have been a member of the royal family, for he had great influence with the leaders of his country.

He was married to a woman whom he called the prophetess. They had two sons. He gave them strange names that expressed his beliefs about his country. One son's name was Mahershalalhashbaz, which in English means "Speed-booty-hasten-prey." By this name Isaiah threatened Judah that unless the country became more honest and just, it would soon become the prey of its terrible enemy, Assyria. His other son's name was Shearjashub, which means "A remnant shall return." It expressed Isaiah's belief that no matter what disaster might overtake Judah, its good part, though a mere remnant, or small piece, would survive. In this way Isaiah dramatically told his people that they must correct their evil ways or else be punished by God. At the same time he said that God would have mercy and not destroy them completely.

Isaiah lived during terrible times of war and the destruction of the northern kingdom of Israel. In that war-torn world he uttered an immortal call for peace:

He [God] shall judge between the nations,
And shall decide for many peoples;
And they shall beat their swords into plowshares,
And their spears into pruning hooks;
Nation shall not lift up sword against nation,
Neither shall they learn war any more.

Isaiah lived past the age of 60. We do not know the date or manner of his death. One belief is that he was put to death in a very cruel way in the reign of King Manasseh.

MORTIMER J. COHEN
Author, *Pathways Through the Bible*

Followers of Islam, called Muslims, gather for evening prayers at the Great Mosque in Mecca, Saudi Arabia. Mecca, Islam's holiest city, draws thousands of pilgrims each year.

ISLAM

Islam is the world's second largest and fastest-growing religion, with more than 1 billion followers. It is based primarily on the teachings of the prophet Mohammed, who was born in Arabia about A.D. 570. The word "Islam" means "submission" in Arabic—("submission" refers to obedience to God) and also signifies peace. In Arabic, God is called Allah, an all-powerful, all-forgiving, merciful, and compassionate being.

One who believes in Islam is called a Muslim. Muslims are found on every continent, but their greatest concentration is in South, Southeast, and Central Asia; the Middle East; and North, East, and West Africa. The largest Muslim population is in Indonesia. There are also many Muslims in Pakistan, India (which is chiefly Hindu), Bangladesh, Turkey, Egypt, Iran, and Nigeria. Today, more than 4 million Muslims live in the United States.

Most Muslims belong to one of two main sects—Sunni and Shi'ite. About 85 percent are Sunnites and 12 to 15 percent Shi'ites. These sects have other divisions within them so that there are various types of Sunni and Shi'ite Muslims, and there are also other groups that are neither Sunni nor Shi'ite.

In addition to belonging to certain sects, many Muslims consider themselves Sufis, which means they try to develop a close personal relationship with God through meditation and other practices. Sufis often belong to special organizations called Sufi orders.

▶ BELIEFS

Muslims believe in a single God that has no gender or form. Their religion is based on divine revelations (statements) from God to various prophets—people thought to be chosen by God to speak for him. These prophets include Abraham and Moses from the Bible's Old Testament. Muslims also believe that Jesus Christ was a great prophet, although they do not agree with Christians that he is the son of God.

According to Islam, the teachings of the prophets were sometimes misinterpreted or distorted until the appearance of the prophet Mohammed (or Muhammad). Muslims believe that Mohammed's teachings are the most accurate and complete.

These teachings were collected and preserved in the **Koran** (also called Qur'an), Islam's most sacred book. Although Muslims also accept the Bible as a holy book, they believe that the Koran is the ultimate source of divine instruction and information. Many familiar biblical events and people, such as the creation, the flood, the Exodus, Abraham, Moses, David, Solomon, and Jesus, are also found in the Koran.

Other sources of Islamic teaching and authority include the **Hadith**, which means "narrative" or "report." The Hadith is a collection of sayings and decisions of Mohammed that were passed down from person to person after his death. They are separate from the revelations in the Koran. There are also other sources of guidance, such as Mohammed's biography (the **sira**), and the lives and actions of men and women called saints, or Friends of God. Many people have been seen as saints in previous centuries, and in some places people still regard holy living individuals as saints.

Muslims believe that life is a brief test requiring total devotion and obedience to God. They also believe in the existence of Satan, who tempts people to sin, and in a final Day of Judgment. On this day, those who have led virtuous lives and sought God's forgiveness for their sins will go to Paradise, while those who have not will go to Hell.

Islam teaches that each individual has a direct and personal relationship with God and that no intermediaries are required. Thus Islam has no priests or other clergy, although Muslims often seek guidance from scholars and those who have led exemplary religious lives and who have much knowledge of Mohammed and the Koran. Among Sunni Muslims, some of these leaders are called imams, jurists, and saints. Imams also preside over worship services, perform marriages, and lead others in prayer. Shi'ite religious leaders

Islam is based on the teachings of Mohammed, who was born in Arabia about A.D. 570.

are called mullahs and ayatollahs. These leaders have great prestige, and Shi'ites respect their judgments and advice.

Although both sects agree on many matters of faith and worship, there are some long-standing differences. The Sunnites believed that Muslim leadership could be passed to elected members of the Muslim community. Shi'ites believed that Muslim leadership should have been restricted to Mohammed's descendants through his daughter Fatima and his cousin and son-in-law Ali. The Shi'ites have a special place for Ali and his descendants in their faith and consider him to be the first imam. Most Shi'ites believe that Ali and eleven imams who followed were especially suited to interpret Mohammed's revelations and lead the Muslim community since they were descendants of the Prophet. According to Shi'ites, the twelfth imam disappeared around the year 873. They believe that God hid him from humans and that someday he will return to lead the Muslim community and the world.

▶ PRACTICES

Muslims are expected to live according to Islamic law, which in some countries is not separate from civil law. The Koran and Hadith are the main sources of Islamic law, al-

Biblical stories such as Abraham's sacrifice of his son are included in the Koran, Islam's holiest book.

though they do not always provide guidance for specific situations. In such cases, Islamic judges will try to base their decisions on similar situations in the Koran or Hadith or by general agreement among learned leaders. The judges may also be guided by their own interpretation if necessary.

Muslims call Islamic law the **Shariah**, or "God's Way." The Shariah includes rules about relations between individuals and groups. It also contains various prohibitions against stealing, lying, killing, adultery, gambling, consuming pork, hoarding wealth, and consuming alcoholic beverages. The laws instruct Muslims to be charitable and to treat each other fairly.

There are also laws governing appearance. The Koran requires both men and women to dress modestly. In some countries this is interpreted to mean that a woman must cover her head or face; in others it is not. Many Muslim men in traditional Islamic societies also cover their heads, and some believe they are following Mohammed's example by having a beard.

Laws regarding the status of women in Islamic countries can vary. While some believe that laws limiting women's rights are rooted in Islam, others say they are more a reflection of various cultural traditions. According to the Koran, men and women are spiritually equal, and women have the right to get an education, obtain a divorce, own and inherit property, hold jobs, and vote. (In some Islamic countries, they have held the highest government position of prime minister.) Women may also retain their family names after marriage and may not be forced to marry without their consent.

Five Pillars of Islam

Besides following Islamic law and accepting certain beliefs, a Muslim must fulfill important duties called the Five Pillars of Islam. These five duties are:

Muslims view the Koran, shown here in Arabic, as the ultimate source of divine instruction and information.

1. **Shahadah**, or profession of faith. Every Muslim must believe that there is only one God, and that Mohammed is his messenger and the prophet. Although Christians and Jews worship the same God, only Islam reveres Mohammed.

2. **Salat**, or prayer. Muslims must pray five times every day: at dawn, noon, mid-afternoon, sunset, and evening (at bedtime). Before praying, which can be done anywhere, Muslims must purify themselves by washing their faces, necks, hands, arms, and feet. At noon on Friday, the Islamic holy day, Muslims traditionally go to pray at the mosque, where they also listen to a sermon.

Prayer consists of reciting short selections from the Koran and bowing, kneeling, and touching the ground with the forehead, to express submission to God. Some Muslims perform these activities on a small prayer rug they carry with them.

When praying, Muslims must face the direction of Mecca (in Saudi Arabia), Islam's holiest city and home to the Great Mosque and the Ka'ba. The Ka'ba, a small stone building within the Great Mosque, is empty inside except for a black stone that is attached to one of its walls. According to Islam, the Black Stone is a holy object that was touched by Mohammed and the prophet Abraham.

3. **Zakat**, or almsgiving. Unless they are poor, Muslims must give a portion of their wealth to the needy. The normal amount is 2.5 percent of one's yearly income or 10 percent of revenue from crops or businesses. Wealthy people are encouraged to give more. It is considered **sadaqah**, or a good deed, to give more than the recommended amount. For centuries, most of the zakat money of each country was given to special endowments to support schools and hospitals, to aid the needy, to maintain mosques, and to fund other charitable activities. Recently, some Muslim countries have made the zakat part

of their tax system, using the revenue for different types of social welfare programs.

4. **Sawm**, or fasting. All Muslims, except children, pregnant women, travelers, and sick people, must fast from daybreak to sunset each day during the month of Ramadan. This means they do not eat or drink anything during those hours. At the end of the month, Muslims end their fast and celebrate Id al-Fitr, or the Festival of Breaking the Fast. Id al-Fitr, a three-day holiday, is one of the two most important Muslim feasts. The dates for this feast and other Islamic holy days are determined by a lunar calendar based on the phases of the moon. This calendar is different from the one based on the solar year. Muslims use both lunar and solar calendars.

5. **Hajj**, or pilgrimage. Muslims who are able to travel and can afford it must make a pilgrimage to the city of Mecca at least once in their lifetime. This pilgrimage must take place during the first ten days of the last month of the Islamic year. The pilgrimage is followed by Id al-Adha, or the Feast of Sacrifice, which is the other great feast in the Islamic year. It commemorates the prophet Abraham's willingness to sacrifice his son as an offering to God.

Each year more than 2 million people travel to Mecca to celebrate Id al-Adha. Dressed in plain white robes, the pilgrims pray at the Great Mosque and walk around the Ka'ba seven times while praying. They also visit other holy sites nearby. Muslims of all racial, national, and ethnic groups make this pilgrimage. A man who does this may be called **hajji**. A woman may be called **hajjah**. These terms mean that the people have fulfilled their hajj duty. Upon their return home, they are greeted with special celebrations.

Muslims observe other holidays as well. Laylat al-Qadr takes place during the final ten days of Ramadan and marks the time of Mohammed's first divine revelation. Al-isra wa-l-miraj, which occurs during the Islamic month of Rajab, commemorates Mohammed's miraculous journey from Mecca to Jerusalem, and then to the heavens, where it is believed he came into God's direct presence. This was also when he first established the practice of praying five times daily. Mawlid al-nabi celebrates Mohammed's birth and is held during the Islamic month of Rabi' al-awwal.

Muslims must pray five times each day, always facing Mecca. Prayer includes kneeling and touching the forehead to the ground.

Like many other religions, Islam has important life rituals. In some parts of the world, a welcoming ceremony—**akikah**—is held when a baby is born. There is also a marriage ritual, when a man and woman formally agree to become husband and wife. When a person dies, the body is washed, wrapped in a shroud, then placed on its side in a grave so that the face is turned toward Mecca. A special prayer is also said before burial.

▶ ORIGINS AND EARLY HISTORY

Although many scholars of religion believe that Islam was founded by Mohammed, most Muslims believe it began with the creation of the world and that Mohammed was simply the last in a series of prophets.

He was born about A.D. 570 in the city of Mecca, an important commercial and cultural center in Arabia. Mecca was also the site of an important annual fair that attracted people from many different Arabian tribes. Each tribe worshiped a different idol-god.

When Mohammed was about 40 years old, he had an experience that changed his life. According to Islamic tradition, the archangel

Ali (center), son-in-law of the prophet Mohammed, is a key figure in Islam. After Mohammed's death, he served as a Muslim leader (caliph) for several years.

to help resolve some disputes among its people. This journey took place in A.D. 622, which became known as the year of **Hegira**, or "migration." It was later made the year 1 of the Islamic calendar.

In Yathrib, Mohammed became a political and religious leader. In time, the city's name was changed to al-Madinah al-Munawwarah (the enlightened city) or Madinat al-Nabi (the city of the Prophet). Today it is known as Medina.

After the Hegira, Mohammed lived the rest of his life in Medina. During that time he had more revelations, many dealing with rules about Muslim society. In 630 Mohammed traveled to Mecca, where many had started to accept his ideas. With the support of Mecca's residents, major tribes throughout Arabia soon converted to Islam. For the first time, many tribes were united in their allegiance to one religion and one God. By the time Mohammed died in 632, Islam was Arabia's major religion.

Choosing a Caliph

After Mohammed's death, the Muslims selected Abu Bakr, a close associate of Mohammed, to be their leader. He was given the title of caliph, which means "the successor." The caliph was Mohammed's successor only as the leader of the faithful, however, not as a prophet. The Muslims who later became known as Shi'ites believed that Mohammed's cousin Ali should have been chosen the leader instead.

The faith of some Muslims was badly shaken by Mohammed's death. Some tribes even abandoned Islam. However, Abu Bakr was able to restore the supremacy of the religion in Arabia.

After Abu Bakr's death in 634, Muslim leaders selected a new caliph, Umar Ibn al-Khattab. Under Umar's leadership, the Muslims of Arabia invaded Syria and North Africa, which were part of the Christian Byzantine empire. The Muslims defeated the Byzantine armies there and continued their advance northward until they were stopped in southern Anatolia (the country of Turkey today). Muslim armies also went east and defeated the Persians and took over their empire. These invasions and conquests were part of a Muslim **jihad**, or holy war, carried out to expand Islam's influence.

Gabriel appeared to him one night while he was meditating and commanded him to spread the word of God. For more than twenty years, the angel continued to appear to Mohammed and give him God's word. These revelations became the foundation of Islam. They included matters related to religious beliefs, human conduct, and government. They also included a narrative of events in the history of the world, similar to those in the Bible.

Mohammed's Preaching

Several years after Mohammed received his first revelation, he began to preach among the people of Mecca. He preached the ideas of equality and charity, and criticized the worshiping of idols. He also spoke against profiting from interest on loans to the poor.

At first the wealthy leaders of Mecca ignored Mohammed. But as he began to attract more followers, they became alarmed. They threatened him and persecuted his followers. Because of this, Mohammed and his followers left Mecca and traveled to the city of Yathrib, where Mohammed had been asked

In 656 Umar was assassinated. This time as well, Muslim leaders disagreed about the selection of a successor. Some thought it should be Uthman Ibn Affan, an elderly Muslim from a wealthy and influential family. Others again preferred Ali. Although Ali was smart, strict, and a devout Muslim, Uthman was chosen instead. Ali accepted this decision, but some of his followers did not. In later years, many groups continued to challenge Uthman's right to be caliph, and a member of one of these groups killed him twelve years later.

After Uthman's death, Ali was chosen to succeed him as caliph. Uthman's relatives and supporters, however, tried to create opposition to Ali. The most powerful person to oppose him was Mu'awiyah, governor of Damascus. Mu'awiyah tried to defeat Ali in battle, but failed. Ali ruled for five years before he too was assassinated.

After Ali's death, Mu'awiyah quickly gathered enough support to declare himself the new caliph. As caliph, he made Damascus the capital of the Muslim empire and suppressed all opposition. When he died in 680, his son Yazid was named caliph. From then on, the position of caliph was passed to the next of kin. Mu'awiyah's family, the Umayyad, became the ruling dynasty, or family of rulers. Muslims who accepted Mu'awiyah as the caliph later became known as the Sunnites.

The division between Shi'ites and Sunnites widened when Yazid was made caliph and the Shi'ites refused to accept his authority. Instead, they wanted Ali's son Husayn to have this position. But Husayn and a small group of relatives and followers were killed by members of an Umayyad army.

The Islamic Empire

Under the Umayyad dynasty, Islamic conquests greatly expanded the territory ruled by Muslims. The Muslims conquered North Africa in 711 and even moved into Europe; they became well established in Spain and Portugal. Although their advance into western Europe was finally stopped, parts of Spain were ruled by the Muslims for about 700 years. Spanish Muslims lived in Spain together with Christians and Jews until 1492, when the Christian conquerors forced the Muslims and Jews to either leave or convert to Christianity.

In 750 the Umayyad dynasty was overthrown by the Abbasids, a dynasty descended from Abbas, one of Mohammed's uncles. The Abbasids moved the capital of the Islamic Empire to Baghdad, a new city they built on the Tigris River, and ruled from there until 1258. Today Baghdad is the capital of Iraq.

With the fall of the Umayyad dynasty, the Muslims in Spain set up an independent state and separated from the Islamic Empire to the east. In the 800's some of the empire's other regions also became virtually independent under their local dynasties.

As different local governments emerged, the Islamic Empire lost much of its unity. But Muslims continued to control a vast area, from Spain and Morocco in the west to India in the east. In India, Muslims founded an empire that remained in power until the British took control in the 1700's. The Ottoman Turks, who originally came from Central Asia, defeated the Byzantine Empire in Greece and Turkey. In time, their Muslim empire expanded to embrace a vast area including southeastern Europe, the Middle East,

As Islam expanded, a distinctive style of architecture developed, as seen in this mosque in Cordoba, Spain. Muslims ruled parts of Spain for about 700 years.

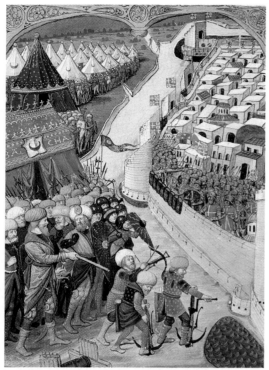

In 1095, Christians launched a series of wars against Muslim Turks in an effort to capture the Holy Land. Known as the Crusades, they lasted until 1291.

and most of North Africa. The Ottoman Turks remained in power until the 1900's. Another Muslim empire, based in Persia (the Safavids), was very powerful during the 1500's and the 1600's.

The Muslims ruled in other places as well. Areas of Southeast Asia, East and West Africa, and Central Asia became primarily Muslim and remained largely in Muslim control until they were invaded and occupied by European colonial powers in the 1700's and 1800's.

From the late 1000's to the 1200's, European Christians invaded the Middle East to capture

This botanical text and astronomical device (astrolabe) are both from a time when the sciences flourished under Islam.

the Holy Land from the Muslims and to gain land and wealth. These Christian invasions were known as the Crusades. By the late 1200's, however, the Muslims had driven out the Crusaders.

This was accomplished under the leadership of the Kurdish general Saladin, whose descendants became known as the Ayyubid Dynasty that ruled over Egypt and the Holy Land.

▶ **THE IMPACT OF ISLAM**

By the 800's, Islam's influence had become greater than that of any other empire in history until that time. This had largely been achieved through conquest. During the centuries that followed, however, Islamic expansion was accomplished primarily through trade and conversion.

As a result of Islamic expansion, people of many different ethnic groups, speaking many different languages, intermingled with each other. Arabic became a common language for religious rituals, trade, and communication. In some parts of the Middle East the population was Arabized, meaning that their language and culture became Arabic. In other areas, people retained their own language and culture, although they often used Arabic script for writing.

Mathematics, natural sciences, literature, and art flourished in the Islamic empire. The Arabs invented algebra. Art and architecture were blended to create beautiful mosques. The unique art of arabesque, a special type of decoration with intricate floral and geometric patterns, was used in building, painting, and embroidery. Calligraphy, the art of writing in artistic styles, was often included in arabesque designs as well.

Islamic civilization influenced many aspects of European culture including the use of irrigation, new types of plants, and the Arabic system of numbers. The Muslims also translated many books from ancient Greek, Sanskrit, Syriac, and ancient Persian languages, and were responsible for the transmission of Greek ideas to Europe.

Since 1900 there have been many changes in the Muslim world. These changes extend from politics and government to Muslims' personal lives. At that time, most of the Muslim world was under the control of European colonial powers. Over time, as Muslims resisted European rule, more than forty independent nations were formed.

Ethnic and national feelings were often as important as religion in launching independence movements and creating the borders of new nations. Nevertheless, religion is still an important element in these countries, and Islam remains a strong force throughout the world.

The Muslim countries today have a variety of governments, including kingdoms, republics, democracies, and dictatorships. In some of these countries, such as Saudi Arabia and Iran, traditional Islamic rules and customs are strictly enforced by the government. In other countries, such as Turkey and Albania, there is a separation between religion and the state.

Muslim countries differ in other ways as well. Some have great wealth, such as the oil-rich Persian Gulf nations. But others are very poor, such as Bangladesh and most of the Muslim countries of western Africa.

As in the past, modern Muslims have differing views on the role of religion in their lives. Some feel it is important to retain older ideas and traditions. These Muslims are considered conservative. Others, called Islamists or fundamentalists, feel that religion should play a greater role in society than it does now. Fundamentalists also revere the past but accept modern techniques and technology. Progressive Muslims, a third group, feel that religion always changes with the times. They believe that Islamic ideals and modern practices such as democracy are fully compatible.

The difference between the fundamentalists and the progressives is that fundamentalists want traditional practices to be implemented in modern societies, while progressives would like to incorporate older ideas into new institutions and practices. Whether conservative, fundamentalist, or progressive, however, all Muslims wish to preserve their religion in the face of growing secularization (society's decreasing emphasis on religion). While their paths may often conflict, all three groups have the same goal: trying to become and remain good Muslims according to the ways in which they understand their faith.

In general, Islam has become more widely recognized in the West since the 1970's. Recently, however, much attention has been fo-

Muslims today have differing views on the role of religion in their lives. Some express these views through their choice of attire.

cused on a small group of Muslims who employ violent means to attain their goals, such as those responsible for the destruction of the World Trade Center in New York in 2001. Although such groups may claim to be acting in the name of religion, Islam explicitly forbids suicide and any unnecessary violence that causes the death of innocent civilians. Thus many other Muslims condemn these destructive actions.

Despite these challenges, Islam continues to expand. One out of every five people on Earth is a Muslim. It appears certain that this religion will continue its rapid growth through both increases in the population of Muslim countries and conversions from other religions.

SHAHZAD BASHIR
Department of Religion
Carleton College

الفَنْ

Above: Calligraphy, or beautiful handwriting, is an important element in Islamic art and architecture. Arabic, the language of most Islamic texts, can be written in a variety of beautiful scripts. The Arabic word for "art" is written here.

Right: Calligraphy and elaborate designs called arabesques decorate a wall in an Iranian mosque. The prayer niche in the wall orients the worshiper toward Mecca. *Opposite page:* Glazed earthenware tiles bear an Arabic inscription.

ISLAMIC ART AND ARCHITECTURE

Islam is the religious faith preached by the Arab prophet Mohammed. During the five hundred years after Mohammed's death in A.D. 632, Islam spread far beyond its place of origin in the Arabian Peninsula. The followers of Mohammed, called Muslims, conquered the rest of the Middle East, as well as North Africa, Spain, central Asia, and north and central India. Most of the conquered people accepted the Islamic religion.

As Islam spread, a distinctive style of Islamic art gradually developed. It was used mainly for religious architecture, book illustrations, and the decoration of pottery, metalware, and other useful objects. Islamic art was influenced by the artistic styles of the conquered regions. These styles included late Roman, Byzantine, and Persian art.

The development of Islamic art was also influenced by two religious restrictions. Mohammed warned artists not to imitate God, the creator of all life, by making images of living things. Most religious art therefore consisted of ornamental designs that did not represent people or animals. The second restriction discouraged the use of costly materials. Islamic artists, therefore, worked mainly with brass, clay, and wood. They learned to decorate objects made of these less expensive materials so skillfully that they looked as beautiful as silver or gold.

DESIGN CHARACTERISTICS

The restriction on making images led to the development of one of the most outstanding features of Islamic art. Artists avoided depicting lifelike forms. Instead, they developed a special kind of decoration, called **arabesque**. An arabesque is a very complicated design. It can consist of twisting patterns of vines, leaves, and flowers. It can be made up of geometric shapes and patterns of straight lines, or

ARCHITECTURE

The religious buildings known as mosques, where Muslims worship, are among the most important examples of Islamic architecture. Other kinds of buildings include madrasahs, or religious schools; tombs; and palaces.

Mosques. The first mosques were simple buildings made of wood and clay. Then, as the world of Islam grew in size and power, large mosques of cut stone and brick were built. Because no Islamic building tradition yet existed, these early mosques were modeled after Christian churches. The oldest existing mosque, the Dome of the Rock in Jerusalem, was built in 691. It has many features of Byzantine Christian churches, including Grecian-style columns and mosaic decorations.

Muslim architects soon began to develop a new type of religious building, designed spe-

it can have curving lines that twist and turn over each other. Sometimes animal shapes were used, but they were always highly stylized and not lifelike.

Another important characteristic of Islamic art is the use of **calligraphy**, or beautiful handwriting. Arabic, the language of most Islamic texts, can be beautifully written in several different kinds of script. These include the straight, geometric Kufic script and the rounded, flowing Naskhi. Islamic artists used Arabic script (which is read from right to left) as part of their designs for religious books, wall decorations, and art objects. Especially beautiful calligraphy and decoration were used for copies of the Koran, the holy book of the Islamic faith.

Right: The Dome of the Rock in Jerusalem, built in A.D. 691, is the oldest existing mosque. Some of its features were modeled after early Christian churches.

cifically for Islamic worship. An early example of the new design is the Great Mosque in Damascus, begun about 705. It is entered through a rectangular court with covered passageways on three sides. In the court is a fountain for washing before prayer. The fourth wall of the court is closest to Mecca, the holy city of Islam. All Muslims face in the direction of Mecca when they pray. The wall is marked by a small, arched prayer niche. Over the aisle leading to this niche is a dome. A tower, or **minaret**, is used to call the faithful to prayer.

Other architects developed variations on this basic style. Some mosques have domes over each end of the aisle leading to the prayer niche. Other mosques have a large central dome. Some domes are ridged on the outside and resemble large melons. Inside, the ceilings of domes are often covered with decorative forms that resemble honeycombs, scales, or stalactites (icicle-like formations found in caves). Many mosques, especially those in

Spain, North Africa, and Persia, are covered with tiles. In the 1500's and 1600's mosques became more complex, with many domes and minarets. The Sultan Ahmed Mosque (also called the Blue Mosque), in Istanbul, Turkey, is a typical example.

Madrasahs and Tombs. Madrasahs, or religious schools, were often built next to mosques. They are four-sided structures built around a central court. Each side has a large arched hall that opens onto the courtyard. Students attended lectures in the large halls and lived in smaller rooms within the structure.

Sometimes the tomb of a ruler was part of a complex of buildings that also included a mosque and a madrasah. The tomb-mosque of Sultan Hasan, built in the mid-1300's in Cairo, Egypt, is such a complex. It is laid out like a cross, with four halls opening off a large square court.

Another well-known tomb is that of the Tatar warrior Tamerlane, which was built in the city of Samarkand about 1400. (Today Samarkand is part of Uzbekistan.) This building has a melon-shaped dome covered with brilliant blue and gold tiles. The tiles are made of glazed earthenware cut into various sizes and arranged in elaborate patterns. Perhaps the most famous Islamic tomb of all is the Taj Mahal in Agra, India. It was built in the 1600's by the ruler Shah Jahan as a tomb for

The Islamic faith spread widely, and examples of Islamic art are found in many parts of the world. *Left:* The tomb of Tamerlane, in present-day Uzbekistan, is notable for its tiled, melon-shaped dome. *Right:* The Blue Mosque in Istanbul, Turkey, has the tall minarets (towers) and clustered domes typical of later mosques. *Below:* The Court of the Lions is one of three courtyards of the Alhambra palace in Granada, Spain.

his wife. The Taj Mahal is so renowned that its very name calls up images of almost unreal splendor and beauty. An article on the Taj Mahal can be found in Volume T.

Palaces. The early Muslim rulers, or caliphs, were used to desert life; they did not like living in crowded cities. They built palaces in the desert where they could go to relax and hunt. The palaces looked like Roman fortresses, for they were built of stone and surrounded by walls with big towers. The throne rooms, prayer rooms, baths, and living quarters were decorated with murals and mosaics.

In the 700's the capital of the Muslim world moved from Damascus, Syria, to Baghdad, Mesopotamia (now Iraq). The architecture of palaces changed as a result of the move. Domed palaces were built of brick covered with thick layers of stucco, and the interiors were decorated with stucco reliefs. In the Jawsaq Palace, built about 850 in Samarra, Mesopotamia, the stucco ornament was of three distinct styles. One type showed deeply carved vine forms, and another added patterns to the surface of the main design. The third style used more abstract patterns, as in the metalwork of Central Asian nomads. These three styles contributed to the development of arabesque decoration, which became typical of Muslim art all over the world.

Of later palaces, the Alhambra at Granada, Spain, built in the 1300's, is the best known. Its many rooms are built around three open courts. The Court of the Myrtles features a long rectangular pool flanked by hedges. In the center of the inner Court of the Lions stands a fountain supported by twelve lions. The lower part of the palace walls are decorated with colored tiles set in geometric patterns. Painted and gilded plaster designs cover the upper part of the walls. Arabic inscriptions in the midst of the ornament say that there is "no conqueror but Allah."

▶**BOOK ILLUSTRATION**

Islamic painting developed mainly in the form of book illustration. Islamic artists produced many beautiful **illuminated manuscripts** (handwritten books decorated with painted pictures and designs). These paintings were created to help explain a scientific text or to add to the pleasure of reading a work of history or literature. Because of the restrictions on making images, illustrations for the

Islamic book illustration reached a high point with the work of Persian artists. This page from a famous Persian epic contains detailed and realistic images.

Koran and other religious manuscripts often consisted of intricate ornamental designs.

Nonreligious manuscripts sometimes contained images of human and animal figures. Figures in early illustrations were simple and painted to look flat or two-dimensional. These qualities can be seen in the illustrations for a famous book of fables, *Kalilah and Dimnah.* Later illustrators painted more detailed and realistic works. Especially skilled were artists working in Persia from the 1300's to the 1700's. One of the best-known Persian painters was Kamal ad-Din Bihzad. This artist combined the ornamental style of Persian illustration with realistic observation of people and animals.

By the end of the 1200's, parts of the Islamic world, including Persia, had been invaded by Mongols from the East. From this time on, the influence of Chinese ink paintings, especially landscapes, can be seen in Islamic painting. The last of the great invaders from central Asia was Tamerlane. He and his followers ignored the dictates of their new religion and encouraged artists to paint pictures of people. These pictures still appeared mainly in nonreligious books, however. Most Islamic

Left: A copy of the Koran, the Islamic holy book, is beautifully decorated with abstract designs. Like many Islamic books, its cover includes a flap to protect the page edges. *Opposite page:* A luxurious carpet, woven of silk and metallic thread, is an outstanding example of the skill of Islamic textile workers.

illustration remained essentially ornamental, uniting many design elements into an intricate pattern.

The Muslims greatly respected the knowledge contained in books, especially in the Koran. Their book covers nearly always include a flap to cover and protect the page edges. The covers were made of beautifully tooled leather, often with added decorations of gold and bright colors.

▶DECORATIVE ARTS

Many different arts were used in the decoration of Islamic mosques and palaces. Arabesque carvings in stone, wood, and plaster adorn the doorways, prayer niches, and pulpits of mosques. The borders of the decorations were often inscribed with quotations from the Koran. Both mosques and palaces were decorated with mosaics—pictures made by pressing tiny pieces of colored glass into wet cement. Painted and glazed tiles covered interior and exterior wall surfaces. Glass lamps decorated with arabesques and Arabic

letters hung by long chains from ceilings.

Beginning in the 1000's, a new class of wealthy merchants arose in cities throughout the Islamic world. They traded ceramics, leather goods, metalware, and textiles as far east as India and China and as far west as Europe. The tastes and spending power of the merchants, as well as the increased contact with other cultures, led to new developments in the decorative arts. Scenes of everyday and popular stories were realistically portrayed on all kinds of objects. These decorative scenes greatly influenced the development of book illustration.

Left: Islamic potters were skilled at making lusterware, pottery covered with a shining metallic glaze. *Below:* A bronze candlestick is engraved with intricate designs.

Metalware. Islamic metalworkers created beautifully worked brass and bronze objects, including pitchers, boxes, and trays. Sometimes they inlaid these objects with intricate designs of gold or silver. Arabesques, scenes with figures, and Arabic writing were all used as decoration. The designs began as detailed drawings, which were then skillfully adapted to a particular object and material.

Ceramics. By the 800's Islamic potters had developed many different techniques for making ceramics and pottery. A major center of pottery production was the city of Kashan, in Iran. The Kashan potters were especially skilled at making **lusterware**, a kind of pottery that is covered with a shining metallic glaze. Luster glaze was also used on tiles that covered prayer niches, wall surfaces, and the outsides of domes and minarets.

Rugs. Luxurious rugs were made by knotting single strands of wool or silk to create intricate patterns. Fine woolen rugs have more than one hundred knots per square inch, while some silk rugs have as many as eight hundred.

Rugs were used in both mosques and homes. Muslims often kneel on rugs to pray. The designs on these prayer rugs were made to resemble the arch of the prayer niche in a mosque. Nonreligious rugs often were decorated with geometric patterns. Other designs featured arabesques of flowers and plants in imitation of gardens. Animal and hunting scenes sometimes were added to the floral patterns. Dragons and other fantastic creatures frequently were part of the design, as were such real-life animals as lions and gazelles.

▶**LATER ISLAMIC ART**

During the Middle Ages, Christians and Muslims fought wars known as the Crusades. The nations of Islam were united in religion and in their common wars against the Christian Europeans. Islamic art was also unified. From Spain to India, the art of the countries of Islam was almost identical.

By the 1400's there was less to unify the Islamic world. Many people in Islamic nations belonged to other religions. The Crusades were over, and Muslim countries sometimes fought against each other.

Artistic activity in the Islamic style continues to flourish. Mosques are still being built; objects of metal, clay, and leather are still ornamented with arabesques; books are illuminated with miniatures; and rugs are still woven in the traditional way. However, after 1500, some Islamic artists began to add elements of European art to their work. Today the art of many Islamic countries has an international character, although the scenes or subjects may relate to a single Islamic nation.

GULNAR K. BOSCH
Florida State University

See also DECORATIVE ARTS; ILLUMINATED MANUSCRIPTS; INDIA, ART AND ARCHITECTURE OF; SPAIN, ART AND ARCHITECTURE OF; TAPESTRY.

ISLANDS

An island is usually defined as a land mass that is completely surrounded by water and that is smaller in size than a continent. (Australia, although surrounded by water, is a continent rather than an island.) Islands vary greatly in size, ranging from tiny coral atolls to huge islands like Greenland, the world's largest island. A chain of islands is often referred to as an archipelago.

Kinds of Islands. Islands can be divided into two main groups—continental and oceanic. **Continental** (or offshore) **islands** lie close to a continent and were probably once connected to the mainland. Changes in the earth's crust may have forced the seabed to rise, forming offshore islands. Or a rise in sea level may have cut off a piece of land and formed an island. Some continental islands are really the tops of submerged mountain ranges. Continental islands have the same geologic origin and structure as the nearby mainland. The

level—often thousands of feet above it. The Hawaiian Islands and Iceland are two examples of volcanic islands.

Coral islands are found in shallow tropical waters. They are the work of tiny sea animals called coral polyps. Many islands in the South Pacific are coral islands. How coral islands, reefs, and atolls are formed is described in the article CORALS in Volume C.

Islands may also take other forms. Mont St. Michel, in France, is an example of a **tidal island.** It is really part of the mainland, but it becomes an island during high tide. **Floating islands** are found in rivers (such as the Nile) or along certain coasts (such as Southeast Asia's). They consist of thickly matted vegetation often mixed with soil. **Barrier islands** are formed by sediment (fine soil and sand) deposited in offshore waters.

Their Diversity. Islands differ not only in their size and origin, but in other ways as well. Some islands have distinctive forms of animal life. The Galápagos Islands in the Pacific

Left: A 4-year-old girl from the Pacific island of Fiji wears traditional dress. Fijians are a mixture of Melanesian and Polynesian peoples.

Right: The Society Islands, a French territory in the South Pacific, are composed of both volcanic and coral islands.

bedrock is similar. Plants and animals are like those on the mainland. Great Britain is an example of a continental island. At one time it was part of the mainland of Europe.

Most of the world's islands are oceanic. **Oceanic islands** were never connected to a continent. They are often located thousands of miles from the mainland. Oceanic islands are classified as volcanic and coral.

Volcanic islands are created by the action of volcanoes deep beneath the ocean surface. Repeated eruptions of lava (hot liquid rock) form a volcanic cone that eventually rises above sea

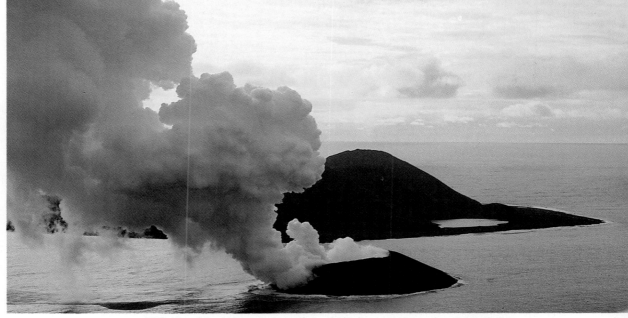

Birth of an island: Repeated eruptions of lava from volcanoes deep beneath the surface of the North Atlantic created the island of Surtsey off the Iceland coast in 1963.

Ocean are home to giant tortoises, rare flightless cormorants and other kinds of birds, and land and marine iguanas. The great lizard known as the Komodo Dragon is found only on a few islands in Indonesia.

In a few cases, islands have become powerful states and centers of empire. Great Britain was for many years the heart of a vast empire. Japan, a nation composed of four major islands, was once a military power. After its defeat in World War II, Japan transformed itself into one of the world's chief economic powers.

Islands have been important as refueling stations and as naval and military bases. For example, the Midway Islands in the central Pacific Ocean are inhabited mostly by U.S. military personnel. Some islands, such as Capri, Majorca, the West Indies, Bali, and Tahiti, are famed for their beauty. Others, such as Devil's Island, were infamous as places of imprisonment.

Some islands, like Hong Kong, Java, and Manhattan (part of New York City), are very densely populated. Others, like most of the islands in the Arctic and Antarctica and the thousands of tiny coral atolls in the Pacific, have few or no human inhabitants.

ANTHONY SAS
University of South Carolina

See also CARIBBEAN SEA AND ISLANDS; PACIFIC OCEAN AND ISLANDS; VOLCANOES.

SOME ISLANDS AND ISLAND GROUPS

Brief descriptions of some of the world's many islands and island groups follow. The countries that the islands are a part of or are colonies of are indicated within parentheses where applicable.

Admiralty Islands (Papua New Guinea) are an island group, part of the Bismarck Archipelago. They are located in the southwest Pacific Ocean, northeast of the island of New Guinea. The largest of the islands is Manus. Copra (dried coconut meat) is the major product of the islands. Area, about 800 square miles (2,000 square kilometers).

Aland Islands (Finland). More than 6,000 islands make up this group, located between Finland and Sweden. The population is Swedish in origin. The people engage in agriculture, fishing, and cattle raising. Area, about 570 square miles (1,475 square kilometers).

Aleutian Islands (U.S.A.) are a group of some 150 volcanic islands, part of the state of Alaska. They extend for about 1,200 miles (1,900 kilometers) southwest from the Alaska Peninsula, between the North Pacific and the Bering Sea. The islands were discovered by Vitus Bering and Aleksei Chrikov in 1741. There are four main groups: the Fox Islands, the Andreanof Islands, the Rat Islands, and the Near Islands. Unimak, one of the Fox Islands, is the largest of the Aleutians. The native inhabitants are Aleuts. The climate is cool, wet, and foggy. During World War II the Aleutians were invaded by the Japanese. Area, about 6,821 square miles (17,666 square kilometers).

The crater of the volcano that formed Amsterdam Island in the Indian Ocean has long since filled with seawater.

Alexander Archipelago (U.S.A.) is a chain of more than 1,000 islands, off the southeastern coast of Alaska, made up of the summits of submerged mountain ranges. The main islands are Chichagof, Admiralty, Baranof, Kupreanof, Prince of Wales, and Revillagigedo. The economy is based on fishing and fish processing and fur trapping. The chief towns are Sitka and Ketchikan.

Andaman Islands (India), a group of five large and many small islands, are located in the Bay of Bengal. The large islands are mountainous, with a heavy cover of tropical hardwood forests. From 1857 to 1945 the islands were used as a penal colony. Most of the inhabitants are now farmers. Lumber is the chief export. Area, about 2,500 square miles (6,475 square kilometers).

Anticosti Island (Canada), located at the entrance to the St. Lawrence River, is part of the province of Quebec. The island was discovered by Jacques Cartier in 1534. Area, about 3,066 square miles (7,940 square kilometers).

Antigua and Barbuda is an island nation in the Caribbean Sea. See ANTIGUA AND BARBUDA.

Antilles are two groups of islands in the West Indies. See CARIBBEAN SEA AND ISLANDS.

Ascension Island (Britain), a small island of volcanic origin in the South Atlantic, is part of the colony of St. Helena. It was discovered by the Portuguese in 1501. Britain gained possession in 1815. Ascension is a breeding ground for birds and turtles. Area, about 34 square miles (88 square kilometers).

Azores (Portugal) are a group of nine islands situated in the Atlantic Ocean, some 800 miles (1,300 kilometers) west of Portugal. The islands are of volcanic origin. The Portuguese navigator Gonzalo Cabral claimed the islands for Portugal in 1431. The economy is based chiefly on farming and fishing. Area, about 890 square miles (2,300 square kilometers).

Baffin Island is a cold, rocky island, part of Nunavut in northern Canada, located in the Arctic Ocean. It is the world's fifth largest island, but it has only a small population. Most of its inhabitants are Inuit, who live along the coastal areas. The main economic activities are hunting, whaling, and fur trapping. The island is named for the English navigator William Baffin, who explored parts of the island in 1616. Area, about 190,900 square miles (507,400 square kilometers).

Bahamas is an island nation in the Atlantic Ocean, southeast of Florida. See BAHAMAS.

Balearic Islands (Spain) are a group of four main islands and several lesser ones in the Mediterranean Sea, east of the Spanish mainland. Most of the people live on the islands of Majorca and Minorca. Citrus fruits, olives, almonds, and wine are the leading products. Tourism is also of importance. Area, about 1,940 square miles (5,025 square kilometers).

Bali is one of the Lesser Sunda islands of Indonesia. See INDONESIA.

Bermuda (Britain) is a small group of islands in the Atlantic Ocean, off Cape Hatteras, North Carolina. See BERMUDA.

Borneo, the world's third largest island, is located at the western end of the Pacific Ocean. See BORNEO.

British Isles include Great Britain and Ireland and adjacent islands.

Above: This boy is from Haiti on the island of Hispaniola in the Caribbean Sea.

Right: Clear waters, white beaches, and palm trees are typical of many South Pacific islands.

Canary Islands (Spain) are a group of seven major islands in the North Atlantic Ocean, off the northwestern coast of Africa. The economy is based on farming and fishing, with tourism increasingly important. Las Palmas on the island of Grand Canary is the major city. Area, about 2,900 square miles (7,500 square kilometers).

Cape Breton Island (Canada) is part of the province of Nova Scotia. The island became a French possession in 1712 but was conquered by Britain in 1758. It was a separate province until 1820, when it was united with Nova Scotia. Cape Breton Island contains valuable coal and gypsum deposits. Fishing is important. The largest city is Sydney. Area, about 4,000 square miles (10,300 square kilometers). See also NOVA SCOTIA.

Cape Verde is an island nation in the Atlantic Ocean, off the west coast of Africa. See CAPE VERDE.

Capri (Italy) is located at the entrance to the Bay of Naples, in the Tyrrhenian Sea. The island is famous as a tourist resort. The Blue Grotto and the ruins of palaces built by the Roman emperors Augustus and Tiberius attract many visitors. Area, about 4 square miles (10 square kilometers).

Caribbean Islands. See CARIBBEAN SEA AND ISLANDS.

Caroline Islands (U.S.A.) are a group of nearly 1,000 small islands and islets in the western Pacific Ocean. See PACIFIC OCEAN AND ISLANDS.

Channel Islands (Britain) are a group of nine islands located in the English Channel, off the Normandy coast of France. Three of the islands—Guernsey, Jersey, Alderney—have been famous for their fine breeds of cattle. Originally belonging

to the dukes of Normandy, the islands became part of Britain under William the Conqueror in 1066. They are British crown possessions, with their own legislatures. Area, about 75 square miles (194 square kilometers).

Christmas Island, located in the Pacific Ocean, is the largest island of the nation of Kiribati. See KIRIBATI.

Comoros is an island nation situated off the eastern coast of Africa. See COMOROS.

Cook Islands (New Zealand) are a group of islands in the South Pacific. See PACIFIC OCEAN AND ISLANDS.

Corsica (France) is located in the Mediterranean Sea, west of the mainland of Italy. Farming, fishing, and livestock raising are the chief occupations of the people. The island's history dates back to 560 B.C. when it was settled by Phoenicians. Napoleon Bonaparte was born in the town of Ajaccio in 1769. Area, about 3,367 square miles (8,721 square kilometers).

Crete (Greece), the largest of the Greek islands, is located in the Mediterranean Sea, southeast of the Greek mainland. Farming, fishing, and the raising of sheep and goats are the chief economic activities. Crete was the center of the ancient Minoan civilization, which flourished from about 3300 B.C. to about 1400 B.C. Area, about 3,235 square miles (8,380 square kilometers). See also ANCIENT CIVILIZATIONS (Cretan Civilization).

Cuba is an island nation in the Caribbean Sea. See CUBA.

Cyclades (Greece) are a group of about 220 islands and islets located southeast of the Greek mainland, in the Aegean Sea. The name is derived from the Greek *kyklos* ("circle"), because the islands form a ring around the central island of Delos. Area, about 1,000 square miles (2,590 square kilometers).

Cyprus is an island nation in the Mediterranean Sea. See CYPRUS.

Devil's Island was part of the penal colony of French Guiana. See FRENCH GUIANA.

Dodecanese (Greece) are a group of 14 large and several small islands, located off the southwestern coast of Turkey, in the Aegean Sea. Only two islands, Rhodes and Kos, have much fertile soil.

Rhodes was the site of the *Colossus of Rhodes*—a huge statue of Apollo (Helios) built in the 200's B.C.—one of the seven wonders of the ancient world. Area, about 1,030 square miles (2,670 square kilometers).

Dominica is a Caribbean island nation. See DOMINICA.

Easter Island (Chile) is a small volcanic island in the South Pacific. People lived on this island before recorded history, but very little is known about them. The present-day inhabitants, mainly Polynesians, are unable to understand the prehistoric picture writing found there, nor do they know the origin of the island's giant statues. The island was named on Easter Sunday, 1722, by the Dutch explorer Jakob Roggeveen. Area, about 46 square miles (120 square kilometers).

Elba (Italy) is located in the Mediterranean Sea off the west coast of the Italian mainland. The island is best known as the first place of exile (1814–15) for Napoleon I. Area, about 86 square miles (223 square kilometers).

The origins of the giant sculptures on Easter Island (*top*) in the Pacific have mystified scientists. They are thought to have been carved by a long-vanished people. Maoris, such as this father and son (*above*), are Polynesians who were the first-known settlers of New Zealand. The desolate Galápagos Islands (*right*), a province of Ecuador in the Pacific, are famed for their unusual forms of animal life, including these iguanas.

Ellesmere Island (Canada), the world's ninth largest island, is part of the Arctic Archipelago of Nunavut, Canada. Cape Columbia on the northern coast of Ellesmere Island is the northernmost point of North America. The remains of Inuit settlements have been found on the east coast, but there are no permanent settlements on the island today. Area, about 75,770 square miles (196,240 square kilometers).

Falkland Islands (Britain; claimed by Argentina) are two large islands and many smaller ones in the South Atlantic Ocean. The islands lie southwest of Argentina, which calls them Islas Malvinas. The inhabitants, mainly of British descent, raise sheep for wool, the chief export. Argentina's claims over the islands led to a brief war (1982) with Britain, which was won by the British. Area, about 4,600 square miles (12,000 square kilometers).

Faroe (or Faeroe) Islands (Denmark) are a group of 21 small volcanic islands located in the North Atlantic Ocean. The islands are hilly, with stony soils. Agriculture is limited, but horse and sheep raising and fishing are important economic activities. From the late 800's until 1380, Norway ruled the islands. Since then, with a few short interruptions, they have been part of Denmark. Area, about 540 square miles (1,400 square kilometers).

Fiji is an island nation in the southwestern Pacific Ocean. See FIJI.

Galápagos Islands (Ecuador) are a group of islands in the Pacific Ocean. See ECUADOR.

Gilbert and Ellice Islands, in the central Pacific Ocean, are parts of the nations of Kiribati and Tuvalu. See KIRIBATI and TUVALU.

Great Britain, the world's fourth largest island, makes up the greatest part of the United Kingdom. It includes all of England, Wales, and Scotland. See UNITED KINGDOM.

Greater Antilles are a chain of four large islands in the Caribbean Sea. They include the nations of Cuba, the Dominican Republic, Haiti, and Jamaica, and the commonwealth of Puerto Rico. See CARIBBEAN SEA AND ISLANDS.

Greenland (Denmark), the world's largest island, is located in the North Atlantic Ocean. See GREENLAND.

Grenada is an island nation in the Caribbean Sea. See GRENADA.

Hawaiian Islands (U.S.A.), a group of Pacific islands, became the 50th state of the United States in 1959. See HAWAII.

Hebrides (Britain) are a group of more than 500 rocky and mountainous islands, located off the western coast of Scotland. About 100 of the islands are inhabited. The people earn a living from farming (barley, oats), fishing, and gathering eiderdown (feathers from eider ducks). Tourism is important in the summer. The islands were under Norwegian rule from the 700's to the 1200's, when they were ceded to Scotland. Area, about 3,000 square miles (7,800 square kilometers).

Helgoland (Germany) is a tiny island in the North Sea. Once an important naval base, it is now a resort. Area, about ¼ square mile (.65 square kilometer).

Hispaniola is the second largest of the islands of the Greater Antilles in the Caribbean Sea. It is shared by the nations of Haiti and the Dominican Republic.

Hong Kong (China) lies off the southern coast of China. See HONG KONG.

Honshu (Japan), the largest of the four major islands of Japan, is the world's seventh largest island. See JAPAN.

Iceland is an island nation in the North Atlantic Ocean. See ICELAND.

Indonesia is a nation of Southeast Asia, made up of numerous islands. See INDONESIA.

Ionian Islands (Greece) are a group of four large and many small mountainous islands located in the Ionian Sea. The largest islands are Corfu (Kerkyra), Leukas, Zante, and Cephalonia. Citrus fruits, grapes, and olives are leading crops. Shipping, tourism, and fishing are important economic activities. Area, about 900 square miles (2,300 square kilometers).

Ireland is the smaller of the two main islands of the British Isles. See IRELAND.

Islas Malvinas. See the entry under Falkland Islands.

Jamaica is one of the islands of the Greater Antilles in the Caribbean Sea. See JAMAICA.

Japan is an island nation in the Pacific Ocean, off the eastern coast of Asia. It is made up of four major islands—Honshu, Kokkaido, Kyushu, and Shikoku. See JAPAN.

Java is the most densely populated island of Indonesia. See INDONESIA.

Kiribati is an island nation in the central Pacific Ocean. See KIRIBATI.

Kuril (or Kurile) Islands (Russia) are a group of about 30 islands located north of Japan. The islands contain many active volcanoes. Economic activities include lumbering, fishing, and fur trapping. The Kurils formally came under Japanese sovereignty in 1875. After World War II the Soviet Union took over the islands. Japan claims the islands closest to Hokkaido. Area, about 6,000 square miles (15,600 square kilometers).

Lesser Antilles are an island chain in the Caribbean Sea made up of the Leeward and Windward Islands. See CARIBBEAN SEA AND ISLANDS.

Manhattan Island is one of several islands that form part of New York City. It is the commercial and cultural center of the United States and one of the world's financial capitals. Manhattan's strong bedrock has made it possible to build the towering skyscrapers for which the city is noted.

Lofoten Islands (Norway) are a group of six islands and several islets located northwest of the Norwegian mainland. The islands are mountainous, and the coastline rugged. Farming is possible only in a few fertile valleys. The major industry is fishing. The Maelstrom, a strait famous for its whirlpool, is located here. Area, about 475 square miles (1,230 square kilometers).

Madagascar is an island nation situated off the eastern coast of Africa. It is the world's fourth largest island. See MADAGASCAR.

Madeira (Portugal) is a group of mountainous islands situated off the northwestern coast of Africa. They consist of two large inhabited islands (Madeira Island and Porto Santo) and a number of small uninhabited ones. Madeira is famous for its wine and is a popular tourist center. Area, about 305 square miles (790 square kilometers).

Magdalen Islands (Canada) lie southeast of Quebec in the Gulf of St. Lawrence. The group consists of nine islands and several islets. Most of the islanders are of French origin. Their main occupations are fishing and sealing. Jacques Cartier discovered the islands in 1534. Area, about 102 square miles (265 square kilometers).

Maldives is a small island nation in the Indian Ocean. See MALDIVES.

Malta is an island nation in the Mediterranean Sea. See MALTA.

Man, Isle of (Britain), in the Irish Sea, is situated about 30 miles (48 kilometers) west of the coast of Great Britain. Farming (oats, fruits, vegetables), fishing, and tourism are the chief economic activities. The tail-less, short-haired Manx cat was cultivated on the island. Britain acquired the Isle of Man in 1765. It is a crown possession and has local self-government. Area, about 221 square miles (572 square kilometers).

Manhattan is one of the islands that form part of New York City. See NEW YORK CITY.

Marianas Islands (U.S.A.) are a group of islands located in the western Pacific. See PACIFIC OCEAN AND ISLANDS.

Marquesas Islands (France) are a group of islands located in the southeastern Pacific. See PACIFIC OCEAN AND ISLANDS.

Marshall Islands consist of numerous coral atolls and small islands in the northwestern Pacific. See MARSHALL ISLANDS.

Mauritius is a small island nation in the Indian Ocean. See MAURITIUS.

Melos, or Milo (Greece) is a small mountainous island of the Cyclades group. The statue known as the Venus de Milo was discovered on the island in 1820. Marble quarrying and fishing are important economic activities. Area, about 58 square miles (150 square kilometers).

Midway (U.S.A.) includes several small islands in the North Pacific Ocean. They were the site of a major naval battle in World War II. Area, about 2 square miles (5 square kilometers).

Nauru is a small island nation in the central Pacific. See NAURU.

New Caledonia (France) is an island in the southwest Pacific. See PACIFIC OCEAN AND ISLANDS.

Newfoundland (Canada) lies east of the Canadian mainland. With Labrador, it makes up the province of Newfoundland and Labrador. See NEWFOUNDLAND AND LABRADOR.

New Guinea (Indonesia; Papua New Guinea), the world's second largest island, is located in the western Pacific Ocean. See NEW GUINEA.

New Zealand is an island nation in the South Pacific Ocean. See NEW ZEALAND.

Nicobar Islands (India) are a group of 19 islands located in the Bay of Bengal, to the south of the Andaman group. The people make their living by fishing and trading in timber and copra. Area, about 740 square miles (1,917 square kilometers).

Orkney Islands (Britain) are a group of about 90

islands, located between northern Scotland and the Shetland Islands. The people are mainly of Scandinavian and Scottish descent. Agriculture and fishing are major occupations, and tourism provides added income. Life on the islands is rapidly changing because of the closeness to the North Sea oil fields. Area, about 375 square miles (970 square kilometers).

Philippines is an island nation situated off the southeastern coast of Asia. See PHILIPPINES.

Pribilof Islands (U.S.A.). The four islands of this group are located in the Bering Sea, north of the Aleutians. The islands came into the possession of the United States when Alaska was purchased from Russia in 1867. They include two large islands—St. Paul and St. George—and two smaller ones—Walrus and Otter. Many of the small population are Aleuts, who engage in sealing. Area, about 180 square miles (466 square kilometers).

Prince Edward Island (Canada) is one of Canada's Atlantic Provinces. See PRINCE EDWARD ISLAND.

Puerto Rico (U.S.A.) is the easternmost and smallest of the islands of the Greater Antilles. See PUERTO RICO.

Réunion (France), a volcanic island in the Indian Ocean off the coast of Madagascar, is one of the Mascarene Islands. Much of Réunion's cultivated area consists of sugar plantations. Area, about 970 square miles (2,512 square kilometers).

Ryukyu Islands (Japan). See JAPAN; PACIFIC OCEAN AND ISLANDS.

Saint Kitts and Nevis is an island nation in the Caribbean Sea. See SAINT KITTS AND NEVIS.

Saint Helena (Britain) is a small island in the South Atlantic Ocean, famous as the place of final exile (1815–21) for Napoleon I. It was discovered by the Portuguese in 1502, occupied by the Dutch in 1600, and first acquired by the British in 1651. It has a limited population and no industry. Area, about 47 square miles (122 square kilometers).

Saint Lucia is an island nation in the Caribbean. See SAINT LUCIA.

Saint Pierre and Miquelon (France) are two small, rocky islands located off the southeastern coast of Canada. The economy is based chiefly on fishing. The islands are a department (state) of France. Area, about 93 square miles (242 square kilometers).

Saint Vincent, an island in the Caribbean, forms part of the nation of St. Vincent and the Grenadines. See SAINT VINCENT AND THE GRENADINES.

Sakhalin (Russia) is a long and narrow island in the northern Pacific Ocean, off the Siberian coast

Sheepherding (*below*) is important economically in the rocky Faroe (Faeroe) Islands in the North Atlantic. San Giorgio Maggiore (*right*) is one of the islands on which the Italian city of Venice is built.

of Russia. The leading economic activities are fishing, forestry, and coal mining. The Russians and Japanese disputed possession of the island for many years. The Soviet Union occupied all of the Sakhalin after World War II. Area, about 30,000 square miles (78,000 square kilometers).

Salamis (Greece) is located in the Aegean Sea. The island was the site of a famous naval battle (480 B.C.), in which the Athenians defeated the Persians during the Persian Wars. Farming is the chief economic activity. Area, about 40 square miles (100 square kilometers).

Samoa, an island group in the South Pacific, includes the nation of Western Samoa and the territory of American Samoa. See WESTERN SAMOA; UNITED STATES (Outlying Areas of the U.S.).

São Tomé and Príncipe is an island nation in the Gulf of Guinea, off the western coast of Africa. See SÃO TOMÉ AND PRÍNCIPE.

Sardinia (Italy), the second largest island in the Mediterranean Sea, lies west of the Italian mainland. The coast has many gulfs and inlets, and the interior is mountainous. The main occupations are farming (olives, citrus fruits, tobacco, grapes, flax); raising sheep, horses, and goats; mining (lead, zinc, copper); and fishing. This island also produces cork. Area, about 9,200 square miles (23,800 square kilometers).

Scilly Islands (Britain) are a group of 140 tiny islands and numerous reefs, located southwest of Land's End on the Cornwall coast. The people make a living by growing vegetables and flowers, by fishing, and from tourism. Area, about 6 square miles (16 square kilometers).

Seychelles is an island nation in the western Indian Ocean. See SEYCHELLES.

Shetland Islands (Britain) are a group of more than 100 rocky, hilly islands located northeast of the mainland of Scotland. About one fourth of the islands are inhabited. Most of the people are of Scandinavian descent. The traditional occupations are fishing and sheep herding. The island's knitted woolen goods are world famous. Area, about 550 square miles (1,425 square kilometers).

Sicily (Italy), the largest island in the Mediterranean Sea, lies just off the southwestern tip of Italy. It is separated from the Italian mainland by the Strait of Messina. The island is mountainous and is subject to earthquakes. The highest point is the volcanic peak of Mount Etna. The people live mainly along the coast. The chief occupations are farming, sheep and goat herding, and fishing. The island was invaded and conquered many times. Greeks, Carthaginians, Romans, Goths, Byzantines, Arabs, Normans, and the Spanish ruled the island at various times in its history. Guiseppe Garibaldi, the Italian liberator, freed Sicily from Spain in 1860, and the island became part of united Italy. The capital is Palermo. Area, about 9,900 square miles (25,500 square kilometers).

Singapore is an island nation of Southeast Asia. See SINGAPORE.

Society Islands (France) are a group of volcanic and coral islands in the South Pacific. See PACIFIC OCEAN AND ISLANDS.

Solomon Islands are a chain of islands in the Pacific Ocean forming parts of the nations of Papua New Guinea and Solomon Islands. See PAPUA NEW GUINEA and SOLOMON ISLANDS.

Sri Lanka is an island nation in the Indian Ocean, located southeast of India. See SRI LANKA.

Sumatra, the world's sixth largest island, is one of the Greater Sunda Islands of Indonesia. See INDONESIA.

Svalbard Islands (Norway). Formerly known as Spitsbergen, this group of five large islands and many small ones is located north of Norway, within the Arctic Circle. The people make their living from mining coal and copper, fishing, and herding reindeer. Area, about 24,000 square miles (62,000 square kilometers).

Taiwan is the island seat of the Chinese Nationalist Government (the Republic of China) and lies about 100 miles (160 kilometers) off the Chinese mainland. See TAIWAN.

Tonga is an island nation in the Pacific. See TONGA.

Trinidad and Tobago is an island nation in the Caribbean Sea. See TRINIDAD AND TOBAGO.

Tristan da Cunha (Britain) is a small island group in the South Atlantic. Tristan da Cunha, the only inhabited island, has an area of about 38 square miles (98 square kilometers).

Tuamotu (France) is a group of about 80 atolls located in the South Pacific. See PACIFIC OCEAN AND ISLANDS.

Tuvalu is an island nation in the Pacific Ocean. See TUVALU.

Vanuatu is a Pacific island nation formerly known as New Hebrides. See VANUATU.

Victoria, the world's tenth largest island, is part of the Arctic Archipelago of Canada's Northwest Territories and Nunavut. It is the site of a joint U.S. and Canadian weather station. Area, about 83,896 square miles (217,290 square kilometers).

Wight, Isle of (Britain), located in the English Channel, is a popular tourist resort. Area, about 147 square miles (380 square kilometers).

Zanzibar, an island off the eastern coast of Africa, is part of the nation of Tanzania. See TANZANIA.

ISOTOPES. See ATOMS.

ISLAND

ISRAEL

Israel is a small nation on the eastern shore of the Mediterranean Sea, in a region of Southwest Asia known as the Middle East. The modern State of Israel was established in Palestine in 1948 as a homeland for the Jewish people. Its founders sought to create a new nation whose ideals, traditions, customs, and way of life would be Jewish.

▶ PEOPLE

About 80 percent of Israel's citizens are Jewish; the rest are Muslim, Christian, and Druze Arabs. Since 1948, Israel's population increased nearly ten times, from about 700,000 to more than 6 million, largely as a result of immigration, mostly from Eastern Europe. Many Jews also came from Iraq, Morocco, Egypt, and other Arab countries as well as Asia.

Jews of European origin are known as Ashkenazim. Those

from the Arab world, Asia, and Africa are called Sephardim, Mizrachim (Eastern), or Oriental Jews. Native-born Jewish Israelis are called Sabras. Most of the country's Arab citizens call themselves Israeli Palestinians or Palestinian Israelis. For more information on the history of the Jewish people, see the article JEWS in Volume J-K.

Language. Israel has two official languages, Hebrew and Arabic. English is also widely used in official circles and is taught as a second language in many schools. All three languages appear on Israeli coins and postage stamps, in many official documents, and on many street signs throughout the country.

Dozens of other languages can also be heard throughout the country, reflecting the multinational origins of the population. For more information, see the articles HEBREW LANGUAGE AND LITERATURE in Volume H and YIDDISH LANGUAGE AND LITERATURE in Volume W-X-Y-Z.

Israel was created in 1948 as a homeland for Jews, many of whom emigrated from Europe after World War II. Most of today's immigrants (*right*) come from Russia as a result of the breakup of the Soviet Union. Hasidic Jews (*below right*), who are Orthodox in their religion, are easily recognized by their distinctive dress. Armed soldiers mingle with pedestrians on Jaffa Road (*below*), Jerusalem's main east-west thoroughfare.

Palestinian children live in Arab communities in the Israeli-occupied Gaza Strip, where Palestinian leaders hope to establish an independent state.

Religion. Israel's Proclamation of Independence guarantees freedom of religion and promises to safeguard the Holy Places of all religions. Because Israel was established as a Jewish State and the majority of the population is Jewish, Saturday, the Jewish Sabbath, is the official day of rest. Jewish religious days and festivals are also observed. Non-Jews are free to worship according to their own beliefs and to observe their own holy days. For more information on the Jewish religion, teachings, holidays, ceremonies, and dietary laws, see the article JUDAISM in Volume J-K.

About 75 percent of Israel's non-Jewish population is Muslim. The rest is made up of Christians (mostly affiliated with the Greek Catholic, Greek Orthodox, and Roman Catholic churches) and Druze Arabs (a small religious community that split from Islam centuries ago). Each of these non-Jewish communities has its own religious courts and religious legal system.

Israel's superb irrigation methods have transformed portions of the Negev desert into some of the world's most productive farmlands (*below*). Crops are also grown in the Jordan River valley (*far right*). An Arabic shepherd (*right*) tends his flock near Bethlehem.

Education. Since 1948, Israel's education system has played an important role in integrating immigrant children from more than 70 countries. Kindergarten is free and compulsory for 5-year-olds. Primary school attendance is required from age 6 to 16 and is free to age 18. Public schools are divided into three groups: state schools, attended by the majority of pupils; state religious schools, emphasizing Jewish studies, traditions, and observances; and Arab and Druze schools, with instruction in Arabic. There are also private schools operated by various religious or international organizations. Where Hebrew is not the language of instruction, it is taught as a second language.

The Ministry of Education is responsible for school curricula and standards. The government finances more than 70 percent of education. Local authorities finance the rest.

Israel's major universities include Hebrew University of Jerusalem, the Technion-Israel Institute of Technology, Weizmann Institute of Science, Bar Ilan University, Tel Aviv University, Haifa University, and Ben-Gurion University of the Negev.

▶ **LAND**

Israel is an irregular narrow strip of land, extending from the hills of Galilee in the north to the port of Elat (Elath) on the Gulf of Aqaba in the south. It is bordered by Lebanon and Syria in the north, Jordan in the

east, Egypt in the southwest, and the Mediterranean Sea in the west.

Land Regions. North of Haifa the country broadens out into one of its most beautiful regions—the Zebulun Valley, which lies along the coast. The Plain of Esdraelon (also called the Valley of Jezreel) runs roughly east to west, and the hills of Galilee overlook the Hula Valley and the Sea of Galilee (also known as Lake Tiberias). South of Haifa stretches the Plain of Sharon and the Judean Plains, a narrow strip leading inland to the Hills of Judea.

The Negev, largely desert, covers roughly the southern half of Israel. In the north it is an extension of the coastal plain. In the east it is a long, irregular valley. In the center the Negev is a plateau, with hills extending westward halfway to the port of Elat.

The Jordan River valley extends from the northeastern corner of Israel, through the Sea of Galilee south to the Dead Sea, the lowest point on the earth's surface. A chain of mountains lying west of the valley stretches about 200 miles (320 kilometers) from Lebanon to the Sinai Peninsula in Egypt. The average height is 2,000 feet (610 meters).

Rivers and Lakes. Israel's principal water source is the Jordan River system, which flows southward along the eastern border from the Yarmuk River in the north through the Sea of Galilee. From there the Jordan flows south into the Dead Sea, the largest body of water in the country. Although rich in minerals, the water of the Dead Sea is too salty to be used for agriculture.

Vacationers flock to the beaches along Israel's Mediterranean coast. Tourism accounts for a major segment of Israel's economy.

Climate. Israel has a Mediterranean climate of warm, sunny summers and cool, rainy winters. Hot, dry winds blow from the east at the beginning and end of summer. The rainy season generally lasts from November to March. Snow occasionally falls in the hills of Galilee in winter.

Natural Resources. Most of Israel's limited mineral resources are found in the Negev. These include phosphates, glass sand, gypsum, ceramic clay, feldspar, copper, and small amounts of oil. Some iron has been found in Galilee. The Dead Sea is rich in potash and magnesium bromide.

Israel's water demands are so great that annual use exceeds average supply by about 15 percent. Some planners have urged that Israel abandon its emphasis on agriculture, which uses more than 75 percent of the water, and shift to industry. Disputes over division of the region's water sources have been one of the major causes of conflict between Israel and its neighbors.

▶ **ECONOMY**

Services. About 60 percent of Israel's working population is employed in public, commercial, financial, and personal services. Tourism, which draws on many service industries, is important to Israel's economy. Historic sites such as Jerusalem, Bethlehem, and Nazareth attract millions of visitors yearly from abroad.

Manufacturing. Since 1948, Israel's industrial development has made it the most technologically advanced country in the Middle East. Major products include medical equipment, advanced optical and other precision goods, and high-technology electronic equip-

ment, particularly computer software and hardware. Israel's largest single employer, Israel Aircraft Industries (IAI), produces combat and civil aircraft, armored cars, missiles, patrol boats, and other military items, many of them for export.

Agriculture. Biblical Israel was "a land of wheat and barley and vines and fig-trees and pomegranates, a land of olive oil and honey." These products are still grown. But today Israel produces mostly dairy and poultry products, cotton, and a large variety of flowers, fruits, and vegetables, including sugar beets, melons, tomatoes, strawberries, mangoes, avocados, and citrus items.

Israel's agriculture is the most scientifically planned, organized, and mechanized in the Middle East and among the most productive in the world. Cultivated areas cover more than 1 million acres (400,000 hectares), about half of which is irrigated. The country's largest water project, the National Water Carrier, conducts water through a 140-mile (225-kilometer)-long network of underground pipes, canals, tunnels, dams, and pumping stations to the arid Negev in the south.

About half the rural Jewish population lives in collective farm settlements called kibbutzim. Other farmers belong to smallholders' settlements called moshavim. Arab farms, located mostly in Galilee, are generally individually owned.

Trade. The United States is Israel's foremost trading partner, and the two countries have agreed to remove customs duties on each others' products. Most Israeli exports are industrial products such as computer software, military equipment, chemicals, and plastics. Agricultural products, especially citrus fruits, are exported mostly to Europe.

Transportation. Automobiles, buses, and trucks are the main means of transportation in Israel. Railroads are used primarily for transporting heavy freight loads. El Al is the national airline for international travel. Ben-Gurion International Airport, located between Tel Aviv and Jerusalem, is the largest air terminal.

Communication. Israel is connected with international communications systems through underwater fiber-optic lines and satellite links. Its conventional telephone network is one of the few in the world with 100 percent digitalization. Nearly one in four Israelis owns a mobile phone.

The government-controlled Israel Broadcasting Authority provides local and international service through *Kol Israel* (Voice of Israel). It operates eight radio networks in more than seventeen languages. *Galei Tzahal* (station of the Israel Defense Forces) operates around the clock, offering news, music, and special interest programs. Television in Israel began broadcasting in 1967. There is a

Israel

STATE OF ISRAEL (Medinat Yisrael in Hebrew and Dawlat Israel in Arabic) is the official name of the country.

LOCATION: Southwest Asia.

AREA: 8,019 sq mi (20,770 km²).

POPULATION: 5,750,000 (estimate).

CAPITAL: Jerusalem.

LARGEST CITY: Jerusalem.

MAJOR LANGUAGES: Hebrew, Arabic (both official), English.

MAJOR RELIGIOUS GROUPS: Jewish, Muslim, Christian, Druze.

GOVERNMENT: Republic. **Head of state**—president. **Head of government**—prime minister. **Legislature**—Knesset.

CHIEF PRODUCTS: Agricultural—citrus fruits (oranges, lemons, grapefruits) and other fruits, vegetables, cotton, beef, poultry, dairy products. **Manufactured**—processed foods, cut and polished diamonds, textiles, chemicals, metal products, military equipment, transportation equipment, electronics. **Mineral**—phosphates, glass sand, gypsum, ceramic clay, feldspar, copper, potash, magnesium bromide.

MONETARY UNIT: Shekel (1 shekel = 100 agorot).

---

state-run channel and one commercial channel that began in 1994.

There are three major and several smaller daily Hebrew newspapers published in Tel Aviv and Jerusalem as well as the English language *Jerusalem Post*. Numerous smaller dailies are published in Arabic, Russian, German, Polish, Romanian, and other languages. More than 1,000 magazines and other periodicals are also produced.

▶ **MAJOR CITIES**

More than 90 percent of Israelis live in urban areas. Among the cities known since ancient times are Jerusalem, Jaffa, Beersheba, Tiberias, and Akko. Modern cities include Tel Aviv and Haifa.

Jerusalem, Israel's capital and largest city, is one of the oldest continuously inhabited cities. King David made it Israel's capi-

tal about 1000 B.C. Today it remains the center of Jewish religious and political life. The city is also sacred to Muslims and Christians. East Jerusalem is claimed by the Palestinians as their capital. For more information, see the article JERUSALEM in Volume J-K.

Tel Aviv, Israel's second largest city, was founded in 1909 as a suburb of the ancient Arab city of Jaffa. Today the twin cities of Tel Aviv-Jaffa form the hub of Israel's commerce, light industry, culture, and entertainment. The population of the greater Tel Aviv metropolitan area, which includes such towns as Ramat Gan, Bat Yam, and Lod, exceeds 1 million.

Haifa, Israel's third largest city, is the country's main port and the center of heavy industry. Haifa is the focus of Israel's international trade and commerce.

▶ **CULTURAL HERITAGE**

Music. Palestine became a music center in the 1930's when hundreds of music teachers, composers, and performers immigrated there from Europe. Internationally renowned Israeli musicians today include the composer Paul Ben-Haim, violinists Itzhak Perlman and Pinchas Zukerman, and conductor Daniel Barenboim. The Israel Philharmonic Orchestra, founded in 1936, is the country's best-known symphony orchestra. The New Israel Opera features performances by local and foreign guest artists. The chamber music tradition, which also began in the 1930's, includes several internationally acclaimed choral groups. World-class musical events are held yearly at the Ein Gev Music Festival on the shores of the Sea of Galilee and at other festival sites.

Tel Aviv is one of Israel's most modern cities. Combined with Jaffa, it forms the country's largest metropolitan area.

Art and Architecture. Israel is an archaeologist's paradise. Among the ancient treasures that have been discovered throughout the land are the Dead Sea Scrolls, the mountain fortress of Masada, and the ruins of Roman theaters at Caesarea. (For more information, see DEAD SEA SCROLLS in Volume D.)

Tel Aviv, today's major arts center, has several art schools, artists' colonies, and museums. The Israel Museum in Jerusalem, the country's national museum, has one of the world's finest collections of art objects.

Literature. After 1920, Hebrew was recognized as one of the official languages of

During Passover, Jews in Jerusalem pray at the Western Wall (known to Christians as the Wailing Wall), which has long been a focus of Jewish pilgrimage.

Palestine, which led to the development of literature in modern Hebrew. In 1966 Shmuel Yosef Agnon became the first Israeli to win a Nobel Prize for literature. Other Israeli writers whose works have been widely recognized are Amos Oz, A. B. Yehoshua, Aharon Appelfeld, David Grossman, Shulamit Hareven, Ruth Almog, and Batya Gurworks.

Theater. Modern Hebrew theater began in 1917 with the founding of Habima (The Stage) in Moscow. In 1931 Habima established its permanent home in Tel Aviv and became the national theater of the Jewish community. Today it produces plays on traditional Jewish themes as well as international classics. Israel also has three other major repertory companies, in addition to a children's theater.

Dance. There are six major professional dance companies in Israel, most of them located in Tel Aviv. Those that have performed in Europe and the United States include the Inbal Dance Theater, the Batsheva Dance Company, and the Israel Ballet. Folk dancing is also popular. The hora, a circle dance adopted from Romania, is frequently performed at social gatherings and during national celebrations.

Arab Culture. The Israeli Arab community has developed its music, theater, dance, and art activities, often integrating popular Palestinian Arab folklore traditions with traditional Western art forms. Several Israeli Arabs such as Anton Shammas (who writes in Hebrew) and Emile Habibi have received international recognition.

▶ **GOVERNMENT**

Israel is a multiparty democracy with more than 20 political parties. Supreme authority is held by the Knesset (or parliament), the legislative body. Members are elected to 4-year terms.

The Knesset elects the president, approves the budget, and enacts all laws. It cannot be vetoed by any other authority. The president, elected for a 5-year term as formal head of state, performs mostly honorary functions. The prime minister (elected by popular vote since 1996) heads the government and appoints cabinet members to direct the various ministries, such as defense, finance, and foreign affairs. Government or cabinet ministers are usually members of the Knesset, but they need not be.

▶ **HISTORY**

Although the State of Israel dates only from 1948, the link between the Jewish people and the "Land of Israel" goes back 4,000 years.

About 2000 B.C., Hebrews began to arrive in Canaan, as the area was then called. They became the dominant group in the area around 1200 B.C. and remained so for nearly 1,000 years. The first Kingdom of Israel—ruled successively by kings Saul, David, and Solomon—was divided into Judah and Israel. Both realms were conquered by the Assyrians and Babylonians. The second kingdom lasted from 167 B.C. to 63 B.C. The area was then ruled in turn by the Romans, Byzantines, Arabs, Crusaders, Turks, and British.

David Ben-Gurion and Golda Meir helped establish the modern nation of Israel. Ben-Gurion served as first prime minister (1949–53; 1955–63). Meir served as prime minister from 1969 to 1974.

Zionism and the Holocaust. During the 1800's, the Jewish nationalist movement called Zionism was founded by Theodor Herzl in reaction to the wave of anti-Semitism in Eastern Europe. Many Jews left Eastern Europe for the United States and Western Europe. A few settled in Palestine, the site of ancient Israel (or Zion), where they hoped to rebuild a Jewish homeland. Palestine, then part of the Ottoman (Turkish) Empire, was largely populated by Arabs, many of whom feared the arrival of European Jewish immigrants.

During World War I (1914–18), the British defeated the Turks and took over Palestine as a mandate (1920–48) under the League of Nations. During this period, the Jewish population in Palestine increased from about 10 to 30 percent. As a result, the Palestinian Arab majority increased its opposition to Zionism, leading to frequent battles between Arabs, Jews, and the British authorities.

As a result of the Holocaust in Europe during World War II (1939–45), in which some 6 million Jews were systematically murdered, Jewish support for the Zionist movement greatly increased. By the end of the war, many Jews remaining in Europe sought to join the growing Jewish community in Palestine. For more information, see the articles ZIONISM in Volume W-X-Y-Z and HOLOCAUST in Volume H.

Independence and War. In 1947, Great Britain brought the dispute between Palestinian Arabs and Jews before the United Nations, which approved a plan to divide the country into independent Jewish and Arab states and an international zone to include Jerusalem. The Jews accepted the plan, but the Arabs rejected it, resulting in a civil war.

On May 14, 1948, David Ben-Gurion, Israel's first prime minister, declared the independence of the State of Israel. Within hours, the armies of six neighboring Arab countries attacked the new Jewish state. After seven months, the fighting ended with a victory for the Israelis, who called the struggle their War of Independence. The war resulted in the flight of over 700,000 Arabs from their homes and land. (For more information on the creation of the State of Israel, see the articles BEN-GURION, DAVID in Volume B and PALESTINE in Volume P).

Armistice agreements were signed in 1949 between Israel, Egypt, Lebanon, Jordan, and Syria. But hostilities continued, caused by differences over the return of the Arab refugees, borders between Israel and its neighbors, and the future status of Jerusalem. These disputes led to a series of wars between Israel and the Arab states in the next decades.

The 1956 and 1967 Wars. In 1956, Egypt nationalized the Suez Canal. This action led to war with Great Britain, France, and Israel. The three countries invaded Egypt, with Israel occupying the Sinai Peninsula and the Gaza Strip. After the intervention of the United Nations, the three nations withdrew.

An Israeli soldier checks a Palestinian's identification card in Jerusalem. Half a century of hostilities between Arabs and Israelis have turned Israel into an armed state.

In May 1967, Egypt mobilized its forces near Israel's southern border and closed the Gulf of Aqaba to Israeli ships, threatening Israel's trade. On June 5, Israel attacked Egypt, which was allied with Jordan and Syria. The fighting lasted only six days, and the Arab forces were defeated. As a result of the war, Israel conquered the Sinai Peninsula, the Gaza Strip, the Golan Heights of Syria, and the West Bank of the Jordan River, including Jordanian East Jerusalem.

The 1973 War. On October 6, 1973—while both Jews and Arabs were observing religious holidays—the fourth Arab-Israeli war began with two simultaneous attacks against Israel, then led by Prime Minister Golda Meir. Egyptian troops crossed the Suez Canal seeking to recapture the Sinai, while the Syrians attacked Israeli positions to regain the Golan Heights. Eventually the Israelis recovered lost ground and pushed across the Suez Canal into Egypt. Israel later withdrew from the canal and in 1975 returned part of the Sinai to Egypt. (See the biography of Meir in Volume M.)

Efforts Toward Peace. In 1977, Egyptian president Anwar Sadat traveled to Israel, seeking an end to the warfare between the two countries. In 1978, Sadat, Israeli prime minister Menachem Begin, and U.S. president Jimmy Carter met at Camp David, Maryland. A peace treaty was signed in 1979, and Israel gradually withdrew from the Sinai. (See the biographies of Begin, Carter, and Sadat in the appropriate volumes.)

Lebanon and the PLO. In 1982, Israel launched an invasion of Lebanon. Israel's aim was to force Lebanon to sign a peace treaty and to destroy bases held by the Palestine Liberation Organization (PLO). At first the PLO wanted to eliminate Israel and replace it with a Palestinian Arab state. But eventually the PLO recognized Israel and sought instead to establish a separate Palestinian state in the Israeli-occupied West Bank and Gaza Strip. The war in Lebanon was criticized by many Israelis and led, indirectly, to the resignation of Prime Minister Begin in 1983. Israel withdrew most of its forces from Lebanon in 1985.

National Unity Government. In the 1984 elections, neither of the two main political groups—Labor and Likud—was able to form a government, so they agreed to a national unity government, with each party's leader alternating as prime minister. Shimon Peres, the Labor leader, took office first. He was succeeded in 1986 by Likud leader Yitzhak Shamir. In 1987 an *intifada* ("uprising") by Arabs against Israeli rule erupted.

The Peace Process. Elections in 1992 brought the Labor Party to power, headed by a new prime minister, Yitzhak Rabin. In 1993, Rabin and PLO leader Yasir Arafat signed the first in a series of accords providing for Palestinian self-rule in the Gaza Strip and parts of the West Bank. The accord also paved the way for a 1994 peace treaty between Israel and Jordan. Rabin was assassinated in 1995 by a religious right-wing Israeli. The following year, Benjamin Netanyahu of the Likud Party won Israel's first direct elections for prime minister.

Neither Netanyahu nor his successor, Labor Party leader Ehud Barak, could reach an agreement with the PLO, and in late 2000 Palestinian frustration erupted into a new *intifada*. Barak resigned, and 2001 elections brought Likud Party leader Ariel Sharon to power in a landslide victory.

Sharon and his conservative Likud Party were re-elected overwhelmingly in 2003 for having maintained a tough position against the Palestinians. Prospects for peace appeared to improve when the Israeli cabinet endorsed the "road map," a step-by-step plan to end the cycle of violence, proposed by the United States. In the first phase of the plan, the Palestinians were to stop their attacks on Israelis, while Israel was to dismantle all Jewish settlements in the West Bank and Gaza Strip. But violence continued on both sides.

Arafat died late in 2004. The following year, Sharon and the new PLO leader, Mahmoud Abbas, called for a cease-fire. Israel then transferred security control to the Palestinians in selected West Bank towns, including the historic city of Jericho. The evacuation of Gaza began in August 2005. Sharon, who remained committed to the road map, quit the right-wing Likud Party that November, as many of it members had objected to the pullout. He formed the more moderate National Responsibility Party and called for new elections to be held in 2006.

DON PERETZ
Professor Emeritus, SUNY Binghamton

See also PALESTINE.

ISTANBUL

Istanbul is the largest city in Turkey, the country's chief port, and the center of its culture, industry, and commerce. One of the world's most historic cities, it has been known by several names—Byzantium, Constantinople, and, finally, Istanbul. As Constantinople, it was a capital of the Roman and Byzantine empires. In 1453 the city fell to the Ottoman Turks, who made it the capital of their own vast empire and gave it its present name.

Istanbul served as the Ottoman capital for nearly 500 years, until the empire was broken up after World War I (1914–18). When the modern Republic of Turkey emerged in 1923, the capital was transferred to the inland city of Ankara.

The City. Istanbul is the only city in the world located on two continents—Europe and Asia. The original city is situated on a hilly, triangular peninsula in European Turkey. It is bordered by three bodies of water: the Sea of Marmara, the Bosporus, and the Golden Horn. The Sea of Marmara extends to the Dardanelles, a strait that connects it with the Aegean Sea, an arm of the Mediterranean. The Bosporus, another strait, is one of the traditional dividing lines between Europe and Asia. It links the Sea of Marmara with the Black Sea to the north. The Golden Horn is one of the harbors of Istanbul. It separates the old city from the newer part of European Istanbul.

The "new" city includes two major districts—Galata and Beyoglu (or Pera). The old and new cities are connected by the Galata and Atatürk bridges and by a circular highway. Üsküdar and Kadiköy, on the eastern shores of the Bosporus and the Sea of Marmara, are major sections of Asian Istanbul. The Asian

and European parts of the city are linked by modern suspension bridges and by frequent ferry service.

Modern Istanbul, however, extends far beyond these limits to include growing suburbs to the west and north. The municipality of Istanbul, which includes the suburbs, has a population of some 8.9 million.

Most of Istanbul's historical places of interest lie within the old city. On the heights overlooking the Golden Horn and the Sea of Marmara is the Topkapi Sarayi Palace, once the center of the Ottoman government. The building is now a museum with world-famous art and jewel collections. Later sultans lived in magnificent palaces overlooking the Bosporus. One of these, the Dolmabahçe Palace, is also a museum.

One of the city's most famous landmarks is Hagia Sophia (Aya Sofya). Completed in A.D. 537, it is considered the greatest example of Byzantine architecture. Originally a church, Hagia Sophia was transformed into a mosque (a Muslim house of worship) by the Muslim Ottoman Turks when they captured the city.

Above: Istanbul is the only city in the world that straddles two continents—Europe and Asia. The two parts are separated by a narrow strait, the Bosporus.

A man prays in the Kara Ahmed Pasa Mosque in Topkapi Palace. Topkapi was the official residence of the Ottoman sultans from the late 1400's until 1856.

It, too, is now a museum. For more information, see the article BYZANTINE ART AND ARCHITECTURE in Volume B.

Istanbul has hundreds of mosques, many noted for their great beauty. Among these are the Süleymaniye Mosque, built in the 1500's, and the Sultan Ahmed Mosque, dating from the 1600's. The Sultan Ahmed Mosque is better known as the Blue Mosque because of the blue tiles used to decorate its interior.

In addition to its many museums, the city has theaters, a symphony orchestra, an opera, an academy of fine arts, and numerous libraries. The University of Istanbul is the country's largest university. Most of Turkey's daily newspapers are published in Istanbul, which is also the country's book-publishing center. Most of Turkey's writers, artists, and musicians also concentrate their activities here.

Economic Activity. The newer sections of Istanbul are the major industrial areas, which employ increasing numbers of Turks who have moved from the countryside. The city's chief manufactured products include textiles, flour, tobacco products, cement, glass, and soap. The great Covered Bazaar, in the old city, with its thousands of small shops, is still an important shopping area. But larger and more modern shopping centers have developed in the newer parts of the city.

History. Istanbul originated as the Greek city of Byzantium in the 600's B.C. The Roman emperor Constantine I (the Great) founded Constantinople ("city of Constantine") on the site of Byzantium in A.D. 324 and made it the new capital of the Roman Empire. With the division of the empire into two parts in A.D. 395, Constantinople became the capital of the Roman Empire in the East. The collapse of the Western Empire in the next century left Constantinople the capital of the surviving part of the Roman Empire. It then became known as the Byzantine Empire.

During its thousand years as the Byzantine capital, the city was often attacked but was conquered only twice. In 1204, Christian Crusaders from Europe on the way to the Holy Land breached its walls and occupied the city. In 1453 the city fell to the growing power of the Ottoman Turks, led by Sultan Mehmed II (the Conqueror). Under Ottoman rule the city was enhanced by the construction of mosques, palaces, schools, and public libraries, and by the development of new areas of industry and commerce. The city was resettled by people from all over the Ottoman lands—Muslims, Christians, and Jews alike. Ottoman subjects were allowed to organize and govern themselves in their own religiously based communities called *millets*.

As Ottoman power declined in the centuries that followed, Istanbul became a prize sought by other countries, particularly by Russia in the middle and late 1800's. In 1915, during World War I, Allied forces tried unsuccessfully to gain control of the vital straits in order to capture the city.

The Ottoman defeat in the war led to the breakup of the empire and the founding of the Turkish republic in 1923. Although Turkey's political life now revolves around Ankara, Istanbul remains the heart of its economic and cultural life.

STANFORD J. SHAW
University of California, Los Angeles
Author, *The Ottoman Empire
and Modern Turkey*
Reviewed by WILLIAM OCHSENWALD
Virginia Polytechnic Institute and State University

See also BYZANTINE EMPIRE; OTTOMAN EMPIRE.

ITALY

Italy is a nation in southern Europe that consists mainly of a long narrow peninsula, shaped roughly like a boot. It extends from the high mountains of the Alps in the north to the shores of the Mediterranean Sea in the south. Italy occupies all of the peninsula, except for two tiny independent states—San Marino and Vatican City. San Marino, located in the Apennines mountain range, is one of the world's oldest and smallest republics. Vatican City, the seat of government of the Roman Catholic Church, lies within the city of Rome, Italy's capital. Italy's territory also includes numerous islands. The two largest are Sardinia, lying west of the peninsula, and Sicily, just off the "toe" of the boot.

Top: Three friends gather on the island of Sardinia.
Below: Saint Mark's Square is a landmark of the city of Venice. Saint Mark's Cathedral, built in the Byzantine (or Eastern Roman) style, was begun in 1063 and took centuries to complete.

The region that is now Italy has played a central role in the history of European civilization. For some 400 years it was the heart of the ancient Roman Empire. After the empire collapsed in the West in the A.D. 400's, the peninsula was broken up into many competing city-states. The Renaissance, the great rebirth of culture that took place in Europe, began in Italy in the early 1300's. During this era, which lasted until about 1600, art and learning flourished in Italy's northern cities more than anywhere else in Europe. Politically, however, Italy remained a fragmented land until 1861, when most of the present-day nation was united under one flag.

▶ PEOPLE

Before the empire of ancient Rome emerged, several peoples of different origins inhabited the Italian peninsula. Of these, the Etruscans in the west central region were cul-

Ethnic Italians are descended from many ancient peoples. *Clockwise from far left:* A woman in Tuscany carries freshly baked loaves of bread. Three women in Florence relax in front of a newsstand. A fisherman operates in the Puglia region, along the Adriatic coast.

turally the most advanced. Various Italic peoples lived in other parts of the peninsula. The Greeks colonized southern Italy and Sicily during the 700's and 600's B.C.

Eventually the new Roman state absorbed these peoples as well as others who were imported as slaves from throughout the growing empire. After the fall of Rome in A.D. 476, invasions from the north brought Germanic peoples, mainly Ostrogoths and Lombards, into the peninsula. Arabs invaded Sicily in the A.D. 700's, followed by Normans and the Spanish, who also established themselves in the south. In recent history, immigrants from North Africa and the Middle East have added to the ethnic variety.

FACTS and figures

ITALIAN REPUBLIC (Repubblica Italiana) is the official name of the country.
LOCATION: Southern Europe.
AREA: 116,305 sq mi (301,230 km²).
POPULATION: 58,100,000 (estimate).
CAPITAL AND LARGEST CITY: Rome.
MAJOR LANGUAGES: Italian (official), German, French, Slovene.
MAJOR RELIGIOUS GROUP: Roman Catholic.
GOVERNMENT: Republic. **Head of state**—president. **Head of government**—prime minister. **Legislature**—parliament, made up of the Senate and the Chamber of Deputies.
CHIEF PRODUCTS: Agricultural—fruits, vegetables, grapes, potatoes, sugar beets, soybeans, grain, olives, bees, dairy products, fish. **Manufactured**—machinery, iron and steel, chemicals, processed foods, textiles, motor vehicles, clothing, footwear, ceramics. **Mineral**—coal, mercury, zinc, potash, marble, barite, asbestos, pumice.
MONETARY UNIT: Euro (1 euro = 100 cents).

Language

Italian is one of the Romance languages, which are derived from Latin, the language of the Romans. It is spoken by almost all of the population, although in many parts of Italy the people take pride in preserving their distinct regional dialects. In the northwestern corner of Italy one finds French speakers. The northern region of the Alto Adige (South Tirol) has many German-speaking inhabitants. See the article ITALY, LANGUAGE AND LITERATURE OF in this volume.

Religion

Nearly all Italians are Roman Catholics, and Vatican City (an enclave within Rome) is the seat of the Roman Catholic Church. Roman Catholicism was made the official religion of Italy in 1929 under the Lateran pacts with the Vatican. This official status ended in 1985, when revisions to the pacts provided for the separation of church and state. See the article ROMAN CATHOLIC CHURCH in Volume QR.

Small communities of Protestants, Jews, and Muslims together make up about 2 percent of Italy's population.

Education

Schooling is free and required by law for all Italian children from the age of 6 to 15. Cities offer kindergartens and day care schools for younger children and for the children of working parents. Required schooling includes five years of elementary education followed by three years of junior high school.

INDEX TO ITALY POLITICAL MAP

Once a student reaches the secondary-school level, he or she may choose to continue in an academic institution or attend a technical or vocational school.

Graduation from a secondary school qualifies a student for admission to a university. Of Italy's many universities, the oldest is the University of Bologna. Founded in 1088, it is considered the oldest university in Europe.

Libraries and Museums

Italy has two national libraries, one in Florence and the other in Rome. Both cities also feature hundreds of historic buildings and museums filled with some of the world's most renowned works of arts. For more information, see the articles on Florence and Rome in the appropriate volumes.

Food and Drink

In Italy breakfast is a simple meal, often consisting of a hard roll, jam, and a mixture of coffee and hot milk (*caffelatte*). The main meal, eaten in the early afternoon, usually begins with pasta, frequently served with a tomato-based sauce or a thick soup and bread. A second course may consist of either meat or fish with a cooked vegetable. Olive oil is used for salads and, in the south, also for cooking. Dessert usually includes whatever fruit is in season, but on special occasions pastry may be substituted. After the meal, a small cup of strong coffee (*espresso*) is often served.

The diet is somewhat more varied in the north than in the south. In Milan, *risotto* (a rice dish) is often preferred to pasta, while in rural areas of the region of Venetia, *polenta* (made from corn meal) is a favorite.

The evening supper is lighter than the midday meal and often begins with broth instead of pasta. Many Italians enjoy wine with their meals. On Sundays in summer many people go out for a dish of ice cream, called gelato.

Sports and Recreation

Italians are enthusiastic sports fans. Vast throngs crowd the stadiums on Sundays for professional football (soccer) matches. Basketball has gained increasing popularity. The game of boccie (lawn bowling) is another favorite. Horseback riding, fencing, swimming, tennis, and skiing are other sports at which Italians excel. Bicycle and automobile racing are also quite popular.

The Piazza del Campo in Siena is home to the *Palio*, an annual horse racing event in which riders representing various city districts compete.

▶ LAND

Italy is bordered by France on the northwest, Switzerland and Austria on the north, and Slovenia on the northeast.

Land Regions

Italy is a mountainous land, with only limited areas of plains. On the north, the great range of the Alps stands like a fortress wall. The Alps include the highest mountains in western Europe. Among them are Mont Blanc (called Monte Bianco in Italy), the Monte Rosa group, and the Matterhorn (Monte Cervino), which Italy shares with France and Switzerland. Monte Bianco de Courmayeur, a secondary peak of Mont Blanc, is the highest point entirely within Italy. It rises 15,577 feet (4,748 meters).

South of the Alps is the valley of the Po River, Italy's largest and most fertile plain.

Sicily, the more southerly of Italy's two large islands, is situated off the "toe" of Italy's boot, in the Mediterranean Sea.

This northern heartland contains the cities of Milan, Turin, Genoa, and Bologna. Smaller areas of plains are found in central Italy, which includes such major cities as Florence and Rome.

In the region of Liguria in the northwest begins a mountain chain called the Apennines, which extends like a backbone down the length of the peninsula to the tip of the "boot." The Apennines bypass the "heel" of the boot, which makes up the generally level plains of the Apulia region in the southwest.

The southern Italian mainland is dominated by the great port city of Naples, from which the active volcano of Vesuvius can be seen. The nearby islands of Sardinia and Sicily are mountainous. Sicily has the highest active volcano in Europe—Mount Etna.

Rivers, Lakes, and Coastal Waters

The long coastline of the Italian peninsula is washed by several arms of the Mediterranean Sea—the Adriatic and Ionian seas in the east and the Tyrrhenian and Ligurian seas in the west.

The Po, Italy's longest and most important river, runs a length of 405 miles (652 kilometers). Rising in the western Alps in the region of Piedmont, it crosses the northern plain eastward, emptying into the Adriatic Sea. The Arno River, in central Italy, flows westward through the city of Florence, before emptying into the Ligurian Sea. The Tiber River flows in a southwesterly direction through Rome, before it empties into the Tyrrhenian Sea.

Northern Italy has a number of spectacularly beautiful lakes, such as Maggiore, Como, and Garda. These resort areas are popular tourist destinations.

Climate

Italy has a generally moderate climate. The Po River valley has damp, warm summers, fairly cold winters with occasional snowfall, and considerable rainfall. In the south and on the islands, winters are cool and rainy and summers hot and dry. The mountainous regions on the mainland have the severest winter weather. The south is subject to severe earthquakes.

Lake Como is one of several spectacular resort areas in the Alpine region of northern Italy, near the Switzerland border.

Italy has a strong and diverse economy. *Clockwise from far left:* A runway model shows off the latest fashions in Milan. Gold jewelry is displayed for the tourists along the Pontevecchio (Old Bridge) in Florence. Hoods for Ferrari automobiles come off a Fiat assembly line.

Natural Resources

The rich soil of the Po Valley makes it the country's most important agricultural region, while the seas surrounding the Italian peninsula abound in a variety of fish. But Italy otherwise has limited resources. Coal is obtained from Sardinia, and modest amounts of petroleum are found in the Po Valley, Sicily, and other regions. Significant amounts of natural gas are also found. But Italy must import fuel to meet most of its industrial needs. Only about 20 percent of Italy's electricity is obtained from hydroelectric power plants, located mainly in the Alps and Apennines.

▶ ECONOMY

In 1951, Italy became one of the founding members of the European Community, an economic union of western European nations now known as the European Union (EU). Beginning in the late 1950's an economic "miracle" transformed Italy, helped in part by aid from the United States.

By the 1970's, Italy had become one of the seven leading industrial powers of the non-Communist world. By the early 1990's its gross national product (the total value of its goods and services) rivaled that of the United Kingdom.

Services

Italy's service industries employ nearly two-thirds of its workforce, from bankers and real estate brokers to teachers and government officials. The largest segment is made up of businesses (such as hotels and restaurants) that support tourism, Italy's single most important industry.

Manufacturing

The industrial sector of Italy's economy employs nearly one-third of Italy's workforce. Principal industries involve the manufacture of machinery, steel, chemicals, processed foods, textiles, motor vehicles, clothing, footwear, and ceramics. Most manufacturing is concentrated in the north, especially around Turin, Milan, and Genoa.

Agriculture

Less than 30 percent of Italy's land is used for farming. Most farms are small and individually owned. The chief crops are fruits and vegetables, especially tomatoes, olives, and grapes. Italy is one of the world's leading wine producers, and vineyards cover many country hillsides. Potatoes, sugar beets, soybeans, and wheat and other grains are grown. Cattle are raised for meat and milk, mainly in the north.

Foreign Trade

Italy's leading trading partners are Germany, France, the United States, the United Kingdom, Spain, the Netherlands, and Belgium. Imported goods include engineering products, chemicals, transportation equipment, fuels, and minerals. Major exports include textiles and clothing, machinery, motor vehicles, chemicals, and foods and beverages.

Transportation

Italy has about 12,100 miles (19,500 kilometers) of railways, and a number of high-speed trains connect Rome and Milan with other major European cities. The country also maintains about 480,000 miles (773,000 kilometers) of highway. A network of superhighways called the *autostrade* runs the length of the country.

Italy supports more than a dozen major ports and harbors. Genoa, Trieste, and Augusta are among the largest. The country has seven international airports. The busiest is the Rome Leonardo da Vinci Airport in nearby Fiumicino. The national airline is Alitalia.

Communication

More than 350 television stations and 4,700 radio stations broadcast throughout Italy. Of the 80 million telephones that are registered, two-thirds are cellular. Italy has 20 million Internet users. More than a dozen daily newspapers are circulated. *Corriere della Sera*, published in Milan, and *La Repubblica*, published in Rome, have the widest readerships.

▶ **MAJOR CITIES**

Nearly three-quarters of Italy's population lives in cities or large towns, especially in the north. Southern Italy and the islands generally have a more rural atmosphere, although there are some major cities, such as Naples and Bari on the mainland and Palermo on the island of Sicily.

Rome, the capital and largest city of Italy, is situated on the Tiber River in central Italy, about 16 miles (26 kilometers) from the coast of the Tyrrhenian Sea. It has a population of about 2.5 million (not including Vatican City) and is the capital of the Lazio region. Once

The Spanish Steps, a famous landmark in Rome, lead up to the Trinità dei Monti church. Rome is the capital and largest city of Italy.

the center of western civilization, Rome is still graced by many architectural treasures from the past. For more information, see the article ROME in Volume QR.

Milan, Italy's second largest city, is the capital of the region of Lombardy and the commercial and financial heart of northern Italy. It has a population of about 1.2 million. A major industrial center, Milan produces textiles, chemicals, and motor vehicles. It is also a world center of style and high fashion. The city's most popular attractions include La Scala opera house and the Milan Cathedral, an elaborate example of Gothic architecture.

Mount Vesuvius overlooks the Bay of Naples and the city of Naples—Italy's third largest city. Vesuvius, a volcano, buried the ancient city of Pompeii in ash in A.D. 79.

Naples, the country's third largest city, is the capital of the region of Campania. A major seaport, it is situated on the picturesque Bay of Naples in south central Italy. Naples was founded in the 600's B.C. by Greek colonists, who called it Neapolis ("new city").

Florence, the capital of the region of Tuscany, lies on the Arno River in north central Italy. Many of its famous buildings, including the Palazzo della Signoria (the city hall), the Uffizi and Pitti art galleries, and the cathedral of Florence, date from the Renaissance period. See the article FLORENCE in Volume F.

Genoa, located on the Gulf of Genoa, is Italy's chief seaport and the capital of the region of Liguria. Genoa reached the height of its power and prosperity as an independent city-state in the 1200's, when it controlled a large empire stretching from the Mediterranean to the Black Sea. See the article GENOA in Volume G.

Venice, known for its canals and grand old palaces, is one of the world's most beautiful and unusual cities. It is the capital of Italy's Veneto region. Built on a lagoon, it lies astride some one hundred small islands that are linked by numerous bridges. From the Middle Ages until early modern times, Venice was a wealthy commercial city-state that dominated trade with the East. See the article VENICE in Volume UV.

Turin, the chief city of the Piedmont region, lies on the left bank of the Po River. An industrial city, it is the home of the giant Fiat automobile works. Turin was the capital of the former Kingdom of Sardinia, whose rulers, the House of Savoy, later served as kings of a unified Italy.

▶ **CULTURAL HERITAGE**

Once the center of Western civilization, Italy has made many lasting cultural contributions to Western art forms, languages, and scientific knowledge.

The Arts

Italy's impact on architecture, painting, and sculpture are incomparable. Art of the late Middle Ages and the Renaissance is dominated by the remarkable talents of Italian artists such as Giotto, Leonardo da Vinci, Michelangelo, Titian, Botticelli, and Raphael. Italians have contributed to modern art as well. Exhibitions by contemporary artists are held regularly. For more information, see the articles ITALY, ART AND ARCHITECTURE OF and RENAISSANCE ART AND ARCHITECTURE and biographies of individual artists in the appropriate volumes.

The Birth of Venus was a masterpiece of Italian Renaissance artist Sandro Botticelli. The painting was commissioned in the 1480's by the Medici, the ruling family of Florence and great patrons of the arts.

Literature

Italians have created great works of literature. During the early Renaissance, the modern Italian language was molded out of the local Tuscan dialect by three brilliant writers in Florence—Dante Alighieri, who wrote the *Divine Comedy*, one of the world's poetic masterpieces; Francesco Petrarch, a writer of sonnets; and Giovanni Boccaccio, author of the *Decameron*, a collection of witty tales. In modern times, the playwright Luigi Pirandello became the first Italian to win a Nobel Prize for literature, in 1934. Salvatore Quasimodo received the Nobel Prize in 1959 for his poems. See the article ITALY, LANGUAGE AND LITERATURE OF in this volume.

Music

Italy has been called the birthplace of music. Some of the greatest music for the church was written there during the Middle Ages and the Renaissance. The first operas were composed in Italy in the 1600's. Today every large city has its own opera house, the most famous being Milan's La Scala and Naples' San Carlo. Most Italians know by heart the melodies and arias of favorite operas by such composers as Giuseppe Verdi and Giacomo Puccini. See the articles ITALY, MUSIC OF; OPERA; RENAISSANCE MUSIC; and biographies of individual composers in the appropriate volumes.

Ruins of the Colosseum still stand in Rome. The largest amphitheater in the Roman Empire, it was completed in A.D. 80 and held 50,000 spectators.

Science

Italy has made significant contributions to the advancement of science. The most famous Italian scientist, Galileo Galilei, lived and worked during the late Renaissance. He was among the first scientists to understand that the sun, not the Earth, was the central body around which the planets revolve.

In modern times, Italy has produced two great physicists. Guglielmo Marconi, the inventor of radio, received the Nobel Prize for physics in 1909. Enrico Fermi received the Nobel Prize in 1938 for his work in nuclear physics, which began the Atomic Age. (See the biographies of Galileo, Fermi, and Marconi in the appropriate volumes.)

▶ GOVERNMENT

Italy has been a republic since 1946, when the monarchy was abolished. Its present constitution went into effect in 1948. The country is divided into twenty political regions, which are further subdivided into provinces.

Italy's legislature is called the parliament (Parlamento). It is made up of two houses, the Senate (Senato della Repubblica) and Chamber of Deputies (Camera dei Deputati), and its members are all elected to 5-year terms. Some half dozen major political parties and a number of smaller ones are represented in parliament. Whenever a government fails to command a majority or a coalition majority, it must resign and a new one must be formed.

The parliament elects the president of the republic, who serves as head of state for a term of seven years. (Former presidents then become senators for life.) But executive power is held by the Council of Ministers, or cabinet. It is headed by a prime minister (known as the president of the Council of Ministers). The prime minister is appointed by the president and confirmed by the parliament. Council members are nominated by the prime minister and approved by the president.

▶ HISTORY

Archaeological excavations show that agricultural settlements existed around Sicily as early as 5000 B.C. By 700 B.C., several distinct peoples—including the Ligurians, Sabines, and Etruscans—were well established on the

Italian peninsula. The expulsion of Etruscan kings from Rome in 509 B.C. marked the establishment of the Republic of Rome.

Ancient Rome

Through alliances and conquest, Romans gradually acquired control over all of the Italian peninsula. Eventually they built an empire that included much of Europe, northern Africa, and western Asia. The Roman Empire in the West finally collapsed in the A.D. 400's, after repeated invasions of Germanic peoples from the north. Imperial power passed to the Eastern Roman (or Byzantine) Empire, centered in Constantinople (modern Istanbul). Italy remained chiefly the center of the Roman Catholic faith. See the articles ROME, ANCIENT and BYZANTINE EMPIRE in the appropriate volumes.

The Middle Ages

While the Byzantine Empire continued to rule southern Italy, central and northern Italy suffered continued invasions. In the A.D. 500's, the Lombards, a Germanic tribe, advanced from the north and took power in central Italy. Resistance to the Lombards came mainly from the Christian popes of the Roman Catholic Church, who would later establish political and military, as well as spiritual, control in the area.

By invitation of the popes, the Franks, another Germanic tribe, descended to end the rule of the Lombards in Italy. In 756, after twice defeating the Lombards, the Frankish king Pepin III (the Short) awarded land to Pope Stephen II, with which he established the Papal States. In 774, Pepin's son Charlemagne ended Lombard rule in Italy completely. In reward for his services, and to extend the authority of the church in Europe, Pope Leo III crowned Charlemagne emperor of the Romans on Christmas Day, 800. (See the biography of Charlemagne in Volume C.)

Meanwhile in the 800's, Muslim Arabs from North Africa and the Middle East, called the Saracens, invaded Sicily. They maintained control until the Normans invaded in the 1000's. The Normans gradually expanded their power to the Italian coast, and in 1130 they united the southern half of the peninsula with Sicily.

The Holy Roman Empire. In the 900's, the German king Otto I (the Great) sought to recreate Charlemagne's empire. Like Charlemagne before him, Otto came to the aid of a pope, John XII, who then crowned him emperor in 962. But future emperors and popes quarreled for many years over religious and political issues.

The struggle for imperial rule was illustrated by a famous feud between two families—the Guelphs (or Welfs of Saxony), who were allied with the popes against the Ghibellines, who supported the rule of the Hohenstaufen dynasty of Swabia. But by the 1200's, the Holy Roman emperors had nevertheless lost control over most of their landholdings in northern Italy. (See the article on the Holy Roman Empire in Volume H.)

The City-States. By the 1000's, far-reaching changes had begun to take place in Italy, as cities in the north grew wealthy from a revival of commerce. Genoa and Venice became sea powers, controlling trade with Asia, while a new class of merchants and bankers emerged in the inland cities of Milan, Cremona, Pavia, Florence, and Siena. These cities became independent city-states with their own form of government, headed by elected councils. Some became large and powerful by conquering their neighbors. Florence eventually controlled all of Tuscany, Milan ruled much of Lombardy, and Venice all of Venetia. In the south, the Spanish king of Aragon took control over Sicily in 1282.

The Renaissance. By the early 1300's, people in the city-states had developed a renewed interest in the classical works of art and literature that had survived from the days of ancient Greece and Rome. Merchants, bankers, and other civic leaders formed governments based on economic interests. The most prosperous families—among them the Medici in Florence, the Visconti (followed by the Sforza) in Milan, and the Este in Ferrara—patronized local artists and scholars, which gave rise to a new birth of learning, called the Renaissance. (See the articles on the Medici and the Renaissance in the appropriate volumes.)

Eventually the elective form of city-state government in many of the northern and central cities was replaced by duchies, governed by dukes, while the popes continued to rule the Papal States. By the mid-1500's, Philip II of Spain had gained control over most of Italy.

Italian Decline

In the early 1500's, Italy experienced a period of economic decline. After the voyages of Christopher Columbus opened up trade to the Americas, the Mediterranean Sea ceased to be the main avenue of commerce, and the Italian states lost much of their sea trade to other countries in Europe that bordered the Atlantic Ocean.

At the same time, more powerful European nations treated Italian territories as pawns in their struggle for supremacy. Spain remained the dominant power on the Italian peninsula until control shifted to Austria in the early 1700's.

When the French Revolution broke out in 1789, some Italians became aware of their own need for political change. But in 1796 the French general Napoleon Bonaparte invaded Italy as a first step in his attempt to conquer Europe. He brought much of the north under French control and gave other regions, including Naples and Tuscany, to members of his family to rule.

Napoleon was finally defeated in 1815, and the nations of Europe met at the Congress of Vienna (1814–15) to restore the balance of power on the continent. Various parts of Italy were returned to rulers the French had displaced, but these divisions would not survive the century. (See the biography of Napoleon I in Volume N.)

Unification: 1815–70

Over time, the feeling of nationalism unleashed by the French Revolution resulted in a movement for national unity, called the *Risorgimento*. This unification movement had three great leaders. The first was Giuseppe Mazzini, who organized a group called Young Italy in the 1830's. Mazzini's goal was to establish an Italian republic. A second leader, Giuseppe Garibaldi, was one of Mazzini's followers. He became a military hero of the republican movement. The third architect of unification was Camille Benso, Count di Cavour, who was prime minister of the Kingdom of Sardinia, ruled by the House of Savoy, that also contained Piedmont, Savoy, and Genoa. Cavour favored creating a constitutional monarchy.

In 1860, in his quest to form an Italian republic, Giuseppe Garibaldi and his army of Redshirts seized Naples and Sicily from Spain.

Cavour skillfully won the assistance of the French emperor Napoleon III in a successful war against Austria in 1859. As a result, the Kingdom of Sardinia annexed Lombardy and parts of central Italy. Then in 1860, Garibaldi led a force of a thousand men—known as the Redshirts—in a daring and successful invasion of Sicily and Naples, then ruled by Spain. Collectively known as the Kingdom of the Two Sicilies, Sicily and Naples were also brought under the rule of the House of Savoy. At the same time, Cavour dispatched an army from Piedmont to seize the eastern half of the Papal States.

In 1861 the new Kingdom of Italy was proclaimed in Turin, with Victor Emmanuel II of

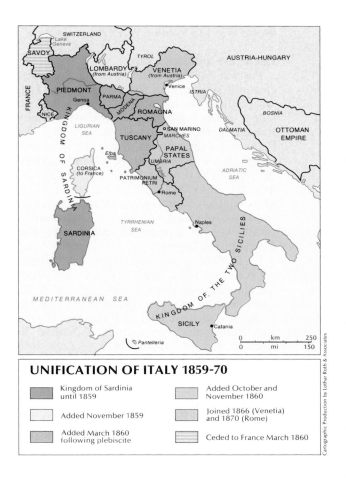

UNIFICATION OF ITALY 1859-70

- Kingdom of Sardinia until 1859
- Added November 1859
- Added March 1860 following plebiscite
- Added October and November 1860
- Joined 1866 (Venetia) and 1870 (Rome)
- Ceded to France March 1860

the House of Savoy as its constitutional monarch. In 1866, in the wake of a new war with Austria, Italy annexed Venetia. Finally, in 1870, Italy took over papal Rome and moved the new Italian capital to that city. (See the biographies of Garibaldi, Mazzini, and Victor Emmanuel in the appropriate volumes.)

Nation Building and World War I

Building an Italian nation proved a difficult task. Many Italians were unable to read or write, and differences caused friction between northerners and southerners. After 1900, however, the situation improved. Industry took hold in the northwest, while in the south, millions immigrated to the United States, relieving poverty and overcrowding.

This progress, however, was interrupted in 1915, when the Italians entered World War I on the side of the Allies against the Central Powers. Italy's leaders hoped to benefit by capturing the Italian-speaking cities of Trentino and Trieste from Austria-Hungary. Instead, the country was drawn into a long, costly, and unpopular war. (See the article on World War I in Volume WXYZ.)

Fascist Era and World War II

Postwar frustrations, combined with a new electoral system, changed the nature of Italian politics. The old liberal leaders could no longer control parliament. Moreover, many Italians feared that the strong new Socialist Party might seize power during the economic unrest of the postwar years. All these developments helped undermine Italy's fragile democracy. In 1922, King Victor Emmanuel III gave control of the government to Benito Mussolini, the leader of the new Fascist Party, whose violent squads of Blackshirts had gained public support.

By 1926, Mussolini had imposed a dictatorship on Italy. Some of his policies were popular. He outlawed labor strikes; negotiated the Lateran pacts with the Vatican in 1929, which ended years of confrontation between church and state; and conquered Ethiopia in 1935–36. But Mussolini's later alliance with Nazi Germany was not popular, and Italy's participation (1940–45) in World War II as an Axis Power left the country devastated. (See the biography of Mussolini and the articles on fascism and World War II in the appropriate volumes.)

Dictator Benito Mussolini, the founder of fascism, rose to power in Italy during the bleak economic decade that followed World War I (1914–18).

A New Republic

Italy's defeat in the war brought an end not only to fascism in Italy but to the monarchy as well. In an election in 1946, in which women voted for the first time, Italians approved a republic, and a new constitution went into effect in 1948. Italy recovered economically with aid from the United States.

The moderately conservative Christian Democratic Party emerged as the strongest political party after the war. For some 45 years it dominated every government, usually in alliance with small parties of the political center.

Recent History. In the early 1990's, financial scandals led to the collapse of the old ruling parties, and voters demanded major political reforms. In 1994 a right-wing alliance, under the leadership of media mogul Silvio Berlusconi, came to power. But the coalition soon fell apart, and an interim government took office. Elections in 1996 were marked by a victory for the left, but budget quarrels in 1998 again brought down the government. In 2001, after two additional but brief changes in power, Berlusconi was returned as premier as head of a new coalition, the House of Liberties and Freedom Alliance (now the Center-Right Freedom House Coalition).

CHARLES F. DELZELL
Author, *Italy in the Twentieth Century*
Reviewed by JEREMY BLACK
Author, *Italy and the Grand Tour*

ITALY, ART AND ARCHITECTURE OF

The artistic traditions of Italy have their origins in the ancient Roman Empire, which was centered in Rome and the Italian peninsula. The classical tradition of ancient Greece and Rome has been an ever-present element in Italian art throughout its history. Its two greatest and most influential periods—Renaissance and Baroque—relied heavily on the style and ideals of classical art. For centuries, artists have traveled to Italy to study both monuments from Roman times and the work of the great Italian masters of the Renaissance and Baroque periods.

Artists visiting Italy also enjoyed painting and drawing the picturesque countryside and cities bathed in brilliant Mediterranean sunlight. Some artists specialized in Italianate subjects.

Before its unification in 1871, Italy was made up of many small independent city-states. The most powerful were Venice, Florence, Naples, and the Papal States centered in Rome. Different styles of art and architecture developed in each city. The major patrons of art in the cities were their wealthy ruling families. These included the Medici in Florence, the Gonzagas in Mantua, and the Farnese and Barberini in Rome. The most influential art patrons in all of Italy were the ambitious popes of the Roman Catholic Church in Rome. They commissioned the leading architects and artists of the day to build and decorate their churches and palaces.

▶MIDDLE AGES (300–1400)

The art of Italy during the Middle Ages can be divided into three periods: Early Christian, Romanesque, and Gothic.

Early Christian Art

In the A.D. 300's, the Roman Empire under Emperor Constantine the Great adopted Christianity as its official religion. Constantine moved the imperial capital to Byzantium and called it Constantinople (now Istanbul, Turkey). This move hastened the decline of Rome as an important center and widened the split between the eastern and western halves of the empire. The eastern half, known as the Byzantine Empire, became very powerful. The western half suffered destruction at the hands of invading Germanic tribes, who gradually took over the region now known as Italy.

During this period, two artistic trends existed side by side and gradually influenced each other. Artists working within the classical tradition, especially those of the court of Constantinople, created realistic, lifelike images. In contrast, artists of the distant provinces of the eastern Roman Empire, and later of the invading Germanic tribes, produced art that was decorative and that stressed the inner meaning of life. When these two traditions merged, the classical image became simplified. Figures were drawn using strong outlines and appeared flat and stiff. Decorative patterns were added to ornament the image.

This change in style reflects a fundamental change in attitude toward the world. During the classical age, people and their lives on

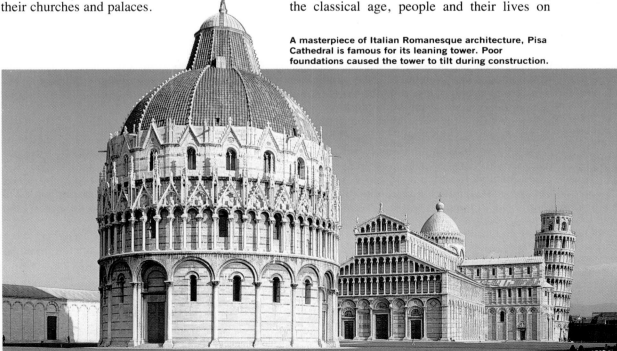

A masterpiece of Italian Romanesque architecture, Pisa Cathedral is famous for its leaning tower. Poor foundations caused the tower to tilt during construction.

The church of St. Sabina was built in Rome about A.D. 425, during the early Christian period. It has a wide central section, or nave, and rows of marble columns.

earth had been of central importance. The early Christian period is marked by an increased interest in the spiritual life. The emphasis on spirituality formed the basis for the art of the Middle Ages and reached its peak during the Romanesque period.

Architecture. When Christianity became the official religion, a church-building campaign was started by Emperor Constantine. Early Christian churches were usually built using either the **basilican** or the **central** plan. The basilican plan had been used for palaces and law courts in ancient Rome and became the model for most churches built in Italy after A.D. 400. A basilican church is shaped like a rectangle. The wide section in the center, called the nave, is separated from aisles on both sides by rows of columns. At one end of the rectangle is a rounded section called the apse, where the altar is located. One of the finest early Christian basilican churches is the church of St. Sabina, which was built in Rome about 425. The marble columns used in this church were taken from the ruins of an ancient temple.

The central plan was developed from the design of Roman baths and tombs. It became especially popular in the eastern Roman Empire. In Italy it was most commonly used in cities, such as Ravenna and Venice, that were in close contact with the Byzantine Empire. In central plan churches, all sections were built around a central dome. A fine example is the Santo Stefano Rotondo (468–83), in Rome.

Although the exteriors of early Christian churches were plain, the interiors were elegant and colorful. The flat wooden ceilings were brightly painted, and the walls were decorated with magnificent mosaics and frescoes that were instructive as well as beautiful.

Mosaics, Paintings, and Sculpture. Mosaics are pictures made by pressing tiny pieces of colored glass or stone into cement. The art of mosaic began in the East. Some of the period's finest mosaics were made in the 500's for the church of San Vitale in Ravenna. They feature portraits of the Emperor Justinian and his court.

Frescoes—paintings on wet plaster—were another type of wall decoration. Frescoes were much less costly than mosaics. They had been used by ancient Romans on the walls of homes and catacombs (burial chapels). The fresco technique was especially popular in Italy, particularly around Rome.

Most early Christian sculpture was made for tombs. Many tombs were decorated with crowded scenes from the Bible. One of the most beautiful is the Tomb of Theodoric (about 520), in Ravenna.

Romanesque Period

With the decline of Rome, a new civilization developed in the empire's northern territories, ruled by the Frankish kings. The first distinct style to emerge by the late 700's was the Romanesque. The subject matter and style of all the arts during this period focused on the spiritual world.

Architects of the Romanesque period were inspired by the remains of ancient Roman buildings that survived throughout the empire.

Romanesque churches were based on the basilican plan of early Christian churches. Architects of northern Italy were probably the first to use rounded stone arches instead of wood in the ceiling of the nave. Thick walls, pierced by only small window openings, were needed to support the heavy stone. This gave Romanesque churches a heavy, solid look.

Another feature that Italian architects added to the Romanesque style was a separate bell tower (campanile) that was built beside the main church. Two examples are the church of Sant' Ambrogio in Milan (begun about 1080) and the cathedral in Pisa with its famous leaning tower (built between 1174 and 1350).

Italian churches during the Romanesque period continued to be decorated with frescoes and mosaics. Saints and other holy figures were portrayed with stiff poses, simplified forms, and staring eyes.

Gothic Period

The Gothic style appeared in Italy during the late 1100's. It came to Italy from France, which at that time was the leader in architecture, sculpture, and manuscript illumination.

Architecture. Gothic cathedrals are high and filled with light. Their soaring walls reach great heights, braced by exterior supports called flying buttresses. The graceful Gothic style contrasts with the heavy, solid look of the Romanesque. The Gothic style never took hold in Italy as it did in France. However, important examples of Gothic architecture can be found in Italy. They include Florence Cathedral, built in the late 1200's, Siena Cathedral, begun before 1260, and Orvieto, begun in 1290. Milan Cathedral, begun in 1386 and completed two centuries later, was designed with the help of French architects. It is one of the largest cathedrals built in Europe during the Middle Ages.

The Venetians, who traded with Islamic countries as well as with countries of northern Europe, combined the Gothic style with Islamic design when decorating their palaces.

Sculpture. A new interest in naturalism (portraying lifelike images) appeared in French Gothic sculpture of the early 1200's. Smiling, lively figures in gracefully draped robes gradually replaced the stiff, stern figures in Romanesque church decoration. Religious subjects continued to dominate, but secular (nonreligious) images appeared with greater frequency.

Italian sculpture showed almost no sign of French Gothic influence until the late 1200's. The change is apparent in the work of Nicola Pisano of Tuscany and his son, Giovanni. Nicola's famous pulpit in the Baptistery at Pisa (1259–60) and Giovanni's carvings on the exterior of Siena Cathedral reintroduced the kind of naturalism found in antique sculpture of the classical period.

Below: Milan Cathedral, built in the Gothic style, is one of the largest churches in Europe. *Right:* Gothic sculptor Nicola Pisano carved this pulpit for the Baptistery of Pisa Cathedral.

Painting. Illuminated manuscripts and stained-glass windows had become important art forms in northern Europe during the Middle Ages. However, painting and mosaic continued to flourish in Italy, as they had since antiquity.

Above: In Giotto's frescoes, holy figures are realistically painted and show human emotion. *Below:* The lavish gold decoration on Simone Martini's *Annunciation* is typical of Sienese art of the 1300's.

The work of one Italian painter, Giotto, marks a dramatic change in Italian painting. His frescoes in the Arena Chapel in Padua, painted in 1305–06, show the extent of his achievement. The figures in the paintings are modeled and shaded rather than merely outlined, and they have the solidity and weight of sculpture. More powerfully than ever before, the figures communicate human emotion through their gestures and facial expressions. Giotto's work looked forward to the painting style of the Renaissance. (A biography of Giotto appears in Volume G.)

Painting on wood panels flourished in Siena and Florence, two rival cities in central Italy. Siena experienced a golden age of art during the 1300's, when it was one of the largest and richest cities in Europe. Sienese painters loved to work with bright colors and gold decoration, and to portray luxurious clothing. Finished paintings were set into richly carved and gilded frames that were capped by pointed Gothic arches.

Among the most innovative Sienese painters were Duccio de Buoninsegna, Simone Martini, and the brothers Pietro and Ambrogio Lorenzetti. The work of these painters incorporated influences from both Byzantine and Gothic art.

Duccio painted a famous altarpiece, called the *Maesta* (1308–11), for Siena Cathedral. The painting, with its expressive figures of the Virgin and Child, was revolutionary for its time. Duccio's pupil, Simone Martini, preferred to work in the International Gothic style of northern Europe. His elegant figures are also emotionally expressive. The Lorenzetti brothers were fresco painters who were skilled at creating the illusion of space in their paintings. Ambrogio's panoramic views of town and countryside in his fresco *The Effects of Good and Bad Government* (1338–40) show his ability to depict large-scale outdoor scenes.

More than half the population of Siena perished in the Black Plague of 1348, and the city never recovered its status. By the late 1300's its rival, Florence, had emerged as the center of the early Renaissance.

▶RENAISSANCE (1400–1600)

The period known as the Renaissance was Italy's Golden Age, during which the country led all of Europe in economic, cultural, and intellectual achievement. *Renaissance* is a French word meaning "rebirth." The period was given this name because there was a rebirth of interest in the learning and arts of the classical age. (An article on the Renaissance appears in Volume R.)

Renaissance scholars broke with the God-centered outlook of the Middle Ages. They focused instead on humans and their world. This movement, called **humanism**, affected all aspects of Renaissance thought.

Renaissance artists sought to return to the ideals of classical Greece and Rome. They often portrayed nonreligious subjects. The human figure dominated Renaissance art. It was often shown nude, as it had been in Greek and Roman art. For the first time, artists studied the human body like scientists. They even dissected corpses to learn more about the body's structure so that they could depict people more convincingly.

Early Renaissance

Florence, the center of the early Renaissance, was ruled by a wealthy and powerful banking family, the Medici. The Medici were generous art patrons and progressive thinkers. Their patronage drew intellectuals and artists from all over Italy to Florence.

Architecture. The Florentine architect Filippo Brunelleschi was the first true Renaissance architect. Inspired by ancient Roman ruins, he introduced classical forms into his own building designs. The dome of the cathedral in Florence is his most celebrated work. Brunelleschi also invented a mathematical method for creating **perspective**, or the appearance of depth, on the flat surface of a painting.

Another important architect of the period was Leon Battista Alberti. A man of many talents, Alberti is best known for his writings on theories of painting, sculpture, and architecture. In creating his building designs, Alberti consulted *De Architectura*, by Vitruvius, the only book on architecture to survive from Roman times.

Sculpture. Italian sculptors were the first to work in the Renaissance style. Lorenzo Ghiberti designed a pair of gilded bronze doors for the Baptistery of Florence Cathedral in 1435. The **reliefs** (raised sculptures) on the doors contain figures that look like classical sculptures.

Another sculptor, Donatello, also studied classical sculpture, as well as human anatomy. He carved the first free-standing statues (those that can be seen from all sides) since ancient times. His bronze *David* (1430–32) and his statue of a solider on horseback, known as *Gattamelata* (1445–50), are realistic and dynamic portraits.

Below: A panel from Ghiberti's bronze doors, designed for the Baptistery of Florence Cathedral. *Right:* Donatello's statue of a soldier, called *Gattamelata.*

In his painting *The Holy Trinity*, Masaccio used perspective to create the illusion of space: The central figures appear to be contained within an arched room.

Painting. Many different painting styles existed in the early Renaissance. The Florentines stressed the importance of drawing in all aspects of art. The art of Florence, therefore, is characterized by graceful lines.

The Florentine master Masaccio established a new direction in painting that lasted for the next 200 years. From his friend Brunelleschi, Masaccio learned how to use perspective to create the illusion of space in his paintings. The sculptural quality of his figures may have been inspired by Donatello, whom he also knew. Masaccio's most famous work is a series of frescoes in the Brancacci Chapel of the church of Santa Maria del Carmine in Florence, painted about 1426. These paintings, which have the realism of Giotto's works, were admired and studied by many later artists, including Michelangelo.

Piero della Francesca continued Masaccio's style. His paintings, with their cool colors, statue-like figures, and simple composition, convey a sense of timelessness and order.

The Dominican friars Fra Angelico and Fra Filippo Lippi painted sensitive depictions of saints and other religious subjects. Their delicate and graceful figures are Gothic in style, but have more solidity.

Antonio Pollaiuolo was one of the first Renaissance artists to paint large-scale scenes from mythology. He often showed nude figures in motion to demonstrate his knowledge of human anatomy. The dynamic movement in his paintings can also be seen in the later work of Sandro Botticelli. Botticelli's elegant portraits, religious paintings, and mythological scenes are typical of the Florentine style of this period.

High Renaissance

After the death of Lorenzo de Medici in 1492, Florence lost much of its power. During the period known as the High Renaissance, Florence was replaced by Rome as a center of culture and learning. Countless artists and architects went to Rome, many to work on projects for popes Julius II and Leo X.

Rome, which contained many surviving works from ancient times, inspired artists to work on a larger scale, to try to recapture the grandeur of the classical period.

Figures in paintings and sculptures were more full-bodied and idealized. Movement and strong human emotion, so important in the Early Renaissance, became less significant. Instead, artists tried to achieve a timeless and quiet serenity that would convey divine perfection. The ideas of the Greek philosopher Plato inspired artists to seek simplicity and balance, harmony and order. Greek and Roman philosophy were combined with Christian beliefs to create a new style.

Leonardo da Vinci. The High Renaissance style of painting first appeared in the work of Leonardo da Vinci. Leonardo was a sculptor, writer, engineer, inventor, musician, and astronomer, as well as a painter. He was revered in his own lifetime as a true "Renaissance man"; that is, someone who developed and used all his talents to full capacity. Leonardo's fresco *The Last Supper* (1495–98) and his portrait *Mona Lisa* (1503–05) are among his most famous works. His technique of using contrasting light and dark areas (called *chiaroscuro*) influenced the development of the High Renaissance style. A biography of Leonardo appears in Volume L.

Bramante, Michelangelo, and Raphael. The ambitious Pope Julius II was fortunate to have in his employment three of the most brilliant artists who ever lived. He hired Donato Bramante to rebuild St. Peter's Basilica, Michelangelo Buonarroti to paint the ceiling of the Sistine Chapel in St. Peter's, and Raphael Sanzio to paint frescoes for the papal apartments in the Vatican Palace. Julius' grand schemes were continued by his successor, Pope Leo X.

Possibly the world's most famous portrait, the *Mona Lisa* is a masterpiece of Renaissance artist Leonardo da Vinci.

Bramante was the first architect of the High Renaissance. His career began in Milan, where he was influenced by Leonardo and by early Christian churches. When he moved to Rome in 1499, his buildings became larger and heavier. His chapel for the church of San Pietro in Rome, known as the Tempietto ("little temple") typifies the basic principles of High Renaissance architecture. The design of the building is based on simple geometric shapes—a rectangle and a circle—that create a sense of harmony and order. Bramante died before he was able to carry out his design for the rebuilding of St. Peter's.

Michelangelo was a sculptor, painter, and architect. His celebrated statue *David* (1501–04) is the Italian Renaissance version of ancient Greek sculptures of athletes. Michelangelo's thorough understanding of human anatomy was unsurpassed. His paintings on the ceiling of the Sistine Chapel, depicting scenes from the Bible, were completed in 1512. They quickly became one of the wonders of the world. Another of Michelangelo's masterpieces is his design for the dome of St. Peter's. The dome dominates the skyline of Rome and has been copied many times over. A biography of Michelangelo appears in Volume M.

Raphael, who was born in Urbino, divided his time between Florence and Rome. The figures in his paintings have an idealized beauty characteristic of the High Renaissance. His frescoes in the Vatican Palace, done between 1509 and 1517, are among his greatest artistic achievements. Raphael also designed ten large tapestries for the Sistine Chapel, depicting the lives of the apostles. The designs were reproduced in engravings and became widely known throughout Europe. Raphael's large studio of assistants and apprentices helped complete many of his projects and continued

Bramante's chapel for the church of San Pietro in Rome is known as the Tempietto ("little temple"), because its design recalls classical Greek and Roman temples.

his style after his untimely death at age 37. A biography of Raphael appears in Volume R.

Other Artists. Another important artist who worked in the style of the High Renaissance was the painter Antonio da Correggio. His greatest work is a fresco, *The Assumption of the Virgin* (1526–30), painted in the domed ceiling of Parma Cathedral. The painting is a masterpiece of perspective, filled with twisting and turning figures who appear to be rising into the heavens. The work looks forward to the baroque style of the next century.

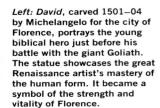

Left: David, carved 1501–04 by Michelangelo for the city of Florence, portrays the young biblical hero just before his battle with the giant Goliath. The statue showcases the great Renaissance artist's mastery of the human form. It became a symbol of the strength and vitality of Florence.

A separate style of painting developed in Venice. The Venetian painters were the first in Italy to work in oil, a medium imported from northern Europe. Other Italian artists used a mixture of oil and egg tempera. While Florentine and Roman artists emphasized line, Venetian artists loved to portray the effects of color and light. They used color and shading rather than lines to define the shapes in their paintings.

Giovanni Bellini, his pupil Giorgione, and Titian were the greatest painters of the Venetian school. These artists took special care in painting the landscapes in the backgrounds of their works. Realistically painted and bathed in mists, the landscapes projected a romantic atmosphere that was to influence later artists.

Late Renaissance and Mannerism

After 1520, some Renaissance artists began to emphasize style over the subject matter of their works. That is, the manner in which a picture was painted or a sculpture was carved became more important than the image it portrayed. These artists were called **mannerists**. Mannerist artists delighted in unusual images. Figures in strange colors and twisted poses were placed in crowded settings. The meaning

Below: Raphael's fresco *The School of Athens* depicts great philosophers and scientists of ancient times, whose works were rediscovered during the Renaissance.

Left: The landscape in the background of *The Tempest*, by the Venetian painter Giorgione, projects a romantic atmosphere. *Right:* Parmigianino's *Madonna with the Long Neck*, with its graceful, elongated figures, is an elegant example of mannerist art.

of a painting's subject would often be intentionally unclear.

Mannerist art reflects the uncertainty of the time. Italy had become a battleground for foreign armies. Much of Rome was destroyed by one of the armies in 1527, and the city lost its powerful position. In addition, the Roman Catholic Church was threatened by the Protestant movement that had begun in northern Europe.

Michelangelo's late work mirrors the questioning mood of the mannerist period. As he grew older, the spiritual nature of his work intensified. A new religious emotionalism can be seen in his painting *The Last Judgment* in the Sistine Chapel and in his later sculpture.

One of the best-known mannerist artists was Francesco Parmigianino. He was much influenced by Correggio and Raphael. His elegant painting of the Virgin and Child known as the *Madonna with the Long Neck*, painted about 1535, is often cited as a typical example of mannerist painting.

Giulio Romano, a pupil of Raphael, was a fresco painter, decorator, and architect who worked in his master's style. His most cele-

brated work was the Palazzo del Te (1526–35), the summer palace of the Duke of Mantua. Giulio designed both the building and its wall decoration. Paintings on the walls of one room, the Sala dei Giganti (hall of the giants), depict a scene from mythology—the rebellion of the Giants against Olympus. The scene surrounds the viewer standing in the room, creating a sensation similar to a modern-day house of horrors in an amusement park.

Other mannerist painters include Rosso Fiorentino and Jacopo Pontormo. Pontormo's pupil, Bronzino, along with Giorgio Vasari, were among the next generation of Florentine mannerists.

▶ 1600'S AND 1700'S

By the end of the 1500's, a new optimism was beginning to replace the uncertainty of the mannerist period. An ambitious rebuilding program was begun to make Rome the most magnificent city on earth. The Roman Catholic Church sought to recover the confidence and faith of the people. Artists received commissions to decorate church interiors with paintings and sculpture that taught church beliefs to the people in a clear and believable way. The mannerist style of confusion and artificiality was replaced by simplicity, clarity, and realism. It was the beginning of a new age, known as the baroque period.

Baroque Period

In general, baroque art and architecture is characterized by a return to the naturalism of the Renaissance, combined with a new element of movement and drama. The vitality of baroque art appeals to the senses. This was the last great period of Italian art.

Architecture and Sculpture. Carlo Maderno was the first architect to work in the baroque

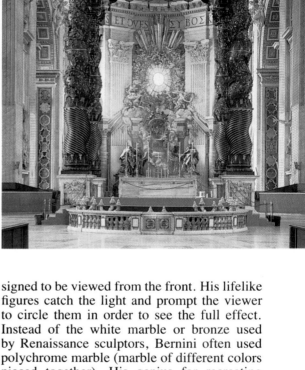

Left: The sculptures of the baroque master Bernini are full of movement and life, as seen in this detail of *Apollo and Daphne.*

Right: Bernini did much of his work for St. Peter's Basilica, in Rome. He designed the bronze canopy over the altar; its twisting columns are characteristic of baroque architecture. In the backgound is Bernini's Throne of St. Peter, with its dramatic sunburst design.

manner and the first to inspire European artists outside Italy to adapt to the new style. In 1607 he completed the facade (front) and nave of St. Peter's.

The greatest of all Italian baroque masters was Giovanni Lorenzo Bernini. A brilliant sculptor, architect, and painter, Bernini was the first to combine all three arts into a single, beautiful whole. No other artist since Michelangelo was held in such high esteem: Bernini was employed by five popes. His most important work was for St. Peter's. For the interior of the church, Bernini designed the Throne of St. Peter, the canopy over the papal altar, and the tomb of Pope Urban VIII. For the exterior, he created the magnificent square, with its stately rows of columns, that welcomes visitors to the church.

Bernini's sculpture was very different from Renaissance statues, which were usually de-signed to be viewed from the front. His lifelike figures catch the light and prompt the viewer to circle them in order to see the full effect. Instead of the white marble or bronze used by Renaissance sculptors, Bernini often used polychrome marble (marble of different colors pieced together). His genius for recreating movement and life in his art can also be seen in the many fountains he designed for Rome. A biography of Bernini appears in Volume B.

Painting. Painting in the 1600's was marked by a return to the values of the Renaissance tradition. The Carracci family in Bologna were instrumental in effecting this change. Their style combined skillful drawing with an emphasis on color. These two elements of painting had remained separate in Renaissance art.

Annibale Carracci and his brother Agostino, together with their cousin Lodovico, shared a

Above: Annibale Carracci's frescoes on the ceiling of the Farnese Palace, Rome, depict mythological scenes.

Below: In *Death of the Virgin* and other paintings, Caravaggio portrayed biblical figures as ordinary people. Theatrical lighting creates a dramatic effect.

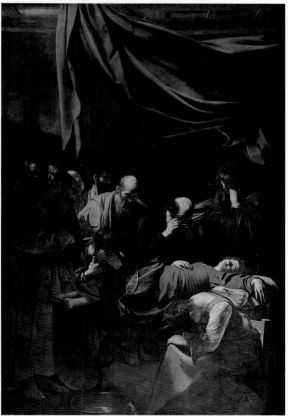

studio. Later they opened a school that taught young apprentices to draw from live models. It was the first time such training had ever been provided. This progressive school produced some of the major figures of Italian painting of the 1600's, including Guido Reni, Domenichino, Lanfranco, and Giovanni Guercino. All these painters worked in the classical style.

Annibale's most important works were produced in Rome between 1595 and 1605. His paintings on the ceiling of the gallery of the Farnese Palace laid the foundation for Italian painting for the next 150 years. Painted in the manner of Raphael and Michelangelo, the paintings depict mythological love scenes from Ovid's *Metamorphosis.* Annibale also made important contributions to the development of landscape painting.

The paintings of Michelangelo Merisi da Caravaggio were as revolutionary as the sculptures of Bernini. In his *Death of the Virgin* (1606), Caravaggio chose to show the Virgin Mary as an ordinary person, with dirty feet and unkempt hair. This portrayal shocked the people of his day, but Caravaggio's brand of realism had enormous influence, as did his use of dramatic lighting. His paintings of fruits and flowers contributed greatly to the development of the kind of painting known as still life. A biography of Caravaggio appears in Volume C.

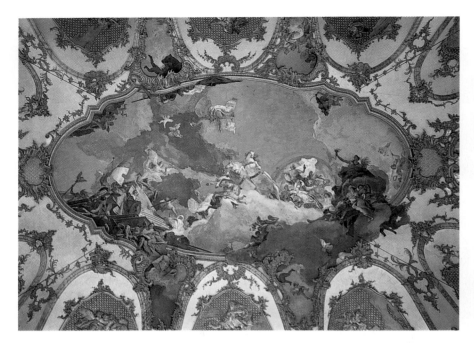

Left: The Venetian painter Tiepolo painted the ceiling of a great hall in the Episcopal Palace, Würzburg, Germany. The paintings, framed by ornate moldings, give the viewer the illusion of looking into the heavens through openings in the ceiling.

Below: Another Venetian painter, known as Canaletto, specialized in views of the canals, gondolas, and buildings of Venice. His paintings, highly detailed and bathed in light, were often sold to the city's many visitors.

Painting in Venice

In the early 1700's, Venice again became an important artistic center. The city was the home of Giambattista Tiepolo, the last great painter of frescoes in the tradition of Raphael and Michelangelo. Tiepolo was a prolific artist whose reputation was as great in Germany and Spain as it was in Italy. He used very light colors that imitated the effects of brilliant daylight and gave his paintings a cheerful optimism. This style of painting is known as **rococo**.

The beauty of Venice attracted tourists from all over Europe. A group of artists known as the *vedutisti*, or view painters, flourished in Venice. They specialized in views—both real and imaginary—of the city, which were sold to tourists. Antonio Canale, called Canaletto, and Francesco Guardi were the most popular and accomplished of these artists.

Left: *The Uncertainty of the Poet*, by the surrealist painter Giorgio de Chirico.
Right: *Unique Forms of Continuity in Space*, by the futurist sculptor Umberto Boccioni.

▶1800'S AND 1900'S

While no longer in the forefront of artistic development in Europe, Italy continued to produce artists of international stature. These included the sculptor Antonio Canova, who worked in the style known as neoclassicism, which tried to imitate classical art.

In the mid-1800's, a group of painters known as the *macchiaioli* (spot painters) emerged in Florence. Like the French impressionists, they painted outdoors and strove to capture the effects of light on figures, objects, and landscape.

At the beginning of the 1900's, Italian artists again led an international movement. The poet and dramatist Filippo Marinetti started a movement called **futurism**. Futurist artists were excited about what the new century would bring, and they wanted to abolish the past. They tried to represent the motion and sound of machinery and modern city life in their paintings and sculpture. Umberto Boccioni and Gino Severini were among the members of the group, which disbanded at the start of World War I (1914–18).

After the war, Carlo Carra, a futurist painter, joined with Giorgio de Chirico to found a movement called *pittura metafisica*. It was part of an international art movement known as **surrealism**. Later, Carra returned to a traditional style based on the old masters. He became associated with Giorgio Morandi, a still-life painter and etcher. Morandi's monochromatic (one-color) studies of bottles have received wide acclaim.

Two important sculptors of the 1900's are Giacomo Manzu and Marino Marini. Manzu created religious sculptures in a refined and elegant style that shows his subject simply and realistically. Marini absorbed a variety of influences, including the sculpture of ancient Greece. The horse and rider is his recurring theme.

As the 1900's drew to a close, Italians continued to contribute to an art scene that was becoming increasingly international. Abstract art (art that does not attempt to represent real objects) was never fully accepted in Italy; the work of Lucio Fontana was an important exception. Most Italians artists have continued to create recognizable images. The works of two leading painters, Sandro Chia and Francesco Clemente, express each artist's very personal vision of life's experiences.

HELEN MULES
Associate Curator of Drawings
Metropolitan Museum of Art

See also BYZANTINE ART AND ARCHITECTURE; GOTHIC ART AND ARCHITECTURE; RENAISSANCE ART AND ARCHITECTURE; ROMANESQUE ART AND ARCHITECTURE; ROME, ART AND ARCHITECTURE OF.

The great Italian poet Dante is pictured with images from his masterpiece, *The Divine Comedy*. In the poem, Dante journeys through Hell and Purgatory to Paradise.

ITALY, LANGUAGE AND LITERATURE OF

Italian, with its romantic and musical sound, has long been a popular language for opera and poetry. The roots of Italian language and literature go back more than 2,000 years—to Latin, the language of the ancient Roman Empire and later the Catholic Church.

▶ ITALIAN LANGUAGE

The classical Latin used by Cicero and Julius Caesar still lives in the sounds and forms of modern Italian. All languages change over time, however, and through the centuries Italian became a distinct language. The Latin that was spoken by the common people of the Roman Empire slowly became different from the classical Latin used in schools and government. When the power of Rome declined in the A.D. 400's, spoken Latin became more important than the classical, written form of the language.

Over the next 600 years, spoken Latin evolved into the Italian language. Actually, it became not one language but many different **dialects**, or regional kinds of speech. Each dialect has slightly different words and rules of grammar and pronunciation. Sometimes a person speaking a dialect from one part of Italy cannot understand the dialect from another part of the country.

Educated people continued to use classical Latin for writing, so that people in different places could understand each other. The first time that Italian was written in an official document was in A.D. 960. Such use of Italian in writing was rare, however. Furthermore, there was no standard for writing correct Italian that everyone would understand.

This situation began to change in the 1200's, when different Italian dialects became popular for writing literature, especially poetry. Later, in the 1300's, three great Italian poets wrote in the dialect of their native city, Florence. The works of these poets—Dante,

Petrarch, and Boccaccio—were greatly respected throughout Italy. As a result, the Florentine dialect became the basis for most future Italian literature. Eventually, this literary language became the standard for modern spoken Italian.

▶ ITALIAN LITERATURE

Italian literature holds a special place among the literatures of the world. In it are found many of the original ideas and movements that shaped the culture of modern Europe. This is especially true of the movement called the Renaissance, the rebirth of classical art and learning. Italian literature also has a special attraction to readers because of the beautiful effects that its writers have been able to create.

Beginnings—the 1200's

For centuries the language of literature in Italy was Latin; no author thought of writing anything in Italian. Not until the 1200's were there enough written compositions to form what could be called an Italian literature. This early literature consists mostly of poems about the basic problems of human nature, especially the experience of love.

Saint Francis. One of the first people to write in Italian was Saint Francis Bernardone of Assisi. Saint Francis gave up a life of wealth to dedicate his love to God and to God's creatures. He expressed this love in a hymn called the "Canticle of the Sun," written about 1224.

The Sonnet. Poets at the court of Emperor Frederick II of Sicily composed some of the first poems about the love between man and woman. These poets generally lacked originality and intensity of feeling. They imitated poetry from southern France and did not create great poetry themselves. But they did give Europe one of its most popular poetic forms, the 14-line poem called the sonnet.

Dante. In the late 1200's, poets in northern Italy breathed freshness and life into the stiff Sicilian poetic forms. The greatest of these poets was Dante Alighieri of Florence. His writing was based on a new poetic ideal that man becomes noble through virtue, not birth. Another ideal was that love is not only a physical experience but also an intellectual and spiritual one. Taken together, these ideas form what Dante called the *dolce stil nuovo*, or "sweet new style."

Dante gave this style a lasting form in his collection of youthful poems called *La vita nuova* ("The New Life"; 1292–93). It tells of his love for a girl named Beatrice, whom he first met when they were both about 9 years old. Combining prose narrative with the poems, Dante records the growth of his love from the time of this first meeting until Beatrice's death 16 years later. Through this ex-

WORDS IN EVERYDAY USE	PAROLE D'USO COMUNE
beautiful	bèllo
book	libro
bread	pane
child	bambino
church	chiesa
city	città
cold	freddo
daughter	figlia
day	giorno
father	padre
half	mèzzo
high	alto
house	casa
low	basso
mother	madre
people	gènte
school	scuola
son	figlio
sweet	dolce
time, weather, season	tèmpo
warm	caldo
way, road	via

NUMBERS	NUMERI
one	uno
two	due
three	tre
four	quattro
five	cinque
six	sei
seven	sette
eight	otto
nine	nove
ten	dieci
twenty	venti
one hundred	cento

MONTHS OF THE YEAR	MESE DEL'ANNO
January	gennaio
February	febbraio
March	marzo
April	aprile
May	maggio
June	giugno
July	luglio
August	agosto
September	settèmbre
October	ottobre
November	novèmbre
December	dicèmbre

DAYS OF THE WEEK	GIORNI DELLA SETTIMANA
Sunday	domenica
Monday	lunedì
Tuesday	martedì
Wednesday	mercoledì
Thursday	giovedì
Friday	venerdì
Saturday	sabato

perience Dante learned to make both his affections and his poetic style more noble. Yet he also realized that he had to become even more noble in spirit before he could properly praise Beatrice in poetry.

Dante succeeded in doing this in a long poem, *La divina commedia* ("The Divine Comedy"; 1307–21). One of the greatest masterpieces of world literature, it is divided into three parts: Hell, Purgatory, and Paradise. It describes how Beatrice, in heaven, sees that Dante has lost his way in life. She obtains divine favor for him so that he may find the proper relationship between love for the world and love for God. To do this, he must make a journey through Hell and Purgatory before arriving in Paradise. There, Beatrice leads him into the presence of God.

Renaissance—the 1300's

During the period, known as the Middle Ages, that preceded the Renaissance, the Christian Church was a powerful force throughout Europe. Most scholarly writings concerned religious issues: God, the afterlife, and the human soul. Then, during the 1200's and 1300's, the direction of European thinking slowly changed. Writers and thinkers began giving more attention to life on earth than to the afterlife.

Petrarch. It was Francesco Petrarch who clearly expressed and organized this new way of thinking. Petrarch's studies and writing, mostly in Latin, are the roots of the period called the Renaissance. The outstanding feature of the Renaissance is the importance given to the human spirit and what it can accomplish with its own intelligence. Because of this idea, the period is sometimes called the age of **humanism**. It is the basis on which Western civilization is built.

Petrarch is also famous for a collection of poems written in Italian for a woman called Laura. These poems differ from those of Dante's "sweet new style." They are more personal and express Petrarch's own feelings of happiness and sorrow. Many later love poems imitated those of Petrarch.

Boccaccio. Giovanni Boccaccio followed in the steps of his friend Petrarch. He, too, was a humanist. His great work the *Decameron* (1353) contains 100 short stories, or *novelle*. In the *Decameron* ten friends leave Florence to escape the plague. For ten days each

of them tells a story a day. ("Decameron" comes from the Greek words for ten days.)

Boccaccio did not make up all the stories, but the way in which he tells them is most original. They are representative of the spirit of the Renaissance and humanism, for they are not concerned with religious or moral ideals. Instead, the subject is the daily human life with all its humor, tragedy, beauty, and ugliness. Boccaccio's work set the pattern of Italian storytelling for centuries.

Renaissance—the 1400's

The Italians of the early 1400's were very attracted to the classical world of ancient Rome, which had been rediscovered and, in part, created by the humanists. It became fashionable to ignore the Italian language and to write in Latin, imitating the style and subjects of classical authors like Cicero.

The Medici Court. Some people fought this new trend and tried to preserve the literary value of Italian. One major patron of art and literature was Lorenzo de' Medici of Florence. Because of his knowledge, wealth, and power, he was called "the Magnificent."

Lorenzo was the patron of Angelo Ambrogini, also known as Poliziano, a humanist and poet who wrote in Greek, Latin, and Italian. Poliziano's *Favola di Orfeo* ("The Fable of Orpheus"; 1480) was the first nonreligious drama written in Italian. His unfinished *Stanze per la giostra* ("Stanzas for the Tournament"; 1475) gives a poetic image of the Renaissance longing for joy amid the beauty of nature and human passions.

Lorenzo's mother was also a patron and supported the poet Luigi Pulci. Pulci's *Morgante* (1483) is an epic poem written in the dialect of Florence. It is based on an old French legend of Charlemagne and Roland.

Sannazaro and Boiardo. Both Jacopo Sannazaro of Naples, with his *Arcadia* (1504), and Matteo Maria Boiardo of Ferrara, with his *Orlando innamorato* ("Roland in Love"; 1487) helped increase the use of Italian as a literary tool. Their works appealed to the aristocratic and humanistic tastes of readers, broadening the interest of noble audiences in Italian poetry.

Renaissance—the 1500's

The efforts of Florentine and other Italian poets of the 1400's helped the Italian language

Near right: Niccolo Machiavelli was a writer and official of Florence. His best-known work, *The Prince*, describes ways of gaining and holding power in government.

Far right: Torquato Tasso was an important poet of the late Renaissance. He wrote *Jerusalem Delivered*, an epic poem with a Christian theme.

become recognized as the equal of Latin in elegance and literary power. Some writers also began to use Italian to create formal elegance with different types of content.

Machiavelli. The Florentine official Niccolò Machiavelli wrote mostly about politics. His most famous work is *Il principe* ("The Prince"; 1513), which examines what a ruler must do to establish and maintain a state. *Il principe* is a fine example of the Renaissance ideal of separating human values from spiritual ones. In it the prince's efforts to create a state are guided by human intelligence and judged by earthly, human values rather than religious or moral ones.

Il principe was one of the great Italian artistic creations of the 1500's. But the country itself was not well. The growing nation states of Europe used Italy as their battlefield, and Italians lost their freedom to Spain and, later, Austria.

Ariosto. Ludovico Ariosto escaped the sad conditions of his country by creating a world of humorous fancy and sublime harmony. In his epic romance *Orlando furioso* ("The Mad Roland"; 1532), he tells the story of the knight Roland's frustrated love for the beautiful maiden Angelica. Numerous characters move from one adventure to another in enchanted forests, and on magical islands, remote continents, and even the moon. Emperors, kings, queens, knights, magicians, a magic ring, a flying horse, and many other fanciful elements

are mixed in charming confusion until all is resolved at the end. *Orlando furioso* was the last great literary work of the Renaissance.

Tasso. Italy's military defeats destroyed her pride and independence. Religious revolutions beginning in 1517 with the Protestant Reformation and continuing through the Catholic Counter-Reformation, which began in 1543, destroyed the country's spiritual freedom. Religious controls on thought and expression crippled the work of Italian writers.

The poetic and emotional results of these developments can be seen best in the work of Torquato Tasso (1544–95). The court poet at Ferrara, Tasso wrote a pastoral comedy, *Aminta* (1573), and a Christian romance epic, *Gerusalemme liberata* ("Jerusalem Delivered"; 1581). *Aminta* portrays the unhappy love of a shepherd named Aminta for the huntress Silvia. His love is frustrated by Silvia's desire for moral purity and honor. *Gerusalemme liberata* tells about the first Crusade and the war between Christians and Muslims for control of the Holy Land.

1600's and 1700's

The 1600's in Italy were a period of showy appearances and extravagant artistic effects. A typical example of this style, known as the Baroque, can be found in Giambattista Marino's poem *Adone* ("Adonis"; 1623). This long poem has a weak plot but is full of pompous verses and extravagant descriptions.

Galileo and Vico. Two great exceptions to the extravagance of the Baroque period were Galileo Galilei and Giambattista Vico. Galileo used a simple writing style to describe discoveries in physics and astronomy. He was also one of the first scientists to write his works in Italian, the language of ordinary people, rather than in Latin, the language of scholars. Vico's study of history and poetry, *La scienza nuova* ("The New Science"; 1725–44), was exceptional in using Italian instead of Latin for a philosophical work.

Arcadian Poetry. A literary reaction against the exaggerations of Baroque poetry appeared in the late 1600's. This poetic revolution was called the Arcadian movement. It promoted simple, elegant language and sincere expression of natural human sentiments. The Arcadian style dominated poetry in the 1700's. It is typified by the work of Pietro Metastasio.

Drama. In the mid-1700's, the playwright Carlo Goldoni of Venice reformed Italian comedy. He developed strong, believable plots about the lives of common people. He also required actors to recite only the lines written by the author and not make up their own lines, as was customary.

Parini, Alfieri, and Foscolo. Three authors of the late 1700's expressed Italy's contemporary problems and their ideals for its future. Giuseppe Parini wrote *Il giorno* ("The Day"; 1763–1801), a poem that pretends to praise noble life but actually exposes the worthlessness of an aristocratic life-style. Vittorio Alfieri criticized the evil effects of corrupt aristocrats and tyrants in his many plays and in his autobiography. The poet Ugo Foscolo rediscovered classic heroism in such verse as *I sepolcri* ("Tombs"; 1807), which encourages people to do great things.

1800's and 1900's

By the end of the 1700's, many Italian writers believed, as did Alfieri and Foscolo, that Italians should restudy their past and try to achieve glorious deeds worthy of it. Above all, they wanted to awaken a moral and civic spirit that might help Italians unite, drive out foreign rulers, and form a united country.

These dreams came true between 1815 and 1871 during a period called the Risorgimento. During this time, revolutionaries fought for and won Italian independence, and the Italian peninsula was united in the Kingdom of Italy.

Leopardi and Manzoni. Two of Italy's greatest writers flourished during the Risorgimento. Giacomo Leopardi wrote moving poems that express the sadness of life and the fact that so few of people's dreams come true.

Alessandro Manzoni wrote a great novel, *I promessi sposi* ("The Betrothed"; 1825–27). Manzoni hoped that his book would serve as an example of the language that modern Italians should use. The story is about the sufferings and dangers a man and woman experience because of their love for each other.

Later Novelists. After Italy's unification, the author Giovanni Verga wrote short stories and novels about the hard life of poor, humble people in Sicily. Verga has his characters speak in a language similar to that of real peasants, as in his novel *I malavoglia* ("The House by the Medlar Tree"; 1881). This realistic use of language and themes, called *verismo* (realism), influenced many later authors.

Another kind of writing was made popular by Carlo Lorenzini, better known as Collodi. His *Le avventure di Pinocchio* ("The Adventures of Pinocchio"; 1882) became a favorite of children all over the world.

Italo Svevo took Italian prose in a third new direction. His novels about family life and middle-class people attempt to describe the reality inside, rather than outside, people's minds. This psychological approach to storytelling can be seen in his entertaining novel *La coscienza di Zeno* ("The Confessions of Zeno"; 1923).

Later Poets. Poets also created a new identity for the young Italian nation. Giosuè Carducci wrote patriotic poems that aroused national pride. He won the Nobel prize for literature in 1906. Giovanni Pascoli experimented with the sounds of language. His poems express a love for nature and for simple, childlike things. Gabriele D'Annunzio also experimented with language, recreating ancient rhythms and forms. His collection of poems, *Le laudi* ("Lauds"; 1903–04), expresses an enchanting image of life between reality and fantasy.

Contemporary Poetry. More recent poets have struggled to deal wih the tragedies of modern life by creating uniquely personal styles of writing. They often use an abstract language that few people can easily understand. Some of the better poets include the

Near right: Luigi Pirandello was one of the most innovative playwrights of the 1900's. His play *Six Characters in Search of an Author* was a landmark of modern theater.

Far right: Umberto Eco is one of the best-known contemporary Italian authors. His novel *The Name of the Rose* became an international best seller.

Nobel prize winners Eugenio Montale and Salvatore Quasimodo, as well as Umberto Saba and Giuseppe Ungaretti.

Drama. The Nobel prize winning author Luigi Pirandello used commonly understood language in his works. His plays explore some of the mysteries of human thought, such as the confusion between fantasy and reality. They reveal the tragic results of human ignorance and foolishness in daily life. Many of his plays, including *Henry IV* (1922) and *Sei personaggi in cerca d'autore* ("Six Characters in Search of an Author"; 1921), have had a lasting impact on world theater.

Prose. With better education and greater wealth, Italians read more novels today than ever before. Alberto Moravia used a realistic style to portray society's moral corruption in the novels *Gli indifferenti* ("The Time of Indifference"; 1929) and *Il conformista* ("The Conformist"; 1951). Cesare Pavese used a realistic style to express the dreamlike experience of memories in *La luna e i falò* ("The Moon and the Bonfire"; 1950).

Vasco Pratolini describes the actual conditions of working-class life in such novels as *Cronache di poveri amanti* ("A Tale of Poor Lovers"; 1947). Leonardo Sciascia exposed the brutality and injustice of life in Mafia-controlled Sicily in *Il giorno della civetta* ("The Day of the Owl"; 1961). The film director, poet, and author Pier Paolo Pasolini used Italian dialect and a focus on low-life

characters to present another aspect of social reality. His novels include *Ragazzi di vita* ("Boys of Life"; 1955) and *Una vita violenta* ("A Violent Life"; 1959).

Women authors became prominent in Italy during the later 1900's. Two of the most important are Natalia Ginzburg, who wrote *La strada che va in città* ("The Road to the City"; 1942), and Elsa Morante, who wrote the enchanting novel *L'Isola di Arturo* ("Arturo's Island"; 1957).

Other Trends. Modern Italian novelists have not concentrated only on realism and the actual conditions of Italian life. Italo Calvino wrote fantasy stories that carry a reader's imagination to new worlds. His works include *T con zero* ("T With Zero"; 1967), *Le citta invisibili* ("The Invisible City"; 1972), and *Se una notte d'inverno un viaggiatore* ("If One Winter Night a Traveler"; 1979). Umberto Eco's mystery novel, *Il nome della rosa* ("The Name of the Rose"; 1979), became a worldwide best seller. Its plot concerns murders in a medieval monastery, but the book also explores the mysterious power of language over people's minds. Calvino and Eco are among the latest authors who have made Italian literature an important part of the Western imagination.

ALFRED F. ALBERICO
San Francisco State University
Reviewed by BRADLEY DICK
New York University

ITALY, MUSIC OF

Italy has made major contributions to the development of Western music. Musical forms, instruments, and performing styles developed in Italy have become well known around the world. The very directions that tell musicians how to perform music are almost wholly in Italian. They include such terms as *presto* ("quickly"), *moderato* ("moderately"), *forte* ("loud"), and many more. Perhaps the most outstanding Italian contribution to the world's music is opera, a form of theater that combines music and drama.

Musical instruments survive from the prehistoric tribes that inhabited Italy in ancient times. When Rome was the center of civilization in the Western world, music occupied an important place in public and private life. However, no written music from ancient times has been preserved, and little is known of Italian music before the Middle Ages.

▶THE MIDDLE AGES

The biggest influence on musical development in Italy during the Middle Ages was the Roman Catholic Church. Christianity had become firmly established in Italy before the end of the Roman Empire. One of the practices introduced with the new religion was the singing of **chants** (also called **plainsong**), religious vocal music with Latin words.

At first, a chant consisted of a single melody, sung without any harmony or instrumental accompaniment. This is called **monophonic** music. Gradually, however, singers added a second voice to the chant. Then over the centuries, three, four, and more voices, each singing a different part, were combined. This kind of music, in which two or more melodies are sung or played at the same time, is called **polyphonic** music.

Italian musicians of the Middle Ages also wrote secular (nonreligious) music. Many of the first secular pieces were monophonic, but Italian composers later made important contributions to the development of secular polyphonic music. Italian musicians traveled throughout Europe, bringing their musical forms and practices with them. Attracted by the rapidly growing fame of Italian music, students from all over western Europe went to Italy to study. One of the finest composers of this period was Francesco Landini, who was also skilled as an organist and lute player.

▶THE RENAISSANCE

By the late 1400's, polyphonic music in Italy had become highly complicated. Mastering its technique required years of hard study and practice. As polyphonic music became more and more complex, understanding the text became more difficult. This was of grave concern to the church, which threatened to ban polyphonic music in its services.

During the period of artistic flowering called the Renaissance, the art of polyphonic music was brought to a magnificent climax by one of the greatest of all church composers, Giovanni Pierluigi da Palestrina. He wrote more than three hundred sacred works, all for voice without instrumental accompaniment. Palestrina's work was praised by the church for its clearly understandable text.

However, Italian music, like music almost everywhere in Europe, continued to move further away from the church. Many leading Italian musicians, such as Luca Marenzio and Carlo Gesualdo, devoted themselves to writing secular vocal pieces called **madrigals**. Others, including Girolamo Frescobaldi, concentrated on music for the organ and other instruments. In Venice, Andrea Gabrieli and his nephew Giovanni Gabrieli wrote some of the earliest music for brass instruments.

Antonio Stradivari headed a family of violin makers that flourished in Italy during the 1600's and 1700's. His violins are considered among the finest ever made.

▶ 1600'S AND 1700'S

The development of music for instruments continued during the 1600's and 1700's. But the major musical event of this period was the invention of opera.

Instrumental Music. During the 1600's, violins gained in popularity, replacing earlier stringed instruments called viols. Italy led in the manufacture of violins and in the writing and performing of music for them. Some of the greatest violin makers of all times flourished in Italy, including members of the Stradivari and Guarneri families. Among composers, Arcangelo Corelli created much outstanding music for violins. Violinist-composers of the 1700's included Giuseppe Tartini, Pietro Locatelli, and Antonio Vivaldi. Vivaldi, a Venetian priest, was a leading composer for orchestra, which also had its beginnings in Italy during this period.

Italians played an important role in the development of the pianoforte, or piano, the first keyboard instrument that could produce a wide range of loud and soft sounds. Where the first pianos were made is unclear. But two instruments labeled *piano e forte* ("soft and loud") were seen at Modena, Italy, in 1598. The first practical piano was manufactured by an Italian, Bartolomeo Cristofori, in 1709. Another Italian, Muzio Clementi, was an important early composer for the piano. He was one of the first composers to develop a style of piano music that was tailored to the characteristics of the instrument.

Opera. About 1600, a small group of artists, poets, and musicians in Florence decided to perform plays as they supposed the ancient Greeks had—with music throughout. They wanted to combine music and theater in a way that would move the souls of their listeners. The result of their experimenting was

Opera, created in Italy, is an important part of the country's musical heritage. *Left:* La Scala, a famous opera house in Milan, was opened in 1778. *Below:* Italian opera star Enrico Caruso performed in a 1910 production of *Pagliacci*.

opera, a musical form that was dominated by Italians for the next two centuries.

The new form soon attracted the attention of a leading Italian composer, Claudio Monteverdi. His opera *Orfeo*, produced at Mantua in 1607, is a masterpiece that is still performed. Like many early operas, *Orfeo* was presented as a private entertainment for aristocrats. Soon public opera houses were opened, attracting both aristocratic and middle-class audiences. Important centers for opera production sprang up in Venice, Rome, and Naples. By the end of the century, opera houses had been built in nearly every Italian city and town. Opera swept Italy and then the rest of the Western world.

One of the foremost composers of serious opera in the late 1600's and early 1700's was Alessandro Scarlatti. Masterpieces of comic opera were composed by Giovanni Battista Pergolesi and Domenico Cimarosa. Both Pergolesi's *La serva padrona* ("The Maid as Mistress"; 1733) and Cimarosa's *Il matrimonio segreto* ("The Secret Marriage"; 1792) are performed widely to this day.

As opera spread, it continued to be written and sung in Italian. The great Austrian composer Wolfgang Amadeus Mozart composed three of his best operas to Italian texts: *Le nozze di Figaro* ("The Marriage of Figaro"; 1786), *Don Giovanni* (1787), and *Così fan tutte* ("So Do They All"; 1790).

▶ **1800'S AND 1900'S**

Opera remained the dominant musical form in Italy throughout the 1800's, and Italian composers of opera won international fame. One of the greatest composers was Gioacchino Rossini. In 19 years, Rossini wrote nearly forty operas, until in many places his name and the word "opera" meant almost the same thing. Rossini is best known for his comic masterpiece *Il barbiere di Siviglia* ("The Barber of Seville"; 1816). After Rossini stopped composing operas, in 1829, other Italian composers began to take their places in the world's opera houses. Two of the most renowned were Gaetano Donizetti, composer of *Lucia di Lammermoor* (1835), and Vincenzo Bellini, who wrote *Norma* (1821). Italian operas by the hundreds filled the stages of theaters around the world.

Also during the 1800's, Italians helped to develop grand opera, a pageant-like opera often based on historical incidents. Among the first true grand operas were Rossini's *Guillaume Tell* ("William Tell"; 1829), and Gasparo Spontini's *La Vestale* ("The Vestal Virgin"; 1807). Both were composed to French texts and first sung at the Paris Opera, but they are both completely Italian in style.

One of the greatest of all opera composers, Giuseppe Verdi crowned the whole history of Italian opera with a series of masterpieces. They include *Rigoletto* (1851), *La Traviata* ("The Wayward One"; 1853), *Il Trovatore* ("The Troubadour"; 1853), *Aïda* (1871), and many others. The most gifted Italian composer after Verdi was Giacomo Puccini. His operas, including *La Bohème* ("The Bohemian Girl"; 1896), *Tosca* (1900), and *Madama Butterfly* (1904), are among the world's most popular operas.

Before the end of the 1800's a new form of Italian opera appeared. It was known as *verismo*, or realism. These operas usually are based on grim, sometimes violent situations from everyday life. The best of the *verismo* operas are *Cavalleria rusticana* ("Rustic Chivalry"; 1890), by Pietro Mascagni, and *Pagliacci* ("Clowns"; 1892), by Ruggiero Leoncavallo.

Modern Times. Although opera has continued to hold an important place in Italian musical life, many modern Italian composers have concentrated on instrumental music.

The best-known Italian composer of the early 1900's was Ottorino Respighi. His orchestral tone poems were written in a musical style, known as impressionism, that originated in France. Later Italian composers also were influenced by musical developments occurring outside Italy. Luigi Dallapiccola used the twelve-tone method of composition developed by the Austrian composer Arnold Schoenberg, while Goffredo Petrassi was influenced by the Russian composer Igor Stravinsky. More recent Italian composers, including Bruno Maderna, Luigi Nono, Luciano Berio, and Sylvana Bussotti, experimented in virtually all contemporary trends, including electronic music.

HERBERT WEINSTOCK
Author, *Rossini: A Biography*
Reviewed by WENDY HELLER
New England Conservatory of Music

See also OPERA.

IVAN

Ivan was the name of six rulers of Russia, who lived between the 1300's and the 1700's. They are sometimes referred to by their English equivalent, John.

Ivan I (1304?–40) ruled the principality of Moscow from 1328 to 1340 and served as grand prince of Russia (from 1331). Ivan owed this throne to the khan (ruler) of the Mongols, who controlled the lands of Russia at the time. He paid considerable attention to courting the khan, and was quick to join in crushing any movement hostile to the Mongols among other Russian princes. A wise money manager, Ivan earned the nickname *Kalita*, or Moneybag. He used his money-making talent to buy other territories, increasing the size of his own principality of Moscow by nearly seven times.

By the time of Ivan I's death, Moscow had emerged as the political and religious capital of all Russia, although it was still subject to the overall control of the Mongols. Ivan established the tradition that princes of Moscow had first claim on the position of Russian grand prince. His heirs held that title almost without interruption.

Ivan II (1326–59), a son of Ivan I, served as Russian grand prince from 1353 to 1359. Known as *Krotkii*, or the Meek, he was not a strong ruler, and was inept as both a political and military leader. He continued to give obedience to the Mongols. Ivan II was strongly influenced by a capable and energetic metropolitan of the Russian Orthodox Church, Alexis. Alexis, in effect, ruled Russia for most of Ivan's reign.

Ivan III (1440–1505), known as the Great, was Russian grand prince from 1462 to 1505. One of only three Russian rulers to be called the Great, he began the unification and centralization of the Russian lands under Moscow. During Ivan III's reign, Mongol rule in Russia declined. In 1480 he repelled an invasion of Moscow by the Mongols, finally freeing Russia from their domination.

During the 1470's and 1480's, Ivan absorbed Moscow's old rivals to the north, the principalities of Novgorod and Tver, as well as other territories, and established a unified rule over what had been a divided Russia. He also fought Lithuania (1492–94 and 1500–1503) in an attempt to reconquer the Ukraine,

The Russian ruler Ivan III is known as the Great. During his reign (1462–1505), he established a unified rule over what had been a divided Russia.

which Lithuania had occupied. But in this he was only partly successful. During Ivan's reign, Moscow was the site of an impressive building campaign, directed by Italian architects and artists.

One of the most important accomplishments of Ivan III's reign was the introduction of a new law code in 1497. This made legal procedures uniform throughout Russia and helped to curb widespread corruption among officials.

After the death of his first wife in 1467, Ivan married Sophia, niece of the last Byzantine emperor, in 1472. Following the marriage, Ivan developed a court ceremony based on that of the Byzantine Empire. He also began to use the title of czar, a variation of the Roman title caesar. By the time of his death, Russia had become a strong nation-state.

Ivan IV (1530–84), known as the Terrible, was crowned czar in 1547, the first Russian ruler officially to hold this title. That same year he married Anastasia Romanov. Although Ivan remarried a number of times after her death, he was never able to recapture the happiness he had enjoyed with Anastasia. The Romanov dynasty, which ruled Russia from 1613 to the overthrow of the monarchy in

Ivan IV was the first Russian ruler to be crowned czar. The first part of his reign (1533–60) was a period of great accomplishment. The second part (1560–84), however, was a time of repression and terror that gave him his nickname of the Terrible. His last years were marked by tragedy. In a fit of anger, he killed his eldest son, Ivan (shown being held by his father).

1917, traces its claim to the throne from their union—through Anastasia's brother, Nikita.

Historians often divide Ivan IV's reign into two periods. The first, from 1533 to 1560, was a period of constructive policies. The second, from 1560 to his death in 1584, was a time of repression and terror that gave Ivan his nickname of the Terrible.

During the first period, Ivan instituted reforms in local government, drew up a new law code, and standardized the duties and responsibilities of the nobility. Russia also began its expansion to the east, beyond the Ural Mountains, and before Ivan's death, had established itself in Siberia. In addition, Ivan opened trade contacts with the English, French, and Dutch.

Anastasia's death in 1560 marked the end of this period of accomplishment. Increasingly powerful, Ivan turned against his advisors. He became convinced that they, backed by the prominent nobility (the boyars), had caused Anastasia's death. By threatening to abdicate (give up the throne), Ivan was given the authority to punish those whom he considered traitors and wrongdoers, executing them if necessary and confiscating their property. His bodyguard, the *oprichniki*, destroyed most of the wealthy old boyar families. Those who were not killed were ruined by Ivan's political and economic policies.

Ivan also began a series of disastrous wars during this period, in an attempt to gain access for Russia to the Baltic Sea. His last years were marked by turmoil and tragedy. In 1581,

in a fit of anger, he lashed out at his eldest son, also called Ivan, and killed him. He probably never fully recovered from the guilt he felt for this act, and he died a broken man.

Ivan V (1666–96) served as co-ruler of Russia from 1682 to 1696. Ivan was feebleminded and partially blind. But he was installed on the throne, along with his half brother Peter I, by his sister Sophia, who governed as regent. When Peter (the future Peter the Great) overthrew Sophia in 1689, he allowed Ivan to continue sharing the throne. Ivan, however, had virtually no power, serving merely as a ceremonial figure.

Ivan VI (1740–64) was emperor of Russia from 1740 to 1741, while still an infant. The great nephew of the Empress Anne (who ruled from 1730 to 1740), Ivan was only 2 months old at the time of Anne's death. Several groups contended for control of the throne. A group centered around Ivan's mother eventually won out.

However, in 1741 a coup led by Elizabeth, Peter the Great's only surviving daughter, overthrew the "baby emperor," and he was imprisoned. A plot to free Ivan in 1764 during the reign of the Empress Catherine II failed, and the former emperor was murdered. He had spent 23 of his 24 years in prison.

DONALD L. LAYTON
Indiana State University

See also CATHERINE; PETER THE GREAT.

IVANOVSKI, DMITRI. See VIRUSES (The Discovery of Viruses).

IVES, CHARLES (1874–1954)

Charles Edward Ives was one of America's most original composers and a pioneer of modern music. He was born on October 20, 1874, in Danbury, Connecticut. He received his first musical training from his father, the director of the town band.

Ives attended Yale University from 1894 to 1898. There, he studied with Horatio Parker, a respected composer. After graduation, Ives went to New York City and began a career in the insurance business, eventually starting his own firm. But he continued to compose in his free time. In 1908 he married Harmony Twichell, a nurse. Harmony was also a poet, and she wrote words for many of Ives's songs.

Ives's insurance business flourished, and he became a wealthy man. Few of his business associates knew that Ives's real interest was music. His financial security enabled him to compose as he wished, without worrying about pleasing critics or the public.

And often his music did not please listeners, for his compositions were very different from the popular music of his day. Ives often based his music on folk songs, hymns, patriotic tunes, and other familiar American melodies. But he transformed these melodies into highly original sounds. He experimented with unusual rhythms and with **dissonance** (clashing musical sounds), anticipating the work of such modern European composers as Arnold Schoenberg and Igor Stravinsky.

Ives was also inspired by memories of his youth in New England. One of his most appealing symphonies is entitled *Three Places in New England* (1903–1914). His second piano sonata (1910–1915), subtitled *Concord, Mass., 1840–1860*, is divided into four movements—"Emerson," "Hawthorne," "The Alcotts," and "Thoreau"—all named for New England authors.

Ill health forced Ives to stop composing in 1926, but he continued to revise his earlier works. Gradually his music gained wider acceptance. His Third Symphony, completed in 1904 but first performed in 1946, won the Pulitzer prize in 1947. By the time of his death, in New York City on May 19, 1954, Ives had earned an honored place in American music.

JOHN KIRKPATRICK
Professor Emeritus and Curator of the
Ives Collection, Yale University

IVORY

For thousands of years, people have valued ivory—the hard, creamy white material that comes from the teeth of certain animals. Over time it has been sculpted into art objects, used in decorative jewelry, and even used as cures for disease.

What is Ivory? All ivory comes from the teeth of mammals. Mammal teeth are made up of three layers: an outer layer of hard enamel, a middle layer of a softer material called dentin, and an inner layer of nerves and blood vessels that feed the tooth. It is the middle layer, the dentin, that is referred to as ivory.

Ivory is not a solid material. It contains a series of very small tubes filled with a waxlike liquid. This structure makes ivory fairly easy to carve. It also gives polished ivory the warm, glowing tone for which it is so prized.

Sources of Ivory. Ivory is most commonly obtained from the tusks of elephants. Elephants use their tusks for digging roots, moving fallen trees, and for fighting. This heavy

A Japanese carver of the 1800's produced this detailed sculpture of a laughing entertainer.

use causes the outer layer of enamel to wear away, exposing the dentin, or ivory. Because carvers do not have to dissolve or chip through a layer of hard enamel to get to the ivory, elephant tusks are an especially desirable source of ivory. Another reason elephant tusks are so valued as a source of ivory is because of their size. The largest elephant tusks ever collected were 10 feet (3 meters) in length and weighed 225 pounds (102 kilograms).

The fossilized tusks of mammoths and mastodons (which became extinct between 10,000 and 50,000 years ago) are another source of ivory. Some of these tusks are much bigger and heavier than the tusks of elephant species living today; but the tusks contain little carvable ivory. Thousands of years of weathering and exposure to water usually reduce the tusks to soft chalk. When hard fossil ivory is found, it is as hard or harder than other types of ivory.

Walruses are the second most common source of ivory. Walrus tusks rarely grow longer than 3 feet (1 meter) or weigh more than 5 pounds (2 kilograms). Native Americans and Inuit of North America often make small sculptures out of walrus tusks.

A rarer source of ivory is the whale tooth. During the 1800's sailors often carved pictures on whale teeth, etching scenes with thin delicate lines. Then they would fill in the lines with ink. This type of art is called scrimshaw.

The narwhal, a type of Arctic whale, is among the most unusual sources of ivory. It has a long, straight tusk that grows out of the front of its mouth. Sometimes this tusk grows to be 15 feet (4.5 meters) long. The narwhal tusk was highly valued during the Middle Ages. People thought it was the horn of the unicorn, a mythical beast. They carved narwhal ivory into spoons that were supposed to turn color when touched with poisoned food.

Uses of Ivory. Although ivory has had many and varied uses, it has most commonly been used to produce decorative pieces and fine art objects. Some of the oldest pieces of carved ivory were found in caves in southwestern France that also contained wall paintings of prehistoric animals. The ivory pieces were made from tusks more than 20,000 years old.

The ancient Egyptians established workshops where ivory was carved into objects for the pharaoh (king). The ancient Greeks also used ivory for large, important works of art. Since Roman times, ivory has mainly been used for small sculptures and for decorating everyday objects, such as combs and jewelry boxes. Although ivory carving had been practiced in the Far East for centuries, especially in China and Japan, it became a very detailed and elaborate art around the late 1600's. Chinese artists were able to carve up to ten concentric balls out of a single block of ivory.

Ivory carving is still part of many different cultures today. However, most modern ivory

Hidden stores of ivory seized from poachers in Kenya make a towering bonfire. It represents hundreds of African elephants slaughtered for their tusks.

products are far removed from the fine art objects once produced. Ivory is most often used for mass-produced knickknacks and sold to tourists as inexpensive souvenirs.

The Ivory Trade. The decline of the African elephant and other ivory-bearing animals has caused great concern about the ivory trade. Since the late 1970's, the size of these elephant herds has been reduced by more than half. Most of the elephants have been poached—killed illegally—for their tusks. The poached ivory, which is smuggled out of the country to ivory-carving factories, commands a very high price.

In 1989, in an effort to reduce the illegal killing of the elephants, the African elephant was classified as an endangered species by the Convention on International Trade in Endangered Species. The action put into effect a ban on all trade in ivory. But some countries openly refuse to follow the ban and continue to import and export ivory.

African countries are also working on ways to save their elephant populations through policies that will protect elephants living in natural reserves and fight the poachers. Once a successful conservation plan is established, the ivory trade can be reopened safely. In the meantime, substitutes for ivory are gaining wider use. These include tagua, an ivorylike substance derived from the nut of two species of South American palm trees, and certain types of plastics. Milk products and potatoes can also be treated to form substances similar to ivory.

ELIZABETH KAPLAN
Author, *Biology Bulletin Monthly*

IVORY COAST
(CÔTE D'IVOIRE)

Ivory Coast (or Côte d'Ivoire) is located in West Africa on the coast of the Atlantic Ocean just north of the equator. The country takes its name from the many elephants that once roamed freely in the territory. Although they are now nearly extinct in the region, the elephant is pictured on the country's coat of arms and stamps, for it symbolizes strength and endurance—qualities that are much admired by the Ivorian people.

▶ PEOPLE

Ivory Coast is a multicultural society. Its population of nearly 17 million is divided into 60 ethnic groups, each belonging to one of five larger cultural groups: the Akan, Krou, Northern and Southern Mande, and Voltaique. Although each group is located in a particular area, there is considerable ethnic intermingling throughout the country. About half the total population is younger than 15 years of age.

More than 4 million migrants from all over West Africa live and work in Ivory Coast as well as thousands of refugees from neighboring war-torn Liberia. Thousands of French and Lebanese nationals have also made Ivory Coast their home.

Language. Ivory Coast was once a colony of France. After gaining its independence in 1960, it retained French as its official language, although it is only spoken among more highly educated people. Most city residents speak "market French," a widely understood dialect that is used in business transactions. Dioula, the language of migrants and traveling traders from the north, is the most widely spoken native language.

Religion. Islam is considered the dominant religion of the north, whereas the south is predominantly Christian. However, most Ivorians are neither strictly Muslim nor Christian but have incorporated traditional African beliefs, including reverence for their creator and the spirits of their ancestors.

The government has financed several impressive mosques and churches, including the magnificent Basilica, Our Lady of Peace, the world's largest Christian church. It is located in Yamoussoukro, the birthplace of Félix

Left: A northern Ivorian wearing a traditional turban. *Below:* Abidjan, nicknamed the Pearl of the Lagoon, is located on the Gulf of Guinea. It is Ivory Coast's largest city and center of commerce.

Houphouët-Boigny, the country's first president and founding father.

Education. Primary education in Ivory Coast is provided free of charge; however, facilities are inadequate and classrooms are overcrowded. Attendance is required, but only three-fourths of school-age children actually go to school, and only the best students can advance to public secondary schools. Private schools are available to those who can pay the tuition.

processing. Child labor is common throughout the country, and children often accompany their parents to the farm or market.

Farmers in the north grow grains, including the local staples of millet and sorghum. Cotton is grown for sale to the textile industry or to local weavers. Cattle herding is another important occupation. Because the northern part of the country faces high unemployment, many young men move south to work in factories, on farms, or as servants in middle-class homes.

Farmers in the south grow a wider variety of food crops, often planting them in between cocoa and coffee trees. A few large-scale farms grow crops for industrial processing. A large number of industries provide jobs to urban workers. But most people in the cities are self-employed or work in small shops.

At night, the cities come to life. Nightclubs offer music and dancing, and street food vendors fill the air with the aromas of grilled fish and chicken. Although dining out in the open air is quite popular, the evening meal, considered the most important meal of the day, is usually eaten at home. Dinner often consists of soup cooked with fish or meat, poured over *foutou* (pounded plantains and boiled cassava) or rice. In middle-class homes, families sit down together for supper. But in the villages, traditionally men eat from one bowl, women from another, and children from a third.

A group of children return to the village of Silikoro after a day of working in the fields. In Ivory Coast, children in rural areas often help their parents work on the family farms or accompany them to market.

University education is provided to students who can pass a highly competitive examination. The number of girls pursuing higher education is much lower than that of boys. The principal university is the University of Abidjan-Cocody (formerly National University of Ivory Coast). Others include the University of Abobo-Adjamé, the University of Bouaké, and Catholic University of Abidjan.

Way of Life. The majority of Ivorians are small-scale farmers living in rural areas. The women are primarily responsible for producing the food for their families. They sell any extra at roadside stands, in local markets, or to marketers from the city. Men typically produce cash crops for export or domestic

▶ **LAND**

Ivory Coast is bounded by Burkina Faso and Mali to the north, Guinea and Liberia to the west, Ghana to the east, and the Gulf of Guinea to the south. In area, it is slightly larger than the U.S. state of New Mexico.

Land Regions. Ivory Coast can be divided into four regions. In the south along the coast, there is a narrow strip of land about 40

miles (64 kilometers) wide that is studded with lagoons. Access from the sea is made difficult by high surf, a long undersea sandbar, and a lack of natural harbors. Beyond this coastline lies the forest region. The rain forest begins gradually and becomes denser farther inland. This interior forest contains some of the world's oldest and most prized species of hardwood. Much of the forest cover has been eliminated by extensive farming, logging, and urban sprawl. To the north lies the savannah, a sparsely populated grassland suitable for grazing livestock.

Overall, the terrain is mostly flat to gently rolling. The ground gradually rises inland from the Gulf of Guinea. Mountains are located in the north and west, along the borders of Guinea and Liberia. At 6,069 feet (1,850 meters), Mount Nimba is the country's highest peak.

Rivers, Lakes, and Coastal Waters. The Gulf of Guinea, which forms Ivory Coast's southern border, is an inlet of the Atlantic Ocean. The gulf includes the bights (bays) Benin and Biafra.

Ivory Coast has four major river systems—the Comoé, Bandama, Sassandra, and Cavally. The Comoé originates in Burkina Faso.

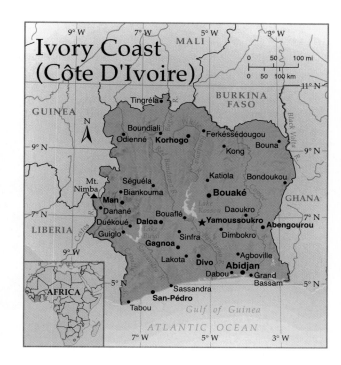

The Cavally flows from neighboring Guinea. All empty into the ocean, except the Cavally. Many rapids and waterfalls make the rivers difficult to navigate. Some sections of the Sassandra are ideal for fishing and seaside tourism. The government has built large dams on several of the rivers for irrigation, flooding control, and electricity production.

Climate. Ivory Coast is tropical and generally hot throughout the country, with some important differences between the southern and northern regions. The south is hot and humid, with temperatures ranging from 72 to 90°F (22 to 32°C). There is almost no difference between daytime and nighttime temperatures. During the long rainy season starting in mid-May, rain falls nearly every day for two months. A dry season follows, then a short rainy season, and another dry season. The total annual rainfall is about 90 inches (2,300 millimeters). The north is dry and hot, with an annual rainfall of only about 54 inches (1,370 millimeters). Between December and February, a dry, dusty wind known as the harmattan blows from the northeast to the coast.

Natural Resources. Ivory Coast once had the most extensive rain forest in West Africa. It provided fertile land for growing cash crops and was a source of valuable timber, including mahogany and iroko (an African

FACTS and figures

RÉPUBLIQUE DE CÔTE D'IVOIRE is the official name of the country.
LOCATION: West Africa.
AREA: 124,502 sq mi (322,460 km²).
POPULATION: 16,800,000 (estimate).
CAPITAL: Yamoussoukro.
LARGEST CITY: Abidjan.
MAJOR LANGUAGES: French (official), Dioula and various other African languages.
MAJOR RELIGIOUS GROUPS: Muslim, Christian, traditional African religions.
GOVERNMENT: Republic. **Head of state and government**—president. **Legislature**—National Assembly.
CHIEF PRODUCTS: Agricultural—coffee, cacao beans, bananas, palm kernels, corn, rice, cassava, sweet potatoes, sugar, cotton, rubber, timber, plantains. **Manufactured**—processed foods and beverages, wood products, refined petroleum, assembled motor vehicles, textiles, fertilizers, building materials. **Mineral**—petroleum, diamonds, manganese.
MONETARY UNIT: African Financial Community (CFA) franc (1 CFA franc = 100 centimes).

mulberry that is similar to teak). But the rain forest's natural resources have been drastically reduced due to development and overuse. The remaining forest and rivers are home to such exotic animals as the pygmy hippopotamus, the bongo (a reddish brown antelope), and the manatee. Ten additional species of antelopes, lions, and a few remaining elephants live in the savanna woodlands.

Ivory Coast's mineral resources include oil and gas (found offshore), diamonds, nickel, cobalt, and manganese. There are additional deposits of gold, iron ore, titanium, and bauxite (aluminum ore), but these have not yet been commercially developed.

Ivorian religious masks are famous throughout the world for their beauty and artistry.

▶ ECONOMY

After gaining independence in 1960, Ivory Coast welcomed foreign investors and promoted many industries, making it one of Africa's most successful economies. It became the manufacturing center of West Africa and a major exporter of cocoa, coffee, and tropical hardwoods. Admirers called it an "economic miracle." However, when cocoa and coffee prices fell in 1979, the economy began to decline. Since then, the country has struggled to regain its earlier economic strength.

Services. Trading is by far the most important service sector activity. Most traders are small-scale retailers who sell in neighborhoods or local markets. Government services are also important, as are public transportation, domestic work, roadside repairs, tailoring, masonry, and carpentry.

Manufacturing. Manufactured goods include processed foods and beverages, wood products, assembled motor vehicles, textiles, fertilizers, and building materials. The Vridi oil refinery, outside Abidjan, produces petroleum products, including gasoline.

Agriculture, Forestry, and Fishing. Thousands of Ivorian farmers produce cash crops for export on small plots of land. Their success has made Ivory Coast the world's leading producer of cacao beans, used in making chocolate. Other important cash crops include coffee, bananas, palm kernels (to make

palm oil), sugar, cotton, and rubber. The main food crops are corn, rice, cassava (a starchy root), plantains, and sweet potatoes. Cattle are raised in the north.

Ivory Coast's forests were once the greatest natural resource of the country, but most of the mahogany and other valuable hardwoods have been cut for export or to clear the land for farming. To help preserve the remaining forests, the Ivorian government has begun a program of reforestation.

Fishing is also an important industry in Ivory Coast, especially in the Gulf of Guinea, where tuna is caught and canned for export.

▶ MAJOR CITIES

Yamoussoukro, the birthplace of former president Félix Houphouët-Boigny, has been the official capital of Ivory Coast since 1983.

Abidjan, nicknamed the Pearl of the Lagoon, is separated from the Gulf of Guinea by a sandbar. With a population of more than

A boy cuts open cacao pods to remove the seeds (beans). Ivory Coast is the world's largest producer and exporter of cacao beans, chocolate's main ingredient.

2 million, it is Ivory Coast's largest city, commercial center, and major seaport. It served as the nation's seat of government until 1983. But Abidjan remains the working capital, and all the foreign embassies are located there.

CULTURAL HERITAGE

Wood carving, gold and brass casting, and weaving have a long and rich history in Ivory Coast. The most common carved objects are religious masks and statues. Their artistic qualities have made them world famous. The Baulé make fine gold jewelry and wooden sculptures. Ivorian textiles are also varied and highly prized.

Ivory Coast has a rich literary tradition in French. The country's most famous writers are Bernard B. Dadié, famous for his autobiographical novels about life under colonial rule, and the playwrights Goffi Jadeau and Amon d'Aby. Other notable playwrights and novelists include Zadi Zaourou and Ahmadou Kourouma. In music, West African reggae singer Alpha Blondy has achieved international renown.

GOVERNMENT

The Ivory Coast is a republic. Its 1960 constitution has been amended many times, most recently in 2000. A president serves as both head of state and government. However, the president also appoints a prime minister who is in charge of the day-to-day running of the government and answers to parliament. The president may serve two 5-year terms. The legislative body is the National Assembly. Its members are also elected to 5-year terms.

HISTORY

For centuries, the area now known as Ivory Coast was protected against invasion by dense forests and a dangerous coastline. Five great African states flourished there, including the Kingdom of Kong, founded in the 1000's. Muslim invaders brought Islam to the region in the 1500's.

Europeans first arrived in the region in the 1600's. Traders bought slaves, palm oil, and gold from the people who lived along the coast. Ivory Coast eventually became a French colony in 1893.

After World War II (1939–45), Ivorian nationalists, who had fought with France against Nazi Germany, demanded a voice in their

Félix Houphouët-Boigny served as president from the time Ivory Coast became independent in 1960 until his death in 1993.

government for their loyalty. They were permitted to elect two deputies to the French National Assembly.

In 1958, Ivory Coast became an autonomous (self-governing) republic within the newly formed French Community. Complete independence was won on August 7, 1960.

Félix Houphouët-Boigny served as president from independence in 1960 until his death in 1993. Henrí Konan-Bédié succeeded him and was re-elected in 1995. In 1999, Bédié was overthrown in a coup, led by General Robert Gueï. Conflicts that had erupted under Bédié between the Muslim north and the Christian south, and between native Ivorians and immigrants from neighboring countries, continued under Gueï.

Gueï ran for president in 2000, but the elections excluded the leading opposition candidates. When Gueï appeared to be losing to Laurent Gbagbo, he halted the vote count and declared himself the winner. A popular uprising forced Gueï to step down, and Gbagbo became president.

In 2002, Gueï was killed in a failed coup attempt, and antigovernment rebels took control of much of the north. Leaders from various African nations tried to coordinate peace discussions, and France sent peacekeeping troops. But despite occasional truces, civil war continued between government forces and rebel groups. In 2003, a power-sharing agreement was signed. But it caused riots by those who believed the French had persuaded Gbagbo to give the rebels too much power. Violence between warring ethnic groups continued until a new government, in which all the political parties were represented, was formed by Seydou Diarra, who was appointed prime minister.

CYRIL KOFIE DADDIEH
Providence College

Index

biological studies   **B:**203–4
blood disorders   **B:**262
cancer   **D:**185, 190
disease prevention   **D:**211
exercise strengthens the immune system   **P:**224
fallout, effects of   **F:**35
immunological diseases   **D:**181, 183–84
interferon   **G:**84
lymphatic system closely associated with   **L:**349–50
medical research   **M:**208e–208f
multiple sclerosis   **D:**196
negative emotions lower the body's defenses   **D:**186
Pasteur, Louis   **P:**98
science, milestones in   **S:**75
severe combined immunodeficiency   **G:**89
vaccination and inoculation   **V:**260–61
Immunity (body's ability to protect itself)   **I:**95
Immunization *see* Vaccination and immunization
Immunoglobulin E (antibody produced in allergic reactions)
   A:190, 191
Immunology (study of the immune system)   **B:**188; **I:**98;
   V:260–61
   Behring, Emil von   **B:**127a
   dermatology, future of   **D:**124
   transplantation of organs and tissues   **M:**208h
Immunosuppressants (drugs that limit the immune system's
   response to transplanted organs)   **O:**226, 227
Immunotherapy (medical treatment)   **A:**191; **C:**95
Impala (antelope)   **A:**297; **M:**70–71
   picture(s)   **M:**68
Impeachment (legal action against a public official)   **G:**276;
   I:99
   Clinton, William, and Lewinsky scandal   **C:**368; **U:**205
   House of Representatives can impeach federal officials
      U:144
   Johnson, Andrew   **J:**115, 118; **R:**118; **U:**186
   limitation on presidential pardoning power   **P:**451
   Nixon, Richard M., resigned instead of facing   **W:**61
   recall   **O:**212
   United States, government of the   **U:**168
   picture(s)
      ticket to Andrew Johnson's trial   **J:**117
Imperfect flowers   **F:**283; **P:**307
   picture(s)   **P:**306
Imperfect fungi   **F:**499–500
Imperial amazons (parrots)   **P:**86
Imperial City (Beijing, China)   **B:**127b
Imperial City (Vienna, Austria)   **V:**332j–333
Imperial gallons (liquid measures)   **W:**115
Imperialism (domination of weak countries by the strong)
   I:100–102; **W:**270–71
   British in Asia and Africa   **E:**251
   McKinley administration   **M:**193
Imperial Palace (Tokyo, Japan)   **T:**219
Imperial Valley (California)   **C:**20; **O:**3; **W:**74
Impetigo (skin disease)   **D:**123, 195
Implants, hormonal (for birth control)   **B:**250b
Implements *see* Tools
Imports   **I:**270–71; **T:**265 *see also* individual country,
      province, and state articles
   tariff discourages imports   **T:**23
   United States food supply   **F:**335
Imposition (arrangement of pages of a book for printing)
   B:332; **P:**470
   picture(s)   **B:**331
Impression: Sunrise (painting by Monet)
   picture(s)   **M:**386
Impressionism (in art)   **I:**103–6; **P:**29
   American art   **U:**131
   art of the artist   **A:**433
   Australian painting   **A:**501
   Cassatt, Mary   **C:**130
   Degas, Edgar   **D:**86
   France   **F:**430, 447

Japanese woodblock prints as influence   **J:**50
   Manet, Édouard   **M:**78
   modern art   **M:**387–88
   Monet, Claude   **M:**411
   painted directly on canvas   **D:**318
   Renoir, Pierre Auguste   **R:**174
   watercolor painting   **W:**56
Impressionism (in literature)   **I:**106
Impressionism (in music)   **I:**106, 412; **M:**398, 544
   France, music of   **F:**447
Impressment (of goods)   **C:**497
Impressment (of sailors)
   Jefferson and the embargo   **J:**71
   War of 1812   **W:**8–9
Imprinting (of birds)   **B:**232; **D:**345; **L:**302
Impromptu (musical form)   **M:**542
Impromptu speech delivery   **P:**520
Improper fractions   **F:**397
Improvisation (composition on the spur of the moment)
   acting   **T:**161
   African and American folk music   **A:**79
   electronic music   **E:**157
   epic poems   **F:**310
   folk music   **F:**321
   India, music of   **I:**143
   jazz   **J:**57, 59, 60, 62, 63, 64
   music   **M:**536
Impulse engines   **E:**229
   picture(s)   **E:**231
Impulse turbines   **E:**229; **T:**341
Impurities (in a material)   **M:**153
Inattention (symptom of ADHD)   **A:**23
Inauguration (of a United States president)   **P:**445
   oath of office   **P:**445
   Twentieth Amendment   **U:**158–59
   picture(s)
      Polk's was in the rain   **P:**376
Incandescence (emission of light from intense heat)
   cold light (bioluminescence)   **B:**205
   electric light bulb, development of   **I:**284
   incandescent filament lamps   **E:**145, 150; **L:**234
   Latimer, Lewis   **I:**283
Incapacitation (isolating criminals from society)   **C:**586
Incas (Indians of South America)   **A:**245; **I:**107–10, 173
   architecture   **A:**367
   blood transfusion   **B:**262
   Chile, history of   **C:**254
   Ecuador   **E:**67, 69
   Heyerdahl, Thor, studies by   **H:**125
   Indians since 1500   **I:**195–96
   knotted ropes as records   **A:**228; **K:**286
   llamas   **L:**278
   mummies   **M:**513
   Peru   **P:**164
   Pizarro, Francisco   **P:**268
   postal service, history of   **P:**397
   Quechuas descended from   **B:**306
   road system   **A:**229
   South America unified over a huge area   **S:**292, 293
   picture(s)
      Atahualpa's meeting with Pizarro   **S:**292
      ceremonial knife   **I:**173
      gold mask   **E:**409
      Machu Picchu ruins   **A:**234, 367; **L:**60; **P:**165
      modern youth in traditional clothing   **S:**284
      mummy   **M:**513
      trail in Peruvian Andes   **S:**275
Incense   **P:**150; **R:**184
Inch (measure of length)   **W:**112
Inchon, Battle of (Korea, 1950)   **K:**305
Incidental infections (which do not contribute to further spread
      of the disease)   **V:**283
Incinerators (to burn solid wastes)   **S:**33
   plastics, disposal of   **P:**327
   treating hazardous wastes   **H:**73

Indians, American (cont.)
    maple syrup and sugar **M:**91
    Maya **M:**184–87
    Mexico **M:**240, 248, 250
    Montana battles **M:**428
    Mormons, relations with **U:**254–55
    music **L:**71–72, 337; **M:**545
    mythology **F:**307; **M:**571–72, 576–77
    natural gas, early use of **N:**60
    New Mexico has highest percentage **N:**184
    Osceola (Seminole warrior) **O:**237
    paintings by George Catlin **U:**129
    Plymouth Colony **P:**346, 347
    Pontiac **P:**382
    Puritans warred with **P:**551
    reservations *see* Indian reservations
    rubber, history of **R:**347
    Samoset **S:**25
    Sequoya **S:**122
    South America **S:**274, 285, 292
    South Dakota colleges and universities **S:**318
    Tecumseh **T:**42
    textiles, history of **T:**143
    tribal governments **I:**190
    wampum **M:**413
    Wanuskewin Heritage Park (Saskatchewan) **S:**47
    What were the consequences of Columbus' voyage in
        1492? **C:**448
    Where are the Indians now? **I:**201
    map(s)
        North American culture areas and tribes in 1500
            I:174
        South American culture areas and tribes in 1500
            I:192
    picture(s)
        Bolivia **B:**306; **L:**47
        ceremonial dances **M:**545; **R:**145
        Cherokee woman working with beads **N:**310
        costume, traditional **C:**373
        folk dances **F:**300
        forced relocation **W:**270
        Ghost Dance **I:**182
        Oklahoma festival **O:**83
        powwow in Nevada **N:**129
        selling handicrafts at outdoor market **O:**86
        Shoshoni sunrise ceremony **F:**141
        South America **S:**284
        United States, population of the **U:**73
        wampum **M:**412
Indians, Asian *see also* Asian Indian Americans; India
    Uganda **U:**4
    United Kingdom **U:**47, 48
Indian summer (warm weather in autumn) **F:**291
Indian Territory (Oklahoma) **O:**94, 95, 96
Indian (Bengal) tigers **T:**198
    picture(s) **A:**438d; **T:**198
Indian wars of North America **I:**202–5
    Apache leader Geronimo **G:**190
    Buffalo Soldiers **B:**431
    French and Indian War **F:**462–65
    gold discoveries led to war **G:**252
    Pontiac **P:**382
    Tecumseh **T:**42
    westward movement **W:**140
Indicator (display screen of a radar system) **R:**38–39
Indictment (in law) **C:**575
Indies, Council of the (colonial Latin America) **L:**58
Indigestion (stomach disorder) **S:**461
Indigo (plant) **D:**373, 376; **S:**310
Indirect taxes **T:**25
Indium (element) **E:**173
Individualists (in Chinese art) **C:**275
Individualized instruction *see* Programmed instruction
Individual proprietorship (type of business) **B:**470
Individual psychotherapy **M:**225

Individuals with Disabilities Education Act (United States, 1975)
    D:180
Indo-America (Indian culture in Latin America) **L:**57
Indo-Aryan languages *see* Indo-Iranian languages
Indo-Aryans (a people of India) **I:**117
Indochina (peninsula in Southeast Asia) **S:**335–36 *see also*
    the names of nations
    French Indochina **C:**38; **L:**43; **V:**334c
    Geneva Accords **G:**93
    Vietnam War **V:**335–38
    World War II **W:**298, 301–2
Indochina War (1946–1954) **S:**335; **V:**335–36
Indochina War, Second (1958–1975) *see* Vietnam War
Indo-European languages **A:**445; **L:**38–39
Indo-Iranian (Indo-Aryan) languages **A:**445; **L:**39
Indonesia **I:**206–12
    Aceh civil war **A:**457
    Borneo **B:**336, 337
    economy **S:**332, 333
    food **F:**332
    food popular in the Netherlands **N:**120
    gamelan orchestra **M:**545
    Jakarta **J:**13–14
    Netherlands, history of the **N:**121
    New Year **N:**208
    nightclub bombing (2002) **T:**115
    Organization of Petroleum Exporting Countries **O:**222
    Papua **N:**148, 149
    population is fourth largest in world **S:**328
    territorial dispute with Malaysia **M:**59
    Timor, East, history of **T:**207, 208
    World War II **W:**303, 304
    map(s) **I:**209
    picture(s)
        batik cloth, hand-dyed **D:**374
        dancer **I:**206
        farmer with water buffalo **I:**207
        flag **F:**232
        Jakarta **A:**449; **I:**206; **J:**14
        liquefied natural gas plant **I:**210
        Malay people **I:**206
        Mount Rindjani **I:**208
        Muslim wedding **W:**103
        Papua **N:**148
        rice crop **A:**92–93, 300, 438e; **G:**281; **I:**208; **S:**328
        Roman Catholic Mass **R:**294
        women carrying goods on their heads **I:**207
Indoor activities *see also* Games; Hobbies; the indoor activities
    listed under Experiments and other science activities
    bulletin boards, how to make and decorate **B:**447–49
    crossword puzzles **C:**597
    decorating a room **I:**260–61
    gift wrapping **G:**206–7
    greeting cards, how to make **G:**376
    jokes and riddles **J:**125–26
    letter writing **L:**158–61
    magic **M:**22–25
    number puzzles and games **N:**389–95
    parties **P:**87–91
    peanut butter, how to make **P:**112
    puppets and marionettes **P:**545–48
    putting on plays **P:**335–38
    puzzles **P:**553–54
    tops **T:**240
    valentines, how to make **V:**266–68
    ventriloquism **V:**302
    video recording **V:**332h–332i
    writing a journal **D:**147
Indoor (Arena) football **F:**364
Induction, magnetic *see* Magnetic induction
Inductive arguments (in logic) **L:**289
Indulgences (papal grants) **C:**291, 292; **P:**492; **R:**130, 290
    Luther's theses against **L:**346
Indus River (Asia) **I:**124; **R:**242 *see also* Harappan
    civilization

Industrial accountants **B:**313
Industrial alcohol **G:**285
Industrial archaeology **A:**351
Industrial arts **I:**213
    machine-made decorative arts **D:**68, 78
    printing **P:**468–79
    woodworking **W:**230–33
Industrial design **I:**213–15
    Bauhaus influence **G:**173
Industrial diamonds **D:**147–48
Industrial diseases *see* Occupational diseases
Industrial engineers **E:**226
Industrial espionage **S:**407, 409
Industrial painting *see* Painting, industrial
Industrial property **R:**113
Industrial Revolution **I:**216–24; **W:**269, 270–71
    advertising **A:**34–35
    building construction, effect on **B:**440
    capitalism became a great force **C:**103
    chemical industry **C:**196
    child labor **C:**227
    cities, growth of **C:**318; **U:**236
    clothing, history of **C:**378
    Communism, origins of **C:**472
    conservation movement, history of the **C:**526
    early childhood education, history of **K:**248–49
    engineering, history of **E:**228
    England **E:**249–50; **U:**59, 62
    Europe **E:**341
    folk music, changes in **F:**325, 327
    guilds, weakening of **G:**405
    home economics, the need for **H:**180
    homes and housing, history of **H:**194–95
    inventions **I:**280–81
    labor movement, history of **L:**11–12
    machine-made decorative arts **D:**78
    manufacturing **M:**87–88
    mining expanded rapidly **M:**324
    Pawtucket (Rhode Island) **R:**221, 226
    science fiction, beginnings of **S:**79
    socialism, history of **S:**224
    technology, development of **T:**40
    textiles, history of **T:**145
    unemployment for first time **U:**28
    wheels, part played by **W:**160
Industrial spies *see* Industrial espionage
Industrial Tool Period (stage in tool use) **T:**235
Industrial unions **L:**16
Industrial wastes
    acid rain **A:**9–10
    air pollution **A:**122–25
    environmental diseases **D:**186
    hazardous wastes **H:**72–73
    wastewater **S:**33
    water pollution **E:**302; **W:**62–63, 64–65
Industrial Workers of the World (I.W.W.) **L:**15
Industry **I:**225–26 *see also* individual country, province, and
      state articles, and names of industries
    acid rain **A:**9–10
    agribusiness **A:**95
    air conditioning, uses of **A:**101
    atmosphere, effects on **A:**480, 482
    automation **A:**529–33
    computer graphics, uses of **C:**484
    corporate and industrial video careers **T:**69
    dairying, history of **D:**10–11
    detergents and soaps used in **D:**139–40
    electronics **E:**162
    environment, problems of **E:**301–6
    factories changed by electric motors **E:**154
    food industry in the United States **F:**333–35, 338
    gases in industry **G:**59–61
    growth affects labor-management relations **L:**4–5
    how people use water **W:**52, 55

Industrial Revolution **I:**216–24
    international trade **I:**270
    jewelry **J:**100
    lasers, uses of **L:**46c
    manufacturing **M:**87–89
    museums **M:**523
    natural gas, uses of **N:**58
    noise, protection from **N:**271
    nursing in industry **N:**419, 420
    personal selling is important to industrial customers
      S:21
    public relations **P:**517–18
    retailing **R:**189
    rivers, uses of **R:**240
    robots, industrial **R:**253–54, 255–56
    Soviet Union **U:**37–38
    special libraries for industry **L:**179
    tariff adopted to protect home industry **T:**23
    technology **T:**40–41
    television, uses of **T:**61
    transportation industry and world economy **T:**289–90
    unemployment **U:**28–29
    United States, history of the **U:**188
    X-rays, uses of **P:**208; **X:**350
Industry and Security, Bureau of (BIS) **C:**455
Indy, Vincent d' (French composer) **F:**446
Inert (chemical term) **C:**204
Inert gases *see* Noble gases
Inertia (in physics) **M:**172; **P:**228, 234
    motion **M:**474
    rockets and Newton's laws of motion **R:**257
    satellites, artificial **S:**53
    work **W:**244
    picture(s)
        pushing a car **M:**173
Inertial confinement (in nuclear fusion) **N:**368
Inertial guidance (navigation system) **N:**76–77
    airplane navigation **A:**119
    gyroscope **G:**436
    missiles **M:**346, 347
    rockets **R:**261
    space navigation **S:**340k
Infantile paralysis *see* Poliomyelitis
Infant mortality
    colonial life in America **C:**411
    countries with highest and lowest rates, list of **P:**387
    Inuit **I:**276
Infantry (of the United States Army) **U:**102
    picture(s) **U:**102
Infants *see* Baby
Infant schools **K:**249
Infection
    drug abuse, harmful effects of **D:**332
    Lister's work **L:**257; **S:**513
    medicine, history of **M:**208c
    preventing wound infection **F:**159
    sanitation measures to prevent **S:**33
    white cells defend body against **B:**260–61
Infectious (Communicable) diseases **D:**181–83
    preventing disease **H:**76
    public health **H:**77; **P:**512, 513
    vaccination and immunization **V:**260–61
    vectors of disease **V:**282–85
Infectious mononucleosis (disease) **B:**262; **D:**195
Inferior planets (in astronomy) **S:**246
Inferior vena cava (large vein that enters the heart) **H:**81
Infertility (inability to have children) **C:**94; **D:**193
Infielder (in baseball) **B:**80
Infield fly (in baseball) **B:**83
Infinite decimals **N:**402
Infinite sets (in mathematics) **M:**169; **S:**128a
Infinity **N:**400
Inflammation (of body tissues) **D:**210
    heart diseases **H:**84
"In Flanders Fields" (poem by John McCrae) **W:**288

Inflation and deflation (of prices) **I:227–28** *see also* Banks
    and banking
    Consumer Price Index **C:**533
    economic cycles **D:**122; **E:**61
    financial panic and bank failures **B:**53
    Nixon's wage-price freeze **N:**262e
    percents, use of **P:**146
Inflation theory (Expanding universe theory) **A:**474–75; **U:**218
Inflections (in language) **E:**265, 267
    Latin language **L:**74
Influenza (virus disease) **A:**457; **D:**195; **I:228**; **T:**152; **V:**261,
    369
Information
    statistics **S:**439–43
Information storage and retrieval systems **A:**532
    computers **C:**480–94
    electronics **E:**161
    interactive database services **A:**32
    use in libraries **L:**186
Infrared Astronomical Satellite (IRAS) **O:**11; **S:**367
Infrared radiation **H:**93; **R:**45
    airborne observatories **O:**10
    fiber optics **F:**107
    light, spectrum analysis of **L:**221
    photography **P:**208–9
    Space Infrared Telescope Facility **O:**12
    Spitzer Space Telescope **S:**368
    telescopes **T:**59–60
    thermometers **T:**164
    diagram(s)
        electromagnetic spectrum, place on **R:**45
INF Treaty *see* Intermediate-Range Nuclear Forces Treaty
Inga Falls (Congo River) **C:**507
Ingalik (Indians of North America) **I:**188
Ingemann, Bernhard Severin (Danish writer) **S:**58i
Ingersoll, Robert G. (American lawyer and lecturer) **O:**191
Ingots, steel **I:**334
    picture(s) **I:**335
Ingres, Jean Auguste Dominique (French artist) **D:**318; **F:**428;
    P:29
    picture(s)
        pencil drawing **D:**317
Inhalation of vapors (drug abuse) **D:**331
Inhalers (to deliver asthma medication into the lungs) **A:**463
Inheritance, genetic **E:**376–77
Inherited diseases *see* Hereditary diseases and disorders
Inhibition by-product (in body chemistry) **E:**307
Initials (used as abbreviations) **A:**4
Initiative, referendum, and recall (in government)
    Oklahoma **O:**91
    Oregon system **O:**214
    referendum and recall are special types of election **E:**129
    referendum defined **G:**276
    Swiss national referendum system **S:**545
Injectable hormones (for birth control) **B:**250b
Injection molding (plastics manufacturing process) **P:**325
    picture(s) **P:**325
Injunction (written court order) **L:**89
Injuries *see* First aid
Ink **I:229**
    ball-point pens **P:**143
    de-inking of paper pulp for recycling **P:**57
    drawing materials **D:**312–13
    inventions **I:**280
    water-based for gravure printing **P:**479
    picture(s)
        drawing materials **D:**310
Ink (defense of mollusks) **M:**407; **O:**50
Inkarrí (Inca legendary hero) **I:**110
Ink-blot tests **T:**119
Inland Sea (Japan) **J:**34
Inland waterways
    Great Lakes-Saint Lawrence system **G:**326–28; **S:**14–15
    Ontario **O:**130

Inlaying (of furniture)
    picture(s) **F:**506
Inman, Henry (American artist) **F:**168
Inner Asia *see* Central Asia
Inner City (Beijing, China) **B:**127b–127c
Inner ear (of the body) **E:**4
    fish **F:**193
    picture(s) **E:**5
Inner Mongolia (a region of China) **M:**416
Innings (in baseball) **B:**81
Innocent III (antipope) **R:**293
Innocent I, Saint (pope) **R:**292
Innocent II (pope) **R:**292
Innocent III (pope) **M:**295 *profile;* **R:**293
    Jews persecuted by **J:**105
    John, king of England, and **J:**112
Innocent IV (pope) **R:**293
Innocent V (pope) **R:**293
Innocent VI (pope) **R:**293
Innocent VII (pope) **R:**293
Innocent VIII (pope) **R:**293
Innocent IX (pope) **R:**293
Innocent X (pope) **R:**293
    Velázquez portrait **V:**294
Innocent XI (pope) **R:**293
Innocent XII (pope) **R:**293
Innocent XIII (pope) **R:**293
Innovation and Improvement, Office of (United States) **E:**89
Inns *see* Hotels; Motels
Innsbruck (Austria) **A:**521
Inns of Court (four legal societies in England) **L:**89
Innu (people of North America) **N:**141
Innuit *see* Inuit
Inodorus melons **M:**214
Inönü, Ismet (Turkish statesman) **T:**349
Inorganic chemistry *see* Chemistry, inorganic
Inorganic fertilizers **F:**97
Inouye, Daniel K. (United States senator) **H:**61 *profile*
Input and output devices (of computers) **C:**481, 491
    picture(s) **C:**482
Inquest (inquiry made by a court-appointed group) **L:**89
Inquisition (jury system instituted by Charlemagne) **J:**163
Inquisition (of the Roman Catholic Church) **R:**290
    Ferdinand and Isabella, revival under **F:**88
    Jewish community expelled from Spain **J:**104
    witches, persecution of **W:**208–9
Insanity *see* Mental illness
Inscriptions, Temple of the (Palenque, Mexico) **P:**558
    picture(s) **P:**558
Insect bites **A:**191; **F:**161; **S:**3
Insect control **I:**249–50
    biological control of **F:**482
    environmental problems **E:**303
    roundworms control pests **W:**321
Insect-eating plants *see* Carnivorous plants
Insecticides
    controlling harmful insects **I:**249
    diseases, prevention of **D:**212
    environment, effect on **E:**303
    gardens and gardening **G:**42
    household pest control **H:**264
    mosquito control **M:**471
    pest control machinery **F:**56
    plant pests **P:**290–91
    water pollution **W:**66
    picture(s)
        sprayed on mosquito nesting sites **P:**515
Insectivora (order of mammals)
    hedgehogs **H:**101–2
    moles **M:**404
    shrews **S:**166
    teeth **M:**72–73
    picture(s)
        mole as example **M:**67

Insect pests *see also* Insect control; Insecticides
  apple trees attacked by   **A:**332–33
  corn, enemies of   **C:**558
  cotton growing   **C:**568–69
  fruitgrowing   **F:**482
  plant pests   **P:**286–91
  vegetable gardening   **V:**288
Insect-resistant crops   **B:**213, 214
Insects   **I:**230–50 *see also* the names of insects
  allergies   **A:**191
  cave dwellers   **C:**158
  compass sense of migrating animals   **H:**202
  dormancy   **H:**128
  dragonflies   **D:**294
  dyes: kermes and cochineal   **D:**373, 375
  estivation   **H:**128
  evolve resistance to insecticides   **E:**378
  experiments and other science activities   **E:**396
  first aid for stings   **F:**161
  glands control molting   **G:**226
  hormones   **H:**228
  household pests   **H:**260–64
  houseplants can be infected by   **H:**267
  metamorphosis   **M:**238
  migration   **H:**198–99
  mosquito control and work of Walter Reed   **R:**128
  mosquitoes spread malaria   **D:**196
  plant pests   **P:**286–91
  pollination of flowers   **F:**286; **P:**308
  rain-forest loss   **R:**100
  reproduction   **R:**177–78
  vectors of disease   **D:**183, 211, 212; **V:**282–84, 285
  zooplankton   **P:**285
Insect stings, first aid for   **F:**161
Inserters (office machines)   **O:**60
Inside Passage (waterway, Washington–Alaska)   **B:**402, 406a; **C:**57
Insignia
  picture(s)
    Boy Scouts and Cub Scouts   **B:**357
    Girl Scouts   **G:**214
    United States Air Force   **U:**108
    United States Army   **U:**103
    United States Marine Corps   **U:**120
    United States Navy   **U:**112
Insomnia (a state of sleeplessness)   **S:**198
Inspection plan (for disarmament)   **D:**181, 182
Inspector General, Office of the (United States)   **J:**166
Inspector General, The (play by Gogol)   **R:**381
Instant cameras   **P:**202
Instant coffee   **C:**397
Instant film (in photography)   **P:**215
Instant messaging   **D:**50
Instant tea   **T:**35
Instinct
  birds   **B:**224
Institute for Advanced Study   **E:**120; **N:**169
Institutional Revolutionary Party (PRI) (Mexico)   **M:**240, 251, 252
Instruction, programmed *see* Programmed instruction
Instructional materials centers *see* Media centers
Instrumental music
  baroque music   **B:**71–72
  Renaissance music   **R:**173–74
Instruments, musical *see* Musical instruments
Instruments, scientific *see* Scientific instruments
Insular Affairs, Office of (United States)   **I:**256
Insular Mountains (submerged chain off Canada)   **C:**56
Insulation and insulating materials
  aluminum   **A:**195
  asbestos   **A:**438c
  building construction   **B:**433, 436
  ceramics   **C:**178
  down of waterfowl   **D:**346, 348

  energy conservation   **H:**97
  fiberglass   **F:**105
  plastics   **P:**323, 326
  poor conductors of heat   **H:**94
  solar energy use in buildings   **S:**239
  wood a good heat insulator   **W:**222
  wool keeps air trapped between its fibers   **W:**234
Insulators, electric   **E:**139, 158; **T:**274
Insulin (hormone used to treat diabetes)   **D:**145, 191–92; **H:**227, 228
  bacteria can produce   **G:**83
  Banting's discovery   **B:**59
  biochemistry   **B:**188
  blood carries through body   **B:**260
  body, human   **B:**292
  endocrine glands   **G:**228
  microbiology   **M:**279
  produced from animal glands   **M:**198
  where drugs come from   **D:**334
Insulin resistance (early stage of diabetes)   **D:**145
Insurance   **I:**251–52
  banks' deposit insurance   **B:**58–59
  doctors' malpractice insurance   **D:**238
  Hartford (Connecticut)   **C:**515
  post office services   **P:**399
  social *see* Social security
  trade and commerce   **T:**265
  unemployment *see* Unemployment insurance
  workers' compensation   **W:**253
Insurance, accident   **I:**252
Insurance, automobile   **D:**327; **I:**251, 252
Insurance, casualty   **I:**251
Insurance, disability   **I:**252
Insurance, fire   **I:**251
Insurance, group life   **I:**252
Insurance, health   **I:**252
  aged, health insurance for the   **O:**99
  Canada's Medical Care Act   **S:**226
  health-care access   **M:**209–10
  picture(s)
    father enrolling son in government-sponsored program   **P:**420
Insurance, liability   **I:**251
Insurance, life   **A:**82; **I:**251–52
Insurance, property   **I:**251
Insurance, social *see* Social security
Intaglio printing   **E:**294; **G:**302; **P:**477
Intaglios (carved gems)   **J:**98
Intake manifold (of an automobile)   **A:**547
Intarsia (inlaying of wood furniture)   **D:**76–77
Integers (numbers)   **N:**399–400
Integrated circuits (in electronics)   **C:**491, 493; **M:**153, 154; **T:**277–78
  automation used in production   **A:**530
  inventions   **I:**285
Integrated construction (of automobiles)   **A:**554
Integration of housing   **U:**234
Integration of schools   **N:**26; **S:**114, 115 *see also* Segregation
  Arkansas   **A:**418–19
  Delaware   **D:**93
  picture(s)
    Arkansas   **A:**419
Intellectual property   **U:**69
Intelligence   **I:**253–54
  artificial intelligence   **R:**254
  brain size not related to intelligence   **B:**364
  effort compared with   **L:**106
  gene interactions   **G:**80
  intelligence quotient   **T:**118
  mental retardation   **R:**189–91
  tests *see* Mental ability tests
  What does it mean to be smart?   **P:**508–9
Intelligence, animal *see* Animal intelligence and behavior

International Federation of Swimming (FINA)   D:228; S:539
International Female Boxers Association (IFBA)   B:353
International Fencing Federation   F:87
International Finance Corporation (IFC)   B:55–56
International Fund for Agricultural Development (IFAD)   F:351;
   U:69
International Gamma-Ray Astrophysics Laboratory (INTEGRAL)
   S:368
International Geophysical Year (IGY)   A:295
International Gothic style (art)   F:423
International Gymnastics Federation (F.I.G.)   G:433
International Historic Site (Saint Croix Island, Maine)   N:55
International Hockey Federation (FIH)   F:120
International Ice Hockey Federation   I:30
International Ice Patrol   I:18; U:124
International Indian Treaty Conference (1977)   A:199
Internationalism (in art)   E:263, 264
International Labor Affairs, Bureau of   L:3
International Labor Day see May Day
International Labor Organization (ILO)   L:18; U:69
International Ladies Garment Workers Union
   picture(s)
      demonstration   L:14
International languages see Universal languages
International law   I:267–68; L:85
   aliens   A:189
   copyright   C:555
   endangered species, protection of   E:209, 210–11
   Geneva Conventions   G:93
   international relations   I:269–70
   passports and visas   P:96
   patent owners, rights of   P:99
   peace movements   P:105–6
   refugees   R:137
   treaties   T:296–99
International Maritime Organization (IMO)   S:154; U:69
International Monetary Fund (IMF)   U:69
International Morse Code see Morse Code, International
International Olympic Committee (IOC)   O:105, 107–8, 110,
   111, 114, 116
International Paralympic Committee (IPC)   O:115
International Peace Garden (North Dakota–Manitoba)   M:85;
   N:322, 331
International Phonetic Alphabet (IPA)   A:303; L:38
International Red Cross see Red Cross
International relations   I:269–70
   Cold War   C:400–401
   disarmament   D:181–82
   foreign aid   F:370
   foreign service   F:371
   Hull, Cordell   H:280
   imperialism   I:100–102
   international law   I:267–68
   international trade   I:270–71
   League of Nations   L:95
   Monroe Doctrine   M:427
   Open Door Policy for China   M:193–94
   Organization for Economic Cooperation and Development
      O:220
   Organization of African Unity   O:221
   Organization of American States   O:221
   Organization of Petroleum Exporting Countries   O:222
   Peace Corps   P:104
   peace movements   P:105–6
   politics and the Olympics   O:111
   powers in foreign affairs of the United States president
      P:451–52
   treaties   T:296–99
   Washington, George: administration of   W:44
   between the world wars   W:292–96
International Science and Engineering Fair (ISEF)   S:78
International Skating Union (ISU)   I:41, 45
International Skeeter Association   I:19
International Ski Federation (FIS)   S:184d

International Space Station (ISS)   S:348, 349–50, 355, 366
   amateur radio station on board   R:62–63
   satellites, artificial   S:54
   space agencies and centers   S:338
   space research and technology   S:363
   space shuttles   S:365
   picture(s)   S:349, 366
International Spy Museum (Washington, D.C.)   M:528
International Standard Book Number (ISBN)   B:329
International style (in architecture)   A:374–75; U:136
   Johnson, Philip   J:123
   Mies van der Rohe, Ludwig   M:306
   picture(s)
      Fagus shoe factory   G:173
International System of Units see Metric system
International Telecommunication Union (ITU)   R:57; U:69
International Telegraph Union see International
   Telecommunication Union
International Tennis Federation   T:95
International Time Bureau   G:374b
International trade   I:270–71
   consumer protection   C:535
   European Union   E:368–69
   free ports   I:270
   General Agreement on Tariffs and Trade   G:76d
   North America   N:303
   North American Free Trade Agreement   N:305
   ships and shipping   S:154–55
   tariff   T:23
   trade and commerce   T:264–65
   triangular trade (New England–West Indies–Africa)
      S:194
   United States   U:94
   What are free ports and foreign-trade zones?   I:270
International Trade Administration (ITA)   C:455
International Ultraviolet Explorer   S:367
International Union for the Conservation of Nature and Natural
   Resources (IUCN)   E:210; N:57
International Union of Pure and Applied Chemistry   E:166, 169
International Whaling Commission   W:153, 155
International Woman Suffrage Alliance   W:215
International Women's Boxing Federation (IWBF)   B:353
International Youth Hostel Federation   H:254
Internet (network of on-line services)   C:486–89, 493, 494
   adoptees' search for birth parents   A:28
   career information   V:376
   communication, advances in   C:468, 470–71
   consumer protection   C:535; F:338
   copyrighted material   C:555
   department stores   D:118
   electronic greeting cards   G:375
   encyclopedias   E:207
   extraterrestrial life, search for   R:70
   fiber-optic cables   L:46c
   genealogical resources   G:76, 76c–76d
   inventions   I:286
   journalism, distribution of information in   J:141
   libraries   L:186
   mail order   M:35
   outlaws and computer crime   O:263, 264
   piracy of commercial recordings   R:124
   postal products and services   P:400
   radio, current and future trends in   R:61
   reference materials   R:129
   science, modern   S:74
   scientific journals   S:68
   telecommunications   C:468; T:49–50
   telegraph systems largely replaced by   T:52
   television   T:71
   United States, communication in the   U:96
   voting online found impossible to secure from hackers
      V:393
   weather information   W:94

Internet (cont.)
   picture(s)
      educational use **C:**462
      wireless Internet connections **R:**51
Interneurons (in the nervous system) **B:**362
Internment (of Japanese Americans in World War II) **W:**304
Interns (in hospitals) **H:**249
Internship programs (in journalism) **J:**139
Inter-Parliamentary Union (representatives of national legislative
   bodies) **P:**84
Interplanetary space *see* Space, outer
Interpol (International Criminal Police Organization) **N:**15;
   P:367
Interpreters (computer programs) **C:**483
Interrogative pronouns **P:**92
Interrupted projections (of maps) **M:**97
Intersection of sets (in mathematics) **M:**158; **S:**128a
Interstate Commerce Commission (ICC) **R:**90; **T:**290, 321;
   U:95, 188
Interstellar matter **U:**211, 212–13
Interstitial fluid (in spaces between body cells) **L:**350
Interstitials (crystal defects) **M:**152
   picture(s) **M:**153
Inter-Testament (apocryphal books of the Bible) **B:**156
Intertropical Convergence Zone (low-pressure region along the
   equator) **W:**189
Interurban railroads **L:**288
Interval (in music) **M:**531–32, 536
Interviewing
   opinion polls **O:**169
Intestate (one who dies without a will) **W:**177
Intestines **B:**281–82; **D:**163, 164–65
   stomach growls **B:**301
   What makes a stomach growl? **S:**461
Inthanon, Doi (mountain, Thailand) **T:**149
In the Black Circle (painting by Kandinsky)
   picture(s) **K:**173
In the Heat of the Night (motion picture, 1967) **M:**495
In the Night Kitchen (book by Maurice Sendak) **S:**116
In the Small, Small Pond (book by Denise Fleming)
   picture(s) **C:**241
Intifada (Palestinian protest movement) **I:**376
Intolerable Acts (Britain, 1774) **C:**82, 536; **D:**59; **R:**197;
   U:176
Intracoastal Waterway (eastern and Gulf coasts, United States)
   N:313
   South Carolina **S:**305
   Texas **T:**127, 133
Intransitive verbs **G:**289; **P:**93
Intrauterine device (IUD) (for birth control) **B:**250b
Intravenous (IV) equipment (to deliver fluid and medicine
   through a vein) **A:**199
Intrinsic factor (stomach secretion) **B:**262; **S:**461; **V:**370c
Intrinsic value (of a piece of jewelry) **J:**94
Introductions (in etiquette) **E:**338
Introvert (personality type) **J:**156; **P:**502
Intrusion (geologic process) **G:**114
Intrusive rocks **G:**117; **R:**265
Inuit (formerly called **Eskimos**) **I:272–76**
   Arctic region **A:**379, 380
   Canada, art and architecture of **C:**71
   Canadian population **C:**51, 52, 85; **N:**141, 341
   Greenland **G:**371, 374–74a
   Indians, American **I:**190–91
   kayaks **C:**101; **K:**199
   Northwest Territories **N:**343
   Nunavut **N:**411–12, 413
   walrus hunting **W:**7
   whaling **W:**155
   picture(s) **I:**272
      boy with salmon **N:**295
      children in caribou furs **C:**50
      costumes, traditional **C:**373
      dogsledding **I:**276; **N:**410

      family **F:**43
      fisherman mending net **N:**293
      girl in fur-lined parka **F:**501
      hunters capturing a seal **A:**300
      hunting **I:**273
      soapstone carving **C:**71; **I:**275
      whale bone carving of polar bear **A:**427
Inuit (Innuit) (word meaning "the people") **I:**272
Inuit-Inupiaq languages **I:**273, 276
Inuit Tapirisat (Inuit Brotherhood) **I:**276
Inupiat (a people of Alaska) **A:**144, 150; **I:**272
   picture(s) **I:**272
Inuvialuit (a people of Canada) **I:**272
Invalides *see* Hôtel des Invalides
Invariants (in topology) **T:**236
Invasive exotics (forest pests) **F:**376
Inventions **I:277–86** *see also* Patents; Technology; the names
   of inventions and inventors
   air conditioning **A:**101–2
   alphabet **A:**194–94c
   Archimedes **A:**363
   aviation **A:**559–72
   Bessemer, Sir Henry **B:**154
   cotton gin **C:**570
   Edison, Thomas Alva **E:**70–73
   engineering, history of **E:**228
   Franklin, Benjamin **F:**455
   Industrial Revolution **I:**218–21, 222
   Kettering, Charles Franklin **K:**236
   Langmuir, Irving **L:**35
   Leonardo da Vinci **L:**152–54
   McCormick's reaper **M:**190
   patents **P:**99
   pottery and American Indians **I:**166
   printing **P:**468, 472, 478–79
   robots **R:**252–56
   science fiction **S:**82
   spinning jenny **I:**218
   technology and inventions **T:**39–41
   Watt, James **W:**77
   wax paper **W:**78
   weaving loom **I:**217–18
   Westinghouse, George **W:**125
   wheels **W:**159–60
   world's fairs bring to the public's attention **F:**17
   Wright brothers **W:**328
Inversion (in music) **M:**533, 536
Inversion, temperature *see* Temperature inversion
Invertebrates (animals without backbones) **A:**265, 267
   circulatory systems **C:**306
   crustaceans **C:**601–2
   Earth's history **E:**26, 27
   fossils **F:**385–86
   jellyfish and other coelenterates **J:**72–77
   prehistoric animals **P:**432
   starfishes **S:**426–27
   worms **W:**319–22
Invert sugar (sweetener) **C:**97
Investigative reporters (journalists) **J:**136
Investment banks **B:**55
Investments (economic activities)
   how to be an entrepreneur **B:**472
   investment banks **B:**55
   stocks and bonds **S:**454–59
Investors (people who buy securities) **S:**454
Invincible Armada *see* Spanish Armada
Invisible inks **I:**229
Invisible Man, The (book by Ellison) **O:**94
Invitations **L:**160a
   for parties **P:**87–88, 90
Invocation (prayer) **P:**430
Involuntary muscles **M:**519
Involuntary smoking (inhalation of tobacco smoke by
   nonsmokers) *see* Passive smoking
Inyangani, Mount (highest peak in Zimbabwe) **Z:**382

Irrigation   I:339–41 *see also* Dams
    Andean civilizations   A:244
    Arizona   A:396
    dams   D:16; D:17, 20, 21
    deserts, future of   D:130
    early Hawaiian system   H:60
    food supply   F:350, 351
    Hohokam people   A:402
    how people use water   W:52
    how rivers provide water   R:240
    inventions   I:279
    Iraq restored ancient Babylonian system   B:5
    Mexican rivers affected by U.S. irrigation   N:293
    Middle East   M:302
    Nebraska's farmlands   N:86, 89, 95
    oases   O:2–3
    orchards   F:482
    prairie farming   P:428
    Sudan's Gezira   S:479
    Sumer   S:487
    vegetable gardening   V:287–88
    water conservation   C:524; W:74
    waterpower   W:69
    picture(s)   D:126; E:100; F:59; I:121; N:86
        volunteer working on project in Ecuador   V:390
        water conservation   C:524
Irving, Washington (American writer)   A:208; I:342–44
    "Legend of Sleepy Hollow, The"   L:129
    "Rip Van Winkle," excerpt from   I:343–44
    short stories   S:161
Irwin, James B. (American astronaut)   S:347 *profile*
    picture(s)   S:347
Isaac (Hebrew patriarch)   A:9; I:345
    picture(s)   B:162
Isaac, Heinrich (Flemish composer)   D:372; R:172–73
Isaacs, Jorge (Colombian writer)   C:407
Isabella I (Spanish queen)   F:88; S:376
    Columbus, Christopher   C:446, 448
    Jews, expulsion from Spain of the   J:104
    Prado   P:423
    picture(s)   S:376
Isabella II (Spanish queen)   S:378
Isabelline Gothic (Spanish art style)   S:382–83
Isaiah (book of the Old Testament)   B:160, 161–62
Isaiah (Hebrew prophet)   I:345
Isamitt, Carlos (Chilean composer)   L:73
ISBN *see* International Standard Book Number
Ise (Japan, site of shrine to sun goddess)   J:40
Isenheim altarpiece (painted by Grünewald)
    picture(s)   G:170
Isfahan (Iran)   I:307, 308
    picture(s)
        Imam Mosque   I:307
        Royal Mosque   A:438d
"I shall find a way or make one" (words of Robert E. Peary)
    P:117
"I shall return" (words of Douglas MacArthur)   M:2
Ishmael (Biblical character)   A:9; B:160; M:199
Ishpeming (Michigan)   M:262
Ishtar Gate (part of Babylonian wall)   A:365
    picture(s)   A:232, 233
Ishtar Terra (continent on Venus)   V:303a
Isinbayeva, Yelena (Russian athlete)   O:120
Isis (Egyptian goddess of magic)   E:108; N:261
    picture(s)   E:107
Islam (religion of Muslims)   I:346–53; R:146 *see also* Arabs;
    Moors
    Abraham honored by   A:9
    Afghanistan   A:43, 45
    Africa   A:57, 65
    Albania   A:160
    Algeria   A:185
    angels   A:258
    Arabic language   L:39

Arabic literature   A:341
Arabs   A:343–44, 344–45
art and architecture *see* Islamic art and architecture
Asian religions   A:448
Bangladesh   B:48, 49, 50
Bible seen to some extent as sacred scripture   B:156
Bosnia and Herzegovina   B:338; G:96
Brunei   B:415
calendar   C:16–17
carnelian talismans   G:72
Christianity and   C:291, 295
Crusades against   C:598–600; R:289–90
early education spread by   E:79–80
Egyptian invasion   E:104
Ethiopia   E:331
European invasion   M:289, 290
family   F:42
France has Europe's largest Muslim community   F:404
Friday is a holy day   R:153
fundamentalism   F:492
funeral customs   F:493
geology, history of   G:109
holy war against Christian world   R:288
India, history of   I:118, 131–32
India, literature of   I:142
Indian festivals   I:122
Indonesia is world's most populous Muslim nation   I:206
Iran's Shi'ites   I:305, 307, 308, 309
Iraq   I:311
Jerusalem   J:80, 82, 84
Jesus Christ   J:85
Judaism and the founding of Islam   J:104
Koran   K:292–93
Kurds   K:307
Lebanese civil war   L:122–23
Lebanon   L:119
Libya   L:187, 190
Malaysia   M:55, 58
marriage rites   W:103
Mauritania   M:179
Mecca, holy city of   M:199
medicine, history of   M:208
Mohammed   M:401
Morocco   M:458
Nigeria   N:253, 254, 257
Ottoman Empire   O:259–61
Pakistan   I:133; P:36, 37, 40, 40a
Palestine   P:40d
Philippine Moros   P:184
prayer   P:430
prayer from the Koran   P:431
Qaeda, Al, Islamic terrorists   Q:2
religion of the Middle East   M:299
religions of the world   R:148
religious holidays   R:153, 155
Russia   R:358
saints   S:18c
Saudi Arabia   S:58a–58b, 58e
science, milestones in   S:69
Southeast Asia   S:329, 335
Spain   M:291; S:370, 375–76
Spanish Inquisition   F:88
Sudan   S:477, 480
sugar use spread through conquered lands   S:484
Syria   S:549
Thailand   T:152
Turkey   T:345
Union of Soviet Socialist Republics   U:35
United Kingdom   U:48
Yugoslavia   Y:364, 365, 369
picture(s)
    Albanian mosque   A:160
    Berber boy holding a Koran   A:54
    children learning traditions   H:283

Islam
picture(s) (cont.)
education, history of   **E:**80
Id al-Fitr celebration   **R:**155
Indonesian wedding   **W:**103
leaving mosque in Delhi   **I:**117
Muslim woman and baby in Germany   **E:**352
Muslim women at Dome of the Rock   **P:**40d
Nigerian Muslims   **A:**57
pilgrims in Mecca   **R:**145
praying   **A:**448; **I:**118, 349; **M:**299
worshipers in Brunei   **S:**329
Islam, Kazi Nazrul (Indian poet)   **I:**142
Islamabad (capital of Pakistan)   **P:**39
picture(s)   **P:**39
Islamic art and architecture   **A:**370; **I:354–59** *see also*
Mosques
Gothic pointed arch derived from   **G:**265
homes and housing   **H:**193
illuminated manuscripts   **I:**78
India   **A:**367; **I:**136, 137, 139
Iraq   **I:**315
Koranic verses used in   **K:**293
Metropolitan Museum of Art collection   **M:**239
pottery   **P:**410–11
Spain   **S:**380–81
Taj Mahal   **T:**12
tapestry   **T:**20
picture(s)
Alhambra   **S:**381
Lima (Peru)   **S:**293
Sultan Ahmed Mosque (Istanbul)   **T:**348
Turkish pottery   **P:**410
Islamic Front for Salvation (Algeria)   **A:**188
Islamists (Muslim fundamentalists)   **I:**353
Island Falls hydroelectric plant (Saskatchewan)   **S:**43
Island of Doctor Moreau, The (novel by H. G. Wells)   **S:**80
Island of stability (range of stable heavy elements)   **E:**167
Islands   **I:360–68** *see also* the names of islands, as Liberty
Island
Arctic Ocean   **A:**379
Caribbean   **C:**112–15
coral islands   **C:**556; **O:**23
Europe   **E:**348
Indian Ocean   **I:**160
Indonesia's major groups   **I:**207–9
Mediterranean Sea   **M:**211
mid-Atlantic ridge, islands of   **A:**478
New York is a city of islands   **N:**226
North American continent, those islands considered part of
N:282
Pacific Ocean and islands   **P:**3–10
Paraguay River's floating islands   **P:**63
Southeast Asia   **S:**328–36
Venice is a city built on islands   **V:**300
volcanic islands   **O:**21
picture(s)
volcanic islands   **O:**20
Islas Malvinas *see* Falkland Islands
Isle of Man *see* Man, Isle of
Isle of Wight *see* Wight, Isle of
Isle Royale National Park (Lake Superior, Michigan)   **M:**262
Isles of Shoals (New Hampshire–Maine)   **N:**152, 160
Isleta (Indians of North America)   **I:**183
Islets of Langerhans (areas in the pancreas that produce insulin)
D:191
Ismail I (Persian shah)   **I:**308
Isobars (lines of weather maps indicating equal barometric
pressures)   **W:**92
Isocrates (Greek orator)   **G:**357
Isodorus of Miletus (Byzantine architect)   **B:**489
ISO (International Organization for Standards) film-speed index
P:204

Isolationism (in international relations)   **I:**269
Minnesota   **M:**339
United States   **U:**195
Isolde (medieval heroine)   **F:**436
Isomers (in chemistry)   **C:**201, 204
Isometry (in geometry)   **G:**125–26
Isoniazid (drug)   **D:**204
Isopods (land-dwelling crustaceans)   **C:**601, 602; **E:**208
Isoprene (liquid hydrocarbon)   **R:**346
Isopropyl alcohol *see* Rubbing alcohol
Isosceles triangles   **G:**121
diagram(s)   **G:**121
Isostatic adjustment   **G:**223–24
Isotherms (on climate and weather maps)   **W:**92
Isotopes (of chemical elements)   **E:**166
atoms   **A:**486
carbon   **C:**106
chemistry of isotopes   **C:**203, 205
defined   **C:**204
nuclear energy   **N:**367
radioactive elements and isotopes   **R:**64, 74
radioisotope imaging   **I:**86
uranium 235 and 238   **U:**229–30
table(s)
radiometric dating   **R:**75
Israel   **I:369–76**
Arbor Day (Hamishah Asar B'Shevat)   **R:**153–54
Begin, Menachem   **B:**127a
Ben-Gurion, David, was first prime minister   **B:**142
Biblical history of   **B:**160–62
David   **D:**43
Dead Sea   **L:**29–30
Dead Sea Scrolls   **D:**47
education   **E:**75
Egyptian-Israeli peace treaty   **E:**105
elections   **E:**130
Galilee, Sea of   **L:**30
history of the kingdom of Israel   **I:**374; **J:**102; **P:**40c
homeland regained   **J:**106–7
immigration   **I:**94
Jerusalem   **J:**80–84
Jordan, relations with   **H:**307; **J:**132
kibbutzim   **F:**43
Lebanon, history of   **L:**122–23
Magen David Adom, equivalent of the Red Cross   **R:**126
Meir, Golda   **M:**212
modern Hebrew language   **H:**99
national dances   **D:**31
New Year of the Trees   **H:**161
Orthodoxy is the only accepted form of Judaism   **J:**149
Palestine   **C:**369; **P:**40c–43
Palestine Liberation Organization and   **A:**456–57
shofar sounded on special occasions   **J:**148
Solomon   **S:**251
Suez Canal   **S:**481
Syria, relations with   **S:**552
world's Jewish population   **J:**149
Zionism   **Z:**386
map(s)   **I:**372
picture(s)
agriculture   **I:**370
banana crop   **M:**303
beach   **I:**371
flag   **F:**233
Jerusalem   **C:**313; **I:**369; **J:**80, 82, 83
kibbutzim   **A:**93
Negev Desert   **I:**370
Negev Desert housing project   **D:**130
Palestinian Arabs in Gaza Strip   **I:**370
Russian immigrants   **I:**369
shepherd   **I:**370
soldiers at checkpoint   **I:**375
Tel Aviv-Jaffa   **I:**373
young woman   **A:**444
Israel Aircraft Industries (IAI)   **I:**372

Israel ben Eliezer (Jewish teacher) *see* Eliezer, Israel ben
Israeli-Arab wars *see* Arab-Israeli wars
Israelites (descendants of the Hebrew patriarch Jacob)
  B:159
Israel Museum (Jerusalem) J:81
ISS *see* International Space Station
Issas (a people of Africa) D:232, 233
Issyk Kul (salt lake, Kyrgyzstan) K:314
Istanbul (formerly Constantinople) (Turkey) I:377–78; M:302;
  T:347 *see also* Constantinople
  picture(s) A:450; I:377
    Galata Bridge M:302
    Hagia Sophia, church of A:369; B:489
    mosque in Topkapi Palace I:378
    Sultan Ahmed Mosque I:356; T:348
Isthmus (geographical term) C:537 *see also* the names of
  isthmuses, as Panama, Isthmus of
István (first king of Hungary) *see* Stephen, Saint
Itabira (Brazil) B:378
Itaipú Dam (Brazil–Paraguay) B:380; L:27; P:64
  picture(s) P:64, 422
Italian Americans (ethnic group)
  picture(s) N:229
Italian greyhounds (dogs) D:246
  picture(s) D:246
Italian Somaliland (now Somalia) S:255
Italian sonnet P:352
Italics (style of type) T:369, 370
Italics (Underlining) (punctuation) P:543
Italy I:379–90
  aquarium (Genoa) A:337
  automobile industry A:555
  Capri I:363
  Christmas customs C:300
  education E:74
  Elba I:364
  Florence F:258–59
  food F:330
  Genoa G:95
  holidays H:167, 169
  Jews, history of the J:105
  lakes L:29, 30, 31
  libraries L:174
  motion pictures M:493
  national anthem N:21
  New Year N:209
  olive production O:101
  puppets and marionettes P:548
  Rome R:305–8
  San Marino, relations with S:35, 36
  Sardinia I:368
  Sicily I:368
  textiles, history of T:144–45
  theater T:161
  Vatican City V:280–82
  Venice V:300–301
  wine W:190
  map(s) I:381
    unification (1859–1870) I:389
  picture(s)
    coastal town C:361
    Como, Lake I:383; L:29
    flag F:233
    Florence F:258
    gardens G:32, 33
    Genoa G:95
    kite festivals K:270
    marble quarry Q:6
    Milan I:393
    Naples I:386
    people I:379, 380
    Rome *see* Rome (capital of Italy)—*picture(s)*
    Sicily I:383
    Siena horse racing I:382
    Venice E:362; I:379

Italy, art and architecture of I:391–403 *see also* the names of
  artists
  art, the meanings of A:428
  baroque period B:64–65
  Bellini family B:140
  cubism C:612
  drawing, history of D:316–17
  Dutch and Flemish art influenced by D:360
  furniture F:509
  futurism (modern art movement) M:391
  humanism in Renaissance art A:430
  painting P:18, 20–21, 23
  pottery P:412
  Renaissance A:371–72; R:160–61, 164–70
  sculpture S:98, 100
  Spanish art, influence on S:383
  Uffizi Gallery U:2–3
  Venetian glass G:231
  Venice V:301
  picture(s)
    furniture F:508
Italy, history of I:387–90 *see also* Roman Empire; Rome,
  ancient
  ancient Roman civilization A:239
  banking B:53
  clothing, history of C:376
  Eritrea E:317
  Ethiopia E:333
  Fascism comes to power F:63
  Frederick II (king of Germany and Sicily) F:459
  Garibaldi, Giuseppe G:56
  Mazzini, Giuseppe M:189
  Medici M:201–2
  Middle Ages M:291
  Mussolini, Benito M:556
  Renaissance R:157–62
  Rome, ancient R:309–17
  Venice V:301
  World War I W:277, 285–91
  World War II W:294, 295, 299, 308, 309, 316, 318
Italy, language and literature of I:380, 404–9
  drama D:305–6
  novelists N:363
  Renaissance period R:159–60
  romanticism in literature R:303
  Switzerland S:540
  Why are so many musical terms written in Italian? M:540
Italy, music of I:410–12 *see also* the names of Italian
  composers
  opera O:139–42, 145
  romanticism R:304
Itasca, Lake (Minnesota) M:334
It Happened One Night (motion picture, 1934) M:492
"I think, therefore I am" (philosophical reasoning of Descartes)
  F:438
Ito, Midori (Japanese figure skater)
  picture(s) I:40
Iturbide, Agustín de (Mexican emperor) M:248–49
IUD *see* Intrauterine device
Ivan I (Russian grand prince) I:413; M:468
Ivan II (Ivan the Meek) (Russian grand prince) I:413
Ivan III (Ivan the Great) (Russian grand prince) I:413; M:468;
  R:357, 369, 375
Ivan IV (Ivan the Terrible) (czar of Russia) I:413–14; R:369
  picture(s) R:369
Ivan V (ruler of Russia) I:414
Ivan VI (emperor of Russia) I:414
Ivanov, Alexander (Russian painter) R:377
Ivanovski, Dmitri (Russian scientist) V:363
Ives, Charles (American composer) I:415; M:398; U:208
Ives, Herbert (American scientist) R:142
Ives, W. & S. B. *see* W. & S. B. Ives
Ivory I:415–16
  African sculpture A:71, 72

PHOTO CREDITS

The following list credits the sources of photos used in THE NEW BOOK OF KNOWLEDGE. Credits are listed, by page, photo by photo—left to right, top to bottom. Wherever appropriate, the name of the photographer has been listed with the source, the two being separated by a dash. When two or more photos by different photographers appear on one page, their credits are separated by semicolons.

117 © R. Koch—Contrasto—Picture Group; © Byron Craders—Root Resources; © John Vacbon—The Image Bank; © Cameramann International Ltd.; © Nick Nicholson—The Image Bank.
118 © David Ryan; © Lorraine Rorke—The Image Works; © Jessie Walker.
119 © Pablo Bartholomew—Liaison Agency; © Larousse—Photo Researchers; © Elisa Leonelli—Bruce Coleman Inc.
121 © David Ryan; © Dan Peha.
122 © Janice E. Burger—Bruce Coleman Inc.
124 © Jagdish Agarwal—The Image Works; © Cameramann International Ltd.
125 © Juergon Schmitt—The Image Bank; © Dan Peha.
128 © Photo Researchers; © Billy Grimes.
129 © Hari Mahidhar—Dinodia Photo Library; © Jeffrey Aaronson—Network Aspen.
130 © SuperStock
131 Victoria and Albert Museum, London/Art Resource, NY
132 National Portrait Gallery, London; The Metropolitan Museum of Art, Purchase, Rogers Fund and Kevorkian Foundation Gift, 1955.
133 UPI/Bettmann Newsphotos; © Baldev—Corbis-Sygma.
134 © Ken Laffal
135 Lauros-Giraudon/Art Resource; Borromeo—Art Resource.
136 Giraudon/Art Resource
137 Giraudon/Art Resource; Lauros-Giraudon/Art Resource.
138 Art Resource; © Randa Bishop; © Cameramann International Ltd.
139 © Tim Gibson—Envision
141 Courtesy of the Freer Gallery of Art, Smithsonian Institution, Washington, D.C.
145 © James Blank—The Stock Market; © Michael Dunn—The Stock Market; © Peter Pearson—Stone.
146 © Frank Cezus—Stone; © James P. Rowan—Stone.
147 © Kitty Kohout—Root Resources
148 © David Umberger—Purdue News Service; © Mary Ann Carter.
149 © Mary Ann Carter
150 Eli Lilly and Company; © Larry Lefever—Grant Heilman Photography.
151 © H. Armstrong Roberts; © Donald C. Johnson—The Stock Market.
152 © Jeff Gnass—The Stock Market; © Cathlyn Melloan—Stone; © Cathlyn Melloan—Stone.
153 © J. D. Pratt—Third Coast Stock Source; © Bob Abraham—The Stock Market.
154 © Steve Solum—West Stock
156 © Gino Domenico—AP/Wide World Photos; Bettmann/Corbis.
157 AP/Wide World Photos; The Granger Collection.
158 North Wind Picture Archives
159 © Richard Day—Midwestock
163 © David Stoecklein—The Stock Market; Roy Morsch—The Stock Market; © Wolfgang Kaehler.
164 © J. Barry O'Rourke—The Stock Market; © Reinhard Brucker.
167 © Buddy Mays; © Lee Boltin.
168 © Reinhard Brucker
169 © William Allen, Jr.
170 © Lee Boltin (all photos on page).
171 © William H. Allen, Jr.
172 Milwaukee Public Museum, Wisconsin; © Allen Russell—ProFiles West/Index Stock.
173 © Reinhard Brucker; The Granger Collection; Michael Holford.
175 © David Stoecklein—The Stock Market; © Bob Coyle.
176 Rochester Museum & Science Center, Rochester, New York; © Reinhard Brucker; The Bettmann Archive.
177 The Granger Collection; National Gallery of Art, Washington, D.C.; Smithsonian Institution—Washington, D.C.
178 Smithsonian Institution—Washington, D.C. (all photos on page).
179 Smithsonian Institution—Washington, D.C.; National Museum of American Art, Gift of Mrs. Joseph Harrison, Jr.
180 © Reinhard Brucker; © Reinhard Brucker; Smithsonian Institution—Washington, D.C.
181 Courtesy of The Newberry Library, Chicago, Edward E. Ayer Collection; The Bettmann Archive.
182 © Topham—The Image Works
183 © Reinhard Brucker; © Reinhard Brucker; Marcia Keegan—The Stock Market.
184 © Manley Publications, Tucson, Arizona; The Bettmann Archive; © Manley Publications, Tucson, Arizona.
185 © Jean-Pierre Laffont—Corbis-Sygma; © Paul Conklin; © Jerry Jacka.
186 National Museum of American Art, Gift of Mrs. Joseph Harrison, Jr.; © Buddy Mays.
187 Smithsonian Institution—Washington, D.C. (all photos on page).
188 © Frans Lanting—Minden Pictures (all photos on page).
189 © Frans Lanting—Minden Pictures
190 The Granger Collection
191 © Robert Semeniuk—The Stock Market; © Tim Thompson; The University Museum, University of Pennsylvania.
193 © Loren McIntyre
194 © Buddy Mays; © Victor Englebert.
196 © Mike Carr—ProFiles West/Index Stock
197 © Loren McIntyre (all photos on page).
199 © Thomas Ives—The Stock Market
200 © Allen Russell—ProFiles West/Index Stock; © John Warner, St. Labre Indian School.
201 © Rick Vargas—Smithsonian Institution
203 Courtesy of Yale University Library
206 © Steve Vidler—Leo de Wys; © Noel Quidu—Liaison Agency; © Jeff Greenberg—Unicorn Stock Photos.
207 © Denis Waugh—Stone; © Abbey Sea Photography—Unicorn Stock Photos.
208 © Steve Vidler—Leo de Wys; © Bowles—Leo de Wys.
210 © Lincoln Potter—Liaison Agency (all photos on page).
211 © Lee Battaglia—Photo Researchers
212 © Reuters/Enny Nuraheni—Archive Photos
213 Courtesy of Ansa Company Inc.—© John Kane
214 The Museum of Modern Art, Peter Schlumbohm. *Coffee Maker* 1941. Gift of Lewis & Conger; Courtesy, AT&T Bell Laboratories; The Museum of Modern Art, Charles Eames *Side Chair* 1946. Gift of Herman Miller Furniture Co.
215 © Ted Morrison; © Tom Hollyman—Photo Researchers.
216 Mary Evans Picture Library
217 The Granger Collection
218 The Granger Collection
219 The Granger Collection
220 © Snark/Art Resource, NY; Mary Evans Picture Library; Mary Evans Picture Library.
221 © Bettmann/Corbis; The Granger Collection.
222 The Granger Collection
223 © Thomas Philip Morgan/Mary Evans Picture Library
224 Michael S. Yamashita—Corbis
228 © Glen Allison—Stone/Getty Images
230 © E. S. Ross; H. Eisenbeiss—Annan.
231 © Alastair Shay—Animals Animals; © Stephen Dalton—Photo Researchers; © Zig Leszczynski—Animals Animals; © Raymond A. Mendez—Animals Animals.
233 © Hugh Spencer; © Green—Annan; © K. G. Preston-Mafham—Animals Animals; © Lynwood M. Chace; © Lynwood M. Chace; Robert Hermes—National Audubon Society; Norman R. Lightfoot—Photo Researchers.
234 © Ross E. Hutchins; © Hermann Eisenbeiss—Photo Researchers; © Ross E. Hutchins.
237 © E. R. Degginger—Animals Animals; © Harry Rogers—Photo Researchers; © E. R. Degginger—Animals Animals.
240 © Herman Eisenbeiss—Photo Researchers; © Harry Rogers—Photo Researchers; Ross E. Hutchins.
242 © Karl Maslowski—Photo Researchers; © Stephen J. Krasemann—Photo Researchers; © Jacques Six.
243 © Robert Fink—National Audubon Society; © Louis Quitt—Photo Researchers.
244 © Lincoln Nutting—Audubon/Photo Researchers; W. J. Jahoda—National Audubon Society; © Lynwood M. Chace—National Audubon Society; © Hugh Spencer; © L. G. Kesteloo—National Audubon Society; © Grace A. Thompson—National Audubon Society; © Lynwood M. Chace.
245 © Treat Davidson—National Audubon Society; © Ross E. Hutchins; © Stephen Collins—Photo Researchers; © Lynwood M. Chace; Eileen Tanson—Audubon/Photo Researchers; © Grace A. Thompson—National Audubon Society; © John H. Gerard.
246 © Ross E. Hutchins; © Stephen Collins—Photo Researchers; © Norman R. Lightfoot—Photo Researchers; © Patti Murray—Animals Animals; © Lynwood M. Chace; © Lynwood M. Chace.
247 © V. E. Ward—National Audubon Society; © Noble Proctor—Photo Researchers; © Ross E. Hutchins.
248 © John H. Gerard; © Ross E. Hutchins; © Ross E. Hutchins; © Annan; © John H. Gerard; © Ross E. Hutchins; © Walter Rohdich—Annan; © Annan; © Herbert Hanks—Monkmeyer.
249 © Pat & Tom Leeson—Photo Researchers; © E. S. Ross.
250 © Garry D. McMichael—Photo Researchers; © E. R. Degginger—Animals Animals.
251 © Ron Frehm—International Stock Photography
252 © John Lamb—Leo de Wys
256 U.S. Department of the Interior
257 The Granger Collection; © Rick Stiller—Liaison Agency; © Patti McConville—The Image Bank.
258 © Alan E. McGee—FPG International; © Kevin C. Rose—The Image Bank.
259 © Nicolas Russell—The Image Bank
261 © Scott Frances—Esto.
262 © Jessie Walker (all photos on page).
263 © Jessie Walker (all photos on page).
267 © Tass—Sovfoto
268 UPI/Bettmann Newsphotos
269 © Fred Ernst—Reuters/Archive Photos
271 © Bob Daemmrich—The Image Works
272 © Lawrence Migdale—Photo Researchers; © Wolfgang Kaehler; John Eastcott/Yva Momatiuk/Photo Researchers; Bryan and Cherry Alexander.
273 © Bryan and Cherry Alexander; © Lowell Georgia—Corbis.
274 © Bryan and Cherry Alexander
275 © Wolfgang Kaehler—Corbis
276 © David Hiser—Photographers/Aspen/PictureQuest
277 © NASA; AP/Wide World Photos; © Lester Lefkowitz/Taxi/Getty Images.
279 © Erich Lessing—Art Resource, NY
280 © E. R. Degginger—Bruce Coleman Inc.
281 Hulton/Archive by Getty Images; The Granger Collection.
282 © Bruce Dale—National Geographic Image Collection; Will and Deni McIntyre—Photo Researchers; © Ken Adreyo of Carnegie Mellon University.
283 U.S. Department of the Interior, National Park Service, Edison National Historic Site; © Julian Wasser—TimePix; © Science Photo Library/Photo Researchers.
284 Hulton/Archive by Getty Images; Taxi/Getty Images.
285 RCA; AP/Wide World Photos.
286 © Peter Menzel
288 © Johnny Johnson—Earth Scenes
289 © Ray Pfortner—Peter Arnold, Inc.
291 © Bill Nellans; David Conklin; © Thomas Hovland—Grant Heilman Photography.
293 © Ken Dequaine—Third Coast Stock Source; © Michael Whye.
294 © Bob Coyle; Pella Chamber of Commerce.
295 © Paul Conklin
296 © Thomas Hovland—Grant Heilman Photography (all photos on page).
297 © Craig Aurness—Woodfin Camp & Associates
298 © Doris DeWitt—Stone; © Bob Coyle; © Michael Whye.
299 © Bob Coyle; © MacDonald—Third Coast Stock Source.
302 The Granger Collection (all photos on page).
303 Courtesy, Grant Wood Art Festival, Inc.; The Granger Collection; The Granger Collection.
305 © Christopher Boisvieux—Liaison Agency; © François Lochon—Liaison Agency; © Christopher Boisvieux—Liaison Agency.
306 © Roland and Sabrina Michaud—Woodfin Camp & Associates; © Alain Nogues—Corbis-Sygma.
307 © Paul Almasy—Corbis; © Alexis Duclos—Liaison Agency.
308 UPI/Corbis-Bettmann
309 © Alain Keler—Corbis-Sygma
310 UPI/Bettmann
311 © Bill Foley—Bruce Coleman Inc.; © Chip Hires—Liaison Agency; © Françoise de Mulder—Corbis.
312 © Laur Van Der Stockt—Liaison Agency
314 © Josef Polleross—The Stock Market; © Grant Smith—Corbis.
315 © Barry Iverson—Woodfin Camp & Associates; © Marc Deville—Liaison Agency.
316 © Bill Foley—Bruce Coleman Inc.
316a © Marco DiLauro—Getty Images; © Laurent Rebours—AP/Wide World Photos.

317 © Arnold Mulcahy—Liaison Agency; © Charles Gupton—The Stock Market; © Le Diascorn/Rapho/Photo Researchers.
318 Courtesy, The Board of Trinity College, Dublin; © Sam Abell—National Geographic Image Collection.
319 © E. Nagle—FPG International; © Steve Vidler—Leo de Wys.
320 © Charles Gupton—The Stock Market
321 © Richard Gorbun—Leo de Wys
322 © D&J Heaton—Leo de Wys; The Granger Collection.
323 The Granger Collection
324 Popperfoto—Archive Photos
326 The Granger Collection
327 © Martha Swope; The Granger Collection.
328 National Picture Gallery, London
329 © Bruno J. Zehnder—Peter Arnold, Inc.
330 © Gerhard Gscheidle—Peter Arnold, Inc.
331 American Iron and Steel Institute; Cameramann International Ltd.
332 Cameramann International Ltd. (all photos on page).
334 Jan Halaska—Photo Researchers
335 American Iron and Steel Institute
336 American Iron and Steel Institute; © Guy Gillette—Photo Researchers.
339 © Jongen—SuperStock; © Joachim Messerschmidt—Leo de Wys.
340 © James Blank—West Stock
342 Historic Hudson Valley
343 Historic Hudson Valley
344 Historic Hudson Valley
346 © Amr Nabil—AP/Wide World Photos
346– Art Resource
347
347 The Granger Collection; The Art Archive/Turkish & Islamic Art Museum, Istanbul/HarperCollins Publishers.
348 © Roland and Sabrina Michaud—Woodfin Camp & Associates
349 © Adrees Latif/Reuters/TimePix
350 The Granger Collection
351 Werner Forman Archive/Art Resource, NY
352 © Bibliothéque Nationale, Paris, France/The Bridgeman Art Library; Werner Forman Archive/Art Resource, NY; The Granger Collection.
353 © François Perri/COS/Woodfin Camp & Associates

354 SEF—Art Resource
355 Victoria and Albert Museum, London; © Nathan Benn—Woodfin Camp & Associates.
356 Lauros-Giraudon/Art Resource; © Sasaki-Scanlon—Comstock; © Zeynep Sunem—Stone.
357 The Metropolitan Museum of Art, Collection of Arthur A. Houghton, Jr.
358 © Francis G. Mayer; Courtesy of the Freer Gallery of Art, Smithsonian Institution, Washington, D.C.; Kuwait National Museum, The Al-Sabah Collection.
359 The Royal Collection, Stockholm
360 © Robert Knight—Leo de Wys; © Nicholas de Vore III—Bruce Coleman Inc.
361 © Regina P. Simon—Tom Stack & Associates
362 *Paris Match*—Pictorial Parade
363 © Carol Lee—Stone; © S. Chester—Comstock.
364 © Wolfgang Hille—Leo de Wys; © Carroll Seghers—Photo Researchers; © Frans Lanting—Photo Researchers.
366 © David Zimmerman—Masterfile
367 © Adam Woolfitt—Woodfin Camp & Associates; © Jessica Ehlers—Bruce Coleman Inc.
369 © ASAP/Yasha Mazur—Photo Researchers; © Van Bucher—Photo Researchers; © Erica Lansner—Stone.
370 © Stephen Ferry—Liaison Agency; © Will Yurman—Liaison Agency; © Richard T. Nowitz—Corbis.
370– © Inga Spence—Tom Stack & Associates.
371
371 © Will Yurman—Liaison Agency
373 © Annie Griffiths Belt—Corbis
374 © A. Ramey—PhotoEdit
375 © David Rubinger—Corbis; © Scott Daniel Peterson—Liaison Agency.
377 © Ed Pritchard—Stone/Getty Images
378 © Ali Kabas—Danita Delimont, Agent
379 © Dallas Stribley—Lonely Planet Images; © Bob Krist—eStock Photo.
380 © Alan Becker—Network Aspen; © Stephen Simpson—Taxi/Getty Images; © Russell Young—Danita Delimont, Agent.
382 © Simeone Huber—Stone/Getty Images
383 © Jon Arnold—Danita Delimont, Agent; ©

Danilo G. Donadoni—Bruce Coleman Inc.
384 © Graziano Ferrari—AP/Wide World Photos; © Michael J. Pettypool—Houserstock; © Horacek—Bilderberg/Peter Arnold, Inc.
385 © SIME s.a.s./eStock Photo
386 © Jose Fuste Raga—eStock Photo; © Scala/Art Resource, NY.
387 © Steve Vidler—eStock Photo
389 © Dagli Orti—Museo Civico, Modigliana, Italy/The Art Archive
390 Photo by Keystone/Getty Images
391 Scala/Art Resource
392 Scala/Art Resource
393 Scala/Art Resource (all photos on page).
394 Scala/Art Resource (all photos on page).
395 Scala/Art Resource (all photos on page).
396 Scala/Art Resource
397 The Granger Collection; © Gian Berto Vanni—Art Resource.
398 Scala/Art Resource (all photos on page).
399 Scala/Art Resource (all photos on page).
400 Scala/Art Resource (all photos on page).
401 Scala/Art Resource (all photos on page).
402 Scala/Art Resource (all photos on page).
403 Tate Gallery—Art Resource; Collection, The Museum of Modern Art, New York. Acquired through the Lillie P. Bliss Bequest.
404 Scala/Art Resource
407 Scala/Art Resource (all photos on page).
409 AP/Wide World Photos; © Frank Origlia—Corbis-Sygma.
410 Art Resource
411 The Granger Collection; Art Resource; The Granger Collection.
413 The Granger Collection
414 © Sovfoto
415 © Lee Boltin
416 © Louise Gubb—JB Pictures
417 © Connie Coleman—Photodisc Green/Getty Images; © Thomas S. England—Photo Researchers.
418 © Bob Burch—Bruce Coleman Inc.
420 © Vanessa Vick—Photo Researchers; © Marc & Evelyne Bernheim—Woodfin Camp & Associates.
421 AP/Wide World Photos